THE U.S.S.R.

FIRST CONGRESS OF PEOPLE'S DEPUTIES

COMPLETE DOCUMENTS AND RECORDS, May 25, 1989–June 10, 1989

Volume IV,

Documents and Media Reports

THE U.S.S.R.
FIRST CONGRESS OF PEOPLE'S DEPUTIES

COMPLETE DOCUMENTS AND RECORDS, May 25, 1989–June 10, 1989

Volume IV,

Documents and Media Reports

Edited by Rolf H. W. Theen

PARAGON HOUSE

New York

First edition, 1991

Published in the United States by Paragon House

Paragon House
90 Fifth Avenue
New York, NY 10011

The material in these volumes was first published or broadcast in Russian by IZVESTIYA, TASS, PRAVDA, or other
Soviet media and was translated into English by the Foreign Broadcast Information Service.

Library of Congress Cataloging-in-Publication Data

Soviet Union S″ezd narodnykh deputatov (1st : 1989 : Moscow, R.S.F.S.R.)
   The U.S.S.R. First Congress of People's Deputies : complete documents and records / compiled and with an
introduction by Rolf H. W. Theen.—1st ed.
      p.   cm.
   ''First published or broadcast in Russian by Izvestiya, TASS, Pravda, or other Soviet media and translated into English
by the Foreign Broadcast Information Service.''
   Translations were first published by the Foreign Broadcast Information Service as supplements to or ''political &
social'' sections of the Soviet Union Daily Report.
   Includes indexes.
   Contents: v. 1. First-eighth sessions, May 25–June 1, 1989—v.
2. Eighth-thirteenth sessions, June 1–June 9, 1989—v.
3. Documents and media reports—v. 4. Documents and media reports.
ISBN 1-55778-469-8

   1. Soviet Union. S″ezd narodnykh deputatov—Congresses.
2. Soviet Union—Politics and government—1985—Congresses.
I. Theen, Rolf H. W., 1937–   .II. United States. Foreign
Broadcast Information Service.   III. Title.
J397.H45S68   1989
354.4703′5—dc20   90-2w4654
                                                        CIP

Manufactured in the United States of America

CONTENTS

TRUD Publishes Bakulin's 31 May Congress Address
PM0306144789 Moscow TRUD in Russian
1 Jun 89 p 2

["Full text" of speech delivered to 31 May afternoon session of the Congress of USSR People's Deputies by V.I. Bakulin, USSR people's deputy from the USSR trade unions and leader of a team of fitters at the "Krasnaya Talka" Spinning and Finishing Factory in Ivanovo]

[Text] Comrades!

It gives me, as people's deputy from the worker city of Ivanovo, great satisfaction to note that our congress coincides with the 84th anniversary of the creation of the Ivanovo-Voznesensk city soviet of worker deputies, the first in Russia. (Applause) It was the first political experiment demonstrating that the workers' voice means a lot in solving major state issues.

Today, aware of the revolutionary spirit embodied in the restructuring of soviets' activity, you have an acute sense of personal responsibility for the country's destiny. The attention and thoughts of all working people, of those who entrusted us with the mandate of full-fledged representatives of the people, are focused on the Congress of People's Deputies. Much is expected of us—above all, answers to questions connected with the future course of restructuring and therefore with the improvement of our living standards. This is the main thing. I have always believed that a real congress cannot be reduced to rally speeches and attempts to stir up trouble, cause confusion and splits, and distract deputies from the discussion of very important matters of domestic and foreign policy. (Applause)

I am in constant contact with the people of Ivanovo, and what worries them in particular is the fact that some deputies are waging an overt struggle for political power, using a variety of methods—even abuse, threats, and name-calling. This causes protests among voters. They believe that such a situation at the congress can only make the situation worse in our country. As an ordinary party member, I am worried by the attitude of those deputies whose speeches and actions are aimed at belittling the role and significance of the CPSU and of the restructuring processes that are taking place. There are attempts to drive a wedge between party and people: Clearly, these people have their own far-reaching political aims. Is it not clear that it is on the initiative of the party, its Central Committee, and the Politburo that changes are taking place in the country's economy and social life, and, comrades, the question of who is to lead restructuring further along the road is not a matter of indifference to us. We can see no other force than the Communist Party, and we will support its policy. (Applause)

What surprises me is: Why are the party workers silent at the congress? Why do they not rebuff the overtly extremist attacks on the party? If we hold dear the ideas of restructuring (Applause), we Communists must not stand aside and avoid debate. In supporting the thesis of Mikhail Sergeyevich Gorbachev's report, I want to confirm that, for all its problems, restructuring is producing positive results. We have seen for ourselves that democratization and glasnost are gaining momentum, people's initiative is being freed, and industry's work is improving, although not as much as it should. Things are improving in agriculture, albeit very slowly. This inspires confidence in the correctness of the chosen course in the party. At the same time, some stagnation phenomena and unsolved problems are also typical of us in Ivanovo. To be frank, there is an urgent need for everyone not just to step up his work, but to strain every muscle to haul himself out of the quagmire, to extricate himself, even if some find it very painful. The working class is very anxious that restructuring not be talked into the ground. Indeed, all the time we hear: The 27th party congress was a breakthrough, the 19th all-union conference was a breakthrough, this plenum was a breakthrough, that plenum was a breakthrough. The present congress is a breakthrough too: That is how we live today. We break through and wage battles. (Noise in the auditorium) As a worker, I want to say that people are tired of multitudes of words and promises—what they want is action and a clearer line in economic policy.

In view of the fact that the Congress of People's Deputies is forming our government's action program I would like to express my views on a number of basic problems of socioeconomic policy, which determines working people's interests. In our view, they need to be solved immediately. As my instructions to the country's Supreme Soviet I want to suggest a deeper, more considered, and more balanced approach to the elaboration and adoption of economic decisions and programs. In the years of restructuring so many resolutions have already been adoopted that their fulfillment would dramatically advance the economy; but in practice we are outlining programs, naming targets and deadlines, and giving the people promises and guarantees while, at the same time, making a mess of them and even going back on them. I will consider two points which are most relevant to my type of work. The textile workers had great hopes for the resolution on fundamentally improving the technical standard of Soviet machine building. They thought that technical progress, at least in textile machine building, would bring them up to world standards, make work easier for our esteemed and dear women. and improve the qwuality of goods. As we can see, this is not happening. Instead of highly productive equipment crammed with electronics we have witnessed the birth of another two resolutions by central organs on unsatisfactory and extremely unsatisfactory fulfillment of previous resolutions. And, as far as we know, no one has answered for this—neither those who drew up the documents, nor those who implemented them. It seems to me that the Supreme Soviet has to find levers to sharply increase responsibility for the implementation of decisions, even to the extent of removing the specific culprits from their jobs. I am firmly convinced that unless executive discipline—from worker to government members—is strengthened and maximum labor productivity is ensured in the very near future, there can be no question of any substantial improvement in the state of affairs in the country. (Applause)

The problem of providing people with goods is as acute as can be. Major state figures have repeatedly referred to last March's party Central Committee and USSR Council of Ministers resolution as a salutary step in the solution of this problem envisaging the construction, reconstruction, and retooling of hundreds of enterprises in our sector. But the first year in which this highly respectable document has been operating has demonstrated its lack of balance. One of the construction projects named was our "Krasnaya Talka" factory. The planning deadline arrived, but neither the State Planning Committee nor the Light Industry Ministry was able to or would promise to decide who was going to reconstruct the enterprise at a cost of tens of millions of rubles in construction and installation work. One cannot understand why, even when one has a government decision, one has to go around demonstrating that it must be implemented. When will there be respect for state decisions? When we stop going cap in hand to the ministries and departments? I think that while there is still time the relevant organs must make a kind of inventory of past decisions. While advocating the priority development of particular sectors in one decision, in another we talk of the need to suspend, mothball, and so on.... This confirms that resolutions which decide the fate of collectives comprising many thousands of people have not been thoroughly examined.

It is important also to stop adopting contradictory documents, which is practically the norm today. There have been a number of resolutions by supreme organs prohibiting the development of industrial construction in the Non-Chernozem Zone, and at the same time there has been a series of resolutions on the construction of new plants, without, what is more, considering local opinion.

I think the country's Supreme Soviet and government should give priority to concentrating material and financial resources on developing the construction industry's material and technical base. Without it we will not solve the food, housing, or any other problems. Even now the oblast's textile workers have over R100 million in production and social development funds and cannot use them for want of material resources and contract organization capacities. Our people have been waiting 15-18 years for apartments. Without developing this sector there is no hope that the stated political task of providing every family with housing by the year 2000 will be solved.

As chairman of the enterprise labor collective council I have to look at economic problems and read a lot of work by Comrades Abalkin, Selyunin, Shmelev, Popov, and others. But what happens, comrade scientists? Whoever the writer is, he criticizes another. One says "there must be an economic reform," another says "the time is not ripe, the masses are not ready for it." What is the answer? Whatever kind of economic reform we have, there must be no decline in the people's living standard. This is apparent to everyone, seemingly, but every day we see empty shelves in stores, rampant speculation, and rising prices. It is time the leading economists switched from debates to devising specific ways of treating our economy. (Applause) And, like doctors, bore the responsibility for healing it as soon as possible. (Applause)

I must also say that the working class is worried at the moment about the development of the cooperative system. Initially we expected the market to be filled with the requisite goods; we expected the problem of scarce goods to be solved and to have healthy competition with the state sector. But what actually happened? We see that the cooperatives have given rise to social injustice, slacker discipline, and more crime; they have picked workers' and pensioners' pockets and created an uncontrolled channel for the conversion of noncash transactions into cash, mostly without extra goods being produced. Against this background, society's stratification is starkly evident. On the one hand, there are a few people with incomes of many thousamds, and on the other millions with not even the bare minimum to live on. Those who kept the country's head above water during extremely hard years feel particularly aggrieved. Legislative legal organs must immediately carry out further work on questions of the development of cooperatives, and ensure that they really do become a necessity rather than a phenomenon in our life.

Comrade deputies! I would like to see the activity of the Supreme Soviet and the government find expression in a constant improvement in the lives of the united Soviet people, in a steady increase in our country's prestige, not only abroad, and, above all, in a revival of the people's pride in their homeland and in our socialist system, which is the most just, humane, and progressive. I am addressing the country's working people and the workers of Moscow and Leningrad: Remember and do not forget Vladimir Ilich Lenin's words: "The proletariat of Moscow, Petrograd, and Ivanovo-Voznesensk...have demonstrated that they will not surrender the gains of the revolution at any price." Today we must firmly adopt this position. (Prolonged applause)

1 Jun Congress Proceedings Reported

Further on Morning Session

LD0206115989 Moscow Television Service in Russian 0825 GMT 1 Jun 89

[Relay of the Congress of People's Deputies held in the Kremlin Palace of Congresses—live; for earlier reports from the morning session see the 2 Jun Soviet Union DAILY REPORT Supplement, pages 7-12]

[Excerpts] [passage omitted] [Academician Boris Paton, chairing the session] The floor is given to Deputy Yuriy Dmitriyevich Chernichenko, commentator of the Agricultural Department of central television. After that will be Comrade Kalish.

[Chernichenko] I am, by birth, from a place where even in the sixties you could hear a grandmother, in comforting her grandson, say: Hush, the Muscovite will come, the Muscovite will come! [preceding phrase in Ukrainian] There is no nationalist underlying cause here; the kind old lady just wants to scare her disobedient pet a little. But when there appeared, before the congress and after the euphoria of the elections, to be 12 most worthy people vying for this place, we got ourselves into turmoil, into a situation of dictated lists and undeclared programs. When it came time for a genuine power struggle, with an authority that had seemingly been openly and honestly elected by the people, there arose then this image of a Muscovite as some sort of scarecrow, charlatan [preceding two words in Ukrainian] from the capital, who had come to seize the quite earnest minds disposed to this. The poor unfortunate house of political education in (?Trubnaya) Square! For 5 weeks it truly became a house both for politicizing and education. People gathered there who were known by the entire country. They forged by night—so to speak—inadmissible things: the idea and program for this congress. It would be awkward to involve the leadership; we have to live with it, after all. But I must tell you in secret that both Lev Nikolayevich Zaykov, first secretary of Moscow, and even Anatoliy Ivanovich Lukyanov met with us there. What we got out of it—forged—what presents such danger for you, was multiplied by us in envelopes and distributed to the deputies. Is that not so? But then without serious opposition in the Russian Soviet Federated Socialist Republic: Who authorized you to do this?

The story of the Moscow group is fear of real political initiative; initiative is, after all, meant to be punishable. Sensitively grasping the semi-vocalized command, one member proposed to the professors a truly (?Zadornov) tactic, so to speak, to forge ourselves once again in the workshop. Another leaned toward an answer to the deficit. A third pointed out: That is where the evil of leasing and cooperatives stems from! Whereas the charming deputy from Kazakhstan even went so far as to deprive them of her womanly favors.

Dutiful indignation—if you recall—only recently spat at Pasternak, branded Tvardovskiy, shouted at Sakharov: Crucify him. And some older people, who are more experienced than the unapproachable female delegate, should well be able to imagine the state of an academician or writer who curses the day and hour when his hand gave in to the weakness and he wrote, signed the base document. But there's nothing one can do! One cannot erase this from the memory of national history. And the result: For some reason or other, in the Supreme Soviet there are no economists such as Abalkin, Bogomolov, Shmelev, Tikhonov, Petrakov, Popov; and of course there are no sociologists such as Zaslavskaya, nor historians like Afanasyev; there are practicaly no lawyers; and not one of the journalists who was read so avidly by the country. What is this? A cultural revolution flaring up? Or is it that the Moor can depart having performed his task? Only please don't give me any speechifying now. Everyone understands that there is no coincidence here and the old collective farm rhyme was right: It's not the tractor that works on its own, the tractor driver has to drive it. [applause]

The young wine of electoral enthusiasm has ben poured into the old wine skins of party diktat. That's the point. I am an old Communist of 40 years' standing soon. The word party can also be translated as part, and when the part becomes more than the whole, then there arises the need for a plot in a time of danger. The elections were unprecedentedly communist! The people clearly divided the party from the ruling bureaucratic apparatus. [applause] But during the congress, at the unpublicized final round of elections, the apparatus took its revenge and confirmed at the Central Committee plenum even

the heads of parliamentary commissions, giving rise to disobedience from even the most obliging. It read out lists that none of those present compiled. Anonymity of initiative and underhanded activity—what an anachronism it all is! How this smacks of the vengeful orators of the April plenum, who appeared to be first and turned out last in the elections!

If the millions awakened to political life reject the constituency meetings as the first link in the bureaucratic chain, then they will never approve the final filtering either—the practice of the broken firing-pin, the reservations of which as a rule and as an exception are cleverly used to produce a joint chorus. Divide and rule does not work anymore: If you want to exercise your power productively, bring them together, and you get where you aim. [applause]

These are not my words. You have elected us. Why? So that we will reason, debate, and decide. But if you see deviations in every dispute and put puppets or dummies on the stage, then who will do the thinking for these dummies? These are words the of Aleksey Ivanovich Rykov, first chairman of the Soviet of People's Commissars after Lenin. [applause]

Restructuring has exhausted its credits, we have eaten up all advances. If we put it on the scale of Lenin's New Economic Policy, which was launched in 1921, we are already in 1925. And by that time the country had been given enough food and clothes; and People's Commissar Krasin barely found time to shuttle between here and there with loads of Russian grain that was sold for gold.

But you must tell Gorbachev to feed us full, exclaims a very ardent devotee of restructuring over there, across the border. Apparently, he entertains tsarist views, he thinks—just as many of us do—that it can be done singlehandedly. We, thank God, have realized that no savior from on high can deliver, no trust have we in prince or peer; and a coercive system of farming will never be able to feed the people.

We have wasted too much time working our way toward grasping the truth that everything is justified, that neither nature, which combines in our regions the entire range of the world's climatic zones, nor our wretched soils, which accommodate almost 190 million hectares of chernozem—the planet's pride—are to blame. There is only one cause of people's poverty and of the destruction of farm land; the reasons for that are solely and exclusively of a political nature. [applause]

Stalinism in agriculture is a political vendee; it is not only capable of torpedoing restructuring, it is already doing so. The word plan should not be overused, the plan which is methodically left unfulfilled, which drags its feet somehow thanks to completely unacceptable borrowing from this or that sector, or thanks to hidden bloodsucking, so to speak—by exchanging our oil for someone else's grain. That plan is no plan. It amounts to something else, we should find the right word for it before adding the prefix gos, state plan. There is no way to explain to a sane person the kind of economy that turns out five times as many tractors per capita, ten times as many combines per capita as the United States, and produces twice as much grain. But that is only half the trouble. [corrects himself] I mean a half of their grain. And as to boots, it produces three times as many—it could have just as well not bothered to produce them at all—as the United States. But there are other things involved here, too. Take sugar, for example. My grandson, thank God, has learned how to line up with the ration card in his hand to buy sugar. We have 31 kg of sugar per capita, whereas in the United States they have 22 and no lines at all, and no ration slips. But now we have these slips even in Moscow.

To take the example of industry, for comparison's sake, we produce six times as much ore as the United States, and as for synthetic resins, our level of production is one-sixth of that in the United States. Who needs an industry like that?

If we turn to electronics, esteemed Comrade Osipyan, our top stock taker who is present here, I learned with horror that he, a leading electronics expert and major expert in physics, uses an abacus to count. That, I think, will go down in history. [laughter and applause]

Right. The system whose elements are the ruble, which was placed under arrest in 1926, and the apparatus which commands but is not held to account, leads to national humiliation. Let us not be children who think that Pinocchio, their favorite wooden puppet, acts of its own accord.

There is a puppeteer above it. We seemed to have reached an agreement—seemingly, because we have been in session for the 7th day running, and not a single word has been spoken yet about the absolute diktat of the party apparatus, about the fact that not a single hair will be shed from a cattle head without the consent of or a command from the agricultural department. We do not look there, although we hit at Murakhovskiy. You have found [a scapegoat]. I am a defender of Murakhovskiy. At 168 meetings with voters or writers I said that Comrade Murakhovskiy is not guilty of anything. As in an American bar, you could put a sign over the door to his study: Do not shoot the piano player; he does his best. That is because up to eight deputies and ministers at a time can be found sitting in the reception hall of a deputy department chief. It is common knowledge, but this must not be said; it is not a proper thing to say in civilized company.

I am very fond of television and at present I am following with a great deal of interest the enlightening broadcasts of Yegor Kuzmich Ligachev. He tours the country and learns a good deal—apparently because it is a new sector for him—and he willingly shares [what he learns] with us. [energetic applause] It is mighty pleasant to me, this kind of dissemination of basic cultural knowledge; he is putting many TV journalists out of a job, and all that is fine. The only thing I want to say, to ask—as I was asked 168 times: Why was a politically essential sector, the sector that is crucial for the potential and the future of restructuring, given to a person who does not know a thing about it and who failed his job in ideology? How could that happen? [applause] I do not see that.

I know; bureaucracy is supranational and the Russian bureaucrat belonged to the same variety as Marx's Prussian careerist, bending his back to his superiors in the very same way. But the specific nation, the present (?society), and the present union of nations can be humiliated by bureaucracy—and in a very productive way. In my old fashioned view, it humiliates it in a minimum of three ways. As for the sum total of nations—well, I do not like to interfere here in these discords because it concerns all of us. But the first thing which, alas, was not discussed in this respect is our shameful exports. We are exporting 200 million tonnes of oil, but whose car is not at a standstill for having an empty gas tank? Two hundred [as heard] tonnes of oil, chiefly crude! Are we dizzy with glory and mimicry? After all, this is squandering the property of our grandchildren! A good manager cannot behave like this. This, my own humilitation before my grandson. I do not know what I shall hand down to him, and that goes for everything else, too.

I am hurt by the humiliation of imports, imports of what is grown on our own lands, of things and materials which are, incidentally, fully renewable. The imports of grain, meat, and butter are extremely advantageous for the seller and destructive for the buyer. Esteemed audience, do not believe, do not believe, deputies, that we are buying second-grade grain. Not at all! According to the Central Statistical Directorate, 18 million tonnes of wheat was purchased last year. Just name one normal person who can explain why these 18 million tonnes were obtained when the country produces 2 and ½ times more of the same wheat than it needs for itself. Where is the schizophrenia and where is the logic? And how can you, after this, call the Gosplan an institution of authority. This has not been going on for just a year; this has been going on for decades. Last year I noted the 25th—a quarter of a century—jubilee of this antinational practice.

When I am asked if Murakhovskiy believes in kolkhozes, I say—between you and I—well, he does not! [laughter] And does he believe in sovkhozes? I say—strictly between ourselves, so don't tell on me—not at all! And why? Well, first and foremost, he would have to pay with his own money. And in 25 years everything would be grown at home, in his own country, because Kazan, Ryazan, Kuban, and Kulunda would already have long restructured themselves on these monstrous billions, and the country of socialism would not have the appearance of an international parasite, which exists beyond the borders of my homeland. [applause]

Last, here is the third and last stage of humiliation: This is technical humiliation. We have become a people backward in all areas. Do you know that the Estonians have in their conversation the words: Russian work. But this can only be a matter between neighbors. It means a bad thing; Russian work means a bad thing. [bell interrupts] I am just going! Unfortunately, Estonian goods and the goods from Karakalpak have also become bad. And so, is this our fault? Are we genetically disposed to this? No! It is the political system, which rules but which itself is not answerable for this, that is guilty. I will not go into all this right now. I joined in a very broad, and in my view very businesslike, agrarian memorandum which was announced yesterday to you by the esteemed agrarian deputies. This, too, is an example of a group and there is nothing bad in it! In these last few seconds I demand one thing only: that we do not become bogged down in talking; that we do not keep putting things off until tomorrow or another day. This is what is said not only by idlers, but by the masters of politics who are able to (?postpone) things so that short circuits will not happen today. And when they do develop they will not be short, they will be very long. We are standing on the verge of such dissatisfaction, on the verge of such irritation, of such long lines, and of conflict within families. The list of nationality conflicts has been loaded to such a point that it is possible to expect the most unpleasant matters. But I am an appeaser. I would like to lead people away from the meeting to their work. I would like to draw a man away from discussions or strikes. You have everything—so get rich! They gave you land. I propose, together with the Moscow group, to adopt a law on land, to return back into circulation the words of Lenin, which were the most revolutionary postscript: Power to the Soviets; the words about lifting the tax on farm produce, in the sense of national salvation and calming down the passions, in the sense of eliminating food shortages in 2-3 years. It must be done now and not sometime later! If we do not adopt the law on land by our next session, our fall meeting in a festive manner with the singing of national hymns—may it be—then the price we will have to pay will be one of no confidence in us. And as for the Moscow group, let us take the wind out of their sails! We already have so many people from Chelyabinsk and Orenburg, and people from Kamchatka, Chukotka, Kursk, and God knows where. They are asking for a human discussion. It seems that a small hall has been given to us here, in the Presidium of the Supreme Soviet. And we invite all, including Meshalkin—what a pity Nina Andreyeva is not here, for we would invite her with great pleasure as an indicator of novelty! [sporadic applause]

[Paton] Thank you. [applause]

[Deputy Vitaliy Nikolayevich Kalish from Zaporozhye] Esteemed deputies, it is a great honor for a worker to get to this rostrum. [passage omitted]

I would like to propose instructing the government, beginning with 1990, to stop bringing the 100 percent order to enterprises of ferrous metallurgy, but to formulate it within the bounds of 80 percent, and to hand over the remaining 20 and everything produced above-plan for the needs of the countryside and first and foremost...[applause] to resolve such fundamental problems as water and gas supply and remaining villages. [applause]

Among the many problems that have swamped our life, one has appeared that in all its acuteness has in a number of places moved to the category of immediate problems. It is the ecological problem. It has already been stated that, in connection with this problem, various informal associations, spontaneous and organized meetings, demonstrations, and various kinds of ultimatums have appeared. This problem is particularly acute in the town of Zaporozhye. According to official data, this town heads a list of the 10 most ecologically-troubled towns in the country. [passage omitted]

I'd like to touch upon the question of social justice. In the press and, as far as can be seen from the debates, at our congress certain comrades are primitively reducing it to depriving so-called bureaucrats of illegal benefits. It suits us that in his report Mikhail Sergeyevich proposed creating a commission to review all of these privileges. I would not like this question to be reduced to just this. I want to ask myself, and you, a question: Why, in spite of persistent propaganda in our press about the various kinds of cooperatives, does the working class regard many of them with hostility? The cooperatives have not produced tangible benefits. The possibility of receiving enormous incomes has been aroused in the minds of many people and we can observe a clear outflow of qualified working people from state enterprises, and, incidentally, qualified, and I would say the most highly qualified because, as has been said here, all of the intelligent ones are going where they can make money.

As a steel founder I can't make such money, and I want to ask you: What would happen if we, the qualified steel founders, all left? In particular, considering the quality metallurgical equipment I operate, what would happen? Who will produce quality metals for you, eh? Where will you get the metal for those planes and satellites? Where, in general, will you get normal equipment so that combines and machines in general aren't cursed here? Cooperatives...I think that here things are going directly in reverse, toward the disintegration of state enterprises. [applause] [passage omitted]

Polarization has taken place as a consequence of this. At one pole more Soviet millionaires are appearing, and at the other end are those who can hardly make ends meet. [applause]

Cooperatives have become a convenient way of legalizing stolen money. [applause] Or here is another question regarding social justice. People here from Moscow, Kiev, and other inhabitants of capitals must not be offended. In Moscow and in other major cities meat and sausage are sold at state prices. Why is it that I, a steel founder, and thousands like me, have to buy all of this at cooperative prices, although I know that all of this is transported here from my oblast? I would like to hear...[applause] from economists about how to feed people in a fair way.

And the last thing: As a Communist and a steel founder of 30 years standing who took an active position in life at all times, I cannot not touch upon one important—in my view—problem: I'm talking about the party apparatus. [passage omitted]

[Deputy Aleksandr Adamovich Grakhovskiy, chairman of the executive committee of the Gomel Oblast Soviet of People's Deputies of Belorussia]

Esteemed comrade deputies, I wish to devote the chief part of my speech to our nationwide tragedy, the accident at the Chernobyl Atomic Energy Station [AES]. And I ask you to forgive me for beginning with what is for us such a sad and, at the same time, shameful fact.

With each day the accident moves further and further away into history, but its acuteness is not lost. Today this is one of the most sore points of our public life, but above all it is the cause of heartache, worry, and ordeals for the population that suffered. For this reason we, more than anyone else, empathize with and understand the alarm and concern that has been heard in the speech by the poet Boris Ilich Oleynik, whom we admire.

I also dwell on this matter because the elimination of the consequences of the accident not only, and not so much, require local efforts, but above all the participation of the whole country. We have suffered this tragedy from the first days of the accident, and today we bear the weight of its consequences on our shoulders. And our burden is not a light one, since proportionately Gomel Oblast is the most contaminated territory in the European part of the USSR.

I want your understanding on the following matter. I am speaking from this high rostrum as one of the direct participants in the work to eliminate the consequences of the accident. I mention this not for the purposes of self-advertisement, but so you will understand and feel close to our daily concerns and worries.

During the initial period we were not left in bitter isolation. The whole country came to our assistance, as a result of which a whole lot of work was carried out in tackling immediate tasks. However, the measures being taken are not reducing the acuteness of the situation. The radiation situation on the territory of the oblast remains complex. Practical experience and scientific forecasts show that no significant improvement in the situation can be expected in the next few years.

We carried out the evacuation of the population in three stages. But there are populated localities in the oblast today where the carrying out of agromeliorative measures in conjunction with decontamination and improvement of facilities do not guarantee safe habitation by people. Another repatriation lies ahead, the fourth. But for it to be the last, the radiation situation and the possible burden of radiation for each separate populated locality must be examined in the most serious manner. Nor can social and living conditions be taken off the agenda. The USSR Ministry of Health must determine... [changes thought] get its bearings on this issue as soon as possible, and provide us with appropriate proposals.

I consider it appropriate to appeal to the scientific community as a whole, and urge you, esteemed comrades scientists, to considerably accelerate all the scientific research work in our Chernobyl testing ground, which—and this is not meant as an offense—was the result of your activities. Here I am in complete agreement with the view of esteemed Vasiliy Ivanovich Belov. Unfortunately, in the 3 years sinc the accident, we have not been supplied with effective technologies, mechanisms, and equipment for decontaminating settlements and agricultural tracts, and a whole range of other proplems and issues remain unresolved. Owing to a considerable part of the land being taken out of commission and the need to supply the area's inhabitants with meat and dairy products from elsewhere, the food problem has been severely aggravated in the oblast. The planning bodies are not taking into account the damage inflicted on the oblast or its requirements for supplying the population with food products in line with scientifically-based medical norms. As you can see, the situation is blantantly abnormal, and this is causing increased social tension.

We are constantly bringing up these issues with the USSR Gosplan and the USSR State Agro-Industrial Committee. There have been instructions from the CPSU Central Committee Politburo, yet still no practical measures have been taken. We believe that the union deliveries must be adjusted in line with our losses and the additional requirements regarding supplies to the inhabitants of the affected region. Our people did not ask for the misfortune that struck them; and their interests must be protected.

Matters connected with the cash allowances being given to people in connection with the restriction of consumption of food products from their private plots have not been fully resolved. People of retirement age have ended up in a particularly bad situation: More than 40,000 retirees receive a pension of less than the average subsistence level. They were affected by the Chernobyl disaster and have an average pension of around R50, or to be more precise, of R47. It is very difficult to survive on such a cash allowance in normal circumstances, let alone in our circumstances. Finding a rapid solution to this issue is our duty and, of course, a matter for our consciences.

You are perfectly aware of just how severe the question of providing our population with highly qualified medical care is. The construction work required to set up the appropriate medical establishments is going ahead, but there is nothing to fill them with; there is still a shortage of medical equipment, instruments, and medicine. The way things are done now, it will be a long time before we are supplied with domestically produced equipment; the only solution is to acquire it abroad. We fully realize and understand that the country has no foreign currency to spare, but given the extraordinary nature of the situation, some must be found. There are problems in improving people's health, particularly that of children. We have begun setting up our own facilities outside the oblast, but without help from elsewhere we will not cope with the task. The question of providing people with extra dosimeters and monitoring devices has been frequently raised, and instructions were also issued on this matter by the CPSU Central Committee Politburo. Yet there are still no dosimeters or devices. We think the time has now come to hold some people responsible for this.

Owing to contamination of considerable tracts of forest peat-bog, procurement of firewood and the production of peat briquettes are falling each year. By the middle of the 13th 5-Year Plan the shortage of fuel produced by the oblast will amount to more than 40 percent. The present circumstances and the medical and hygene conditions in the area make it essential to make gas available throughout the oblast immediately.

In order to tackle Chernobyl and other severe social problems in a good, timely way, we must considerably accelerate the construction of housing and sociodomestic amenities. We are not asking for builders to be sent from other parts of the country, but given the situation, we consider it essential that as of next year we be released from housing construction in Tyumen, and that industrial construction in the oblast be virtually stopped.

The list of unresolved issues and problems is a long one, but it could have been considerably shorter if the USSR Government commission for eliminating the consequences of the Chernobyl Nuclear Electric Power Station accident had worked harder, if it had concerned itself not only with the atomic power station but with the entire affected region. This list must now be systematized, with measures, deadlines, those responsible, and the means to be used specified for each point.

Given that clearing up the aftermath of the Chernobyl nuclear electric power station accident is a long-term business, it is essential for the union bodies to be involved. We believe that it is most essential to draw up this year in the country a comprehensive USSR state program for eliminating the consequences of the Chernobyl nuclear electric power station accident, on the basis of an analysis of what has been done and a scientific prediction. [applause] And in order for this document to be binding on all, it must be confirmed by the USSR Supreme Soviet. A major measure like this would have a positive effect on the population's safety, and the sociopolitical feelings in a large part of the country would rule out diverse approaches—above all, profiteering from the Chernobyl disaster—and would make it possible to advance more concretely along the path of radical social, economic, and political transformations.

Comrades, the way in which our congress is developing and the processes underway in the regions invite each of us to do some very deep thinking. On the one hand, one can understand that deputies are eager to guarantee the stable and irreversible devlopment of democracy and glasnost and the quickest possible solution to social, economic, interethnic, ecological, and other problems. On the other hand, one cannot fail to notice—and on a number of issues this is causing concern—that some deputies are attempting to divert us from finding cardinal solutions to urgent matters by trying to impose their own, at times dubious, points of view. Instead of profound analysis of the basic causes of various adverse processees and the drawing-up of practical measures for solving them, we are hearing calls for mass rally democracy and unnecessary and lengthy debates and discussions that are sometimes of little benefit. I accept democratization and glasnost only where there is strict self-discipline, organization, and responsibility for the task with which one has been entrusted, where people are aware of the individual's role in society. In all their other manifestations they take on demagogical forms with elements of anarchy and slackness. [applause]

Therefore, I would like to support the appeals heard in this hall for more constructive work, consolidation of all forces, and a responsible attitude from deputies toward the tackling of the problems faced. This, comrades, is of exceptional importance; our congress should serve the people as a model, a school, of businesslike creativity and a profoundly intelligent approach to getting the country out of its present state.

I cannot agree with individual deputies who have proposed that we get down to adopting laws and decrees right away, without even forming the congressional bodies and the government. We do, of course, need laws, but I believe that drawing up good draft laws is no easy matter. Speed is not of the essence here. It is perfectly obvious today that in the past, too, many fine plans were deformed in their development due to the hasty adoption of a whole series of decisions and underestimations of possible socioeconomic repressions. This applies to the weak points of the law on the state enterprise and the law on cooperatives, and indeed to the measures for combating drunkenness and alcoholism. Therefore, when drawing up draft laws it would be more sensible to rely on qualified legal thinking, on national traditions and territorial peculiarities, on the wisdom of all peoples of our country, and on experience in the regions. This is why I am in favor of broad representation of all social strata of the population in the USSR Supreme Soviet. Setting it up only on the principle of the deputies' level of professionalism can be no guarantee of the perfection of its functions. [applause] Each of us can continuously participate in the work of the Supreme Soviet by maintaining contacts with our representations, and this should not by any means offend or insult any of us.

As a Communist and a citizen I am particularly concerned by the wholesale slander of party cadres that has got underway. They were subjected to massed attacks during the election fight, and we should not close our eyes to this. Their adversaries stopped at nothing; false rumours, falsification of the true state of affairs, and other techniques were brought into play. I do not consider them or any other category of worker clear of blame for the existing failings and major shortcomings in society: We are all guilty together, and it is up to us jointly to bring society up to a qualitatively new level. But the method that has been selected may lead to a loss of businesslike cadres. It is inflicting great damage on the party as a whole, and our common cause can only suffer because of this. Thank you.

[Paton] On the instructions of the Presidium of the congress, the floor is given to Deputy Lippmaa, Endel Teodorovich, from the Estonian Soviet Socialist Republic [SSR].

[Lippmaa] Esteemed Congress and esteemed visitors! The issue of the 1939 treaties with Nazi Germany has been raised by many delegations and in many speeches. In this connection we submit a draft decision for the analysis of these most complicated problems. It reads as follows:

Decision of the Congress of USSR People's Deputies on forming a commission to legally assess the 1939 Soviet-German Nonaggression Treaty—the so-called Molotov-Ribbentrop Pact—and the secret additional protocol to the pact. The Congress of People's Deputies of the USSR decides:

1. To form a commission to formulate a political and legal assessment of the 1939 Soviet-German Nonaggression Treaty and the secret additional protocol—that is to

say, the protocol on the territorial and political reorganization of Eastern Europe, and the Baltic countries and Poland, and documents linked with it. The members of the commission are to be Lyudmila Akopovna Arutyunyan, head of a department at Yerevan State University in the City of Yerevan; Georgiy Arkadiyevich Arbatov, director of the USA and Canada Institute; Yuriy Nikolayevich Afanasyev, rector of the Moscow State Historical Archives Institute, city of Moscow; Ilmar Olgertovich Bisers, professor at the Stucka Latvian State University of the City of Riga; Mavrik Germanovich Vulfson, senior teacher at the Latvian Academy of Arts, city of Riga; Igor Nikolayevich Gryazin, head of a department at the Institute of Philosophy, Sociology and Law of the Academy of Sciences of the Estonian SSR, city of Tartu; Aleksey Ivanovich Kazannik, faculty lecturer at Omsk State University, city of Omsk; Vitaliy Alekseyevich Korotich, chief editor of OGONEK, city of Moscow; Vitautas Vitautovich Landsbergis, professor at the Lithuanian SSR State Conservatoire, city of Vilnius; Maryu Yokhannesovna Lauristin, head of a department at Tartu State University, city of Tartu; Endel Teodorovich Lippmaa, director of the Institute of Chemical and Biological Physics of the Estonian SSR Academy of Sciences, city of Tallinn; Kazimir Vladislavovich Motieka, lawyer at the Vilnius No. 1 legal consultation office, city of Vilnius; Nikolay Vasilyevich Neilands, Latvian SSR deputy minister of foreign affairs, city of Riga; Edgar Elmarovich Savisaar, deputy director Maynor special planning and design office of the city of Tallinn; (?Zita Leonovna Snicyte), lawyer at the Klaipeda legal consultation office, city of Klaipeda; Aleksey Mikhaylovich Ridiger, metropolitan Aleksiy of Leningrad and Novgorod, city of Leningrad; Valentin Mikhaylovich Falin, head of the CPSU Central Committee International Department; and in addition one deputy each on representation from the delegations of the Ukraine, Belorussia and Moldavia. As chairman of the commission, we propose Chingiz Aytmatov, writer, city of Frunze. That was the first point.

2. To make it incumbent upon the Foreign Affairs Ministry... [Lippmaa corrects himself] I beg your pardon—we also had proposals about these three possible candidatures from the Ukraine, Belorussia, and Moldavia, although this is, of course, a matter for their delegations: These were Vladimir Ilarionovich Shinkaruk, director of the Institute of Philosophy; Vasiliy Vladimirovich Bykov, writer; and Ion Panteleyevich Drutse, writer.

So: 2. To make it incumbent upon the USSR Foreign Affairs Ministry and other departments and archives to make all necessary material available to the commission.

3. The commission will present its conclusions to the USSR Supreme Soviet by the end of June this year and will make the results of its activity public.

The question arises: Why such haste? This is because the 50th anniversary of this agreement with Hitler on the division of Europe falls on 23 August this year, and for that reason we must do something immediately. Besides this, there were proposals that this pact should be denounced from the moment it was signed. That is not a bad proposal, but many of our deputies do not know the text, in the first place, and in the second place that is not enough. Conclusions must be drawn from this. The

reality alone is not enough; from this new ones emerge. It is essential, therefore, to set up a commission. The draft includes deputies from the Estonian delegation, with active participation by Lithuania and Latvia and primarily our Presidium.

[Paton] Comrade deputies! If there are no objections let's confirm the proposal that has been put before us and vote on it. Are there no objections?

[Gorbachev] No, the question... [drowned by noise from the floor] [passage omitted]

[Gryazin] Gryazin, national-territorial constituency No 473, Parnu. This question of what to do with these treaties and protocols has already been broached. It is a juridical matter, whether to denounce or not denounce, whether to annul or not annul them. Incidentally, just now a rather original idea was expressed that in 1941 some of the treaties became invalid. This idea is an original one and also merits examination. This is precisely why the commission is being set up. What is to be done with them? What are we talking about? Forgive me, these eight lines of printed text merit being read aloud. Let me read them: 23d August 1939. Moscow. Point one: In the event of territorial and political reorganizations [preobrazovaniya] in areas belonging to the Baltic states—Finland, Estonia, Latvia and Lithuania—the northern border of Lithuania will represent the line dividing the spheres of influence of Germany and the USSR. In this connection, Lithuania's interest in the region of Vilnius is acknowledged by both sides.

Second: In the event of territorial and political reorganizations in areas belonging to the Polish state, the spheres of influence of Germany and the USSR wil be delimited approximately along the line of the rivers Narew, Wisla, and San.

The next bit is very interesting: The matter of whether the preservation of the independence of the Polish state and of the borders of that state is desirable in the interests of both sides will be finally decided only by the course of future political events. In any case, both governments will resolve this matter by means of friendly accord.

Third: Concerning southeastern Europe, the Soviet side has indicated its interest in Bessarabia. The German side clearly stated its complete lack of political interest in these territories.

Fourth: This protocol is considered by both sides as strictly secret. Signatures: Joachim von Ribbentrop for the German Government; Vyacheslav Molotov, USSR Government plenipotentiary. This is the text that we are talking about. Is it correct or incorrect; what should be done? This is why we need a commission. It is impossible for a decision to be taken now. A commission is needed. I ask you to vote for this commission. Thank you. [applause]

[Paton] Esteemed comrades, one moment. I see another nine people wishing to speak. [noise in hall] Let's give each person up to 1 minute. [uproar] Please, go ahead Roy.

[Medvedev] Well, I won't introduce myself since I am known here. Comrades, I think our stormy reaction is related not so much to the fact that the commission has been proposed—and I have no doubts whatsoever that such a commission is necessary—but to the fact that the commission has been proposed in this particular composition. As a historian, I must tell you that we Soviet historians are not ashamed to say that Russia conquered the Northern Caucasus. We are not even ashamed to display in our museums the famous picture of the conquest of Siberia by Yermak. But to this day, in our official historical works, in our articles and in our publications appearing in Moscow, we write that Estonia, Latvia and Lithuania voluntarily joined the Soviet Union; that this was a popular revolution, that there was no force and there were no threats, whatsoever, and that this was the completely voluntary will of the Lithuanian, Estonian, and Latvian peoples. This is not true. It was, of course, an act taken while the imperialist war was already underway, and at a time when not only the Soviet Union, but all the others as well—Germany, Japan, Britain, and France—had no respect at all for the rights of small countries and peoples and solved their problems taking no account either of the neutrality of Belgium, Holland, Finland, or other countries. Therefore, such a commission must be set up and we must, finally, arrive at a correct evaluation of these pacts. But the commission should include not only authoritative representatives of Estonia, Latvia and Lithuania. The commission should also include statesmen of our country, and I am surprised that our comrades have proposed, for example, that Chingiz Aytmatov, who is respected by me and by all of us, be made chairman of the commission, and not USSR Foreign Minister Shevardnadze, for example.

That is, I propose that a decision be adopted on setting up such a commission, but that the members of the Estonian and Latvian delegations work further on the individual composition of the commission along with the Presidium and members of the Soviet Government and the Politburo. [applause]

[Gorbachev] Comrades, can I ask to introduce, out of turn, some clarity into this problem? This problem has been on the agenda for a long time. It is being discussed. It is being studied. It is being studied by historians, political scientists, relevant departments alike. And I must say that while we are holding scientific discussions within specific departments, all the documents, including the secret appendix to the treaty, have already been published everywhere, including the Baltic press, which has published all that.

However, all the attempts to find this original of the secret treaty [as heard] have been unsuccessful. If there are those who deal with these questions, they would have noticed that I had touched upon this question both during the conversation with the Polish comrades and the Polish press, as well as in my concluding remarks following the meeting with Poland's intelligentsia.

We have been dealing with this question for a long time. There are no originals There are copies. It is not known what they are copies of, but they bear signatures. What gives rise to a particular [as heard] among us is that Molotov's signature is written in German letters.

When Chancellor Kohl was here... [Gorbachev changes thought] Maybe it was a one-to-one conversation, as they say, but once it assumes this sort of dimension here, so to speak, it is, apparently, worthwhile and Mr Chancellor will surely not be quick to take offence, as it were, because I will reveal this secret of the talks.

There were particularly confidential issues, one-to-one issues to the exclusion of everyone else altogether. And, in particular, I asked him: Do you have the originals of these treaties, with the appendices? He said: We do; that they do have them. I say: In that case please give them to us. And we sent Foreign Ministry representatives, right, Eduard Amvrosiyevich? [barely audible yes heard in reply] And we did send them on the basis of this accord, and the originals were not to be found there, either.

That is why I... [Gorbachev changes thought] this information is for reflection, as it were. But, all in all, the issue is a serious one, requiring a scientific and political analysis. I do not want to simplify it. But the fact is that it must be discussed and a evaluation of it must be arrived at, as the comrade suggested.

That is why I would favor setting up the commission, since this is a request, as it were, from several delegations. But I would [as heard] in this commission, apart from the fact that I asked comrades to see who else should be included, I think this commission must be expanded. That is why the Presidium which proposed it should ask the congress for permission to have time granted. And competent people, so to speak, should become members of it, on the basis of consultations both with our scientists and the Academy of Sciences and another one. This is because the matter is a very serious one. This is the first thing.

Here is the second point: Since I have given you this particular piece of information, including details of my conversation with Mr Kohl...[Gorbachev changes thought] I would not talk in advance about deciding to set up a commission—and first of all, there are different interpretations here—to make a political and legal evaluation, to carry out a legal evaluation of the Soviet-German nonaggression treaty and the secret supplementary protocol to the pact.

The secret protocol is not at hand yet and we cannot assess it. Generally speaking, I think that it should be a commission—I would indeed agree with this—to draw up a political and legal evaluation of the nonaggression treaty, without mentioning...since this...all the archives of ours that we have turned upside down...although I can tell you that the historians there know, and could tell you about this now, that something did happen: Two powerful forces were heading toward each other and at a certain point these adjoining forces stooped completely, and so something must have been at the basis of it. But for the moment these are still only arguments. So an investigation is needed here, an analysis of all the documents and of the whole situation as it evolved, including the way the Soviet Government treated the treaty when the war started. And what we did was deem it invalid.

I think that this whole set of questions must be evaluated, because the Baltic region is seething as these issues are debated. In connection with this, doubt is cast on whether the will of the people was involved at all in the incorporation into the Soviet Union. That is scarcely the truth. All this must be studied. Thus I would have the congress set up a commission to carry out a political evaluation and legal evaluation of the Soviet-German treaty, and afterward it should be constituted at the appropriate level, and let them get on with it, let them get on with it and give us their qualified view of this matter. I do not even know if they will get at the truth on the first attempt or not. No doubt it is no simple matter. But since the question exists, we should not try to evade or duck it, I believe. As we have said, in the course of restructuring there are many acute problems. All the same, let us not duck them; let us approach them and get down to studying them. If the comrades deem it necessary before the adoption [of a decision] on the composition of the commission for some kind of information or preliminary considerations to be given on behalf of the Foreign Ministry, we could ask Comrade Shevardnadze to speak and tell us something on this matter, some preliminary [details], so that the comrades, so to speak...if this is necessary. [sentence as heard] But I think, I think that the most important thing is to set up a commission of this sort; I think this is right. It should get down to work, and this will no doubt all come either to the Supreme Soviet or...then all deputies will know the results of the proceedings of this commission.

That is the clarification I wanted to give. We could thus now confine ourselves to this view, and if the comrades support the view that the commission should be set up, then let us give the Presidium time to continue the consultations and put qualified people on the commission. Yes, comrades? [shouts of approval] Fine, that is settled. [replying to indistinct shout from hall] No, comrades, Eduard Amvrosiyevich is not a deputy. Ministers are not deputies; they are not deputies. Let us instruct two of our international affairs experts from the Central Committee and the Politburo. Let us have Yakovlev; let us have Yakovlev on the commission. [applause] Let us have him. Fine.

[Paton] Comrade deputies, as I understand it, everyone has approved the proposal regarding the desirability of setting up a commission. And as far as its membership is concerned, Mikhail Sergeyevich has proposed—and I think that we will all adopt that proposal—that the Baltic delegations and the Presidium be instructed to give this matter additional consideration, as a large number of professionals and experts on this question still need to be included. Is that proposal adopted? [affirmative shouts] Thank you. [passage omitted]

Lithuania's Landsbergis Speaks

LD0206164489 Moscow Television Service in Russian 1340 GMT 1 Jun 89

[Speech by Deputy Vitautas Vitautovich Landsbergis from Lithuania at the Congress of People's Deputies, held in the Kremlin Palace of Congresses—live]

[Text] Esteemed congress, respected chairman. All of us here must try to understand each other, to see the general aims, to appreciate the noble aspirations of everyone, and to display this political culture as part of the people's general culture.

The striving of the Baltic republics to strengthen their sovereignty, to develop and to have statehood restored, is also the path to the liberation of the people's creative forces, one of the aims of restructuring. A gain on this path is essentially a gain for all—for example, the concept elaborated in the Baltic region of economic independence of republics. In Lithuania and in Estonia it has already acquired the force of law and is now proposed to the congress in the form of the draft of a union law which, as we see it, is useful for all republics. It would be a pity if it were to lie too long in a heap under the inscription: miscellaneous.

The problem of the survival of mankind, put by Mikhail Gorbachev above private, state, class, and ideological interests, is being recognized increasingly deeply. It is, nevertheless, being resolved in a concrete place. This is happening, for example, in Lithuania, which has already been placed on the brink of an ecological disaster. The problem of survival is becoming comprehensible for people of all nationalities, just as are financial autonomy, the struggle against inflation, and a more stable, more secure life. That is why the attempts by the anti-restructuring forces in our republic to sow suspicion, fears and dissension between nationalities are relatively ineffective. The heavy load of the old domestic political thinking accompanies restructuring. The new thinking is still, rather, for export. Perhaps the domestic market, which is in the stranglehold of limitations, has not yet ripened for it, or else it, too, has withered away in the protracted stagnation. The old thinking weighs particularly heavily on the gamut of ideas connected with the rights of peoples and republics. It is not in vain that this sphere of problems is most neglected concerning theory, while the practical pronouncements of the central leaders are not, unfortunately, devoid of psychological errors. The wisdom of the Russian people has long grasped that method of thinking, characterizing it with the bitter irony of proverbial sayings: The penetration and the generalizing capacity of these sayings as applied to state policy with regards to, for instance, the convulsions of the economy, or the tragedy of Afghanistan, are worth the work of many years standing of some social sciences institutes.

The relations between the center and the republics, which by habit are realized according to the command administrative method, have long since become obsolete—morally, practically, and politically. Democratization cannot manifest itself just in the sphere of human rights or of the work collective's rights, or in the sphere of freedom of conscience, speech, or economic freedoms. It inevitably also poses questions of the freedom of peoples and of the rights of republics. But if we have a distorted understanding of democracy as the power of the majority over the minority, it will also set its traps for restructuring.

That is why the democratization of such a complex country should presuppose guarantees that the republics will not be encroached upon by any kind of pseudo-democratic procedure of voting by the majority. Guarantees are necessary, since we are moving from a strong-arm to a law-governed state, so that no union republic feels itself to be in a situation of constant danger in the question of its vital rights to its land and its laws. For this, bearing in mind poorly developed legislation, the inertia of the great power thinking, and other defects of the current union, it is essential to immediately work out a parliamentary defense mechanism for the union states and their peoples. For instance, a chamber of the Soviet of Nationalities, set up on the basis of parity, could carry out a legislative and control function. Moreover, for the adoption of a law binding to all republics, the agreement and approval of each would be demanded with registration of the law by the republic's Supreme Soviet. So far there is no such union parliamentary mechanism. It is only natural that the repbulics which tackle the issue of self-determination with greater independence have set about creating a mechanism of legal self-defense on their own territory. For instance, on 18 May the Lithuanian SSR [Soviet Socialist Republic] Supreme Soviet adopted, among others, an amendment to Article 70 of the Lithuanian Soviet Socialist Republic Constitution which now says in particular: The laws of the USSR and the legislative acts of the bodies of state power and government of the USSR are in force on the territory of the Lithuanian SSR only once they have been approved by the Lithuanian SSR Supreme Soviet and registered according to the set procedure. I am quoting from the newspaper SOVETSKAYA LITVA, which was published the following day. Also stressed in a declaration of the Lithuanian SSR Supreme Soviet on the state of sovereignty of Lithuania, which was adopted on that same day. I quote: Henceforth, from the moment of adoption of the amendment ot Article 70 of the Lithuanian SSR Constitution, only laws adopted or ratified by its Supreme Soviet have force in the Lithuanian SSR.

Thinking about how long collisions with the obsolete Brezhnev union constitution and unnecessary political tension can be avoided, we propose to the congress that an amendment be introduced to Article 74 of the present USSR Constitution so that it read in full: The laws of the USSR have force on the territory of the union republics after their adoption and registration by the Supreme Soviet of the union republic. [applause] Availing myself of the opportunity, I submit to the congress this proposal from a group of deputies from Lithuania as a legislative initiative. [bustle in hall]

The country's democratization should presuppose also the defense of the process of democratization. In connection with this, I would like to recall the address directed here to the Congress of People's Deputies on the threat of a war between a state and its own people, which was adopted in Tallinn on 14 May this year by the Baltic Assembly of People's Fronts, including the Lithuanian Sajudis. It is to be read out separately and distributed as a document of the congress calling for the functions of the Armed Forces to be defined as exclusively defensive, and to be used only in the event of an external attack. These proposals are also included in the more detailed address to the USSR Congress of People's Deputies signed by 50 deputies from Latvia, Lithuania, and Estonia, which proposes as a legislative initiative a USSR Supreme Soviet decision which includes Point 4: to

disband the military units which took part in the murders and violence on the civilian population in the city of Tbilisi, as having disgraced themselves. [applause]

You will again be convinced from these documents that our hopes and cares concern everyone. It is our wish that the people never have experience of battle gases, even in peacetime. But the congress, which today is responsible for the destiny of democracy, must ensure that it gets rid of, well beforehand, any semblance of legislation peculiar to the coups of Napoleon and Pinochet.

Permit me to remind you that we are talking about the formal right of the minister of internal affairs, and his personal decision to set special forces in motion, and about the right of the USSR Supreme Soviet Presidium to declare a special situation even on the territory of the whole country at one and the same time. In other words, let us say, Mikhail Sergeyevich is taken prisoner and a ruling junta is openly announced. Are we really agreeing to provide them with such emergency powers without any control by the people? Do you really agree with a phantom appearing at each of your doors with a poor Constitution in one hand and a bloody shovel in the other, that kind of power of the law? [whistles, yells and applause from within the hall]

Lithuania, at any rate, does not agree! Accept these remarks as a proposal to the congress that every deputy personally should think carefully about this, return to the debate, and once again vote for the abolition of these decrees and subsequent addenda to the criminal legislation, especially on the section on state crimes. You must also think about what has already been done and what positions you have taken.

On the 3d day here, Deputy Rodionov went on nostalgically about 1937, and many deputies happily applauded him. Just think, comrade deputies, what you were applauding! All of us here are affected by such a dark and bloody stain on the history of the USSR as the Stalin-Hitler pact, about which a very serious debate has alrady begun here. The existence of secret protocols has been proved not only in the Nuremberg documents, but also by the scrupulous execution of secret protocols in 1939-41. The fact that they existed is, in my view, not doubted by Mikhail Sergeyevich, either. I propose that the commission's task be defined at least by such a title as "on the pact and the problem of secret protocols." The purpose of it has been clearly set out in the address to us by the Lithuanian Soviet Socialist Republic Supreme Soviet—to condemn the aforementioned secret deals signed by the Soviet Government of that time, and to proclaim them illegal and ineffective from the moment of signing. There is no doubt that this will be done. It is better for all of us if this ambiguous rubberband is not stretched any further.

In which way should we be looking today, in what direction? Restructuring also means going back to the words with their proper meaning. The term union means neither compulsion nor subordination [soyuz eto ne pri-yuz i ne pod-yuz]. Union is an amalgamation of allies which, not forcibly but voluntarily, have joined for the common purpose on the basis of consent and benefit. Such a union is not close at hand but it can come. It can do this thanks to restructuring and by helping restructuring. New concepts derived from the best of Lenin's legacy and deriving nothing at all from Stalin's are necessary. May ours become a union of states and a union of fatherlands! If the spiritual rebirth of nations strengthens and produces material results it will again acquire the form of fatherlands, including Russia—self-governing states of the people, growing from the principle of people's sovereignty, impregnating the will of the people, the owners of their land. Then it will be they—the peoples and the states—who will decide which mutual treaties their unions will conclude. Such a concept is capable of embracing whole regions, be they in the east or in northern Europe, joining them together and opening up more realistic prospects for the celebrated European home.

Who knows, perhaps there will even be an additional road of the spiritual drawing together of Europe and Asia and of Christianity and Islam.

Of course, the "European home" will then cease to be in the form of a hostel under the authority of an all-knowing and all-suspicious commandant, but rather in the form of a peaceful village where no one fears anyone and where one can share work, goods, assistance, and the joys of goodneighborliness without formality. Thank you. [applause]

2 Jun Congress Proceedings Reported

Georgian Education Official Speaks

LD0206191189 Moscow Television Service in Russian 0643 GMT 2 Jun 89

[Speech by Shalva Aleksandrovich Amonashvili, director general of the experimental science-production association of the Georgian Soviet Socialist Republic Education Ministry, at the Congress of People's Deputies, held in the Kremlin Palace of Congresses—live]

[Excerpts] Esteemed chairman of the Supreme Soviet, esteemed deputies, yesterday deputies from Georgia had a meeting with Mikhail Sergeyevich Gorbachev. It was an extremely frank [otkrytaya] meeting, straight talking, where we were able to express our thoughts, our feelings, explain certain phenomena and, for his part, Mikhail Sergeyevich also explained a lot to us. I am convinced that the commission which you, the congress, set up will sort out everything superbly and will make the necessary, true, only true decisions, and this truth will be spoken. We all need truth—you need it, and we need it, for in our country which is being built on the basis of new principles, principles of humanization and democratization of society, glasnost, this truth of ours will be as a weapon to fight for the salvation of people's souls. But it is very complicated for us now.

I shall not now dramatize the situations which have happened to us, and perhaps it is no longer worth talking about all the events. But I want to speak about it from the viewpoint of the upbringing of the future generation. First, I should like to say that the telegrams which were read out were not known to us, but, most importantly, I simply want to tell you, dear deputies, that the idea that it was allegedly drug addicts and alcoholics who had gathered on the square does not correspond to the truth, for in the thousands of people who were standing there may have been extremists and people of other tendencies, but mainly they were talented young people who were aiming to achieve sovereignty for the republic. [sounds of animation in the hall]

I want to say a few words about the state of the schools which is causing many of our problems, and will continue to cause them. Our schools have become extremely authoritarian. Clearly this is a logical phenomenon, since over a period of many years authoritarianism itself affected our whole country, and this authoritarianism was reflected, mirror-like, in our schools as well. [passage omitted: expanding on this theme; more needs to be spent on education; Georgian language is used in schools and this is okay, but the history taught is too lop-sided, not enough Georgian history; one must be very sensitive to national feelings]

I know that my speech is being listened to in Tbilisi, and there are various event happening there. And so I want them to know, and I also want to tell you, that the article which was referred to by General Rodionov was written during the military curfew, and I ask you, please do not think that it was on the basis of those events which happened there. And let us allow the commission to determine fully the whole picture of what happened there. [passage omitted: the union must be kept together not by force, but by common spiritual values and friendships; appeal to deputies speaking at congress to show restraint in dealing with ethnic matters; different minority languages should be allowed to be used at the congress]

Allow me to say a few words in Georgian, and they will be addressed to our young children in Tbilisi, and I ask you also to listen to it. I assure you that I shall not be saying anything that could split us and destroy our common purpose and our love. But, forgive me for one thing. I want you all, dear comrades, to be fully aware that Georgia has never gone for nationalism, and never will. And those words alleging that [applause] there were anti-Russian actions there, alleging that there were calls for secession and so forth—there are individual happenings, but they are not a reflection of the Georgian soul. It is free. It strives for friendship, and if you go there, you will find hospitality, you will certainly be embraced and, perhaps I'll offend our government if I say that there will be wine and vodka standing on your table! [laughter and applause] [passage omitted: brief address in Georgian] [applause]

Aytmatov Addresses Congress

LD0206214589 Moscow Television Service in Russian 0655 GMT 2 Jun 89

[Speech by Chingiz Aytmatov, chairman of the board of the Khirghiz Soviet Socialist Republic Union of Writers and chief editor of INOSTRANNAYA LITERATURA, to the Congress of People's Deputies session at the Kremlin Palace of Congresses—live]

[Excerpts] There is an expression: We meet at last [Vot my i svidelis]. [audience laughs] This phrase refers to a certain stage in a conversation, a difficult conversation, between people. I would like to say this today to you: We meet again. Here at this building site, where we are erecting together the buildings of a new democracy, there is quite a lot of crowding, disorganization, and lack of restraint. Naturally, you worry. Throughout these days I have felt both pain and hope; nevertheless, I have never stopped hoping. Whatever happens, the work goes on; walls are being built and this is the main thing.

From the first minutes, the issue of the forum of the people's deputies has worried us all. Should it have the unconditional mandate of a supreme body in an independent democracy? Or will it again be an obedient and convenient tool in the hands of the ruling bureaucracy? It can already be stated with confidence that in overcoming the thorny skirmishes of polemics and inner struggles, interpreting and re-interpreting its past and present, the congress has gained the appearance of a democratic phenomenon which is fundamentally new in our history, in our consciousness, in our...in world public opinion. After decades of the people keeping silent, after decades of abstract promises and the triumph of abstract communism, after severe spiritual enslavement, after ideological and economic totalitarianism, self-deception and lies, our democratic aspirations are being reflected in a civilized law-making setting. And let this be just the beginning.

But it is already difficult to overestimate the significance of the phenomenon in question—not only for the fate of the fatherland but, on the whole, for the entire world as well, for we are a part of the human race.

How surely we are able to find a way out of a very serious economic crisis; how far we will be absorbed with constructive activities in the organization of a law-based state and freedoms of the individual; how far we will flourish in the settling of interethnic relations; how harmoniously we will be able to integrate with the living, interacting structure of the world community; how far we will be able to develop in ourselves an understanding of the priority of universal human values and get rid of the barbarism of the teaching of world revolution; and how far we will be less dogmatic and less aggressive in our discussions and ideological confrontations with other societies—will depend on the extent to which we lighten the fate of contemporary humanity and, of course, of ourselves.

Everywhere people are now glued to their television sets, worrying and concealing in their hearts hope for better things. And this is how it should be. We are a great multinational state and positive impulses should emanate from us—as well as positive experience—even when we are preoccupied with exclusively internal business and even when our social calamities are being discussed. How will we live in the future? How will we find our way out in full view of the whole world?

Every economy has—allow me to have my say on this—the economy...[Aytmatov changes thought] In this country there are no clear economic conceptions. And this is the stumbling block. A very dangerous state of affairs has gone too far. Against a background of mass dissatisfaction and censure, it is not of course especially difficult to trot out criticism, attracting the attention of television viewers. In this sense, we will all succeed. But

no one really knows how to practically increase the quantity and quality of output, how to achieve this on a nationwide state. Inspired by the spirit of restructuring and glasnost, we are now beginning to see clearly the material crisis which is just around the corner. And if we suppose, fairly, that the cause of our misfortunes lies mainly in our shortsighted and incompetent leadership, the ineffectiveness of reforms and the inconsistency of restructuring, then this is still far from being the whole story. You cannot travel on a cart without wheels, however much you whip the horses.

The transition from labor which is essentially forced, from the legacy of barrack-like socialism, which categorically excludes an individual's initiative, enterprise, and ability to compete, from considering the transition to be intolerable from the class point of view and from expressing unacceptable opposition to its levelling, unifying, and faceless policy—all this cannot happen in any other way. It gave birth to the most terrible evil. Its name is universal alienation. The total alienation of everyone from everything. The government from the people, the people from the government. Up to the most recent times, the people were pushed aside from living politics and here, before our very eyes, a break, a mass break is taking place in interpreting the situation of society by the people themselves. [Passage omitted: need to overcome alienation in society, musings on the nature of socialism]

While we were surmising, judging, and laying down the law as to what socialism must and cannot be, other people already have it, have built it, and are enjoying its fruits. Moreover, with our experience, we have done them a good service in showing them how not to build socialism. I have in mind such prosperous, law-based societies as Sweden, Austria, Finland, Norway, the Netherlands, and finally Spain, Canada across the sea, not to mention Switzerland, which is a model. Workers in those countries earn an average of four or five times as much as our workers. We can only dream about the social security and level of prosperity enjoyed by workers in those countries. This is indeed real, if you like, trade union socialism, although these countries do not call themselves socialist; however, they are none the worse for that. [passage omitted: criticizing shortages in USSR; Stalin's idea of socialism is hopeless]

If we ourselves do not know how, we must learn how others know how to live and work under truly genuine socialism. In this connection, I have two small specific proposals, comrades. First, and this is enforced, but unavoidable: We must borrow from the West large sums in credits to alleviate the shortages. I understand that debts are bondage, but we have enormous potential. We will settle them in time; we will pay them off. We should borrow before it is too late. That is the most important emergency measure. [sounds of animation in hall]

To continue, yesterday we heard the appeal and speeches about agriculture. It was a universal cry for the countryside. Anyone who grew up in a peasant family would want to cry even more. We must help the peasantry with all our might. I propose, by analogy with the alternative offered to military service in European countries—when a conscientious objector does his military service by working at cancer hospitals as a medical orderly, for example—something similar could be done if recruits willing to serve their Army term in the countryside were allowed to do so. The more so, in that universal conscription is also not our finest adornment. [applause] At any rate, it seems to me that it is worth thinking about this matter.

After the economy, the second most acute problem is our inter-ethnic relations. It is a good thing that a commission on Tbilisi has been set up. Whatever happens, a legal guarantee against violence should be worked out for the peoples of our country. Overall, I agree with the idea of full socialist sovereignty for the union republics. Without that, the federative status becomes a fiction. However, in my view the improvement of sovereignty should be pursued in a methodical, considered, and consistent way, by means of statute and not emotion. And there should be no rush to dot the i's and cross the t's at the first attempt. What we have is too precious, and what we want too crucial. The problems of ethnic languages are closest to me, and I would like to dwell on them briefly. There is talk of a concept of state languages in the republics and of imparting a legal basis to this process. This is correct. A general model must be thought out. I think that the federated status of the state should also be integrated with the federated status of the country's languages, in the sense that the languages of the indigenous peoples of the union republics should function as state languages. Again sensible consistency and sensible and cogent coordination should, it seems to me, be observed in this area, too. Put briefly, the ethnic languages of the republics, ignored locally for so long, should be given "most favored" linguistic status in order that, revived, they may take their legitimate place. [applause]

This is a very difficult matter, and in particular in Central Asia. Many of our fellow citizens, unused to the presence of the languages of the indigenous peoples in official circles, see them as something that is in opposition to the Russian language. Let us get to the bottom of this. The genius of the Russian language has served us all to the full, and I cannot imagine our lives without this common cultural asset of ours in the future. The Russian language in this sense is unshakeable and universal. Nothing threatens it within the confines of the entire country. But it should not, because of its historical distribution, drive out other languages of the indigenous peoples existing side by side.

It is necessary to realize in this regard that every people is a people for so long as it has a command of its own language, and herein lies its cultural sovereignty. And as soon as, for one reason or another, it is deprived of the opportunity to use and cultivate its language, it ceases to be what it was and what it should be. This gives rise to the task of the harmonization of languages, principally on the basis of the concept of bilingualism, with preference being given under a "most favored" system to the language of the indigenous population, enshrined in state law. Thus far, not all of us are prepared to recognize this truth. We must opt for compromise, dialogue, and mutual rapprochement, and everything must be tackled on the basis of mutual advantage and mutual respect. [bell rings] Please forgive me, I need a couple more minutes.

[Lukyanov] Let us give him 2 more minutes, 2 minutes.

[Aytmatov] We must agree to compromises. Regrettably, the news media do not always promote this process, and this applies particularly to the central press. It has become all but a fashion to accuse of nationalism and regionalism any citizen standing up for his natural national needs. And at the same time, by encouraging nihilism and a denial of one's people as a people and by accusing normal, patriotic people of nationalism, these articles in the press, whether they want to or not, artificially stoke up undesirable and negative sentiments locally, in places where people have lived peacefully and could peacefully understand each other's common cares and problems. When nationality questions are involved, the press and television should look before they leap. For instance, KOMSOMOLSKAYA PRAVDA said quite seriously that the events in Alma-Ata were all but generated by the fact that many young people attending [word indistinct] schools still have classes in their own language. How is this to be understood and what should it be called? The sovereign rights of a socialist republic should not pass Kazakhstan by. This republic should not be made an exception to the rule, since the Kazakh people, one of the most ancient nations of the region, were not to blame for the fact that the country needed bread, and that numerous millions of people had to be resettled from the European part to the virgin lands, something which exerted a negative influence on the proportional demographic correlation. And now, at every convenient opportunity, the indigenous people are put in the corner and reminded of their place. [slight applause] The law and the Constitution should protect the cultural uniqueness of every people, out of consideration for the fact that the indigenous peoples, for instance in Central Asia—and that includes the Kazakh people—have no ethnic counterparts of their own outside their regions to enable a theoretical supposition to be made that if not here, then somewhere else abroad, the language and culture of a given nation will be preserved. Every people is unique.

Our press and television are also tactless regarding the Uzbek people, with the notion of the so-called Uzbek affair constantly being savored to please the man in the street. What does it have to do with the Uzbeks? Why the insult? Is it because this uniquely hardworking people has devoted its life to a thankless task such as the cultivation of cotton, and that for decades cotton has, apart from everything else, been one of the main items that earn net hard currency for the state purse? If organized crime does exist in particular areas, let the law deal with it without wounding the national honor of a people. [applause] [bell rings again] I wish to say the same thing in defense of the Crimean Tatar people. Excuse me - time is against me.

[Lukyanov] Finish what you have to say. Go on.

[Aytmatov] How long will we avoid tackling the crying shame of this tragic ethnic destiny? And in this state of affairs, our news media continue to sometimes present things as if this people all but deserved such an inhuman act of genocide. It is ludicrous. By what right is the opinion formed and judgment passsed on a whole people? Who possesses such a right? Even the Good Lord does not have the right. In the war years, was it really only the Crimean Tatars among whom traitors and turncoats were found and the others remained untainted? Things do not happen that way. War is war; it is a battle, it is heroism and suffering, it is chaos and cruelties, it is captivity and betrayal, it is victory and defeat. And all this can affect any people, and a dialectical attitude must be taken toward this, without degrading the dignity of a whole nation. [applause] I cannot fail to say that an injustice toward our country's German population is taking place to this day. Banished, scattered, and humiliated in the war years, they continue to this day to suffer political discrimination and homelessness. Cultural and administrative autonomy for Germans would help to perform a service not just to them, but to all of us. I do not doubt that German autonomy would be a model for all of us. [applause] Let us draw conculsions from the terrible past, so that it is not repeated in the future. It is necessary to draw up constitutional guarantees of the categorical inviolability of peoples as ethnic units and the categorical impermissibility of deportations of peoples for whatever political, state, or racial reasons and motives—for the sake of equal justice for all. The place of every people should be where it historically sprang up. [applause]

Lukyanov on Procedural Matters
LD0206212189 Moscow Television Service in Russian 0758 GMT 2 Jun 89

[Remarks by Anatoliy Lukyanov, candidate member of the CPSU Central Committee Politburo and first deputy chairman of the USSR Supreme Soviet, to the Congress of People's Deputies session at the Kremlin Palace of Congresses—live]

[Text] Comrades deputies, before declaring an interval I have the following to report to you. A question has been received from Deputy Shamikhim: I ask the presidium to announce the order of business of the congress-...[Lukyanov corrects himself] er Supreme Soviet on Saturday. Many people are interested in this.

What are the plans for Saturday? The congress has been working very strenuously, and so we think that the majority of the deputies taking part in the congress should take a rest on Saturday. Tomorrow, on Saturday, in line with requests many deputies have come up. Visits are being arranged for people's deputies, if they wish to go to a number of districts, enterprises and institutions in Moscow and Moscow oblast and meetings with representatives of labor collectives. I should tell you that many labor collectives would like to meet deputies from different parts of the country and hear your views.

It is proposed to organize a visit to the housing estate and sports complex at Krylatskoye, and also a number of enterprises and organizations in the Moscow region, several rayons. There are notices about this at the registration points. You've seen them. During the interval, please express your views so that we can organize these trips. In addition, there will be a notice about an exhibition of space technology where, by the way, deputies—deputy Kiselev came up to me about this—will get explanations about how much it costs in the first place, what the money is spent on and what our space technology is designed to do. Deputies who wish to take part in all these events should put their names down.

After the interval, Deputy Kiseleva will be the first to speak. A 30-minute interval is declared. [audience noise] Just a minute, comrades, pardon me. People are asking

about the Supreme Soviet. It is planned tomorrow to hold a session of the Councils of Elders of the chambers. That is 60 deputies, as you know, a small group. And in the afternoon the idea is to hold a session of the Soviet of the Union—the first organizational session. It'll be in the afternoon, at 1400 [1000 GMT].

Belorussian Deputy on Chernobyl
LD0206224189 Moscow Television Service in Russian 0837 GMT 2 Jun 89

[Speech by Zoya Nikolayevna Tkacheva, departmental head in Slavgorod Rayon hospital of Mogilev Oblast in the Belorussian Soviet Socialist Republic, at the Congress of People's Deputies in the Kremlin Palace of Congresses—live]

[Excerpts] Esteemed comrade deputies: I have been instructed to speak by deputies of Mogilev and Gomel oblasts, and also by deputies of other oblasts—by Momosova, Zhukovskaya, Golovnev, Kiskov and others; and I am also speaking on behalf of our electorate who live in the polluted areas of these oblasts. Briefly about myself: I am a doctor, a pediatrician. I have 20 years of work experience. I would have ceased to respect myself if from this podium today I had failed to raise the following questions: Today clean land, water, air, forests and meadows—something without which man cannot live but can only exist—have been taken away from us, inhabitants of these areas. The official resume of the Health Ministry published in the press, PRAVDA on 29 May 1989 are lacking in appropriate concern about the health of people and about the fate of future generations, in the concern that exists in reality. After all, this accident [Chernobyl] is the first of its kind and therefore there is no experience in the world in observations of this kind.

No! No substantial changes have yet occurred in the general sickness rate structure, although there are already the first omens: Children are being born with congenital cataract, reduction in the sharpness of sight, strained immune systems, increases in the number of anemia and myorcardic infarctions. Although it is too early for us today to speak in terms of figures, we will be doing so in 10-15 years.

Now it is necessary to pay attention to the qualitative side of diseases, in other words, to their progress. And I believe that up until now this question has not been studied at all. For not a single report-back reflects it. Biologists move in and live for years next to animals to study their behavior. This is what medical scientists should do. After all the complaints that the population of these areas present to us—indisposition, heightened fatigue, headaches, dry mouth—do not fit into any single nosology unit of diseases. [passage omitted: Tlacheva thinks that scientists could have done better. Would it not be a good idea to turn to foreign expertise]

It is necessary to say that the assessment by practicing doctors of the state of the health of the population living in the polluted areas diverges increasingly from that of medical scientists and leaders of the country's health care. I can compare this divergence as I have lived for many years now on this territory and I can see changes in the state of health of people before and after the accident. The experts that visit us, especially of high ranks, having stayed a few hours or days, try to prove to us that the people's state of health is not deteriorating. [passage omitted: examples of how they explain the changes, among which no mention is given to radiation. The Academy of Sciences could have done more to tackle the problem. No help has been given to the area in the form of healthy food or offering methods to diagnose lukemia early]

We believe that it is desirable to carry out planned stage-by-stage resettlement from the polluted areas. For life shows that it is not us who rule the situation, however much we might wish this, but we are ruled by it. At meetings with the electorate, people demanded that the question of settling people out should be resolved. After all at present people continue living in the areas where the total radiation dose exceeds the safety conception of 35 becquerel. [passage omitted: the electorate demands immediate evacuation and that the state should pay damages for the Chenobyl accident and that the retirement age should be brought back in the sphere of production: detail of this is given]

We are completing the elaboration of a state program for 1990 to 1995 envisaging moving people away from the areas where it is impossible to live without carrying out a range of measures for changing over to an ordinary way of life. We hope that the newly created government will consider and ratify this program. In order to implement it, a great deal of capital investments will be needed, which the republic is not able to raise in the situation that has arisen. In this connection we request the CPSU Central Committee and the USSR Ministers Council to give us the necessary help. [passage omitted: creation of a permanent body is needed to tackle the elimination of the consequences of the Chernobyl accident within the USSR Supreme Soviet so as to avoid tackling these problems on a voluntary basis as it is done now; Tlacheva wishes to submit for discussion by congress Likhanov's proposal on help for Chernobyl children and also children in other disaster areas; applause; Tkacheva hands over the address of her electorate to the presidium of the congress, which reflects all the questions she mentioned; she concludes by thanking people for attention; applause]

Abkhazia's Ardzinba Gives Address

LD0206225189 Moscow Television Service in Russian 0848 GMT 2 Jun 89

[Address by Vladislav Grigoryevich Ardzinba, director of the Abkhaz Institute of Language, Literature, and History under the Georgian Academy of Sciences, to the Congress of People's Deputies session at the Kremlin Palace of Congresses—live]

[Excerpts] Esteemed deputies: [passage omitted] The official condemnation of the personality cult at the 20th party congress did not result in the legacy of Stalinism being scrapped. This legacy continues to make itself felt. Serious offenses against the Abkhaz people in the sphere of the nationalities policy were spelled out in collective and private letters sent to the central party and Soviet bodies by representatives of various strata of the Abkhaz people—the intelligentsia, the working class and the peasantry—in 1947, 1957, 1967, 1978, and 1988. For a while after these appeals steps were taken to improve the state of affairs in the autonomous republic. But just a short while later there would be a return to the situation about which the representatives of the Abkhaz people had complained. In particular there was something that occurred at the end of 1988: rallies in Tbilisi heard calls for the abolition of the already truncated Abkhaz Autonomous Republic. One unofficial society drew up a special program to combat the Abkhaz people and its cultural institutions. It is noteworthy that this society, whose members consider themselves champions of democracy, declares in the program written by them that in 1936 and 1954 the supremacy of the separatists and the coercion by the (?Absuytsy)—that is what they call the Abkhazians—of the other nations living in the Abkhaz Autonomous Soviet Socialist Republic [ASSR] were ended. In other words, the way these democrats see it, the best years were those in which the annihilation of the Abkhaz people was in progress.

Representatives of the democrats came to Abkhazia, where they incited anti-Abkhaz feelings among the local Georgian population. They succeeded last December in organizing an unsanctioned rally in Sukhumi and a procession through the city.

Not just the Abkhazians, but also the other denizens of the republic, are seriously concerned over the preparation and discussion of the draft state program for the development of the Georgian language, which raises the question of the use of Georgian as the only official language, in all establishments, and of the compulsory study of Georgian by every person in the republic. This has reopened unhealed wounds, recalling the crude distortions of the history of the Abkhaz people and the flouted rights of the Abkhaz Autonomous Republic. The Abkhaz public was particularly upset by the fact that these actions did not call forth the principled assessment they deserved from the leadership of the union republic.

The culmination of all this was that on 18 March 1989 a sanctioned rally was held in the village of Lykhny, on the historic square where, from time immemorial, matters of importance to the destinies of the people had been resolved. At this rally an appeal addressed to the CPSU Central Committee general secretary, the chairman, USSR Council of Ministers and a number of academic institutions was adopted. It was signed by around 32,000 people, including the leaders of several higher party and soviet bodies, and all deputies of Abkhazian extraction. Moreover, the message was signed by more than 5,000 Russians, Armenians, Greeks, Georgians, and others. It made the request that Abkhazia should have restored to it the status of the Soviet Socialist Republic, which it had in 1921, in the lifetime of Lenin. Contrary to some assertions, this would mean not a withdrawal, but the restoration of the status of Abkhazia, as once agreed. Under the 1921 treaty between the Abkhaz Soviet Socialist Republic [SSR] and the Georgian SSR, this status would give the Abkhaz SSR the opportunity to decide its own destiny independently should the matter arise of the withdrawal of the other union republics from the USSR, because the Abkhazian people believes their presence in the USSR to be the only possible way of maintaining national identity. [applause]

I believe that this experience of a union treaty could be utilized in drawing up documents regulating the relationships between other autonomous formations and the republics in which they are contained. The sense of the appeal was that the extension of the rights of the republic in the interests of the entire multinational population of the Abkhaz ASSR would not create any advantages for any people.

In no way is the appeal directed against the Georgian people, with whom we wish to continue to live in peace and friendship. The assessments of this appeal—expressed from the podium of the Georgian SSR Supreme Soviet on 29 March 1989—as contradicting the spirit of the decision of the 27th party congress and the directives of the 19th all-union party conference are absolutely illegal. Apparently, then, the Abkhaz people did not have the lawful right to voice its opinion, while the organs of the union republic had decided the fate of the Abkhaz Autonomous Republic long before the CPSU Central Committee plenum on interethnic relations. The assessments of the leadership of the union republic had the effect of further stoking up the campaign, which has not died down to this very day. Evidence of this are the articles that have appeared in the press even as this congress has been working. At their meeting with the leaders who came to Tbilisi following the tragic events, the representatives of the Georgian intelligentsia tried to make out that the Lykhny appeal was the reason for what has happened, even though other causes lay behind the Tbilisi events, which pursued other aims. We are desperately sorry about the tragedy that ocurred in Tbilisi. We have deep sympathy, and we believe that these events should be fully and thoroughly investigated, and the guilty parties brought to book. [applause]

On 26 May 1988 [as heard] the restoration of Georgian statehood was marked in the Abkhaz ASSR. It is for the historians to assess th significance of this event in the life of the Georgian people. However, in the history of the Abkhaz people, these events are bound up with a statehood that in 1918 drowned an Abkhaz Bolshevik commune in blood, and subsequently carried out terrorist acts in the villages of Abkhazia. This celebration brought the Abkhazian and Georgian populations of the autonomous republic to the verge of conflict. According to the many telegrams that have reached and continue to reach us... [bell rings] I am just finishing ... telegrams, telephone messages, and other messages, the situation in Abkhazia remains very disturbing to this day. If urgent steps are not taken, something quite irreparable could occur.

Unfortunately, the CPSU Central Committee and the USSR Council of Ministers are maintaining their silence, despite a written question from the deputies of the Abkhaz ASSR submitted on 25 May this year. We

insistently beg all USSR people's deputies to back our proposal to set up a special commission from among the people's deputies to study the state of interethnic relations in Abkhazia.

Preferably there should be a standing commission made up of USSR people's deputies to discuss the problems of autonomous formations, to remove the tension in the most complicated regions and prevent things reaching the stage of conflict. Our request concerned with the Abzhaz ASSR is dictated by the fact that extremist forces have shifted the epicenter of the tension to Abkhazia in order, so we believe, to provoke people to conflict, and then to accuse our people of this. It would not be difficult to portray us as the guilty parties, since the mass media give one-sided information, while the representatives of the Abkhaz people are deprived of their right to voice their point of view. I would like to note that people understand the need for maximum restraint and calm, for the future of restructuring and the future of our great country are dependent on this. We deputies are doing, and are obliged to do, everything we can to ensure this.

A few specific proposals: first, a system of public hearings and scientific expert consultations should be instituted in the chambers and commissions of the USSR Supreme Soviet on matters of interethnic relations in the USSR; second, commissions on national groups and national minorities should be set up in the USSR Supreme Soviet's Soviet of Nationalities and in the Supreme Soviet Soviet of the Union; third, it is essential to return to the fundamental principles of Soviet power and to Lenin's solution to the nationalities question, which is based on the declaration of the rights of the peoples of Russia.

A decision to set up a commission of deputies to study the situation in the Abkhaz ASSR will bring peace of mind to people, and will restore their belief in the triumph of justice. Thank you and my apologies.

Latvian Writer Addresses Congress
LD0206213189 Moscow Television Service in Russian 0904 GMT 2 Jun 89

[Speech by Yanis Yanovich Peters, chairman of the board of the Latvian Soviet Socialist Republic Union of Writers, to the Congress of People's Deputies session at the Kremlin Palace of Congresses—live]

[Excerpts] Esteemed chairman, fellow-thinkers, dissenters, comrade deputies! [laughter, applause] In the very center of Moscow there is a banner greeting the participants of the Congress of People's Deputies and Muscovites, which proclaims "Restructuring and the revival of the Leninist face of socialism!" I read that pithy phrase and shuddered. [passage omitted on Lativa suffering from actions of all-union monopolies] I look at Latvia and think not so much of a revival of the face of socialism as how to stop the death of the people, since the results of the pragmatic, economically ill- founded actions are already to be seen. The numbers of the indigenous nation in its own territory are through spontaneous emigration nearing the critical point of becoming a minority. [passage omitted: aggressive planning is harming Latvia]

It should be acknowledged that the USSR Government and the Government of the Latvian Soviet Socialist Republic have for decades been violating Article 76 of the USSR Constitution, which states very simply that a union republic is a sovereign Soviet socialist state, which has amalgamated with other Soviet republics to form the USSR. [passage omitted: highlighting the negative things occurring in Russia] I consider that the all-union administrative team, including the USSR State Planning Committee, is also infringing on the sovereignty of the Russian Soviet Federated Socialist Republic and the interests of all the peoples of Russia. [passage omitted: Latvia should not be compared with undeveloped regions]

Let us really turn to a radical restructuring also with regard to matters relating to interethnic relations and the status of a union republic as a sovereign state. It is clear to every schoolchild who has studied grammar that sovereignty is a synonym for the notion of independence. So why are we so afraid of this word? Why is Russia afraid to become independent from the all-union dictatorship? Why does official Latvia fear this, while unofficial Latvia is already unafraid of anything or anybody? [passage omitted]

I think that the time is not far distant when Article 81 of the USSR Constitution will be brought into operation. That article proclaims that the sovereign rights of the union republics are protected by the Union of Soviet Socialist Republics. I am convinced that the USSR must not be reticent about looking into the defense of the sovereignty—that is, the independence—of the union republics. But what then is the USSR? It is, after all, you and I and each of the 15 constitutionally—but as yet regrettably only declared so for effect—independent states. Only genuinely independent states with some limitations on their independence, as can be observed in all federal unions, can at this historic moment lead us out of the political, economic, ecological and national crisis and out of the impasse of the moral slump. [passage omitted] If the center is strong, it should defend us strongly against arbitrariness. [passage omitted]

The new USSR Supreme Sovieet should base the deployment of the army in the union republics on legal principles. If the opportunity has not yet arrived to reduce to a minimum the numbers of army subunits and naval bases in Latvia, Lithuania, and Estonia, or for the purposes of disarmament altogether to bid them farewell, the situation can only be improved by an open treaty between the USSR Ministry of Defense on the one hand and the Council of Ministers of a union republic on the other. The treaty must openly provide for the army of troops, their locations, their numbers and the duration of their deployment in the republic. The concluded treaty must be submitted for ratification to the republic's Supreme Soviet. Accordingly new articles should be inserted in the USSR Constitution and the constitutions of union republics on the relationship between the army and the supreme power in each union republic. In addition, official rules should be drawn up on the economic,

ecological and cultural conduct of army subunits, establishments, departments, soldiers and officers. I believe the military should be given a minimum knowledge of the history, traditions and way of life of the people among which they will find themselves for a certain period of time under the treaty. The treaty must guarantee a prohibition on the display of strength to psychologically intimidate the citizenry. Otherwise there develops among the servicemen the psychology of the citizen of a military district and not of a country. [passage omitted]

Congress Discusses Afghan War
LD0206184189 Moscow Television Service in Russian 0947 GMT 2 Jun 89

[Discussion of war in Afghanistan, at the Congress of People's Deputies, held in the Kremlin Palace of Congresses—live]

[Excerpts] [Lukyanov] The floor is given to Deputy Chervonopiskiy, first secretary of the Cherkassy town Komsomol [Leninist Communist Youth League] committee in the Ukraine, an internationalist serviceman [applause] and representative of the Komsomol [strong applause]. Deputy Gorbunov, Irkutsk, to get ready.

[Chervonopiskiy] Comrades, first of all I must express thanks for the fact that they have at long last, after how many days, started giving the floor to representatives of young people. This is one, as they say, carry forward of those reproaches which our voters phone in to us and send to us. [passage omitted: being in the hall makes him think more and more of a phrase used by a hero in a popular film—for the state, it is a shame] It is a shame about coupons in the 72d year of Soviet power. It is a shame about the disintegration of the economy. It is a shame about ruined villages. It is a shame about the at times savage interethnic relations. It is a shame about rivers with no fish and towns with chemical smog. True, I see that we already have something to be proud about, too. In my view, apart from the largest computers in the world, we also have the largest unconstructive criticism in the world. [passage omitted: digression]

But the most shameful thing is that you, the older comrades, fathers and grandfathers, have not left for us, for young people, at least some kind of acceptable ideals on which one could build one's life, for which one could strive, for which one could struggle and on which one could educate young people. [applause] As far as the Komsomol is concerned, comrades who are criticizing it indiscriminately are obviously judging from those times when they worked there themselves or, rather, did not work. Now, even in the last 5 years, the situation has changed greatly. [passage omitted: lists the clubs, centers and complexes which exist today] The Komsomol has taken a course for concrete deeds. True, don't think that it's already like that everywhere—rather the opposite—but nonetheless it is a reality.

Exactly a year ago, in Sevastopol, a town of everlasting Russian glory, representatives of 100,000 Afghans of the Ukraine elected me the chairman of the republican council of reserve servicemen. They named me, as is the usual way for us to put it in the Ukraine, their father [svoyim bat'kom]. So I am speaking rightfully, on their behalf, today.

First, in Mikhail Sergeyevich Gorbachev's report we did not hear a political appraisal of the Afghan war, which we were all waiting for, and possibly the whole country and the whole world.

Second, bringing tears to the eyes of those who, completely out of turn, walked under dushman bullets, on Italian mines and under U.S. Stingers, at times one has to hear from the lips of bureaucrats belonging to the party, local soviet, Komsomol and other bodies, the words: "I didn't send you to Afghanistan"—which has already almost become a catch-phrase—in the so-called privilege lines in which one has to wait for a baby's pram until the child is going to school, for an apartment—realistically—until the year 2,000, and for furniture and other items of domestic luxury evidently until the time when everyone starts to live well in Russia. I have not even mentioned my brothers who have been maimed, for our artificial limb industry remains at the level of the stone age. Comrades, I am not exaggerating: My artificial limbs were manufactured on equipment at one of two artificial limb works which were presented to us after the war by Churchill's wife. Yes, esteemed scientists, it is possible to cut with a scythe of a 12th century model, and it's even not too bad to do so: But to move around with the help of this kind of rubbish at the end of the 20th century is something I would not wish even upon my enemies. [applause]

Thirdly: The people have already expressed their trust in us, former internationalist servicemen. Present in the hall today are 120 people's deputies who have passed through the school of deprivation, difficult courage, and military valor in the long-suffering land of Afghanistan. As you know, our children are the most upright people there have been in the world. Tens of thousands of young people, snatched from the claws of drunkenness, drug abuse, and crime—including organized crime—and we have specific examples of this—are engaged in military and patriotic clubs of their own volition—of their own volition, note. Let me give an example here. In our own small town of Cherkassy we have nearly 15 clubs in which 800 youngsters are undergoing courses. These clubs turn out more internationalist servicemen. In these clubs they engage not in the production of cannon fodder, as some people try to accuse us of, but in the raising of physically strong, mentally tough citizens of our socialist motherland, ready for any difficulties, whose hands will build the society whose foundations we, comrade deputies, are now laying. These clubs have many problems. And often there is no understanding or support in any way from the bureaucrats of the Voluntary Society for the Promotion of the Army, Aviation, and Navy [DOSAAF] and national education, the sport bosses, who under the most varied pretexts stubbornly do not want to put at the disposal of these really effectively functioning clubs even the wretched sports facilities which are under their management. And in the meantime, the kids often exercise on an ad hoc basis in school sports halls, old sheds, and basements, totally against any sanitary requirements and norms. There is a surprising paradox: At the dawn of Soviet power children were given palaces, and now we are chasing them into basements. The clubs do not have the elementary material basis, equipment, or educational aids. The leaders are mainly workers and students. Working 4 or 5 days a week with adolescents gives them nothing but nervous tension and unpleasantness at home and at work. So I propose that the most serious attention should be paid to this question at state level. And the Armed Forces should not be restricted by ambiguous directives, but efficient leadership should be organized.

As for the Tbilisi tragedy, I as someone who—God forbid that any of you should have to live through the same—has had to say farewell forever to my brothers, my combat friends, including Belorussians, Lithuanians, Gagauzes, Tatars, Dargans, and Russians; to the bottom of my heart I hate death in war. Today I still cannot express a definite opinion on this clearly most shameful and disgraceful provocation in our contemporary history. But one thing gives me special doubt—the assault regiment from Kirovabad, which was mentioned as one of the last to leave Afghanistan, to end that contradictory war. The boys who, even in battle, saved Afghan women and children, could never become killers and punishers, as they were called here [interrupted by applause]...by the politicos from Georgia and the Baltic republics, who have themselves long been busy with training their own storm-troopers [shturmovyye otryady] [interrupted by applause]...whose role in the history of some states is well known to us. They are not wearing their USSR People's Deputy badges today, preferring the symbols of their own People's Fronts. [applause] I certainly support the idea of republican financial autonomy, but, when shops sell goods only to people registered as living in the Baltic republics, it seems to me that that should be called republican nationalist selfishness. [applause]

We are also seriously concerned by the unprecedented hounding of the Soviet Army which has developed in the mass media. [applause] The aim and the meaning of the irresponsible statements by Deputy Sakharov on Afghanistan are totally incomprehensible. I will now read the malicious insults uttered by those dashing fellows on the TV program "View". Excuse me for interrupting my speech to read you one brief appeal:

To the Presidium of the Congress of USSR People's Deputies; to Comrade Mikhail Sergeyevich Gorbachev, chairman of the USSR Supreme Soviet, general secretary of the CPSU Central Committee and chairman of the country's Defense Council.

Esteemed comrade members of the Congress Presidium. Esteemed Mikhail Sergeyevich. We soldiers, sergeants, and officers of a servicemen's collective of many thousands, the 60th Anniversary of the USSR Red Banner Orders of Lenin and Kutuzov Second Grade Air Assault Unit, which carried out its internationalist duty for 9 years in the Republic of Afghanistan, earnestly request you to give the people's deputies from the congress rostrum an explanation of the basis on which, or on whose instructions, USSR People's Deputy Sakharov gave an interview to journalists from the Canadian newspaper OTTAWA CITIZEN about how Soviet airmen supposedly shot their own Soviet soldiers who had become surrounded, so that they could not surrender.

We are incensed to the depths of our souls at this irresponsible and provocative escapade by an eminent scientist, and regard his inhuman accusation as a malevolent attack on the Soviet Armed Forces in order to disparage our people, and as yet another attempt to cause a rift in the sacred unity between the Army, the people, and the party. We view this as a debasement of the honor, dignity, and memory of those sons of the motherland who fulfilled their orders to the end—Heroes of the Soviet Union, assault troops Mironenko, Chebik, Karyagin, Zadorozhnyy, and Yurasov. Their example is for us a symbol of patriotism and selfless devotion to their serviceman's and internationalist duty. The delegates to the congress must know that, despite the attempts by Sakharov and the like, the assault troops will continue to reliably defend the interests of our multinational homeland. [prolonged applause]

I associate myself with this message because I am myself a former major in the air assault troops and I myself served in that unit. It was signed by Major General Botcherov, Lieutenant Colonel Popov, Major Petrov, Lieutenant Colonel Yerko, Captain Turchak, Sergeant Petitov, Sgt Martynov, Private Solovyev and Senior Lieutenant Batyuk—all decorated with orders and medals of the Soviet Union. [prolonged applause]

Comrade delegates! I am prepared for a discussion about the thoughts that I have expressed today, but I warn that it must be a discussion and not shouts as has already been the practice here with us. And my final point: More than 80 percent of the people in the hall are Communists. Very many of them have already spoken. But none of them—including the report—have used the word communism. I am a convinced opponent of slogans and show, and today I will say the three words for which I consider we all together have to fight: These are the state, the homeland and communism. [applause] Comrade chairman, since I have saved several minutes in my speech—just a second--I have saved several minutes in my speech and I ask you to give 2 minutes from my own speech to (Pavel Zhidko), my brother from Belorussia:

[(Zhidko)] Thank you. Esteemed people's deputies! Esteemed invited guests to the congress! What Sergey has said from the platform here today, I confirm, and that phrase which even today continues to be heard from bureaucrats—I didn't send you to Afghanistan—perhaps it will continue to be heard. How could it be otherwise? What one glimpses on the newspaper pages today brings us no peace—Yevtushenko's verses, the Sorcerer, the Afghan ant, and others. We internationalist servicemen demand that an all-around assessment be made of the introduction of troops into Afghanistan. We know the truth about Afghanistan and we ourselves want all of you to know it, too. We know that it will not be easy to do this, taking into consideration the whole complexity of that situation, but one cannot take too much time over it. The CPSU Central Committee's closed letter gave rise to differing interpretations of the essence of the issue, and the most dreadful thing might be loss of trust in the state which sent us to war abroad. We do not want to be the victims of a political mistake. We will strengthen the struggle for peace, the struggle to ensure that no one dares to send our children outside our homeland's borders without a decision of the supreme organ of power. [applause] [passage omitted: we know that the defense ministry is working on a memorial book, but we insist that a list of those killed be published; the selflessness of the men who fought in Afghanistan; now help is needed in the form of good artificial limbs, pensions for young people, who have been maimed, and housing] [Video shows Sakharov coming to rostrum and conducting brief, indistinct exchange with Lukyanov before being allowed to address congress]

[Sakharov] The last thing I wanted to do was to insult the Soviet Army. I deeply respect the Soviet Army and the Soviet soldier who defended our motherland in the Great Patriotic War. But when we are dealing with the Afghan war, then, again, I am not insulting the soldier who shed his blood there and heroically fulfilled his orders. That is not what it is about. It is about the fact that the very war in Afghanistan was criminal, a criminal adventure undertaken nobody knows by whom: It is not known who bears responsibility for that immense crime of our motherland. And that crime cost the lives of almost 1 million Afghans. A war of annihilation was waged against an entire people. A million people perished. And that is what lies on us as a terrible sin, a terrible reproach. We must wash ourselves clean of that very disgrace, that terrible disgrace which lies on our leadership. That act of aggression was performed aganst the people and against the Army.

[Lukyanov interrupting] Andrey Dmitriyevich, Andrey Dmitriyevich....

[Sakharov interrupting] I spoke against introducing Soviet troops into Afghanistan and was banished to Gorkiy for it. It is precisely that which served as the main cause, and I am proud of it. I am proud of that banishment to Gorkiy as an award which I received.

[Lukyanov interrupting] Andrey Dmitriyevich....

[Sakharov interrupting] That is the first thing I wanted to say. And the second thing is that when there was that interview, and the subject was not at all the one about which...[changes thought] I have already explained it in KOMSOMOLSKAYA PRAVDA, but I will repeat it. It was about the return of Soviet POW's who were in Pakistan. And I said that the only means of solving that problem was direct negotiations between the Soviet side and the Kabul government and the Afghan partisans, who it is necessary to recognize as a party in the war: They were defending the independence of their motherland and that gives them the right to consider themselves the defenders of their motherland. Only in that way can this problem be solved, only through exchange and direct recognition of their [word indistinct due to bell ringing in hall] and after that question I mentioned of those foreign reports with which I was familiar from foreign radio broadcasts, about cases of execution, with the aim—as written in the letter which I received—of avoiding capture. The word, directly, was exclusion of capture. That was a slip by those who wrote to me, a purely stylistic slip, simply recopied from secret orders. This question is now being investigated, and until this question has been investigated nobody has the right to accuse me of telling an untruth, until this question has been subjected to objective and strict investigation.

And I am constantly receiving new cases. [bell rings] That, for the time being, is all that I wanted to say. I am not making apologies to the Soviet Army. I have not insulted it. I have insulted neither the Soviet Army nor the Soviet soldier. But I have insulted...[applause] those who gave that criminal order to send Soviet troops into Afghanistan.

[Lukyanov, addressing soldier at the podium] For information? Three minutes, up to three minutes.

[Ochirov] Comrades, I am a deputy representing the 548th national-territorial constituency, Colonel Ochirov, air force regiment commander. Some time ago, when I was a captain and then a major, the regiment had occasion to be in Afghanistan twice. I have read the information given by Comrade Sakharov. I, too, was indignant, also on behalf of those who served with me. Empowered by those who failed to return and those who may have failed to return, I state that these are slanders and lies about our soldiers, about the honor of our people and our Soviet Army. [lengthy applause] [passage omitted]

[Eyzan] Comrade deputies, 1 minute. I am Deputy Eyzan, 300th national-territorial constituency, Latvian SSR. On behalf of the Baltic republics I am duty-bound to make the first statement for the congress to the effect that the pain suffered by the Afghan veterans is felt in the Baltic republics just as strongly as in all the other corners of the USSR. And secondly, I assure you with all responsibility that not in a single Baltic republic has there been even an idea of forming storm-trooper units. There are none, nor will there be any. Thank you. [applause]

[Akhromeyev] Comrades deputies! Akhromeyev, territorial constituency No 697, Moldavia. I happened to take part in this discussion with Academician Sakharov. I fulfilled the duties of first deputy chief of the General Staff and chief of the General Staff during the whole period of the events in Afghanistan. I report to you with all responsibility, that never—yes, and I was 2 years in succession, and in the course of 2 and ½ years I carried out my military duty in Afghanistan—and I report to you that not a single order of that kind was sent out by the General Staff or the defense ministry. We did not receive any such savagely cruel instruction from the political leadership of our country to destroy our own troops who had become surrounded. All this is a pure lie, a shocking untruth, and Academician Sakharov will not find any documents to support his lie! [applause]

[Unidentified speaker] Comrade deputies!

[Lukyanov, interrupting] Name yourself.

[Kravchenko] Galina Ivanovna Kravchenko, 134th territorial constituency. I address our great scientist, Comrade Sakaharov. Who gave him the right to insult our children? I have two sons. One served for a year. The other one will soon enlist. Well, what I want to find out precisely is this: Who gave him the right to insult our children? Indeed, they have regard for nothing, neither for their lives, nor for their families, nor for their youth! How can a statement like that be made? Well, I suppose a workman could have said it, a workman who, well, who indeed fails to understand. [shouts of indignation from

hall] Well, maybe he could have heard it and believed this rumor in view of his illiteracy, but, comrades, such a major scientist—this made me very indignant! During one preelection campaign I was asked: What is your attitude toward Comrade Sakharov's activities and his policies? Well, with some difficulty I replied that it was difficult for me to judge his activities and his policies as a working woman. But now, here, present at the congress, I understood precisely that I have a completely different view of this man. [applause]

[Polikarpov] Comrade deputies. I am Nikolay Aleksandrovich Polikarpov, deputy representing the 253d constituency in the town of Penza. My younger brother, age 23, died in Afghanistan. He was a military pilot. Why did he die? Under what circumstances? Neither I nor anyone else knows to this very day. The proposal made here is correct: May Soviet soldiers never again in the future die for interests we do not understand! [applause] But, comrades, the statement just made about our Soviet Army I regard as slanderous. Thank you for your attention. [applause]

[Kazakova] Kazakova, 603d territorial constituency, Uzbekistan. Comrade Academician, by your single action you have reduced to nothing all your previous activities! You insulted the entire Army, the entire people, all of our fallen who gave their lives! And I bring you universal contempt! You should be ashamed! [lengthy applause, bell ringing, and shouts of approval]

[Lukyanov] A recess until 1600 is announced.

2 Jun Concluding Session
LD0306094589 Moscow Television Service in Russian 1158 GMT 2 Jun 89

[Relay of the third session of the 2 June Congress of People's Deputies from the Kremlin Palace of Congresses—live]

[Excerpts] [passage omitted] [Lukyanov] Comrade deputies! Comrade deputies! We are continuing the work of the congress. The floor is given to Deputy Gorbunov, Gennadiy Nikolayevich, director of the Irkutsk 60th Anniversary of the USSR aircraft works. [passage omitted: Gorbunov, Atdayev address congress]

[Lukyanov] Deputy Karyakin, Yuriy Fedorovich, senior scientific staff member of the Institute of the International Workers' Movement of the USSR Academy of Sciences. And let Deputy Dzasokhov get ready.

[Karyakin] Comrade president! People's deputies! Voters! What has happened to the days when our general secretary and president became three-time Hero of the Soviet Union and received the Order of Victory because his exploits were depicted excellently in a film by an actor who also received the title of Hero of Socialist Labor for his performance? What has happened to the days when people wrote books for Brezhnev and for them he received the Lenin prize for literature? The days when that prize was presented to him by Markov, and later Markov himself received the title of Hero of Socialist Labor from the freshly-made laureate? What has happened to the days when people made careers out of books about general secretaries, when even Chernenko published a work about the triumph of human rights in the Soviet Union, and when one of the most famous of journalists entered a state of frenzied rapture on account of that work? If someone who did not know about all of that were suddenly to come into our congress now, I think he would be flabbergasted by the conclusion that there is no one more to blame for all our misfortunes than our general secretary.

A dangerous trend has come into being—this has already been demonstrated by our congress—it is an unprecedented breakthrough in the establishment of normal relations between authority and the people through the deputies. Now, for the first time, everything is taking place in front of the eyes of the whole people. It is a real forum. The process of the removal of the mystery from authority has been accelerated. However, a dangerous trend has arisen. People used to be so accustomed to sucking up to the old general secretaries that they now consider themselves under an obligation to be rude to the new one. [applause] Although even now there are a lot of obsequious people. Moreover, one of them, having seen Mikhail Sergeyevich shaking hands with me as we said good-bye, immediately decided to offer me the job of editor in chief of a very serious journal. [applause]

I give you my word of honor that when I speak about rudeness I do not have anyone in particular here in mind. I simply see and feel this trend and I am very, very frightened of it. It would be a good thing to spot it and put an end to it from the very beginning. The criterion of one's progressiveness lies not in wholesale criticism of Gorbachev but in the constructive help one gives to the cause in a businesslike way, the more so since we have convinced ourselves with our own eyes that there really are no zones that are closed for criticism.

I would support very strongly indeed the initiative—if I understand it correctly—put forward by Gorbachev at the April plenum that the sessions of the Central Committee should be published in full. [applause] If I understand things correctly the party does not have secrets from the people, and the Central Committee cannot have secrets from the party and the people, just as the Politburo cannot have any from the Central Committee, and so on, with the exception, of course, of certain state secrets. It seems to me that this will help us find ways of uniting in a constructive way—it is a difficult thing to do—the power of the people and the soviets on the one hand, and the power of the party on the other, because the division is a problem that exists and there is no getting away from it. Let us not be under any illusions that we are the power. So who then are you, comrades of the Politburo? No doubt there has to be some very constructive and not legalistic solution here.

I have a great deal of respect for Yuriy Vlasov but the demand for impeachment quite honestly seems to me to be something out of a dream world. In bygone centuries our impeachment was defined like this in our country: monarchy was restricted by a slipknot; you remember? But our present-day impeachment is something like what happened on 14 October 1964—and that was it at its best. And if one is to tell the whole story, then I do not think that we should forget that. At any rate, at the Leningrad plenum in April and at this one I have mentioned, there were elements of 14 October visible to the naked eye. And as I understood it, our congress elected Gorbachev to be president in orde to both defend and speed up restructuring. [applause]

Mikhail Sergeyevich, I have a request to put to you as president. I would like our congress to support it. My request is as follows: that our Russian citizenship be returned to Solzhenitsyn, that aged writer of the Russian land, that great humanist, the man who first dared to say the truth about the rule of Stalin, who was the first to call upon himself and upon us not to lie. [applause] You found a common language with the Iron Lady. You found a common language with Bush and Reagan. You found a common language with the Pope. They did not cease to be anti-Communists. And you found this common language on the soil of humanism. Surely, we will find a common language with Solzhenitsyn, the great humanist, on this soil? Let's think about the fact that if Pushkin, Dostoyevskiy, and Tolstoy were living now—would we really be to their liking? And would that be a good reason to exile them? It seems to me that we will not be able to forgive ourselves—it's not my own original thought—we will never be able to forgive ourselves, and our descendants will not forgive us if we do not do this.

There is another question which has long tormented me. They tried to persuade me not to talk about it. Forgive me, but, of course, I'm going to do so. During my childhood I learned one quite little fact that we have almost completely forgotten. Lenin himself wanted to be buried near the grave of his mother at the Volkhovo Cemetry in St Petersburg. And naturally Nadezhda Konstantinovna and Mariya Ilichna, his sister, wanted the same thing. Neither he nor they were listened to. This was yet another element, not immediately noticed and not immediately recognized, in our dehumanization. What was flouted was not just Lenin's last political wish; what was flouted was his last personal wish as a human—in the name of Lenin, of course. Just imagine what he himself would have said, how he would have dealt with those who did this. He lay there down below. Above him walked the butcher in soft boots who afterwards lay down himself beside him. There was also a buffet there which they later removed. That's the devilry of the fanatic. The mausoleum that contains Lenin's body is not Lenin's mausoleum. It's still Stalin's mausoleum. You can gather ideological and political arguments against this by the thousands; there isn't a single human argument for it. They warned me that the people wouldn't understand. The people will understand; I assure you. One thing they will understand is this quiet fact that we have forgotten, that Lenin wanted to lie in rest like a person—surely we can understand that? The tanks move across Red Square; the body shudders; scientists and artists mould this fact—it's a nightmare—to create the appearance, and it isn't there. It's dreadful to talk about this, but we should let this body rest in peace where he, Lenin, wanted it to. And if I were a believer and if the soul were immortal, it would say to you: Thank you. [applause]

My third thought is even more heretical. If we have not lost our memory, if we have not killed our conscience—and conscience means 'con' and 'science,' ['with the knowledge']—then we must write the names of the 40 million or so people—we do not know the exact figures—who died on account of, as a result of, and on the orders of Lubyanka, write them on Lubyanka, indeed on the building. If blood has flowed that was spilled by order in Lubyanka, then Lubyanka should be demolished. Our national, social, and human honor demands this, and I am convinced that it will happen.

And—how much time do I have? [indistinct voices from the floor] Three minutes? Three minutes! I have received a letter: I propose that the congress adopt a resolution comdemning Academician Sakharov. The letter writes as follows: Mr [Gospodin] Sakharov. All the services rendered by you have been crossed out by your blasphemous statement alone. Yes, you are one of the creators of the hydrogen bomb, without which the might of our great power would not exist. Yes, you have rightly worn the awards of the homeland, which three times made you a Hero of Socialist Labor. Yes, you are one of the initiators of the banning of nuclear tests in three media. Yes, you were opposed to the entry of our troops into Afghanistan. Yes, you were a defender of democracy and glasnost. But all of this has now been struck through. Give thanks that we are not exiling you either to Gorkiy or abroad.

I received a second letter as I made my way here: Every day during the Afghan war, dozens of our people and hundreds of Afghans were maimed and killed. Shortening the war by just 1 day saved many from that fate. On behalf of all those who are still alive, their mothers, their wives, and girl-friends, on behalf of their future children—both Russian and Afghan—we give you great thanks, Mikhail Sergeyevich, and you too, Andrey Dmitriyevich. [applause] The Brezhnev clique began the war in Afghanistan. Now, in order to conceal its criminal role, it is switching the attention of the people away from itself. That's everything. [applause] [passage omitted: Dzasokhov from North Ossetiya on Gorbachev report, and Shcherbakov, Moscow trade union, on socialist achievements]

[Lukyanov] Comrades! Several notes come in mentioning the fact that we have normally been dragging out the congress beyond 1900, beyond 1800, in violation of standing orders. We still have Comrade Boris Vartanovich Dadamyan, from Nagorno-Karabakh Autonomous Oblast [NKAO] registered, but perhaps we shall ask him to speak tomorrow, I mean at the next morning session. But now let us turn to those questions which are of an organizational nature and to the general points of information which people are requesting. You don't object? [cries from hall] Boris Vartanovich, the morning, then?

The first instruction which the deputies handed to the presidium, together with the delegations of the union republics, is the formation of a commission on a political and legal appraisal of the 1939 Soviet-German nonaggression.

The presidium, together with the delegations and with the deputies of the Baltic republics, the Ukraine, Moldavia, and a number of other republics, agreed upon the composition of this commission. Permit me to read out the prepared draft decision on this question.

A decision of the Congress of USSR People's Deputies on the formation of a commission for a political and legal appraisal of the 1939 Soviet-German nonaggression pact.

The Congress of USSR People's Deputies decrees:

For the working out of a political and legal appraisal of the Soviet-German nonaggression pact, which was concluded in 1939, and the documents connected with it, to set up a commission comprising the following USSR people's deputies:

Chairman of the commission: Aleksandr Nikolayevich Yakovlev, Politburo member and CPSU Central Committee secretary.

Members of the commission:

Chingiz Aytmatov, writer and chairman of the board of the writers union, Kirghiz Soviet Socialist Republic [SSR].

Arbatov, director of the United States and Canada Institute.

Lyudmila Okopovna Arutyunyan, a department head at Yerevan State University.

Yuriy Nikolayevich Afanasyev, rector of the Moscow State Historical Archives Institute.

Vasiliy Vladimirovich Bykov, writer and secretary of the board of the USSR Writers Union, Minsk.

Mavrik Germanovich Vulfson, senior teacher of the Latvian Academy of Arts, Riga.

Igor Nikolayevich Gryazin, head of a department of the Institute of Philosophy, Sociology and Law of the Estonian SSR Academy of Sciences, Tartu.

Ion Panteleyevich Drutse, writer, Moldavia SSR, Moscow.

Grigoriy Sidorovich (?Yeremey), chairman of the Moldavian Republic Trade Union Council.

Aleksey Ivanovich Kazannik, faculty lecturer at Omsk State University.

Ivar Yanovich Kezbers, secretary of the Latvian Communist Party Central Committee.

Vitaliy Alekseyevich Korotich, editor-in-chief of OGONEK magazine.

Vladimir Alekseyevich Kravets, foreign minister of the Ukrainian SSR.

Sergey Borisovich Lavrov, a department head of Leningrad State University.

Vitautas Vitautovich Landsbergis, professor at the Lithuanian SSR state conservatory.

Maryu Yokhannesovna Lauristin, a department head at Tartu State University.

Endel Teodorovich Lippmaa, director of the Institute of Chemical and Biological Physics of the Estonian SSR Academy of Sciences.

Yustinas Moteyevich Martsinkyavichyus, writer, Lithuanian SSR.

Kazimir Vladislavovich Moteka, lawyer at Vilnius No 1 legal consultation office.

Nikolay Vasilyevich Neyland, deputy foreign minister, Latvian SSR.

Aleksey Mikhaylovich Ridiger, Metropolitan Aleksey of Leningrad and Novgorod.

Edgar Elmarovich Savisar, deputy director of the Mainor special planning and design office, Tallinn.

Valentin Mikhaylovich Falin, head of the International Department of the CPSU Central Committee.

Vladimir Ilarionovich Shinkaruk, director of the Institute of Philosophy of the Ukrainian SSR Academy of Sciences.

Zina Leonovna Shlichite, lawyer with the Klaipeda legal advice office.

Comrades, all the delegations fully agreed on this list. And, as you can see, it comprises representatives of all the Baltic republics and those towns, for example Klaipeda, which were the first to suffer in 1939. Then, Belorussia, the Ukraine, Moldavia and, finally, the Russian federation and the union as a whole. The presidium considers that this composition of the commission will be able to deal with this most complex historical and political question which the commission is proposed to study. Are there any proposals to approve this composition? [stirring in the hall] Then, I will put it to the vote. Those in favor of this proposal please raise your mandates. Against? I want to see who is opposed, comrades. There are some against. Therefore, please.... [pause for counting]

[Teller] Esteemed deputies, six have voted against.

[Lukyanov] Who has abstained? [pause for counting]

[Teller] Seven deputies have abstained.

[Lukyanov] Therefore, comrades, the decision of the Congress of USSR People's Deputies on the formation of a commission for a political and legal appraisal of the 1939 Soviet-German nonaggression pact has been adopted by a majority of votes.

Comrade deputies, the presidium has charged me to dwell on one more matter. A week of the work of the congress has passed. As is common knowledge, and you have heard this for yourselves, a number of deputies, when speaking at the congress, have made deputies' inquiries. Some inquiries were conveyed to the secretariat in writing. In accordance with the Constitution and with the practice which has formed, a deputy's inquiriy is construed as meaning an inquiry addressed by a deputy or by a group of deputies to a body or to an official. It is a demand for an official explanation to be given or for a position to be outlined on a certain problem which comes under the competence of the corresponding state body. A deputy's inquiry should, naturally, be distinguished from questions, and I will say that, in the overwhelming majority of cases, it is difficult even for a lawyer to decide where there is a question and where there is an inquiry. But we took a sufficiently serious look at this, attempting to distinguish in some way inquiries from questions, remarks and proposals which are addressed to state bodies, the information media, the presidium itself, and so on.

What do I wish to say about inquiries? About 20 such documents in all have come in from the people's deputies to date, documents named deputies' inquiries. They touch upon a broad range of problems of an economic, social, and ecological nature, and the development of the branches of the national economy. Many people's deputies—Comrades Vasnetsov, Igityan, Kurbanov, Tolpezhnikov, and others—have made inquiries connected with the events of 9 April 1989 in the city of Tbilisi. Seeing as a deputies' commission has been set up by the congress to consider this question, it is proposed that the documents be conveyed for that commission to examine. The presidium of the congress considers it expedient to act in the same way with the inquiries that have come in with regard to the Soviet-German treaty—we have only just established a commission—and with regard to the activity of the group of investigators headed by deputy Gdlyan, we have formed such a commission. Although I ought to say that a protest has been made by the Orenburg delegation that we have not included in the commission representatives of their delegation. It seems to me that, with our already having published the composition of that commission, is there any sense in our reviewing it? [voices from the hall cry no] No.

The next question. I want to inform you about the fate of the other deputy documents which are inquiries or questions. A group of people's deputies—Lukyanenko, Demchuk, Matveychuk, and Sidor—made an inquiry about the legitimacy of increasing the capacities of atomic power engineering in the Ukrainian SSR, notably at the Rovno and Khmelnitskiy nuclear electric power stations [AES's]. That is a grave question, indeed a major question. A group of people's deputies from the Crimean Oblast—Ivanov, Baranovskiy, Koltsov, and others—made an inquiry about the expediency of the construction of the Crimean AES. It is proposed that these inquiries be sent to the government and that Lukonin, the USSR minister of atomic power, should reply to them. Deputies Merkulov, Aksenov, and Mironova made an inquiry about the prospects for the functioning of the Semipalatinsk range. You also heard about this in the speech of Olzhas Suleymenov. This inquiry has been sent to Comrade Yazov, USSR defense minister, and to Marchuk, president of the Academy of Sciences.

Third. The inquiry of a group of deputies from the Kirgiz SSR and from some public organizations—Comrade Komarov, Aytmatov, Kruchinin, Shipitko, and others—is about the exceptionally unfavorable ecological situation which has come about in the city of Frunze. It has been addressed to Comrade Maslyukov, chairman of the USSR Gosplan, and to Chernomyrdin, minister of the gas industry.

A group of deputies from Nikolayev Oblast—deputies Lisnichiy, Opolinskiy, Pogorelov, and Lisitskiy—have an inquiry about the reasons for crude violations of environmental protection legislation in the oblast and the continuation of work to build the South Ukraine power complex. The inquiry has been passed on to the USSR Council of Ministers, while an inquiry from Deputy Sokolov, from Tikhvin Territorial Constituency No 64, on the Kirishi biochemical works and the Leningrad pumped-storage power station has also been sent on to the USSR Council of Ministers.

You are aware of how much has been written about Kirishi. A group of people's deputies—Comrades Gelman, Zalygin, and others—are making an inquiry to the USSR Council of Ministers on suspending the construction of the second stage of the Trans-Volga chemical works. I must say that the relevant commission of the old Supreme Soviet already studied this matter closely, and this was published. Deputies Goncharik, Kashperko, and others made an inquiry about the elimination of consequences from the accident at Chernobyl atomic power station. All these inquiries have also been forwarded to the government. Deputies Studenikin, Klimov, Kolesnikov, and others have an inquiry for Ministers Bykov, Ministry of the Medical and Microbiological Industry; Shkabardnya, Ministry of Instrument Making, Automation Equipment, and Control Systems; and Panichev, Ministry of the Machine Tool and Tool-Building Industry, about the timetable for resolving the problem of the manufacture of the requisite amount of disposable syringes and blood-transfusion systems. The comrades read about the disgraceful state of affairs concerning this, and the deputies' concern is justified. Deputy Filshin from Irkutsk Oblast has an inquiry for Gladkiy, chairman of the State Committee for Labor and Social Problems, about the reasons for the delay in dealing with the matter of bringing in length-of-service allowances in southern areas of east Siberia and increasing the relevant factor to take into account the different standards of living in these areas. An inquiry from Deputy Shcherbak on the state of financing of the health service will be sent to Comrade Chazov, USSR health minister. Deputy Korotich sent an inquiry to the USSR Council of Ministers on raising low pensions. Well, you've heard several deputies speak on pensions here. Deputy Mukishev's inquiry about the reasons for unsatisfactory work by the Ministry of Railways in providing open wagons for Ekibastuz was passed to the USSR Council of Ministers. Deputy Vasilyeva's inquiry about the reasons for price increases for services for individuals in private housing construction was passed to Comrade Batalin, chairman of the USSR State Construction Committee.

I tell you, comrades, the inquiries, questions, and wishes of this kind are still coming in. If we include all these inquiries into the congress agenda, as is laid down in our standing orders, we will not be able to discuss problems connected with the report nor the forthcoming issues which are included on the congress agenda; we will depart a long way from the agenda. That's why the presidium proposes that it would be more appropriate if the government and ministers were to provide written answers to all the deputies, and that these answers, because it is required of the entire congress to know them, be made known to all the deputies participating in the congress through the distribution of the appropriate documents. [applause]

Let me also brief you on questions and other submissions from deputies. To these may be ascribed applications and other submissions addressed specifically to the leaders of specific ministries and departments on particular questions. We did not consider it necessary to announce or hold back such applications; we passed those on, through the secretariat, directly to the appropriate ministers, ministries, and departments.

All these are being conveyed to the appropriate ministries and departments for measures to be taken, and they will then be examined in the Supreme Soviet we elected, in its committees and commissions, so that the committees and commissions are a means of monitoring, so to speak, the questions presented by deputies. The deputies will then be appropriately informed.

What problems have been raised here? They are the problems of radical economic reform, improving the political system, increasing the level of prosperity of people, and developing the social sphere. Particular isolated problems were raised as well on environmental protection and so forth. Questions relating to the life of certain regions of the country are being raised, the life of collectives, of groups of people, of individual citizens. Urgent help, say, is asked for someone—such telegrams have arrived and we have taken immediate measures. None of these problems can be left unattended, and suitable instructions are being given with respect to all applications to the congress that are being received, have been received, or will be received. All documents are being thoroughly considered, they are being sent to the executive people, and the deputies must be informed about them in accordance with the existing law on status.

A significant number of applications have been made by the people's deputies on matters of ethnic relations. For instance, a group of deputies from the Abkhaz Autonomous Soviet Socialist Republic [ASSR]—you heard today a speech by Ardzinba, but several other deputies also made applications—considers it necessary to establish a comprehensive commission of the Supreme Soviet to study the situation that has formed in this area. Delegates from Latvia—deputies Ivans, Konev, Zakis, and others, 10 in all—make a number of proposals about restoring historical justice with respect to Soviet Germans and the Crimean Tartars. There was discussion of that here today. Applications to the congress from their voters on these same questions were handed in by deputies Yarin and Tso. Deputy Forgiyev asked the congress to examine the question of establishing an Ingush ASSR. You heard that, too. Deputy Anufriyev spoke about the position of the Gagauz people in the Moldavian SSR. That, so to speak, was entered. What decision is proposed? All these proposals and questions require, as you understand, lengthy and most substantial and tactful study. It is proposed that they be sent for the examination of the USSR Supreme Soviet which we have elected and of the commission which is currently preparing for a plenum of the Central Committee on interethnic issues. [noise in the hall]

There is a proposal by Deputy Veprev about accelerating the passing of a program for the scientific and technical development of KATEK [Kansk-Achinsk fuel and energy complex] and other questions of the social and economic development of the region have been sent on to Shchadov, minister of the coal industry.

A group of deputies, including deputies Stadnik, Kurtashin, and Levykin, among others, demand that the volume of felling of forestry in Moscow Oblast be reviewed. The Moscow press and central press have written a great deal about this question. They are the green lungs of the capital.

Deputy Petrakov proposes a review of the procedure for adopting major economic decisions, especially concerning the construction of major national economic installations requiring significant capital investment. Deputy Zbykovskiy asks, justifiably in our view, a question about further improving the law on state enterprise. A very large group of questions concerns the social sphere, particularly the life of war and labor veterans. People's deputies Gromov, Temnogrudova, Konkov, and others have come forward here. Over 60 persons have sent in these proposals. They propose examination and implementation of measures to increase the standard of living of older citizens, which has just been spoken about from the rostrum at the congress.

A group of deputies—Ryzhov, Belyayev, Kartashov, and others—propose that the proportion of resources allocated to the development of public education be increased. The presidium has discussed this matter. We think that it will be correct to pass it on to the Supreme Soviet and the relevant commissions for study and for monitoring of its implementation, as the deputies wish. A significant proportion of the appeals from deputies contain proposals on improving Soviet legislation. In particular, Deputy Bogdanov proposes the elaboration of a law on protection of children and on youth. This has also been put forward here by speakers.

A group of deputies from the Ukraine proposes the elaboration of a draft law on nuclear power and its submission for nationwide discussion. Deputies Likhanov, Semenko, and others submit a proposal on adopting a law on protecting children's rights. Many deputies raise questions in other spheres of social and economic development and the field of economic activity. We suppose that all these and other issues will become the subject of thorough study by the Supreme Soviet and its commissions and committees. This has nothing to do with inquiries; I am talking about the proposals that have been submitted by deputies.

I want to say, and I draw your attention to the fact that a number of deputies—Babchenko, Luchenok, Pamfilova and Safiullin—have asked very acute questions in connection with crime in the country and its growth, and they have raised the issue that the government should adopt urgent measures in this area. Evidently, we ought to support their opinion and to instruct Interior Minister Bakatin to report on this matter and the planned measures to the USSR Supreme Soviet. This is a matter of paramount importance.

That, comrades, is some brief information from the presidium and secretariat of the congress on the flood which has come in to us during this week.

[Gorbachev] You still need to....

[Lukyanov, interrupting] I would like to add what has happened to the cables we have received. We have received 64,300 letters and cables to date from labor collectives, individual voters, etc. That is, an average of 9,500 citizens address the congress every day. In a number of cases, deputies suggest reading these cables out loud, but that would be impossible.

Interesting cables have started to arrive in which voters demand that their deputies be included in the list of speakers. The only thing I would like to say, comrades, is the following: We should probably limit ourselves in this case. A kind of synopsis of the letters and cables that have arrived is compiled every other day for the benefit of the congress deputies. We are just physically incapable of reading out these cables. [shouts of agreement from the hall]

I would also like to report to you that between 25 May and 2 June, 407 speeches were made on various issues at the Congress of People's Deputies—a fifth of the total [of the number of delegates]. Sixty-five deputies have spoken to date in the debate on the report. Some of the deputies came up to the rostrum several times in connection with the discussion of various issues, and one of the deputies has worked it all out thoroughly that the ratio per delegation—I don't want to read out which—was quite uneven. The only thing I would like to say to you is that in connection with this we in the presidium will have to adjust that matter a bit somehow to allow both the regions and the republics to be represented. I will only say that about 20, no, 30, delegates have emerged who spoke twice or more.

So, we have reported to you everything that is taking place. If you have no objections and support that policy, we could take that into account and continue our work in the same spirit.

Just a moment. If there are, all right, if there are proposals on these issues, let us now agree on bringing our session to a close in an organized manner.

So, up to 3 minutes, no more, for each person presenting information or proposals. [sounds of protest] No. I cannot disregard the standing orders. It says here: Up to 3 minutes are allowed for speeches on the procedure for conducting sessions and on voting issues, and for information. So don't take offence. [to the next speaker] Go ahead. [sounds of protest] Turn on the microphone.

[Khodyrev] Khodyrev, deputy from territorial constituency No 163, Gorkiy Oblast. Anatoliy Ivanovich set out a clear-cut system for work with electors' mandates and inquiries. That's quite right. The registering and processing of them were organized correctly. But I would like to draw the attention of Anatoliy Ivanovich, the presidium, and the secretariat to departmental replies that are hasty and not exactly of high quality. In particular, the deputies of Gorkiy Oblast, 18 in all, forwarded an inquiry to the Council of Ministers about what is to happen to the nuclear heat-supply station that is being built 5 km from the city of Gorkiy. Here is our reply from Comrade Shcherbina: The supplying of heat to inhabited localities by means of nuclear fuel has been carried out in our country for more than 10 years. Moreover, its high level of efficiency and total safety have been demonstrated.

As though Chernobyl had never happened! As though there were no public anxiety—as it were—about nuclear power! So it seems to me that the leaders of ministries and departments must adopt a more responsible approach to answering of deputies' inquiries. [passage omitted: Khodyrev on the inadequacies of media coverage; Sazonov, from Naberezhnyye Chelny, on autonomous republics]

[Medvedev] Esteemed President, esteemed chairman, I'm Nikolay Medvedev of the National-Territorial Constituency No 237. We declare a resolute protest against the insulting attacks against the delegations of the three Baltic republics—which are at the same time attacks on the people these delegations represent—that have been voiced from the elevated congress tribune. We censure the session chairman, who let these insults pass without comment on his part. We believe that such attacks are designed to split and wreck the congress. We came here for cooperation. However, the whipping-up of anti-Baltic chauvinism could make such cooperation impossible. I can only add that when there was talk here of shock detachments, I considered myself to be one of them. As distinct from voluntary people's militia groups, we can be roused at any time of day or night, and we hurry on our way having learned that somewhere someone is being offended—a Russian, a Lithuanian, a Jew, a Tatar. We are armed from head to toe. Our weapon is words. We have unlimited rights. We can put ourselves in the path of the blows when someone is being offended—moral and physical blows. This may be the reason why we have rallies, attended by 200,000 people, that are not surrounded by the militia. Esteemed Secretary Brazauskas and Second Secretary Berezov join us. We argue, are reconciled, disagree, and agree again, and we seek the truth. We have no drunks at these rallies, and we don't have hooligans at these meetings. Thank you for listening. We do this on Saturdays and Sundays. [applause]

[passage omitted: Yerevyanko from Odessa and unidentified female deputy from Tashkent speak]

[Lukyanov] Your name, please.

[Leontyev] Leontyev, territorial constituency No 208, center of Russia, Kuybyshev Oblast. I was asked—and here are 16,000 signatures—by our electors to appeal to the congress. The question is as follows: Here clash the vital interests of each of us and of the most important political decisions of our state.

Esteemed comrades, USSR people's deputies! The inhabitants of the town of Chapayevsk and other inhabited localities stituated near the plant for the destruction of chemical weapons that is being built appeal to you. We support the party and government policy of struggle for peace, disarmament, and the destruction of weapons of mass destruction, including chemical weapons. This policy expresses the will of all honest people of the planet. It is dictated by the concern for man and for the future of our civilization. The concern for man must always be shown, including in the erection of such important facilities, as is the plant for the destruction of poisonous gases.

Even when carrying out a superficial analysis, however, it is clear that concern for people's interests was taken into account last during the design and selection of the place of construction. The situation has arisen in such a way that three quite big chemical enterprises, at which there are works producing explosives, have been working directly in the town for many years. These enterprises are systematically polluting the environment. Over the last 3 years three accidents with explosions and human casualties occurred here. The last explosion, which thundered on 27 November 1988, cost six human lives. [murmur in the audience]

Only one plant has purification equipment. It is extremely overloaded. Uncleansed waste flows in the Chapayevka River and then into the Volga. In comparison with the average data of the oblast, child mortality is 2.5 times larger in the town. The number of blood, upper respiratory tract, heart, and oncological diseases are typical among the inhabitants of the town of Chapayevsk.

Under these complex ecological conditions, a plant for the destruction of poisonous gases is being prepared for a start-up 10 kilometers from town, in a quite densely populated zone. The information about this plant is very contradictory, and this naturally arouses alarm among the local inhabitants. During his first meeting with the inhabitants of the town of Chapayevsk on 2 February 1989, Academician Kuntsevich said that the plant will destroy the poisonous gases which were produced by local enterprises. [bell rigns, followed by noise and sporadic applause]

[Lukyanov] We can have this telegram sent around, comrades. [passage omitted: Deputy Solovyev speaks]

[Yaroshinskaya] Deputy Yaroshinskaya from the town of Zhitomir, territorial constituency No 446. Esteemed comrades, I have a big request for our presidium and also for you. What I have to say concerns not only myself and my electorate. It is spoken of as a general human problem. The fact is that Narodichi Rayon in Zhitomir Oblast comes within the zone of particularly severe silence. As a journalist I have not been able for a year and a half to publish truthful material anywhere about what has been occurring there. It is interesting, comrades, that, whereas at first there were 18 villages within the zone of particularly severe radiation, now after 3 years there are about 90 such villages. Whereas earlier only Narodichi Rayon was affected by radiation, now there are four more such rayons.

Comrades, Ukrainian Health Minister Romanenko has until today been telling all of us who live there in that zone that it is almost a Swiss resort. Comrades, this is simply disgraceful. If you were to view the footage shot by Moscow documentary filmmakers, you would see what is in actual fact happening there. It is what concerns all of us. Tbilisi, yes. Other events, yes. But what is happening there. Comrades, it is very important, and I make a big request of the presidium. Here is a video cassette. I would very much like you to listen to me, and for the presidium to make it possible for the whole congress and all of us people's deputies to view this video cassette. Here is the truth about Narodichi Rayon. Thank you. [applause] [passage omitted: Deputy Kasyan from the charity fund on lineup of speakers]

[Lukyanov] Comrades, I believe that we should take a vote. Those in favor of ending the debate for the time being, go ahead please. Those against? Let us call it a clear minority. No?

In that case, permit me to brief you on the work tomorrow, the day after tomorrow, etc. To start with, our cosmonauts and Comrade Ryumin invite you to visit an exhibition of space technology, which says: those who wish to visit the exhibition of application of achievements of space rocket technology to the national economy should put their names today on a list at the congress desk for the issue of documents run by Deputy Ryumin. And the departure is tomorrow at 0930 from the Moskva Hotel. The excursion will last until about 1600. An additional tour is offered on Sunday for the delegates working on Saturday. So, we would like you to have a look at the kind of technology, what it costs, and what it gives us. That is the first thing.

Second, I would like to remind the deputies who have been included in the composition of the Councils of Elders of the chambers that a session of the Councils of Elders of the chambers will be held tomorrow at 1000 in the chambers' conference hall, where the Supreme Soviet Presidium is found; you pass by the (?Spasskaya) Tower on the way here. The first organizational session of the Council of the Union will take place tomorrow at 1500, also in the conference hall of the USSR Supreme Soviet chambers. And on Monday, a session of the Council of Nationalities will take place. The next session of the congress will take place on Monday, 5 June at 1000 here, at the Palace of Congresses. And as to the scheduled finishing time, ask me another one! [laughter]

All the best to you!

2 Jun CPSU Central Committee Plenum on Congress

Ryzhkov Comments on Plenum
LD0206173689 Moscow TASS International Service in Russian 1430 GMT 2 Jun 89

[TASS correspondents Vladimir Isachenkov and Sergey Karmalito report from the Kremlin]

[Text] Moscow, 2 Jun (TASS)—The critical mood of the USSR Congress of People's Deputies reflects the high-level political activity by the Soviet People, Nikolay Ryzhkov, chairman of the USSR Council of Ministers, stated today. In a conversation with Soviet and foreign journalists during a break between sessions, he noted that this great political intensity was reflected both during the pre-election campaign, the elections themselves, and at the congress.

Nikolay Ryzhkov, who in the event of his being elected chairman of the Council of Ministers at the session of the newly elected Supreme Soviet will deliver a report at the congress, expressed some thoughts on the state of and tasks for the development of the Soviet economy. Answering a question about the proposal made at the congress to start a new 5-year plan in 1990—not in 1991—and give up the previous plan, he stated that such a decision might do "more harm than good." After all, all the economic norms have already been approved for enterprises, which have designed their plans around these quotas. "It is necessary to see this 5-year plan through to the end," Nikolay Ryzhkov said. This does not mean that we should not prepare, for example, for territorial financial autonomy, some elements of which should be tried even in 1990."

On the subject of the proposals advanced by deputies from the Baltic republics concerning the introduction of republican financial autonomy, Nikolay Ryzhkov remarked that to some extent they depart from the guidelines already drawn up together. They contain some good ideas that need to be carefully examined again. But there are points that give rise to very grave doubts, for instance the introduction by the republics of their own currencies.

Asked about the expediency of cutting the number of ministries even more, Nikolay Ryzhkov emphasized that this matter must be approached in a balanced way. "As conditions mature in the primary links—in enterprises and organizations—when there really is more independence there, when all economic relations between enterprises are running smoothly, we will not need so many ministries," he said.

Speaking about the attitude towards the experience of other socialist states in resolving economic issues, Nikolay Ryzhkov acknowledged that they are being carefully studied in the USSR, in particular the experiences of Hungary and Czechoslovakia. Everything useful is (?being noted).

Asked about today's CPSU Central Committee plenum—which is expected to take place after the evening session of the congress concludes—Nikolay Ryzhkov replied that it would be discussing the work of the Congress of People's Deputies. "The party must analyze the course of the congress," he said. "That is a natural process."

There was also a question about whether there were Politburo members complaining about the criticism heard at the congress, and in particular how Yegor Ligachev, member of the Politburo and secretary of the Central Committee, had reacted to it. According to Ryzhkov, Yegor Ligachev categorically denies the accusations made against him. Nikolay Ryzhkov declared that the Politburo is prepared to express its opinion should that be necessary. Yegor Ligachev would also probably have his say. "But we are firmly convinced that these are not true," emphasized Nikolay Ryzhkov.

Gorbachev, Ryzhkov Address Plenum
LD0206201989 Moscow TASS in English 2012 GMT 2 Jun 89

[Text] Moscow June 2 TASS—A plenum of the Soviet Communist Party Central Committee was held here today to discuss the Congress of People's Deputies and the upcoming session of the Soviet Supreme Soviet.

Soviet Communist Party leader Mikhail Gorbachev made a report on these issues.

The plenum was also addressed by Nikolay Ryzhkov, chairman of the Soviet Council of Ministers, Vitaliy Vorotnikov, Russian Federation Supreme Soviet president, Vadim Medvedev, Communist Party Central Committee secretary, several regional party leaders and ministers.

The plenum recommended Nikolay Ryzhkov for the post of chairman of the Soviet Council of Ministers.

Mikhail Gorbachev made the closing speech.

CPSU Plenum Participants Listed
LD0206212989 Moscow TASS International Service in Russian 2015 GMT 2 Jun 89

[Text] Moscow, 2 Jun (TASS)—A CPSU Central Committee plenum devoted to the Congress of USSR People's Deputies and the upcoming session of the USSR Supreme Soviet took place today.

M.S. Gorbachev, CPSU Central Committee general secretary, spoke on these matters at the plenum.

The plenum was addressed by: N.I. Ryzhkov, chairman of the USSR Council of Ministers, E.K. Pervyshin, minister of the USSR communications equipment industry, V.G. Afonin, first secretary of the Kuybyshev Oblast CPSU committee, B.M. Belousov, USSR minister of machine-building, V.K. Mesyats, first secretary of the Moscow Oblast CPSU committee, I.K. Polozkov, first secretary of the Krasnodar Kray CPSU committee, V.P. Mysnichenko, first secretary of the Kharkov Oblast committee of the Ukrainian Communist Party, N.A. Nazarbayev, chairman of the Ministers Council of the Kazakh Soviet Socialist Republic, A.I. Volskiy, chairman of the Committee for Special Administration of the Nagorno-Karabakh autonomous oblast and head of a section at the CPSU Central Committee, V.I. Potapov, first secretary of the Irkutsk Oblast CPSU committee, B. Ye. Paton, president of the Academy of Sciences of the Ukrainian Soviet Socialist Republic, V.K. Foteyev, first secretary of the Checheno-Ingush Oblast CPSU Committee, Yu. A. Manaenkov, first secretary of the Lipetsk Oblast CPSU Comittee, N.I. Malkov, first secretary of the Chita Oblast CPSU Committee, B.M. Bolodin, first secretary of the Rostov Oblast CPSU Committee, P. Ya. Slezko, deputy chairman of the party control committee under the CPSU Central Committee, Yu. I. Litvintsev, first secretary of Tula Oblast CPSU committee, Ye. D. Pokhitaylo, first secretary of the Omsk oblast CPSU Committee, V.V. Karpov, first secretary of the Board of the USSR Union of Writers, G. Ch. Shirshin, first secretary of the Tuva Oblast CPSU committee, V.A. Kuptsov, first secretary of the Vologda Oblast CPSU committee, M.F. Nenashev, chairman of the USSR State Committee for Radio and Television Broadcasting, A.G. Melnikov, first secretary of the Kemerovo Oblast CPSU Committee, L.I. Khitrun, first secretary of the Ryazan

Oblast CPSU Committee, V.I. Vorotnikov, chairman of the Presidium of the RSFSR Supreme Soviet, and V.A. Medvedev, secretary of the CPSU Central Committee.

The plenum recommended N.I. Ryzhkov for appointment as chairman of the USSR Council of Ministers.

In conclusion, M.S. Gorbachev, CPSU Central Committee general secretary, addressed the plenum.

Thereupon, the CPSU Central Committee plenum ended its work.

PRAVDA Lists New USSR Supreme Soviet Members
PM0206120089 Moscow PRAVDA in Russian 1 Jun 89 Second Edition pp 4-5

["USSR Supreme Soviet Elected by the USSR Congress of the People's Deputies"—PRAVDA headline]

[Text]

Soviet of the Union

Russian Soviet Federated Socialist Republic [RSFSR]

Alekseyev, Sergey Sergeyevich, corresponding member of the USSR Academy of Sciences, director of the USSR Academy of Sciences Urals Department Institute of Philosophy and Law, Sverdlovsk City.

Blayev, Boris Khagutsirovich, director of the Tyrnyauz Tungsten-Molybdenum Combine, Kabardino-Balkar Autonomous Soviet Socialist Republic [ASSR].

Bliznov, Leonid Yevgenyevich, fitter-repairman at Moscow's Kerchief Production Association, Pavlovskiy Posad City.

Bobyleva, Yevdokiya Fedorovna, director of the Odoyev Secondary School, Tula Oblast.

Bogdanov, Igor Mikhaylovich, director of School No. 94, Gorkiy City.

Bogomolov, Yuriy Aleksandrovich, director of the "Yevlashevskiy" State Farm [Sovkhoz], Kuznetskiy Rayon, Penza Oblast.

Borovkov, Vyacheslav Aleksandrovich, machine assembly works fitter at the "Kirovskiy Zavod" Production Association, Leningrad City.

Borodin, Yuriy Ivanovich, chairman of the USSR Academy of Medical Sciences Siberian Department Presidium, Novosibirsk City.

Bocharov, Mikhail Aleksandrovich, director of the Butovskiy Construction Materials Combine, Moscow City.

Burlatskiy, Fedor Mikhaylovich, political observer for LITERATURNAYA GAZETA.

Velikhov, Yevgeniy Pavlovich, vice president of the USSR Academy of Sciences.

Veprev, Arkadiy Filimonovich, director of "Nazarovskiy" Sovkhoz, Nazarovskiy Rayon, Krasnoyarsk Kray.

Vlazneva, Mariya Ivanovna, milkmaid at the "Rossiya" Collective Farm [Kolkhoz], Torbeyevskiy Rayon, Mordovian ASSR.

Vnebrachniy, Ivan Semenovich, diesel engine driver at the Velikolukskiy Locomotive Depot, Velikiye Luki City, Pskov Oblast.

Volkov, Vladimir Anatolyevich, secretary of the party committee at the M.I. Kalinin Sverdlovsk Machine Building Plant.

Volodichev, Viktor Vasilyevich, leader of a team of construction workers on the "Angarstroy" Construction Administration's Construction-Work Train No. 274, Irkutsk Oblast.

Voskoboynikov, Valeriy Ivanovich, Mi-8 helicopter flight engineer of the 25th Flight Detachment of Novyy Urengoy Combined Air Detachment, Tyumen Oblast.

Gamzatov, Rasul Gamzatovich, writer, chairman of the Dagestan ASSR Writers Union Board, secretary of the RSFSR Writers Union Board, secretary of the USSR Writers Union Board.

Glazkov, Nikolay Semenovich, foreman and team leader at the Moscow Decorative Timepiece Plant.

Golik, Yuriy Vladimirovich, dean of the law faculty at Kemerovo State University.

Golyakov, Aleksandr Ivanovich, first deputy chairman of the All-Union Council of War and Labor Veterans, Moscow City.

Gorbatko, Viktor Vasilyevich, chief of faculty in the N.Ye Zhukovskiy Air Force Engineering Academy and chairman of the board of the All-Union Society of Philatelists.

Grachev, Nikolay Petrovich, troubleshooter at the "Tretiy Gosudarstvennyy Podshipnikovyy Zavod" Production Association, Saratov City.

Gritsenko, Nikolay Nikolayevich, rector of the All-Union Central Council of Trade Unions [AUCCTU] Higher School of the Trade Union Movement named for N.M. Shvernik, Moscow City.

Gross, Viktor Ivanovich, general director of the "Bryanskiy Avtomobilnyy Zavod" Production Association.

Grudinina, Anna Kornilovna, chief of section in the Borisoglebskaya Central Rayon Hospital, Voronezh Oblast.

Gubarev, Viktor Andreyevich, deputy director of the "Neftetermmash" Prototype-Experimental Machine Building Plant, Krasnodar Kray.

Gudilina, Valentina Grigoryevna, chief of department in the Solnechnogorskaya Central Rayon Hospital, Moscow Oblast.

Gutskalov, Nikolay Ivanovich, captain-director of the Murmansk Trawler Fleet Administration's large autonomous trawler "Marshal Yeremenko."

Denisov, Anatoliy Alekseyevich, professor at the M.I. Kalinin Leningrad Polytechnical Institute.

Dikul, Valentin Ivanovich, director of the Center for the Rehabilitation of Patients Suffering From Spinal and Brain Injuries and the Consequences of Infantile Cerebral Palsy, Moscow City.

Dorokhov, Ivan Vasilyevich, first secretary of the Bobrovskiy Rayon CPSU Committee [Raykom], Voronezh Oblast.

Druz, Petr Antonovich, pensioner, Belovo City, Kemerovo Oblast.

Drunina, Yuliya Vladimirovna, poetess, secretary of the USSR Writers' Union Board, secretary of the RSFSR Writers' Union Board, Moscow City.

Dyakov, Ivan Nikolayevich, first secretary of the Astrakhan Oblast CPSU Committee [Obkom].

Yegorov, Oleg Mikhaylovich, second officer aboard a refrigerator transport ship, Kaliningrad City.

Yezhelev, Anatoliy Stepanovich, chief of IZVESTIYA's Leningrad Correspondent Center.

Yemelyanov, Aleksey Mikhaylovich, chief of the Agricultural Economics Faculty at the M.V. Lomonosov Moscow State University.

Yermolayev, Gennadiy Mikhaylovich, director of Kormilovskiy Rayon's "Mikhaylovskiy" Livestock Breeding Sovkhoz, Omsk Oblast.

Yefimov, Nikolay Vasilyevich, leader of an installation workers' team at the "Stalkonstruktsiya" Trust's Vyksa Construction and Installation Administration, Gorkiy Oblast.

Zhdakayev, Ivan Andreyevich, bulldozer operator at the Pervomaysk Timber Industry Enterprise, Sakhalin Oblast.

Zubov, Yuriy Ivanovich, director of "Oktyabrskiy" Sovkhoz, Rybinskiy Rayon, Yaroslavl Oblast.

Ivanov, Kliment Yegorovich, general director of the "Sever" Agro-Combine, Yakutsk City.

Ivchenko, Ivan Mikhaylovich, link leader on the "Oktyabr" Kolkhoz, Chertkovskiy Rayon, Rostov Oblast.

Iovlev, Dmitriy Mikhaylovich, fitter at the Lenin Komsomol [All-Union Leninist Communist Youth League] "Moskvich" Production Association automobile plant, Moscow City.

Kazarin, Aleksey Aleksandrovich, carpenter and concrete worker at the "Sharyadrev" Timber Processing Production Association, Sharya City, Kostroma Oblast.

Kazachenko, Petr Petrovich, chairman of "Voskhod" Kolkhoz, Uzlovskiy Rayon, Tula Oblast.

Kalmykov, Yuriy Khamzatovich, chief of department at the Saratov Law Institute Named for D.I. Kurskiy.

Kasyan, Vladimir Vasilyevich, section chief at Anapskiy Rayon's "Pervomayskiy" Sovkhoz, Krasnodar Kray.

Kim Yen-un, senior scientific staffer at Omsk State University.

Kisin, Viktor Ivanovich, chief of Moscow's I.A. Likhachev Automobile Plant New Technology Administration.

Klimov, Mikhail Valeryevich, deputy chief physician at Vyshnevolotskiy Central Rayon Hospital, Kalinin Oblast.

Konkov, Pavel Ivanovich, pensioner, Krasnoyarsk City.

Kopylova, Aleksandra Vasilyevna, chief of the Mtsensk City Soviet of People's Deputies Executive Committee [Gorispolkom] Public Education Department, Orel Oblast.

Kopysov, Nikolay Mikhaylovich, controller at the Izhevsk Radio Plant, Udmurt ASSR.

Korenev, Aleksandr Anatolyevich, drivers' team leader at the Kurgan Motor Transport Production Association.

Koryugin, Nikolay Nikolayevich, chief of the economic research laboratory at the Cherepovets 50th Anniversary of the USSR Metallurgical Combine, Vologda Oblast.

Krasnokutskiy, Boris Ivanovich, chairman of the Ya.M. Sverdlov Kolkhoz, Sysertskiy Rayon, Sverdlovsk Oblast.

Kryuchenkova, Nadezhda Aleksandrovna, teacher at the Inzhavinskiy Secondary School No. 2, Tambov Oblast.

Kuzovlev, Anatoliy Tikhonovich, chairman of the Kalinin Kolkhoz, Kanevskiy Rayon, Krasnodar Kray.

Kulikov, Viktor Georgiyevich, general inspector of the USSR Defense Ministry General Inspectors' Group.

Kurtashin, Vladimir Yegorovich, general director of the "Kriogenmash" Science and Production Association, Balashikha City, Moscow Oblast.

Laptev, Ivan Dmitriyevich, chief editor of the newspaper IZVESTIYA.

Leonchev, Vladimir Aleksandrovich, fitter team leader at the Novokuybyshevsk "50-Letiye SSR" Petrochemical Combine, Kuybyshev Oblast.

Lubenchenko, Konstantin Dmitriyevich, reader on the Moscow M.V. Lomonosov State University law faculty.

Lunev, Viktor Andreyevich, lathe operator at the Moscow "Kompressor" production association's "Kompressor" refrigeration machine building plant.

Lushnikov, Vladimir Petrovich, drifter at the "Intaugol" production association's "Vostochnaya" Mine, Komi ASSR.

Mayboroda, Viktor Alekseyevich, cutter-polisher at the Ust-Katavskiy Freightcar Building Plant, Chelyabinsk Oblast.

Malkova, Yevgeniya Kirillovna, foreman of workshop No. 5 at Clothing Production and Repair Factory No. 1 of the Moscow City "Siluet" Production Association.

Maltsev, Innokentiy Ivanovich, planer at the Moscow Yefremov "Krasnyy Proletariy" Machine Tool Manufacturing Plant.

Manayenkov, Yuriy Alekseyevich, first secretary of Lipetsk CPSU Obkom.

Markov, Oleg Ivanovich, arc welder at the "Sibenergomash" Production Association, Barnaul City.

Matviyenko, Valentina Ivanovna, deputy chairman of Leningrad Gorispolkom.

Medvedev, Roy Aleksandrovich, writer, historian, current affairs writer, Moscow City.

Medikov, Viktor Yakovlevich, prorector of the Siberian Metallurgical Institute, Novokuznetsk City, Kemerovo Oblast.

Menshatov, Aleksey Dmitriyevich, director of the "Azinskiy" State Pedigree Stud Farm, Chernushinskiy Rayon, Perm Oblast.

Militenko, Svetlana Aleksandrovna, department chief at the "Lesnaya Polyana" Sanatorium, Pyatigorsk City, Stavropol Kray.

Minin, Viktor Mikhaylovich, chief of shop at the Glebovskoye Poultry Breeding Production Association, Moscow Oblast.

Mikhedov, Fedor Fedorovich, leader of a drift miners' team at "Primorskugol" Production Association's "Tsentralnaya" Mine, Partizansk City.

Mukhametzyanov, Aklim Kasimovich, general director of the "Tatneft" Production Association named for V.D. Shashin, Almetyevsk City.

Naumov, Sergey Yakovlevich, chairman of Argayashskiy Rayon's "Marksist" Kolkhoz, Chelyabinsk Oblast.

Neyelov, Yuriy Vasilyevich, chairman of Surgutskiy Rayon Ispolkom, Tyumen Oblast.

Neumyvakin, Aleksandr Yakovlevich, chairman of All-Russian Society for the Blind Central Board, Moscow City.

Nikanorov, Igor Alekseyevich, lathe operator at Ryazan Machine Tool Plant.

Nikolskiy, Boris Nikolayevich, chief editor of the journal NEVA, Leningrad City.

Nuzhnyy, Vladimir Pavlovich, lease collective leader at Apanasenkovskiy Rayon's "Rossiya" Kolkhoz and Breeding Plant, Stavropol Kray.

Orekhov, Anatoliy Pavlovich, chairman of Karymskiy Rayon Soviet of People's Deputies Executive Committee [Rayispolkom], Chita Oblast.

Ostroukhov, Viktor Alekseyevich, secretary of the "Sibkabel" Production Association party committee, Tomsk City.

Pamfilova, Ella Aleksandrovna, chairman of the trade union committee at the "Mosenergo" Production Association's central mechanical repair plant.

Panteleyev, Nikolay Vasilyevich, lathe operator at the Lepse Kirov Electrical Machine Building Plant, Kirov City.

Penyagin, Aleksandr Nikolayevich, refractory maker at the Chelyabinsk Electrometallurgy Combine.

Pivovarov, Nikolay Dmitriyevich, chairman of the Rostov Oblast Soviet of People's Deputies Executive Committee [Oblispolkom].

Piryazeva, Nina Mikhaylovna, electrical assembly worker at Novosibirsk's "Sibselmash" Production Association.

Postnikov, Viktor Ivanovich, general director of "Stavropolskoye" Broiler Production Association.

Pokhodnya, Grigoriy Semenovich, shop chief of the Frunze Kolkhoz, Belgorodskiy Rayon, Belgorod Oblast.

Pribylova, Nadezhda Nikolayevna, department head and professor at the Kursk Medical Institute.

Primakov, Yevgeniy Maksimovich, director of the USSR Academy of Sciences Institute of World Economics and International Relations.

Pukhova, Zoya Pavlovna, chairman of the Soviet Women's Committee.

Rakhimov, Murtaza Gubaydullovich, director of the 22d CPSU Congress Ufa Oil Refinery.

Rakhmanova, Marina Nikolayevna, department head at the Orenburg Medical Institute.

Reshetnikov, Anatoliy Vasilyevich, deputy shop chief at the Kaluga Engine Building Production Association.

Rogatin, Boris Nikolayevich, chairman of the AUCCTU Voluntary Physical Education and Sports Society.

Rogozhina, Vera Aleksandrovna, senior scientific assistant at the USSR Academy of Sciences Siberian Department Institute of the Earth's Crust, Irkutsk City.

Ryzhov, Yuriy Alekseyevich, rector of the Moscow Aviation Institute named for S. Ordzhonikidze.

Ryumin, Valeriy Viktorovich, deputy chief designer at the "Energiya" Science and Production Association, Moscow City.

Savitskaya, Svetlana Yevgenyevna, deputy chief of department at the "Energiya" Science and Production Association, Moscow City.

Savostyuk, Oleg Mikhaylovich, secretary of the USSR Artists' Union Board, chairman of the board of the Moscow Organization of the RSFSR Artists Union.

Sazonov, Nikolay Semenovich, party committee secretary at the Kama Motor Vehicle Plant automatic lathe production unit, Tatar ASSR.

Sapegin, Aleksey Andreyevich, electric locomotive engineer at the Smolensk Locomotive Depot of the Moscow Railroad.

Sarakayev, Archil Totrazovich, chairman of the Kalinin Kolkhoz, Irafskiy Rayon, North Osetiyan ASSR.

Svatkovskiy, Vladimir Vasilyevich, chairman of the V.I. Lenin Fishing Kolkhoz, Kamchatka Oblast.

Skvortsov, Vladimir Vitalyevich, chief of a shop at the Vyazniki Motor Vehicle and Tractor Lighting Equipment Plant, Vladimir Oblast.

Sleptsov, Sergey Yefimovich, machine operator at "Churovichskiy" Sovkhoz, Klimovskiy Rayon, Bryansk Oblast.

Smorodin, Ivan Mikhaylovich, controller at Novgorod "Volna" Production Association.

Sobchak, Anatoliy Aleksandrovich, chief of department at the Leningrad State University Law Faculty.

Sokolova, Yuliya Yuryevna, senior instructor at the Soviet Army and Navy Main Political Directorate.

Sotnikov, Nikolay Ivanovich, director of the Leningrad Ceramics Plant.

Stadnik, Vladimir Yakovlevich, workshop chief at the Lukhovitsy Machine Building Plant, Moscow Oblast.

Stepanov, Vladimir Nikolayevich, director of the "Vidlitskiy" Fur Sovkhoz, Olentskiy Rayon, Karelian ASSR.

Stoumova, Galina Ivanovna, workshop chief at the "Gatchinskiy" Sovkhoz, Leningrad Oblast.

Tetenov, Valentin Afanasyevich, first deputy chief of the Perm branch of the Sverdlovsk Railroad.

Timchenko, Vladimir Mikhaylovich, milling machine operator at the "Azovskiy Optiko-Mekhanicheskiy Zavod" Production Association, Rostov Oblast.

Timchenko, Mikhail Andreyevich, director of the "Marushinskiy" Sovkhoz, Tselinnyy Rayon, Altay Kray.

Tutov, Nikolay Dmitriyevich, secretary of the Komsomol committee of a military unit, Orenburg City.

Usilina, Nina Andreyevna, chief veterinarian at Shakhunskiy Rayon's "Komsomolets" Sovkhoz, Gorkiy Oblast.

Filshin, Gennadiy Innokentyevich, department chief at the USSR Academy of Sciences Siberian Department's Economics and Organization of Industrial Production Institute, Irkutsk Oblast.

Finogenov, Vladimir Vyacheslavovich, tool shop foreman at the "Elektroavtomat" Plant, Alatyr City, Chuvash ASSR.

Frolov, Konstantin Vasilyevich, vice president of the USSR Academy of Sciences, director of the A. Blagonravov USSR Academy of Sciences Machine Science Institute.

Khadzhiyev, Salambek Naibovich, general director of the "Grozneftekhim" Science and Production Association.

Khmura, Valeriy Vasilyevich, chairman of the Olginskiy Rural Soviet Executive Committee [Ispolkom], CPSU member, Primorsko-Akhtarskiy Rayon, Krasnodar Kray.

Tsyplayev, Sergey Alekseyevich, scientific secretary at the S.I. Vavilov State Optical Institute, Leningrad City.

Tsyurupa, Viktor Aleksandrovich, head of the Opthalmology Department at City Hospital No. 15, Moscow City.

Chernyayev, Nikolay Fedorovich, machine operator at the "Krasnoye Znamya" Kolkhoz, Karsunskiy Rayon, Ulyanovsk Oblast.

Chichik, Yuriy Mikhaylovich, director of the "Krasnorechenskiy" Sovkhoz, Khabarovskiy Rayon, Khabarovsk Kray.

Shaydulin, Midkhat Idiyatovich, pensioner, Ufa City.

Sharin, Leonid Vasilyevich, first secretary of Amur CPSU Obkom.

Shashkov, Nikolay Vladimirovich, manager of the Nikitinskoye department of the "Vasilyevskiy" Sovkhoz, Shuyskiy Rayon, Ivanovo Oblast.

Shekhovtsov, Viktor Afanasyevich, deputy dean of the Far Eastern State University Law Faculty, Vladivostok City.

Shishov, Viktor Aleksandrovich, director of the "Vazhskiy" Sovkhoz, Velskiy Rayon, Arkhangelsk Oblast.

Shmal, Yuriy Yakovlevich, director of the "Maslyaninskiy" Sovkhoz, Maslyaninskiy Rayon, Novosibirsk Oblast.

Shtepo, Viktor Ivanovich, general director of the "Volgo-Don" Specialized Production Association, Kalachevskiy Rayon, Volgograd Oblast.

Shukshin, Anatoliy Stepanovich, grinder at the Far East Power Machine Building Plant, Khabarovsk City.

Yudin, Vladimir Dmitriyevich, chief of the Northeastern Geological Production Association Central Geochemical Group, Magadan Oblast.

Yakutis, Vladislav Stanislavovich, comprehensive team leader at the "Boguchanles" Timber Association Timber Station, Krasnoyarsk Kray.

Yarin, Veniamin Aleksandrovich, operator at the Nizhniy Tagil V.I. Lenin Metallurgical Combine, Sverdlovsk Oblast.

Yarovaya, Olga Pavlovna, milkmaid at the "Krasnaya Zvezda" Training Farm, Atkarskiy Rayon, Saratov Oblast.

Ukrainian Soviet Socialist Republic [SSR]

Amosov, Nikolay Mikhaylovich, honorary director of Cardiovascular Surgery Scientific Research Institute, Kiev City.

Babchenko, Nikolay Ivanovich, chairman of Dnepropetrovskiy Local Industry and Municipal and Consumer Service Enterprise Workers Union Obkom.

Breurosh, Boris Sergeyevich, combine operator at the "Druzhba" Kolkhoz, Maloviskovskiy Rayon, Kirovograd Oblast.

Vakarchuk, Ivan Aleksandrovich, head of department at the Lvov Iv. Franko State University.

Vasilets, Aleksandr Nikolayevich, electric engine driver at the 25th CPSU Congress Southern Railroad Kupyansk locomotive depot, Kharkov Oblast.

Vasilchuk, Nikolay Parfenovich, chairman of the Board of the Khmelnitskiy Oblast Consumer Cooperative Union [Potrebsoyuz].

Vologzhin, Valentin Mikhaylovich, general director of the 60th Anniversary of the Great October Socialist Revolution "Konveyer" Production Association, Lvov City.

Vuychitskiy, Anatoliy Stanislavovich, chairman of "Druzhba" Kolkhoz, Novomoskovskiy Rayon, Dnepropetrovsk Oblast.

German, Natalya Fedorovna, team leader of the "Shabo" Sovkhoz-Plant, Belgorod-Dnestrovskiy Rayon, Odessa Oblast.

Gil, Yaroslav Yakovlevich, chief physician at the Kremenetskiy Central Rayon Hospital, Ternopol Oblast.

Grib, Aleksandr Vasilyevich, blast furnace attendant at the "Zaporozhstal" Metallurgical Combine, Zaporozhye City.

Danilov, Valeriy Nikolayevich, foreman at Pridneprovsk Railroad Sinelnikovo Refrigerated Freight Car Depot, Dnepropetrovsk Oblast.

Demchenko, Fedor Mikhaylovich, leader of a team at Poltava Housing Construction Combine.

Zelinskiy, Igor Petrovich, rector of Odessa I.I. Mechnikov State University.

Kasyanov, Anatoliy Fedorovich, chairman of Novoazovskiy Rayon's Karl Marx Kolkhoz, Donetsk Oblast.

Kravets, Vladimir Alekseyevich, Ukrainian SSR foreign minister.

Kucherenko, Viktor Grigoryevich, chairman of Donetsk Oblispolkom.

Lesyuk, Yaroslav Stepanovich, chairman of the Gnezdychevskiy settlement soviet ispolkom, Zhidachovskiy Rayon, Lvov Oblast.

Matveychuk, Sergey Ivanovich, fitter-repairman at Vladimir-Volynskiy Cannery, Volyn Oblast.

Matiyko, Lidiya Timofeyevna, team leader at Fastov No. 37 Construction and Installation Administration, Kiev Oblast.

Moskalenko, Galina Semenovna, link leader at Pogrebishchenskiy Rayon's Lenin Kolkhoz, Vinnitsa Oblast.

Moskalik, Mariya Nikolayevna, cook at the Gorodenkovskiy Rayon Potrebsoyuz Canteen, Ivano-Frankovsk Oblast.

Motornyy, Dmitriy Konstantinovich, chairman of the S.M. Kirov Kolkhoz, Belozerskiy Rayon, Kherson Oblast.

Nozdrya, Viktor Alekseyevich, leader of a team of fitters and installation workers at the "S. Ordzhonikidze Sevastopolskiy Morskoy Zavod" Production Association, Crimean Oblast.

Opolinskiy, Vladimir Aleksandrovich, team leader at Chernomorskiy Ship Building Plant, Nikolayev City.

Pavlevich, Ivan Borisovich, leader of the Kamenetsk-Podolskiy housing operation association trade union committee's "Desantnik" military sports and patriotic club, Khmelnitskiy Oblast.

Pavliy, Aleksandr Andreyevich, senior consultant of the Donetsk Oblispolkom.

Plyutinskiy, Vladimir Antonovich, chairman of the "Zarya" Agrofirm's "Zarya Kommunizma" Kolkhoz, Rovenskiy Rayon, Rovno Oblast.

Prikhodko, Zinaida Semenovna, first secretary of the Perechinskiy Ukrainian Communist Party Raykom, Transcarpathian Oblast.

Revenko, Grigoriy Ivanovich, first secretary of the Kiev Ukrainian Communist Party Obkom.

Ryabchenko, Sergey Mikhaylovich, laboratory chief at the Ukrainian SSR Academy of Sciences Institute of Physics, Kiev City.

Saunin, Anatoliy Nikolayevich, faculty lecturer at the Makeyevka Engineering Construction Institute, Donetsk City.

Sbitnev, Anatoliy Mitrofanovich, steelworker at the Kommunarskiy Metallurgical Combine, Perevalsk City, Voroshilovgrad Oblast.

Sidorchuk, Tatyana Vasilyevna, upholsterer at the Carpathian Furniture Combine, Ivano-Frankovsk City, Ivano-Frankovsk Oblast.

Smirnov, Dmitriy Genrikhovich, engineer and designer at the "KhEMZ" Production Association, Kharkov City.

Sukhov, Leonid Ivanovich, driver at the Kharkov 16301 Motor Transport Enterprise.

Sushko, Boris Ivanovich, smelter at the 50th Anniversary of the USSR Pure Metals Plant, Svetlovodsk City, Kirovograd Oblast.

Trefilov, Viktor Ivanovich, vice president of the Ukrainian SSR Academy of Sciences, director of the Institute of the Problems of Materials Science of the Ukrainian SSR Academy of Sciences, Kiev City.

Tyminskiy, Grigoriy Aleksandrovich, chairman of Kelmenetskiy Rayon's "Druzhba Narodov" Kolkhoz, Kelmenetskiy Rayon, Chernovitsy Oblast.

Kharchenko, Grigoriy Petrovich, first secretary of the Zaporozhye Ukrainian Communist Party Obkom.

Tsavro, Yuriy Stanislavovich, head of department at Yalta City Hospital, Crimea Oblast.

Tsarevskiy, Aleksandr Leonidovich, faceworker at the 22d CPSU Congress "Stakhanovugol" Production Association Mine, Voroshilovgrad Oblast.

Tsybukh, Valeriy Ivanovich, first secretary of the Ukrainian Komsomol Central Committee.

Chabanov, Alim Ivanovich, general director of the "Rotor" Science and Production Association, Cherkassy City.

Chentsov, Nikolay Ivanovich, arc welder at the "Shakhterskugol" Production Association's "Komsomolskoye" Mine Administration, Kirovskoye City, Donetsk Oblast.

Chepurnaya, Margarita Aleksandrovna, organizer of extracurricular and extramural educational work at Popovskiy Secondary School, Konotopskiy Rayon, Sumy Oblast.

Chervonopiskiy, Sergey Vasilyevich, first secretary of the Cherkassy Ukrainian Komsomol Gorkom.

Shabanov, Vitaliy Mikhaylovich, USSR deputy defense minister.

Sharyy, Grigoriy Ivanovich, chairman of the "Zapovit Lenina" Kolkhoz, Chutovskiy Rayon, Poltava Oblast.

Shust, Anna Andreyevna, livestock unit chief at the "Mayak" Kolkhoz, Sumskiy Rayon, Sumy Oblast.

Shcherbak, Yuriy Nikolayevich, writer, secretary of the Ukrainian Writers Union Board, Kiev City.

Yakimenko, Anatoliy Nikolayevich, chairman of the "Zhovten" Kolkhoz, Novgorod-Severskiy Rayon, Chernigov Oblast.

Belorussian SSR

Bobritskiy, Nikolay Grigoryevich, deputy general director of the "Bobruyskshina" Production Association, Mogilev Oblast.

Dudko, Tamara Nikolayevna, chairman of Partizanskiy Rayispolkom, Minsk City.

Kalashnikov, Sergey Fedorovich, deputy director in charge of youth work at the Bobruyskiy Sewn Goods Factory Named for F.E. Dzerzhinskiy, Bobruysk City, Mogilev Oblast.

Luchenok, Igor Mikhaylovich, composer, chairman of the Belorussian SSR Composers Union Board, Minsk City.

Miloserdnyy, Anatoliy Kirillovich, director of Orsha "Krasnyy Borets" Machine Tool Building Plant, Vitebsk Oblast.

Piskunovich, Georgiy Petrovich, machine operator on the "Geroy Truda" Kolkhoz, Glubokskiy Rayon, Vitebsk Oblast.

Semukha, Vladimir Iosifovich, chairman of the Belorussian SSR Red Cross Society Central Committee.

Sokolov, Yefrem Yevseyevich, first secretary of the Belorussian Communist Party Central Committee.

Feskov, Nikolay Stepanovich, director of Kochishche Secondary School, Yelskiy Rayon, Gomel Oblast.

Shetko, Pavel Vadimovich, lecturer at the Minsk Belorussian Komsomol Obkom Propaganda Department.

Uzbek SSR

Akbarov, Yuldash Tadzhiyevich, driver with the No. 2 motor vehicle combine, Tashkent City.

Arslonov, Aliyer Kumriyevich, team leader at the 22d CPSU Congress Papskiy Rayon Kolkhoz, Namangan Oblast.

Zhurabayeva, Tozhikhon, chief of the rural medical outpatient clinic of the Nayman Kishlak Soviet, Tashlakskiy Rayon, Fergana Oblast.

Kirgizbayeva, Tukhtakhon Bazarovna, team leader at Syrdarinskiy Rayon's "Malik" Sovkhoz, Syr-Darya Oblast.

Kucherskiy, Nikolay Ivanovich, director of the 50th Anniversary of the USSR Navoi Mining and Metallurgical Combine, Samarkand Oblast.

Mirkasymov, Mirakhmat Mirkhadzhiyevich, first secretary of the Tashkent Uzbek Communist Party Obkom.

Mukhtarov, Akhmedzhan Gulyamovich, chairman of the Uzbek Journalists Union Board, editor of the republic newspaper KISHLOK KHAKIKATI (RURAL TRUTH), Tashkent City.

Ogarok, Valentin Ivanovich, first deputy chairman of the Uzbek SSR Council of Ministers.

Pavlov, Aleksandr Sergeyevich, chief of the CPSU Central Committee State Law Department.

Rakhimov, Azim, deputy manager of the "Bukharaoblagropromstroy" No. 2 Oblast State Cooperative Association.

Salykov, Kakimbek, first secretary of the Karakalpak Uzbek Communist Party Obkom, Nukus City.

Ubaydullayeva, Rano Akhatovna, deputy director of the Uzbek SSR Academy of Sciences Economics Institute, Tashkent City.

Ergashev, Bakhromzhon Makhmudovich, chairman of the Engels Kolkhoz, Leningradskiy Rayon, Fergana Oblast.

Yusupov, Erkin Yusupovich, vice president of the Uzbek SSR Academy of Sciences.

Kazakh SSR

Dzhanasbayev, Azhibzhan Tokenovich, leader of a team of drillers at the "Kazvolfram" Production Association's Akzhal Mine, Dzhezkazgan Oblast.

Donchak, Yaroslav Antonovich, leader of a drift-mining team at the 60th Anniversary of the October Revolution Mine, Karaganda City.

Iskakova, Bayan Seilkhanovna, chief of department at the Kzyltuskaya Rayon Hospital, Kokchetav Oblast.

Kolbin, Gennadiy Vasilyevich, first secretary of the Kazakh Communist Party Central Committee.

Krivoruchko, Yekaterina Vasilyevna, machine operator at the Chimkent Cement Plant.

Milkin, Anatoliy Vasilyevich, first secretary of East Kazakhstan Kazakh Communist Party Obkom, Ust-Kamenogorsk City.

Pal, Oskar Maksimovich, director of the "Sovetskaya" Agricultural Firm, Vozvyshenskiy Rayon, North Kazakhstan Oblast.

Sagdiyev, Makhtay Ramazanovich, chairman of the Kazakh SSR Supreme Soviet Presidium.

Semenikhin, Aleksandr Vasilyevich, electric locomotive driver at Tselinograd station's locomotive depot on the Virgin Lands Railroad.

Suleymenov, Olzhas Omarovich, writer, first secretary of the Kazakh Writers Union Board.

Fominykh, Viktor Nikolayevich, arc welder at the "Aktyubinskselmash" Plant, Aktyubinsk City.

Chursina, Pavlina Mikhaylovna, weaver at the Karagaylinskiy Cloth Combine, Alma-Ata Oblast.

Shakhanov, Mukhtar, writer, chief editor of the journal ZHALYN, secretary of the Kazakh SSR Writers Union Board.

Shopanayev, Kayyrly Amenovich, leader of an integrated team at the "Almaatakultbytstroy" Trust No. 17 Construction and Installation Administration.

Georgian SSR

Amaglobeli, Nodar Sardionovich, rector of Tbilisi State University.

Kvaratskhelia, Gucha Shalvovna, senior scientific staffer at the Georgian SSR Academy of Sciences Linguistics Institute, professor of Tbilisi State Pedagogical Institute.

Kontselidze, Marina Rizayevna, citrus fruit grower on the Khala Village Kolkhoz, Kobuletskiy Rayon.

Kublashvili, Vakhtang Vladimirovich, assembly fitter at the Dimitrov Tbilisi Aircraft Production Association.

Mgaloblishvili, Nodar Mikhaylovich, chairman of the Georgian Architects' Union Board.

Azerbaijan SSR

Amanov, Akif Mami ogly, drilling foreman at the Ali-Bayramly Drilling Work Administration.

Gilalzade, Dzhangir Gadi ogly, team leader in No. 32 Construction Administration in No. 3 Construction and Installation Trust, Kirovabad City.

Melikov, Arif Dzhangir ogly, composer, department chief at the Azerbaijan U. Gadzhibekov State Conservatoire.

Rzayev, Anar Rasul ogly, writer, first secretary of the Azerbaijan Writers Union Board.

Salimov, Alibala Khanakhmed ogly, chairman of the N. Narimanov Kolkhoz, Neftechalinskiy Rayon.

Lithuanian SSR

Antanaytis, Vaydotas Vito, head of department of the Lithuanian Agricultural Academy, Kaunasskiy Rayon.

Brazauskas, Algirdas-Mikolas Kaze, first secretary of the Lithuanian Communist Party Central Committee.

Burachas, Antanas Yonovich, chairman of the Scientific and Technical Information Council attached to the Lithuanian SSR Academy of Sciences Presidium.

Prunskene, Kazimera Danute Prano, rector of the Lithuanian SSR Council of Ministers Institute for Improving the Qualifications of Senior National Economic Officials and Specialists.

Moldavian SSR

Akhromeyev, Sergey Fedorovich, adviser to the chairman of the USSR Supreme Soviet Presidium.

Grossu, Semen Kuzmich, first secretary of the Moldavian Communist Party Central Committee.

Katrinich, Vasiliy Antonovich, team leader at the 50th Anniversary of October Sholdaneshtskiy Rayon Kolkhoz.

Mokanu, Aleksandr Aleksandrovich, chairman of the Moldavian SSR Supreme Soviet Presidium.

Latvian SSR

Vagris, Yan Yanovich, first secretary of the Latvian Communist Party Central Committee.

Gorbunov, Anatoliy Valeryanovich, chairman of the Latvian SSR Supreme Soviet Presidium.

Skulme, Dzhemma Otovna, painter, secretary of the USSR Artists Union Board, chairman of the Latvian SSR Artists Union Board.

Kirghiz SSR

Druzhinina, Lyubov Nikolayevna, sewing machine operator at Frunze's 1 May Sewn Goods Production Association.

Kerimbekov, Teldibek Abdiyevich, driver at Talas Passenger Motor Transport Enterprise.

Masaliyev, Absamat Masaliyevich, first secretary of the Kirghiz Communist Party Central Committee.

Tajik SSR

Kanoatov, Muminsho, first secretary of the Tajik SSR Writers Union Board.

Makhkamov, Kakhar, first secretary of the Tajik Communist Party Central Committee.

Saydaliyev, Saidkul, plasterers' team leader at No. 14 Special Construction Administration of the "Dushanbestroy" Trust.

Armenian SSR

Arutyunyan, Suren Gurgenovich, first secretary of the Armenian Communist Party Central Committee.

Voskanyan, Grant Mushegovich, chairman of the Armenian SSR Supreme Soviet Presidium.

Kirakosyan, Armenak Balasanovich, lathe operator at "Luys" Production Association's Kirovakan Lighting Engineering Plant, Kirovakan City.

Turkmen SSR

Amanova, Maral Bazarovna, department head at the Turkmen A.M. Gorkiy State University, Ashkhabad City.

Niyazov, Saparmurad Atayevich, first secretary of the Turkmen Communist Party Central Committee.

Shaklycheva, Dzhumagozel, leader of a team of plasterers and painters in the Maryoblagropromstroy No. 22 interfarm mobile mechanized column, Sakar-Chaginskiy Rayon.

Estonian SSR

Vare, Vello Iosifovich, leading scientific staffer at the Estonian SSR Academy of Sciences Institute of History.

Lauristin, Maryyu Yokhannesovna, Tartu State University department head.

Soviet of Nationalities

From the RSFSR

Belov, Vasiliy Ivanovich, writer, secretary of the RSFSR Writers Union Board, Vologda City.

Bosenko, Nikolay Vasilyevich, chairman of the All-Russia Council of War and Labor Veterans.

Vorotnikov, Vitaliy Ivanovich, member of the CPSU Central Committee Politburo, chairman of the RSFSR Supreme Soviet Presidium.

Gayer, Yevdokiya Aleksandrovna, junior scientific staffer of the Institute of History, Archeology, and Ethnography of the USSR Academy of Sciences Far Eastern Branch, Vladivostok City.

Yeltsin, Boris Nikolayevich, CPSU Central Committee member, Moscow City.

Likhanov, Albert Anatolyevich, writer, chairman of the V.I. Lenin Soviet Children's Fund Board.

Lukin, Vladimir Petrovich, oxyacetylene cutter at the Kolomna diesel engine building plant named for V.V. Kuybyshev, Moscow Oblast.

Matyukhin, Leonid Ivanovich, chief of the Gorkiy Railroad, Gorkiy City.

Nevolin, Sergey Innokentyevich, chief physician at Novokuznetsk City Hospital No. 11, Kemerovo Oblast.

Podziruk, Viktor Semenovich, lieutenant colonel, senior instructor, navigator-researcher in a military unit, Ivanovo City.

Falin, Valentin Mikhaylovich, chief of the CPSU Central Committee International Department.

From the Ukrainian SSR

Venglovskaya, Vanda Sergeyevna, weaver at the 60th Anniversary of the Great October Socialist Revolution Zhitomirskiy Flax Combine.

Gnatyuk, Viktoriya Vyacheslavovna, physician at the Kalinovskiy Central Rayon Hospital, Vinnitsa Oblast.

Zabrodin, Ivan Aleksandrovich, Ukrainian SSR minister of finance.

Ivashko, Vladimir Antonovich, second secretary of the Ukrainian Communist Party Central Committee.

Kapto, Aleksandr Semenovich, chief of the CPSU Central Committee Ideological Department.

Katilevskiy, Sergey Mikhaylovich, team leader at "Voroshilovgradteplovoz" Production Association, Voroshilovgrad City.

Kurilenko, Viktor Trifonovich, machine operator at the "Ukraina" Kolkhoz, Pologovskiy Rayon, Zaporozhye Oblast.

Lezhenko, Grigoriy Filippovich, tunneler at the V.I. Lenin "Krivbassruda" Production Association Mine, Krivoy Rog City.

Oleynik, Boris Ilich, poet, secretary of the Ukrainian SSR Writers Union Board.

Romanenko, Viktor Dmitriyevich, director of the Ukrainian SSR Academy of Sciences Institute of Hydrobiology.

Shevchenko, Valentina Semenovna, chairman of the Ukrainian SSR Supreme Soviet Presidium.

From the Belorussian SSR

Bolbasov, Vladimir Sergeyevich, chief scientific associate, deputy chief of laboratory at the Belorussian SSR Academy of Sciences Electronics Institute.

Golovnev, Vasiliy Yefimovich, military unit aviation technician, Bykhov City, Mogilev Oblast.

Dubko, Aleksandr Iosifovich, chairman of the "Progress" Agro-Industrial Kolkhoz-Combine, Grodnenskiy Rayon, Grodno Oblast.

Ignatovich, Nikolay Ivanovich, investigator for especially important cases under the Belorussian SSR Prosecutor's Office.

Kiseleva, Valentina Adamovna, machine operator at Grodno's "Khimvolokno" Production Association named for the 60th anniversary of the USSR.

Kucheyko, Aleksandr Petrovich, multi-skilled team leader at Construction Trust No. 19 Construction Administration, Lida City, Grodno Oblast.

Labunov, Vladimir Arkhipovich, chief of the Minsk Radio Engineering Institute Microelectronics Department.

Mateushuk, Zinaida Kondratyevna, shop chief at the 25th CPSU Congress Brest Electromechanical Plant.

Momotova, Tamara Vasilyevna, deputy chief engineer at the Zhlobin Artificial Fur Production Association, Gomel Oblast.

Tarazevich, Georgiy Stanislavovich, chairman of the Belorussian SSR Supreme Soviet Presidium.

Yakushkin, Viktor Vladimirovich, head of physical education at the No. 147 Secondary Vocational and Technical School, Vitebsk City.

From the Uzbek SSR

Adylov, Vladimir Tuychiyevich, lathe operators' team leader at the Tashkent V.P. Chkalov Aircraft Production Association.

Atadzhanov, Alikhan Rakhmatovich, first deputy chairman of the Uzbek SSR Council of Ministers, chairman of the Uzbek SSR State Planning Committee [Gosplan].

Badalbayeva, Patima, chief physician at Shakhrisabzskiy Central Rayon Hospital, Kashka-Darya Oblast.

Davranov, Narzi, physician at the Sverdlovskiy Central Rayon Hospital, Bukhara Oblast.

Yefimov, Anatoliy Stepanovich, chairman of the Uzbek SSR People's Control Committee.

Zokirov, Munavarkhon Zakriyayevich, chief of the Kasansayskiy Rayon Voluntary Society for the Promotion of the Army, Aviation, and Navy [DOSAAF] Sports and Technical Club, Namangan Oblast.

Korshunov, Aleksandr Aleksandrovich, team leader at the Tashkent V.P. Chkalov Aircraft Production Association.

Nishanov, Rafik Nishanovich, first secretary of the Uzbek Communist Party Central Committee.

Sefershayev, Fikret, leader of a cotton-growing team on the "30 Let Uzbekskoy SSR" Kolkhoz in Chinazskiy Rayon, Tashkent Oblast.

Khudaybergenova, Rimadzhon Matnazarovna, first secretary of the Khorezmskiy Uzbek Communist Party Obkom.

Tso, Vasiliy Ivanovich, general director of the Akhunbabayevskiy Cotton-Wool Production Association, Andizhan Oblast.

From the Kazakh SSR

Auyelbekov, Yerkin Nurzhanovich, first secretary of the Kzyl-Orda Kazakh Communist Party Obkom.

Akhmetova, Rushangul Sunurovna, teacher at the Ch. Valikhanova Secondary School, Enbekshikazakhskiy Rayon, Alma-Ata Oblast.

Veyser, Ledzher Marovich, secretary of the Komsomol Committee of the Secondary School Named for Masanchi, Kurdayskiy Rayon, Dzhambul Oblast.

Vidiker, Vladimir Ivanovich, director of the "Suvorovskiy" Sovkhoz, Irtyshskiy Rayon, Pavlodar Oblast.

Dzhumatova, Menslu Duisenbayevna, head physician at the Chapayevskiy Rayon's Dzhambul Rural District Hospital, Uralsk Oblast.

Klishchuk, Petr Martynovich, team leader at the Chistopolskiy Rayon's "Salkynkolskiy" Sovkhoz, Kokchetav Oblast.

Kozhakhmetov, Ibraimzhan, chairman of the Kirov Kolkhoz, Panfilovskiy Rayon, Taldy-Kurgan Oblast.

Medeubekov, Kiylybay Usenovich, chairman of the V.I. Lenin All-Union Academy of Agricultural Sciences Eastern Branch Presidium, Alma-Ata City.

Rakhmadiyev, Yerkegali, composer, first secretary of the Kazakhstan Composers Union Board.

Romazanov, Kabdulla Zakiryanovich, steelworker at the Karaganda Metallurgical Combine, Temirtau City.

Shtoyk, Garri Gvidovich, director of the East Kazakhstan Copper and Chemical Combine of the "Kazpolimetall" Production Association, Shemonaikhinskiy Rayon.

From the Georgian SSR

Advadze, Valerian Sergeyevich, director of the Georgian SSR Gosplan Scientific Research Institute of Economics, Planning, and Management of the National Economy.

Amonashvili, Shalva Aleksandrovich, general director of the Georgian SSR Ministry of Public Education Experimental Science and Production Teacher Training Association, Tbilisi City.

Bakradze, Akakiy Viktorovich, artistic leader of the K. Mardzhanishvili State Academy Theater in Tbilisi.

Guguchiya, Dzhoto Iosifovich, chairman of the kolkhoz named for K. Marx, Zugdidskiy Rayon.

Gumbaridze, Givi Grigoryevich, first secretary of the Georgian Communist Party Central Committee.

Dikhtyar, Anatoliy Dmitriyevich, leader of a multipurpose team at "Tbilgorstroy" Association's No. 5 Housing Construction Combine.

Kurashvili, Zeynab Giviyevna, sewing machine operator at the "Gldani" knitwear production association in Tbilisi.

Menteshashvili, Tengiz Nikolayevich, secretary of the USSR Supreme Soviet Presidium.

Spanderashvili, Tamaz Mikhaylovich, steelworker at the Rustavi Metallurgical Plant.

Stepnadze, Telman Sergeyevich, team leader at Khashurskiy Rayon's Alskiy Viticultural Sovkhoz.

Tabukashvili, Revaz Shalvovich, leader of the "Gruziyafilm" Movie Studio Screenplay Association, Tbilisi City.

From the Azerbaijan SSR

Abbasov, Yashar Isag ogly, steelworker at the Azerbaijan V.I. Lenin Pipe Rolling Mill, Sumgait City.

Azizbekova, Pyusta Azizaga kyzy, director of the Azerbaijan History Museum, Baku City.

Aleskerova, Rukhi Mursal kyzy, chairman of the Lagich Settlement Soviet of People's Deputies Ispolkom, Ismaillinskiy Rayon.

Barusheva, Lyubov Vasilyevna, seamstress at the Volodarskiy Sewn Goods Factory, Baku City.

Vezirov, Abdul-Rakhman Khalil ogly, first secretary of the Azerbaijan Communist Party Central Committee.

Gadzhiyev, Mazakhir Nushiravan ogly, adjusters team leader at the Baku S.M. Kirov Machine-Building Plant.

Ibragimov, Guseyn Rustam ogly, driller at the "Neftyanyye Kamni" Maritime Drilling Operations Administration of the 22d CPSU Congress Oil and Gas Recovery Administration of the "Kaspmorneftegaz" Production Association, Baku City.

Ismailov, Tofik Kyazim ogly, general director and chief designer of the USSR Main Administration for the Creation and Utilization of Space Technology, Space Research Science and Production Association.

Kafarova, Elmira Mikail kyzy, deputy chairman of the Azerbaijan SSR Council of Ministers.

Mamedov, Veli Guseyn ogly, first secretary of the 26 Baku Commissars Azerbaijan Communist Party Raykom, Baku City.

Namazova, Adilya Avaz kyzy, faculty chief at the Azerbaijan Medical Institute, Baku City.

From the Lithuanian SSR

Bichkauskas, Egidiyus Vitautovich, investigator for especially important cases under the Lithuanian SSR Prosecutor's Office.

Vilkas, Eduardas Yono, director of the Lithuanian SSR Academy of Sciences Institute of Economics and chief scientific secretary of the Lithuanian SSR Academy of Sciences Presidium.

Genzyalis, Bronislavas Konstantinovich, professor at the V. Kapsukas Vilnius State University.

Gudaytis, Romas Vitautovich, writer, literary consultant to the Lithuanian SSR Writers Union.

Zaletskas, Kyastutis Vatslovovich, first secretary of the Vilnius Lithuanian Communist Party Gorkom.

Kudarauskas, Sigitas Yuozovich, chief of the electrical engineering department of the Kaunas Polytechnic Institute's Klaypeda faculties.

Kuplyauskene, Yurate Yono, chairman of the Vilnius Engineering and Construction Institute students union committee.

Medvedev, Nikolay Nikolayevich, sector chief of the Kaunas Scientific Research Institute of Radio Measuring Eguipment.

Moteka, Kazimir Vladislavovich, lawyer at the First Vilnius Legal Consultation Office.

Olekas, Yuozas Yuozovich, senior scientific staffer at the Vilnius V. Kapsukas State University Microsurgery Problems Institute.

Uoka, Kazimeras Kosto, secretary of the "Sajudis" Social Movement, Kaunas City.

From the Moldavian SSR

Doga, Yevgeniy Dmitriyevich, composer, first deputy chairman of the Board of the Moldavian SSR Union of Composers.

Drutse, Ion Panteleyevich, writer, Moscow City.

Zamanyagra, Mikhail Fedorovich, truck drivers' team leader at the "Beltsytrans" Production Association.

Kanarovskaya, Anna Matveyevna, deputy director and chief economist at the Dzerzhinskiy Sovkhoz-Plant, Dubossarskiy Rayon.

Kiriyak, Nellya Pavlovna, secretary of the Moldavian SSR Supreme Soviet Presidium.

Kostishin, Nikolay Anatolyevich, fitter and assembly worker at the "Pribor" Plant, Bendery City.

Moshnyaga, Timofey Vasilyevich, chief physician at the republic clinical hospital, Kishinev City.

Palagnyuk, Boris Timofeyevich, director of the 60th Anniversary of the USSR Pedigree Poultry Breeding Sovkhoz, Rybnitskiy Rayon.

Pashaly, Mikhail Konstantinovich, chairman of the Chadyr-Lungskiy Rayon Agro-Industrial Association.

Platon, Semen Ivanovich, chairman of the Kagul Gorispolkom.

Chimpoy, Mikhail Ilich, writer, secretary of the Moldavian SSR Writers Union Board.

From the Latvian SSR

Bisher, Ilmar Olgertovich, professor at the P. Stuchka Latvian State University, Riga City.

Vulfson, Mavrik Germanovich, senior lecturer at the Latvian Academy of Arts Social Sciences Department, Riga City.

Klibik, Valentina Sergeyevna, secretary of the Latvian SSR Supreme Soviet Presidium.

Kostenetskaya, Marina Grigoryevna, writer, Riga City.

Kukayn, Rita Aleksandrovna, director of the Latvian SSR Academy of Sciences A. Kirkhenshteyn Institute of Microbiology, Riga City.

Lutsans, Yanis Petrovich, chairman of the Limbazhskiy Rayon "Ladezers" Kolkhoz-Agrocombine.

Neyland, Nikolay Vasilyevich, Latvian SSR deputy foreign minister.

Nyuksha, Konstantin Ivanovich, fitter and toolmaker at the "Rizhskiy Elektromashinostroitelnyy Zavod" Production Association.

Peters, Yanis Yanovich, writer, chairman of the Latvian SSR Writers Union Board.

Rubiks, Alfreds Petrovich, Riga Gorispolkom chairman.

Shamikhin, Albert Mikhaylovich, responsible organizer of the Automotive and Agricultural Machine-Building Workers Union Central Committee, Riga City.

From the Kirghiz SSR

Aytmatov, Chingiz, writer, chairman of the Kirghiz SSR Writers Union Board, chief editor of the journal INOSTRANNAYA LITERATURA.

Akayev, Askar, president of the Kirghiz SSR Academy of Sciences.

Akmataliyeva, Urukan Kalilovna, silk reeler at the Osh All-Union Komsomol Silk Industrial and Trade Association.

Akmatov, Tashtanbek, chairman of the Kirghiz SSR Supreme Soviet Presidium.

Barabanov, Vyacheslav Ivanovich, livestock unit chief at Dzheti-Oguzskiy Rayon's "Kommunizm" Kolkhoz, Issyk-Kul Oblast.

Beyshekeyeva, Zayna, senior shepherd at the Dzhety-Oguz State Special Farm, Dzhety-Oguzskiy Rayon, Issyk-Kul Oblast.

Zanokha, Aleksandr Ivanovich, chairman of the Lenin Kolkhoz, Alamedinskiy Rayon.

Isakov, Ismanali Ismailovich, face worker at the Khaydarkan Mercury Combine, Frunzenskiy Rayon, Osh Oblast.

Kiselev, Gennadiy Nikolayevich, second secretary of the Kirghiz Communist Party Central Committee.

Kuldyshev, Mamidali Sagimbekovich, "Tash-Kumyrstroy" Trust Mobile Mechanized Column No. 370 Komsomol-youth team leader.

Orozova, Umtul Sheysheyevna, chairman of the Kirghiz SSR State Committee for Television and Radio Broadcasting.

From the Tajik SSR

Britvin, Nikolay Vasilyevich, member of the Military Council, chief of the USSR KGB Border Troops Political Directorate.

Gulova, Zulaykho Sokhibnazarovna, field crop cultivation team leader on the "XXII Partsyezd" Kolkhoz in Ordzhonikidzeabadskiy Rayon.

Kodyrov, Barakatulo Kamarovich, senior herdsman at the Khasan Sovkhoz, Leninskiy Rayon.

Manko, Nikolay Mikhaylovich, installation worker at Construction and Installation Administration No. 3 of the "Dushanbezhilstroy" Planning and Construction Administration.

Odzhiyev, Rizoali Kadamshoyevich, chairman of the "Internatsionalist" Cooperative Association, Dushanbe City.

Pallayev, Gaibnazar, chairman of the Tajik SSR Supreme Soviet Presidium.

Rakhimova, Bikhodzhal, secretary of Leninabad Tajik Communist Party Obkom.

Safarov, Bozorali Solikhovich, shift engineer at the Kulyab Airport Aviation Technology Base.

Safiyeva, Gulrukhsor, poet, chairman of the Tajik Republican Branch of the Soviet Culture Foundation, Dushanbe City.

Fatullayev, Mirbako, deputy chief physician at the Ura-Tyubinskiy Central Rayon Hospital.

Khusanbayev, Mutallim Abdumuminovich, caster and molder at the Nauskiy "Leninabadselmash" Plant, Leninabad Oblast.

From the Armenian SSR

Abramyan, Khoren Babkenovich, artistic leader of the Sundukyan Academy Drama Theater, chairman of the Armenian Theater Workers Union Board.

Ambartsumyan, Viktor Amazaspovich, president of the Armenian SSR Academy of Sciences.

Ambartsumyan, Sergey Aleksandrovich, rector of Yerevan State University.

Arutyunyan, Lyudmila Akopovna, head of department at Yerevan State University.

Arutyunyan, Elmir Tatulovich, leader of a team of toolmakers at Yerevan's "Elektropribor" Production Association.

Vardanyan, Rafik Petrosovich, chairman of the St. Shaumyan Araratskiy Rayon Ararat Village Kolkhoz.

Yenokyan, Goarik Agabekovna, general director of Yerevan's "Garun" Sewn Goods Production Association.

Igityan, Genrikh Surenovich, general director of the Republican Aesthetic Education Center, director of the Armenian Museum of Modern Art.

Mnatsakanyan, Bavakan Gagikovna, chairman of the Arshaluys Rural Soviet of People's Deputies, Echmiadzinskiy Rayon.

Oganesyan, Rafik Gevorkovich, bricklayer at the "Lenstroy" Trust No. 46 Construction Administration, Leninakan City.

Khanzadyan, Sero Nikolayevich, writer, Yerevan City.

From the Turkmen SSR

Akmamedov, Geldy Mamedmuradovich, master baker at the No. 1 Bakery of the "Ashkhabadkhleb" Production Association.

Allayarov, Redzhapbay Allayarovich, chairman of Tashauzskiy Rayon's Kalinin Kolkhoz, Tashauz Oblast.

Annamukhamedov, Atakhodzhamengli, deputy commander of the Turkmen Civil Aviation Administration head enterprise first flying division air squadron, Ashkhabad City.

Atdayev, Khodzhamukhamed, blacksmith at the 50th Anniversary of the USSR Ashkhabad Petroleum Machine Building Plant.

Bazarova, Roza Atamuradovna, chairman of the Turkmen SSR Supreme Soviet Presidium.

Baleshev, Nikolay Fedorovich, first secretary of the Ashkhabad Turkmen Communist Party Gorkom.

Gundogdyyev, Yazgeldi Potayevich, first secretary of the Turkmen Komsomol Central Committee.

Ishanov, Khekim, chief engineer at the "Turkmenneft" Production Association, Nebit-Dag City.

Kurbanova, Amangozel, carpetmaker at the "Turkmenkover" Production Association in Ashkhabad, Ashkhabad City.

Meleyev, Kaka, chief agronomist of the "Leningrad" Kolkhoz, Takhtinskiy Rayon, Tashauz Oblast.

Shalyyev, Atabally Bapbayevich, drilling foreman at the South Turkmen exploratory drilling administration of the "Turkmengazprom" Production Association, Mari Oblast.

From the Estonian SSR

Aare, Yukhan Yokhannesovich, commentator of Estonian Television's Chief Propaganda Editorial Office.

Bronshteyn, Mikhail Lazarevich, head of department at Tartu State University.

Vooglayd, Yulo Vakhurovich, scientific leader at the Raplaskiy Rayon Agro-Industrial Complex Data Processing and Computer Training Center, Tallinn City.

Gryazin, Igor Nikolayevich, chief of department at the Estonian SSR Academy of Sciences Philosophy, Sociology, and Law Institute, Tartu City.

Kallas, Siym Udovich, deputy editor of the newspaper RAHVA HAAL, Tallinn City.

Kakhn, Yuriy Kharriyevich, senior scientific staffer at the Estonian SSR Academy of Sciences Economics Institute, Tallinn City.

Kyabin, Tiyt Reynkholdovich, academic secretary of the Estonian SSR Academy of Sciences Presidium Social Sciences Department, Tallinn City.

Nugis, Yulo Iokhannesovich, general director of the "Estoplast" Production Association, Tallinn City.

Pupkevich, Tadeush Karlovich, mobile excavator operator at the "Estonslanets" Production Association's "Narvskiy" open pit, Sillamyae City.

Ryuytel, Arnold Feodorovich, chairman of the Estonian SSR Supreme Soviet Presidium.

Khallik, Klara Semenovna, leading scientific associate of the Estonian SSR Academy of Sciences Philosophy, Sociology, and Law Institute, Tallinn City.

From the Abkhaz ASSR

Ardzinba, Vladislav Grigoryevich, director of the Georgian SSR Academy of Sciences Abkhaz Institute of Language, Literature, and History named for D.I. Gulia, Sukhumi City.

Arshba, Ruslan Ardevanovich, shaft-sinker at the "Tkvarchelskoye" Mining Administration Mine No. 2.

Salukvadze, Revaz Georgiyevich, director of the Sukhumi I.N. Vekua Physicotechnical Institute.

Cholokyan, Karzui Sarkisovna, kolkhoz member at the Rustaveli Kolkhoz, Gulripshskiy Rayon .

From the Adzhar ASSR

Badzhelidze, Nino Usupovna, tea grower at Khutsubani Village Kolkhoz, Khutsubani Village, Kobuletskiy Rayon.

Buachidze, Tengiz Pavlovich, chairman of the Georgian Culture Fund, Tbilisi City.

Gogeshvili, Aleko Rafayelovich, transformer assembly worker at the Batumi Transformer Plant.

Sakandelidze, Iamze Binalovna, tobacco grower on the Merisi Village Kolkhoz, Kedskiy Rayon.

From the Bashkir ASSR

Nikolayev, Vasiliy Vasilyevich, machine operator at the Sterlitamak "Kaustik" Production Association.

Prokushev, Vladimir Ivanovich, PRAVDA correspondent for the Bashkir ASSR.

Safin, Minikhalaf Mustafaivich, chairman of the Lenin Kolkhoz, Krasnokamskiy Rayon.

Sharipov, Yuriy Kamalovich, general director of the Ufa S.M. Kirov Production Association.

From the Buryat ASSR

Angapov, Semen Vasilyevich, pensioner, Ulan-Ude City.

Kalashnikov, Vladimir Yakovlevich, director of "Erdem" Sovkhoz, Mukhorshibirskiy Rayon.

Litvintseva, Galina Nikolayevna, interior decorator team leader of the "Zhilgrazhdanstroy" Trust's No. 7 Construction and Installation Administration, Ulan-Ude City.

Stepanova, Galina Sambuyevna, organizer of extracurricular and extramural education work at Onokhoy Secondary School.

From the Dagestan ASSR

Gorbachev, Aleksandr Grigoryevich, director of the "Rossiya" Sovkhoz, Kizlyarskiy Rayon.

Zaynalkhanov, Dalgat Gadzhiyevich, docker-machine operator at Makhachkala Maritime Commercial Port.

Kakhirov, Kurbanmagomed Zulfikarovich, team leader at Magaramkentskiy Rayon's "Leninskiy" Sovkhoz.

Magomedov, Gadzhimurad Magomedovich, first secretary of the Sergokalinskiy CPSU Raykom.

From the Kabardino-Balkar ASSR

Zhigunova, Lyudmila Tazretovna, chief of the children's department of the city first-aid clinical hospital, Nalchik City.

Karpenko, Valentin Filippovich, leader of a team of fitters at the Nalchik Remote-Control Equipment Plant.

Kuliyev, Sultan Oyusovich, livestock unit chief at the Lenin Kolkhoz, Chegemskiy Rayon.

Umerenkov, Aleksey Mikhaylovich, chairman of Prokhladnenskiy Rayon's Zhuk Kolkhoz.

From the Kalmyk ASSR

Burayev, Ivan Zambayevich, head of the "40 Let Oktyabrya" Kolkhoz machine workshops, Sarpinskiy Rayon.

Kugultinov, David Nikitich, writer, chairman of the Kalmyk ASSR Writers Union Board.

Nikitin, Vladilen Valentinovich, first deputy chairman of the RSFSR State Agro-Industrial Committee, RSFSR minister.

Ochirov, Valeriy Nikolayevich, colonel, air force regiment commander.

From the Karakalpak ASSR

Abdimuratova, Shukir, family contract worker on the "Pravda" Sovkhoz, Shumanayskiy Rayon.

Ibragimov, Mirzaolim Ibragimovich, chairman of the Uzbek SSR Supreme Soviet Presidium.

Kaipbergenov, Tulepbergen, writer, chairman of the Karakalpak ASSR Writers Union Board.

Pershin, Andrey Leonidovich, excavator operator at the Kungradskiy Rayon Production Repair and Operation Association.

From the Karelian ASSR

Afanasyeva, Lyudmila Vladimirovna, chief physician at the No. 1 maternity home, Petrozavodsk City.

Genchev, Anatoliy Aleksandrovich, senior engineer and flight safety inspector with the Petrozavodsk Aviation Enterprise.

Demidov, Mikhail Vasilyevich, first secretary of Kalevalskiy CPSU Raykom.

Pilnikov, Stanislav Vasilyevich, teacher at the No. 1 secondary school, Pitkyaranta City.

From the Komi ASSR

Ignatov, Stepan Vladimirovich, chief economist on the "Pomozdinskiy" Sovkhoz.

Lushchikov, Sergey Gennadyevich, Komi ASSR deputy minister of justice.

Maksimov, Valeriy Nikolayevich, team leader at the "Vorkutaugol" Production Association's "Severnaya" mine.

Chernykh, Galina Aleksandrovna, director of the Obyachevo Secondary School, Priluzskiy Rayon.

From the Mari ASSR

Vedenkina, Zinaida Alekseyevna, trolleybus transport administration trolleybus driver, Yoshkar-Ola City.

Karpochev, Vladimir Andreyevich, chairman of Volzhskiy Rayon's "Put Lenina" Kolkhoz.

Nikitin, Rudolf Ivanovich, general director of the "Izotop" Production Association, Yoshkar-Ola City.

Samsonov, Nikolay Alekseyevich, lathe operator at the Mari 50th Anniversary of the USSR "Kontakt" Plant, Yoshkar-Ola City.

From the Mordovian ASSR

Aliluyev, Nikolay Ivanovich, electric locomotive engineer at the Kuybyshev Railroad Ruzayevka Station locomotive depot.

Kulikov, Yevgeniy Andreyevich, chairman of the Lenin Kolkhoz, Dubenskiy Rayon.

Levakin, Vyacheslav Alekseyevich, general director of the Saransk "Svetotekhnika" Production Association.

Maslakova, Anna Polikarpovna, team leader at the Saransk "Rezinotekhnika" Plant.

From the Nakhichevan ASSR

Abasov, Kurban Abas Kuli ogly, general director of the "Kaspmorneftegaz" Production Association, Baku City.

Isayev, Geydar Isa ogly, first secretary of the Nakhichevan Azerbaijan Communist Party Obkom.

Kerimov, Dzhangir Ali Abbas ogly, head of a department at the CPSU Central Committee Academy of Social Sciences.

Nagiyev, Ramazan Shamy ogly, engineer at the Azerbaijan Railroad's Dzhulfa Locomotive Depot.

From the North Osetiyan ASSR

Aguzarova, Stella Borisovna, fitter at the Ordzhonikidze 50th Anniversary of the Komsomol Electric Lamp Plant.

Byazyrova, Valentina Timofeyevna, teacher at the No. 5 Secondary School, Ordzhonikidze City.

Ikayev, Georgiy Dzambulatovich, first secretary of the Digorskiy CPSU Raykom.

Nyrkov, Anatoliy Ivanovich, machine setter at the Ordzhonikidze Glass Plant.

From the Tatar ASSR

Buravov, Gennadiy Vladimirovich, diesel locomotime engineer at the Bugulma Locomotive Depot of the Kuybyshev Railroad.

Kamenshchikova, Galina Nikolayevna, chief physician at the children's association of the Zelenodolskiy Rayon Central Hospital.

Minnullin, Tufan Abdullovich, writer, Kazan City.

Mukhametzyanov, Mukharam Timergaliyevich, chairman of Buinskiy Rayon's "Iskra" Kolkhoz.

From the Tuva ASSR

Kara-Sal, Damdyn Bazyyevich, director of the "Tuvinskiy" Sovkhoz, Dzun-Khemchikskiy Rayon.

Komarov, Yuriy Trofimovich, general director of the V.I. Lenin "Tuvaasbest" Combine, Ak-Dovurak City.

Lapygin, Vladimir Lavrentyevich, general designer and director of an automation and instrument-making science-production association, Moscow City.

Sanchat, Aleksandr Sandanovich, first secretary of Tes-Khemskiy Komsomol Raykom.

From the Udmurt ASSR

Danilov, Sergey Nikolayevich, livestock farmer and lessee on Yukamenskiy Rayon's "Shafeyevskiy" Sovkhoz.

Korobkin, Vladimir Vladimirovich, chief of the normalization and standardization department at the "Izhevskiy Motozavod" Production Association.

Murashov, Vladimir Konstantinovich, team leader at Seltinskiy Rayon's Lenin Kolkhoz.

Engver, Nikolay Nikolayevich, leading scientific staffer at the USSR Academy of Sciences Urals Department Physicotechnical Institute, Izhevsk City.

From the Chechen-Ingush ASSR

Darsigov, Musa Yusupovich, team leader at Malgobeksiy Rayon's "Alkhanchurtskiy" Sovkhoz.

Nemtsev, Yevgeniy Ivanovich, leader of a repair team at the "Orgtekhnika" Production Association's "Elektropribor" Plant, Groznyy City.

Umalatova, Sazhi Zayndinovna, leader of an integrated team at the Groznyy "Krasnyy Molot" Machine Building Plant.

Foteyev, Vladimir Konstantinovich, first secretary of the Chechen-Ingush CPSU Obkom.

From the Chuvash ASSR

Valentinov, Leonid Fedorovich, road grader operator with the "Spetsstroymekhanizatsiya" Trust, Cheboksary City.

Dmitriyev, Aleksey Aleksandrovich, machine operator at Yalchikskiy Rayon's "Slava" Kolkhoz.

Mikhaylova, Lidiya Ivanovna, teacher at the Shorshely Secondary School, Mariinsko-Posadskiy Rayon.

Fedorov, Nikolay Vasilyevich, senior lecturer at the Chuvash State University.

From the Yakutsk ASSR

Boykov, Sergey Vladimirovich, leader of a fitters' team from the No. 154 Mechanized Column of the "Bamstroymekhanizatsiya" Trust, Aldan City.

Larionov, Vladimir Petrovich, deputy chairman of the USSR Academy of Sciences Siberian Department Yakutsk Scientific Center Presidium and director of the Institute of Arctic Physical and Technical Problems.

Mikheyev, Mikhail Alekseyevich, leader of an integrated team at the "Yakutuglestroy" Combine's "Uglestroy-1" Construction Administration, Neryungri City.

Osipov, Prokopiy Dmitriyevich, secretary of the party committee of enterprises and associations in Chernyshevskiy Settlement, Mirninskiy Rayon.

From the Adyge Autonomous Oblast

Dmitriyev, Vladimir Vasilyevich, worker at Maykopskiy Rayon's Pervomayskiy Timber Procurement Establishment.

Mashbashev, Iskhak Shumafovich, writer and responsible secretary of the Adyge Writers Organization, Maykop City.

From the Gorno-Altay Autonomous Oblast

Yerelina, Valentina Kuzukovna, director of Sugash Secondary School, Ust-Koksinskiy Rayon.

Mironova, Dagmara Sergeyevna, weaver at the Barnaul Cotton Textile Combine.

From the Gorno-Badakhshan Autonomous Oblast

Navruzov, Sherkhonbek, team leader on Ishkashimskiy Rayon's "Vakhon" Sovkhoz.

Khudonazarov, Davlatnazar, first secretary of the Tajik SSR Cinematography Workers Union Board.

From the Jewish Autonomous Oblast

Danilyuk, Nikolay Nikolayevich, chairman of the Khabarovsk Krayispolkom.

Khitron, Pavel Abramovich, director of "Amurskiy" Sovkhoz, Oktyabrskiy Rayon.

From the Karachayevo-Cherkess Autonomous Oblast

Kangliyev, Andrey Yakhyayevich, truck driver at the "Erken-Shakharskiy" Fruit Sovkhoz, Adyge-Khablskiy Rayon.

Petrova, Lyudmila Nikolayevna, general director of the "Niva Stavropolya" Science and Production Association, Stavropol City.

From the Nagorno-Karabakh Autonomous Oblast

Dzhafarov, Vagif Dzhafar ogly, first secretary of Shushinskiy Party Raykom.

Pogosyan, Genrikh Andreyevich, pensioner, Moscow City.

From the Khakass Autonomous Oblast

Batynskaya, Lyudmila Ivanovna, IZVESTIYA correspondent for Krasnoyarsk Kray and Tuva ASSR, Krasnoyarsk City.

Botandayev, Iosif Nikiforovich, driver at the "Tuimskiy" Sovkhoz, Shirinskiy Rayon.

From the South Osetiyan Autonomous Oblast

Tedeyev, Lev Radzhenovich, machine operator at Znaurskiy Rayon machinery and tractor pool repairs and operations enterprise.

Khugayeva, Diana Varlamovna, leader of a lease collective at the Kirovskiy Sovkhoz Chasavalskiy Stock Unit, Dzhavskiy Rayon.

From the Aga Buryat Autonomous Okrug

Nimbuyev, Tsyren, general chairman of the "Mogoytuyskoye" Agro-Industrial Association.

From the Komi-Permyak Autonomous Okrug

Khomyakov, Aleksandr Ivanovich, chairman of the "Rodina" Kolkhoz, Kochevskiy Rayon.

From the Koryak Autonomous Okrug

Kosygin, Vladimir Vladimirovich, correspondent of the Kamchatka Oblast Committee for Television and Radio Broadcasting.

From the Nenetsk Autonomous Okrug

Vyucheyskiy, Aleksandr Ivanovich, chief of the rolling and repair shop of the Khoreyver Oil and Gas Prospecting Expedition, Arkhangelsk Oblast.

From the Taymyr Autonomous Okrug

Palchin, Semen Yakovlevich, director of the "Tukhard" Sovkhoz, Ust-Yeniseyskiy Rayon, Krasnoyarsk Kray.

From the Ust-Orda Buryat Autonomous Okrug

Batorov, Oleg Borisovich, second secretary of Osinskiy CPSU Raykom, Irkutsk Oblast.

From the Khanti-Mansiysk Autonomous Okrug

Aypin, Yeremey Danilovich, writer, chief of department at the Okrug House of Creativity of the Northern Ethnic Groups, Tyumen Oblast.

From the Chukotsk Autonomous Okrug

Yetylen, Vladimir Mikhaylovich, postgraduate student at the CPSU Central Committee Social Sciences Academy.

From the Evenki Autonomous Okrug

Mongo, Mikhail Innokentyevich, chief of the Krasnoyarsk Krayispolkom Department for Northern and Arctic Ethnic Groups' Affairs.

From the Yamalo-Nenetsk Autonomous Oblast

Rugin, Roman Prokopyevich, writer, senior methodologist at the Okrug House of Culture of Peoples of the North, Salekhard City.

USSR Supreme Soviet of the Union Meets 3 Jun

Council of Elders Meets First

LD0306065189 Moscow Domestic Service in Russian 0600 GMT 3 Jun 89

[Excerpt] A report on the work of the Congress of People's Deputies of the USSR:

The session of the Council of Elders of both chambers is starting in the USSR Supreme Soviet at this moment. The first organization session of the Soviet of the Union will open at 1500 [1100 GMT], which will be broadcast by Mayak Radio and by Central Television channel 2. [passage omitted]

Gorbachev Chairs Councils of Elders

LD0306113789 Moscow TASS International Service in Russian 1109 GMT 3 Jun 89

[Text] Moscow, 3 Jun (TASS)—A joint session of the Councils of Elders of the Soviet of the Union and the Soviet of Nationalities of the USSR Supreme Soviet chaired by Mikhail Gorbachev, chairman of the USSR Supreme Soviet, took place today in the Kremlin in the conference hall of the chambers of the USSR Supreme Soviet.

The councils examined the questions on the procedure of opening the session and the agenda of the USSR Supreme Soviet and on permanent commissions of the chambers and committees of the USSR Supreme Soviet.

Gorbachev Opens Soviet of the Union

LD0306142689 Moscow Television Service in Russian 1100 GMT 3 Jun 89

[Opening speech by Mikhail Gorbachev, chairman of the USSR Supreme Soviet, at session of Soviet of the Union of the USSR Supreme Soviet in the Kremlin—live]

[Text] I already announced information about registration, therefore allow me to open the first meeting of the chamber of the Soviet of the Union of the USSR Supreme Soviet. First of all, I want to congratulate you cordially, dear comrades, on your election to the Supreme Soviet, to this Supreme Soviet that is assuming obligations at a very important stage of the development of restructuring.

Perhaps I am repeating myself, but I am repeating myself consciously. Today, when the concept of restructuring is coming into touch with life, when restructuring the political area, is transforming itself into practical activity, has moved into the spheres of life in our society, and is engaging the living, vital interests of all of us, there are very many important problems before us. And the most important one among them is how to act so that everything that we have started becomes more dynamic, deeper and stronger and so that this gives positive results. We have felt this during the election campaign. The people have shown great support, trust in all of us. At the same time it has brought to the elections, to this election campaign, I would say, a spirit of healthy criticism and great exactingness. This is all explicable, because we all want restructuring to move more quickly and be fruitful.

We have not only not yet solved the many problems that we inherited. And, also as a result of our work, we have committed a number of blunders and miscalculations which also need to be perceived, borne in mind, and taken into account in our work.

At the present time when a situation is taking shape whereby through the Congress of People's Deputies, we are getting new bodies of supreme power in the country and a more clear-cut distribution of legislative and executive power—and this is being accompanied at the same time by processes of decentralization in the government, the economy, and also in the spiritual sphere and the process of democratization—it is very important for all of these bodies, and in the present instance our Supreme Soviet, to find their place in order to carry out in the best way their very responsible role.

In the days that the congress has been at work, I have seen for myself how restructuring is quickly changing people, how many remarkable people there are, who are different and dissimilar from each other, but very interested in things changing for the better in the country, and how these restructuring processes are throwing up and already, so to speak, crystallizing new cadres.

This, moreover, is the way toward restructuring production and forming its cadres, because this cannot be achieved in a laboratory somewhere outside the restructuring processes. We must be realistics. I have become convinced of this.

As it turns out, I have figures showing that we have had a large renewal of cadres. Nevertheless, we have seen that the new echelon, and the second and third ones, that have come along also require time and cannot yet comprehend and find their places. They still do not have enough experience to conduct affairs in a new way. This applies to the political process and to the economic process and also to the sphere of management. In just the same way, in the new conditions our people—the workers, peasants, and intellectuals—have to construct their lives and organize their work in a new way. We are in general in the process of mastering new forms. It is very important for this process to take place quicker, more effectively, more wholeheartedly, and with fewer mistakes so that we may put into operation the strong mechanisms that our social system has at its disposal.

In this respect I am a committed optimist since through the mechanisms of democracy we are leading our people, the working people, into the main areas of restructuring. This is the greatest guarantee of the fact that we will nevertheless take the situation in hand, people will be found for all spheres of activity, and we will solve the tasks. However, let us not oversimplify. The debates have shown how complex the situation is and how much we have to accomplish. I want to wish you, dear comrades, fruitful activity and as chairman of the Supreme Soviet I want to say immediately that I am open for contacts, for conversations, for discussions, so that we have here a comradely situation, a democratic situation, so that we can harmonize all the work in the interests of business. I congratulate you. I wish you great success. [applause]

As I make my speech, 261 people are present. I am making use of my powers to launch your chamber, the Soviet of the Union, and to help you conduct the first organizational conference, or rather sitting, at which it is intended to elect the chairman of the chamber and to exchange opinions on the basis of the short report Anatoliy Ivanovich [Lukyanov] will give on the list of the commissions and committees. These are the two questions we must decide today. Are there no objections to this agenda? No.

Primakov Elected Chairman

LD0306220189 Moscow Television Service in Russian
1058 GMT 3 Jun 89

[Relay of Soviet of the Union of the USSR Supreme Soviet session from the Kremlin—live]

[Excerpts] [video shows scene inside chamber, with assembled delegates and Gorbachev and Lukyanov seated on platform] [Gorbachev] Not to embarrass anyone in case someone still has to come up and sit down, they still have 2 minutes. I will give you the information that of 271 deputies, 238 have registered.

In the meantime, we could discuss the following question: We have many different traditions. When I was chairing sessions at the congress, I was sent notes saying: Mikhail Sergeyevich, why do you stand all the time? As if to say that I dominate the proceedings and some kind of pressure is exerted. In general world practice the chairmen stays seated and in some places they have a hammer in addition. Well, let us do without the hammer for the moment but let's just agree how to do it. It not only affects me, but there will be chairmen of the chambers sitting as well. It is the generally-accepted parliamentary tradition. [words indistinct from a deputy] Yes, they will be getting up too. There you are. We have spent the time usefully. Yes, of course, I think we will have many of our own (?traditions). [passage omitted]

Comrade, Velikhov, [Gorbachev corrects himself], Deputy Velikhov has the floor to speak about the proposal on behalf of the Council of Elders on the matter concerning the candidature for the post of chairman of the chamber.

[Velikhov] Esteemed comrade chairman, esteemed deputies: The Council of Elders met this morning, and we discussed proposals on the chairmanship of the Soviet of the Union. After an hour-long discussion many questions were posed and a number of remarks were made. We unanimously concluded that the most appropriate candidate recommended to us is Yevgeniy Maksimovich Primakov, academician and director of the Institute of World Economy and International Relations of the Academy of Sciences. He is academician-secretary of the academy...er, International Department of the Academy of Sciences, and he also holds a number of other public positions. It is natural that for us, for the academy, this will be a serious problem but the academy also supports this decision.

During the discussion, Yevgeniy Maksimovich replied to questions, and from his replies and his brief speech I can try to summarize that, as we understood it, he intends... He understands the difficult and exceedingly responsible task involved in heading the work of the Soviet of the Union, in fulfilling its constitutional obligations and rights in the legislative sphere and in the area of supervision, above all through the budget, and also through other functions. He realizes that this now has to be done on a completely different basis, on a businesslike basis, in the spirit of restructuring, with democratic reliance on the deputies in the Soviet of the Union and the people's deputies in the congress and, through them, a direct dialogue with voters.

The remarks expressed were from Siberian and Lithuanian deputies. They mainly concerned matters of style. It must be said that the fact that Yevgeniy Maksimovich is well-known helped the discussion, and it was recommended to him that in the future he should hold more dialogues and listen to more views, so to speak, in his contacts with deputies. After an hour's discussion, we all reached the unanimous view that his candidacy should be recommended.

[Gorbachev] Are there any questions for Comrade Velikhov? No? Go ahead.

[Unidentified speaker] Were other candidacies considered?

[Velikhov] In the process leading up to that point, various candidacies were considered, but here we all reached a view on Academician Primakov's candidacy.

[Unidentified speaker] Can I ask a question? You said that Yevgeniy Maksimovich had many public commitments and a heavy work load. Won't this, in the course of his work...

[Velikhov interrupts] This matter was raised during the discussion. And he said quite clearly that he will divest himself of all his public posts and his principal work. [words indistinct] At the meeting of the Council of Elders we only discussed his candidacy, yes.

[Gorbachev] Other proposals were not submitted, even though I did ask whether there were any other proposals. People who attended—and I can see many people here who attended—can confirm that is what happened. Sit down, Yevgeniy Pavlovich. We can proceed by letting Comrade Primakov speak. Take a look at him and hear what he has to say, and ask him questions. Is that all right? [affirmative mumurs from hall] Over to you, Comrade Primakov. Then we will continue the exchange of views. [passage omitted]

[Gorbachev] My feeling is that you want me to put the question [of your chairmanship] like this: Are there any objections? [indistinct murmuring from the floor]

[Deputy Khadzhiyev] If the Supreme Soviet seeks the admission of our 13 remaining republics to the United Nations as members of the United Nations will you be in favor or against?

[Primakov] I will be in favor, but I can tell you in advance that it would be very difficult.

[Khadzhiyev] Thank you, that is all that needs to be said, that is another question. I wanted to know and I am going to vote for you. [laughter]

[Gorbachev] Comrades, can we complete the discussion? [cries of "yes" from the floor] I put it to the vote: Who is in favor of electing Comrade Yevgeniy Maksimovich Primakov as chairman of the house? Please raise your documents. Please put them down. Are there any against? No. Abstentions?

[Unidentified Speaker] One. Three.

[Gorbachev] Three people have abstained. So Comrade Primakov is elected by an overwhelming majority. [applause]

[Primakov] Well, I am surely starting from the most useless [words indistinct] Well, comrade deputies, first and foremost, allow me to thank you cordially for the trust that has been placed in me and to assure you that I will, indeed, do everything so that you are not disappointed in the choice you have made. We will now deal with a procedural question. [indistinct interjection] As far as deputies are concerned, I want to say that Mikhail Sergeyevich proposed a fairly democratic procedure at the Council of Elders today to the effect that the chairmen of both our chamber and of the Soviet of Nationalities should, following consultations with all the union republics, should themselves put forward their own deputy chairmen following that. And then this issue will be debated and passed by the relevant chambers. Two deputy chairmen are proposed for here and for the Soviet of Nationalities, according, naturally, to the constitution. The question of setting up standing commissions and committees is put forward for the examination of this session. The floor is given to Comrade Anatoliy Ivanovich Lukyanov to speak on this question. [passage omitted]

[Unidentified speaker] Anatoliy Ivanovich, you have just named 14 commissions and 4 committees. I would like to know about the way their work is organized. How large are the commissions expected to be? How many deputies will belong to them and will the members of the commissions have to be released from their main jobs? (?Or only those who) are in charge?

[Lukyanov] I will only speak about what is being proposed. Once we have passed the resolution on the formation of the commissions, after that the chairmen of the chambers, along with the deputies and on the basis of what you yourselves have written, will create the skeleton of these commissions. And you will vote. It is proposed that half those included will be members of the chamber, and half deputies, people's deputies of the USSR who are members of the congress. It is quite clear that the chairman of the commission or committee, the secretary of the committee and a few, perhaps three or four persons, at the beginning, will have to be released from all their duties, and to work in the committee. The remaining comrades will combine their own work with work in the committees and commissions, and I will tell you that if we create only purely professional committees, who do not touch earth for practical experience, we will make them lifeless. [shouting] And the composition will be about 40-45 persons, perhaps 35-40 persons: It all depends on what the deputies themselves propose. I must say that it immediately became clear that a lot of people wanted to join some committees, while a number of committees are not yet filled. For example, we have suddenly gotten a Committee for Nature Protection. It needs a clever collective farm chairman and a works director. It needs a political figure and a party leader. We must look, and I think there is enough wisdom among the delegates to form committees of a sort that will work. [passage omitted]

[Unidentified speaker] Anatoliy Ivanovich, has there not been discussion of the issue of having the planning and budget committee under the Supreme Soviet and of leaving the finance committee here—the planning and budget committee under the Supreme Soviet and not in the Soviet of the Union—dividing out the finance element, leaving the finance committee in the Soviet of the Union?

[Lukyanov] I would like to tell you, comrades. No, we have discussed this question. The fact is that detaching finances from the plan in our country is impossible. The budget is the formulation in financial terms of our plan targets and for that reason two commissions have been set up: one commission on general questions, so to speak, in the Soviet of the Union, and the other on particular issues. They will, of course, be working in contact with each other, but we have to approach plan and financial issues as a single set of issues. If we confine ourselves to budget questions alone—as is done in a number of bourgeois countries—we will be forgetting a very important specific feature of the socialist economy, the plan. [Passage omitted]

[Primakov] The floor is given to Comrade Samarin, a deputy who is not a member of the USSR Supreme Soviet.

[Samarin] Esteemed members of the Supreme Soviet: This is what I would like to say, I believe there have been proposals aired both at the congress and in what many of our electors have had to say, to the effect that a commission or a standing committee must be set up to monitor the work of the organs of the Ministry of Internal Affairs, the Committee for State Security, and the Armed Forces. The problem is that the commissions on defense, state security and—I have forgotten what it is on. Some other commission are concerned with, let's say drawing up either military concepts, or else concepts, let us say, to combat antistate manifestations or what have you. But I believe that there really must be monitoring by deputies of the work of these executive bodies. You see my point? [hubbub from hall]

The Committee for Law and Order? No, the Committee for Law and Order is quite a different matter. It draws up suggestions for tabling and amending legislation, and so on. But what I mean is a committee that would monitor and, if you like, protect more extensively the rights of citizens, you see? And of the state, too. You see? Protect them against possible developments. And incidentally, the events today that are occuring, that have occured. You see my point? Including in Tbilisi and Armenia. They suggest that there must be the strictest control here by the Supreme Soviet. And not general control, but specific monitoring by a commission. That is my proposal. Thank you for you attention.

[Golik] Golik, constituency No 190, city of Kemerovo. Comrades, I know that very many proposals are being expressed regarding the setting up of commissions to monitor the activities of KGB bodies, the procuracy, and the Ministry of Internal Affairs. One such proposal has just been made here. I do not believe that there is a need for us to do that. It is not necessary for this reason: Let us try to get away not from the old world but from the old psychology of trickery as I would call it, where we are trying to let some things through and monitor some things. Any commission and any committee that we set up will have the right to monitor the activity of any department which falls within the sphere of activity of that committee. Therefore, it is superfluous to set up some special monitoring body. Doing so will dissipate our energy and our attention. Furthermore, I cannot agree with the proposal of my colleague (?Shakhovtsov) that a change is needed to the wording of the committee on questions of legislation, legitimacy and law and order.

[(Igor Afanasyevich)], I consider your proposal simply to be wrong wrong if only for the fact that in the form in which you propose it the question of law and order, whether we like it or not, is taken away from the activity of this committee. And that should not be done in any event. Furthermore, the same issues concerning monitoring the activities of the law enforcement bodies will disappear, and I, for example, would be opposed to that in the extreme. I therefore, propose that we retain the name that exists here and confine ourselves to that.

Primakov Addresses Supreme Soviet

LD0306183589 Moscow Television Service in Russian 1112 GMT 3 Jun 89

[Speech by Yevgeniy Primakov, nominee for chairman of the Soviet of the Union of the USSR Supreme Soviet, in the Kremlin, with interjections by Gorbachev and questions from deputies speaking from the floor of the hall—live]

[Text] [Primakov] Esteemed comrade deputies: I understand that if I am elected chairman of the Soviet of the Union, I will have to devote my whole activity, my whole life if you wish, to the work in this post. Therefore, this is out of the question. I will naturally resign from all my other duties and all other work which I am now instructed to carry out on behalf of the institute, the department, and on behalf of the Soviet National Committee for Asian-Pacific Economic Cooperation. I proceed from the fact that the Supreme Soviet is of exceedingly great importance for transforming our political structure in the process of restructuring. I proceed from the fact that both chambers must take a place appropriate for them in the structure of the people's power which is now being formed before our eyes.

I do not think that you are awaiting any statements from me which can, in their totality, signify a program or my concept of the Supreme Soviet's activity. It would be foolish of me to make statements like this now. The concept can be worked out only as a result of contact, only as a result of discussions, only on a collective basis, and undoubtedly with the participation of all the deputies of our chamber, and including everyone who wishes to take part in this most responsible work and who have failed to become Supreme Soviet members.

But I would like to say that undoubtedly the Supreme Soviet and our chamber must not repeat in its work that which used to happen before. It cannot and must not be a voting machine. It must be a mechanism for law making, including for introducing amendments in already existing laws, in that section of them where they have failed to justify themselves in action. At the same time, the Supreme Soviet and our chamber must undoubtedly be custodians of the interests of Soviet people in the process of restructuring. And I see this in that both chambers, and our chamber in particular, must implement supervision, real supervision over the activities of executive bodies.

These functions were not, of course, characteristic of the old Supreme Soviet. We are now forming a new Supreme Soviet, a new parliament which should also work in a new way. If I am elected, I will apply all of my strength to justify, to some extent, your choice. Thank you for your attention.

[Gorbachev] Will there be any questions, comrades? Perhaps you will speak a little about yourself for the deputies?

[Primakov] I was born in 1929. I grew up, I finished secondary school in Tbilisi and started at the Institute of Oriental Studies. I finished at the Institute of Oriental Studies in 1953 and after this I studied at Moscow University, in the Economics Faculty, as a postgraduate. I finished my postgraduate studies and worked for the radio. Then I worked for a long time at PRAVDA where among other things I was a Near East correspondent from 1965 to 1970. I defended my doctoral dissertation while working for PRAVDA and I went over to working for the Academy of Sciences. I worked as the deputy director of the Institute of World Economics and International Relations where I am now continuing to work. After this I went over, was moved, to the post of director of the Institute of Oriental Studies and I returned to the institute where I am working at the present time, as director. I joined the party in 1959.

[Gorbachev] What questions do you have, comrades? Go ahead.

[Unidentified deputy] What is your attitude to the decisions taken on 18 May by the Supreme Soviets of Lithuania and Estonia? And a second question. What is your attitude toward the proposals to make changes in the existing constitution?

[Primakov] I will begin by answering your second question, if you will allow me to. I think it is necessary to make changes in the existing constitution but this must not be done, as they say, on the spur of the moment, not directly in accordance with the proposals which are arriving immediately now and then holding a vote. This is complicated law-making activity, to the highest degree, but it should be implemented unconditionally and a committee or a commission should be working which would concern itself with the elaboration of the constitution. As far as... [changes thought] moreover it should take into account, unconditionally—I want to emphasize this—it should take into account those proposals and remarks which have already been expressed at the congress and which will be received from various places.

All that needs to be taken into account in the most thorough manner imaginable. Generally speaking, I cannot imagine the work of the Supreme Soviet without real feedback, feedback from the voters, from people's deputies who were not included in the Supreme Soviet, feedback from all working people in our country, and naturally, feed back from the republics. The reason for this lies in the fact that there is the other chamber—the Soviet of Nationalities—but that chamber too should base its work on feedback from the republics.

In this connection, allow me to answer your second question. I believe that the proposals which are being put forward by the Baltic republics contain many useful things. That usefulness is in the framework of redressing the deformations which were observed in relations between the center and the periphery in the past. I believe that the situation should, certainly, be reversed because the republics—or rather, individual republics because this applies not only to the Baltic republics—work better but do not see any, so to speak, real improvements in their living standards as a result of their better work.

That is the chief principle, one of the main principles that should be unfailingly laid as a basis when getting rid of the deformations that existed between the center and the periphery. At the same time, on many specific things, I think that serious discussions are needed involving experts, specialists in this or that field, in order to attain results which would satisfy us all—not only as residents of individual republics or representatives of individual republics, but also as citizens of the great Soviet Union....[Primakov pauses due to interruption by unidentified deputy] Go ahead, please.

[Unidentified deputy] Could you tell me, please, Yevgeniy Maksimovich, which particular concept of developing socialism at the present stage you consider to be the most viable in your capacity as an economist—out of all the existing concepts?

[Primakov] As an economist I believe I can tell you that the most viable concept of developing socialism in the economic field is, in my view, the concept which leads to a self-regulating economy.

[Gorbachev] Comrade Medvedev?

[Medvedev] My question is of a purely procedural nature. [words indistinct] The Supreme Soviet is supposed to be working permanently. Is it going to be in session as soon as the Congress of People's Deputies is over?

[Primakov] Well, certainly, because it is going to work on a permanent basis.

[Medvedev] For how long?

[Primakov] Ask me these questions if you elect me. Then I will give you an answer. [laughter]

[Unidentified deputy] Comrade Primakov, opinions of the delegates at the congress have diverged. It is likely that in our chamber these opinions will diverge too? Are you going to side unconditionally with this or that group, or do you favor finding compromise?

[Primakov] To start with, it is my belief that the main task of a chairman is to conduct business in such a way that he does not have to take any stands immediately and does not have, therefore, to cut short or to prevent the exchange of opinions which take place in the chamber

from taking its course. He must conduct matters in a democratic way in order to try to find a healthy compromise between various positions.

[Unidentified deputy] Yevgeniy Maksimovich, as you know, at the congress we heard a proposal to review the status of the country's Supreme Soviet, on turning it into the working executive body of the congress. What is your attitude to this proposal?

[Primakov] I consider—again I apologize for the fact that I am beginning all my answers with the words I consider, but I am being asked questions...

[Gorbachev interrupts] It is precisely your viewpoint that is required at present.

[Primakov] My personal viewpoints?

[Gorbachev] Yes.

[Primakov] One needs to take a dialectical approach to this. On one hand it is definitely a continuation of the congress and it is an organ of the congress. On the other hand, it must have a number of powers which makes it a constantly functioning parliament. That is my answer to your question.

[Gorbachev] Yes, Comrade Ryzhov, if you please.

[Ryzhov] Yevgeniy Maksimovich, I would like to know what your attitude is in principle to procedural issues or [words indistinct] in particular what your attitude is to roll-call, open, or more secret voting? [words indistinct]

[Primakov] I rather think that it is necessary to use all forms of voting—secret voting, open voting, and roll-call voting depending on what form in each particular instance will produce the maximum effect and facilitate the adoption of correct decisions.

[Gorbachev] If you please.

[Unidentified deputy] [words indistinct]

[Primakov] Comrades, I think you will regard me as a frivolous person if I were now to explain to you all the hierarchy regarding these draft laws which are to be discussed. It seems to me that this should be the result of our collective discussion, taking into account the views of all deputies, and afterwards, if I am elected, I shall make definite proposals in this regard.

[Gorbachev] If you please.

[Unidentified deputy] I would like to draw your attention to certain things you have said. I consider that a formulation such as the center and the periphery [words indistinct] in the future. This is somewhat humiliating to the republics and predetermines the priority of developing the center.

[Primakov] I agree with you.

[Unidentified deputy] [words indistinct] the decision of the Supreme Soviet on the creation of commissions and also the Soviet of the Union. My question is to Primakov, but not only to him. The word culture has been dropped and absolutely does not exist. As a composer, I do not agree with this, and I regard culture as a very important factor. The word has disappeared [words indistinct]

[Primakov] The word culture is present in one of the commissions, but... [Gorbachev interrupts] This is our second issue and we shall be discussing it.

[Unidentified deputy] Yevgeniy Maksimovich, we supported your candidacy at the Council of Elders but I would like to ask whether you consider that we should develop interparliamentary links more actively, not only on the level of the leadership of chambers of the Supreme Soviet and the Committee on International Issues but in other of our parliaments as well.

[Primakov] Of course I consider that we should actively develop interparliamentary links, especially as, comrades, it is exactly in that sphere of restructuring where we have achieved very large, indisputably large and positive results. We have moved away from the boundary which we approached and we have now directly eliminated the threat of nuclear catastrophe which was hanging over the whole of humanity. And under these conditions we need to consolidate our hold on these boundaries and to move on. Interparliamentary activity should be called upon to be one of the channels which allows us to resolve this task. Yes? [words indistinct]

You have noted, comrades, it seems to me that if the spectrum of opinion on the issues which are now being brought up for discussion is taken into consideration, and we want it to be taken into account by a genuine, functioning parliament which will be qualified to examine all the issues professionally and which will not later be ashamed of the decisions which it has taken, it seems to me that it is not necessary for this to be resolved by means of voting, but only after serious discussion nevertheless with the proposal of voting after some time has passed and we are able to have serious discussions taking everything for and against into consideration. For this reason it seems to me, this is my personal opinion, I do not know what Mikhail Sergeyevich and Anatoliy Ivanovich think, but it seems to me...

[Gorbachev interrupting] I am forming the opinion that we probably altogether need to create at the congress—and perhaps this will be the most important thing—to form a constitutional commission.

[Primakov] And I think precisely this as well, not because I...

[Gorbachev interrupting] Yes.

[Primakov]...simply mechanically stay with the opinion of the chairman of the Supreme Soviet but because I also adhere to this same point of view...and to then to bring out some first results of this commission at the next congress which will take place in the fall. Yes?

[Unidentified deputy] [words indistinct]

[Gorbachev] It is not advantageous to speak about one's weaknesses at such a moment. [laughter]

[Primakov] What can I say? I have only one real hobby—work. I have been concerned with this all my life and I have put all of my strength into trying to work responsibly. This is the model which I was taught. If you are interested in my personal life then I will tell you personally. [laughter] Yes?

[Unidentified deputy] Yevgeniy Maksimovich, I would just like to ask you how you view the proposal that the constitution should in the future be approved by nationwide voting, that is, changing Article 174. We are preparing a proposal here and then we will submit it to nationwide voting, on each separate article. The article would then be passed by a majority of votes. Why is it that... if you analyze all of our constitutions which have been passed during the years of Soviet power—the four major changes including those of 1956, (?1958)—indicate on the whole that this does not work?

[Primakov] I believe your proposals merit the greatest attention, since sometimes we submit less significant bills to nationwide discussion. Naturally, the constitution will be submitted for nationwide discussion, but as regards the voting procedure—I believe these proposals should be heeded.

[Unidentified deputy] Yevgeniy Maksimovich, I have two questions: Your opinion, please, on the formation and organization of a committee on agricultural affairs. I can find no mention of any such committee in the Supreme Soviet's draft decision. And my second question, how would you view the principle of the formation of the committee. [words indistinct]

[Primakov] I'm sorry?

[Speaker] The principle of the formation of committees and commissions?

[Primakov] Committees and commissions? That is the next thing we will be discussing. But jumping ahead, I can tell you that the question of a committee on agrarian policy and foodstuffs was, as it happens, resolved at the Council of Elders. Yes, go ahead.

[Unidentified deputy] Yevgeniy Maksimovich, your opinion, please, on the number and mix of the deputies who work full time in the Supreme Soviet.

[Primakov] Generally speaking, it would be better if there were more people...

[Gorbachev interrupting] We had a figure at the Council of Elders—80-90 percent should work full time.

[Primakov] Yes, that will then create the backbone which one can rely upon all the time.

[Gorbachev] Go ahead.

[Unidentified deputy] Tell me please, at the congress yesterday a deputy from the Ukraine uttered a (?slogan) that was connected with [words indistinct]—For the state, homeland, and communism. Does this accord with your ideals? If so, then I have a second question. How can the concept of a state be combined with the democratization of the union?

[Primakov] I believe indeed that only the concept of a modern-day state can have a such a combination, because a modern-day state must rely on a democratic structure. Concerning my ideals, naturally I advocate liberty and communism. I am a communist and proud of it. And I have never denied the description.

[Unidentified deputy] How effective do you think nationwide discussion of bills of law is? What is your opinion.?

[Primakov] Let us call a spade a spade. At the moment this discussion is not effective enough. I believe the reason why it is not effective enough stems from the fact that we do not have a structure—and in particular not in the Supreme Soviet—that can genuinely provide analysis and general conclusions, and engage in the feedback process that I was speaking about. As I see it, services such as these must be set up in the Supreme Soviet.

[Gorbachev] Comrade Lauristin, please.

[Lauristin] Following on from [word indistinct] question, I would just like to draw your attention to the fact that in many languages [word indistinct] the word derzhava is given in the dictionary as an concept, and therefore it seems to us unconvincing if you say that a state is a democratic union. And in this connection, I would like to ask: We have two chambers—the Soviet of the Union and the Soviet of Nationalities. The Soviet of Nationalities is built on the republican principle. The Soviet of the Union, though...well, how will you see to it that precisely those demands will be aired in it [words indistinct]

[Primakov] Well, first the semantics, right? There exist quite set definitions, for example that of great powers, and this definition exists in international practice too. And I don't think, by and large, that when someone says that a power [derzhave] must be democratic, (?that does not make the USSR) [word indistinct] that the power is an empire. Of course not!

Now, you are asking me... Sorry, your second question was...?

[Lauristin] (?The right) of the Soviet of the Union...

[Primakov interrupting] How to separate out the fuctions. of course, the Soviet of Nationalities must be involved mainly with questions of relations between nationalities and, running ahead, I can say on this subject—evidently Comrade Lukyanov will be making a report—that here at the Council of Elders a commission on relations between nationalities was even proposed as the first commission to be appointed by the Soviet of Nationalities. This is the profile, the main profile, or the main function of the chamber of the Soviet of Nationalities. The Soviet of the Union, according to its functions, will tackle a number of other questions of all-union significance.

But the structure of the Soviet of the Union provides for—and we had elections, as you know—provides for the representation of all the union republics. And when questions of the budget and so on are discussed, I am convinced that this must be on the basis of a serious discussion with representatives of all the union republics, aspiring to achieve a consensus and agreement.

[Gorbachev] Comrade Gamzatov.

[Gamzatov] Mikhail Sergeyevich, it seems to me that there are many questions which are already beginning to [word indistinct] an inquiry. In my opinion, there will be no end to questions.

[Gorbachev] Quite correct.

[Gamzatov] (?Let us vote) on the basis of (?these questions) [words indistinct]

[Gorbachev] [words indistinct] who particularly wants to ask a question? Just a few more and then we will wind up.

[Unidentified deputy] Two questions. First question: Please say clearly which of these concepts you support: The USSR as a federation of sovereign states, or the USSR as a federation of sovereign republics?

[Primakov] Sorry, what is the second one?

[Deputy] The USSR as a federation of sovereign republics. Your attitude (?to this too). And the second question: What specific steps do you see to raise the role of the Supreme Soviet. Not general ideas, but specific steps. How (?you see them).

[Primakov] The first question. If you have in mind that a federation of sovereign states implies the existence of state formations that are completely based, so to say, on some sort of purely independent, autarkic, if you like, base, then I am against that. At the same tinme, however, I am for our republics having all the attributes of sovereignty which do not run counter to the principles of their being united within the single entity of a federal state. In connection with this, comrades, I want to add that if you talk of the economy then, in principle, there are some things which are being proposed which undoubtedly are in keeping with the requirements of developing the national economy of the Soviet Union as a whole and these are being proposed by individual republics.

At the same time, however, there are also some kinds of general concepts and ideas which consist in the fact that productive forces now require major markets in order to develop, while Europe will, after 1992, develop supranational structures. The thinking there is that these structures will make it possible for them to implement, so to speak, an up to 8 percent increase in the national income through the elimination of patchwork economies alone. One must approach all these things in a very sensitive manner. They must be studied very attentively and the existing state of relations among many republics must be taken into account to a very big extent, and, at the same time, one must proceed from the premise that it is essential to eliminate the deformations that had existed in the past in the relations between various republics.

[Unidentifed speaker] [words indistinct]

[Primakov] With respect to the United Nations, this is a somewhat naive question. This is because, after the war, the United Nations was joined by—apart from the USSR—the Ukraine and Belorussia and this was achieved as a result of an agreement, on the basis of an analysis of the results of the war. I am not certain that the United Nations will now be ready to accept a further 13 representatives from the Soviet Union, sovereign republics.

[Unidentified deputy] Is that your own view?

[Primakov] If you elect me here, I will be responsible for the work of the Soviet of the Union, together, to a certain extent, with you—but not for the work of the United Nations. Please go ahead.

[Unidentified deputy] Yevgeniy Maksimovich, (?do you consider it expedient) to review or to amend the 1989 budget in view of the results of the first half of the year and (?thus) to resolve the topical questions of social development, the same questions mentioned during the congress?

[Primakov] I think that corrections of this kind are essential. You began to put your question.

[Unidentified deputy] [words indistinct]

[Primakov] When this question is discussed you will see that a certain modification has been incorporated and that transportation issues have been marked out in the work of one of the commissions. As to the question of being equal or not—if I am elected I would like to work in precisely that kind of way, on an equal basis with all deputies. Therefore, ask me questions and criticize both until such time as you elect me and if you elect me.

[Gorbachev] Perhaps—just a minute, please—given that there is the desire that we should perhaps conclude this part here and ask the comrades to express their opinion. How do we feel, comrades? [shouts of "yes" from the floor] You want to put the last question—that's your opinion that it will be the last! [laughs] I would like to discuss my proposal, although in fact it is not my proposal, it's yours. Shall we end the questions, comrades? Who's in favor of doing that? Please vote. Thank you. Who's against? That's adopted. Thank you. Yevgeniy Maksimovich. We will now start to discuss you. Who would like to speak? Please do so.

TASS Provides Primakov Biography

LD0306135589 Moscow TASS in English 1318 GMT 3 Jun 89

[Text] Moscow June 3 TASS—Deputy Yevgeniy Primakov, who was elected chairman of the Council of the Union (one of the two equal houses of the new Soviet full-time parliament—the Supreme Soviet), is a Russian born on October 29, 1929.

In 1953 he graduated from the Moscow Institute of Oriental Studies. He began his working life—after completing post-graduate studies at Moscow State University in 1956—was a correspondednt for the state Gosteleradio committee handling radio and television broadcasting uner the USSR Council of Ministers.

In 1962-1970 he worked as a columnist, a deputy editor and a correspondent for the national daily PRAVDA, a newspaper of the Soviet Communist Party Central Committee. This included tours of duty in a number of Middle East countries.

For the following seven years Primakov was a deputy director of the Institute of the World Economy and International Relations, a think-tank under the Soviet Academy of Sciences.

In 1977-1985 he was director of the Institute of Oriental Studies, also under the academy.

From November 1985 Primakov has been directing the Institute of the World Economy and International Relations.

A Communist Party member since 1959, he was elected an alternate member of the party Central Committee at the 27th party congress and promoted to full membership at the April 1989 Central Committee Plenum.

A deputy of the Supreme Soviet since 1987, he served as a member of the Council of the Union's Foreign Relations Commission. Primakov was elected to the new Supreme Soviet at the inaugural session of the Congress of People's Deputies.

He is a widower, with a daughter and a granddaughter.

Primakov Interviewed on Chairmanship

LD0306202689 Moscow Domestic Service in Russian 1800 GMT 3 Jun 89

[Text] [Correspondent Ruvinskiy] Immediately after the session [of the Soviet of the Union] our correspondent interviewed Yevgeniy Maksimovich Primakov, chairman of the Soviet of the Union.

[Begin Recording] [Vasilenko] Yevgeniy Maksimovich, all the deputies have probably already asked you these questions. Allow me first of all to congratulate you on your appointment as chairman. This is All-Union Radio's latest news and Moscow Radio. Tell us, Yevgeniy Maksimovich, how much of a surprise was your nomination?

[Primakov] To me or to the voters?

[Vasilenko] To you and the deputies!

[Primakov] I had hoped that when the deputies were going through the possible candidates that I would have been among those possible candidates. It was a surprise to me, but my decision to agree to being nominated, when it was proposed to me, is linked with the fact that I understand the importance of restructuring. I understand that now all sorts of personal interests must be even pushed aside. Of course, it would perhaps have been easier for me to stay in the institute and carry on all my academic functions. The work here, as I can already imagine, is enormous. But if we really want this parliament to be a parliament, if we really want restructuring to be restructuring, then I think everyone should at least try and fully give all his efforts and potential.

[Vasilenko] With what are you starting, Yevgeniy Maksimovich?

[Primakov] With giving you an interview!

[Vasilenko] Then what?

[Primakov] Then I will be working! The democratic atmosphere is evident, and there are so many wise people, so many wise questions, so many wise things said. All this, however, was until very recently out of sight in some dark fertive soil, and now all this is coming to the surface. This that is the main result of restructuring: That fact that we, that people are now set free, people are coming to the surface of public life. That is the main thing.

[Vasilenko] We have been meeting you in this hall for very many years now. You have participated in the sittings of the Soviet of the Union. How do you think your work will change now? What direction will it take? And not only your work as chairman, but that of the deputies, too?

[Primakov] When we worked before in this hall, in the Soviet of the Union, the main thing was that there was one main program. This program was directed toward there being a unanimous vote. To stick to such standpoints now would—if you want to give things their proper names—mean ruining the Supreme Soviet and failing to understand the place it should occupy in the general system of a people's democracy [narodovlastiye] which is developing in the Soviet Union. We must now therefore strive to increase the activity of all the deputies to the maximum, to raise to the surface, to drag out, all the existing potential possibilities of each deputy to take part in the leadership of the country.

[Vasilenko] I was unable to make my way through to you for about 15 minutes. What questions were the deputies asking you just now, after the session, even though very many questions were asked during the session, too?

[Primakov] The deputies are mainly interested at the moment in issues such as the following: How will their work here be organized? Will they be able to devote themselves fully to this work? How will they be able to combine work in Moscow with work in the localities?— for the majority of them have been elected from the territorial constituencies. These are all very important questions, and they must of course be tackled. Many of them are pretty hard to resolve immediately, but they must be resolved in the near future, I think.

[Vasilenko] A very large number of questions were raised at the congress on the status of a deputy. The deputies say that it is impossible to start work without having this document. What is your point of view on this matter? And when do you think these matters will be resolved?

[Primakov] I think we should have this document by the next congress.

[Vasilenko] Another question: I cannot imagine that a scientist would tear himself away from his scientific research, from his scientific work. How have you decided this question, for yourself, within yourself, as a man and as a scientist?

[Primakov] I have walked my own path, if you like, but I think that at least one night I will be able to write something, work on some things.

[Vasilenko] That is clear! Many thanks, Yevgeniy Maksimovich, we wish you successful work!

[Primakov] Thank you very much. [end recording]

Deputy Chairman Lukyanov Speaks

LD0306224989 Moscow Television Service in Russian 1205 GMT 3 Jun 89

[Speech by Anatoliy Lukyanov, deputy chairman of the USSR Supreme Soviet, at session of Soviet of the Union of the USSR Supreme Soviet in the Kremlin, with interjections by Primakov, questions from deputies in the hall—live]

[Text] [Lukyanov] Comrade deputies: The Soviet of the Union and the Soviet of Nationalities elect from among the members of the Supreme Soviet and also from among other people's deputies of the USSR standing commissions of the chambers to carry out legislative [corrects himself] work drafting laws, to preliminarily examine and prepare questions within the remit of the USSR Supreme Soviet and also to facilitate the implementation of the laws and other decisions adopted by the Congress of People's Deputies and the USSR Supreme Soviet and to control the activities of state bodies. This is what Article 122 of the USSR Constitution proclaims.

It must be stated that for the same purposes the chambers of the USSR Supreme Soviet can set up committees of the USSR Supreme Soviet on an equal basis, as well as other commissions and committess. In order to resolve the question of setting up commissions and committees and of the commissions of the Soviet of the Union above all, the congress presidium has carried out a great deal of analytical work. All deputies were handed a questionnaire and they were also handed a draft decision with a list of commissions which it could be possible to set up and, at the same time, every deputy was given an opportunity to make his views known as to what commission he would like to serve on.

More than 1,800 deputies responded to this questionnaire and it must be said that 80 percent of them fully supported the proposals regarding commissions which had been put forward and they spoke in favor of participating in one commission. Some suggested [corrects himself] said they could take part in, say, two commissions. Others named two commissions but said it is only possible to work in one of these commissions, and that they would be ready to choose.

Approximately 12 percent of the replies contained elaborations with regard to the list of the commissions, proposals regarding various structures of the commissions, and so on. What premise did we proceed from in our appraisal of these proposals? First and foremost from the fact that the composition of the chambers is not large. Each of them has 271 deputies. If we bring up the number of the commissions to a very large number, then we will simply be unable to make sure that each commission is composed of equal halves made up of members of the chamber and the deputies, USSR people's deputies who make up the congress. On the other hand, we started from the position that the commissions cannot be tied to the industries. Otherwise they will coincide in name with the ministries and departments, and that too will hinder their parliamentary activity, profile, and functions.

Third, there will certainly be subcommissions or subcommmittees within the commissions in which it will be possible to tackle whatever questions may arise of a narrower type.

And finally, we started off from the position that in setting up commissions in one chamber we have to bear in mind that commissions of a different type will be set up in the other chamber, and that the committees will be set up jointly. So we have to have an all-round approach to this problem.

For this reason, at the session of the Councils of Elders of both chambers today, we went very carefully through all the commissions and committees. You have those documents. And I just want to tell you, inform you, how the work on these documents went, what amendments we introduced and are presenting for your consideration.

First of all, the commissions, the standing commissions of the Soviet of the Union, of this chamber. It is being proposed that an equal number of standing commissions, four each, should be set up in each chamber, but the Soviets of the Union should take the main type of these commissions, the all-union questions, and the Soviet of Nationalities the questions of more, so to say, [corrects himself] relating to the development of the nationalities, the national republics, issues of autonomy, and so on. Therefore it is being proposed to create in the Soviet of the Union: a planning and budget-finance commission; a commission on the problems of industrial development, covering power engineering, technology, and many other questions—evidently there will be subcommissions there; a commission on the questions of transportation and communications—it is down here to have a commission on food questions, but we decided to suggest to you the setting up a committee on agrarian questions and food, and here the questions of transportation and communications, you will understand, is a real all-union question, and it should thus be under the jurisdiction of the Soviet of the Union. And finally, a commission on questions of labor, prices, and social policy. This question was discussed in detail since this is a matter of how a person's labor rights must be defended regardless of where he lives in our territory, and ensured. Prices have the most fundamental all-union significance, and finally a strong social policy is a most important component in the policy of our state as a whole.

In connection with this it is intended to set up four permanent commissions of the Soviet of the Union and this is being presented for your consideration. As far as the Soviet of Nationalities is concerned—so that it is clear how the commissions of the Soviet of the Union stand out in this sense—here we have proposed that a commission on inter-ethnic relations be brought into the foreground—and call it the first one. The next commission is here. Clearly it will have a number of subcommissions, in particular a subcommission on questions concerning the development of numerically-small peoples, which is extremely important, not just the ethnic groups of the north but the numerically-small people of our country overall. The next commission is a commission on the social and economic development of the union and autonomous republics, the autonomous oblasts and okrugs. It is a matter of this being approximately the same kind of planning and financial-budgetary commission, only this time applied to the republics and our autonomous entities. This is extremely important, although it is clear that these commissions will work together quite often.

Next, the commissions linked with those branches of the economy which are now being handed over in full to the management of the republics. These are a commission on consumer goods, retail trade, everyday municipal and other services for the population; and a commission on the development of culture, language, national and internationalist traditions and the protection of historical monuments. We have proceeded from the premise that the roots of our culture of many nationalities lie here in the development of every people. Our multinational culture is indeed put together from the cultures of all the peoples. A commission on culture, therefore, has indeed been included among the commissions in the Soviet of Nationalities of our Supreme Soviet. That completes the commissions of the Soviet of Nationalities.

Finally the committees. The committees will be created by the chambers on the principle of parity. They, too, were the subject of certain changes introduced during discussion at the session of the Council of Elders of the chambers and I would like to comment on them. Each of you has them in your hands—the list. It is proposed that we form a committee on international affairs, which will comprise both foreign economic links and inter-parliamentary links to a certain extent and humanitarian relations and so on; and a committee on defense and state security. We discussed this for a long time and we decided that these issues are so closely linked that they have to be determined together. The next committee, a committee on legislation, legitimacy and law and order—and although this committee will be engaged to the maximum degree with work on draft bills and sharpening the formulas used in legislation, it is nevertheless very important that it also be linked with legitimacy and law and order because it can then have an opportunity to observe how the laws are implemented and to monitor this, to monitor the activity of law enforcement bodies. Without this, purely legislative work would not have any point, especially since other committees, too, will be dealing with legislation.

The next committee has also been introduced after many proposals by the deputies. It is a committee on the work of soviets of people's deputies, the development of management and self-management. It must be said that many proposals came in on this question, and the deputies support this committee.

The next committee has been introduced on the basis of proposals by deputies and those remarks, those proposals that were formulated in the report by Mikhail Sergeyevich Gorbachev at the congress. I am talking of a committee on economic reform. In practice the Planning and Budget Committee and the Committee on the Development of the Republics and on Economic Reform will work in the closest contact.

And now the next committee that was deemed expedient at the Council of Elders to be introduced on to this list is a committee on agrarian questions and food. We decided...[unidentified deputies shout: on agrarian policy] No, we discussed that question. Policy is the business in general, perhaps, of the party and state. We are talking precisely of agrarian questions and food. That is what we agreed.

[Primakov] So, comrade, you are making a remark about the word policy?

[Lukyanov] Yes.

[Primakov] The (?name) of the problem or question?

[Lukyanov] Yes. The next committee is a committee on questions of construction and architecture. There were many proposals. Some said that we need only town planning. Others said rural construction would then be deprived of our attention. Others said it should simply be on questions of construction without architecture. But we believe that the proposals put forward by the chairman of our Union of Architects, Comrade Platonov, are correct: This committee must be called on construction and architecture.

The question of a committee on science and popular education was carefully discussed. As a result of the discussion at the session of the Council of Elders, we are proposing that this committee should be called the Committee for Science, Popular Schooling, and Education. Probably that is right, it makes sense.

The next committee: on protecting the people's health. A proposal on this question was made by the Academy of Medical Science. In my opinion it covers the whole complex of questions on health care.

The question of what to call the committee on women's affairs was discussed. It turns out that the concept of family is lost here, and our constitution records the protection of our families by the state, the strengthening of the family. So it is proposed to call this committee: The Committee for Women's Affairs, Protection of the Family and Children.

The next committee: on the affairs of veterans and invalids.

Another committee is the committee on youth affairs; the committee on the ecology and the rational use of natural resources; and finally the committee on the rights and appeals of citizens. I have to say that here an examination was made of what we should do here. Perhaps we should have a separate committee on rights, but the deputies concluded that the kind of committee that must be set up will be closely linked with the proposals and complaints that will come in to the Supreme Soviet—and about 500,000 of these are received annually—so that the possibility is there for a direct response to possible violations of citizens' rights and so that the Supreme Soviet may stand guard, stand guard in every way, over the legitimate rights and interests of the Soviet citizen.

Those are the committees which, it is proposed, should be formed jointly. If, therefore, it is possible to decide on the commissions, the permanent commissions, of the Soviet of the Union now, then the committees, if the chamber approves this list with the amendments that I have mentioned, then these proposals must be passed [break in transmission of a few seconds at this point] and if it adopts your proposals, then the two chambers together will decide which committees have to be formed in the USSR Supreme Soviet.

The only thing I want to add, of course, is that there will be a whole series of commissions, both commissions of the congress and investigation and auditing and other commissions and groups which will be formed by the Supreme Soviet in its activity.

One further consideration: It is practically impossible to draw a dividing line between the commissions. It is also impossible to set up many of them, but as a rule they work, as experience shows, together and they resolve a whole range of closely related issues. Setting up barriers between them, therefore, is virtually impossible in our view. Those are the proposals that I put forward for your consideration on behalf of the USSR Supreme Soviet Presidium, proposals which have been drawn up on the basis of deputies' proposals and on behalf of the Council of Elders of the Soviet of the Union and the Soviet of Nationalities.

Gorbachev Suspends 5 Jun Congress After Tragedy
LD0506072389 Moscow Television Service in Russian 0601 GMT 5 Jun 89

[Speech by Mikhail Sergeyevich Gorbachev, general secretary of the CPSU Central Committee and chairman of the USSR Supreme Soviet, at the 5 June session of the USSR Congress of People's Deputies in the Kremlin Palace of Congresses—live]

[Text] Comrade deputies, as you know, on the night of 3-4 June, a major accident happened on a liquified gas pipeline near the Chelyabinsk-Ufa railway in the territory of the Bashkir Autonomous Soviet Socialist Republic, on the border with Chelyabinsk Oblast. The catastrophe resulted in great human casualties. According to preliminary data, this is several hundred people. Among them are a group of children travelling to the south for a holiday. I propose, in the name of...[sentence incomplete] I propose that our congress pay its respects to the memory of those who died with a minute of silence. [deputies observe minute of silence]

I propose, in the name of our congress, that profound condolences be expressed to the families, relatives, and dear ones of those who died as a result of the catastrophe.

Yesterday, Comrade Ryzhkov and I flew there, but the local population had already come to help there in the very first minutes; let us say this right away. It is a very remote place, far from major settlements. The biggest settlement is the town of Asha in Chelyabinsk Oblast, 15 km away. All this happened; the local population, having heard and seen that something had happened, set off for the site of the explosion. When they saw it all, they passed on all the information to Ufa and to the rayon centers, and to Chelyabinsk. All night the local population was working. In literally the first minutes, the first hour, 100 first aid teams travelled out from Ufa. Those who are still alive—it is still difficult even to take stock of everything, so to speak—but when we were there yesterday, 580 people or so remained alive, but many of them were in grave condition. Even yesterday, several people passed away during the day.

Everything is being done there, but the tragedy is serious. It is even difficult to imagine. The pipeline is a kilometer away from the railway. We have been there and had a look around. One cannot approach the scene yet. The flame is still ablaze. The product [gas] has been cut off, and it is burning out, but obviously there was a breach in the pipeline where this is burning and this product was coming down the sloping section toward the railway track. Because of the temperature—the weather has been warm recently—it started rising, filling the entire depression. And obviously it filled a large expanse, for the explosion was so terribly strong that the forest there has been destroyed over a large territory. All the rails have been dislodged there. In a word, people were involved in such a calamity there that it is even terrible to imagine.

This was at 0200 local time. Most people were asleep, but there were some of them—those who were in a condition to, and there are several dozen people, too, who received a small amount of help and went out, and some were capable—and we talked to them and to people from both the latter and the former group, who told us about this, about everything that happened.

Now I do not wish to take it upon myself to pass judgement on the causes. For this would mean that by expressing these opinions we would be anticipating the work of the government commission and the work of the bodies of inquiry which are already there and engaged in their work. However, at 2000 [1600 GMT], 3 hours before this happened, a drop in pressure was discovered in this product pipeline. I do not know, nor do I wish to pass judgement, but evidently, as even common sense suggests, this required investigation, according to regulations, of what was going on and why.

According to the first information—but all this is also subject to revision—the bodies of inquiry have now imposed on all the equipment which registers the work...[sentence incomplete] All these parameters are being written down and studied. However, as we have been told, the pumps were switched on to raise pressure without having sorted out what was going on. Obviously, they were pumping it into the pipe, and they were pumping it here, as it were, and it accumulated. When it had accumulated and reached the level where passing trains were coming into contact with power, a spark was enough, and everything exploded. So this is what happened there.

At the beginning, I was very greatly concerned about why the two trains were together, but it turns out they were not supposed to meet at that station, but there was some sort of a hitch there so they met in another place. In other words, this was not a planned stop, according to the schedule, but a passing place, with trains passing in opposite directions.

At any rate, however, one has to sort this out. We have talked to local people, too. People say that one has to inquire into all this, so as to prevent things being affected again by incompetence, irresponsibility, poor management, and all the disgraceful things I have discussed, comrades, as well; and all the residents there said that things will not go well in our country if this lack of discipline keeps causing this sort of human, let alone economic and other, tragedy in various places.

Anyway, the commission is at work now. There are medics there, headed by Comrade Chazov. All the country's major burn-treatment centers have been mobilized; the major specialists have been mobilized and are all working there. People are donating blood. So everything has been set up and everything is being done there, though the situation is a very severe one. We will have to learn some very harsh lessons from this in every respect. Before flying out there yesterday we consulted our comrades from the Politburo and agreed that they should go to the hotels to inform the deputies and have a talk. During these conversations many deputies expressed the wish that all the deputies, out of charitable feelings, should pay their day's earnings as deputies into the charity fund for the provision of assistance to the families. Well, to the extent that this can help...[sentence incomplete] You cannot replace dear ones or children, but to stand beside people, I think...we will respond to this, I think. [murmurs of assent from hall]

Another thing: We have declared today a day of mourning. The view among us is that we should have a day's break in our work. How could we hold a debate at the moment? And then tomorrow, at 1000, we will hold the first session of the congress, and at 1600 [1200 GMT], the session of the Soviet of Nationalities, so that that chamber can decide on some issues. During the time available today, the deputies could visit the government, the Central Committee, the ministries, or wherever anyone has any unresolved issues, or else on the contrary, where they have been in contact, to check how issues are being tackled and use the time, to speak, for this. I think from the moral point of view as well, this is what we ought to do. Do you agree, comrades? [assent from hall]

Then I will wind up this part, but I want to...[sentence incomplete] There's an appeal here from a group of deputies. The deputies probably are troubled by the situation in Fergana and Nagorno-Karabakh, and a group of deputies has called upon those involved—to read out this letter on behalf of the congress—that we, the USSR people's deputies, call upon those involved in clashes on an interethnic basis to heed the voice of reason and put an end to the bloodshed. Injustices and problems have accumulated in interethnic relations and been ignored for years, but this does not mean that painful issues cannot be resolved in principle. Think about those innocent people against whom has been raised the hand of...[changes thought] about the women, children, and elderly. Stay that hand and prevent injustices from being committed. We call upon you to resolve the problems that have arisen by peaceful means, by means of the law. Well, there you are.

I did not understand everything here, but I have read out practically all of it. There is a large group of deputies here from Leningrad, Moscow, and other places, the Baltic republics, and I would support this appeal from our congress. This is also something that disturbs us all. We all feel it, the congress, and this topic is at the center of our discussions and we seek now to go on solving these issues. How do you feel, comrades? [indistinct murmuring from the floor] And publish? People are listening to us and I believe they will also hear our voice and the call for reason, and this appeal will be published on behalf of the congress. Then we bid farewell at this point today.

General Gromov Interviewed on Afghanistan War

PM0406183189 Moscow SOTSIALISTICHESKAYA INDUSTRIYA in Russian 4 Jun 89 p 1

[Interview with USSR People's Deputy Colonel General Boris Gromov by Yu. Kurbanov: "This Must Never Happen Again"; date and place of interview not given—first paragraph is SOTSIALISTICHESKAYA INDUSTRIYA introduction]

[Text] We think there is no need to introduce USSR People's Deputy Colonel General Boris Gromov. He commanded the Limited Contingent of Soviet Troops in Afghanistan. At the moment he is the commander of the Red Banner Kiev Military District.

[Kurbanov] Boris Vsevolodovich, the congress is in its 2d week. In general, what are your impressions?

[Gromov] My impressions are very positive. The main thing is the totally frank and unbuttoned nature of the discussion of the most acute questions and the critical attitude of the people's deputies. We are witnessing the birth of a new democracy. The congress can be said to be living its own unpredictable life. We are all learning, we are mastering the rudiments of political debate. Although there are certain difficulties: A lack of political culture on the part of many deputies is clearly felt, and much time is taken up with the counting of votes. The absence of voting equipment is simply astounding. Sometimes emotions triumph over common sense. However, I do not believe that there is any need to get alarmed about this. After all, this is the first time we have held a congress like this.

[Kurbanov] Why do you think a whole series of military leaders who put forward interesting programs during the election campaign nonetheless lost?

[Gromov] I think that this was partly due to our inconsistency. For many years and even decades we painted Army life only in rosy colors. Now, in the age of glasnost, we have swung to the other extreme and we are being very lavish with black. But after all, the Army merely reflects the present state of our society as a whole. In addition, it has its own specific shortcomings, of course. Whether we like it or not, a negative attitude to the Army has gradually taken shape. And this was reflected in the fate of certain of our candidate deputies. Incidentally, many party officials found themselves in a similar position.

Nonetheless, the Armed Forces are represented at the congress by 80 people's deputies, ranging from a military school cadet to an Army general.

[Kurbatov] In M.S. Gorbachev's report our military budget—R77.3 billion—was made public for the first time. Moreover, specific figures were also cited for its reduction—R10 billion in 1990-1991. What is your attitude to this?

[Gromov] It may seem paradoxical to some people, but questions concerning the reduction of the military budget featured in the election programs of virtually all the candidate deputies representing the Armed Forces. We are perfectly well aware of the strained situation concerning our state budget. I support those people's deputies who spoke from the congress rostrum about the need to increase pensions and assistance to low-income families. After all, in no civilized society are old people in such a pitiful position.

As I see it, the main ways to reduce the military budget are to decrease the size of the Armed Forces and bring troop subunits back home from abroad. But the defense of the fatherland is my profession. Therefore I am convinced that cuts in the military budget must not be carried out mechanically. The Army must attain a qualitatively higher technical level. I would formulate this problem as follows: Less, but considerably better.

[Kurbatov] I was among those who welcomed you on the banks of the Amu Darya River. Tell me, what is the significance of Afghanistan for the Army, young soldiers, and you personally?

[Gromov] For everyone who was there, Afghanistan is a memory. A memory of events and of the people with whom he served. A memory of courage and of the strength of human spirit. We discharged our duty honestly and we are able to look people squarely in the face. The overwhelming majority of the "Afgantsy" [veterans of the Afghan war] continue to faithfully serve the homeland. I believe that it is no accident that there are many former internationalist servicemen here at the congress.

[Kurbatov] It has been claimed at the most varied levels lately that the introduction of our forces into Afghanistan was not just a strategic but also a political mistake....

[Gromov] It is not within my competence to judge this. Clearly, one would have to have been in that situation at the time. I believe that it is wrong to make such categorical statements so lightly. It is necessary to take a close look at what happened and how. I fully agree with those who say that at that time Afghanistan was in dire need of help. It is another question as to what kind of help was required and by what methods and means.

[Kurbatov] It is claimed that the decision to send in troops was taken behind closed doors and that even some members of the Politburo did not know about it. Are there any guarantees that this will not happen again?

[Gromov] I believe there are. The question of the use of our forces abroad has already been raised at our congress. And what is more, it was raised by the chairman of the USSR Supreme Soviet M.S. Gorbachev himself. However, as I see it, the very tenor of our life and the approach to the solution of the most acute problems will prevent this from being done in the future.

[Kurbatov] Now to the problem of the "Afgantsy." Does it exist, in your opinion, or does it not?

[Gromov] This is a complex question. On the one hand, I believe, there is no such problem. Fortunately, most of our people view the former internationalist servicemen with understanding and sensitivity. The state has granted them considerable benefits.

But on the other hand, it appears that it is not that easy for them to avail themselves of these benefits. I am worried at the indifference with which invalids and the families of dead servicemen are treated in some places. It seems to me that this is cruel, to say the least. I know from my own experience how difficult it is for "Afgantsy" who have looked death in the face to adapt to peaceful life. Frequently this is a painful process. We have to understand this and be more tolerant of the maximalism of the "Afgantsy" and their sharp rejection of many of our realities.

There are also problems of a purely material nature. Above all the provision of the "Afgantsy" with housing. I am aware of the acuteness of these problems in the country as a whole. But they must be resolved.

Of late I have crisscrossed virtually the whole of the Ukraine; I receive hundreds of letters from former internationalist servicemen. I would like to stress once more that in them restructuring has tempered, courageous fighters who will never act against their conscience.

[Kurbatov] Boris Vsevolodovich, if we moved our congress 10 years back in time and the question of introducing our forces into Afghanistan was raised, would you personally vote "for" or "against"?

[Gromov] I will answer unequivocally: "Against." It must never happen again!

Contacts With U.S. Army Desired

LD0306062589 Moscow in English to North America 2200 GMT 2 Jun 89

[Text] Among the deputies to the congress there is a large number of military men. Colonel-General Boris Gromov is among the most recognizable officers. On 15 February, as commander of the Soviet military contingent in Afghanistan, he became the last Soviet military man to leave that country under United Nations-mediated Geneva accords. The event was widely publicized, and at the congress he is treated as a celebrity. He shared his general impressions about the congress with reporters in his new capacity as commander of the Kiev Military District and, of course, as a deputy to the congress. Boris Gromov:

[Begin Gromov recording in Russian with superimposed English translation] My general impression? It seems to me that at first, particularly in the first days, the congress was going hard, now it is getting into a working order, in my view. As I understand it, the congress must deal with major issues, global questions which relate to the whole nation. However what we saw in the first days were minor, trivial issues being raised. I don't mean that those people have no right to raise such questions, but I think it would be more appropriate to deal with them elsewhere, such as for example in commissions in subsequent sessions of the Supreme Soviet, but not here at the first congress of the people's deputies. [end recording]

[Announcer] Last Tuesday, in his keynote address at the congress, Soviet President Mikhail Gorbachev disclosed the country's actual defense spending and announced that in 1990 and 1991 the USSR will slash this spending by 10 billion rubles. Earlier he announced at the United Nations this country was reducing its armed forces by 500,000 men. How do the Army people regard these defence cuts? Col Gen Gromov comments.

[Begin Gromov recording in Russian with superimposed English translation] On the whole, Army people take them positively. Our only wish is that these cuts should not affect the quality of our armed forces, but work in the opposite direction. For me, like for anyone else in our country, the state of the national economy and the living standards are of major concern and we should find a way out of our current problems. I support the proposed defense cuts. At the same time, I expect and hope for broadening our ties with other military men. Not only our traditional ties with other members of the Warsaw Treaty organization, but I would like to see more contacts with U.S. Army men. We need more such contacts with representatives of other armies. [end recording]

[Announcer] Col Gen Boris Gromov speaking to newsmen in the Kremlin Palace of Congresses.

31 May Congress Proceedings Reported

Tajikistan's Makhkamov Speaks
*PM0506155189 Moscow IZVESTIYA in Russian
2 Jun 89 Morning Edition p 9*

[Speech by K. Makhkamov, first secretary of the Tajik Communist Party Central Committee, Dushanbe City (Dushanbinsky Territorial Electoral Okrug, Tajik SSR) at 31 May afternoon session of the Congress of USSR People's Deputies]

[Excerpt] [passage omitted] Comrade deputies! In the course of the congress we have all become aware of how many complexities and acute problems have accumulated in interethnic relations. All this is a result of the fact that we were prisoners of complacency, when wishes posed as deeds. These are the serious consequences of previous times which we must all overcome together. We are convinced that this must be done by joint efforts, in an atmosphere of amicability and the ability to listen to and understand one another. In particular, we in Tajikistan are still running up against the consequences of an inadequately conceived solution for questions connected with national-territorial demarcation in Central Asia. The mistakes made then are still affecting us. There are problems which we are solving on the spot. And there are problems which we cannot solve on the spot. Here is one of them, a tiny example. Many Tajiks and some Uzbeks who live in Tajikistan and Uzbekistan have long been asking about the correcting of passport entries on nationality, because distortions were committed in the past. This problem could have been sorted out a long time ago just by amending the 1974 provision on establishing national affiliation. Back in November last year Tajik and Uzbek leaders petitioned the USSR Council of Ministers on this score. A positive conclusion was apparently arrived at by the competent bodies, but the problem still has not been resolved. At the same time we and the leaders of Uzbekistan are doing all we can so that our peoples strengthen their friendship and solve together the issues that arise. We have begun to implement a joint program of practical measures to develop interethnic links between our republics, including both economic and cultural aspects. But now, in our opinion, it is time for a more profound approach to questions of improving the national state structure on an all-union scale. In order to broaden legal guarantees and meet the national-cultural needs of citizens living outside their national state formations, or if such formations simply do not exist, it seems necessary to resolve the issue of creating, in places where there is a concentration of inhabitants of a particular nationality, national regions with their own soviets and their own representation in the republics' highest state organs. As a whole the newly formed USSR Supreme Soviet should pay particular attention to questions of interethnic relations by resolving all the arising problems in a timely and considered manner.

Comrades, yesterday a Georgian deputy raised the question about the institution of second secretaries of union republic Communist Party central committees. I support Deputy Ishanov on this issue. I believe that if our Georgian comrades have a problem, then let them solve it for themselves. It is not necessary to spread the problem to other republics.

In the course of the congress some deputies' speeches from this platform have contained reproaches—undeserved in my opinion, and, I hope, not just in mine—against our party. Have there been mistakes and errors on the part of the party? Yes, there have. But was it not the party that led the October revolution? Was it not the party that raised up the entire multinational Soviet people and led them to victory in the Great Patriotic War? Today it has once again started a revolutionary restructuring of society. So, comrade deputies, let us all together help the party win a new victory which will determine the future of our country and of all socialism. Thank you for your attention. (Applause)

Kazarezov Addresses Congress
*PM0506152589 Moscow IZVESTIYA in Russian
2 Jun 89 Morning Edition p 7*

[Speech by V.V. Kazarezov, first secretary of the Novosibirsk Oblast CPSU Committee, (Tatarskiy Territorial Electoral Okrug, Novosibirsk Oblast) at the 31 May afternoon session of the Congress of USSR People's Deputies under the general heading "Congress of USSR People's Deputies"]

[Text] Comrade deputies! As a party worker, I should perhaps talk more today about the political aspects of restructuring, but I will be dwelling on the economic aspects, because there has unquestionably been progress in the political sphere.

It is quite obvious to me that if there is no improvement in the people's standard of living in the near future and if urgent social programs are not implemented, people will start to lose faith in the possibility of any positive changes at all. And this would mean the end of restructuring, from whichever direction it came—from the left or from the right. (Applause).

The economy is ill with a serious, chronic disease and I, at least, can see no signs of improvement at present. It seems to me that we have not properly assessed the real depth of the economic crisis. As far as the most recent period is concerned, official assessments have clearly tried to embellish the true state of affairs. This is quite intolerable. Studies conducted by Siberian economists have shown that in the first 3 years of the 5-year period the growth in industrial output has not been 13 percent, as statistical reports would have us believe, but only just over 4 percent—and only 1 percent in 1988. It seems that the remainder of the increase, or, to be more precise, the appearance of an increase has been achieved through concealed price rises and flawed statistics. (Applause).

It is possible that our scientists are overdramatizing the situation, but I do not think that this is to any significant degree. So, I would like to conclude this theory in my speech with an appeal for a totally accurate assessment of the socioeconomic situation in the country, and consequently feel it possible to instruct the newly elected Supreme Soviet and the appropriate commissions to look more deeply into the situation and inform deputies and the population. But it seems more important to establish the reasons for the increasing deterioration in the situation, and more important still to look for ways out of this situation. I could, at this point, talk about our national economy's unreceptiveness to scientific and technical progress, or about how economic reform is marking time and so forth, but a great deal has already been said on the subject and, I am sure, will be said yet. I do not want to deprive scientists and economists of their living. I would like to talk about something else—and on this I am in agreement with the previous speaker—namely, about the low level of competence and weak scientific study when substantiating major decisions in our country, and also about the half-hearted, timid, inconsistent approach to putting these decisions into practice.

You can judge for yourselves the kind of impression that could have been created by the formulation of the task ahead 3 years ago: To ensure that 80-95 percent of basic output is manufactured to world standards by 1990, or, in other words, ensure the kind of leap forward that would make your head spin. It was a bitter, painful experience for the country's leadership when, at every step, people showed amazement at such an unrealistic task, to put it mildly, and, after all, we have been obliged to motivate party organizations and collectives to fulfill this task. Where is this incompetence coming from? I would like to ask you, Mikhail Sergeyevich, to consider what kind of advisers suggest these kind of decisions. Take a really recent decision. The state order for agricultural output is to be conveyed to republics and oblasts but not to individual economic units. In my view, this approach is not only incorrect and illogical, it is also immoral. There must be either one thing or another: Either we abandon the state order from top to bottom, if we are ready for this, or we retain it for a while—again from top to bottom. Otherwise we end up with a conflict between oblast- and rayon-level leadership, on the one hand, and the direct producers of agricultural output on the other, while the center takes a highly respectable democratic position.

There is more. It seems to me that we are causing problems by our ill-considered approach to changing investment policy under the guise of reorientation toward the social sphere. Here, too, I have an example. It is planned to reduce investments in the development of the heat and electric power industry together with other industrial ministries. I will not attempt to judge the situation in the country as a whole (although it is now our duty to think of the country as a whole), but for Novosibirsk Oblast this will mean an impasse situation

in social development. Look at what is happening. Last year a USSR Council of Ministers resolution was adopted on the development of the power industry in Novosibirsk Oblast, which envisaged almost doubling capital investments in the Ministry of Power and Electrification in 1990 in comparison to the 1988 level. It has been estimated that the shortage of heat for Novosibirsk alone amounts to 1,000 kilocalories. There is also a considerable shortage of electricity. But it is in fact planned to reduce investments for 1990 to below the present level. Anatoliy Ivanovich Mayorets, minister of power and electrification, explains this as a reduction in capital investments in the power industry within the framework of the general reduction of industrial construction in the country. I would not just call this a shortsighted policy—it is something worse. We are talking about the social sphere, but just try to name a more social sector than heat and electricity generation! When there is no meat you can substitute potatoes and pasta for it for a while; when there is no soap you can get by for a few days, washing without it. (A stir in the audience). But how, in Siberia, with temperatures of minus 40 degrees, can you live if it is cold in your apartment and at work? How are we to heat new housing, schools, kindergartens, and hospitals, which we are now building in greater numbers (and we are indeed building them in greater numbers, comrades), if there is not enough heat to go around, once they are built? We will be forced to curtail our social programs. And the reality of building 1 billion square meters of housing per year across the country, which Mikhail Sergeyevich talked about in his report, is a great problem in this connection. That is why I talk of an impasse situation and urge deputies, particularly those who will be working on the relevant commissions, to help to speed up the development of the heat and electric power industry.

Furthermore. A paradoxical situation has developed in our country. On the one hand, there is excessive centralization in economic management and, on the other, the center is completely powerless when it comes to organizing the division of labor and integrating production and scientific potentials. I see this as one of the main reasons for our lagging behind. After all, in my opinion, in terms of the degree of cooperation and specialization in industry, particularly in machine building, and in terms of certain other indicators, we are at the level of premonopolist capitalism. Take a look at our country's machine-building plants. Each one represents a combine with a selection of virtually every technology available. There is everything here: casting, forging, welding, machine-tool, and other production operations. They have virtually every type of instrument, spare part, industrial holder and fastener, and standard fitting; each one makes them for itself. I am sure that if all this were produced at specialized enterprises, the prime cost of machine-building output would be sharply reduced, the quality and technical standard of this output improved, and the amount of materials used in the process reduced. Comrades, I have studied the documents of party congresses, beginning with the 23d congress. Like an incantation, they have repeated the thesis on the need to develop production specialization and cooperation, but the process has in fact gone in the opposite direction. Four years of restructuring have produced nothing and the situation has only got worse.

Or take this situation. Realizing that it is futile to hope for the centralized organization of the production and supply to villages of machinery and equipment they so need, such as silage combines, hay-making equipment, cranes, and so forth (agricultural workers here in the hall know that they certainly do not have enough of all these things—not to mention supplies of new equipment for agriculture), we decided to organize the production of all these things ourselves in the oblast, scattering assemblies and components to dozens of plants. Moscow has given us a pat on the back for this. But what kind of pat on the back do they deserve, when the machinery is going to be several times more expensive and the quality several times more inferior? This is quite barbaric: Each oblast making its own agricultural machinery when the country has such a powerful machine-building potential! And I know that Sverdlovsk, Voronezh, and other oblasts are doing the same as us. But we are ruining the country, comrades, with this kind of approach! How can we talk seriously of restructuring in the economy in view of this? On the whole, as I see it, this is restructuring back to front.

I would like to say a few words about regional economic accountability and self-management. I, like the overwhelming majority of people, am categorically in favor of this. I can understand how this is viewed at union republic level. But what about us, the krays and oblasts—are we each supposed to withdraw into our own cocoon? It seems to me that we should be thinking about making the transition to a region-based administrative system—for example, the Urals, West Siberia, the Far East, the Center, and so forth—and, perhaps, give these regions the rights enjoyed by the union republics in economic respects. (Applause).

A few more words about regional economic accountability. It should be total. It is thought, for example, that investments in science yield the greatest effect. If that were so with regard to the region where science is located, Novosibirsk Oblast would be the most prosperous in the whole country, because in terms of strength of scientific potential we cede place only to Moscow and Leningrad—and possibly Kiev. We have three academy branches here: the USSR Academy of Sciences, the V.I. Lenin All-Union Academy of Agricultural Sciences, and the USSR Academy of Medical Sciences. The fact that they are concentrated in one city is, in my opinion, wrong, but it is too late to talk about that now. We will take the view that history has ordained it so. But in that case it should be to our advantage to develop science, receiving an appropriate percentage for the local budget from the results of scientists' work (and, what is more, work financed from the budget and work based on an

economic contract) introduced not only here but elsewhere in the country and sold abroad. Then, firstly, it would be clear exactly what kind of feedback we are getting from our three branches. And, secondly, if the feedback from investments in science really proves to be the most profitable, we will give it priority development at the expense of other sectors and programs, meaning by this that we will resolve many local social problems by using the dividends from science.

A few more words about science. It really does need to very seriously review its attitude to itself. We have outstanding scientific cadres and scientific results of world standard. But it is a thorny path from ideas to practice. The main thing here, apart from the ineffectual economic mechanism, is the weakness of our experimental base, which has already been much discussed. How can the situation be put right? The presidium of the Siberian Branch of the USSR Academy of Sciences takes a traditional approach to this: It is proposing the construction of new institute buildings (the same old extensive course of action again), which means a further increase in the number of new building projects. What can I say? I myself have an allergy to new construction work. And with regard to this particular issue, the position is this: First, building new premises and fitting them out with equipment, thereby investing millions and millions of rubles, is not the same thing as creating an experimental base for institutes. And who is going to work in these premises? Second, for us it will mean setting aside the solution of vital social problems, which, naturally, is something we cannot agree to.

So what is the solution? A solution does exist. In connection with the cuts in arms expenditure and the conversion of defense enterprises, a number of plants in defense sectors should be placed at the disposal of science for use as an experimental base. (Applause). These plants' output would then be redistributed among other enterprises. This is no simple matter, of course, but it would be the sensible thing to do from the state's point of view and would also represent a restructuring of attitudes in these very important areas.

And the last point, esteemed comrades deputies: I would like to say a few words about Siberia. We have already heard the words of our great ancestor, Mikhail Lomonosov, in this hall, about how Russian might would be increased by Siberia. What can I add to this? The accelerated development of Siberia's productive forces is an important component of CPSU strategy, but this strategy is not being implemented satisfactorily. The main thing is that there is no mechanism to stimulate the accelerated development of regions of Siberia. But if we recall the end of the last century and the beginning of this one, there was a massive resettlement to Siberia—voluntary, not forced—from the center of the country, the Ukraine, Belorussia, and other regions. It was Stolypin, a now undeservedly forgotten Russian statesman, who initiated the reform which ensured this resettlement, without which Siberia's present level of development would not have been possible.

Where are the statesmen of today who could offer something similar, which would make it possible for our country to more actively engage Siberia's powerful potential to the benefit of all the people? (Applause). Many incentives could be considered. But the main point is that only a substantially higher standard of living in Siberia can ensure an influx of fresh forces and stop the indigenous population from leaving for the country's western regions.

Siberian scientists now estimate that at present the level of consumption and use of the most important benefits and services in Siberia, including food, housing, and units in the non-production infrastructure, is below average for the republic. The shortfall will be even more serious if you consider the need to compensate for the harsher natural and climatic conditions, which require a minimum increase of 20-40 percent in the consumer budget in Siberia's southern regions and an increase of 1.5-2 times in its northern regions in comparison to the country's central regions. I ask you to see my speech as raising the question of increasing Siberia's zonal differentiation coefficient. I am sure that giving priority to raising the population's living standard in Siberian regions not only accords with the principles of social justice but is also an essential condition of implementing very important all-union economic programs. Thank you for your attention. (Applause).

Metropolitan Aleksiy Gives Speech
PM0506124189 Moscow IZVESTIYA in Russian 2 Jun 89 Morning Edition pp 6,7

[Speech given by A.M. Ridiger, member of the Russian Orthodox Church Holy Synod, Metropolitan Aleksey of Leningrad and Novgorod, Leningrad City (from the Soviet Charity and Health Foundation) at the 31 May afternoon session of the Congress of USSR People's Deputies]

[Text] Esteemed presidium, Esteemed people's deputies! I believe this is the first time a religious figure has spoken from this high rostrum of our country. I would like to first thank Mikhail Sergeyevich for his report and the concept he proposed to us as a way out of the crisis situation. Of course, this concept will be enriched by deputies' speeches, and we should by common efforts find a means of escaping from the crisis situation in which our country and our society find themselves.

From this high platform I would like to say that Orthodox people and all our country's believers not only wholeheartedly support restructuring in the broad sense of the word but also see the processes of renewal being implemented as the real embodiment of their hopes and aspirations. We realize the complexity of the restructuring process, which must affect all spheres of our life—it

is sometimes easier to build anew rather than restructure. The progress of restructuring presupposes radical economic reform designed to turn the economy toward man, the democratization of internal life, and the moral renewal of our society. I would like to dwell on this last point in somewhat more detail.

The most important lesson that our country has derived from its recent past is the realization of the underlying linkage between morality and society's social development. As is well known, our history has confirmed the ancient truism that you cannot implement the most splendid social ideas by coercion without appealing to man's morality, his conscience, reason, moral choice, and inner freedom. That is why the grave situation in which our economy has found itself, and many aspects of public life, have their initial cause not only in someone's ill will and mistakes by specialists but also in the spiritual impoverishment that has afflicted our society. Our century has seen an unprecedented acceleration in scientific and technical progress—a sphere of mankind's activity which is on the whole exempt from morality. And look what has happened. Today as never before people are spiritually alienated from one another. They are indifferent to one another. This is in a world where man is receiving a hitherto unprecedented amount of information about the life of his colleagues in every part of the world via the most diverse technical channels and means of communication.

Ethics and moral principles are called upon to be that powerful means which will enable us to overcome people's disunity and spiritual alienation and will thus unite us as brothers and sisters to build a happy future for ourselves and our descendants. It is our restored sense of morality that is rendering us tolerant toward one another, charitable to all those who are suffering, the sick, invalids, the elderly, and the lonely, charitable to nature—a scornful and predatory attitude to the latter is a direct consequences of egoism and the unhealthy state of the human soul. (Applause)

I would like to urge all people's deputies from this rostrum to consolidate our efforts to resolve together the common questions with which we are faced. Crises in contemporary society are linked with the moral crisis, and because of this responsibility for moral education falls on all of us, on our entire society. Each person should build his relations with those around him, with society, and with nature on the foundation of a general human moral code. We must all realize that there is a direct link and a direct dependence between morality and survival. That is why the question of the moral education and improvement of all members of our society is very acute today. Academician Dmitriy Sergeyevich Likhachev put this very well from this rostrum; he was speaking about culture, but culture and morality are interconnected.

The church and religious associations are prepared to take part in this process of ensuring the moral renewal of our society, and we await with hope the adoption in the near future of a law on freedom of worship which would give the church greater opportunities for taking part in the social life of our society. (Applause).

Our congress is taking place at a remarkable time which may fundamentally change the course of the country's development. The international situation today is also promoting this. Two days before our congress began I returned from the Swiss city of Basel where the European Christian Ecumenical "Peace and Justice" Assembly had taken place. This meeting was virtually beyond compare. Representatives of all European Christian churches gathered together to discuss burning issues of the day—peace, disarmament, justice, and the preservation of our natural environment. We discussed these questions for a week and reached a unanimous decision, after setting out our solutions in a general document. It touches on all problems facing mankind today. Europe's Christians expressed readiness to work together without procrastination, as Prof Carl von Weizsaecker urged them: "There's no time to lose." We have to work together to ensure mankind's survival and the preservation of peace, justice, and our natural environment. Permit me to convey this assembly's documents to the head of our state. (Applause) (He hands documents to the presidium.)

Congress Debates Molotov-Ribbentrop Pact 1 Jun
PM0506115189 Moscow IZVESTIYA in Russian 3 Jun 89 Morning Edition pp 1, 5-6

["Stenographic Record" of 1 June Congress of the USSR People's Deputies proceedings]

[Excerpts] Eighth Session

Kremlin Palace of Congress, 1000, 1 June 1989.

Session chaired by USSR people's deputy B. Ye. Paton, president of the Ukrainian Soviet Socialist Republic [SSR] Academy of Sciences and director of the Ye.O. Paton Institute of Electric Welding. [passage omitted]

B.Ye. Paton: Let us move on. On the instructions of the congress presidium, deputy Endel Teodorovich Lippmaa of the Estonian SSR will take the floor to make a proposal.

E.T. Lippmaa, director of the Estonian SSR Academy of Sciences Institute of Chemical and Biological Physics, Tallinn (Tallinnskiy-Tsentralnyy Electoral Okrug, Estonian SSR): Esteemed Congress and Esteemed Guests! Many delegations and many speeches here have raised the question of the 1939 treaties with Nazi Germany. We are submitting a draft resolution for the analysis of these most complex problems. The draft runs as follows: "Congress of USSR People's Deputies resolution on setting up a commission to legally appraise the Soviet-German nonaggression treaty of 1939, the so-called Molotov-Ribbentrop pact, and the secret additional protocol to the pact." The Congress of USSR People's

Deputies decrees: First, to make a political and legal appraisal of the Soviet-German nonaggression treaty of 1939 and the secret additional protocol—that is, the protocol on territorial and political reorganization in Eastern Europe, in particular in the Baltic area and Poland—and related documents, a commission should be set up comprising the following USSR people's deputies: Commission members: Lyudmila Akopovna Arutyunyan, department head at the Yerevan State University, Yerevan; Georgiy Arkadyevich Arbatov, director of the United States of America and Canada Institute; Yuriy Nikolayevich Afanasyev, rector of the Moscow State Historical Archives Institute, Moscow; Ilmar Olgertovich Bisher, professor at the Latvian Stuchka State University, Riga; Mavrik Germanovich Vulfson, senior teacher at the Latvian Academy of Arts, Riga; Igor Nikolayevich Gryazin, department chief at the Estonian SSR Academy of Sciences Institute of Philosophy, Sociology, and Law, Tartu; Aleksey Ivanovich Kazannik, department lecturer at Omsk State University, Omsk; Vitaliy Alekseyevich Korotich, chief editor of the journal OGONEK, Moscow; Vitautas Vitautovich Landsbergis, professor at the Lithuanian SSR State Conservatory, Vilnius; Maryu Yokhannesovna Lauristin, department head at Tartu State University, Tartu; Endel Teodorovich Lippmaa, director of the Estonian SSR Academy of Sciences Institute of Chemical and Biological Physics, Tallinn; Kazimir Vladislavovich Moteka, lawyer at the 1st Vilnius Legal Consultancy, Vilnius; Nikolay Vasilyevich Neyland, Latvian SSR deputy foreign minister, Riga; Edgar Elmarovich Savisaar, deputy director of the "Maynor" Special Planning and Design Bureau, Tallinn; Zita Leonovna Shlichite, lawyer at the Klaypeda Legal Consultancy, Klaypeda; Aleksey Mikhaylovich Ridiger, Metropolitan Aleksiy of Leningrad and Novgorod, Leningrad; and Valentin Mikhaylovich Falin, chief of the CPSU Central Committee International Department. Also one representative each for the Ukrainian, Belorussian, and Moldavian delegations. Incidentally, we also had suggestions on three possible candidates from the Ukraine, Belorussia, and Moldavia. Although, of course, it is a matter for their delegations, they were: Vladimir Ilarionovich Shinkaruk, director of the Institute of Philosophy; Vasiliy Vladimirovich Bykov, writer; and Ion Panteleyevich Drutse, writer. We propose Chingiz Aytmatov, writer, Frunze, as chairman of the commission. That is number one.

Two, the USSR Foreign Ministry and other departments and archives are to make available to the commission all the essential materials.

Three, the commission is to present its conclusion to the USSR Supreme Soviet by the end of this June and publish the results of its activity.

The question remains: Why such haste? Because 23 August this year is the 50th anniversary of the agreement with Hitler on the partitioning of Europe. Therefore we must do something right away. Moreover, there were proposals that the pact should be immediately denounced from the moment it was signed. This is not a bad proposal but, in the first place, many of our deputies do not know the text and, in the second place, this is not enough. Conclusions must be drawn fromn this. Declaring invalidity alone is not enough. Much flows from this, so the commission must be set up anyway. This draft was drawn up by deputies from the Estonian delegation with the active participation of Lithuania and Latvia, but, above all, our presidium.

B.Ye. Paton: Comrade Deputies, if there are no objections, let us approve the proposal put to us and vote. Any objections?

From the floor: No.

B.Ye. Paton: And the title of the commission? Deputy Yarovoy.

V.I. Yarovoy, director of the " 'Dvigatel' State V.I. Lenin Union Plant," Tallinn (Tallinnskiy-Lasnamyaeskiy National-Territorial Electoral Okrug): Comrade Deputies! There is much talk about this pact in the country as a whole and particularly in the Baltic region. For 18 months the indigenous population has actually been indoctrinated concerning this pact and distrust has been aroused if the Estonian section of the population. As a result the non-Estonian part has been turned into "occupiers," "colonialists," and who knows what else. I believe that the commission which has been drawn up on the initiative of the Estonian deputies should not be allowed to consider the issue, because they have a stake in the solution of this question. (Applause)

B.Ye. Paton: Any more proposals, any one else want to speak?

M.S. Gorbachev: There was a question comrades wanted to ask.

B.Ye. Paton: They ask for the title of the commission, the aim of the commission.

E.T. Lippmaa: The commission's aim is simple. So that there are no misunderstandings, so that we can move forward well and effectively. Not to kindle disagreements, but to solve the question, so that there is no superfluous discussion and we can work in a businesslike way.

B.Ye. Paton: Question, please.

Academician Zh.I. Alferov, director of the USSR Academy of Sciences A.F. Ioffe Physical and Technical Institute, Leningrad (from the USSR Academy of Sciences). I have a purely legal question about the treaty having lost its validity. I understood that the Molotov-Ribbentrop treaty lost its validity with the start of the war, on 22 June. (Applause).

One can forumulate one's attitude to the treaty very clearly. Like many others, I believe that the treaty was a disgraceful phenomenon in our history. But do we really need to discuss whether it has ceased to be valid or not? It ceased to be valid on 22 June, when the war started. (Applause).

Doctor of Philological Sciences V.V. Ivanov, sector chief at the USSR Academy of Sciences Institute of Slavic and Balkan Studies, Moscow. (From the USSR Academy of Sciences). I want to make a proposal on the procedure for discussing this question. The question is extremely important—perhaps one of the most important we are discussing at this session, and I would like to draw attention to the actual discussion procedure. Delegations from three republics have made a proposal. Of course, we could reject it by an absolute majority and thereby plunge ourselves into yet another very significant conflict within our federative state. I suggest using the method of consensus, which we use too little anyway. We do not need to bother with majority and minority. It is a method that has historically shown itself to be incorrect. We must seek a consensus. And it seems to me that proposals from three republics are enough for the Congress to adopt this proposal by consensus. (Applause).

V.M. Semenov, secretary of Grodno Belorussian Communist Party Oblast Committee [Obkom], Grodno (Grodnenskiy Territorial Electoral Okrug, Belorussian SSR): Comrades! As you can see, I am from Western Belorussia. I am speaking on a procedural issue. We could end up with too many proposals, including urgent, serious, and important ones. We must not put all questions to the Congress alone. I have a proposal: Instruct the newly elected Supreme Soviet to consider this issue.

Deputy (he did not give his name): Esteemed Deputies, Esteemed Comrades in the presidium. I support the comrade from western Belorussia and I want to say that we must set up a commission on Chernobyl, on the tragedy that occurred. And these secondary issues can wait. Because it was not only Belorussia and the Ukraine that were affected, but Russia too. The Supreme Soviet Presidium could decided these issues and submit them to our Congress for its decision. And let us be constructive and businesslike in our approach to issues. Let us solve these issues. After all, the electorate expects really concrete action from us.

V.A. Berezov, second secretary of the Lithuanian Communist Party Central Committee, Vilnius (Tauragskiy National Territorial Electoral Okrug, Lithuanian SSR): I am a Russian. I ask you, Deputies, to support this commission. It is the most painful issue for the Baltic peoples. And these problems must be solved. Because we are not discussing the Molotov-Ribbentrop pact. You have received the Lithuanian SSR Supreme Soviet's appeal. It has been distributed to everyone. The Lithuanian SSR Supreme Soviet is calling for a solution to this problem. It is a question not of the pact itself, but of the secret Molotov-Ribbentrop treaties. These secret treaties are being talked about all the time: They do not exist, they have been lost, and so on. And we deputies from Lithuania, Latvia, and Estonia cannot go home without solving this question. I beg you to back the commission. (Applause)

B.Ye. Paton: Please, go ahead.

I.Ya. Kezbers, Latvian Communist Party Central Committee Secretary, Riga (Kuldigskiy Territorial Electoral Okrug, Latvian SSR): Esteemed colleagues, ther are many urgent questions, urgent issues. I represent Latvia. As we often say, that is one percent in many indicators. That is true. But our history is as dear to us as the entire history of our socialist homeland. I believe that it is necessary to back this commission and the idea of investigating this question and we must at last give our people an answer: Yes, there have been black spots and blank spaces, but we are assessing them fairly. Therefore I ask you to support the proposal that has been made. (Applause).

I.N. Gryazin, department chief at the Estonian SSR Institute of Philosophy, Sociology, and Law, Tartu (Pyarnuskiy National Territorial Okrug, Estonian SSR): This question has already been touched on: what to do with these treaties and protocols? It is a legal question. Denounce or not denounce? Annul or not annul? Incidentally, some suggested the rather original idea that part of the treaties lost its validity in 1941. An original idea, which also deserves consideration. And that is why the commission is being set up.

What are we talking about? Excuse me, but these eight lines of text need to be read out loud. "Moscow, 23 August 1939. Point one. In the event of teritorial and political transformations in areas belonging to the Baltic states—Finland, Estonia, Latvia, Lithuania—the northern border of Lithuania will be the line separating the spheres of influence of Germany and the USSR. In this connection Lithuania's stake in the Vilno area is recognized by both sides. Second, in the event of territorial and political transformations in areas belonging to the Polish state, the spheres of influence of Germany and the USSR will be demarcated approximately by a line following the Narew, Wisla, and San rivers."

Further on there is a very interesting bit: "The question whether it is desirable in the interests of both sides to preserve the independence of the Polish state and the question of the borders of that state can only be finally decided by the course of future political events. In any case, the two governments will resolve this question by means of a friendly agreement. Third. Concerning Southeast Europe. The Soviet side has indicated its interest in Bessarabia. The German side has clearly stated its total lack of interest politically in these territories. Fourth. This protocol is regarded as strictly secret by both sides. Signed by Jochen von Ribbentrop for the Government of Germany and by Vyacheslav Molotov, plenipotentiary representative of the Government of the USSR."

There is the text. That is what we are talking about. Correct or incorrect? What do we do with it? The commission is needed for this purpose. We cannot decide now; we need a commission. I ask you to vote for the commission. Thank you. (Applause. Noise in the hall).

E.E. Inkens, senior editor in the Latvian SSR State Committee for Television and Radio Broadcasting main television news editorial office, Riga (Tsesiskiy National-Territorial Electoral Okrug, Latvian SSR): I want to talk about the special significance these treaties have for the Baltic region. What we are saying here today is unprecedented. The whole world knows full well that these protocols exist. We in the Baltic area have also know this for a long time. And the reluctance to examine them here is like covering your ears when the truth is being told. And another thing. This treaty has not been eliminated, because, despite the outbreak of war in 1941, the Soviet Union concluded a special treaty with the emigre Polish government (in London) on the partial denunciation of this treaty. So, unfortunately, it still has some influence. And most important, the pernicious part of the treaty relates to the period 1939-1940. That is the period of annexations in the Baltic area.

Yu.Yu. Boldyrev, senior engineer at the Central Scientific Research Istitute of Marine Electrical Engineering and Technology, Leningrad (Moskovskiy Territorial Electoral Okrug, Leningrad, RSFSR): Esteemed Comrades! I do not have a vested interest. I doubt whether there is any need at all to persuade you of the importance of this issue. But I want to draw your attention to the results of today's and yesterday's sessions. What we are doing is absolutely intolerable. Esteemed Deputies, none of us, in my view, has the moral right to assess and challenge other deputies. Only our voters should have the right to assess us. Passions are being fueled here at the moment, yet in fact a perfectly concrete and clear proposal has been made: Decide nothing here; set up a commission to examine the issue and have the results of the commission's work submitted for your perusal. In this situation, it seems to me, it is quite out of order to challenge these people and say that they have a vested interest. I believe that if anyone sees fit to add their own representatives to the commission, this must be done. Thank you for listening.

B.Ye. Paton: Esteemed Comrade, just one moment. I can see nine more wanting to speak. Let us give them each a minute. Please.

R.A. Medvedev, writer (Voroshilovskiy Territorial Electoral Okrug, Moscow): Comrades, I think our tempestuous reaction is due not only to the fact that a commission has been proposed. I have no doubt that the commission is necessary. It is a matter of the membership of the commission. As a historian, I must tell you that we Soviet historians are not ashamed to say that Russia conquered Central Asia. We are not ashemed to say that Russia conquered even the North Caucasus. We are not ashamed to hang the celebrated picture "Yermak's Conquest of Siberia" in our museums. But hitherto, in our official works of history, in our articles, in our publications appearing in Moscow, we have written that Estonia, Latvia, and Lithuania joined the Soviet Union voluntarily, that it was a people's revolution, that there was no violence and there were no threats, and that it was a full, voluntary expression of the will of the Lithuanian, Estonian, and Latvian peoples. This is untrue. It was, of course, an action that occurred when an imperialist war was taking place and when no one—not just the Soviet Union but Germany, Japan, Britain, and France—showed any respect for the rights of small countries and peoples and when problems were being tackled without regard for the neutrality of Belgium, the Netherlands, Finland, or other countries. So the commission must be set up and we must finally make a correct assessment of these treaties. But the commission must include not only authoritative representatives from Estonia, Latvia, and Lithuania. The commission must have other state figures from our country on it. I am surprised to hear comrades proposing, for example, Chingiz Aytmatov, a man respected by me and by all of us, as chairman of the commission and not Foreign Minister Shevardnadze, for example. That is, I propose that the decisions be made to set up the commission but that its membership be looked at again by the deputies from the Estonian and Latvian SSR's, in conjunction with the Congress presidium and members of the Soviet Government and Politburo. (Applause).

M.S. Gorbachev: Comrades, may I speak out of turn? Just to make this issue somewhat clearer. It is an old problem, one that has been discussed and studied by historians, by political scientists, and by the relevant departments. And I have to say that while we have been holding scientific discussions in certain departments all the documents, including the secret appendix to the treaty, have been published everywhere. The Baltic press has published everything. But all efforts to find the original of the secret treaty have failed. Those who are dealing with these matters will note that I broached the matter in conversation with the Polish comrades and with the Polish press and in my concluding remarks on the topic following my meeting with the Polish intelligentsia.

We have been dealing with this question for a long time. There are no originals. There are copies, but it is not known what they are copies of. They are signed, but what creates doubts, particularly for us, is the fact that Molotov's signature is in German letters. When Chancellor Kohl was here—it was, as they say, a one-on-one discussion, but since the issue is turning out this way it obviously must be said, and I do not think the chancellor will be very offended if I reveal this secret—there were

matters of a purely confidential nature, one-on-one. In particular, I asked him: Do you have the originals of these treaties, the appendix? He replied that they had them. I said: Then would you please give them to us. And on the basis of that understanding we sent Foreign Ministry representatives. Eduard Amvrosiyevich? Yes. But the originals were not found there either.

This is, so to speak, information to mull over. A serious question that requires scientific and political analysis. I do not want to oversimplify the issue, it must be discussed and evaluated, as the comrades have proposed. So I would advocate the creation of a commission, since it has been requested by several delegations. But I would ask the comrades to look again at who should be on the commission. I think this commission should be expanded and therefore the Congress and the presidium, which made the proposal, should be asked to provide the time for this. On the basis of consultations with our scientists and with the Academy of Sciences competent people should be placed on the commission, because it is a very serious question. That is number one.

Number two: In view of the special information I have provided, including the conversations with Mr Kohl, I would not at this early stage call the proposal "On the formation of a commission..." In the first place there are different interpretations. The proposal is on the elaboration of a political and legal appraisal, and it is called: "on a legal appraisal of the Soviet-German nonaggression treaty and the secret additional protocol to the pact..." We do not have the secret protocol at the moment, so we cannot evaluate it. But I do think there should be a commission, I would certainly go along with that. It must elaborate a political and legal appraisal of this nonaggression treaty without mentioning the secret protocol, since all the archives we have rummaged through here have not provided an answer. Although I will tell you that the historians know and would tell you: What happened was that two powerful forces were moving toward one another and at some point this coming into contact came to a complete halt. Something lay at the basis of it. But all we are doing is debating at the moment. So it requires an investigation, an analysis of all the documents, of the entire situation as it occurred, including the way the Soviet Government dealt with the treaty when the war started... What we did was deem it invalid.

This full range of issues, I think, must be evaluated, because the Baltic republics are frantically discussing these issues, and, as a result, it is being questioned whether the will of the people came into it at all when they joined the Soviet Union. That is scarcely the case. All this must be studied. So I would have the Congress set up a commission to provide a political and legal appraisal of the Soviet-German treaty, and after it has been formed at the relevant level let it get down to work and give its competent judgment on this issue. I do not even know if it will get at the truth at its first attempt. It is no simple matter, but since it exists I believe that we must not try to duck it. Let us not duck it, let us get on and study it. As we have said, in the course of restructuring there are very many acute problems. If the comrades consider it necessary to obtain some more information before making a decision on the composition of the commission, to have some preliminary ideas from the Foreign Ministry, we can ask Comrade Shevardnadze to speak on the matter. But I think the chief thing is to set up the commission correctly, for it to get to work, and then either the Supreme Soviet or all the deputies will be informed of the results of the commission's work. That is my clarification. We might confine ourselves to it now and if the comrades support the idea of creating a commission, then the presidium shgould be given time to continue consultations, to provide it with competent people. Is that right, Comrades?

From the hall: Right!

M.S. Gorbachev: Fine, Settled, then.

From the hall: (Inaudible).

M.S. Gorbachev: No, Comrades, Eduard Amvrosiyevich Shevardnadze is not a deputy. Ministers are not deputies. Let us instruct some deputies. There are two international affairs experts from our Central Committee and from the Politburo there is comrade Yakovlev. Let us have Yakovlev on the commission. OK? (Applause).

B.Ye. Paton: Comrade Deputies! As I see it, the proposal on the advisability of setting up a commission is therefore accepted by everyone. As for the membership, Mikhail Sergeyevich has made a proposal. I think we all accept this proposal: to instruct the Baltic delegations and the presidium to consider the matter further, since the commission must include more professionals and experts on this issue.

Is the proposal accepted? Thank you.

(Noise in the hall).

B.Ye. Paton: You want a vote? Vote for what? For the advisability of setting up a commission? I mean, we cannot vote for the members as they stand. So it is just the advisability of a commission. I think no one objects to that? Accepted?

From the hall: Accepted.

B.Ye. Paton: Esteemed Comrade Ceputies! The presidium has received many requests and comments on the fact that many deputies have not been given the floor, that lists are being changed, and so on. I am authorized by the presidium to announce that around 500 requests to speak in the debate have been received. That is number one. Number two, the presidium looks at the lists of speakers twice a day to ensure that all regions, republics, public organizations and so on are represented, so that no one is offended. During the dinner break the list will be drawn up for the evening session. It seems to us that this is the only possible solution in such a complex situation.

I also want to announce that the presidium receives memoranda that are more or less identical. I will read out a very short one. It is from Valentin Fedorovich Romanov of Magnitogorsk: "Notes on debate procedure: One. It seems to me that during the debates we often display particular inspiration and a splenetic single-mindedness in exposing shortcomings by the spadeful. Although criticism cannot be made in strict doses, the time has come to change the emphasis from the viewpoint of seeking proper ways out of the present situation and not simply stating shortcomings which are familiar to us all. And the criticism must be courteous and benevolent. Second, the tactic of trying to intimidate the Congress, where certain speeches end with the words 'there could be unforeseen consequences,' must be abandoned. We are building a state in which the consequences must be foreseeable, so ultimatums are not our way." (Applause). There have been similar memoranda from groups of deputies and I am not going to read them out.

Since the situation concerning those wishing to speak is so strained, let me read out a memorandum to the Congress presidium from deputy Vasilyev: "Please read out the proposals. For the USSR people's deputies who, because of the lack of time, do not have the chance to speak from the Congress platform, but would like the pages of the central newspapers to be used as a platform and these newspaper items published during the Congress to be regarded as speeches at the Congress itself and entered in the stenographic record for the relevant day." This is not a bad idea, I think.

Let me make some very brief announcements now, Comrades.

First, since there have been questions about registering to speak on the USSR Council of Ministers chairman's report, the presidium has authorized me to inform you that registration will begin after the Council of Ministers chairman's speech.

Editorial commission chairman Vadim Andreyevich Medvedev has asked me to inform the commission members that the editorial commission will meet at the start of the break in the Faceted Room and asks the commission members to make their way there.

A request from the doctors: To announce a meeting of all doctor-deputies here, in the hall, at the start of the long interval. There is a similar request from people's deputies working in industry. But it does not specify where and when they want to meet.

Finally, what is in my view a very interesting memorandum to the effect that people's deputy Nikolay Andreyevich Kasyan, whom we all know very well, is prepared to give medical assistance to any participant of our Congress. (Applause).

Allow me to announce that we are taking a break until 1600 hours. [passage omitted].

2 Jun Congress Proceedings Reported

Moscow Union Leader Speaks

*PM0506120389 Moscow IZVESTIYA in Russian
5 Jun 89 Morning Edition pp 1-3*

["Congress of USSR People's Deputies. Stenographic Transcript"—IZVESTIYA headline]

[Excerpts]

Ninth Session (end)

[passage omitted]

Kremlin Palace of Congresses, 2 June 1989, 1600 hours.

USSR People's Deputy A.I. Lukyanov is in the chair. [passage omitted]

A.I. Lukyanov. Deputy Shcherbakov has the floor. Deputy Dadamyan should get ready.

V.P. Shcherbakov, chairman of the Moscow City Trade Unions Council, Moscow City. (From USSR trade unions). Esteemed comrade deputies! We all know the enormous attention with which Soviet people are following the course of the congress. We are saying a lot about where things are bad and why. But we are keeping shamefacedly quiet about the achievements of socialism, to which there is no alternative in any social system. And proof of this is to be found primarily in the political biographies of all those sitting in this auditorium, beginning with the president. These biographies are impossible under any other political system.

Soviet people are proud of the very great gains of October and the equality and fraternity of all peoples. This alliance must be safeguarded and strengthened. And it is particularly painful today that the potential of socialism is not being used. It is becoming increasingly hard to explain why, despite the decisions which have been taken and the measures which are being implemented for the economy's social reorientation, the working people's living standard is declining. Some people are trying to speculate on these difficulties, to justify their political claims, like, for instance, the leaders of the Democratic Union, openly calling for civil disobedience to the authorities, for demonstrations and strikes. They stated: "When the stores are empty, when the plants come to a halt, the authorities will fall of their own accord."

The rapid increase in wages, which is outstripping labor productivity growth, is now being cited as one reason for the crisis phenomena in the economy. It is understandable that this phenomenon is abnormal and perturbing, but to seek here the root for economic disorders, for the imbalance in the market, and for the shortage of goods is wrong, to say the least. The real reason is that the main element of the economic reform—economic accountability [khozraschet]—has not worked. It does not exist in teams, on sectors, or in shops. Enterprises have no real independence. Many of the decisions taken formerly to normalize the economy have done nothing to help this, rather the reverse. One example is the transition of industrial enterprises to the new conditions of remuneration of labor, rates, and salaries. In the process of preparing for this crucial step, the labor collectives accumulated a wages fund. Was there no calculation of what this resolution would cost the state when wage rates and salaries were raised? All the Moscow enterprises took an active part in elaborating the "Progress-95" program, which is to ensure the solution of many tasks, including social ones. It will use its own funds here. The implementation of this program has already begun. Many enterprises, using economic independence, are on their own initiative paying for additional leave and child care leave, and are giving grants to badly off families and labor veterans—that is, they are beginning to implement an active social policy without counting on aid from above. But the finance organs are subjecting this policy to criticism.

It is an erroneous opinion that Moscow lives at the expense of other regions. I can say that the capital puts R16 billion in profit into the state budget every year, yet its own budget is R4.2 billion. Today the growth of wages is being artificially limited at many state enterprises. At the same time income in the cooperative sector is not restricted by anything. Why should similar sanctions not be applied to cooperative members? Or does the law so important for state enterprises not operate here?

Everyone knows the story of the "Tekhnika" cooperative which caused such a sensation. Producing nothing, playing mainly on shortages and prices, people there receive wages sometimes hundreds of times greater than the wages of academicians and scientists and statesmen and politicians. I am not opposed to high wages, but one way or another the remuneration of labor should comply with its outlays. The development of the cooperative movement is undoubtedly a necessary matter, but it is a bad thing when this development proceeds without control, with direct connivance from the Ministry of Finance, not unbeknownst to whom the cooperative members are now so successfully transforming state enterprises' noncash funds into cash. Last year Moscow's cooperative members took R311 million out of Moscow's banks and invested R12 million. In the first 5 months of this year they have taken R976 million and invested R38 million. Unless their appetites are moderated then in the course of the year they will take over R4 billion from Moscow alone. Incidentally, the monthly wages for all workers in Moscow is R1.1 billion, and I remind you that the annual budget for Moscow's municipal economy is R4.2 billion.

I am worried not only by this fact in itself, but by why the financiers and economists are keeping silent, why they are not shouting for help. The working class is directly asking: Who stands to gain? Who is pandering to this? (Applause).

PRAVDA wrote that eight staffers of the USSR Ministry of Justice institute, including a close relation of O. Soroka, USSR deputy prosecutor general, took part in sharing out the revenue from the "Tekhnika" cooperative. Does that not answer the question of why the cooperatives are under such heavy legal protection? (Applause).

The money which the cooperative members have taken from the banks would be enough to increase the minimum pensions for 20 million badly-off pensioners or to institute 24 days of paid leave right now for all the country's working people. Yet we are seeking funds in terms of crumbs, of kopeks, to help badly-off families, invalids, and pensioners. Here attempts are still being made to reduce appropriations for social needs. Unless the siphoning of funds from enterprises to cooperatives is halted there will be a financial catastrophe. There is already a common saying to the effect that we have achieved the highest labor productivity in printing money. But what have the cooperatives given the working class? In their mass they have engaged in middleman activity, buying up reserve raw material, semifinished materials, and consumer goods. This aggravates the shortage of commodities, leaves store shelves empty, and intensifies corruption, bribery, speculation, and the growth of organized crime. People are asking when this will be stopped.

In this connection I cannot but share the alarm of the group of people's deputies from the trade unions at the aggravating situation with regard to crime in the country voiced in their request to the government. After all, a favorable economic base has now been created for the growth of crime.

Today there is an increasingly acute ring to the question of why we have not achieved the pace for restructuring on which we were counting. Of course, it is impossible to predict the full depth of problems, but there is much which we were obliged to envisage and resolve more vigorously. Here, too, it is appropriate to ask not only our government but also our economic science: Where have you taken us? Behind the keenly critical speeches addressed to the management and apparatus we have somehow forgotten that no adequately clear economic model for the future has been elaborated. New economic methods, before they have even gone into operation, are being sharply criticized, including from this rostrum, and are being recognized as imperfect. Practical workers

have been caught up in experiments. Can our economic science really offer nothing more suitable than purely market relations, the transfer of state enterprises into private hands, and the creation of a free manpower market, which some well-known scientists are advocating? The representatives of the Moscow group of delegates do have such proposals, although they are 25-30 people out of Moscow's 195 deputies. I should like to draw your attention to this, because not all that group's proposals and opinions can represent the opinion of all the capital's deputies. (Applause).

Everything the economists are proposing now is not new; it has been solemnly borrowed from capitalism's experience, but where are the laws of development of the socialist economy? Unfortunately, today we have no scientifically substantiated economic concept of restructuring. Many people understand restructuring in their own way, each as they choose, but there should be no different interpretations here. Economic scientists must pool their efforts in elaborating the economic concept of restructuring, and not waver. Measure seven times and cut once. That folk saying should become the principle of the economists' work. (Applause).

Specific measures are needed to normalize the economy. In addition to the sensible reduction of expenses on defense, the maintenance of the apparatus, and capital construction, the foremost, the main task is financial normalization. It is essential to immediately carry out a monetary reform which will not affect the interests of the honest worker but which will remove from circulation funds acquired by unjust means, to introduce more rapidly a progressive tax on income, and to put state enterprises and cooperatives on an equal footing, giving them the opportunity to compete openly. We must immediately forbid state enterprises from settling accounts with cooperatives out of the production development and social development funds and capital repair funds, whatever arguments may be cited. Accounts should be settled with them only from the material incentive fund. That will increase economic leaders' responsibility to the labor collectives for every ruble spent. (Applause).

The market cannot be saturated with high-quality goods if light industry receives only 3.7 percent of all fixed capital for the entire country. It is essential to redistribute state budget funds and to alter substantially, not by 1 percent but several times over, the correlation of capital investments in favor of the development of group "B" sectors. We should not appeal for this, which is what we have done for years, but introduce an economic mechanism which would interest machine-building and defense enterprises and enterprises of other sectors; we should have a state order for the production of consumer goods in volumes no lower than the annual wages fund. Otherwise the Karacharovo mechanical plant will produce consumer goods worth just 5 kopeks for every ruble of wages, the Sergo Ordzhonikidze plant will produce goods worth 6 kopeks, the Vladimir Ilich plant goods worth 35 kopeks, and so forth. Is it not clear to the leaders of the State Planning Committee and the Ministry of Finance that until there is a direct connection between these concepts, and until economic leaders' wages depend on an increase in the volumes of consumer goods production, we will never get out of this vicious circle.

I support Mikhail Sergeyevich's proposal to create a special Supreme Soviet commission which would revise all benefits and privileges and examine the problems of the fair distribution of social consumption funds. We cannot fail to see that they have gradually become the means for redistributing benefits in favor of the most affluent groups of the population. On average, receipts from these funds for workers and employees per member of the family with an income of under R50 are nearly three times smaller than in affluent families. We talk too much about the plight of our health care and about social injustice in the use of various benefits. We must ask: Why do some people enjoying position and power have the opportunity for treatment in a sanatorium every year while others, if you take the travel vouchers normatives, wait for years for such an opportunity? Some people are fed in hospitals for R1.50, others for R3. I think we should decide to redistribute social consumption funds in favor of the badly off.

During the congress the question of resolutely improving pension provisions has been frequently raised. This axiom requires no proof. One of the first laws which should be adopted is the Law on Pensions. Funds are needed for that. I believe that the R10 billion which are being released as a result of the reduction of expenses on armament should be purposefully given to pensioners. The state has the duty to pay its debt to those who have given their labor for the benefit of the motherland. (Applause).

I suggest instructing the Supreme Soviet to finally find out what the minimum living wage is in our country, and to make these figures public. As a whole we must review the entire system of social and legal protection of working people. The existing system provides no protection against inflation and the rise in prices (as though it did not exist in our country). It is essential to introduce a cost of living index and to amend wages, grants, benefits, and pensions when it changes. I consider it absurd and economically harmful to impose restrictions on the payment of pensions and wages to working pensioners. We are short of manpower, and thousands of enterprises are working just one shift, yet we are excluding from social production millions of highly qualified workers and specialists, doctors, and teachers. (Applause). And restrictions for invalids look quite flagrantly unfair. After all, it is not enough that they cannot always find work, the total sum of their wages and pension is limited by law. It is time to remove these restrictions; invalids have a hard life as it is. (Applause).

The congress must take decisions which would enable every person to feel that social justice is being restored. (Applause).

Georgian Deputy's Speech Published

PM0506171389 Moscow TRUD in Russian 3 Jun 89 p 2

[Speech by S.A. Amonashvili, USSR people's deputy from USSR trade unions, general director of the Georgian SSR Ministry of Public Education Experimental Educational Science and Production Association, Tbilisi city, delivered 2 June at Congress of USSR People's Deputies; excerpts of the television version of this speech appeared in the 5 June Soviet Union DAILY REPORT Supplement, page 12]

[Text] Esteemed Chairman of the USSR Supreme Soviet! Esteemed deputies! Yesterday the deputies from Georgia met with Mikhail Sergeyevich Gorbachev. It was an extremely open meeting, a direct conversation where we were able to express our thoughts and feelings and to explain certain phenomena. For his part Mikhail Sergeyevich also explained a great deal to us. I am sure that the commission, which was set up by you, the congress, will sort out everything thoroughly and will make the necessary truthful, only truthful decision. And this truth will be spoken. We all need the truth: You need it, and we need it, for in our country, which is being built on the basis of new principles—the principles of the humanization and democratization of society and glasnost—in our hands this truth will be like a weapon in order to struggle to save people's souls.

We are currently going through a very complex time. I am not going to dramatize the situations which have taken place in our country. Perhaps it is no longer worth talking about all the events, but I want to look at them from the viewpoint of educating the future generation.

I would like to say first that the telegrams which were read out were unknown to us. And the main point is that I would simply like to assure you, dear deputies, that allegations that drug addicts and alcoholics had gathered in the square do not accord with the truth. Perhaps there were extremists among the thousands of people who were standing there, and people of other persuasions, but they were mainly talented young people who were striving to achieve sovereignty for the republic.

I would like to say a few words about the state of the schools, which have caused many of our problems and will continue to do so. Our schools became extremely authoritarian. Evidently this a predictable phenomenon, for over a period of many years authoritarianism itself prevailed throughout the country. And this authoritarianism was reflected, as in a mirror, in our schools as well. Pressure on the children, an end to freedom, no ideas, no fresh ideas. And the teacher as the main figure, as an authoritarian, stands in front of his children. And it is appropriate to say that a paradox arises here: On the one hand, the teacher is the most frightened person in our country, for a very broad network and system has always hung over him: inspectors, commands, resolutions. All this restricted the teacher's movement toward lively thought. And on the other hand—this frightened person intimidates his pupils in the classroom.

We must free ourselves from this situation in the schools. And if there is no democracy or glasnost in schools, if there is no human approach to the child, to the child's personality, schools will become soulless.

Currently we are talking a great deal about restructuring schools, about providing new equipment for our schools. This is essential. It is essential to give significantly more funds to education—to double, treble, quadruple them. But at the same time it should be taken into account that without a good teacher who knows how to approach a person, there will be no education in schools. And occasionally this good person can just sit under a tree with his pupils and mold their soul.

It was evidently authoritarianism which also influenced the events which are taking place both in Tbilisi and in other places, for the child brought up under these conditions is now finding that free rein is being given to his feelings, and this is shown in diverse aspects, in diverse spheres.

There is one more huge problem concerning national schools. We often say that in our schools teaching is conducted in our native language. This is correct. This is an achievement of the revolution, and the national language is the language of instruction for every republic. But at the same time it should be taken into consideration that instruction, let us say, in the Georgian language does not at all mean that this school of ours is both a national and a Georgian school, if it is taken into account that all the rest of instruction is nothing other than a translation from Russian into Georgian.

Let us take the problem of teaching history in schools. What history do our children study? We mainly study Soviet history as applied to Georgia. And what does this history mean? Our Georgian children know more about events in Russia, about what happened from ancient times to modern times, than about events and phenomena in Georgia itself. And Georgia's history barely squeezes into the school curriculum; it was even forbidden to devote more hours to this subject. I think that each republic has its own great culture, its own great past. This is also our country's property. For this reason not only history, not only literature, but also, perhaps, all other subjects must be built precisely on these principles. Our schools are being ruined by uniformity: the uniform program, the uniform text book, the teacher's uniform training—everything is uniform, and so we ultimately get a person who is also molded in the spirit of uniform thinking. And now that freedom is given, we are surprised that the person is perhaps revealing himself in less than restrained forms.

National sentiments are the most sensitive cords in a person, the most sensitive; they must be approached extremely carefully. I know that people are now listening to my speech in Tbilisi, and diverse events are taking place there. So I want people in Tbilisi also to know what I am saying now to you. The newspaper article cited by General Rodionov was written at the time of the military curfew. I ask you, please do not think that the events took place exactly as set out in the newspaper. A commission has been set up. It precisely will establish fully the entire picture, everything which went on there.

At the same time I would like to say the following. Under present conditions—what I would call the courageous conditions of restructuring—many complex problems came to light in mutual relations. And you will probably agree with me if I say that in the future our country must adhere not to strength but to spiritual unity and friendship. And if this friendship is infringed to a certain degree, very great complications may arise between us, and this will not be for the better.

So my appeal to the deputies—please forgive me for daring to say this—is that anyone who will speak from this platform be extremely careful: May he weigh his words when they refer to nationality. I have received many telegrams recently—from Armenia, from Azerbaijan, and from Georgia. They contain many such lines: Every word needs to be weighed very carefully, so as not to affect that deep structure which so concerns man. (Applause)

And in conclusion. Perhaps what I shall now say will not be supported, but all the same I want it to be supported. We have a multinational country, but there are main languages in our country, for example those languages in which our republics live, talk and work. And; evidently it would not be a bad thing if the congress worked in these diverse languages. May the Azerbaijani, Armenian, Georgian, Latvian, and other languages be heard occasionally from this platform. We must accustom our ear to the sound of national languages. This would not harm our mutual relations. (Applause)

And now, so that this is done for the first time today, allow me to say a few words in the Georgian language. This will be addressed to our young people in Tbilisi. You, too, please, listen to this sound. I assure you that I shall not say anything which could bring about a split between us and destroy our unity and our love. I want everyone to know, dear comrades, that Georgia has never harbored nationalism and this will never happen. (Applause) They say that during the events in Tbilisi there were anti-Russian actions, that allegedly there were calls for secession and so on. It is possible that were some such calls, but this is not a reflection of the Georgian soul: It is free, it strives for friendship. And if you come to us, our hospitality will surely embrace you. Maybe I will offend our government, but let me say that there will be both wine and vodka on the table. (Applause) And these are the Georgian words which I address to my compatriots. (The speaker speaks in the Georgian language.)

Dear compatriots, young people! I am addressing each of you on behalf of the deputies from Georgia. The congress is taking our problems to heart. A commission has been set up which will establish the truth. We had a meeting yesterday with Mikhail Sergeyevich; he also believes that all those who are guilty must be punished most severely. I ask you to keep calm, and to be patient. And let us together—the young and the older generations—build Georgia's future, its sovereignty with our common efforts. (The author's own translation from the Georgian language to Russian.)

Many thanks for your attention. (Tumultuous applause).

Congress Presidium Makes 6 Jun Statement on PRC
LD0606084689 Moscow Television Service in Russian 0600 GMT 6 Jun 89

[Relay of first session of the 6 June Congress of People's Deputies from the Kremlin Palace of Congresses—live]

[Excerpts] [passage omitted] [Gorbunov] Comrade deputies, before we declare a break, the presidium offers the draft of the following statement. May I read the statement? It is a statement on the events in China:

In neighboring China, dramatic events have taken place. Soviet people have been informed broadly and in timely fashion about them. The situation has become particularly acute in the last few days. As the Chinese mass media report, clashes have taken place in Beijing, the PRC's capital, between participants in mass demonstrations of young people and troops. Weapons have been used. There are human casualties. Now is not a time for unconsidered, hasty conclusions and statements. Whatever the heat of passions may be, it is important to patiently seek adequate solutions which would be determined by the aims of consolidating society. Naturally, the events which have just unfolded in China are an internal affair for the country. Any attempts at pressure from outsiders whatsoever would be inappropriate. Such attempts merely heat up passions, but do nothing at all to stabilize the situation. We hope that wisdom, common sense, and a considered approach will prevail and that a way out, worthy of the great Chinese people, will be found in the situation that has formed. We sincerely wish for the friendly Chinese people that they will turn this tragic page in their history, as soon as possible, and will go ahead along the path of economic and political transformations, the path of construction of a strong, peace-loving, free, socialist China—a great country which enjoys the respect and sympathies of its neighbors and of all mankind.

Do you have any objections or proposals in connection with this, comrades? The proposal is to adopt such a statement on behalf of the congress. Are there any comments on the wording?

[Unidentified deputy] [Words indistinct]

[Gorbunov] Yes?

[Unidentified deputy] [Words indistinct]

[Gorbunov] I see. If there are no other wishes or comments, then I ask you to vote for the text of the statement. Please raise your mandates. Thank you. Who is against?

[Unidentified speaker from hall] One.

[Gorbunov] Any abstentions? An overwhelming minority. So, the congress adopts the statement. The overwhelming minority abstained. And so, the congress adopts the given statement. We declare a break for 30 minutes.

Supreme Soviet Soviet of Nationalities Meets 6 Jun
LD0606063289 Moscow Domestic Service in Russian 0000 GMT 6 Jun 89

[Text] The Congress of People's Deputies of the USSR will continue its work in the Kremlin at 10 am [0600 GMT] on 6 June. Central Television's second all-union program and "Mayak" radio program will start transmitting from the Kremlin.

At 1600 [1200 GMT] there will be a session of the Soviet of Nationalities of the country's Supreme Soviet.

1-2 Jun Congress 'Stenographic Record' Continues

PM0606140089 Moscow IZVESTIYA in Russian
4 Jun 89 Morning Edition pp 1-7

["Congress of USSR People's Deputies: Stenographic Record"—IZVESTIYA headline]

[Excerpts]

Eighth Sitting (Continuation)

[passage omitted]

B.Ye. Paton: Comrade deputies, on your instructions the congress presidium has drawn up a proposal on the composition of the commission to investigate materials relating to the activity of the USSR Prosecutor's Office investigation group headed by Deputy Gdlyan. Deputy Rafik Nishanovich Nishanov has the floor on this question.

R.N. Nishanov, first secretary of the Uzbekistan Communist Party Central Committee (Leningradskiy National-Territorial Electoral Okrug, Uzbek Soviet Socialist Republic [SSR]): Esteemed comrade deputies! In the course of the preparation of this proposal a number of comrades withdrew. At the same time a total of 30 new candidates were proposed. The congress presidium held consultations with deputies from various union republics and regions, including comrades Telman Khorenovich Gdlyan and Nikolay Veniaminovich Ivanov. All the comrades are agreed that the commission should include deputies from various union republics and regions who have not previously associated themselves in any way with assessments of the work of the investigation group. For this reason it is not expedient for the commission to include either representatives of the former commission, which has played its part, or those deputies who have made various statements on the work of the investigation group.

It is deemed expedient also to refrain from including on the commission workers of the USSR Prosecutor's Office, since this department's work is in question. At the same time we must support the proposal that the commission should be able to involve in its work (in the capacity of experts) consultants and specialists in various spheres. So that is the general principle, and now the composition of the commission:

Chairman of the commission: Roy Aleksandrovich Medvedev.

Members of the commission: Vladimir Tuychiyevich Adylov, lathe operators' team leader at the Tashkent V.P. Chkalov Aircraft Production Association; Valeriy Grigoryevich Aleksandrin, chairman of Yoshkar-Ola City People's Court, Mari autonomous republic; Aleksandr Ivanovich Baranov, chairman of the "Izhorskiy Zavod" Production Association trade union committee, Leningrad City, Kolpino City; Ilmar Olgertovich Bisher, professor at the P. Stuchka Latvian

State University; Egidiyus Vitautovich Bichkauskas, Lithuanian SSR Prosecutor's Office investigator for important cases; Yuriy Vladimirovich Golik, dean of Kemerovo State University Law Faculty; Nikolay Ivanovich Ignatovich, Belorussian SSR Prosecutor's Office investigator for important cases; Konstantin Dmitriyevich Lubenchenko, lecturer at Moscow State University Law Faculty; Vello Paulovich Pokhla, member of the editorial collegium of the "Estonskiy Telefilm" Main Editorial Office, Estonian SSR State Committee for Television and Radio Broadcasting, Tallinn City; Vitaliy Aleksandrovich Semenov, senior scientific staffer at the Ukrainian SSR Academy of Sciences Institute of Technical Mechanics, Dnepropetrovsk City; Igor Viktorovich Sorokin, senior superintendent of criminal investigations at the Kuybyshev Station railroad internal affairs department; Nikolay Alekseyevich Strukov, senior investigator of the Kursk Oblast Prosecutor's Office; Olzhas Omarovich Suleymenov, writer, first secretary of the Kazakhstan Writers' Union Board, Alma-Ata City; Svyatoslav Nikolayevich Fedorov, general director of the "Mikrokhirurgiya Glaza" multisector scientific and technical complex; Viktor Nikolayevich Shorokhov, fitter at the Tula V.M. Ryabikov Machine Building Plant; and Veniamin Aleksandrovich Yarin, operator at the Nizhniy Tagil V.I. Lenin Metallurgical Combine, Sverdlovsk Oblast.

Both on the congress presidium and on the secretariat, we considered this matter very carefully and selected these 17 candidates, and I would ask you to approve this composition.

B.Ye. Paton: Any questions for Rafik Nishanovich? (Disturbance in the auditorium.)

B.Ye. Paton: No questions?

Voices from the floor: No.

From the floor: I have a question.

B.Ye. Paton: Go ahead. (Disturbance in the auditorium.)

From the floor: We nominated Yakovlev. The Yakutsk delegation proposed Yakovlev. Why was he excluded? (Disturbance in the auditorium.)

B.Ye. Paton: Go ahead, please, your question.

From the floor: (Inaudible.)

From the floor: Please listen to me, comrade deputies, for a minute. Our delegates agree entirely with the opinion on the selection of this commission. But we think that the working class is equally conscious, and moreover there is not a single Komsomol [Leninist Communist Youth League] representative here. I therefore propose—as was proposed earlier in a note—that

Vladimir Norikhin be included—he is a controller, from Vladimir City. He is a deputy from the Komsomol and a principled comrade. I ask your support for our proposal.

R.N. Nishanov: Let me answer the question about Comrade Yakovlev from Yakutia. When we were drawing up the list, Comrade Yakovlev's candidacy was also proposed by Comrades Gdlyan and Ivanov. But there were six people on the list. We agreed on the basis of parity that those whom we are investigating cannot form the commission themselves. Therefore I asked for three people to be chosen. The comrades proposed three names, which I included on the list—it is all very logical.

One last point. All the deputies on this list have good credentials, they are all upright, no one has discredited any of them, they are all conscientious, and I am convinced that they will study any question objectively. (Applause.)

From the floor: Let us vote! [passage omitted]

V.S. Shevchenko, chairman of the Ukrainian SSR Supreme Soviet Presidium, Kiev City (Kiyevskiy Rural National-Territorial Electoral Okrug, Ukrainian SSR): Esteemed comrade deputies! This morning many deputies found notes to this effect at the doors of their hotel rooms: "Comrades, we ask you to support comrades Gdlyan and Ivanov." We regard this as an attempt to put pressure on deputies.

The decision to form a commission was decided at the congress on Saturday. On Sunday, at 1000 hours, the entire body of deputies from the Ukrainian SSR, and there are 262 of us, met almost in full, and we discussed this question. The delegation decided together whom to recommend for the commission. Several candidacies were put forward. The entire delegation settled on Comrade Semenov's candidacy. And we gave him this instruction: Examine everything honorably and conscientiously. Vindicate the innocent, punish the guilty. We have every trust in the deputy whom we recommended for the commission, and we believe that neither Comrade Gdlyan nor Comrade Ivanov has the right to withdraw a deputy who was recommended by an entire delegation. (Applause.)

E.Yu. Yusupov, vice president of the Uzbek SSR Academy of Sciences, Tashkent City (From the All-Union "Znaniye" Society.)

An organization in defense of Gdlyan and Ivanov is at work in Moscow. It is operating very efficiently. There is not one deputy who has not received an anonymous letter and message in praise of Gdlyan. Drunken young people are walking around everywhere carrying placards, stopping delegates and claiming that if Gdlyan is vindicated, the Food Program in the country will be resolved. When we asked one of them, why are you campaigning

for a man you have probably never set eyes on, he replied: I do not know him, but I have been instructed to do this. This is not honest, I think it is a provocation.

Moreover, comrades, you have doubtless read a lot about the activity of the investigation team in Uzbekistan. The facts you have learned are only the tip of a huge iceberg, and we have not yet studied what lies beneath the surface. Let the commission examine it and tell us everything. And another comment. I am opposed to Roy Medvedev's candidacy as chairman, because he is one of the handful of journalists who are involved in creating the myth of Gdlyan and Ivanov. (Applause.)

N.A. Strukov, senior investigator of the Kursk Oblast Prosecutor's Office (Kursk Territorial Electoral Okrug, RSFSR): Comrades, we are talking now about a man's guilt. But you have forgotten the most important thing: In accordance with our Constitution, guilt can only be established by the court (Article 151 of the Constitution). Therefore, in order to discuss the formation of a commission, we must think about making an amendment to the Constitution on the question of forming a commission. On this basis I, as a specialist, do not refuse to participate in the commission, but I request that its formation be given constitutional backing.

Moving from the general to the particular, I propose that the question of the actions of the investigation group be examined from the viewpoint of the imposition of law and order. The examination of the question should proceed in two dialectically interconnected directions. First, to establish whether the group operated on the basis of the principles of the rule of law, or of lawlessness. After all, in 6 years Gdlyan and the others entangled many officials, up to the level of the USSR Supreme Soviet, in an endless, irresponsible chain of impermissible methods. For the sake of their political career, they are prepared to do anything in the guise of the protection of law and order, spurred on by the journalists' loathsome praise, in the past, of Gdlyan and his deputy, not of all 209 members of their group. Incidentally, a number of them have already expressed their opinion on the matter. Let us not annoy the people with superfluous talk.

Second. The mafia is still the mafia, and if Gdlyan had not wounded the very foundations of its existence, no violations of the rule of law on his part would be under examination now; it would all have remained in the shadows. (Applause.) If we are to debunk the Gdlyan phenomenon, let it be only through the court in accordance with the Constitution. Our parliament is not professional in this respect. There are only a very small number of representatives of legal science on the proposed commission.

But we cannot allow the verdicts that were pronounced, and their legality, to be discredited—that is the most important thing. There were millions of rubles, there were givers and receivers of bribes. There were bribers and bribe-takers, and this campaign is, in my view, aimed at distracting public opinion from the problem of the mafia and preventing investigation of the so-called "sharks."

We will only preserve faith in the rule of law by observing the due process of criminal law. Not many people know that criminal proceedings have now been instituted in the case of the Gdlyan group. But neither he nor the general prosecutor is in any hurry to inform the congress of this. I consider it unlawful to conduct a judicial investigation and an unprofessional investigation by people's deputies in parallel. You cannot build the framework of a rule-of-law state on unlawful foundations. Clearly incompetence of this kind is what leads to casualties in Tbilisi and other regions.

The Constitution must not be violated, and therefore only on condition that an amendment to the Constitution is adopted to provide for the creation of a commission, am I prepared to take part in the examination of this question.

B.Ye. Paton: Comrades, one moment. I want to remind you that the proposal to set up a commission was put forward by the deputies themselves. Questions that come under the jurisdiction of the court may arise in the course of the commission's work. Naturally, these will be handed over to the court. I think that is quite clear.

Voice from the floor (the deputy did not introduce himself): Comrades, I did not want to seize the microphone, but in the course of the election campaign, at every meeting the voters asked me the same question: Are Gdlyan and Ivanov right or wrong? This is a very serious question, and should not be settled by the methods appropriate to a collective farm [kolkhoz] meeting. (Applause.)

Embezzlement and bribery have reached a large scale in our state. You know this very well, and we have to combat this evil. This evil is eating like rust into the moral foundations of Soviet man. And people want to know the truth. Therefore I ask that this question be approached seriously, without fuss or protestations. And if Comrades Ivanov and Gdlyan want to ask the deputies for help to find justice, once again I say—let us approach this seriously. And if Gdlyan and Ivanov are guilty, they should be punished. But if they turn out to be right, the consequences, comrades, will be unpredictable. There is a mafia at work here. Let us approach it seriously. (Applause.)

A.G. Mukhtarov, editor of the republican newspaper KISHLAK KHAKIKATI ("RURAL TRUTH"), Uzbek SSR, Tashkent City (from the USSR Journalists' Union): Interesting things are happening here, comrades. To form one congress commission, a commission of deputies, has taken so many debates, so much fuss, so many votes, and so forth. But why were tens of thousands of innocent people from Uzbekistan arrested and put in prison, where they languished for a year, 2, 3, 5, 6 years? I have a telegram here: A man from Tashkent Oblast has been in prison for 8 years.

Comrades, if Gdlyan and Ivanov are not guilty, they should not be opposed to the formation of a commission. I wholly support the composition of the deputies' commission. I have only one proposal: The commission chairman should be elected from among the commission by those who are part of it. But not Comrade Medvedev. That is my earnest request. We have our reasons for this.

Z.K. Rustamova, member of Syr-Darya Oblast People's Court, Uzbek SSR, Syr-Darya Oblast, Gulistan City (from the USSR trade unions): On the question of the formation of the commission, since the deputies have decided to form one, we must approach it with the utmost seriousness.

I am very well aware that the lawyers—investigators and attorneys—who are present here know very well that in 6 years Gdlyan's group did an enormous amount of work. They were investigating criminal cases in a particularly complex category, and each criminal case is not just one or two volumes—it is a criminal file of dozens of volumes. In the oblast courts we have received criminal files of 150 volumes. If a commission is set up it will have access to the numerous complaints made against the investigation group. Let us assume it is to study the complaints. But that will mean that it will be necessary to study the actual criminal cases. Yet the deputies nominated to the commission, our Comrade Adylov, for instance, who works in an entirely different sphere, and then a writer, an apparatchik—from what angle will they approach the study of a criminal case? I am an experienced lawyer, but even for me, it would take a very long time. It is necessary to have a thorough knowledge, by heart, of the norms of the criminal procedure code and the norms of the criminal code. You do not simply open the file, take a look, leaf through it, and decide: Here there was a violation, here Comrade Gdlyan did so-and-so, and so forth. No, even with practical experience you simply cannot do that. And even we lawyers often come unstuck, most often precisely when it comes to the norms of criminal procedure legislation. Yet you want to include heaven knows who on the commission. They will not be able to form their own opinion, offer their own conclusions; they will rely on competent comrades, and they themselves will only nod their heads obediently. I do not understand why we need such a commission. If there really are a vast number of complaints of abuses on the part of Gdlyan's group, as many inhabitants of Uzbekistan assert, then in that case I support the previous comrade's proposal that the matter should be investigated not by a deputies' commission, but by a special investigation group. If abuses are found, then criminal proceedings must be brought and the case investigated and handed over to the court. And only the court can determine their guilt. If the court does not establish guilt, the case will be dropped. The results will be reported to the congress. But what can our incompetent commission decide? (Applause.)

S.V. Belozertsev, senior teacher at the Karelian State University, Petrozavodsk City (Kalininskiy National-Territorial Electoral Okrug, Karelian Autonomous SSR [ASSR]): I wish to say a few words. Today I submitted to the secretariat an appeal from 419 inhabitants of Karelia to the effect that Gdlyan and Ivanov should be given space in the newspapers and time on television to justify themselves. Some kind of one-sided game is going on in the newspapers. If you look at it, it is not surprising that those who are defending them—informal groups and other support groups—are trying to support them by some means of their own. Including pamphlets. That is only natural.

And about the commission. Lawyers are indeed needed, but not only lawyer deputies; independent lawyers must be brought in from outside. The secretariat has two telegrams from Petrozavodsk and Murmansk. I hope you will heed them.

A.U. Khusanov, executive secretary of the oblast newspaper KOMMUNA, Fergana City (Ferganskiy National-Territorial Electoral Okrug, Uzbek SSR): Esteemed deputies! Esteemed chairman! First the deputies who are defending Gdlyan and Ivanov themselves proposed setting up a commission and investigating everything thoroughly. Now they do not want the commission to work. I wish to say that I approve the proposed composition of the commission. Let this commission investigate, as well as Gdlyan and Ivanov, the case of investigator Galkin, who in the course of 1987 was conducting cases at the Fergana Oblast Prosecutor's Office and in the course of a year unlawfully jailed 20 innocent people.

I wrote an article on this. It was 100 percent confirmed, but this Galkin was not punished in any way. They presented him with flowers and sent him off to Sverdlovsk. In Sverdlovsk he is working as prosecutor, and also, doubtless, working with equal "success."

I request that the commission investigate the case of investigator Galkin.

Yu.A. Levykin, scientific staffer of the USSR Academy of Sciences Institute of Spectroscopy (Podolskiy Territorial Electoral Okrug, Moscow Oblast): It was said here recently that certain deputies have received anonymous letters calling on them to help Gdlyan. I have received letters from my voters, workers at Podolsk plants. The letters have hundreds of signatures. People demand that this case be objectively examined. I will hand these letters over to the presidium, but now I want to talk about something else.

This is the point. We are now forming our third commission, but we are forgetting the most important things. Namely, the powers of the commission and its standing orders. But this is very important, because these things will determine how effective the commission is. What do I have in mind? Well, even such a simple thing as this—who actually goes to whom: the commission to the official, or the other way round, the official to the commission? And another thing. If someone is summoned and fails to attend the commission session, what will happen to him? What enforcement measures can be applied? And again. The people participating in the commission must be able to obtain access to documents, and I do not rule out secret documents. Here, obviously, conflict situations of some kind could arise. it seems to me that the standing orders and powers of the commission should rank above departmental norms, since they are set by the USSR Congress of People's Deputies.

And many other questions must be decided before setting up such a commission. Therefore I have a proposal: Before discussing the personnel of the commission, it seems to me, a working party should be set up; after all, we do not yet have experience of the formation and utilization of such groups and commissions. And only after we have defined and approved the powers and standing orders of the commissions' work will it be possible to set them up. Otherwise the commissions will be simply futile. They will be shown various out-of-date materials, and perhaps they will be favored with interviews by a few of the chiefs. And that is all.

A.A. Sobchak, department chief at the Leningrad State University Law Faculty (Vasileostrovskiy Territorial Electoral Okrug, Leningrad City): Comrade deputies! I have mounted this platform in order to give some explanations, and first of all to express my disagreement with the two colleagues, the judge and the investigator, who have already expressed their attitude to the formation of this commission. Let us be clear about this. We are setting up a parliamentary commission, not a commission to investigate the case of Gdlyan and Ivanov. And they are USSR people's deputies, and we have to decide the question of whether to deprive them of their deputies' immunity or, conversely, to refuse to do so. Therefore we will have to set up a commission in any case.

A second question. What are we creating this commission for? I think the commission must be set up first and foremost to investigate the accusations that Comrades Gdlyan and Ivanov made against a number of state and party workers. That should be the purpose of the commission's work, and not to investigate what violations, if any, were committed in the course of the activity of Gdlyan and Ivanov. (Disturbance in the auditorium.)

Your attention, please. Only after investigation—this will be quite correct legally—only after investigation of the accusations made by Comrades Gdlyan and Ivanov, and depending on the results of that investigation, should the commission investigate the activity of the investigation group itself. And to that end the commission, like any parliamentary commission of investigation, should be invested with the widest powers, the right to study any documents, and the right to summon any official. And from that viewpoint I now propose that we discuss only the proposed composition of the commission. If there are specific objections to specific individuals—let us discuss them. If not—let us approve the commission, and make it possible for it to work. (Applause.)

B.Ye. Paton: Comrades, I would like.... (Disturbance in the auditorium.) Please, let me speak, let me speak.... I would like to remind you that provision was made for the possibility of obtaining any documents that the commission demands. And now, please, go ahead.

G.M. Kurochka, chairman of the permanent session of the Komi ASSR Supreme Court (Vorkutinskiy National-Territorial Electoral Okrug, Komi ASSR): People have said here that various charming anonymous "documents" have been sent to various people, and that someone is behind Gdlyan. I speak on behalf of the miners of Vorkuta City. In our presidium now, if they look, they will find at least 10 telegrams from Vorkuta alone to the congress and to me, expressing indignation that we cannot form an objective commission and decide the question of the protection of two investigators. If we are to form a commission, it must include specialists, otherwise people will not understand us. We do not claim to check on how medics carry out operations, we do not investigate teachers. Why should a teacher investigate the work of investigators?

N.A. Kutsenko, jurisconsult at the Kremenchug House Building Combine No 3, Kremenchug City (Poltavskiy National-Territorial Electoral Okrug, Ukrainian SSR): This is my proposal. Everyone is tired of the arguing, and it seems to me that there is a simple solution. We should wait a little while for the formation of the Constitutional Oversight Committee at the USSR Supreme Soviet, and hand over in full to this committee the powers to investigate both the events in Tbilisi and the Gdlyan case. That would be according to the Constitution. And it would at the same time be a test of the reliability of the new committee. Otherwise all the ballyhoo will simply continue here.

S.S. Sulakshin, laboratory chief at the Scientific Research Institute of Nuclear Physics, Tomsk City (Tomskiy Territorial Electoral Okrug, Tomsk Oblast): Emotions have flared up, not only in this auditorium, but countrywide. Do not forget the millions of Soviet citizens who are even more concerned about this question than we are. I think everyone is too tired now to resolve this serious question. Therefore I propose: First—that the question be postponed until tomorrow. Second—that the proposed list be regarded as a working group to prepare the brief for the commission, and third—to grant Gdlyan and Ivanov the right, not to nominate members of the commission, but to reject

them. The point is that the whole country should have confidence in this group, so that emotions do not flare up later in the country and so that people do not start saying that once again an unlawful and inadequate commission has been set up. (Applause.)

Deputy (did not introduce himself): Comrade deputies! I did not take Deputy Ivanov's speech to mean that he is opposed to the formation of a commission. I do not think he is opposed to it. From his speech, or rather, from the part of his speech we were able to hear, since the rest was interrupted by rude shouting from the left, we understood that he is in favor of a commission, but a commission that should include people whose objectivity and impartiality he does not doubt.

The esteemed Ukrainian delegation spoke just now and said that they discussed and discussed for a long time the person they are proposing for the commission. But how did the others get there? (Disturbance in the auditorium.)

Excuse me! For instance, Comrade Aleksandr Ivanovich Baranov, representative of the Leningrad delegation, was not discussed at the group meeting. And I do not know how Comrade Baranov came to be on the commission. You understand, comrades, Ivanov and Gdlyan should, of course, have a right of consent, so that only objective, impartial people get onto the commission. We cannot hurry this matter now. They should speak, they should be given the right to speak without interruptions or noise and to express doubts, if they exist, on each candidacy. I think that is the right way to resolve the question. (Applause.)

From the floor: Comrades! Give me a minute. Ivanov was elected for a national okrug, from Leningrad City. We are receiving many telegrams, telephone calls, and letters asking us to support Gdlyan here. I wish to say that Comrade Sobchak was on the previous list. We did not object to that. But a proposal came in: Since Comrade Ivanov was elected from our okrug, we proposed to add another, alternative candidacy from the trade unions, from the workers. From the workers who supported Comrade Ivanov by electing him deputy from our national-territorial electoral okrug. That is why I support Comrade Baranov's candidacy, and I ask you, too, to support his candidacy.

B.Ye. Paton. Understood. Comrades, let us put the question to the vote, since our congress has every right to form a parliamentary commission, first. Second, provision has been made for the possibility of obtaining the necessary materials to enable the commission to operate. Third, the commission has the right, as necessary, to bring in professionals whom it considers necessary to its work. Consequently there are no infringements of rights here. So it is proposed that a vote be taken. But, as we did yesterday, not to elect the commission chairman, but to give the commission itself the right to elect its own chairman.

M.S. Gorbachev: Has someone withdrawn?

B.Ye. Paton: Comrade Shorokhov has withdrawn, since he considers himself unqualified to work on the commission; he asks that his place be taken by a professional lawyer. "I have no other reason," he writes. I think we can accept this withdrawal.

So, if there are no objections, let us put to the vote the composition of the commission, without preliminary election of the chairman. Those in favor of this proposal, please raise your credentials cards.

B.Ye. Paton [resuming]: Against? Count those against, please.

A.D. Sakharov (from the floor): I was waving, waving my hand. Why has what I proposed yesterday not been discussed? I have two questions.

From the floor: The list was discussed.

From the floor: Comrade chairman! We nominated a lawyer, why was the Orenburg delegation's candidate, Comrade Miroshin, not taken into account? I request that he be included, instead of Shorokhov.

M.S. Gorbachev: What does the comrade have to say?

R.N. Nishanov (from the floor): I can answer that question. Comrade Miroshin—chairman of Sovetskiy Rayon Executive Committee [rayispolkom] in Orsk City, people's deputy—was included on the list submitted to the presidium by Comrade Gdlyan and Comrade Ivanov. Comrade Miroshin does not yet have his legal education; he is studying at the law institute. When I proposed to Deputies Gdlyan and Ivanov that three of the six be selected for the commission, Comrade Miroshin's candidacy was dropped. There is nothing unnatural about that. It is all legitimate.

B.Ye. Paton: Comrades, I say again, first those who are in favor of the proposed composition of the commission voted, and then those who are against. We asked the commission to count those against, since the overwhelming majority, it was plain to see, are in favor.

A.G. Kostenyuk: Esteemed comrade deputies! There were 61 votes against.

B.Ye. Paton: Who abstains?

From the floor: I simply have an announcement to make. The Supreme Soviet Presidium cordially invites the Moscow delegation and all those wishing to attend, to assemble in the Malyy Hall. That is what I wanted to say. In the Malyy Hall in the Supreme Soviet Presidium building, by the Spasskaya Tower. Half an hour after the end of the sitting.

B.Ye. Paton: Have the abstentions been counted?

A.G. Kostenyuk: There were 93 abstentions.

B.Ye. Paton: Thank you. So, comrades, the commission is approved by congress. [passage omitted]

Ninth Sitting

Kremlin Palace of Congresses, 2 June 1989, 1000 hours.

A.I. Lukyanov, first deputy chairman of the USSR Supreme Soviet, in the chair. [passage omitted]

A.I. Lukyanov: Deputy Sergiyenko has the floor. Deputy Trudolyubov should get ready.

Sergiyenko, V.I., chairman of Krasnoyarsk Kray Soviet Executive Committee [ispolkom] (Minusinskiy Territorial Electoral Okrug, Krasnoyarsk Kray): Comrades! While supporting in principle the basic guidelines for domestic and foreign policy presented in Comrade Gorbachev's report to the Congress of People's Deputies, I would like to put forward some thoughts on my own understanding of the problems facing our society that we have to tackle. Recently, at the congress and elsewhere, we have heard a good many very harsh assessments of our history and reality. I think we have had quite enough of this to be able to move on to formulating proposals for rectifying the situation. In considering the question of power, many people see the main evil in the machinations of the apparatus. But since it is impossible to do without the apparatus entirely, and replacing some apparatus workers with others is hardly likely to amend matters significantly, I see it as one of the main tasks of the USSR Supreme Soviet and our congress not simply to formulate individual laws, however good and however necessary, but radically to improve our legislation with a view to creating a genuine mechanism of people's power, and to separate the legislative, executive, and judicial powers.

As an agrarian specialist I share and sympathize with the concerns and needs of our peasantry. Of course, I support the appeal of the group of people's deputies to the congress on this matter. But I cannot share the enthusiasm or the arguments of Comrade Chernichenko or many of his assessments and conclusions. I do not understand why such a serious journalist has to embellish his speech by accusing a party Central Committee secretary, in passing and without any serious arguments, of incompetence. (Applause.)

From the congress platform there have unfortunately been many offensive remarks about individual deputies. And if in some cases apologies have followed, this is to some extent understandable. But the direct and as yet unsubstantiated accusation of a grave crime that was leveled again yesterday by Comrade Ivanov against a Politburo member is a more than serious matter. I know well Comrade Ligachev's selflessness, purposefulness, and energy in his work, and his modesty in personal life. I think the congress has a right to demand serious, substantiated arguments on the basis of which Comrade Ivanov makes this accusation. Otherwise it can be assessed not only as outright defamation of a party leader, but as another attempt to cast aspersions on the party itself. (Applause.) On a party that has assumed full responsibility for the past and has proposed and taken the lead in the policy of restructuring and renewal. [passage omitted]

Ya.Ya. Peters, writer, chairman of the Latvian SSR Writers' Union Board, Riga City (Valmiyerskiy National-Territorial Electoral Okrug, Latvian SSR): Esteemed chairman, people of like mind, people not of like mind, comrade deputies! (Stir in the auditorium, applause.)

In the very center of Moscow, greeting the participants in the Congress of People's Deputies and the Muscovites, there hangs a banner which says: "Restructuring—the rebirth of the Leninist face of socialism." I read this fine phrase, and shuddered. What if this is just another flight of poetic fancy—a watchword that we will regard tomorrow with the same bitter irony as the promise that the present generation of Soviet people will live under communism?

I look at the sole historical territory of my forebears, my homeland—Latvia, and I think bitterly: How can it be made into a state that is not even Leninist, but simply normal, not humiliated by all-union monopolies, not poisoned by irresponsible economic activity on the part of irresponsible authorities that are subordinate to no one? How can we ensure that the USSR Council of Ministers allocates, for instance, to the city of Ventspils a mere 1 percent of the currency from the huge proportion of income that it contributes to the all-union budget, paying for it with terrible diseases and deaths among its inhabitants, including abnormalities in pregnant women and their offspring?!

I look at Latvia and I think not so much of "rebirth" as of how to stop the death of my people, because the results of pragmatic, economically invalid actions are already visible. Because of spontaneous migration, the numbers of the indigenous nation in their own territory are approaching the critical minority point. Each people belongs not only to itself. Each people belongs to the world, and the peoples have a shared blood supply.

When this blood supply is disrupted, the entire organism falls sick. That this is so, is indicated by a telegram I received the other day, which I consider it my duty as a deputy to read out:

"To USSR People's Deputies Yanis Peters and Valentin Rasputin, Congress of People's Deputies, Moscow. Please raise the question of the expediency of the construction of the Katunskaya Hydroelectric Power Station, which is a threat to the survival of the Altai ethnic group. [Signed] V. Kydyyev, journalist; Gyuzel Yelemova, poet; S. Kergilov, teacher; M. Tolbina, scientific staffer; A. Tolkachekov, trainer; A. Tadinov, artist; V. Tolkachenov, physician; A. Tyukhteneva, physician."

It is terrible to read such a text, but it is even more terrible to realize that aggressive planning is continuing its crusade against the existence of peoples.

In speaking of the tragedy in Latvia we should, of course, seek the roots in the tragedy of the Russians, Belorussians, Ukrainians, the tragedy of other peoples of the Soviet Union. It is not just for the fun of it that people leave Russian or Belorussian socially oppressed territories, their own sacred lands, and take refuge in the Baltic region, where, without being personally culpable, they are drawn against their will into the creation of a demographic imbalance and an ethnopsychologically unhealthy climate, and the destruction of the national identity and statehood of the union republics. All this destabilizes the political situation and reduces the prestige of the communist parties of Latvia, Lithuania, and Estonia.

It must be admitted that for decades the USSR Government and the Latvian SSR Government violated Article 76 of the USSR Constitution, which states very simply: "A union republic is a sovereign Soviet socialist state that has united with other Soviet republics in the Union of Soviet Socialist Repbulics." I can already hear people saying: "But things are even worse in Russia—Baykal is dying, the birth rate is falling, disease is on the increase, morality is dying...." Yes; I do not deny it, and I believe that the all-union administrative team, including the USSR State Planning Committee [Gosplan], also violates the sovereignty of the Russian Soviet Federated Socialist Republic [RSFSR] and the interests of all the peoples of Russia, including the interests of the Russian people and the aforementioned Altai. But the fact that things are even worse in Russia is no consolation for the Latvians, Lithuanians, and Estonians, and no reason to expect equally bad times in the Baltic region. Why should we be compared with less developed regions? Compare us with Finland, Sweden, Norway, Denmark. And if we do not want anti-Russian, anti-Latvian, anti-Lithuanian, anti-Estonian, anti-Semitic, anti-Armenian, anti-Georgian, even anti-Islamic, or anti-anything else feelings to develop, let us really carry out radical restructuring on questions of interethnic relations and the status of the union republic as a sovereign state.

Every schoolboy who has studied grammar knows that sovereignty is virtually synonymous with "independence." So why are we so afraid of this word? Why is Russia afraid of becoming independent of all-union diktat? Why is official Latvia afraid of it? (Unofficial Latvia is no longer afraid of anyone or anything.) Why have we begun to be officially afraid of each other? Why are we afraid of what we ourselves wrote into the Constitution—I quote Article 80: "A union republic has the right to enter into relations with foreign states, conclude treaties with them and exchange diplomatic and consular missions, and participate in the activity of international organizations"?

We are not used to it? Let us admit that at the moment this is true. But I think the time is not far off when Article 81 of the USSR Constitution will also be brought into play—it states: "The sovereign rights of the union republics are protected by the USSR." I am convinced that the USSR should not shrink from coming out in defense of the sovereignty, that is, the independence of the union republics. After all, what is the USSR? It is you and I, each of the 15 constitutionally—but unfortunately, as yet only theoretically—independent states. Only the true independence of these states, with certain restrictions on independence, as is observed in all federal unions, can bring us out of the political, economic, ecological, and national crisis, out of the impasse of moral decline, at this historic moment. The national potential of each people could give a decisive boost to a general economic revival, because national self-awareness, national statehood consists first and foremost of the devout feelings of sons and daughters toward their mother, the motherland, the people who are your family. But the family has the right to lay down order in its own home, and to define the place in that home for its dear relatives, who are, moreover, not relatives at all according to the ethnic principle. In the Baltic family this principle has never dominated. Russian, Belorussian, German, Jewish, Polish, Swedish, and Finnish blood flows in our veins. All we want is not to become lodgers in our own home.

If the center is strong, it should protect us strongly against tyranny, otherwise all it does is to demonstrate strongly its weakness. The new USSR Supreme Soviet should justify on legal principles the stationing of the Army in the union republics. If it has not yet become possible to reduce to a minimum the strength of Army subunits and naval bases in Latvia, Lithuania, and Estonia, or to do away with them entirely in the name of disarmament, then the situation can only be improved by means of an open [glasnyy] contract between the USSR Defense Ministry on the one hand and the union republic Council of Ministers on the other. This contract should stipulate openly what category of troops, in which places, in what numbers, and for what period are deployed in the republic. The concluded contract should be submitted to the republic Supreme Soviet for ratification. New articles should be introduced accordingly into the USSR Constitution and the union republic constitutions, on the relations between the Army and the supreme power in each union republic. Official statutes should be drawn up in addition on the economic, ecological, and cultural behavior of Army subunits, institutions, and departments, soldiers, and officers. I think the military should pass a test in the minimum basic knowledge of the history, traditions, and way of life of the people among whom they will be living for a certain time under the contract. The contract should guarantee a ban on the show of strength for the purposes of psychological intimidation of citizens. Otherwise the mentality of a citizen of the military district, rather than the country, develops among servicemen.

Comrade deputies! As a result of the February and October 1917 revolution, Latvia, Lithuania, and Estonia acquired national statehood. In 1940 Stalin and his emissaries, Vyshinskiy, Dekanozov, and Zhdanov, the butchers of the peoples, including the Russian people, promised us socialist happiness. It turned out that this was the crude, savage Stalin-Hitler deal on the distribution of spheres of influence. We all are very well aware that you cannot go back to 1939 and start over, but we also are aware that socialism should be synonymous with self-determination for nations and independence for states. It is characteristic that on 25 May, the opening day of the Congress of People's Deputies, PRAVDA published the theses drawn up by the commission of scientists from the USSR and Poland, which say: "In the process of adoption and implementation of decisions, including the 28 September treaty, the Soviet Government committed serious violations of international legal norms. First and foremost we note that the 28 September treaty, which stipulated the extreme eastern limit of the Wehrmacht's advance with a commitment on the part of Germany at state level, was called not only a treaty on the 'border,' but also a 'friendship' treaty, which provided grounds for speaking of 'friendly' relations between the USSR and fascist Germany, in effect whitewashed fascism, distorted class principles in the public and individual consciousness, and had grave consequences for both Poland and the USSR; the treaty flouted Leninist principles and struck a blow against the international workers' movement."

Comrades! Our delegations simply have no right to go back to Riga, Vilnius, and Tallinn without a promise that the USSR's highest legislators will instruct the USSR Government to take all the necessary measures to denounce the unlawful international legal document of 1939, because it is a question of Mankurtism, that phenomenon that was so precisely defined by Chingiz Aytmatov. Remember, a Mankurt is a man who has lost his memory, and is therefore ready to shoot his own mother dead, because he does not recognize her.

The whole world is watching today to see whether the Latvian will shoot his mother Latvia, whether the Lithuanian will shoot his mother Lithuania and the Estonian his mother Estonia, by renouncing their own true history under pressure. The whole world will also watch the commission we have set up, which is called upon to restore the historical memory of the peoples, not in the name of the glorious gains of Russia, but in the name of the preservation of life and the rights of national self-determination for the three peace-loving peoples on the shores of the Baltic Sea.

I appeal to Comrades Gorbachev, Yakovlev, and Shevardnadze right now, at the time of the rebirth of the new society that we all so badly need, to become personally involved in unraveling this historical knot.

And in conclusion—although this is not a congress of Communists—about the party. Yes, the party won a victory in the elections, but it also suffered a defeat. It is characteristic that the vast majority of those who became people's deputies are those Communists who linked their future with the people's and civil movements for democracy, and also with the idea of national rebirth.

Why was Mikhail Sergeyevich Gorbachev elected president of the USSR almost without an alternative candidacy? Obviously the secret is very simple—the leader of the Soviet Union's Communists has resolutely taken the people's side and occupied a position of democratic transformations, and is trying to turn the party into a champion of the peoples' interests and to make the party's activity an integral part of the people's movement. Obviously this is the only way for Communists if they wish to claim the role of a progressive political force.

This is also indicated by the phenomenon of the disobedient Communist, Boris Nikolayevich Yeltsin, for whom we found a place on the Supreme Soviet after all.

But how can we say that the nonparty candidates lost the elections? When we see today among the most respected and genuine people's deputies the conscience of the Russian intelligentsia, Andrey Dmitriyevich Sakharov, what right do we have to speak of a defeat for the nonparty people? So who won, in the end? I will dare to take the responsibility for saying that for the first time after decades of humiliation, it was a victory for the people, democracy, and the desire to begin the creation of an association of independent rule-of-law states.

One last thing. I would like to remind the presidium that a question from Latvian SSR deputies on the fate of the Crimean Tatars has been in the presidium for some days now. Thank you. (Applause.)

A.I. Lukyanov: Deputy Viktor Amazaspovich Ambartsumyan has the floor. Comrade Khudonazarov should prepare himself.

V.A. Ambartsumyan, president of the Armenian SSR Academy of Sciences (Ashtarakskiy National-Territorial Electoral Okrug, Armenian SSR): Comrade deputies! At the end of last year Soviet Armenia suffered a disaster on a gigantic scale. An earthquake of enormous destructive power afflicted the whole area from Leninakan to Kirovakan and all the adjoining regions. Nearly half a million people were left homeless as a result of the tragedy. Winters in the Leninakan region—I say this for the benefit of those who have no idea that Armenia is terribly diverse in terms of climatic zones—can be severe, and the situation was extremely grave. In that difficult, troubled time we received generous assistance from all the republics and oblasts of the Soviet Union. All the peoples of the world, states, and governments gave Armenia moral and material support, which we will never forget.

Since the whole of our country and the whole world are watching our first Congress of People's Deputies closely, I will take this opportunity to express most profound gratitude to all the Soviet peoples and the citizens of the world for this mighty and, I would say, unprecedented manifestation of human solidarity. (Applause.)

The city of Spitak—the epicenter of the earthquake of which nothing remains—has become a symbol of human goodness.

Armenia bows to you, people of the planet. Unfortunately, we also experienced much else that was distressing last year, we had other grave trials, too. In early March 1988 we received thousands of refugees who were fleeing not an earthquake, but the violence in Sumgait. Many people see the name of that city as a symbol of national enmity. I do not want it to be like that, because I very much respect the labor of many thousands of Azerbaijanis, Russians, and Armenians who together built this young industrial center, which, incidentally, has its problems, too. But we must ensure that Sumgait does not happen again.

Esteemed Deputy Azizbekova has sketched a picture of Azerbaijani-Armenian friendship. This friendship has indeed had a long history, but she omitted to say how the events in Sumgait fit in with this friendship. It must be recognized that internationalism is not only a matter of words; it only gains strength from real deeds.

Throughout last year and the early part of this year we learned daily of the troubles of the people of Nagorno-Karabakh, whose oppression has lasted for decades, and which was removed unlawfully from Armenia.

All this is a grave blow against the unity of the Soviet Union's peoples. Yet that unity is the guarantee, the main guarantee, of our country's future. And comrades, let us cherish and strengthen this unity. And although what I have said also implies criticism of our country's central organs, which do not do enough to protect our society against interethnic clashes and oppression, all the same I do not advocate the weakening of central organs. But I demand that they work better and stop helping those forces that seek to weaken the unity of our peoples.

Furthermore, it seems to me that the argument about the rights that should belong to the center and to the periphery—the great discussion about this—is not being conducted quite correctly. After all, the leadership and the apparatus of power are created solely to serve the people. That is their sacred duty. And in order to fulfill their duties well they should be clearly defined and separated. A clear and precise allocation of duties and functions is absolutely essential. We must know precisely what each of us is responsible for.

And what happens? When any shortcoming is uncovered in our work, when anything bad happens, as is so frequently the case, the same question always arises:

Who is to blame? If everyone knew precisely what he is responsible for, that is, knew his duties precisely, then after such an event we would see a resignation, the resignation of the civil servant concerned, that is, the one with the relevant duties. Incidentally, for some reason we regard "civil servant" ["chinovnik"] as a rude word. But no a civil servant is first and foremost a person who carries out quite specific duties that are entrusted to him. For some reason we have come to accept their renaming. And they have begun increasingly to forget that they have duties; they are glad that they are no longer called civil servants, and they think more about their rights than their duties.

At the same time the distribution of duties should be in accordance with the people's needs, and should not arouse their suspicion. When a clear demarcation of duties is set between the center and the republics, then it will be possible to distribute rights in accordance with duties—and this should be done. I do not mean that duties alone are needed first, and rights only later. This is, of course, a single process. But duties should be clarified first and foremost with regard to the people. And then it should be decided, so to speak, what rights are necessary for the fulfillment of these duties, and only these duties.

If you go into the Karabakh question, the reason for the dispute becomes clear. In the consciousness of the Armenian people the unlawful, unconditional removal of Karabakh from Armenia in the twenties was also based on the principle that the most important thing is to gain rights. To begin the de-Armenianization of that territory. And when the de-Armenianization is completed, as has already been done in Nakhichevan, then let them say what they like. All the same, it will be a fait accompli by then. The question of the final normalization of the situation in Nagorno-Karabakh can only be resolved on the basis of the principle of the peoples' self-determination. Life itself has shown that the Leninist principle of self-determination of nations is the only means of resolving such issues. And this will, of course, be in the spirit of restructuring.

Comrades, great significance is attached to the foreign policy questions to which the second part of Mikhail Sergeyevich's report was devoted. Here our country has achieved successes on a truly worldwide scale. These arose from the introduction of the new thinking. This thinking and its introduction led to the lessening of tension throughout the world. That is greatly to our country's credit.

Our troops have been withdrawn from Afghanistan. I believe that throughout this sphere full approval of our government's activity can be expressed. (Applause.) But we ask our government also constantly to take into account the fact that not only the Union as a whole, but each of the Union's peoples, has its own external interests, not only economically, but also politically. Some examples.

First. When Foreign Minister (former, of course) Molotov once declared on behalf of the Armenian people that they renounce their claims to the restoration of the Kars region [now in Turkey] and the territory where, as the whole world knows, the 1915 genocide was carried out, he was not telling the truth. He mercilessly flouted the feelings and interests of one of the peoples of the Soviet Union. The Armenian people are in favor of peace. No one proposes to use force on this matter, but we hope that the question will find a peaceful solution in the future.

Another example. A number of foreign states, as well as the European Parliament, have officially acknowledged and condemned the genocide of Armenians in 1915 by Ottoman Turkey. The Armenian SSR Supreme Soviet recently adopted a decision to request that the USSR Supreme Soviet officially condemn the extermination of the Armenian people in Turkey in 1915. That would be as just as the condemnation of the deportation of the Tatars from the Crimea.

I wish to make one more brief, but important observation here. Many of us representatives of outlying republics have spoken here about our peoples' national feelings, and in particular of cases where national consciousness has been injured. Yes, there is much suffering and many injuries in our shared history. But in this atmosphere of justified demands and reminders of our own grief, it is incumbent on us to pay due tribute to the amazing staunchness of the Russian people—the people who suffered numerous losses in the Great Patriotic War and endured the horrors of depeasantization and de-Cossackization, showing exemplary industriousness, creative initiative, and love for other peoples. Whether we like it or not, the Russian people are placed in a position where they bear the heaviest burden, the heaviest duties, which they cannot shrug off, by virtue of their position. At a congress such as the present first Congress of People's Deputies, this observation on the part of representatives of all the peoples living in the union republics will, I hope, be deemed entirely apposite. (Applause.)

Comrades, allow me to express the hope that at least some of the questions we have raised will be resolved in the process of this congress' work. (Applause.) [passage omitted]

6 Jun Congress Proceedings Reported

Morning Session Begins Work

LD0606142989 Moscow Television Service in Russian 0600 GMT 6 Jun 89

[Relay of the first session of the 6 June Congress of People's Deputies proceedings at the Kremlin Palace of Congresses—live; this item incorporates the excerpt from this broadcast already published in the Soviet Union DAILY REPORT Supplement of 6 June on page 14 under the heading "Congress Presidium Makes 6 Jun Statement on PRC"]

[Excerpts] [Gorbunov] Comrade deputies, we shall continue with the work of our congress.

Allow me to announce the results of the registration of deputies for the morning sitting on 6 June: 2,119 deputies have registered.

We shall continue to discuss the issue of the main directions of USSR domestic and foreign policy. In accordance with our tradition, there is a proposal to announce the program of the morning session, listing the speakers determined by the presidium of our congress:

Dadamyan, director general of Stepanakert Motor Transport Production Association, Nagorno-Karabakh;

Sokolov, chairman of the Gorkiy Oblast Soviet of People's Deputies Executive Committee;

Khallik, senior scientific employee of the Estonian Soviet Socialist Republic [SSR] Academy of Sciences Institute of Philosophy, Sociology, and Law;

Mongo, head of the Krasnoyarsk Kray Executive Committee department for northern and Arctic nationalities;

Kasyan, head of department at the Leshchinovskiy boarding school, Poltava Oblast;

Minnullin, chairman of the board of the Tatar Autonomous Soviet Socialist republic [ASSR] Union of Writers;

Seleznev, first secretary of the Kursk Oblast CPSU Committee;

Kugultinov, writer, chairman of the board of the Kalmyk ASSR Union of Writers;

Lizichev, chief of the Main Political Administration of the Soviet Army and Navy;

Alekseyev, director of the Institute of Philosophy and Law;

Rasputin, writer;

Yarovoy, director of the Dvigatel Production Association, city of Tallin;

Sharin, first secretary of the Amur Oblast CPSU Committee;

Borovik, writer, chairman of the Soviet Committee for the Defense of Peace;

Lavrov, artist of Leningrad Gorkiy Theater, chairman of the Board of the USSR Union of Thespians;

Arbatov, academician, director of the USSR Academy of Sciences United States and Canada Institute;

Bykov, artistic leader of the Mosfilm Yunost Association, secretary of the USSR Union of Cinematographers;

Suleymenov, writer, first secretary of the Board of the Union of Writers of Kazakhstan; and

Comrade Ugarov, artist, president of the USSR Academy of Arts.

This is the program planned by the presidium for our morning session—[whispers in the background] for the whole day of our work here together.

[Gorbunov] And so, Comrade Dadamyan, Boris Vartanovich, general director of the Stepanakert production and transport association, Nagorno-Karabakh, has the floor. Comrade Sokolov will get ready. [passage omitted: brief interruption from floor]

[Dadamyan] [passage omitted on condolences on Urals disaster]

Esteemed chairman, esteemed deputies! In his speech at the congress on national problems, Mikhail Sergeyevich used the image of a plow: If we're going to set boundaries, if we start plowing up our land, this will be a ruinous road. That's all so. But let's ask ourselves honestly: Who was it who plowed up the destiny of the people of Nagorno-Karabakh? [passage omitted: historical outline of formation of the Nagorno-Karabakh Autonomous Oblast]

Those who drew the boundaries knew very well what they wanted. What was behind this? Short-sightedness, or a policy of divisions, separations, and incorporations? But what was the result? What came afterwards? There came a policy of discrimination against the Armenian population of the Nagorno-Karabakh Autonomous Oblast [NKAO], of driving them out of their native land. The leaders of the Azerbaijan SSR changed, the words and slogans changed, but this policy remained immutable. Discrimination encompassed all spheres: the economy, cadres, education, culture. The NKAO was turned into a raw material appendage of Azerbaijan. The people have been leaving their lands. There are currently about 300,000 Armenians originating from Karabakh living outside of Nagorno-Karabakh, having been compelled to leave. During the period of the 70's and the 80's only every 10th Armenian born in Nagorno-Karabakh remained there; the remaining 9 were forced to emigrate. Any attempts to establish cultural and spiritual links wth Armenia were cruelly curtailed. In the cultural and spiritual spheres they tried to take from the Armenians not only their future but also their past. The history of Armenia was banished from Armenian schools. The most ancient monuments of Armenian culture and architecture were destroyed and desecrated. These are the stone witnesses to our land's belonging to our people. Even the ancient Armenian khackhar, that is, stone crosses, were declared to be monuments of the Azerbaijani forefathers. Things went so far that they started to tell Armenians that they weren't Armenians at all but Armenianized Albanians. Such hysterics and ideological aggression had only one aim: to prove that the Armenians were newcomers, foreigners in this land. Not for a day, not for 2 days, but for decades, the national dignity of the Armenians of Karabakh has been trampled on. And still there is not the national peace that was promised by the (?coordinating) bureau. Before the eyes of the Armenians of Nagorno-Karabakh is the example of the tragic fate of Nakhichevan. This ancient Armenian land, at the demand of Turkey and in a accordance with a treaty between Russia and Turkey in 1921, was handed over to Azerbaijan, which dealt with it in its own way.

There are in this autonomous republic, entirely located on the territory Armenia, without any border with Azerbaijan but part of it, practically no Armenians today. The idea of the national liberation movement held the minds of the Karabakh Armenians throughout these decades. The people of the NKAO have on more than one occasion risen against ethnic oppression, but all efforts were cruelly put down. Restructuring generated hope. Expressing the will of its people, in February 1988, the oblast soviet of the NKAO appealed to the supreme soviets of the Azerbaijan and Armenian SSR's, and also to the Supreme Soviet of the USSR, and requested that the question of reuniting Nagorno-Karabakh with Armenia be examined and resolved. There is some sad truth in the view that, when complex problems arise, our country makes decisions at the very outset which are far from the best ones, or it follows the golden rule of the period of stagnation: shove the problem aside and not address it. That's how it happened with the problem of Nagorno-Karabakh. The country's leadership, in beginning restructuring, understood of course that it would not be able to bypass national problems. Difficulties were expected. This is the reason why events in the NKAO weren't taken for themselves, in their actual essence, but as a dangerous precedent, as a possible threat to restructuring. This explains the first reaction of the authorities to prohibit; this explains the Politburo's erroneous decision of 21 February 1988; this explains the presidium's half-measure decision of 18 July. These decisions failed to take account of the complexities of the real situation, and, in artificially prolonging the delay in addressing the problem, sharply aggravated interethnic relations in the region. Only many months later did they start to acknowledge that there was a problem, and that it arose on the basis of a discriminatory, even inhuman—as Mikhail Sergeyevich Gorbachev accurately described it—attitude to us on the part of the former leadership of Azerbaijan.

Attempts have been made and are being made to replace the political problem of Nagorno-Karabakh with economic problems. Of course, the economy of the NKAO is in an extremely neglected state, and we are in favor of lifting the economy and regional financial autonomy. But the main thing for us is the resolution of the political problem within the framework of self- determination. The fact that the economy will remain lame in the absence of a political solution is proved by the R450 million which was allocated by Moscow for the NKAO,

but which got stuck in Baku on the way; we haven't seen them yet. Moreover, all of you understand that money ceases to be mere paper only when it is backed up by resources, in particular resources of building materials and equipment. And the lion's share of resources should come to us from Baku—should but doesn't.

The Karabakh movement has raised many questions that still remain unanswered. The main one of these lies in the following: Do we recognize Lenin's principle of the self-determination of nations? We say, Lenin stressed, that it would be a betrayal of socialism to abrogate implementation of the self-determination of peoples under socialism. Today, at the end of the 20th century, in spite of the commonly accepted international norms of the law and practice of self-determination of peoples, a clear and unambiguous expression of the people's will for the reunification of Nagorno-Karabakh with Armenia is interpreted as an impermissible and illegal aspiration to redraw the borders as something that is in essence intolerable and anti-social. Should we in Nagorno-Karabakh understand this as the effective departure of the party from the principles of self-determination of nations? In his report to the congress, Mikhail Sergeyevich Gorbachev said: The principle of national self-determination, as put forward by Lenin, has been and remains one of the main elements in the national policy of the Communist Party. How are the people of Nagorno-Karabakh to understand these words? As assent to the reunification of the two parts of the Armenian people, or as a political slogan of the kind: yes, but? Eighty-five percent of those in this hall are Communists, and we, to a certain degree, represent the face of the party. So let's ask ourselves: For the sake of what lofty principles should the Armenian people of Karabakh suffer? What kind of self-determination is this if a small nation has to ask permission for self-determination from a bigger nation; and that bigger nation can kindly grant permission, or arrogantly forbid? What kind of great power-permissive self-determination is this?

The time has come to bring our Constitution in line with Lenin's concept of self-determination. Esteemed deputies! I would like to focus your attention on the practice of selective de-Stalinization. Why is it that while freeing ourselves from Stalin's legacy in other areas of the country's life, we are leaving untouched arbitrary decisions in the area of the principles and structure of the federative system adopted under pressure from Stalin? The existing status of autonomy is in essence a semi-feudal institution, a form of consolidating the hierarchy of nations. Under these conditions the very concept of equality of nations becomes fiction. And now, from the proud slogan of self-determination, let's go on to the reality, and see what has Nagorno-Karabakh gained instead of self-determination. It has gained a special form of administration. The powers of the oblast soviet of people's deputies, labor collective councils, and the oblast party committee have been suspended. Local soviet power has in effect been abolished. The decision to set up the committee for special administration was presented to the public as a compromise, infringing upon no one's interests and capable of stabilizing the situation in the region. However, this is not the case. The special form of administration relies upon a strong military presence which unfortunately hampers the Azerbaijan leadership from conducting an ever harsher line on discrimination against the Armenian people. The interethnic conflict is continuing to become more profound. Do we realize that in the NKAO, the Azerbaijani leadership is carrying out a (?division) on the Cyprus model? The oblast is being split along ethnic lines into two opposing communities. That is the result of the desire to push aside settlement of the Nagorno-Karabakh problem. We ought to have foretold such a development of events and spoken of the unpredictable consequences, instead of whipping up passions.

The Sumgait crime is a special issue. Without going into that, I want to point out that a political evaluation of the Sumgait crime is important not only for the Armenian people, but for the Azerbaijani people, too. [indistinct shout in hall]

For my own part, I would like to assure you that we are far from placing the responsibility for this misdeed upon the Azerbaijani people, and we profoundly regret that the real inspirers and organizers of that misdeed have not been uncovered even yet.

To conclude my address, I would like to convey to the congress, upon instructions by my voters, the demands of the Armenian people in Nagorno-Karabakh. We demand, first, that the CPSU oblast committee and the NKAO oblast executive committee be restored immediately. Bring back soviet power to the Karabakh land! Second, that the Politburo decisions of 5 July, 1921 be annulled as unlawful. Third, that a Supreme Soviet committee be set up on a schedule for procedure on reunification of the NKAO.

If you would allow me 2 more minutes, I want to read out the decision of the Congress of People's Deputies, the draft of this which we are proposing...[bell rings; stir in hall]

[Gorbunov] Esteemed colleague, you should ask me if you want extra time.

[Dadamyan] I want to read just three points of the draft....

[Gorbunov, interrupting] Boris Vartanovich asks 3 minutes to read out....

[Dadamyan, interrupting] No, 2 minutes!

[Gorbunov] Two minutes to read out the decision. [noise in hall]

[Dadamyan] About the situation in the Nagorno-Karabakh Autonomous Oblast. This is the draft decision we are proposing: To set up a commission of deputies for an all-round and objective study of the situation and to draw up a nationwide referendum in the NKAO on the basis of points 2 and 13 of Article 108, and of point 12 of Article 73. The USSR Supreme Soviet, in accordance with point 6 of Article 119 of the USSR Constitution, is to organize and conduct a referendum in the Nagorno-Karabakh Autonomous Oblast. Second, before a referendum is conducted, the Committee for Special Administration of the NKAO is to be given powers to bring the oblast under the real jurisdiction of the center. Third, it is to be considered expedient to restore the functions of the local organs of power.

This has the signatures of 33 deputies. Here you are. [hands paper to Gorbunov] [applause]

[Passage omitted: address by Sokolov, chairman of the executive committee of Gorkiy Oblast]

[Gorbunov] I call on Comrade Khallik, Klaris Semenovna, a leading member of the academic staff at the Institute of Philosophy, Sociology, and Law of the Academy of Sciences of the Estonian SSR. After her will be Deputy Mongo.

[Khallik] Esteemed comrade chairman, comrades deputies. After a break of 66 years since the 12th party congress, our congress is hosting a frank discussion, for the first time, about ethnic relations in our country. This discussion is showing that all the fears Lenin warned about in his testament have come true. The congress has already identified the causes of what has happened: the vices of state bureaucratic socialism, and the abnormal and antidemocratic nature of the tenacious habis of imperial rule. This is a system that infringes the rights of all nations, including the biggest of all—the Russian nation. When the restructuring got under way, neither its main architects nor the general public were prepared for the possible emergence of ethnic movements, and even today not everyone regards them as proper. We experienced this ourselves after the Estonian Supreme Soviet's famous declaration of sovereignty on 16 November last year. On the one hand, there was support from the democratic public, and on the other, we were branded with the words creeping counter-revolution, separatism, nationalism, and antisocialism. Practically at the beginning of our congress, the authors of the document distributed to the deputies today called for the introduction of a special form of administration in Estonia. In November we were told: What are you playing at with these ethnic affairs of yours? Let's do the restructuring first and then it will be your turn. Here at the congress, too, people are saying that we should resolve state affairs first and then ethnic ones. We now realize that there must be no state affairs that are not the affairs of the people as well.

In analyzing ethnic policy we are discovering many bitter truths which many are psychologically unprepared to accept. Nevertheless, it is essential to try and understand the causes of the present ethnic tensions.

This alone will enable us to determine the place of the national-democratic movements in the restructuring.

First, the main cause of our ethnic contradictions today is the failure of Lenin's attempt to set up a federative union. Stalin recreated the empire, stooping even to the methods of imperial foreign policy. A unitary state was set up in a federative shell, with no local self-administration and with the periphery subordinated to the center in everything. This reality and nothing else explains both the ethnic injustice and, by way of reaction to this, the constant reproduction of centrifugal forces.

What action should be taken now under conditions of democratization? We have been reminded here, in a perturbing combination, of the concept of power [derzhava], but I think it's now clear to everyone that the state cannot be kept intact by the methods used for this purpose in the past. These methods will come up against increasing resistance from all the peoples. We have no other choice but to genuinely restore the nations' right to self-determination, to make the union—in both content and form—a union of equal sovereign states, and to ensure broad national-territorial and national-cultural self-administration for peoples who have no statehood. It is this right to self-determination, as opposed to leftover rights granted by the center, that must be the source of the republics' sovereignty, and a treaty must become the source of federal law. In other words, we must carry out the constitutional reform of the union to guarantee a return to Lenin's ideas of federalism.

In this connection, I'll say a couple of words about the reverse side of the so-called Russian coin already mentioned by Deputies Oleynik and Belov. The truncate structure of Russian national statehood and the administration of Russia, not as a country but as a conglomerate of oblasts, are causing the erosion of national self-awareness and supplanting it with a union-wide sameness. Under contemporary conditions this is a break on ethnic revival, and as a result, many people in Russia perceive the struggle against bureacratic centralism in the other republics as a struggle against Russia. If all the political institutions were set up in Russia, most of the union departments and organizations would become superfluous and would be replaced by direct, mutually beneficial, and equal ties between the republics. And perhaps then we might succeed in working out how many Russian nations there are in this country—1, 15—taking into account the union republics—35—and taking into account the autonomous formations. This confusion is the source of the strained ethnic relations in the republics. Incidentally, yesterday's SOVETSKAYA ESTONIA wrote about the real support enjoyed by certain comrades who claim to fully represent the entire non-Estonian or so-called Russian-speaking population

of the republic. The constitutional reform of the union should not only resolve the ethnic problem, but also change the face of socialism in the direction of the self-governing democratic society. All nations, whether large or small, are in need of this to some extent or other. [passage omitted on cultural and religious differences]

The domination of the monopolies in the national republics and krays has disrupted the social integrity of a whole range of nations. Some of them, as a result of monopolistic management, have ended up in the position of a social stratum employed in agriculture or other auxilliary spheres. Unbridled extensive development of industry has also placed the inner equilibrium of the structure of the Estonian national in jeopardy: It is turning into a people with an incomplete social structure. In order to stop this process, there must be a sharp change in the concept of economic development in the regions and republics, and the ethnic implications of all economic measures must be taken into account. This, incidentally, is the ethnic significance of our concept of republican financial autonomy.

Particular mention should be made of the small peoples of the north and the east. Over many centuries, they have adapted to harsh, while at the same time, fragile and easily damaged, natural conditions, and have created a unique and caring culture of interaction between man and nature. They have preserved a flourishing natural environment for present generations and for the country. In gratitude for this, our state has repeated one of the biggest disgraces of European civilization, which destroyed the American Indians. And we have repeated this on the eve of,the 21st century, in a country which calls itself socialist. Before all is lost the state must redeem its guilt before the small peoples of the north, and not just the north. A special body for the protection of small ethnic groups should be set up in the Soviet of Nationalities of the Supreme Soviet, a state program should be drawn up, and the public should be mobilized in order to revive a normal working life, and through this the human and ethnic dignity of the small ethnic groups. I would like to propose as a congress document an appeal from the small ethnic groups, from an international meeting of writers of the Ugro-Finnish peoples, from the Kurdish people, from the Crimean Tatars, from the Gagauz, and certain others. [passage omitted on reviving cultural and linguistic diversity]

[Gorbunov] Next to speak is Deputy Mikhail Innokentyevich Mongo, chief of the department for the affairs of the ethnic groups of the northern Arctic of Krasnoyarsk Kray Executive Committee, from the Evenki National-Territorial Okrug No 749. After that will be Deputy Kasyan.

[Mongo] [Passage omitted on respecting the rights of nations and ethnic groups]

While leaping centuries, in the sense of social system and education, the indigenous population of the northern regions has fallen behind in social development by decades. For instance, the average life expectancy of the ethnic groups living in this area is 16-18 years below the country as a whole. Cases of TB are five or six times more frequent. Child mortality is two or three times the all-union rate. The average housing space per indigenous inhabitant is 3 or 4 square meters, which is not much more than a person needs in the nether—as the Evenkis put it—world beyond the grave. Over 3,000 families, more than 13,000 people, continue to lead a nomadic way of life. They live in animal-hide tents, and canvas tents in temperatures of up to 50 degrees below freezing. And this is not just because their work compels them to do so: All these families have neither hearth nor home, as the saying goes, in the settlements. Teachers, doctors, agricultural and cultural workers, aviation workers, builders, geologists, war and labor veterans, and others who live or work under these harsh conditions are acutely in need of housing and basic amenities. Throughout the north, and that includes the Tyumen area where the country's main drilling rigs are to be found, only 3 percent of settlements have been connected to the gas supply, 4 percent have piped water, and 0.1 percent have central heating. The majority of settlements lack wastewater disposal and water-intake systems. In a word, the people of the taiga and tundra live in primitive conditions, but they have television—as was said in an article in the Soviet press. Thank you to those who set up the Orbita system, thanks to which our voters can confirm that we, the people of the north, are telling the truth, bitter though it is, from this rostrum. [passage omitted on veterans' benefits, raw materials, and resources]

In my view, it is high time to draw up and adopt a special law to cover accountability for mismanagement and negligence. How long can explosions such as the one that occurred a few days ago continue to rock the country? A law of this sort is needed for the whole country, but above all for its most vulnerable regions like the far north and Arctic. [passage omitted on preserving the northern habitats]

Comrades, we have adopted effective measures to protect the bear and the polar bear, and other rare species of animals and birds, whic are entered in the list of protected species. But a law should also be passed to protect the right of the indigenous ethnic population in outlying parts of our state to live on their native soil. All the small ethnic groups of Siberia, the far north, and far east, numbering 180,000 people, are inexorably approaching the dangerous point of full assimilation. Take the Evenki, for instance: At the end of the 19th century there were more than 70,000; according to the latest census, there are only a little more than 20,000 left. [passage omitted urging the improvements of living conditions and Kasyan's remarks]

[Gorbunov] Deputy Tufan Abdullovich Minnullin, board chairman of the Union of Writers of the Tatar Autonomous Soviet Socialist Republic [ASSR] has the floor. Next to speak will be Deputy Seleznev.

[Minnullin] [passage omitted on condolences for the Urals accident victims]

We Tatar deputies and our electorate have reached a single view on general issues of ecology, but they are less inclined to consider this subject in an abstract manner. They are worried about the death throes of the great Volga River and the construction of a nuclear power station on the Kama. It is being built in the middle of a densely populated industrial area in the republic. In spite of the numerous protests from scientists about the extremely unfortunate selection of the site from the geological and geographical point of view, construction work is going on. It is true that after a request from the republic's leadership and the public, an expert commission was set up by the USSR Council of Ministers. But it is in no hurry to get down to business. Meanwhile, there is a shortage of building organizations' capacity for hospitals and schools. [passage omitted on self-financing]

In the election manifesto of the Tatar deputies, there was also the question of nationalities. I would like to dwell on this problem in some detail, because it is especially topical today and requires urgent solution. We have all seen that these days the childish, emotional interpretation of the friendship of people is coming into collision with the real conditions of the peoples of our country. Today, as the result of a dogmatic attitude to the problem and through violations of the Leninist nationalities policy, a crack has appeared on the monolith of the unselfish friendship gained by the October revolution, which was our main weapon in the years of the Great Patriotic War. This phenomenon requires deep scientific study. To me, it seems that one of the main causes is non-observance of equality.

We all know the truth that only equals can be friends; that is why this truth is included in our constitution and backed by Article 36. But in the very same basic law, in articles 109, 111, and 118, doubts are cast on this truth. Why, for example, the union republics elect 32 deputies from national-territorial constituencies, while the autonomous ones only 11? Why are some republics represented by 11 deputies in the Soviet of Nationalities, while others by only 4? Where is logic here? How are the union republics essentially different from the autonomous republics? Even at our congress, the union republics are singled out and given a special position, while for us the role of listeners is reserved. Why has such setting off been continuing for so many years?

This is not just a question of prestige. Such inequality, like a dangerous latent disease, is widespread in our life. It is particularly noticeable in the field of national culture. A territorial-administrative attitude to culture has led to a privileged position for some peoples and a humiliating attitude toward others. Why, say, are the 7-million-strong Tatar people deprived of their own cinematic art? Is the republic's economic development weak? I wouldn't say so. At present, the republic's national product is worth R23 million. Is there no national personnel? There's any number you like. Why, say, have the Tatar or Bashkir, Chuvash, Mari, and other autonomous radios and televisions much less air time for their programs than those in the union republics? I am speaking here now, and my voters can watch my speech. But had I been speaking on the republican television, they would not have been able to watch their deputy. One-hundred-and-twenty-one kilometers from the capital of their republic, the people are deprived of an opportunity to watch their own television programs, because of—or so it is explained—production, technical, and economic reasons. But I am compelled to see other reasons here, and I view this phenomenon from a political point of view. That is precisely how the issue is put by tens of thousands of the republic's rural population.

If we take the issue of the publication of books, newspapers, magazines—all right, I am going to stop enumerating things, I don't want to seek pity.

What do we propose to do to get out of this humiliating situation. The administrative-territorial barriers which stand in the way of full equal rights for all people of the Soviet Union must be eliminated through legislation. We consider it necessary to equate the status of all national republics, without splitting them into union and autonomous. [applause] Perhaps there are other options. They have to be thought through and discussed, but we must not leave the question open, or rather closed. Friendship and unity are more precious than anything else in the world. They are not washing powder or soap; to keep our souls clean we need more effective detergents. We are going to get out of the economic crisis, but if a crisis begins in our relations, it is doubtful that we will come out alive and in good health.

The ruinous nature of the administrative-territorial attitude to culture is especially evident in the case of our people. The point is that only one-quarter of the Tatar population lives within the boundaries of its republic. The rest are practically cut off from the center where the main forces of national culture are concentrated and where the nation's social ideas are formed. The natural desire of the Tatars living outside the republic to preserve their originality was previously regarded almost as frenzied nationalism, while our striving to introduce them to their own culture was viewed nearly as interference in the internal affairs of a foreign state. I think that even the Ministry of Consumer Services had a greater scope of activity than the republic's Ministry of Culture and Ministry of Public Education.

Today things appear to be getting better. But how much are words worth without material basis and legal backing? Over the last few days, I have been constantly harassed by Tatar Muscovites. There are more than 200,000 of them living in the capital. For several years now they have been asking for their own cultural center in Moscow. The municipal authorities hear them but do not listen to them. The Tatar Muscovites demanded that I say this at the congress, and so I am saying it. I hope that the comrades from the Moscow Soviet can hear me and are thinking about a solution for this very important issue.

There is also a problem which has no administrative-territorial boundaries. It worries every nationality. Although it has already been spoken about in the report and in speeches, I cannot pass over Hamlet's question: To be or not to be? I am not going to philosophize on the subject of the necessity to know one's own language. After all, can one debate whether or not one needs one's own language? Neither is there any need to prove that it is necessary to know the Russian language as the language of communication between the nationalities. But how is this to be combined? It is not easy to provide prescriptions for this, but something has to be done and it has to be done in the immediate future at the state level. In our republic we are trying to take some measures, but these are no more than emergency oxygen. This problem cannot be solved through educational or amateur methods. We need all-union legislative acts protecting the national languages and promoting their development. Interethnic relations in our republic are not as exacerbated as in some regions, but this does not give us a right to rest content. Every fact connected with this problem requires special attention and study. For example, just before my departure for the congress a voter asked me the following question: Why in the capital of the republic, in Kazan, with its six constituencies, wasn't one representative of the indigenous nationality elected deputy? The question is far from simple. But we, deputies, are obliged to find an answer to it. And we will return to the very best things pronounced by the October revolution, and in the future our unity will continue to be our main strength.

Last week in our republic there were the Bashkir culture days. For the peoples of two large republics, this event was a festival of friendship and a concrete approach to strengthening the sacred traditions of fraternity. In connection with this I have to reproach the organs of the central press and the radio and television. They do not show proper interest in such events. Principles of friendship are not sufficiently propagandized on the basis of positive examples. I understand our friends the journalists. For a long time we engaged in praising paper internationalism. But the times are changing and the festivals are acquiring different significance. This too should be noted.

These days we have a great many angry and dissatisfied people, and we talk a lot about them. That is natural and normal in today's conditions. But we should also not forget that anger and dissatisfaction should serve not destruction, but creation. How we love extremes. Just 10 years ago in forums, speakers competed against each other in self-glorification. Today a number of deputies are competing in delivering the angriest and most painful speech. Regretfully, some speakers have even got almost as far as speaking about our inferiority. I think that in any case, if we are aspiring to objectivity, we have to know how to make balanced appraisals of our deeds, both bad and good. We have to restore the lost faith in our future, otherwise it's going to be difficult for us to live a normal life. And we do have to go on living, dear comrades.

Thank you for your attention. [applause]

[Gorbunov] Deputy Aleksandr Ivanovich Seleznev, first secretary of the Kursk Oblast party committee, has the floor. Deputy Kugultinov will be the next to speak.

[Seleznev] Esteemed comrade deputies! If one carefully looks and listens to the work of our congress, one can say without question that the congress reflects the processes of democratic renewal and revolutionary transformation which are taking place in our society today. Numerous meetings with voters show that our people give the party and the central committee their due for getting society out of its apolitical, lethargic sleep and support the policy of restructuring. At the same time, it is quite justified that one should strictly call to account party committees and specific workers for mistakes that have been made, for lagging behind in economic and social development, and demand radical decisions to eliminate difficulties and problems.

There are complex processes taking place locally at the present time in the party committees in our country. There have been people there with an unclean conscience who abuse their official position, and it is possible that they will make their appearance. But people see that the party cleanses itself and its body becomes more healthy. And in my view the actions of those who whip up groundless suspicion of party members and attach all kinds of labels are dangerous here. And the accusations make from this platform against Yegor Kuzmich Ligachev, secretary of the Central Committee, are motivated by nothing other than a desire to cast a shadow over the Politburo. In my view, such actions cannot be seen other than as a desire to undermine the people's trust in party workers. Without sorting out who is working in what way there is one task being set here—that of compromising people. And a deputy from our oblast, speaking on 29 May, suspected me, too, of some kind of intrigues with regard to the congress and—to put it bluntly—embarked upon a path of fabrication and publication of things that had allegedly been heard that is unacceptable in relations between people. Words of accusation have been heard here against the Committee of State Security. Of course, there is not, nor can there ever be, forgiveness by the people for those workers who are guilty of the downfall of people who have been tormented and maimed, not just physically but primarily morally. But to say that and then stop will be to tell only part of the truth. The whole truth amounts to the fact that thousands of Chekists and intelligence officers, dedicated to their people, dedicated to the cause of the revolution, have given and are giving their knowledge, and not infrequently their lives, too, for the sake of saving people. It is thanks to their efforts that many large-scale misfortunes have been averted. Surely there are not some people who really want to forget all of that? Believe not words, neither your own nor those of others; put your trust in deeds, both your own and those of other people. This was the call of Lev Nikolayevich Tolstoy.

I also want to mention the following detail: During the congress's work, the words president and parliament of the country have been heard not infrequently. Even the newly elected chairman of the Soviet of the Union constantly used the word parliament at the first session. But these words in no way reflected the essence of our power; if it was a case of naive error or the desire to use a foreign word, then it was a small matter. You and I are proud of the power of the Soviet born of the October revolution; we are proud of our people's deputies. [applause] [passage omitted on agrarian problem]

A system of measures has to be implemented for the radical and necessarily integrated social rearrangement of the countryside, and I want to draw attention to the fact that this concerns, first and foremost, Russia. It is indeed in Russia that rural problems have stuck out in the most acute and blatant way. A lot has been said about this, both before the congress and during the congress. By way of illustration, I will give just a few figures relating to our own Kursk Oblast, not the most decayed oblast of Rusisa, but one situated on the richest lands in the center of Russia. Over the past 20 years, the population here has fallen by nearly one half. About 300 villages have ceased to exist. The age of the people living in the countryside has gotten much older: The average age of its inhabitants has risen to 50. We now have fewer work-capable people than we have pensioners. And the most alarming fact is that the number of children has fallen by three times. I imagine that this situation is also characteristic of many other oblasts in Russia. [passage omitted on the deterioration of the Russian countryside]

And my final point, comrades, is that many problems in the development of agriculture in the Russian federation are tackled in a way that is inferior to that in other union republics, because—I believe—the existing pattern of state and economic management is not in keeping with its scale and the different levels on which it exists. It cannot fully take into consideration and embrace all the special features of that territory. It is considered expedient, therefore, to ask the Central Committee and the Supreme Soviet to think out a pattern of state and economic management for Russia.

In conclusion, I want to say that the deputies from the Kursk Oblast, expressing the mood of their voters, have taken deeply to heart the concern over the state of affairs in the country which has been expressed in the report by Mikhail Sergeyevich Gorbachev and share the constructive proposals contained in it. Thank you for your attention. [applause]

[Gorbunov] Comrade deputies, before we declare a break, the presidium offers the draft of the following statement. May I read the statement? It is a statement on the events in China:

In neighboring China, dramatic events have taken place. Soviet people have been informed broadly and in timely fashion about them. The situation has become particularly acute in the last few days. As the Chinese mass media report, clashes have taken place in Beijing, the PRC's capital, between participants in mass demonstrations of young people and troops. Weapons have been used. There are human casualties. Now is not a time for unconsidered, hasty conclusions and statements. Whatever the heat of passions may be, it is important to patiently seek adequate solutions which would be determined by the aims of consolidating society. Naturally, the events which have just unfolded in China are an internal affair for the country. Any attempts at pressure from outsiders whatsoever would be inappropriate. Such attempts merely heat up passions, but do nothing at all to stabilize the situation. We hope that wisdom, common sense, and a considered approach will prevail and that a way out, worthy of the great Chinese people, will be found in the situation that has formed. We sincerely wish for the friendly Chinese people that they will turn this tragic page in their history, as soon as possible, and will go ahead along the path of economic and political transformations, the path of construction of a strong, peace-loving, free, socialist China—a great country which enjoys the respect and sympathies of its neighbors and of all mankind.

Do you have any objections or proposals in connection with this, comrades? The proposal is to adopt such a statement on behalf of the congress. Are there any comments on the wording?

[Unidentified deputy] [Words indistinct]

[Gorbunov] Yes?

[Unidentified deputy] [Words indistinct]

[Gorbunov] I see. If there are no other wishes or comments, then I ask you to vote for the text of the statement. Please raise your mandates. Thank you. Who is against?

[Unidentified speaker from hall] One.

[Gorbunov] Any abstentions? An overwhelming minority. So, the congress adopts the statement. The overwhelming minority abstained. And so, the congress adopts the given statement. We declare a break for 30 minutes.

Lizichev Addresses Congress

LD0606112489 Moscow Television Service in Russian 0846 GMT 6 Jun 89

[Speech by Army General Aleksey Dmitriyevich Lizichev, chief of the Main Political Directorate of the Soviet Army and Navy, at USSR Congress of People's Deputies session in the Kremlin Palace of Congresses 6 June—live]

[Text] Esteemed comrade chairman, esteemed comrade people's deputies: The Armed Forces are called upon to ensure strategic stability in the world and to guarantee the security of the Soviet state and its allies from aggression. I am now in my 4th year as a member of the country's Defense Council, and I can report to the people's deputies that throughout these years the Defense Council, with the involvement of major specialists, scientists, and designers, has examined the fundamental issues of the country's defense and of military construction from all sides, profoundly and in a competent fashion, and that the decisions adopted on restructuring in the armed forces are both well considered and profound.

Judge for yourselves: Over these years, a new defensive doctrine has been developed and adopted. The principle of reasonable sufficiency for defense has been adopted and has come into effect. More than 1,200 medium- and intermediate-range missiles have been destroyed, the Armed Forces are being reduced, the withdrawal of our troops from friendly countries has begun, the Vienna talks on conventional weapons cuts are in progress, and the quantitative make-up of the Army and Navy, the numbers of servicemen in the branches of the Armed Forces, and also the country's defense budget have been made public. Observers and inspection groups travel to major military exercises, both others coming here and ours going elsewhere. That is the reality today. It is the result of the new political thinking in the sphere of defense policy, and of firm day-to-day leadership of the Armed Forces by our party and its Central Committee and Politburo.

Within the Armed Forces themselves, on the basis of a considered assessment of the military-political situation and the realistic capabilities of the country, the main stake in restructuring has been made on the qualitative parameters of their development. Measures are being implemented to enhance combat readiness, equipping of troops and fleets with modern weaponry is in progress, amendments are being made in operational arts and tactics, and operational combat and political training is being further improved. A solid legal foundation is laid for all military restructuring work. I am confident that the committee which is being formed on issues of defense and security, and the drafting and adoption of a USSR Law on Defense will strengthen even further the legislative base of restructuring in our armed forces. Party principles of the style and methods of work of cadres, and of selection and placement of them, are being firmly implanted. The cadres corps of the central apparatus of the Defense Ministry and the absolute majority of commander-in-chief and commanders have a younger average age and half of them are new. Almost 1,400 posts with general's rank and 11,000 posts with colonel's rank have been abolished. These processes have not been painless nor easy. They have affected people's futures. But we have embarked upon them, and we can now see that the right choice was made.

The Armed Forces are today also taking an active part in the country's economic life. In particular, the volume of our capital construction amounts to almost R4 billion. Our subsidiary farms and military sovkhozes [state farms] provide meat and vegetables for all our personnel for 3 months of the year. We are carrying out a lot of road construction with our own resources, with more than 20 units in the Russian non-chernozem zone. Railway troops carry out big national economic jobs. The Army and Navy participate in the harvest every year. Our military construction engineers carry out tasks in the interests of more than 10 union ministries, often in the most difficult conditions, or even extreme ones. A tendency has taken shape for galvanization of party work and for improving the observance of regulations and of discipline. Demands for the latter have become stricter. Over the last 3 years, we have managed to reduce criminality by more than one-third.

We are rooting out bullying [dedovshchina]. An inquiry is being carried out by the procuracy into each case, and we have seriously got down to preventing bullying. There has been a reduction of more than 50 percent in the number of those convicted by military courts.

However, the radical improvement of discipline demanded of us today by the Party Central Committee and by restructuring has not been achieved. Public criticism of us in this regard is wholly justified. On one hand, all-around analysis of the demographic situation in the country shows, comrades, that today we have in effect no possibility of selecting those called up for military service. It was thought that such an opportunity would emerge in connection with the reduction. However, we had to opt for deferring call-up for students. This decision is undoubtedly correct, but we are once again calling up quite a sizeable proportion of young people, primarily into the construction troops, who already have a criminal record, have moral and physical defects, and who are already familiar with both drugs and alcohol. But they are also our people, after all, and therefore we—as we say in the Army—will make soldiers of them, too. At the same time, we ask ministries and departments, not to treat these troops as outcasts, but to show real concern for their every-day life and labor organization.

On the other hand, comrades, the soldier and officer's work is in general becoming increasingly strenuous intellectually and harder both psychologically and physically, by virtue of the fact that we are arming ourselves with new technology equipped with complex electronic systems, audio, and video technology, and new direction and control systems. Furthermore, it must be borne in mind that in our country more than two-thirds of the servicemen serve on the entire perimeter of our country and beyond its boundaries, often in areas as yet uninhabited, while the personnel, through operational readiness and combat duty, are for days at the control panels of missiles and radar and at the control columns of aircraft, helicopters, and ships. Not all withstand the nervous and physical burden of such service.

However, despite all the shortcomings which exist in our Armed Forces, as chief of the Main Political Directorate, I can with full justification report to the congress that the Armed Forces live together with the people and live the life of the people; that they fully support the party's policy of restructuring; and that the main body of soldiers, sailors, and officers are conscientiously fulfilling their duty. Hundreds of thousands of them went through the war in Afghanistan; there were no cowards; no one dodged fulfilling an order. And they returned from there as patriots of the motherland, not snivelling about shortcomings, but as fighters for justice, fighters for restructuring. Officers, too, did not hide behind soldiers' backs; one in every five killed and one in every six wounded there was an officer. And no one has the right to sully their military biography with bad language. [applause]

Comrades, I think the Ukrainian and Belorussian deputies will have fine memories of the servicemen involved in clearing up the accident at the Chernobyl atomic power station; as will the people of Sverdlovsk, Gorkiy, and now Bashkiria regarding clearing up the aftermath of the transport explosions; and the Armenian and Tajik peoples regarding the servicemen's actions during the hours and days of the earthquakes and the recovery work. It is true that in the Army, as in any school, there are disobedient pupils, and there are not only inexperienced but also even negligent teachers. The aircraft that got through to Moscow, Navy accidents, incidents in the Air Force, and bullying, particularly in construction units, have not enhanced our authority. For this reason, there has not yet been much improvement in discipline. But I would like to assure you that policy of reinforcing combat readiness and discipline, of reinforcing unified command, and of improving political and educational work has been correctly taken up and will be firmly conducted.

We accept positive criticism, comrades, and from it we will draw conclusions and put things right. I must, however, express distinct concern here over the fact that in a number of regions of our country agitators have appeared who see only the dark side and who are endeavoring to compromise the Army and its veterans and to undermine the armed forces' authority among the people. Prophets have also appeared, declaring that the Army is unnecessary and that it is going to recruit on a professional basis. Demands have even emerged for the

Armed Forces to be compartmentalized according to nationality, with no thought whatsoever to the implications of such talk. In some places things are going as far as gross violations of legality against officers and their families. Soldiers, sailors, and officers are frequently being called occupiers and told to head for home. Housing is not allocated; obstacles are placed in the way of obtaining residence permits, treatment in local hospitals, jobs and education for members of their families. It is hard in the services, comrades, when the rise in the cost of living is compounded by moral oppression and vilification. The problem is that in the regions these insinuations, slanders, and vilifications are not always given a mature party assessment. All of us, including military men, are concerned by the events in Tbilisi. The congress has set up an authoritative commission; we will supply it with all the documents we have, and are willing to answer any questions. Let us wait for its findings instead of placing wholesale blame for everything on the Army alone, as some are seeking to do.

Our main objective is to teach the troops what is essential during a war, and we fully support the policy that the Army must do its own business, as stated here by Mikhail Sergeyevich Gorbachev. [applause] It is not self-interest, but the most exalted responsibility for the fatherland's destiny and security that has always defined the aim of military men's service. This stance will continue to form the basis of all our educational and party-political work. We consider that our army should be a regular army, educated in the spirit of patriotism, friendship of the peoples of the USSR and socialist internationalism, in the spirit of glorious combat traditions, and recruited on the basis of universal and extra-territorial military service, as a socialist army closely bound together with the people and devoted to the cause of the party, the cause of restructuring.

We are for the unity of the country and the army, and for the consolidation of the Soviet socialist state. [applause]

Dear comrades, reality demonstrates that our theoretical front today lags substantially behind the rate of the politicization of society. Our social scientist are failing to keep up with the pace of change both in our country and in the countries of our friends and allies. The opinion is sometimes formed in the public mind, and particularly as far as young people are concerned, that everything in the country is bad. On such a soil, as one knows, creative might and patriotism do not grow particularly well. Attempts to erode Marxist-Leninist teaching on war and the Army and Leninist tenets about the role of the armed forces and defense of the socialist fatherland have become more frequent. There is too much at stake to be hasty with such conclusions.

Comrades, the Army has now started to be reduced. Of the 500,000, almost 150,000 are officers and warrant officers. Counting women and children, there are more than half a million people involved. For them, the process of reductions is far from straightforward; sometimes it is a painful one. People have to be resettled and provided with work, housing, and other such things. The government has adopted the relevant decisions. We would ask the people's deputies that matters to do with the provision of housing and jobs for those being transferred to the reserves should always be the object of your concerns, so that their futures should be decided on the principles of our social justice—in the way that in the Ukraine, Belorussia, and Azerbaijan, for instance, matters of rendering assistance to internationalist servicemen and war invalids are already being tackled. So much for those being released. Those who are continuing to serve have many problems, too. Hundreds of thousands of officers do not as yet have a place of their own. Many wives of officers and warrant officers cannot find work. There is an acute shortage of preschool facilities. Many people's deputies have included the tackling of these matters in their programs. My thanks to you. I shall say for my part, comrades, that the leadership of the Ministry of Defense and the Main Political Directorate and our commanders and the more than 1-million-strong party organization of the Army and Navy will perform all the tasks determined for them by our Congress and will do everything they can to make our Army always modern and reliable and strong. Thank you. [applause]

6 Jun Session Continues
LD0606163189 Moscow Television Service in Russian 0827 GMT 6 Jun 89

[Relay of the Second Session of the 6 June Congress of People's Deputies proceedings at the Kremlin's Palace of Congresses—live]

[Excerpts] [Passage omitted: Gorbunov announces reopening of session: Deputy Kugultinov of Kalmykiya speaks; Lizichev address]

[Gorbunov] The floor is given to writer Valentin Grigoryevich Rasputin. Next to speak will be Deputy Yarovoy.

[Rasputin] Esteemed comrade deputies! A contrast beween us has unwillingly emerged here, between those who have been through the competitive fights with many candidacies, and those who have come from the public organizations. I have repeatedly heard these days that some are the people's chosen ones, while others have been imposed in order to put brakes on the momentum of restructuring. I also consider that the Law on Elections is not perfect, and that it should eventually be changed in favor of the constituency system only. Can it really be right when one person votes twice or even three times, and as can happen four times—in his own constituency, maybe in the culture fund, in the Union of Writers, and then in the Academy of Sciences, too? Of course, such things could not happen. [applause] However, the further our debates go, the more I become convinced that at the initial stage of democratic elections, representation of public organizations has been necessary for the sake of pluralism, about which we say a lot as a condition of democratic existence. [passage omitted on pluralism to counter antirestructuring forces without excesses]

Pluralism is possible as a variety and multifariousness of public and political opinion. You have imposed on the country a pluralism o morality. That is more dangerous than any bomb. A society either supports morality or does not support it. There is no third way. The timid voices that have broken through here about the supreme importance of culture and spirituality in any civilized country have, it seems to me, been lost on people's ears. We are more involved in various legislative hocus-pocus. Heaven preserve me from being against sensible amendments to the constitution and to laws, but I would be amazed if the new constitution, following Stalin's and Brezhnev's ones, were to be Yevtushenko's one. [applause] I repeat I am not against all kinds of sensible amendments—that is what we are here for—but so far there is nothing in the name of the soul, the dignity, and the cultural and moral outlook of the people. Bread and circuses—that is what has now been surreptitiously prescribed to replace restructuring. We have already prospered in circuses, and circuses of the most dubious kind. There is almost open propaganda for sex and violence, for liberation from all moral norms. Now is a time of tragedies which for some reason follow one on the other, but have you noticed one regular thing? The voice of the announcer telling us about human misfortunes and victims has only just died away, when the screen and the airwaves are filled with the cacophony of musical ravings. But it makes no difference to us; we are free of morality and of compassion.

Where do we go from here? The journal of the Lenin Children's Fund, the magazine SEMYA, is publishing from one issue to another a children's sexual encyclopedia in pictures which even make an adult ill at ease. Probably the chairman of the fund and the editor of the magazine see their mission for the salvation of children deprived of such education. [passage omitted: classics call for moderation; beauty queens compete with minute of silence for victims of events in Georgia]

I recall somebody here attacking Comrade Lukyanov for the growth of crime. There are many reasons, whatever one may say. But one of the main ones, perhaps the most important, is the lack of moral control, the lewdness, the lack of discrimination, and the muck-raking of the mass media, especially publications and programs for young people. [applause] All this has washed into books, the cinema, and the theater in a murky stream, and has started servicing the entertainment industry which parasites on human failings. Our young people died pointlessly in Afghanistan, and they are being equally senselessly crippled by the undeclared war against morality. Appeals to become better are not enough in such cases. We need a law which would consolidate and protect morality, and would ban the propaganda of evil, violence, and vice. [passage omitted; more nihilism and arrogance in today's society]

During the election campaign, the mood of certain groups was felt by some candidates with sensitivity of a barometer. All one of them needed to do was tear up his party card and his popularity would have taken off as if on wings. [applause] I am not a party member and consciously did not join it, observing how many kinds of self-seekers make their way into it. It was an advantage to be a party member, and that is why it lost its authority. Now it has become disadvantageous to be in the party, and moreover dangerous; to leave it at such a moment is by no means courageous, as it is presented to the (?uninitiated), but is the same calculation that previously brought them into the party. [applause] It would have been courageous to do so 10, or even 5 years ago; but haven't you deserted the ship a bit early? Aren't those who reckon the ship is doomed being led astray by their sensitivity? [applause]

More than once lawyers have explained to us here the subtleties of their subject and have shown such an intricate knowledge of laws that it has warmed the heart. If there are such specialists, then we are not far from a law-governed state. However, comrade lawyers, how are we to deal with such tricks, which are far from subtle, as when your colleague, in the interests of being elected a deputy, causes a sensation, connecting a name in the very top echelons of power with crime? Does the confidentiality of investigations no longer exist? Has presumption of innocence, or whatever you call it, been abolished? [applause] Not in the law-governed state which has been in existence for a long time, where perhaps the general and the Politburo member can feel secure, but in the law-governed state toward which, by all accounts, you are leading us—won't the highest-ranking personage and even the most ordinary person, if he has displayed dissident thinking or has displeased someone, be free, if not from physical, then from moral destruction, from slander and the libel machine which is no better than the quartering [as in execution] machine that already seems to be in action? [applause] Does it matter what the condemned man dies of, whether it is from state terror or from the terror of an environment in the state where perhaps the written laws will begin to be observed?

Unfortunately, you did not reply, Mikhail Sergeyevich, to the statement by Deputy Roy Medvedev that every time you have been absent from Moscow, if your absence has coincided with the absence of Aleksandr Nikolayevich Yakovlev, then a situation close to a coup d'etat has arisen. I would like to ask you, is this so? Was there another risk of a coup d'etat during your latest visit to China, when Aleksandr Nikolayevich was also with you? If such an evil person exists in the Politburo, then why does the Politburo put up with him? If Deputy Medvedev's accusations are groundless, why don't you say so? Is it really not obvious that in the struggle for power, which is no secret to anybody here, the first figure, against whom an organized campaign has long been waged, is marked for elimination? There is no need to remind you who will be next. [applause]

All this, esteemed comrade deputies, has alas already happened. Too much of the atmosphere of our congress is recognizable. Vikterinskiy, Milyukov Guchkov and Chkheidze are appearing here. I hope that the Georgian delegation, sorry deputies, will not link that Georgian surname with themselves. With time others will appear, too. The appeals for the period of the State Duma are ridiculous, as is all the prancing about on procedural questions which is frustrating discussion of important matters—not to mention attempts to force one's standpoint on others and a passion for strong expressions. Remember, first the military minister was accused of state treason, and when they got away with this they accused the empress of the same. The rest was a technicality. These are not my words, but it is relevant to repeat here a small edited version of the famous words: You, sirs, need a great shock, we need a great country. [applause]

About the country. Not once since the war has its stability as a power been subjected to such ordeals and shocks as today. We Russians respect and understand the national feelings and problems of all peoples and nationalities of our country, without exception. But we also want others to understand us. The chauvinism and blind arrogance of Russians is the fabrication of those who are playing on your national feelings, esteemed brothers. And one has to say that they are playing on them very skillfully. Russophobia has spread in the Baltic and Georgia, and it is penetrating other republics also, in some less, in others more, but noticeably almost everywhere. Anti-Soviet slogans are being combined with anti-Russian ones, and emissaries from Lithuania and Estonia travel with them to Georgia, creating a united front, and from there local agitators set off Armenia and Azerbaijan. This is not a struggle against the bureaucratic mechanism; it is something else.

Here at the congress we can clearly see the activeness of the Baltic deputies who, by parliamentary means, are trying to obtain the inclusion of amendments to the Constitution which would allow them to say farewell to this country. It is not for me to give advice in such cases. In accordance with the law and your conscience, you will, of course, deal with your own fate. But, in accordance with the Russian habit of rushing to help—I am thinking aloud here—perhaps Russia should come out of the Union if in all your misfortunes...[interrupted by applause] Perhaps you will demand this, if you accuse it of all your misfortunes, and if its underdeveloped and cumbersome nature burden your progressive aspirations. Perhaps that would be better. Incidentally, this would help us to resolve many problems, both of the present and of the future. Oh, what resources, both natural and human we still have! Our hands have not withered. Without fear of being nationalists, we could then pronounce the word Russian, speak about national self-awareness, and before you know it, the mass corruption of the souls of the young would be stopped, we could finally set up our own Academy of Sciences which would back Russian interests, and we could deal with morality and help the people to gather into a single spiritual body.

Believe me, we are fed up with being the scapegoat and enduring mockery and insults. We are told that this is our cross. [applause] However, this cross is becoming increasingly unliftable. We are very grateful to Boris Oleynik and Ion Drutse and other delegates from the republics who have spoken kind words here about the Russian language and Russia. They are permitted to do this; we are not forgiven for doing so. It is not possible at the moment to explain in detail—and anyway you should know this yourselves—that it is not Russia that is to blame for your misfortunes but that general yoke, that general yoke of the administrative-industrial machine, which has been for all of us more terrible than the Mongol yoke, and which has also humiliated and pillaged Russia to such an extent that it can barely breathe. There is no need for detailed explanations, but we would ask you, whether we are to live together or not, not to behave conceitedly toward us. Do not bear malice against him who truly does not deserve it. And it would be best for all of us to correct the situation together. There is, it would seem, every opportunity to do so. [applause]

It is also true that this industrial machine that is destroying nature is much to blame for the difficulties in relations between nationalities. I agree with those who have suggested that here we should not needlessly frighten deputies—and that means the whole country, which is glued to the television—with the gravity of our situation. [bell sounds] There is no need to frighten people. Just a moment. But there is one most important, primordial aspect of our existence in which nothing will be enough, whatever you say and however hard you try to exaggerate the picture, and that is ecology. Nature has long since traced this word not in green but in black. We are trying to build a new and just state, but what is the point of building it if, as a result of our treatment of nature, our years are numbered? Goskompriroda [State Committee for the Protection of Nature] is failing to cope with its functions and, given its subordination, cannot cope. Before it is too late, it must be rescued from its condition possessing no rights, and handed over to the Supreme Soviet. [applause] All wide-scale nature-transforming projects should be discussed by a Supreme Soviet Commission and submitted for final approval to the Congress. (?Otherwise it is a lost cause.)

Otherwise we will continue adopting government resolutions in secret away from the people, such as, for example, the resolution on the construction of five oil and gas chemical complexes in Tyumen Oblast, which are ruinous for the country and excessively destructive for nature, but probably profitable for foreign firms. Otherwise it will be impossible to halt the practice of adopting projects without calling in ecological experts.

And as I come to the end, I would like to address Nikolay Ivanovich Ryzhkov. Nikolay Ivanovich, when you were in Altay Kray, you were, it seems to us, misled by the those pushing for the construction of the Katun hydro-electrical power station, and you publicly agreed, for the whole country to hear, that yes, it must be built. Then at a meeting with the kray party committee, you made the proviso: on condition that a positive ecological expert ecological examination is carried out. But your words were heard only by those who did not want to hear them [as heard], and the first ones, pronounced on television, were taken as a guide to action. For that reason, many deputies are being showered with telegrams and letters with thousands of signatures by the native Altay people, and by tens of thousands of people who are deeply concerned about the Altay. They are being inundated because it is precisely at this time that the expert commission of the Siberian section of the Academy of Sciences and the RSFSR Gosplan is making a decision to approve the construction, and in this way destroy the last unique natural complex in Siberia. We are asking you to examine the Katun case attentively.

Some of us deputies who took part in setting up the Baykal movement for preserving fresh water had to leave the congress for 2 days in order to hold a routine meeting of that international movement on Lake Sevan. We saw a film about the Minomata disease that the Japanese had brought, a disease caused by organic mercury. A fearful film; the terrible pictures showing the torments and the scale of the disaster make your hair stand up on end. There are mercury deposits in the area of the Katun GES [hydroelectric power station], which up to now have aroused doubts in scientists, which I fear disappeared after your unintentional intervention, Nikolay Ivanovich.

For several years now the water at the Angara GES has been (?falling); there is nowhere for the electricity to be sent. Perhaps, instead of ruining the Katun, that electricity should be sent to the altay, but there are other ways, too.

I am just finishing. I should like to end by saying that if we are bringing nationwide referendums into use, it would be good to hold the first referendum on the question of the existence of atomic power stations. Thank you. [applause]

[Gorbunov] Deputy Vladimir Ivanovich Yarovoy, director of the Dvigatel production association, city of Tallinn, has the floor.

[Yarovoy] Esteemed comrade deputies! Esteemed presidium! In seeing us off on our way to the congress the voters handed us a mandate of confidence. At the same time they placed responsibility upon us for working out a program of action for overcoming the difficult economic and political situation in which our country finds itself as a result of the long period of stagnation. Many of those who have spoken have proposed their own models for overcoming this situation, and each deputy has built his own model in accordance with his own vision of the

restructuring concept. Some see a way out of the situation through radical economic reform. Others see the root of the evil in the existing bureaucratic apparatus. A third group places the sovereignty of the republics above all else.

All these are important topical issues which require solution. But I would not be completely honest and principled if I did not—on behalf of my voters—draw the deputies' attention to the situation in our common home, the Union of Soviet Scoialist Republics, and to the need to protect it against a possible split into individual, isolated, national states. The implementation of any models being proposed would then be impossible. I might be asked whether I am not now dramatizing the situation; does that kind of danger exist? No, comrades, I am bold enough to assure you that these are the views of my voters, the working people of major associations and enterprises belonging to the United Council of Labor Collectives of Estonia, of which I have been elected chairman of the presidium.

Let's look: Pressure is falling so quickly on the country's political barometer. More and more regions find themselves in a situation which is heated and unstable. Conflicts are breaking out in various places, in the main on nationality grounds. The chorus of voices putting utimatums to the center for a revision of the country's state establishment, the union treaty, the USSR Constitution, and other acts of legislation controlling relations between the republics and the USSR is sounding more and more loudly in the country. Even at our congress a representative of the Lithuanian delegation tried to organize a demarche on discussing the issue of elections to the USSR Supreme Soviet. Using restructuring as a shield and confusing democracy with demgagogy, numerous groups and organizations of an extremist nature are operating increasingly openly and audaciously. United under the banners of the national liberation movement, they instigate mass demonstrations by the indigenous population—and are essentially unimpeded as they do so—striving to sow a lack of confidence among the people in the existing system, the party and the government, and to inspire hatred against the population that speaks another language.

From whom—or rather from what—do they want to free themselves? From the dictate of central departments and industrial ministries? Or from a part of their own people which speaks a different language? The republican legislative acts that are being passed and the course of events suggest that it is the latter. Not content with successes in their own republic, the latter-day missionaries actively propagandize their views and aspirations in many regions of the country. They also carry it out here at the congress; they do it in the hotel; they do it on the streets of the city of Moscow. Powerful pressure is put upon party and state bodies, and the supreme soviet of the republic, which forces the latter to make concessions even where it is essential for firmness to be displayed. In turn, constant tractability by the leading echelon and its loss of the initiative have led to a situation in which restructuring in Estonia has been turned into a one-way street, where there is no room for the majority of the non-Estonian part of the population which does not support the cult of the priority of nationality. [applause]

Legislative activity has begun to acquire a character which is increasingly in contradiction to the law. The republic violated the USSR Constitution for the first time—part of the article 74—on 16 November last year, when a session of the Supreme Soviet of the Estonian SSR [Soviet Socialist Republic] adopted well-known amendments to the Constitution, and the declaration on sovereignty. The USSR Supreme Soviet Presidium deemed them to be invalid, thereby making a negative appraisal of similar actions. It would be logical if the leadership of the republic were to insist that the anticonstitutional article should be repealed, but that did not happen. The decision by the presidium was merely noted. A legal conflict arose between a union republic and the union state, which remains unsolved to this day. Not only that: On 18 May this year, this conflict was worsened when the Estonian Supreme Soviet adopted a law on the bases of the financial autonomy of the Estonian SSR, based on the aforementioned amendments, and went yet further on the path of rejecting the Constitution of the Soviet Union, and of blocking the application of the union codex of labor laws, the legislation on state enterprises, and a number of other legislative acts on the territory of the republic.

A paradoxical situation has arisen, when we, citizens of the Soviet Union, do not know under whose laws we live. Under these conditons, can one speak seriously of aspiring toward a state based on law, which is constantly proclaimed when the government of the republic needs to adopt this or that decision? Can we seriously believe in the leadership's assertions on the socialist nature of the transformations being implemented, on their desire to develop and strengthen the socialist federation, if we can see the opposite happening in front of our eyes—the creative unions, public organizations, and voluntary societies of Estonia breaking their links with their central organs? An alternative structure is arising. The pioneer organization has ceased to exist in Estonia; the Komsomol is on the verge of being dissolved; the question of the autonomization of the Estonian Communist Party is being persistently thrown around.

And now look how quickly the mass media have been restructured. The propagandizing and extolling of petty bourgeois ideals and values are being conducted on an enviable scale among the population. At the same time, people are being encouraged to despise everything that is Soviet. I can give an example of the anti-Soviet, anti-Russian mood that is being whipped up. Here you are, as an example: an article by Herbert Vaino, from 30 May, literally during the time when the congress has been working, in the paper of the Tallinn party town committee, [word indistinct] VERCHERNYY TALLINN. I quote: If Stalin—his nationality is irrelevant—replaced

the Lenin plan for a federation with a unitary Russian central power, and if the Russian people allowed him to do that and to proclaim themselves throughout the whole Soviet Union to be unique and great, this means that in the eyes of the little peoples responsiblity for the distorted Stalinist nationalist policy lies not only with the Stalinist regime and the stagnation regime, but with the Russian nation. Perhaps people don't like this, but it is a fact, and if the responsiblity for the crimes of the Stalinist period, of marking time in the period of stagnation, falls on us Communists, as members of the ruling party, regardless of what our personal role was, then the Russian Communists bear double responsibility for the distorted Stalinist national policy.

Over the last year and a half you can find any number of such articles.

The idea is constantly being expressed that Estonia's entry into the Soviet Union was an act of violence and occupation, which brought grief to the Estonian people, who could be living better today than in next-door Finland. This is why some of the ideologists of the People's Front are trying persistently to get Moscow to admit that the Molotov-Ribbentrop Pact of 23 August 1939, and the secret protocol attached to it, were invalid from the moment they were signed. No, it is not for the sake of establishing historical truth that they are showing such persistence, but with the aim of returning the republic to the situation of 1939, and if people used to talk about this before in whispers in cosy cafes, and in the quiet of creative workshops, now it is being spoken out loudly so that the whole world may hear.

On 14 May this year, the so-called Baltic Assembly which took place in Tallinn, attended by heads of the National Fronts of Lithuania, Latvia, and Estonia, definitively dispelled the myth of the true aims of these movements. And although one of the resolutions addressed to Mikhail Sergeyevich Gorbachev gives him an assurance of their devotion to the policy of restructuring, and expresses support for the Soviet leader, the main idea lying in another document—and I quote—is: The Baltic Assembly expresses the aspiration of its nations for state sovereignty in a neutral and demilitarized Baltiskandia.

Comrades, why I am saying all this? First of all, so that every deputy here in the hall should feel the real threat to our federation, and should realize that in the shape of those who dream of a return to the times of the bourgeois republic, we have serious and well-organized force which is capable of extreme steps to achieve its aims.

Let me note, by the way, that there are about 60 people's deputies here among us who took part in the work of the Baltic Assembly and voted for its decisions. The CPSU Central Committee and the Supreme Soviet Presidium are well aware of how events are developing in the Baltic states.

However, the numerous messages from labor collectives, primary party organizations, and private citizens expressing alarm and disquiet over the future of Estonia continue to be ignored. One gets the impression that drowning people are supposed to be rescued by other drowning people. Can you really believe this standpoint to be the correct one, when you remember the sad experience of Sumgait, Nagorno-Karabakh, and now Tbilisi and Fergana?

In view of the limited time I have to speak, I cannot present all the facts, materials and documents that would serve to back up our anxiety over the destiny of the Soviet state. And therefore I shall pass the material over to the presidium, and at the same time submit the following proposals for the congress: First, at this very congress, to draw up and adopt a declaration on the fundamental principles and stages of strengthening the Soviet socialist federation, and to this end form a special commission from among deputies representing all union and autonomous republics, krays and oblasts, and including the leading Soviet scholars and experts in the field of the state and law.

Second, to commission the USSR Supreme Soviet to draw up and put forward for nationwide discussion a USSR draft law on a federation, and simultaneously the text of amendments and additions to the Constitution, the fundamental law, the law to be adopted at the Second Congress of People's Deputies.

I believe it would be expedient for the draft law to have a provision that would promote equality of conditions, rights, and actual opportunities in republics, including the Russian Soviet Federated Socialist Republic [RSFSR], and that would guarantee the dynamic and all-around development of regions in proportion to their economic potential and the size of their population. It should clearly record the legal status of ethnic minorities living outside their national territorial lands.

Third, to speed up the elaboration of a USSR draft law on citizenship and delineation of the powers of the Union of Soviet Socialist Republics and the Union Republics, strengthening the legal status of autonomous republics, krays and oblasts, and the free development and equal use of the languages of the peoples of the USSR. The new Supreme Soviet body is to guarantee the urgent drawing up legal documents, covering the whole of the country, that would provide the opportunity for all union and autonomous republics, krays and oblasts to discuss and agree with them at the study stage.

Comrade deputies—another thought: Earnest debate is going on at our congress. Criticism is being levelled at certain people. Lack of confidence is being voiced. That was directed at our esteemed Chingiz Aytmatov, at our president, and at the Politburo. And as confirmation of what has been said today, I support the blasphemy levelled at the Vladimir Ilyich Lenin mausoleum. [as heard] However, the deputies who spoke immediately

afterwards restored the balance of fairness, and we in this hall rallied round to support them. I consider it my duty and the demand of my electors to restore the balance of fairness after a speech by a deputy from the Estonian group. That was on 27 May, while I was striving to get to this podium.

At the time, unsubstantiated and unfounded criticism was levelled at Academician Gustav Naan and the newspaper PRAVDA. We have received a flood of messages from our electors on this point. They are disgusted at this speech [by the Estonian deputy] and the theses it contained about confrontation as the norm in relations. An example of this norm was given as restructuring in Estonia, where confrontation supposedly does not impede the maintenance of normal relations. Yes, to some extent that is true: We do not have direct clashes, pogroms or refugees. There are no tanks, armored personnel carriers or black tickets [as heard]. But there is genuine opposition. There is a growing alienation and mistrust between the two large sections of the populace. Strike committees have been set up that demand active measures. Civil committees are being set up that demand our withdrawal from the Soviet Union. And now we hear more and more calls for the creation of an administrative-territorial unit in the northeast of Estonia, where the majority of the non-Estonian part of the population is concentrated. Is this really what we should be striving for? That is the other side of the truth, about which the speaker [Estonian deputy] kept silent. And incidentally, he said nothing about how in fact the confrontation is combined with respect for Gustav Naan, one of the few who put forward a scientifically-based position on the demographic situation that gives the lie to all the fabrications regarding the demise of the Estonian nation. Without finding any arguments to prove Naan wrong, as though on command, the local press has started persecuting the academician, making him out to be an enemy of the Estonian nation. The reaction was not far behind: The academician has been literally deluged by numerous telephone calls, letters, threats and insults. And for this reason, standing here on this podium, I declare my disagreement with the speech of one of our deputies, and I speak out in defense of the Estonian academician Gustav Naan. [applause]

The newspaper PRAVDA hardly needs the defense of my electors, and therefore I am extremely grateful, and on behalf of my electors I congratulate Afanasyev, PRAVDA's editor-in-chief, and also the newspapers KOMSOMOLSKAYA PRAVDA, IZVESTIYA, and TRUD, for having found the courage to cover the pages of their newspapers with the truth about the events that are taking place in Estonia.

Comrade deputies. I came to the podium with one aim in mind. My main point is that the voice of electors, the voice of the majority of working people, and the voice of the majority of the working class working at enterprises that belong to the Associated Council of Labor Collectives, is not being heeded in the republic. It was not desired that the voice of my electors should be heard from the podium today.

Vladimir Ilich Lenin once wrote that a state law must be published by which any measure that involves any sort of privilege for one nation, and that upsets the equality of nations or violates the rights of a national minority, should be declared illegal and invalid, and that any citizen of the state should have the right to demand that such a measure be scrapped as anticonstitutional, and that those people who tried putting it into effect should be liable to criminal prosecution. Today, as we strive to remove the distortions in the nationalities policy that were allowed to occur in the period of Stalinism and of stagnation with regard to the union republics, we have immediately—even earlier than expected—allowed distortions to occur in interethnic relations within the republic itself and within the region, since we have not taken into account the altered demographic situation and the structure of the population. It is no longer just one man, but tens of thousands of his electors, more than 100,000 of whom work in enterprises of the Associated Council of Labor Collectives—and if their families are counted, then that amounts to hundreds of thousands, presumably—who must now be reckoned with. Thank you for your attention. [applause] [passage omitted: Yarovoy reads out telegram from veteran soldiers about lack of housing; Godlanskiy speaks about need for deputies to be polite to each other]

[Gorbunov] I call Comrade Shakhanov, Mukhtar. The next to speak will be Comrade Aydak, Arkadiy Pavlovich.

[Shakhanov] Exalted congress, I would like to make the following statement on behalf of the 19 USSR people's deputies from Kazakhstan, to prevent renewed outbursts of interethnic strife in the acute situation which exists in the republic. Since the question of the events in Georgia was raised at the congress, the group of deputies from Kazakhstan have received a multitude of telegrams and collective letters from their voters. They are dissatisfied that even with this level of glasnost and openness at the congress we have not raised the issue of the Alma-Ata events of December 1986, when, for the first time in the country, trenching shovels and official dogs were used against peaceful protestors, and girls were beaten up with truncheons and leather boots.

All this happened before the well-known decree on demonstrations and rallies. The number of protestors who died is being concealed from the public to this day. According to incomplete data, around 2,000 people were arrested, many of whom have been sentenced to lengthy terms of imprisonment. Thousands were expelled from academic establishments or dismissed from their jobs.

On coming under attack for the first time the era of stagnation bared its ferocious teeth, to which hundreds of politically-unprepared boys and girls, their lives ruined forever, fell victim.

For the sake of justice it has to be noted that the republic's party organizations, led by that outstanding internationalist figure Koblin, Comrade Kolbin, went to great lengths to improve the situation. But the truth about the events in Alma-Ata and the unlawful actions of the soldiers and internal troops remains secret to this day. This is why there are a number of unhealthy rumors in the republic, which cast a shadow on the friendship of the peoples and give rise to ethnic hostility. In connection with these we firmly request that a commission consisting of people's deputies representing different regions and nationalities be set up to establish the real truth about the events in Alma-Ata that December. After those events the CPSU Central Committee issued a decision on the work of the Kazakh republican party organization in the internationalist and patriotic education of the working people. That decision describes the events as a manifestation of Kazakh nationalism. One can accuse 5,000 people, 10,000 or 100,000 people, but one cannot accuse the entire Kazakh people of nationalism. The words Kazakh nationalism are an accusation against the entire Kazakh people. Therefore we request that justice be restored, that the harsh and undeserved accusations be withdrawn from the people. By their history and with their blood, the Kazakh people have frequently demonstrated their loyalty to the friendship of the peoples.

A CPSU Central Committee plenum is scheduled for the near future, but many of the people's deputies concerned will not be able to take part in that forum, since they are not members of the Central Committee. Therefore the group of Kazakhstan deputies proposes that here at our congress we should adopt a decree giving state status to the languages of the indigenous nationalities of the union and atuonomous republics, the autonomous oblasts, national territories, and small ethnic groups before the plenum, and also resolve the now very strained issue of the destiny of the Soviet Turks and Crimean Tatars, who to this day feel exiled in their own country. Allow me to hand over to the presidium some of the voters' demands, including letters to the congress signed by well-known writers, scientists, and young people in the republic. Thank you. [applause] [passage omitted: Deputy Aydak on need for agrarian commission]

[Plotnikov] Comrades, I'm Plotnikov, deputy from the Komsomol. Esteemed comrade chairman, esteemed deputies, the Supreme Soviet is soon to resolve what seems to me to be a very important matter—the membership of the standing commissions and committees. During the congress, we have already witnessed the way in which a number of candidacies were lost in elections to the Soviet of the Union. Aside from that, the name of Yuriy Chemodanov, who disappeared from the secret-vote ballot-paper, is well known to us all today. In drawing up the list of candidates, the views of oblast delegations regarding the candidacies of our young deputies Tsigelnikov and Uvarov were ignored. Individual details are being added to this picture even now. It turns out that during the drawing up of the membership of the committee on youth affairs, the names of a number of deputies have again been lost. They include Gubin and Minin. This may be accidental, but one could do without such accidents. This is all the more relevant in that in filling out the forms for commissions and committees, a whole number of deputies wrote down several at one go. Thus, the principle of duplication is in operation, and this is on no account acceptable when such important matters are being dealt with. [passage omitted: we must learn from our mistakes]

[Unidentified female deputy] I want to say, esteemed comrades, that since Friday we have had a terrible tragedy in the country, which has disrupted the functioning of our congress. We all remember how our congress ended on Friday evening—nationwide contempt for Academician Sakharov was publicly voiced. On what grounds can one person speak on behalf of the entire people? I have received telegrams, heaps of telegrams from the Far East, asking me to convey support, respect, and admiration for Sakharov. [applause] I want to state, on behalf of the people of the Far East, that it is wrong to slander the people's conscience at this congress, and I ask that if he has been guilty of something, you should allow him to speak in peace, without clapping him down or shutting him up.

[Gorbunov] Comrades, I now have some very brief but very important messages. First, it is proposed that we all now go to pay our respects to Lenin, and to lay wreaths to the Vladimir Ilyich Lenin Mausoleum and the tomb of the Unknown Soldier on behalf of our congress. [applause] It is proposed that the wreaths be laid now, immediately after our session ends. [passage omitted: procedural announcements; session declared closed]

Gorbachev Meets People During Congress Interval
LD0606223289 Moscow Television Service in Russian 1430 GMT 6 Jun 89

[Video report from Moscow's Red Square of wreath-laying ceremony at Lenin Mausoleum and the Tomb of the Unknown Soldier attended by Gorbachev and other members of the CPSU Central Committee Politburo on 6 June during a break in the USSR Congress of People's Deputies proceedings; including recording of Gorbachev meeting and speaking with inhabitants and guests of Moscow; from the "Vremya" newscast—opening paragraphs read by announcer]

[Text] Today in the interval of the morning session, the participants in the Congress of USSR People's Deputies paid a visit to the mausoleum of Vladimir Ilich Lenin, the founder of the Communist Party and creator of the first socialist state in the world, and laid a wreath. [video shows group of leaders approaching mausoleum behind a large wreath carried by two soldiers; visible in the first shot are, from right to left of screen: Nikonov, Vorotnikov, Shcherbitskiy, Talyzin, Chebrikov, Ligachev, Slyunkov, Ryzhkov, Medvedev; video then shows the wreath being laid and the leaders lined up on the steps of the mausoleum; in the first row, standing from left to right are: Lukyanov, Gorbachev, Ryzhkov; in the second row Zaykov, Biryukova, Medvedev, Ligachev, Slyunkov, Vorotnikov; visible behind these are Chebrikov, Shcherbitskiy, Nikonov, Talyzin; other participants are seen behind, tailing off away from the mausoleum]

On the crimson ribbon of the wreath is the inscription: to Vladimir Ilich Lenin, from the Congress of USSR People's Deputies.

A wreath was also laid at the tomb of the unknown soldier. [video shows leaders bowing their heads, then a march past of troops; as they march past the leadership lineup may be seen from left to right of screen: Vorotnikov, Zaykov, Slyunkov, Gorbachev, Lukyanov, Ryzhkov, Medvedev; video then shows small crowd gathered in Red Square]

Here also on Red Square, there was a conversation between Mikhail Sergeyevich Gorbachev and the inhabitants and guests of Moscow. [video shows Gorbachev speaking]

[Begin recording] [Gorbachev] The fact that you are raising the topic of the position of a deputy—I accept it completely, and in my view that is the mood of all of us. And so even before the elaboration of our new status, we have to register such things....

[Lukyanov, interrupting] [words indistinct] must be adopted.

[Gorbachev] Adopted. And we want to introduce this, simply at the congress, where on the one hand one part of this decision is an instruction to the Supreme Soviet to prepare, in time for the fall congress, a law on the status of the deputy and to distribute it on the eve of the congress, but actually at the present congress, in issuing the instruction to do the elaborate work, to actually state some of the points of the clauses. Ones such that it is clear that the position of a deputy is different. And that is.... [Gorbachev changes thought] But, you know, if we do things like this, and the session lacks the reason to turn the country round in such a way that it starts working [passage indistinct].

[Unidentified woman] Yes, and they were working in the regions.

[Unidentified man] So that we in the regions can show we do not trust those leaders who are not working.

[Gorbachev] Well, that's nonsense. Such a formulation is already common. Such rights do exist. We held a meeting in (?Asha).

[Unidentified man] Yes.

[Gorbachev] And they were standing like this there, and everyone was having a talk. It's clear they had undergone a terrible ordeal; before one's eyes. People see all that, one has to say. Our people (?endured) such a difficult situation. I am surprised: so much endurance and self-possession that they even started to give us support. Well, such things happen, and probably will again. Mikhail Sergeyevich it's necessary. [as heard], Well, so we discussed all this, and then they say, there is our town. The town is like this. And these little towns—this is a special problem—little towns in Russia, and in the Ukraine, I've come across them....

[Lukyanov] [words indistinct].

[Gorbachev] And there were even Demidov enterprises there [reference to 18th and 19th century Russian industrialists], and the fate of these little towns is difficult, often even more difficult than the villages. You know, they began to raise a question: Well, we are now giving you greater opportunity to do things like this. Suddenly the question arises, well, what are you talking about, Mikhail Sergeyevich, eh? You understand that something or other, here in the regions isn't working out. When will it work out? Well, as you know, and they just don't want to change the order as it used to be. And here we are speaking, making a noise, and things in the meantime fail to change. This was discussed directly in the presence of the first secretaries who were there.

And so I say, ok, listen, you see who enjoys real authority here. You gather in your own soviets; elections will take place, they took place in a party meeting; there will be elections to local soviets, and you decide there who you have confidence in, who enjoys real authority. You arrange things so that these people now are put in charge.

[Unidentified man] But there are also people who go for cheap authority.

[Gorbachev] Yes, they do exist; they are loud-mouthed, just loud-mouthed, loud-mouthed.

[Unidentified man] But it is necessary for legal-...[corrects himself] for leaders to be protected by law, through the Supreme Soviet.

[Gorbachev] I think that once a person has been elected, once trust has been shown in him, once all that has taken place, all laws, everything, should back him up, so that he dos not go around like a poor relation, even after he has been elected.

[Unidentified man] In the role of a supplicant.

[Gorbachev] Yes, indeed. He should be put forward in a democratic manner; singled out as a person in whom the people now show [trust]. But, subsequently, it is his powers that come into play and he should go about his business in a confident manner—this is the only possible way. It is here, so to speak, that there is a coincidence between, on the one hand, democracy in the process of putting forward and selection, so that the people know; all the more so because we say to everyone: Well, you will live within the collective through financial autonomy, so how will you go about your business? But then working people within each collective have the right to say: Then give us the rights, too. Why have we come to this? Give us also the right to determine for ourselves what the collective should be like. Through financial autonomy you wish to make us carry the yoke of responsibility—let us agree to call it that—but you will not give us any rights at all? Oh, no, give them to us, so that the council of the labor collective can step in, and you should have a circle of specialists in whom we can believe and trust. Well, this has taken place. And subsequently, this should be put to use: Once trust has been vested in one, one should enjoy sovereignty. One cannot rule in fits and starts.

[Unidentified man] Mikhail Sergeyegich, how do you react to the terrible events in China?

[Gorbachev] What? We made a statement on this through the congress.

[Same man] (?more terrible than) [word indistinct]

[Gorbachev] Moreover...you've heard, isn't that so?

[Same man] Yes, yes.

[Gorbachev] Well, you know, I spoke there; we happened to be in China at a moment when there was, so to speak, some sort of beginning of these events and they were acquiring a mass character. There were letters to us, to the delegation.

Well, of course, I think that any delegation and any country and any government should, of course, above all proceed from this: that within each state there are processes of its own under way and each should bear responsibility for the fact that, naturally, we do, after all, worry and see and are watching the course these processes are assuming. [sentence as heard] And we said there—I also said at a news conference—we are for dialogue between state and party bodies alike with the working people and also with the student fraternity. It is, nevertheless, only upon a path of dialogue that answers can be found to all questions. I am in favor of this, now, too.

[Unidentified man] President Bush, he (?acted)....

[Gorbachev interrupting] Well, let President Bush act the way he sees fit. We won't incessantly (?chastise) the United States! [laughter]

Soviet of Nationalities Holds First Session 6 Jun
*LD0706123989 Moscow Television Service in Russian
1200 GMT 6 Jun 89*

[Relay of the Soviet of Nationalities first session held in the Kremlin on 6 June—live]

[Excerpts] [Gorbachev] Until we have been told how many people have been registered—because we have to start our work from this—perhaps we should act in the same as they did in the chamber of the Soviet of the Union. Requests have already been voiced and sent to the congress that the chairman should not stand up and loom over the speaker and the Presidium. In general, this is a tradition at all gatherings, especially at those functioning on a permanent basis—take, for example, the United Nations, or the parliamentary tradition, and so on. I myself have attended many of them and have seen that, therefore I think we can come to an agreement about this, so to speak, because this is a matter of work, a working process, and a working situation. Well then, we will agree upon this. When you start working here, this is the way it will go. In the absence of new data, 239 deputies have been registered, though comrades are still coming. Later I will make an additional announcement.

[Lukyanov] How many?

[Gorbachev] Two hundred fifty-two. First of all, before the opening, I would like to cordially congratulate you all, dear comrades, on your election to the USSR Supreme Soviet by the first Congress of People's Deputies, and to the chamber of the Soviet of Nationalities. I would also like to note, to voice two thoughts, perhaps, two ideas. First of all, this relates to both the congress and the Supreme Soviet and the new government. Of the new bodies of power, Soviet people expect serious work improvements by all bodies of the upper echelons and link serious improvements, solutions to urgent problems, an advance of restructuring, and real changes in our society with the improvement of their activity and their more efficient work, both in the legislative area and the exectuive area.

You may perhaps have noticed and felt currently how attentively the people have been following all the sessions of the congress and what response it evokes; it is rumored, however, that there is a negative point, to the effect that the situation is such that many people have left their work places and are not working in the country. This is not very good. We have advised our media to broadcast in the evenings and at night so that people can make up for what they miss while they work.

Well, this emphasizes once again how our (?people) are interested in having the new organs of supreme power operate fruitfully and function effectively. That's the first thing. Second, the specifics in the work of the Soviet of Nationalities as one of the chambers of the Supreme Soviet to a significant, to a decisive extent, are linked also with another circumstance: It is a question of the Supreme Soviet, of one of its chambers in a federated state, where there are so many nations and nationalities living, where such a huge world over a period of many decades has been seeking ways for the better, for the benefit of each people, by means of cooperation and interaction. Life, and what the congress also shows, convincingly shows, is that we have achieved much together in a federated state, helping each other, strengthening and developing our cooperation; but also, by reason of known causes again connected to a significant extent with the deformations which were committed on our path following October. I mean in both the economic, social, and political processes, it has had a grave effect both on interethnic relations and also on the conduct of nationalities policy.

It has turned out that on the one hand, as a result of the implementations of the aims of October, our peoples emerged on to a broad road of development and advanced far in their socio-economic development and cultural development, particularly in education. The apperance of national intelligentsias is connected with this, as is the development of feelings of dignity of every people, every person, representatives of every nation, and nationality. The existence of a large number of intellectuals, scientific intellectuals, is accompanied by the fact that all people are deeply studying the roots of their historical past, all the upheavels which have been encountered by this or that people. This is fully understandable. The people are concerned and want to know their past; they are concerned by the problems of the present and want to dream about and forecast the future of its own people from the viewpoint of life, living standards, from the viewpoint of cultural development, language and so forth.

All of this is living reality and we are seeing how everything here is not simple, how many problems have emerged. Naturally, to a significant extent, this will determine responsibility, and it also assumes a high level of work of the Soviet of Nationalities at this state of perestroyka, when we have embarked on the path of really giving, as it were, a genuine sound to Lenin's nationalities policy in conditions of the-present achievements and the present stage of development in our society.

That is probably one of the main areas of restructuring, so crucial that when I heard people say at the congress, let us not speak only of the union and relations among the nationalities and ethnic groups but also of restructuring, of the economy, I must say that such a way of formulating the issue is incorrect. It is a component—the main, inalienable, organic, crucial component of restructuring. Without it our union cannot live, develop, or move forward. Without restructruing we cannot live or gather momentum.

I wanted to make these two brief remarks to give immediately a kind of direction, so to speak, to both our work and our session today. That is why, permit me, once I have said these words and welcomed you in your capacity as members of the USSR Supreme Soviet Soviet of Nationalities, to declare our work open. At this session, we should resolve the issue, in accordance with the constitution, of the chairman of the Soviet of Nationalities and his deputy. However, as we discussed at the Council of Elders—and those who took part will remember that we had agreed to act as follows: To proceed in a more democratic way in that respect, and that is what we did at the Soviet of the Union, namely that we should resolve the issue of the chamber's chairman at this session, and then let the chairman of the chamber talk to and establish contact with the delegations, to work out some ideas, so to speak, and present them at the subsequent session, as to the best way to proceed, how to make the presentation. I think we should also do the same. It would be more correct and this would enable us to immediately channel it all back, so to speak, to the chamber itself from the very outset. We have agreed that deputy Khudaybergenova of the Council of Edlers will speak on the nomination of a chairman of the Soviet of Nationalities, of your chamber. Is she her or not; we shall ask her: Go ahead, please, comrade Khudaybergenova! A deputy from Uzbekistan, first secretary of an oblast party committee.

[Khudaybergenova] Comrade deputies! on instructions from the Council of Elders, I am submitting for your examination the motion to elect deputy Rafik Nishanovich Nishanov as chairman of the USSR Supreme Soviet Soviet of Nationalities.

Comrade Nishanov was born in 1926. He is an Uzbek. He has been a member of the CPSU sicne 1949. He has a higher education. He is a candidate of historical sciences. He possesses extensive work experience in party and Soviet bodies. He was elected chairman of the Uzbek Soviet Socialist Republic Supreme Soviet Presidium and deputy chairman of the USSR Supreme Soviet Presidium. Comrade Nishanov has been involved in diplomatic work for many years. At present he is first secretary of the Uzbek Communist Party Central Committee. He is a man of principle, exacting both to himself and his subordinates. He knows how to listen to others and how to draw correct conclusions. As a person he is responsive. He is distinguished with kindness, simplicity, and understanding.

[Gorbachev] Very well, are there any questions? So, the mission is accomplished. The desire of the Council of Elders has been ascertained and now.... [Gorbachev changes thought] Thank you! What do the members of the Soviet—deputies—think about it? [chorus of "endorse, endorse"] Comrade Nishanov, go ahead please; perhaps you will be asked something or told something, or perhaps you would like to say something yourself? To start with, are there any questions?

[Voice] Go ahead, please.

[Unidentified speaker] I have a question on the events in Fergana.

[Gorbachev] Go ahead, please!

[Same unidentified speaker] A question on the events in Fergana.

[Gorbachev] Yes, here you go. This is exactly your role, and [words indistinct].

[Same unidentified speaker] What was your role in this?

[Nishanov] First of all, one must say that the events that have acquired an interethnic nature of late started with insignificant commonplace disagreements. Touching upon the history of the Meskhetian Turks' inhabitation of the Fergana Valley, I would like to stress that 45 years ago the Uzbeks received Meskhetian Turks like brothers and sisters and provided for them all the conditions necessary for life, well-being, work, and education.

[Unidentified speaker] How many of them reside there?

[Nishanov] There are 60,000 Meskhetian Turks residing in Uzbekistan, including 12,000 residing in Fergana Valley. They all are provided with corresponding work and care, and they actively participate in all the organs of state power and government. There are members of party committees and local soviets among them. Everything was going all right. In the last few years, on more than one occasion, Meskhetian Turks voiced the demand that they be returned to their native places.

Recently, in connection with the convocation of the Congress, such calls have become somewhat more active but clashes began from an absolutely insignificant and commonplace event at a market place, during the sale and purchase of agricultural produce. Because of the high prices, a Meskhetian Turk adressed a female vendor who was selling the produce she had grown in a rude manner. In the end, he overturned a plate with strawberries, and citizens who were at the scene took that as an insult and a fight broke out. It was possible to end the fight but some time later, a small group of Meskhetian Turks attacked a group of local youth and killed one of them. Measures were taken and everything calmed down, and for almost a week everybody was in a normal state. But one week later, unexpectedly for the local organs and for the Meskhetian Turks themselves as well as for the Uzbek part of the population, a large group of young people aged from 15-16 to 20-22, some of them in a somewhat intoxicated state from alcohol or drugs, having armed themselves with sticks and so on, started attacking dwellings of the Meskhetian Turks. And the Uzbek youth having armed themselves with sticks, chains, axes, and rods, went on a rampage and beat those who they met on their way, setting fire to some houses belonging to Meskhetian Turks. This tragic incident, which was in fact a manifestation of vandalism, ended in a somewhat tragic way. According to our data, about 50 have died so far, including 35 or more Meskhetian Turks—this is being clarified now—10 Uzbeks, 1 Tajik, and 1 Russian, the latter being among those who were establishing order and happened to be in the area. The event concerned strictly Uzbek and Meskhetian Turks. For some time, the situation was out of control, and during that time several houses were set on fire. Thanks to the urgent measures taken by Union organs, republican organs, and also by the forces of the Republican and union Ministries of Internal Affairs, the situation is now fully under control, the Meskhetian Turks are either in their permanent residences or in the military garrison where we evacuated some of them yesterday and the day before; they were lodged in barracks, provided with room and board, and they are now safe.

By decree of the Presidium of the Supreme Soviet of the Uzbek Soviet Socialist Republic, a curfew has been imposed in all rayons where these clashes flared up. Order is being maintained. Yesterday and today, there have been no further complications. The situation is under control, and we hope that the local party and Soviet bodies, the administrative bodies, will fully succeed in isolating the situation and in ensuring proper order.

I have been there and have spoken to the Meskhetian Turks where there are concentrations of them, and also with those whom we have accomodated in a military garrison. On behalf of the Party organization and all working people of the republic, I condemned the vandalism of the Uzbek youth, and expressed profound condolences and apologies to our meskhetian Turk brothers and sisters. I believe we will carry out our internationalist duty to the end, and will create the conditions they require. By and large, the working people of Uzbekistan—Uzbeks, Russians, Tajiks, Kazakhs, Karakalpaks, Turkmens, and Kirgizians who live there—are hospitable, hard-working, and modest people. I believe the acts of vandalism meet with universal condemnation, and it is fitting that we should draw the proper lessons from this, so that nothing similar should ever happen again.

[?Gorbachev] Please go ahead, Comrade [name indistinct]

[Speaker, name indistinct] Tell us please, Rafik Nishanovich, have any conflict situations arisen before on ethnic grounds, and if so how did you manage to settle those?

[Gorbachev] The question is: have ethnic-based conflicts flared up before, and if so how were they settled?

[Nishanov] Isolated clashes have flared up before, but exclusively over run of the mill matters. There have not been such cases on ethnic grounds before. And therefore, that is the first such instance on ethnic grounds. Yes, please.

[Unidentified speaker] You have been nominated to a very important post. The person should be very objective. You are just such a man, and we respect you. But in this connection I have for you several...well, I would say one question: On the subject of...[speaker changes thought] this mistake was committed neither by you, nor by us, nor by our generation, but the mistake falls on us to rectify, because glasnost and restructuring gives us this opportunity to speak loudly about this. I am talking...you know this very well... about the fact that (?some) Tajiks of Bukhara and Samarkand once had 'Uzbek' written in their passports. You know of this matter. You and our leaders have had many meetings on this subject, but the question remains... unresolved. What do you think, how will this matter be resolved. Is it an issue or not? What do you think about the further progress of this?

[Nishanov] I understand the question. That some members of the Tajik population living in Uzbekistan have had 'Uzbek' written in their passports under nationality, and that some of the Uzbeks living in Tajikistan had 'Tajik' nationality written in their passports is known to all. On this subject, the leadership and the working people of Tajikistan and Uzbekistan, we all have the same attitude toward this. Everyone should have the complete right to write anything he wants under the heading 'nationality'. In particular, we did this during the census. Furthermore, Comrade Makhkamov, first secretary of the Central Committee of the Communist Party of Tajikistan spoke of this from the podium of our Congress...we and the Tajik leadership have asked the government of the USSR to allow this on a legal basis, by some directive. Therefore, I do not consider this to be an issue. We have complete mutual understanding. Everyone has the complete right to give his nationality as anything he wants.

[Unidentified speaker] We are well aware that, citing Lenin and the constitution, in our country equal rights of all nations and peoples living on our territory is declared. At the same time, again citing the constitution, we differentiate four different political and legal statuses of nations and peoples. How do you conceive a solution to this question, a definite political and legal nonsense? That is the first question. The second question is of a more private nature: At our congress some union republics have already reached the second and third rank of representatives of union republics, while a whole number of autonomous republics have not yet spoken once.

[Nishanov] To the first question, without speaking of any juridical or other aspects of the question you have raised, I would limit myself to the following reply: All nations and ethnic groups of the Soviet Union must be guaranteed equal rights. In what form this needs to be further elaborated is a matter for our chamber. At the congress there is naturally very acute and principled talk about the ways of our future development. Proposals are being worked out. Naturally, each wants to expound all the sore questions which in fact do exist in all regions, in all republics, in all autnomous formations. And the comrades; wish to ascend the tribune and expound their views is completely explicable. Second, I would not say that some national formations have been restricted by anything. Nothing has restricted them. It is simply that time does not permit everyone to speak. Some republics have been represented in the debates by two speakers, others by one speaker, and some republics by five or six. It is simply that our machinery has not yet been developed. The comrades who have spoken from the congress tribune have rightly said that we need to develop the machinery so that any autonomous formations, any national formations may feel themselves in all respects as having full rights. I think our chamber in this respect needs to accumulate the experience of all republics, all autonomous formations, all nations, and work out some kind of rules which would be listed as standing orders, and we would not bear a grudge against one another.

[Gorbachev] Any more questions, comrades?

[Unidentified speaker] I read and heard about full national rights back in 1924, but since 1924 nothing has been done. How will you correct this? These are terrible mistakes.

[Nishanov] Well, first of all I would like to say that it is not I who will correct them, but together with you we shall work it out and amend it. As regards the year 1924, I would like, if you will permit me, to divide our nationalities policy into the period of the life of Vladimir Ilich Lenin and after Lenin. The big mistake consists in the fact that after the death of Vladimir Ilich Lenin, the nationalities policy was deformed. One thing was said in words but in practice a different [word indistinct] was implemented. Apart from what we have achieved—each republic, each nation, and each ethnic group has its achievements—there were the most blatant deviations, mistakes, and distortions. I think that our chamber, as Mikhail Sergeyevich has just stressed, too, in his introductory speech, faces simply enormous work in order to elaborate the juridical and legal and legislative basis, and work out ways of economic, social, and cultural development in order that whatever the population of the nation or ethnic group it should possess all rights to full enjoyment of its sovereignty, its independence, and its uniqueness. That is how I would reply.

[Unidentified speaker] Rafik Nishanovich, this question is directed to you—and probably to all of us, too, generally. The nationalities' questions are much too complicated. it is namely they which prevent us from being seriously involved in restructuring, and in a dynamic and active manner. We all have a whole host of problems, of all-union problems. All that pulls us back. And so, when we address these questions, it is said that there are 19 such problems in the Soviet Union, or perhaps even 119, even 1,119. It is as if 19 sick people were gathered together and all treated with one and the same medicine—let's say Aspirin. But the problems are various. That is why it seems to me that one cannot adopt a stereotype approach to this. Just as we approach

each individual person, so we should approach the fate of every people, regardless of its size, regardless of how large the population, and proceed from the Leninist self-determination of nations. That is why I address you. What is your view? In the process of our work, will we be able to fulfil this very important mission all together? And of course, on the basis of good decisions, and just ones, too. Or will we, as was usually the case in our country for many years, constantly apply cosmetic treatment to the wounds? Wounds have to be healed. Because if we don't heal the wounds there will be complications and our ship won't get very far. You have probably recognized the reality and the complexity of those tasks and difficulties which will in the main lie on your shoulders. I think this because what we would want least of all is for us to play the role of some kind of extras. Do you understand? It is not for this that the people elected us. And so, I want you to tell us how you really view the dynamics of the solution to these questions. Thank you.

[Nishanov] Dear colleagues, first of all I would like to take your question as your wish for the work of our chamber. If I were immediately from this platform to expound ways of resolving this question I would not be adopting a serious approach to this highly serious problem. I agree with you completely that these questions are very hard and difficult. The wounds are deep. We need to treat them not just with Aspirin but by using every means at our disposal. I think that our chamber, which in fact represents all nations and ethnic groups of the Soviet Union, will be capable of working out these paths. Of course, some immediate questions might arise, some might require some time for elaboration. But I think that we, if we are united, will seek prctical ways. We've got the Statistical Board—which unfortunately works badly—to gather statistics; While we, as political figures, will seek ways toward a political solution of these questions which are rather delicate and which trouble everyone so much.

[Voice] Please go ahead.

[Unidentified speaker] My question is this. In your opinion, what signs differentiate a nation from an ethnic group, and given the successful implementation of the leninist nationalities' policy, can an ethnic group, during its development, become a nation within the framework of the Soviet Union?

[Nishanov] Thank you colleague. Now this question you all know well. For many long years we lived according to the Stalinist definition. And naturally this approach is now being reviewed. It is being reviewed by both scholars and social scientists, and by you and I together as well. That is why, I think, how should it be defined? Obviously the chamber will assist; scholars and social scientists must work on this question a bit; While you and I will actively join in so that it is not the old dogma that is in operation, but so that there is a creative approach to the examination of this highly complicated and highly delicate question.

[Gorbachev] Now, first of all, I will all the same give (?the floor) to a comrade who asked, who raised.... [voices from hall] Alright, alright.

[Mashbashev] Rafik Nishanovich, I am Deputy Mashbashev from the Adygey autonomous oblast. When we were discussing your candidacy in the Soviet of Elders, we, the representatives of numerically small peoples of Russia, put questions to you. After several such questions one of the deputies—I don't remember the name—from from the Baltic republics stood up and said: Let them first decide their questions in their own republic. Will there not be pressure on the deputies of numerically small peoples of Russia? How do you view that?

[Gorbachev] Incidentally, I apologize, let's just give Rafik Nishanovich a minute or a half to think, but I'll say that we at the Soviet of Elders and then, I think, in the Soviet of the Union, reached agreement not use the term small peoples, but numerically small. Looking at the documents there appears even in a resolution of our congress it says small peoples. We were used to it.

[Mashbashev] Yes, Mikhail Sergeyevich, That's how it was.

[Gorbachev] Clearly we needed to adopt that [sounds of agreement in hall], because if one says small has quite a different connotation, you know. It has, so to speak, a certain element of [word indistinct]. Please carry on, Rafik Nishanovich.

[Nishanov] I fully understand your disquiet. It seems to me tha the comrade who had raised that question made a slip of the tongue, made a mistake.

[Mashbashev] I also think so.

[Nishanov] Yes. If you please.

[Mashbashev] Thank you.

[Unidentified speaker] Comrade deputies, allow me to put a question in my own language, if you do not object. [Question put to Nishanov in vernacular]

[Unidentified speaker] That was a Kazakh speaking Uzbek! [laughter]

[Nishanov] Yes, yes. comrades, the esteemed colleague deputy, speaking Uzbo-Kazakh—that's how I'd describe it—put a question with a foreword that we are electing you, or will be electing you to high office. How do you regard the idea that every nation and ethnic group should speak in its own native tongue, and will there be a possibility in parliament, either in the Supreme Soviet or at the Congress, for them to speak in their native languages? Now, should I reply in Uzbo-Kazakh or Russian? [laughter, shout] I think that first—and this was mentioned at the congress both in the report and in many speeches—all nations, all ethnic groups should be

ensured the sovereign right to speak in their own native language. There should be no obstacles, no labels on this matter. As for our speeches in our native languages in the Supreme Soviet, at sessions of the chambers or the congress, you know that the presidium, when our session opened, gave an instruction to the apparatus to carry out the appropriate work in order to install the technical devices for synchronized translations of the speeches. I think that this desire of yours is correct, and it will be carried out.

[Unidentifed speaker] Esteemed Mikhail Sergeyevich, my first question is addressed to you. We are electing a chairman of the Soviet of Nationalities without an alternative, do you see that?

[Gorbachev] The council of Elders proposed a candidature.

[Same speaker] So, but other deputies can propose another, do you see?

[Gorbachev] Well look, if you have a proposal...

[Same speaker, interrupting] Well, fine, that's the first question, I've understood, and so the second question; Dear deputies, well let me address you in the Nanais language [three phrases in Nanais]: Hello dear deputies, may you be healthy and happy, and may success accompany you in your work. The Nanais word has been heard for the first time within the walls of the Palace of Congresses, but my question is as follows—I address you: I very much want to ask you about your attitude to the International Convention which was adopted in 1957 in Geneva, on an indigenous (?hostile) population leading a tribal way of life, which was not ratified in our country, and therefore in the nationalities policy in our country, on minority peoples, it was in no way considered. That's the first question. And I want to ask you how will you—if you become chairman of the Soviet of Nationalities—how will you contribute to resolving nationalities questions with regard to indigenous peoples of the Far East and the North, the European North and the Far East North, for you see a mass of nationalities problems there has not been settled for decades.

So I have the two questions. The convention which was adopted in Geneva in 1957 will be reviewed this year in June. There will be a partial review of this convention. Problems feature in this convention about minority peoples, indigenous peoples, which lead a tribal way of life, and so on, and they are considered to be vitally important for all indigenous peoples, and I would very much like to know how you will... [changes thought] your position on ratification—will the question of ratification stand before us, and naturally, on the articles. We will consider... [changes thought] yes, please.

[Nishanov] Thank you. Your anxiety is fully understandable. To the first question I would answer in the following way: Those tasks and functions on which we must work are laid down exactly in the working out of the statutes on the Chamber of Nationalities in this composition and in the definition of the functions of our chamber with you. Our chamber will study this declaration of 1957 and if the chamber considers it essential, it will work out recommendations and put them forward to the Supreme Soviet, and the Supreme Soviet, at a Congress of Deputies, if such a level is necessary, and if not, the Supreme Soviet will consider the matter in the prescribed manner. Our task is to study these documents and if they are acceptable to all nations and ethnic groups of the Soviet Union, to work out recommendations. I am ready to take part actively in this matter.

The second question: Well, small ethnic groups have problems everywhere. They exist both in the north and in the south, and in the east, and in the west. Therefore I will not divide, that I (?will not) busy myself with the north while I will omit the south, otherwise I will be accused of a one-sided approach. We all need to busy ourselves with small ethnic groups so that they too should feel sovereign and worthy in our great brotherhood of peoples.

[Unidentified speaker] I have two questions. The first: It is known that both chambers are equal and therefore it is not only relations between the nationalities which will be of interest to us. What kind of questions do you think need to be referred to the competence of the union and what kind of questions to union republics? That's one question, and the second is: We are making ready for a common European home and in connection with this I want to ask you to comment on the European Economic Community's plans for integration from 1992.

[Nishanov] [passage omitted: Agrees fully on question one—both chambers involved in great range of matters] Second, we will be working in close contact with the Soviet of the Union and we will even be resolving many questions together. [passage omitted: says functions of union and republican bodies are now being worked out—unidentified speaker interrupts to tell him to stick to answering the question] As far as the program for the economic integration of the European Community is concerned, then I think that when we have a bit more free time, we will devote one of our sessions to studying the experience of the European Community. We have the experience of CEMA, we have our internal experience, and the European Community indeed has interesting experience, and it deserves attention. In this respect I support you. [passage omitted: Gorbachev sorts out who is to speak next].

[Unidentified speaker] I want to express my dissatisfaction with your replies, since you have not given a concrete answer to a single question. For instance, I should like to ask the following. When you were asked about the events in Fergana, you started by pointing to an incident that took place there nearly a week ago involving strawberries, and then a few days later some people intoxicated by drugs and alcohol started some

sort of march; then all this found expression in killings of population of another nationality. You said that you went to sort things out, and were there on the spot. Now, I want you to answer quite specifically what it was that you sorted out there, and what causes you ascertained. And I want you to say what the cause was, was it strawberries, or alcohol and drugs, or was it after all national enmity? If it was national enmity on a national basis, tell us specifically what the issues were that sparked off this incident? Thank you.

[Nishanov] I consider that I gave a wholly reasonable objective reply. Whether or not you are satisfied with my reply is another matter. As for an investigation of the more profound causes of this phenomenon, the Uzbekistan Communist Party Central Committee and the government of the republic have set up a government commission led by Comrade Kadyrov, chairman of the republican council of ministers, which is currently on the spot and is investigating the situation. These are matters which demand most painstaking and carefully- considered investigation and political and fundamental evaluation. I have expressed my fundamental evaluation in my first reply. I condemn this vandalism. What it is that you find unsatisfactory here, I do not understand. Who else, please?

[Unidentified speaker] Good afternoon. My distinguished colleague, I have two questions to ask you but not questions of substance generally speaking. That is because the national questions of substance, as you have said correctly—I am totally at one with you—are going to be tackled by everyone. And your position is to chair—and to be honest, I would like to draw the attention of all colleagues to the calm way in which you are doing it. That is one of the most important functions in this future stormy chamber. That is why I shall put two questions—not proposals but exactly questions—that relate more to the form.

First, what is your attitude to the very idea of establishing the right of veto by republics, national okrugs, and others, on the issues which touch on their vital interests—republics, autonomous republics.

Second, what is your attitude to the following idea: We are going to have one chairman with two deputies. We have 15 union republics. What about introducing a yearly rotation - i.e. 5 years—and each time, as three people are replaced, all republics have the chance of being represented. Your attitude, please. Thank you.

[Nishanov] Thank you, esteemed colleague. To start with, about the right of veto. We can hold counsel on that issue of course. However, relying on international practice I may tell you that as far as I know the right of veto has so far been applied in international organizations, since major forces are represented there which represent various countries with various social state order, various visions of life, and various approaches to the resolution of these or other issues. And when the Un

Charter was being developed, that principle was elaborated in order not to infringe on someone's rights because of a class approach or some kind of a regional approach. But so far it has never happened that we were unable to reach an agreement on a voluntary basis and that we would have some kind of a right of veto looming above us. That is why, for the moment, as long as I am here on this rostrum, I believe that that issue—well that there is no special need for that issue. But if someone has some kind of approaches or justifications and will stand by them, we shall discuss it at the chamber.

[Gorbachev] It seems that I have, probably, to look to the left now. Go ahead, please. Ah, there is also a second question!

[Nishanov] Second question?

[Gorbachev] Rotation, rotation.

[Nishanov] Oh, yes, rotation. We are legislators here, me and you. For the time being we have one law which stipulates that a chairman is elected and things. That is why we shall take it as a guidance. However, theoretically, I accept and may support that approach. Rotation can exist. That is because all republics enjoy equal rights—the autonomous ones do too—and any can be [incharge—FBIS]. Any of those sitting in the hall can become chairman of the chamber; I support that idea too.

[Gorbachev] Go ahead, please.

[Unidentified delegate] The issue of small peoples, such as Crimean Tatars...

[Gorbachev, interrupting] Small in numbers!

[Delegate] Small in numbers, yes, excuse me, has been repeatedly raised at the congress.

[Gorbachev] A habit.

[Delegate] The peoples who are small in numbers, such as Crimean Tatars, Baltic Germans, Gagauzes, and others. A great number of interethnic problems are also observed in the Baltic republics. Could you please tell us, do you have your own concept of how these issues should be resolved? That is my first question. Here is the second question: In the Baltic republics, in the interests of protecting their own language—because of the existing economic malfunctioning, and since diverging opinions have emerged there on ethnic grounds—the Baltic republics have declared their languages to be state languages. Could you explain your attitude to that state of affairs?

[Nishanov] Your first question. Naturally, the ethnic groups or peoples which lost their home areas or some kind of their formations should have them restored. That is the approach of principle. As to when and in what

particular way, we should probably relate here to real conditions. But the issue exists, and the ways should be looked for, including in our chamber.

[Voice from the floor] That's right!

[Nishanov] The second question—as to who, how, and where one should proclaim one's own language state language, to use it in official proceedings or on other occasions,—that is a full sovereign right to each republic. I do not believe that any limitations or transferring a particular form from one republic to another are expedient here. Let each republic decide for itself. This is my general appraoch of principle. If you have declared your own language a state language, other republics have promulgated their draft laws on declaring their languages state languages, etc. That work is in the process of being done. But as a matter of principle, I support that process. Second, at the same time, I would like to stress that when any republic declares its language a state language, no discrimination against any other language should be tolerated. Each republic should provide maximum space for free use of any languages whatsoever—in education, in cultural communication, at work, in official state proceedings, etc. I believe that if these two aspects are dealt with, to, it seems to me that the interests of all nationalities and ethnic groups, no matter where their domicile is, will be taken into account.

[Gorbachev] You have been wanting to ask a question for a long time already. Yes, you.

[Unidentified speaker] Evidently I should, to begin with, make a very small introduction. Very many of our electors liked the way you chaired one of the sitting of the congress. On Saturday and Sunday we had meetings with Muscovites, young and middle-aged, they liked it too and many even voiced the intention to recommend you as chairman of the chamber of the Soviet of nationalities. In connection with this, I cannot help wondering if that is your permanent style of dealing with people or did your position as congressional chairman over us oblige you to be like that? [laughter in hall] You know, my second question boils down to this: We, as my colleague from the Baltic area said, apparently do not just have to deal with relations between nationalities, but also with the socioeconomic development of the republics, and, well, krays etc. What is your attitude toward the the development of power engineering today? Today, atomic power engineering was condemned, hydro-electric power stations were condemned, heat and power stations were condemned. So are we now to light candles then? Are we now to harness oxen? How do you regard this development, is it right or not?

[Nishanov] As for the need to communicate with people, to find contacts, not to exacerbate any relations but to live in friendship, in harmony, this is my internal need. In general, I believe that one of man's greatest merits is never to lose the feeling of the need to learn, to learn from another, to learn from people, to learn from life. If this process takes place any person will feel himself free and his interlocutor will also feel free in his presence. Thanks you for the compliment. At the congress I fulfilled the duties of a Presidium member and proceeded from this: that the interests of all who were present in the hall were represented, so that nobody was offended. [word indistinct] if it was a success, thank you very much.

As for the development of power engineering and so on, some errors have of course, been allowed to be made. probably our scientists and economists and power engineering specialists, with the involvement of state plan specialists, of specialists of all republics and regions must study this question very thoroughly. but on the one hand, all our development is founded on power engineering and we cannot cast it aside. On the other hand, we must resolve this problem in such a way that no damage is done to our nature, ecology, to people's life. But, on the contraty it is still happening here and there in our country that people are suffering from energy in some places. People should receive joy from energy. That is the formulation of the question. We will participate in this process as far as we can, so that sensible paths can be worked out.

[?Gorbachev] Please. Go ahead.

[Unidentified speaker] Mikhail Sergeyevich. In connection with the fact that very many questions have been put to Rafik Nishanovich. I think this is probably the first time in his whole life that he has stood like this and answered question. Because there never has been anything like it before. I know him well, Rafik Nishanovich, we are neighbors. I must honestly admit that before him, we had, you know, great problems between the Tajik republic and the Uzbek. [another unidentified speaker says "Yes."] Very great problems. In connection with [words indistinct] the appointment, or to be more precise he was, to begin with, elected chairman of the Presidium and then first secretary of the Central Committee. He came twice to our republic in that short time. He came twice. Once we even held a large meeting together in the city of Dushanbe. There he answered almost half of the questions with his speech. He is a very sociable man. We know him as a good comrade. [bustle in hall]

[Gorbachev] You know, no oratorial art will help at all if a person has nothing to say...

[Unidentified speaker] Yes.

[Gorbachev] ...has no position.

[Unidentified speaker] Of course.

[Gorbachev] Or on the contrary, if he has such a position which he does not take into account, which denies all others' opposition.

[Unidentified speaker] These are the kind of questions we had in the big hall. We had more than 1,200 people there. The questions were like these. He answered all the quesions. In general, to put it briefly, we resolved half the problems at that meeting, half the problems. That is why I know him as... [passage omitted]

[Unidentified speaker] [words indistinct]

[Gorbachev] So what is your question?

[Unidentified speaker] I do not have a question.

[Gorbachev] So, that is a question you put to Mikhail Sergeyevich...[laughter]

[Unidentified speaker] I do have a wish. I mean. My wish is this: that all deputies should lend their support to the proposal of the Council of the Elders to, I mean, elect him chairman of [words indistinct] of the Supreme Soviet.

[Gorbachev] That is understandable and this is already a hint for me as the person in the chair. [laughter] All the same, I did promise someone, where is he, yes, yes, yes, I mean you, yes, yes, please go ahead. Presently we will exchange views; Will we continue further or will we exchange views.

[Unidentified speaker] National-territorial constituency no. 510 in the Bashkir ASSR [Autonomous Soviet Socialist Republic]. We have been sitting for a long time now in the Congress and listening to everything. To a certain extent we regard ourselves as not having equal rights. Why is this? Because we have asked to speak many times, but things are not going well. There are 4 million people living in Bashkiria, but only one of our representatives has spoken at the Congress. Questions are being posed at present but only by certain Baltic republics. For some reason there has been favoring of those republics. But there are here representatives from autonomous republics which have populations of 4, 5, and 6 million. So, I think...

[Gorbachev interrupting] You have changed this.

[Speaker continuing] ... that this is a question definitely for you, Mikhail Sergeyevich. Secondly, Rafik Nishanovich, I would like to say that there are only four representatives from our republic in the Soviet of Nationalities while we have a population of 4 million people. The union republics have 11 representatives. We would very much like to know your precise position on how in the future autonomous republics with such large indigenous national populations will be represented.

[Unidentified voiced interrupting] In the Ukraine there are 50...

[Speaker continuing] What is your position in this regard and how shall we settle this question for the very near future? We would very much like to know this.

[Nishanov] May I?

[Gorbachev] Yes, of course.

[Nishanov] You touched on a question concerning the constitutional situation, and for that reason I could not now give you an answer outside the framework of the constitution. Probably, since the question has arisen, a problem does exist and it is necessary to sort out in a calm situation the best way to resolve it. I, of course, understand. Bashkiria is, like Tataria, a large republic. The Tatar autonomous republic has a population of 7 million...

[Gorbachev interrupting] But Comrade Ivashko is saying that Ukraine has 52 million people and has 11 representatives, not to mention Russia.

[Nishanov] Yes, Bashkiria has a population of 4 million. There are 140 million people in Russia, and in our own republic there are 20 million. We need, of course, somehow to study this as calmly as possible. If our approach is simply from the point of view of numbers, many question will arise. Well, some kind of problem does obviously exist, and we here in the Soviet of Nationalities need to study this in more depth. [passage omitted: Deputy Oleynik speaks briefly on importance of language and brotherhood]

[Unidentified speaker] In general I have been studying your calmness and restraint and your ability to smooth things out from the way you have chaired a whole day at the congress. Our congress is proceeding in a new way and I would like to ask whether you have your own personal proposals about how the Soviet of Nationalities will work in its new manner, and what is your role as chairman in the procedure with regard to us? That is, there it is. [sentence as heard] Thank you.

[Nishanov] First of all, if I am elected, I see my role to be to ensure full democracy in the life of our chamber, full coordination of actions, and to take maximum account of the proposals and interests of everyone. Of course, perhaps not all the proposals will be adopted. But if there is a rational kernel which satisfies everyone and our harmonious and united community then, of course, we shall adopt it. But if there are proposals which rush ahead too fast or which in some way do not correspond with the interests of our community then, naturally, we shall consult with you. I simply promise to ensure full-blooded activity in the chamber to any member of our chamber.

[Gorbachev] Well then, comrades, should we end at that point for a while? [confused shouting from hall] No, wait a moment. We shall not dictate. We shall come to a decision. If people want to continue, then we will continue. I see comrade [name indistinct] Quite simply, there are still questions in all sectors, I see. Are we to continue or shall we restrict ourselves to this? Who is in favor of ending the questions to Comrade Nishanov at this point and changing over, please? Please lower your hands. Who is against? Abstentions? Well, clearly a minority. Now, who wants to take the floor and say something? I shall now give the floor to this comrade and then you can speak.

[Samsonov] Mikhail Sergeyevich, may I have a word?

[Gorbachev] OK!

[Samsonov] I wanted to ask what, in my opinion, was a serious question, but I wasn't allowed to. I am Samsonov, a deputy from Mari Autonomous Soviet Socialist Republic.

[Gorbachev] Well, Comrade Antonov [name as heard], it wasn't I who wouldn't let you. We have already agreed on that.

[Samsonov] As I understand it, the Supreme Soviet will be a permanently active one. And my question is that this: If Comrade Nishanov, who as I understand it is Uzbek first secretary, is elected chairman of the Soviet of Nationalities, he will not be able to work in his usual way. And I have this question: How will he combine the office. [murmering in hall] he won't combine, is that right—then everything's understood!

[Gorbachev] No, he's coming here to work—if he's elected!

[Darsigov] Nazranskiy rayon, Chechen-Ingushetiya, Constituency No.674. We, the deputies of Chechen-Ingushetiya, support the candidature of Nishanov as chairman of the USSR Soviet of Nationalities. But I have something here comrades, which I must read because it concerns [word indistinct]. Throughout the Congress I have received about 140 (?letters) addressed to me. How can the people's deputies of the USSR avoid voting on the question of the restoration of the Ingush autonomy which was abolished by Stalin in 1934? The foundations of the genocide against the Ingush people, as that against other peoples, were laid down long before the implementation of the act on forced evacuation back in 1944. The constitutional rights of the people were first violated in 1934 when, without due regard for the national interests of the Ingush people and without due regard to their opinion, the Ingush autonomous oblast was abolished.

At the present time the opinion of the Ingush people on the need to eliminate the aftermath of the Stalin-Beria tyranny was expressed in October 1988 and April 1989.

The appeals were signed by 60,000 people—the over-whelming majority of the adult population. These appeals were submitted to the CPSU Central Commit-tee, the Supreme Soviet and the USSR Council of Ministers.

In connection with this, I ask that the question be reviewed of the creation of the Ingush Autonomous Soviet Socialist Republic [ASSR] within the composition of the Russian Soviet Federated Socialist Republic [RSFSR], thus uniting the historically developed terri-tory of Ingushetiya as it was before the abolition of Ingush autonomy in 1934. The decision to create the Ingush ASSR would be an act for the complete and actual rehabilitation of the Ingush people and the com-plete elimination of all the harmful consequences of the Stalinist tyranny and would restore the Leninist norms of nationalist policy. Deputy Darsigov.

I have one another question for Rafik Nishanov. When Lenin was alive, Ingushia was entered (?in red) in the Kremlin book. Later, after Lenin died, this name was removed. I ask that this name of the Ingush people be personally restored. Because Vladimir Ilyich Lenin's name is part of us—we have a museum and a [word indistinct] which he gave. [passage omitted] I will not go on any more about the difficulties which we have suf-fered; and the electorate—20,000 people—said to me, that if you get the chance, present this letter to Gor-bachev personally. So here I present it, if you would be good enough to receive it. Thank you for your attention.

[Gorbachev] I think we have listened to the question which bothers you. But now I would like to speak about the candidature for the office of chairman of the cham-ber. Comrade [name indistinct], if you please? [pause] No, wait a moment, comrade [word indistinct], then I'll pass to you. [passage omitted]

[Medvedev] Esteemed chairman, esteemed deputies: Nikolay Medvedev, National Territorial Constituency No 237. You understand, we very often confuse the grounds for ethnic dissentions with their reasons. A question was put to Comrade Nishanov here which he did not reply to completely...it did not completely satisfy us. You understand that when we discussed this candi-dacy I was among others in the Council of Elders. We were really pleased with the way he conducted the session flexibly and delicately and the way he answered those questions. Do not think that I now wish to reject his candidacy. I want us to think very carefully.

What happend in Uzbekistan shows that this drunken brawl was the basis for the conflict. The reasons, obvi-ously, are much deeper. No extremist can incite people into an ethnic conflict unless the ground is favorable. Therefore, we suppose that there, obviously, just as in other republics that ground exists.

Not wishing to remove Comrade Nishanov's candidacy and sensing how delicately he is able to manage pro-cesses, we only took thought after having heard the opinion of other republics and having spoken yesterday evening with many representatives of other republics. Yesterday evening we discussed this question for a very long time. It was a very difficult discussion. Now, when such a situation exists there, are we able—obviously the ground exists—can we tear him away from there? That really is a very serious question. I certainly don't want, and I don't think that any of us want a new hot-bed of tension to appear there like the one in Karabakh. It would be desirable to extinguish it now using all possible means. You understand that this is very important because, I know, that when there is blood between two peoples it is very, very difficult to extinguish, especially, most likely, among more southern people.

On the other hand, I very much liked the way that Rafik Nishanovich said that we should construct everything on the principles of consent. We shall not impose things on you because it sometimes turns out as if the people from the Baltic area are trying to impose something. No, we shall only propose. You will be able to discuss your proposal and adopt it or not adopt it.

However, the question of relations between nationali-ties; whereas in the solution of economic questions logic and energy are needed, here what is needed primarily is delicacy and agreement. That is the difference between our two chambers. Therefore, we propose—we the USSR peoples deputies from Lithuania, Estonia and Latvia—consider that the work of the Supreme Soviet should be restructured starting with the chamber of the Soviet of Nationalities where what should be used primarily is the principle of agreement at the level of the 15 union republics. This principle is applicable right now in put-ting forward candidacies for the post of chairman of the chamber. The person in whom confidence is expressed by each union republic by a majority of votes during separate discussions can then be put forward for a general vote of the members by chamber. In the absence of such an agreement—the confidence of all 15 union republics—a new candidacy is to be put forward.

We consider that voting by simple majority for a candi-date proposed from above is outdated in principle and particularly unacceptable for the election of the chair-man of the Soviet of Nationalities. Let us think about this theme. This does not mean that we are sweeping aside Rafik Nishanovich's candidacy, but when we were discussing the matter, we gave thought to who could be chairman of the chamber of the Soviet of Nationalities. It is most likely the sort of person about whom any republic could say: Aha, he thinks the way I do. That means that in a conversation with Georgians, he is a Georgian; with Armenians, an Armenian; with Lithua-nians a Lithuanian; with Kirgiz a Kirgiz; that is, he understands people's souls. So, we discussed and took thought, and such people do exist in our union. Take, say, Chingiz Aytmatov. In our native Lithuania he is loved as a Lithuanian, as the most Lithuanian Lithuanian, you understand. I think that there are similar people in other republics. There is Oleynik, we accept him in exactly the same way. Ion Drutse, Peters. You understand, we do have such people. We have to learn to make use of this potential. Now Comrade Nishanov: Previously I knew him less, and now I know him better. We do have such people. Let us think deeply about this. Our chamber must display maximum tact. Thank you for your attention. I hand over the floor.

[Unidentified speaker] I have a question for my colleague from Lithuania.

[Medvedev] Go ahead.

[Unidentified speaker] Why do you stress the union republics, the 15 union republics. What is this, observance of a paragraph or your world view?

[Medvedev] I can answer you. You understand, we are accustomed to respecting the law. Are you satisfied with my reply? The law and the Constitution state 15 republics. If the Constitution were to be drawn up in some other way and we adopt it in some other form, then we shall respect it in exactly the same way. Are there any other questions for me?

[Gorbachev] I think that there may be but we shall not take them, comrades. Let everyone express his own opinion, or else...a question sprang into my mind but I managed to restrain myself in time. I, in particular, must ask less questions. I am already receiving a lot of criticisms, because if one recognizes that there are 15 republics in the Constitution I fully agree. However, when we have legal norms, on the basis of which we are conducting this session of the chamber and draw them up, you respect them but at the same time you are introducing them. So thus it is possible, it is a real snowball. All the same, we shall discuss them. Comrade Shevchenko, then Comrade Tarazevich. [passage omitted]

[Bichkauskas] Deputy Bichkauskas, the 254th national territorial constituency, Lithuania. Esteemed Mikhail Sergeyevich, esteemed Anatoliy Ivanovich, esteemed deputies!

I would still like to go back to and put to a vote the proposal of the Baltic republics, on discussion of the nominations made by each union republic.

[Gorbachev] It is said that there are no Baltic republics.

[Bichkauskas] From Latvia, Estonia, and Lithuania.

[Gorbachev] Yes. [voices in the hall]

[Bichkauskas] So, I would like to say—please hear me out! I would like to say that the proposal in question does not run contrary to the Constitution, since Article 11

specifies that—Article 111—that each chamber of the Supreme Soviet elects the chamber's chairman and two deputies to him. The procedure of electing the chairman is not specified. That, for sure, should be specified for certain in the standing orders for the work of the Supreme Soviet which we still do not have. And Article 115 dealing with the adoption of laws by the chambers does indeed make mention of a mechanical majority of votes, but referring to the adoption of laws, and not to the election of a chamber chairman. Do not discard that proposal, try to see it as, perhaps, the first step toward a democratically necessary mechanism for the protection of a parliamentary minority, think well about it. Would you be so kind as to put that proposal to a vote? Thank You. [angry voices]

[Gorbachev] Are you insisting on.... [incomplete sentence as heard]

[Gorbachev aside] No, I know. Go ahead, please. Go ahead, please.

[Unidentified speaker] I am going to abstain during the vote on Comrade Nishanov, and if you have enough patience, I shall put forward my considerations. But are you going to let me finish? It is a different opinion. All opinions have been more or less to the same effect. Well, the deputies of the Baltic republic are often reproached for being very active—too active. That comes as a result of the fact that we, perhaps, also have a different idea of what a nation is. But, much as we read Lenin's works, it is in tune with Lenin's concept of a nation. And in no way does it contradict the rights of autonomous republics, or the rights of the republics which—oblasts and a national okrugs. [sentence as heard]

I have seen many breaches of democracy during the work of the congress and thought it was because there were so many people, making it simply impossible to work in a very democratic way. But here we are not very numerous, and it is already possible to work democratically. Nevertheless, I can see that the desire to listen to someone else's opinion is not much in evidence here, whereas each of us has the voters of a given nationality standing behind him, if not the entire nationality—as in case of small nationalities. That is why I am asking you not to discriminate against any speaker from this rostrum in any way, because that makes a guarantee, a guarantee of just ethnic relations here, in this chamber, as well as in the whole of the union.

I was horrified at the congress when the union—the union's Supreme Soviet, the Congress of People's Deputies—forgot about the affairs of an entire nationality, the Mari ASSR. The congress applauded Comrade Chemodanov for what he did, but it applauded one person. As they did so, all forgot about the fact that they still had forgotten about the nationality—that made me feel horrified. I was horrified when Kazakh Deputy Suleymenov spoke and one could hear voices from the hall: Let's speak on matters of substance! Why, Suley-menov spoke of the rights of small nationalities, and someone was yelling, let's speak on matters of substance. And is small nationalities not a matter of substance? I am horrified when the concepts of region and republic are still being confused here. And now a new concept is being introduced, some kind of autonomy—that concept is not Lenin's at all. Lenin did not use that concept. And that is why, if this chamber, too, lacks the capacity to listen to what each deputy here has to say, and I stress, each deputy, because interests of his nationality stand behind him, then I feel justified in speaking of a possible departure [as heard] from the Union of Soviet Socialist Republics of my homeland, Lithuania. That is a constitutional right, and I do not want—if it is going to continue this way—I do not want my homeland, Lithuania, to be part of such an unbecoming union.

[Voice] Were you not horrified on hearing the speech of your comrade?!

[Speaker] Which particular comrade?

[Voice] The one who spoke today.

[Speaker] Remind me who it was, please, I just don't remember.

[Voices] The association director! [words indistinct]

[Speaker] Ah, the association director. Very well, let us bear in mind the fact that....

[Voice interupting, followed by more heckles from the floor] Just answer the question, that will be all!

Very well, more than 90 percent of workers at the Dvigatel Association are of non-Estonian origin. The director himself conducted his work in such a manner that Estonians did not enroll there, not asking so much as by your leave from the Estonian people [more heckles]. And that is why I am not horrified at all. Thank you.

[Voice] And what about defending [word indistinct]?

[Gorbachev] Point taken.

[Another voice] and you don't think that you are going to have a kind of Karabakh in Estonia, too? [heckles]

[Speaker] I am from Lithuania and not from Estonia, or else I shall note that the Russians residing in ethnic republics have their own land, Russia, whereas the republics which are nurtured by—which live on their own land—have no other land to go to! That is all, thank you. [chorus of heckles, followed by the chairman's bell]

[Gorbachev] Point taken.

[Voice] Let's vote.

[Gorbachev] Dear comrades, may I sum up a bit the conversation which has taken place here and try and lead you, so to speak, to a final conclusion.

In the first place, despite the fact that at our first session there already are some elements which have aroused anxiety, I consider that the discussions in the chamber are being conducted, even with making an organizational decision on an organizational matter—but after all at issue is the leader of a chamber, this very important chamber—let's say it straight, the discussion pleases me. It pleases me because the discussion is proceeding in an informal way. It means the deputies and the members of the Soviet of Nationalities understand the kind of responsibility that falls on this chamber at the present stage of restructuring in the country, the implementation of political reform, and the solving of varied problems in interethnic relations. From this viewpoint I always think the same thing: It is hardly possible to hope that this chamber can expect easy work, that here there will be no discussions, and that there all will be a bed of roses, so to speak. No; so complex are the problems that have accumulated, so complex have they grown that they need to be carefully studied, that great work—and it is possible to predict this right away—awaits the chamber.

All of you need to arm yourselves with great respectfulness, with great love for work, with an ability to listen to the most varied opinions, and here is represented a multitude of voices of the entire union. It is impossible to escape this. We want to pursue a realistic policy. We are saying that our restructuring was born as an evaluation of the reality in which we found ourselves, both within the country and in the context of the realities which surround our country. This is how both internal and foreign policy were born; therefore in this respect, too, it is not possible to make headway without relying on these realities, without taking them into account, and without removing or casting away a single one of the problems which today form the worries of our peoples. I think that in no case should we take a path if one does not like the problem, when it is so uncomfortable that it is necessary to clear it away from the path.

This wouldn't do, comrades. This is the life of the peoples and it can be only approached in a serious way. Otherwise the sense of all the work is being lost. Therefore, and this is how I understood that the comrades spoke—Comrade Arutyunyan, Comrade Medvedev, and also in my view, Comrade Starovoyotora.

They said that it seemed to them as if Comrade Nisha-nov aspired not to the role of leader of this chamber, which would make it possible to gather all the powers and potential of deputies and all the experience which they brought in here, but to the role of a kind of Luka—the comforter from Gorkiy's play "The Lower Depths." I did not understand it in this way. I simply understood that this is a man who is well disposed toward a joint quest for answers to all these decisions.

If someone now wished to reproach Comrade Nishanov to the effect that on some problems he did not provide clear answers, it seems to me that some of us are still unable to answer many questions. But I did detect, I did indeed—that is what impresses me, I have a feeling that this found your response, too—that this man believes in the necessity of conducting affairs in such a way that all peoples may live better, that the policy which matters will not progress if we do not tackle these problems, and if we are following the policy of toasting each other. No, we have reached a stage when all things must be done. And this is his position, his responsibility. Someone said, Comrade Shevchenko indeed, that he endeavours to find and to achieve compromise at this stage so that the problem would be solved in a particular way, and so that it would find a solution which it is able to find today, although sometimes we would like to tackle it in a better way. Well, I have been listening to comrade Nishanov, and quite apart from the fact that I know him, he is, in my view, well disposed toward this.

I do not want mistrust or suspicion to arise. I beseech you, I beseech you. That is the basis, really. Let us not suspect each other of insidious schemes. Let us investigate, if something has to be investigated, then let it be investigated precisely, both in one region and in another. Information from a deputy of one region or another may even be introduced into practice when something reaches Moscow and the Supreme Soviet here—and when something begins as it were to worry deputies, those in charge of the chamber can be asked to release the information, to receive all that from first hand, as it were. To put it more briefly, a very good democratic situation must be created. There is no other alternative, comrades. Great work lies ahead for the chamber.

Well, strictly speaking, all that is left for us to do is to examine whether we have a common approach on the basis of which we reach decisions both at the congress and which we put to use at the Soviet of the Union. This is what arose, so to speak, in our country from practice, what ensues from the constitutional statutes. This is one approach. The second approach—comrades from the Baltic region propose that it be discussed. It boils down to this: Deputies from Lithuania, Estonia, and Latvia believe that the work of the Soviet of the Union should be restructured, and of the chamber of the Soviet of Nationalities primarily. Above all, the principle of consensus at the level of the 15 union republics must be applied. This is the proposal. I will not read all of it out further. Objections ensued here, we also heard dissatisfaction, but the proposal remains. essentially....

[Unidentified speaker] [words indistinct directed at Gorbachev]

[Gorbachev] What?

[Voices from hall] Information!

[Unidentified speaker] We deputies from Latvia are sitting here and we are not the authors or co-authors of the statement that was read out by the comrade deputy allegedly on behalf of all three Baltic republics. [words indistinct from hall] And altogether, I ask that such a category as a speech on behalf of deputies from a number of republics be used with great care. [bustle in hall]

[Gorbachev] All the more so since everyone here has the opportunity to speak and set forth his position. [indistinct voices from back of hall; bustle in hall]

[Unidentified speaker] I am sorry I did not come up to you to ask.

[Gorbachev] Nonetheless, I want to invite you and here is what to do. So, the first thing is either we will follow the approaches which have emerged on the basis of those principles according to which the congress is run, or we must accept the proposals of the comrades which the people's deputies signed here, and there are real signatures here. Therefore, then, will we change or (?not) change approaches now? [voices from hall shout "no"; bustle in hall; unidentified speaker shouts, "What about the rights of the electorate?"] I ask you to remain where you are please. I ask you to remain where you are.

[Unidentified speaker] Mikhail Sergeyevich, [words indistinct]

[Gorbachev] Excuse me. Do not put me in an awkward position when I, making use of my rights of chairman, must return you to your seat.

[Unidentified speaker] It is just that I did not hear. [bustle in hall]

[Gorbachev] Alright, sit down. [bustle in hall; indistinct words]

[Gorbachev] Comrades, begin with the culture of social intercourse. [indistinct voices in hall] I apply this to myself also, to myself. From my own experiences I know how difficult that is to achieve. But we have no alternative. We will begin from that. We will seek and find the answers to the most difficult questions. Will we change our approach? [voices in hall shout, "no"] Do you have a question for me?

[Unidentified speaker] It is just that from my experience, I do not know the essence of the proposals put forward by these comrades. What are they proposing? Can you [words indistinct]

[Gorbachev] If they do not agree [bustle in hall] if the deputies of at least one republic, or the majority, do not agree, then the candidacy is considered to be rejected. [bustle in hall, voices say "oh," "that is not constitutional, that cannot be," words indistinct]

[Gorbachev] Yes, that is precisely how it is, just like that. [bustle in hall] If, so to speak, one does not go into details, I quickly realized what the crux of the matter was here. [bustle in hall] Well, incidentally, I consider that other questions which have been posed here and are listed may be discussed more thoroughly later and that something may be introduced into working practice, so to speak, to be introduced into discussions and so forth. But the main question here is that if one of the republics or the majority of deputies fail to support the candidature that candidacy is not accepted. That is the explanation.

[Unidentified speaker] Mikhail Sergeyevich, that should not be done, because the autonomous republics will become second-class.

[Unidentified speaker] Although the questioning of Rafik Nishanovich is over, nevertheless, I think that he is still in the minds of not just the people who are in this hall but also perhaps of those who are at their TV sets. I would like, not as it were to ask Rafik Nishanovich, but I would like it to receive clarification here because I think it is a delicate question, and also a difficult question and very important one.

[?Gorbachev] Well, ask then, ask.

[Unidentified speaker] If possible, I would like to ask for the microphone.

[Gorbachev] Well, please go ahead. [Bustle in hall]

[Announcer] You are listening to a direct relay from the first organizational sitting of the Soviet of Nationalities of the USSR Supreme Soviet. The deputies are continuing to ask questions of deputy Nishanov.

[Unidentified speaker] Deputy from Orsk territorial constituency no (?206). I am here as a deputy with consultative rights, but according to the standing instructions, as I have understood them, I have the right to be present. I would not like under any circumstances to cast suspicion on Rafik Nishanovich or on the representatives of the republic, but the population and our electors know about the recent events which took place there, connected with the name of Rashidov. Therefore, I think that, in order that there are no misunderstandings at all, and particularly that no questions should arise when we return to our homes, I would think that there would be grounds for Rafik Nishanovich to touch upon this question today because we know that there was a large turnover of cadres there, but to explain a little for the electors, so to say, the situation and his position in those years, what he was engaged in those years and what position he occupied.

[Gorbachev] O.K. Two minutes, Rafik Nishanovich. It is a big question. But just give us the essence.

[Nishanov] Of course, what happened in Uzbekistan is called negative phenomena by some people. I consider that these are ugly phenomena: the degeneration of cadres, corruption, and dishonest practices. This deserves universal condemnation and the republic's party organization is conducting this policy.

Some elements of violation of the Leninist principles of cadre selection, the positioning of compliant people in posts, and then the gradual sounding out of the possibilities of violating socialist legality and the Leninist morals of our morals and life appeared at the end of the 1960s. At that time I was secretary of the party Central Committee and was in charge of questions of ideology. I frequently spoke out against these phenomena both officially and in individual conversations with Rashidov. I even raised these questions in the CPSU Central Committee. This ended with my being offered the post of ambassador extraordinary and plenipotentiary. I spent 15 years continuously in this post. Then, at the suggestion of the CPSU Central Committee I returned to the republic and actively got involved in the work which the republic's party organization is conducting to morally cleanse the cadre corps. In my speech at the congress I said: The Central Committee bureau is conducting a principled struggle in this direction and it will carry it through to the end. At the same time, I would like to reply here to what was said by esteemed Deputy Starovoytova. She asked about the theme of the candidate's dissertation that I defended. I am a candidate of history. The defense took place in the Academy of Social Sciences under the CPSU Central Committee in 1969. The theme of the dissertation was the activity of the Communist Party of Uzbekistan on the internationalist education of the working people. Thank you.

[Gorbachev] A good theme. OK. Is it possible to consider that we have had a detailed discussion? [voices in hall shout, "yes."]

So, in this position, I can put to the vote the question of electing Comrade Rafik Nishanovich Nishanov as chairman of the chamber. [voices in hall shout, "Yes"] I can? [voices in hall shout, "yes."] Did you want to say something?

[Unidentified speaker] This means that the comrades have imposed a veto. That is, during an election, naturally, I think that it is undesirable to do this but those questions which concern, say, the republics, oblasts...

[Gorbachev] Excuse me, comrade. I did not manage to finish, I was interrupted. Yes, yes, yes. You were right to remind me.

[Same unidentified speaker] It is necessary to ensure the rights of the minority, because we cannot, like the union as a whole, decide for any separate region, you understand.

[Gorbachev] One can say this, comrades, in connection with the discussion of this situation. Taking account of the moods and the way we have been working over these past days, I would operate on the principles and approaches as have arisen amongst us by today and, relying on which we take decisions. I am referring to the principle of democratic...discussion and democratic decision by adoption by the majority. However, along with this instruction on this proposal, an instruction which may well be one of a kind, a decision could, perhaps, be adopted either to forward it to a commission, or else it may be regarded as necessary to subsequently—well, that's a short decision—examine in detail all the questions of procedure, of how the work in the chamber, the Soviet of Nationalities, should be organized.

[Gorbachev] Well, can it be like that? [bustle in hall, voices shout, "yes"] Perhaps the comrades who introduced (?the proposal) agree with this, too?

[Unidentified speaker] The first proposal was that republics should vote in the voting for the chairman. But you introduced a second proposal to vote as had been adopted. Then let us take a vote on which proposal will be adopted.

[Gorbachev] Yes, alright. But we know that it will not be...but I think that the first proposal is what is contained in our Constitution. [bustle in hall] It all comes from there. Comes from there.

[Unidentified speaker] The procedure for electing the chairman is not written in the Constitution.

[Gorbachev] Here, everything that has been decided so far on everything—both in the congress and in all chambers, and in all bodies—is decided on the basis of the Constitution. That is, within the framework of the principle of democracy on the basis of the adoption of majority decision. So, on the basis of this, debates are held here and are discussed. So, the first is a constitutional approach. [bustle in hall; voices shout, "yes."] All the rest are already subsequent proposals. [bustle in hall] Who is favors preserving that approach, which ensues from our constitutional statutes and on the basis of which we work within the framework of this congress? I ask that you raise your cards. I ask you to lower them. Who is against? [bustle in hall] Who abstained? [bustle in hall] And three.. four, five, six abstained. Six So then, the question is decided. We will follow....

[Unidentified voice] Thirteen.

[Gorbachev] So then, the question is decided. We will follow....

[Unidentified Speaker] Thirteen against and six abstained.

[Gorbachev] Abstained. Now I can put the matter to the vote. Yes, the second part, nevertheless, from this follows...there are interesting thoughts there which might be used in work in the future. Therefore, perhaps this could be done—charge the chairman of the chamber together with deputies, including those who introduced these proposals, to work on this group of questions and then to inform the chamber of their ideas on that account. From the point of view of examining what useful things can be extracted from that for the organization of the chamber's work. Can such a decision be adopted, comrades? [bustle in hall] I ask those in favor of adopting such a decision to vote. I ask you to lower your cards. Who is against? Who abstains? No one. It is adopted.

Now I pose the question of voting for the election of Comrade Nishanov, Rafik Nishanovich, as chairman of the chamber of Soviet of Nationalities. I ask you to raise your credentials or your pass. I ask you to lower them. Who is against? [bustle in hall]

[Unidentified teller] One, two, three. Three are against.

[Gorbachev] Three are against...four. Are you against? Yes? Four, five. Five are against. Five are against. [bustle in hall] Who abstained? [bustle in hall]

[Unidentified teller] One, two, three, four, five, six, seven, eight, nine, ten, eleven.

[Gorbachev] Five against and eleven abstained. Comrade Nishanov is elected chairman. Let us greet him and congratulate him. [applause] Please, Rafik Nishanovich [words indistinct] But I think that since (?the post of chairman suits you so well) we will declare a break for 20 minutes. [bustle in hall]

[Unidentified speaker] Thank you. [bustle in hall]

[Gorbachev] Because we will now have to form, not form, but to speak about committees and commissions. [bustle in hall] Twenty Minutes for the break. [bustle in hall]

[Announcer] So you have been listening to a direct relay from the first organizational sitting of the Soviet of Nationalities of the USSR Supreme Soviet. The candidacy of Nishanov, of Deputy Nishanov, first secretary of the Communist Party of Uzbekistan Central Committee was put forawrd for the post of chairman of the chamber of the Soviet of Nationalities, of the Council of Elders. In the course of almost 2 hours, around 40 different questions on relations between nationalities, on national characteristics were put to him by tens of USSR People's Deputies. He answered all questions thoroughly, soundly. In my opinion, all deputies received (?the answers).

PRAVDA Publishes 31 May Mutalibov Speech

PM0206092189 Moscow PRAVDA in Russian
1 Jun 89 Second Edition p 3

[Account of speech by Deputy A.N. Mutalibov, chairman of the Azerbaijan Soviet Socialist Republic Council of Ministers, under the general heading "Time of Analysis and Decision: Team of PRAVDA Journalists Reports From Kremlin Palace of Congresses": "From the Speech by Deputy A.N. Mutalibov (Kubatlinskiy National Territorial Okrug No 211, Azerbaijan Soviet Socialist Republic)"; speech delivered at 31 May first session of Congress of USSR People's Deputies]

[Text] Hardly anybody doubts today that the democratization and glasnost engendered by restructuring have become irreversible. This is borne out by the whole atmosphere, the whole ambience in which our congress is taking place. The working people of Soviet Azerbaijan, the people's deputies, and our delegation perceive the report of M.S. Gorbachev as a thorough, self-critical analysis of what has been accomplished during the years of restructuring and as a program of our future joint work. Irrespective of the complex and very difficult problems which exist in the country, restructuring—and this is a fact—has set our society in motion. It is merely a question of the pace and efficiency with which it is proceeding, a question of what we should focus our attention on in the coming period and where we should begin.

The problems which have arisen in the country and all its regions apply, in one way or another, also to Azerbaijan. The disproportions and mistakes which were tolerated in the past have created a strained economic situation in the republic. Azerbaijan is characterized by single-crop [monopolnyy] agriculture and by industry geared to the extraction of raw materials and the production and delivery of semimanufactures. The republic has quite a high indicator for per capita national income, yet at the same time regarding all social security problems, or rather everything that determines people's living standards, we are lagging seriously behind the average union indicators, which fail to satisfy the people. This structure of the economy, naturally, does not ensure today the most vital tasks, which are connected in particular with consumer goods production and the provision of a wide range of services, and this has given rise to an imbalance in money circulation and caused other negative phenomena.

This social backdrop has made it necessary for us to elaborate and adopt effective measures and take unorthodox decisions. Within a relatively short time a decisive breakthrough has been achieved in implementing tasks in the social sphere, which is the most backward and causes the most concern among Azerbaijan's working people. The volume of individual housing construction has doubled, for instance, and we are determined to further step up its pace. Changes for the better are emerging in food supplies and the provision of medical services, and a computerization program is under way, along with efforts to improve the structure of industrial production in favor of the development of those sectors capable of absorbing surplus labor resources. The struggle against corruption, the black economy, and all types of crime has been stepped up. And these are only the first signs of restructuring, only the very beginning of our work.

Higher targets can only be achieved by efficiently assimilating new methods of management and implementing the measures proposed in M.S. Gorbachev's report. We regard territorial economic accountability as the shortest way to the development of the republic's productive forces and therefore we fully support the policy aimed at expanding the economic independence and giving expression to the sovereignty of union republics. In this context I propose that the elaboration of the law on union republic self-management and self-financing be speeded up, that no experiments be carried out, and that instead, these principles be assimilated in all republics as a whole because, as I see it, they are interested in this.

At the same time I would like to emphasize that the new system of economic relationships must not be allowed to erode the principles of Soviet federalism but must promote their consolidation. The union republics cannot be strong without a strong center, and vice versa. At the same time there have been attempts of late to use the concept of regional economic accountability as a sort of cover for autarkic tendencies, for a desire for self-isolation. This is fraught with the curtailment of economic ties between union republics. Incidentally, I must say that long before the switch to territorial economic accountability in 1989, when, as you know, more than 50 percent of the production of national economic output is being based on direct contracts, we are having tremendous difficulties which can be expressed in a single phrase—diktat by labor collectives: I conclude a contract if I like, if I choose not to, I don't. As a result the industry in our republic is already in a chaotic state. No doubt this also applies to other regions. This cannot be tolerated in conditions of a state that is built on the principles of a voluntary union of sovereign republics that are closely linked by economic and cultural ties and have a common history and political system. The integrated national economic complex is a tremendous asset of our social system and it must not be squandered. This is our position. Integration processes are a general world trend today. Is it possible to depart from it?

Development is unthinkable without large-scale equivalent exchanges of goods and sensible specialization and production sharing. At the same time one-sided development of the national economies of specific republics or their transformation into a raw material appendage are impermissible. It is necessary in the interests of resolving internal republican problems such as, in particular, saturating the republican market with goods and solving the problem of balance, to examine regional rights and to permit republics (and here I back the statements of my colleagues) to market goods produced over and above the state order as well as raw materials and production waste.

We are now trying to solve these problems by relying on our own resources and to rid ourselves of freeloading attitudes. However, there are also problems where support from the center is necessary, for instance, problems such as improving the structure of the republic's industry and creating new jobs in view of the highly critical demographic situation. In this context I would like to take this opportunity to express particular disagreement with the decision to mothball a number of industrial construction projects such as, for instance the Baku personal computer plant or the Kirovabad automobile plant, where two-thirds of the capital investments have already been assimilated, or the Nakhichevan carpet combine, which is essentially finished. Such actions on the part of central departments in the spirit of administrative-edict methods of leadership are no longer acceptable today. The commissioning of these projects would make it possible to reduce goods shortages and provide jobs for tens of thousands of people. After all, we must provide work for more than 65,000 able-bodied people who have arrived in the republic from Armenia as a result of the well known events.

By common efforts we must also solve the problem of sore points in the sphere of interethnic relations, including the problem of Nagorno-Karabakh. For all the specific nature of each of the numerous problems of this kind, they are essentially typical of many regions of the country. They stem from deformations allowed to occur in the past in the system of social relations and from a failure to resolve socioeconomic and moral and psychological issues. And they have to be tackled in a calm atmosphere rather than by means of strikes, pressure tactics, and violation of republics' sovereign rights. As is known, as a result of the CPSU Central Committee and USSR Council of Ministers resolution to cardinally improve the situation in the Nagorno-Karabakh Autonomous Oblast, considerable funds have been appropriated for this purpose. It is necessary to spare no effort to utilize this aid. However, there are forces—and I say this with pain in my heart and with much regret—which, in the pursuit of certain aims, are blocking the first signs of positive changes and are not allowing interethnic confrontation to subside. The time has come to draw a sharp distinction between those who really seek to improve interethnic relations and strive for the socioeconomic transformation of this region and those who only make territorial claims. How much trouble, how much damage have they already caused! It is necessary to strictly observe the laws and with their help to ensure order and guarantee security and protection to all people, no matter where they live and irrespective of their nationality. M.S. Gorbachev especially emphasized this idea in his report and we fully support it. Our voters demand that we switch from appeals to resolute actions to apply the laws adopted by the Soviet people to protect their interests.

Ecological problems have become particularly acute of late. They are causing us much concern, too. The makers of a film shown recently on central television described Sumgait as a dead zone. Chemical installations have pushed people into the background here and have brought the city to the brink of an ecological crisis. There are quite a few such cities in the republic and the country as whole. The situation which has developed in these cities stems from departmental egoism and disregard for people's interests, but at the same time it is also due to the irresponsibility of the labor collectives themselves, their immediate managers, and us all. A great deal has already been said about this, it is concrete actions that are needed.

We are carrying out a tremendous amount of work, which, incidentally, is being closely watched by the republic's entire public. At the same time we do not steer a course of confrontation with union ministries, a course of shutting down chemically harmful or ecological harmful production facilities, since, as I understand it, the country's national economy cannot manage without them. As an example I would like to mention the interesting work which we have been doing of late with leaders of ministries and the Council of Ministers. I would like to mention Comrade Gusev, who has visited our republic many times in connection with these questions and Ministers Comrade Bespalov and Comrade Olshanskiy. We are aware that only together can we find a solution to all questions.

Since these problems hold the attention of our entire public today, our delegation deems it necessary to put forward a proposal that a special commission be formed at the Supreme Soviet, a commission on the environment which would assist the State Committee for Nature Conservation to exercise its rights more fully and in a more principled fashion.

The solution of ecological problems demands interregional integration. Take the Caspian Sea, for instance—we will never resolve the problems connected with cleaning it up single-handed without the cooperation of the oblasts of the Volga region, Dagestan, and the Kazakh and Turkmen Soviet Socialist Republics. We propose that a Caspian Institute be set up for this purpose with the functions of a subcommittee, with directive functions, whose instructions would have the force of a law to be implemented by all republics.

The number one problem is food supplies to the population. Its solution depends on many factors. Today I would like to highlight the problem of land reclamation. Of late a mood opposed to land reclamation has been developing in the country. I would in no way justify the many distortions, but it is quite obvious that without land reclamation the guaranteed conduct of agriculture is impossible today.

The restructuring under way in the country has reached another stage which is significant for us—the elaboration of laws defining the rights of the USSR, the union republics, and autonomous formations. Can it be regarded as normal when, among the countless legal acts regulating the sphere of economic relations, only an insignificant quantity, literally a handful, take the form of a law?

Now about our attitude toward improving the work of the Soviet of Nationalities. It has been proposed that all problems relating to interrepublic and interethnic relations submitted to the Congress of People's Deputies be examined by the USSR Supreme Soviet. We believe that these questions must first of all without fail be agreed with union republics, especially those of them relating to changing borders or forming new subdivisions. These questions must be examined only with them, on the basis of Article 78 of the constitution.

USSR Supreme Soviet of the Union Meets 3 Jun
PM0706105189 Moscow IZVESTIYA in Russian
5 Jun 89 Morning Edition pp 4-7

[Unattributed report: "First USSR Supreme Soviet Session"]

[Excerpts]

First Sitting of the Soviet of the Union

The sessions hall of the chambers of the USSR Supreme Soviet in the Kremlin, 1500 hours, 3 June 1989.

Comrade M.S. Gorbachev, chairman of the USSR Supreme Soviet, is in the chair. [passage omitted]

[Primakov] Comrades! Let us begin with questions. Are there any questions? Please.

[From the floor] More than 200 delegates representing public education in the USSR met together to discuss questions, and a decision was adopted to create a separate joint committee of the Soviet of the Union and Soviet of Nationalities on public education and upbringing. Was this question raised, and how was it resolved?

[Lukyanov] This question was discussed very carefully, because many deputies expressed this stand: It would be wrong now to separate public education from the higher educational institutions [VUZ]—this means science, for more than half of our science is concentrated in VUZ's. Therefore it has been deemed expedient to call it the committee on science and public education.

It was pointed out in the chambers' Councils of Elders that although we teach, we educate rather badly. This is why it was proposed to call this committee the committee on questions of science, education, and upbringing. But this does not prevent us from setting up three subcommissions on these questions within this committee.

[Primakov] Please, a question.

[From the floor] [Inaudible].

[Lukyanov] This question, too, was discussed carefully, the question of the political reform. If we said: a commission on questions of the political reform, that would be just the same as a commission on creating the new USSR Constitution. At the congress it is proposed to form a commission to revise the Constitution—Mikhail Sergeyevich spoke of this today—and, naturally, all questions of the political reform will be included here for examination by the commission on revising the Constitution and its creation. Although certain questions of the political reform—for example, the soviets of people's deputies and management and self-management, questions of the protection of citizens' rights and legality—are already enshrined in these commissions.

[Primakov] Please, a question.

[From the floor] Anatoliy Ivanovich, briefly with regard to the commission on transport and communications, in outline. The main resources and the main return in developed countries now come from information science. It would be expedient to have a commission on information science, transport, and communications. This is an extremely important package of questions.

[Lukyanov] This is an interesting question in general. It would be possible to call it the commission on transport and telecommunications. Or on transport, telecommunications, and information.

[From the floor] Right, on information.

[Lukyanov] Well, it must be discussed. That is why we put this proposal to you.

[From the floor] We have discussed interethnic problems in the corridors here. As is known, they are very complex. The idea has emerged that there is clearly no way we can avoid constantly discussing these questions in both chambers. Would it not be expedient to set up a committee on national problems not at chamber level but at Supreme Soviet level?

[Lukyanov] I think that many questions will be discussed together—for example, economic questions, questions of local soviets and nationalities, and so forth. But still, from my viewpoint, the profile of the Soviet of Nationalities must be sustained. This is very important; it is a great advance made at the 19th party conference.

[Primakov] So, please.

[From the floor] Anatoliy Ivanovich, what prompted you to accommodate the consumer goods commission precisely in the Soviet of Nationalities, and not in a committee? These are statewide questions after all, are they not? We regard them as national....

[Lukyanov] We were guided by three elements above all: By the concept which has already been published for nationwide discussion, which hands these questions over to the republics. That is the first point.

Second. The union will still be involved in introducing economic accountability, self-financing, and so forth. Budget planning and financial questions will be here. But, all the same, the responsibility and, most importantly, the management of these questions—and here comrades from the Baltic republics have repeatedly proposed this—have, in my opinion, been resolved correctly. This must be in the republics. And whoever ensures himself better will be in the vanguard.

[Primakov] Comrade Ryzhov, please.

[Yu.A. Ryzhov, rector of the Moscow S. Ordzhonikidze Aviation Institute (Leningradskiy Territorial Electoral Okrug, Moscow City)] Which of the committees or subdepartments will deal with the question of the mass media?

[Lukyanov] We discussed this question and decided for the time being not to make a special note of this, because the mass media will be a question running through a whole series of commissions. Take, for example, the commission on legality and legislation. It will have to create a law on the press. Then another committee will tackle a whole series of questions of protection of citizen's rights. That is, by specially creating this committee now, we would artificially wrest this topic from a whole series of commissions. We will see. If this is necessary, the Supreme Soviet or its chambers will always be able to create such a commission. Let us see in practice. Perhaps we can create a subcommittee or subcommission somewhere.

[From the floor] Anatoliy Ivanovich, a group of Leningrad deputies submitted a proposal to create a committee on appointments to top state posts. As far as I know, that proposal was also supported by a number of Moscow and other deputies. Was this question discussed? If it was not discussed, I resubmit this proposal.

[Lukyanov] The question was discussed most carefully. The point is that the committee on appointments to top state posts is, in fact, every committee and every commission. It is perfectly clear that the appointment of the chairman of the State Planning Committee will be linked with the commissions, with two commissions—on budget-planning financial questions and the commission on the republics' development. It is perfectly clear that the committee on questions of defense and state security will be linked with top appointments to these posts, and so forth. Likewise, the committee on international questions will be linked with the appointment of a whole series of officials for work both in the Soviet Union and abroad. That is, we have made it possible to examine these questions in greater depth and in broader outline. And this is recorded both in the Constitution, as you know, and in the decisions of the 19th party conference.

[Primakov] Do you have a question? Please.

[From the floor] I received a reply to a question connected with culture, but I am not satisfied.

[Primakov] You know, I will only ask you to ask questions, comrades, and to make statements later. You will have an opportunity to express your viewpoint. If you have a question, please ask it.

[From the floor] A commission only on questions of culture in a package with other questions, only in the Soviet of Nationalities, does not satisfy me.

[Primakov] But that is not a question, it is a statement.

[From the floor] [Inaudible].

[Primakov] Fine. Please.

[Lukyanov] I will only say at once that at first we made this decision: a commission on science, education, culture, and upbringing. But then during the discussion the deputies themselves nonetheless proposed moving culture from here to here—to the national question. That includes art, culture, protection of monuments, and so forth. This should be emphasized. On the other hand, it will always be possible to discuss this in any other commission. For example, appropriations for culture will, of course, be discussed by the budget-planning commission, and a whole series of other questions will be discussed in other commissions and in Supreme Soviet committees.

[Primakov] Please.

[From the floor] Was this question not discussed? Well, we know about the role of scientific and technical progress, its place and significance. We have somehow ended up with a commission on science—that is, a committee on science—and a commission on problems of industrial development. We have split up this question. For there is also fundamental, sectoral, and VUZ science. Somehow these questions were not discussed before....

[Lukyanov] I must say that in this case we would increase the number of commissions but would resolve little, because the Supreme Soviet Committee on Science and Technology that used to exist, for all my respect for it, was still forced to incorporate a commission on industry, a commission on transport, and so forth. Clearly, questions of technology and scientific-technical progress are concentrated in the commission called the industrial development commission.

And second. Commissions on the economic reform. These two aspects must be here.

[Primakov] Please.

[From the floor] [Inaudible].

[Lukyanov] I will speak only about what is proposed. After we have adopted the resolution on the formation of the commissions, the chairmen of the chambers together with the deputies will create the backbone of these commissions on the basis of what you yourselves have written, and you will vote. It is proposed to include in them half the members of the chamber and half the USSR people's deputies making up the congress. It is perfectly clear that the commission or committee chairman, the committee secretary, and, perhaps, another three or four people must initially be released from all duties and must work on the committee. The remaining comrades will combine their work with work on committees and commissions. I will say that if we only create purely professional committees divorced from practice and the land, we will drain them of blood. The composition will be approximately 40-45 people, or perhaps 35-40 people. It all depends on what the deputies themselves propose. I must say that I at once ascertained, for example, that very many people wanted to join a number of committees, while some committees are still not full. For example, such a committee was the committee on nature conservation. An intelligent collective farm chairman and a plant director are needed on it, and it needs a politician and party leader. We must have a look. And I believe that deputies will have sufficient wisdom to form such committees, so that they work.

[Primakov] Please.

[From the floor] [Inaudible].

[Lukyanov] During the last break I was subjected to an attack by the women's committee, which said that "childhood" must be set apart, because "childhood" must be tackled separately. Still, comrades, it is hard to tear "childhood" away from the family and the mother. Therefore we would like to create a single commission for women's affairs and protection of the family and children, so as to have subcommittees there. I have no doubt that there will be a subcommittee for children there.

[From the floor] I have a question. All the commissions begin in a specific way: the commission or committee for questions of.... And just one: on construction, on problems of industrial development.

[Lukyanov] Well, in my opinion, "question" and "problem" are one and the same. Let us call it this: on questions of industrial development.

[From the floor] And another question. The question is not clear whether there is a commission or a committee on the power industry.

[Lukyanov] Yes, in industrial development there will definitely be a subcommittee or a subcommission on the power industry, as there was. But I want to say to you, comrades: Why "on questions"? Perhaps we can dispense with questions altogether? No. The point is that

there is, all the same, a parliament with its own sphere. Name a committee without "questions," and you will almost repeat the name of a certain ministry.

[Primakov] Please.

[From the floor] Anatoliy Ivanovich, please tell me. You have spoken of setting up a constitution commission, too. What will this be?...

[Lukyanov] I believe that it must be a commission of the congress, not of the Supreme Soviet. The question is too big. A constitution commission formed by the Congress of USSR People's Deputies. Because only the congress can alter the constitution.

[Primakov] Just a moment.

[From the floor] [Inaudible].

[Lukyanov] A commission is so named only because it is formed by a chamber, whereas a committee is an organ created by the two chambers along lines of parity. Only for that.

[From the floor] [Inaudible].

[Lukyanov] The point is that in a considerable part of the country credentials commissions tackle questions of immunity, and you have seen that our Credentials Commission has tackled this immunity. In addition, under the Law on the Deputy's Status, the Supreme Soviet Presidium stands guard over immunity. Further. The Supreme Soviet, too, is now involved in ensuring the deputy's legitimate rights. During a session the Supreme Soviet alone can deprive a deputy of immunity. And finally. I wish to say that the question of a committee on the ethics of relations was also discussed. At a session of the chambers' Council of Elders we agreed for the time being not to create this committee after all, because in many of the world's parliaments this is dealt with by the chambers' chairmen and deputy chairmen, and where such committees on ethics do exist relations among deputies are quite bad. I believe that our democracy will create a mechanism of good, cultured, and ethical relations among deputies. But, if necessary, we will create one and do something.

[From the floor] [Inaudible].

[Lukyanov] I have already answered that. Both the commission on culture and the commission on human rights and other commissions will tackle this. It was proposed not to create a special committee on this question in the chambers' Council of Elders.

[Primakov] Please. One moment, comrades. Keep in order.

[Lukyanov] No. You will recall that this proposal has already been made.

[From the floor] I remember the proposal, but it was not discussed.

[Lukyanov] How was it not discussed? A proposal was submitted to have a special committee. I read it out: a special committee on questions of the press. Not on questions of information and glasnost, but on the press. This is the second time I have answered you on this.

[Primakov] Comrades, let us reach exact agreement, because we have a huge number of questions to discuss. Let us do this—only those whom I ask to speak will rise and ask questions. Otherwise it will be hard for us to work. Please.

[From the floor] [Inaudible].

[Lukyanov] I agree with you that the name of the commission on problems of industrial development is not very precise. Let us think, because there is here....

[From the floor] [Inaudible].

[Gorbachev] That is a pretty good name.

[Lukyanov] Yes. Although it does not include power engineering, and that is very important to us.

[From the floor] [Inaudible].

[Lukyanov] Well, industry does not always mean the power industry. Do you understand? And, second, as regards the commission on standing order: I am perfectly sure that as soon as the chambers embark on joint work they will set up a commission to prepare standing orders, and the chambers' chairmen and the Supreme Soviet Presidium will monitor their fulfillment.

[Primakov] Who else wishes to put a question? Please.

[From the floor] [Inaudible].

[Lukyanov] I would like to say, comrades, that we discussed this question. The point is that in our country it is impossible to separate finances from plans. The budget is the financial formulation of our plan outlines. And so it is proposed to create two commissions: one commission for general questions, so to speak, in the Soviet of the Union, and the other—for questions of profile—in the Soviet of Nationalities. They will, of course, work in contact with each other, but we must take a comprehensive approach to planning and financial questions. If, as is done in a number of bourgeois countries, we confine ourselves just to budget questions, we will forget about the very important specific nature of the socialist planned economy.

[From the floor] [Inaudible].

[Primakov] No, comrades, if someone insists on questions, they must be given an opportunity to put them. Please.

[From the floor] Comrades! Our press—newspapers and magazines—and also radio and television publish and transmit a lot of materials every day, containing very valuable and businesslike suggestions and criticisms. There is not a single institute in our country where articles in the press are defended. They are mainly the opinions of working people. What about creating a commission where these very valuable working people's suggestions would be studied and even approved.... [Inaudible].

[Lukyanov] From my viewpoint, all commissions must work for this if they want to be linked with the public.

[Primakov] Questions, please.

[From the floor] If there are 30-40 people on a commission, as can be seen from your reply, will 5 or 6 deputies be working permanently?

[Lukyanov] No. As Mikhail Sergeyevich Gorbachev said, 80-90 percent of the deputies elected to the Supreme Soviet will work on it permanently.

[From the floor] We must—perhaps not today but over the coming week—define how we will work in order to know what those who will not be working permanently are to do.

[A.I. Lukyanov] I believe that this question will be resolved as soon as the question of the commissions' personnel and numerical composition is resolved.

[Primakov] Comrades, I urge everyone to ask questions now only on the commissions, if possible, and on the committees. Please.

[From the floor] Please say how many USSR people's deputies not elected to the Supreme Soviet will be incorporated in the commissions and committees. How will rotation by one-fifth and early withdrawal take place in them.... [Inaudible].

[Lukyanov] I can say that according to my calculations, at first the commissions will include approximately 400 USSR people's deputies elected to the congress. Subsequently they will be rotated.

[Gorbachev] That is, in all approximately 800 deputies come to light on the commissions and committees.

[Lukyanov] Yes, 800.

[Gorbachev] Half of them are members of the Supreme Soviet, and half USSR people's deputies. And, in addition, remember that I have said that since we plan for USSR people's deputies to be involved in work all the time, we must, perhaps, ensure that one of the deputy chairmen of a committee or commission is a people's deputy. For they have an equal voice on the commissions, but they no longer have the casting vote when participating in sessions of the chambers.

[From the floor] [Inaudible].... Then third-class deputies will also appear.

[Lukyanov] In general, I am categorically opposed to any division of deputies into first, second, and third classes. Then I must remind you here that in addition to these commissions, there will also be others operating. We have already created at the congress 3 commissions, each of approximately 20 people. And all kinds of groups have been created at the congress.

[Gorbachev] A Constitution commission, for example, will be created.

[Lukyanov] Yes, there will be a Constitution commission, and there will be a mass of other assignments. As far as I know and as we propose, three deputies' commissions will be created under the Supreme Soviet Presidium: on pardons, on awards, on citizenship. That is, no one is more interested in involving deputies in all this work than the Supreme Soviet Presidium. And no one is more interested than we in ensuring that deputies are not divided up into any categories.

[Primakov] So, does anyone else want to ask questions? Well, please put them.

[From the floor] [Inaudible].... The committee on questions of defense and state security. Please say whether this committee will control the activity of state security organs, or will the KGB remain uncontrolled?

[Lukyanov] Definitely, because questions of state security come within its competence, and the KGB will come under the control of that parliamentary committee.

[Gorbachev] In this connection, clearly, it will have a special status, as in all parliaments.

[Lukyanov] That is, the nature of this committee's sessions, too, let us say, and it will, perhaps, have somewhat fewer members [sentence as published].

[From the floor] I have this question: Proposals to create a commission or committee to study public opinion have been heard in speeches at the congress. What about them?

[Lukyanov] I believe that this question concerns all commissions and all committees. A special data bank will be created for this, and it will have access to the data banks of ministries, departments, and institutes. The study of public opinion must be placed on the very highest level. Both a direct link and feedback between the Supreme Soviet and the population must function very well.

[Primakov] Please.

[From the floor] [Inaudible].

[Lukyanov] From my viewpoint, people will address these questions to the committee on rights and citizens' appeals—first. Second, to the committee on questions of the economic reform. Third, industrial cooperatives to the commissions on these questions. Cooperatives connected with services for the population—to the corresponding commission. Complaints will be made to the committee on safeguarding the people's health against cooperatives in the sphere of health care. And so forth. That is, specialists must take a concrete look at every case every time.

[Primakov] Well, some will complain, and some will support.

[Lukyanov] Of course, because I believe that it would be wrong to take an unequivocally negative attitude to cooperatives.

[Primakov] Comrades, perhaps two more comrades will ask questions, and we will end there? Do you agree?

[Deputies] We agree.

[Primakov] Please.

[From the floor] [Inaudible[.

[Lukyanov] There are two commissions: the commission on questions of labor, prices, and social policy—all-union questions; and a second commission, which will examine questions of the economic and social development of republics and regions. And, finally, the committee on questions of the work of soviets of people's deputies and the development of management and self-management, that is, the regional plan will be included here in full. Although Mikhail Sergeyevich rightly said that the committee on questions of the economic reform will tackle these matters in particular detail.

[Primakov] And the final question, please.

[From the floor] Which commission will resolve the question of export-import collaboration?

[Lukyanov] If they are international questions, they will be resolved in the committee on international affairs, which will create a number of subcommittees for this.

[Primakov] So, comrades, before proceeding to the discussion, I would like to reach agreement on the following. Perhaps we will introduce this procedure, which exists in many of the world's parliaments: We allocate a definite time to questions and to discussion and keep clearly to this schedule?

[From the floor] [Inaudible].

[Primakov] Because like this we will have endless disputes, and no one is interested in that. Let us now allocate a definite time to discussion, because the answers to many questions have already been received and, in general, the discussion has already taken place to some extent. How much time do we need to continue it?

[From the floor] Half an hour.

[Primakov] Half an hour for discussion. Are there other proposals? Obviously there is no need to vote. If we conduct the discussion for half an hour, we will vote on these questions, and then we will have nothing more on the agenda. Then it will be possible to dispense with a break. Please.

[From the floor] [Inaudible].

[Primakov] Please, you can come up here if you want.

[Shekhovtsov, deputy dean of the law faculty of the Far Eastern State University (Vladivostokskiy Territorial Electoral Okrug, Russian Soviet Federated Socialist Republic [RSFSR])] The point is that I submitted a proposal at the session of the Council of Elders, but it was not taken into account. I would like to reason and cite arguments.

Comrades! You understand that the very name predetermines the functions of an organ of a committee or a standing commission. I draw your attention to the third committee—the very important committee on questions of legislation, legalities, and law and order. I have already explained that legislation is the sum total of laws and normative acts. What will this committee tackle? Will it really analyze existing legislation? No.

You understand, the corresponding commissions and committees will in their own sphere look at which law to adopt, discuss, and prepare a draft law, and see which must be altered. Then the constitutional oversight committee will verify the norms of current legislation from the viewpoint of their compliance with the Constitution—this layer of relations is also being tidied up. Right? That is, what do I propose? I believe that it must be formulated somewhat differently—the committee on questions of legislative work or on questions of legislative activity. Precisely that committee will receive proposals from the commissions and other committees, and it will be necessary to hone legal formulas here. Because the quality of the law will depend on these formulas. You and I have been convinced, I hope, that the essence suffers, the cause suffers because of all these "as a rule's" and various reservations. Right? Therefore I believe, Anatoliy Ivanovich, that this amendment relating to questions of legislative work must, all the same, be adopted.

[Lukyanov] Unfortunately, I cannot agree, because all the committees and all the commissions will tackle legislation with the participation of this committee. If we write only "legislative work," then it alone will legislate.

Do you see? We have already had the Legislative Proposals Commission, which considered its right to legislate to be a monopoly. All committees and all specialists must participate. The legislation commission, which participates in this work, and others will be responsible for honing formulas.

[Shekhovtsov] Then I propose another option. On questions of improving legislation. That is, it will not examine legislation there in a static state, but questions of altering legislation.

[Primakov] Fine, it will be possible to examine this. I give the floor to Comrade Samarin, a deputy not on the USSR Supreme Soviet.

[Samarin, own correspondent of the newspaper ORLOVSKAYA PRAVDA (Orlovskiy Territorial Electoral Okrug, RSFSR)] Esteemed members of the Supreme Soviet, this is what I would like to say. In my opinion, suggestions have been made both at the congress and by voters that it is necessary to create a commission or a standing committee to monitor the activities of organs of the Ministry of Internal Affairs, the KGB, and the Armed Forces.

The point is that the committee on defense and state security and another committee—I have forgotten now what it is called—are connected with the elaboration either of certain military concepts or of the concepts of combating certain antistate manifestations, and so forth. But I believe that deputies must definitely have control over their work.

The law and order committee is quite another matter. It formulates proposals for making changes to legislation, and so forth. I mean the committee which will monitor or, to put it more broadly, protect the rights of citizens and the state against manifestations which might appear. Incidentally, the events which occurred in Tbilisi and in Armenia indicate that the Supreme Soviet must, without fail, exercise very strict control here. And not general control, but precisely control by a commission. This is my proposal.

[Primakov] Thank you. Please, Deputy Revenko has the floor.

[Revenko] [First secretary of Kiev Ukrainian Communist Party Oblast Committee [obkom] (Belotserkovskiy Territorial Electoral Okrug, Kiev Oblast, Ukrainian Soviet Socialist Republic [SSR])] I believe that we are all now agonizingly seeking how best to organize the work of the Soviet of the Union. These are my views.

First. Not to be in a hurry with the number of commission members. To reserve the right to ensure that it is not a rigid number. Time will suggest to us how each commission will begin its work and how busy it will be. This is important, because many comrades think that by remaining in Moscow they have lost their voters. I am afraid that those deputies who remain in Moscow will find themselves under the same pressure as we find ourselves today from our voters. Therefore a very balanced approach must be taken to the question of who will be here and who will be there. And I would ask the chairman—you, Yevgeniy Maksimovich—to observe this flexibility for the time being, so that we are not in a hurry to define 45, 50, 70, and so forth.

Second: I would consider it necessary for the time being to proceed from smaller to larger, and not from larger, so as not to return later to smaller.

Further, I believe that such a number of commissions must show today that we are in a businesslike mood, because if we increase their number people will say: They are approaching in number the same ministries. Therefore I submit a proposal, which I impose on no one: to confine ourselves for the time being to what we have created. The possibility of work on subcommittees (there will be as many of them as life dictates) will enable us later to orient ourselves correctly in those questions which are of concern to many people. I favor such a number of commissions and committees.

Ye.M. Primakov: Thank you.

Yu.V. Golik, dean of Kemerovo State University Juridical Faculty (Tsentralnyy Territorial Electoral Okrug, Kemerovo Oblast, RSFSR): Comrades, I know that very many proposals have been voiced regarding the creation of commissions to monitor the activity of KGB, Prosecutor's Office, and Ministry of Internal Affairs organs. One has just been heard here. I do not think that we need to do this, and here is why. When we make up our minds to ask for something and to take control of something, let us try to renounce not the old world, as such, but what I would call the old, servile mentality. Any commission and any committee that we set up will have the right to monitor the activity of any department that falls within that committee's sphere of activity. That is why there is no point in creating a special monitoring body. That would disperse both our forces and our attention.

Moreover, I cannot agree with my colleague Shekhovstov's proposal regarding the need to change the formulation of the committee on legislation, legality, and law and order. Viktor Afanasyevich, I consider your proposal simply unsatisfactory, for the simple reason that, according to your proposal, questions of law and order will, whether we like it or not, fall outside this committee's activity. That should not happen on any account. Moreover, the very questions of monitoring the activity of law enforcement organs will also fall outside its activity. I would be extremely unwilling for this to happen. That is why I propose retaining the present title and confining ourselves to that.

Ye.M. Primakov: Please.

From the floor: I was thinking of the Committee on Legislative Work, Legality, and Law and Order, that is, the two remaining functions are to be retained.

People's deputy (unintroduced): Esteemed Chairman! Esteemed Deputies! Women's and children's have traditionally been linked together for many years. That seems quite natural. There has always been a single commission responsible for the protection of mother and child.

Many questions relating purely to women have indeed accumulated today. These include international cooperation involving Soviet women, Soviet women's participation in political and social activity, the social status of women of various groups involved in production, working women's working and living conditions and health, and so on.

Moreover, children's problems form a very vast range of problems and they are, incidentally, not only linked with women and mothers.

Last, there is a vast expanse of problems relating exclusively to children, ranging from upbringing to ecology, crime, and so on. That is why we have upheld very ardently indeed here at the session of the two chambers' Councils of Elders the idea of creating two independent committees—a women's committee and a committee for the family and children. But since it has already been proposed to set up 14 committees, it is senseless to increase their number even further. That would complicate the work of the Supreme Soviet. Evidently it makes sense to agree that there should be a single committee dealing with the affairs of women, the family, and children but that it should be divided without fail into subcommittees dealing with women's affairs and the affairs of the family and children.

There is another request asking for these committees to be formed so as to ensure that women alone do not have to shoulder all the aforementioned problems and their solution.

Ye.M. Primakov: Good. Please.

Yu.N. Shcherbak, writer, secretary of the Ukrainian Writers Union Board, Kiev City (Shevchenkovskiy Territorial Electoral Okrug, Kiev City): Esteemed Yevgeniy Maksimovich! Esteemed Deputies. I spoke at the session of the Council of Elders and I simply want to repeat what I said, because my proposal was not accepted. I did not, like my colleague who spoke here, agree with the name of the commission on problems of industrial development. I comsider that a rather outmoded title. I propose creating a commission on problems of industrial and power engineering development. Since I proposed creating a nuclear regulation committee there, it might be advisable to create a subcommission for nuclear regulation and the security of technological systems under the commission for industrial and power engineering development. There would then be an independent organ within the Supreme Soviet to monitor these high-tech systems. After Chernobyl we know the consequences of lack of monitoring in these matters. It is absolutely essential to ensure that this organ is outside departmental jurisdiction and independent of the Council of Ministers.

I have another proposal: All the proposed commissions make no mention of the word "religion" or "faith," although this is a very serious question that cannot be ignored. I propose creating a commission for questions of the development of culture, language, national and international traditions and the preservation of historical monuments and faith. Thank you.

Ye.M. Primakov: Please.

Voice from the floor: We have completely overlooked transport. Yet this involves motorized, railroad, river, maritime, air, and even space transport. That is why I am asking for the commission to be called "Transport and Communications." It should prevail. If there are any doubts, put this question to the vote.

Ye.M. Primakov: Good. We will create a commission entitled as follows: the commission on problems or questions of the development of industry, power generation, machine building, and technology. Another commission will also be created. It will be called the commission for questions of transport, communications, and information science. Are you satisfied? Good. Thank you. Who else wants to speak? Go ahead.

V.I. Kirillov, senior scientific staffer at Voronezh Polytechnical Institute, Voronezh City (Leninskiy Territorial Electoral Okrug, Voronezh Oblast): I am not a member of the Supreme Soviet. I am a congress deputy. I come from Voronezh. I want to say that information science generally incorporates the problems of the country's computerization and creation of a unified data and program bank. I think that this question, which is, so to speak, in a quite embryonic state in our country, should be assigned to a single individual committee or commission on information science.

Ye.M. Primakov: Comrades, before I give the floor to the next speaker, I want to provide the following clarification. First, we will, of course, have subcommittees and subcommissions. That is why many questions will be designated in the form of existing subcommissions and subcommittees. If we create either individual commissions or individual committees on each of the important questions we have raised here, we will either duplicate the executive structure or we will have such an unbelievably large number of committees and commissions that all the Supreme Soviet's work will dissolve utterly and completely.

That is why I am asking you merely to take this into consideration. I am also asking you to take another element into consideration—the fact that corrections and amendments will be made and this system modernized

after we begin our work. We will come to all of this. For now, let us start to work, and don't let us begin now by breaking down what has been proposed. In view of the comments that have been made, the proposal enables us to create a good foundation to begin our work.... Thank you.

A.S. Yezhelev, chief of the IZVESTIYA Leningrad office, Leningrad City. (From the USSR Union of Journalists): My proposal is in the spirit of your recommendations. Since Anatoliy Ivanovich Lukyanov told us at the Council of Elders that no unanimous opinion was reached on the question of creating a committee on questions of glasnost and the work of the press and the mass media, I subscribe to Deputy Lauristin's proposal at this session to extend the functions of the committee on questions of economic reform designated here, make it a committee on questions of economic and political reform, and have a subcommittee within the framework of this committee on glasnost and the work of the press and the mass media.

In this instance I am also fulfilling the instructions of all deputies from the Union of Journalists and many deputies from other creative unions. I ask you to examine this proposal and urge you to support it.

Ye.M. Primakov: I am afraid that we are "throwing out the baby with the bath water" in this formulation of the question, Comrades, because economic reform is the main thing now, it is what we need. And... What are you saying?

Voice from the floor: Don't breach the standing orders. You do not have the right...to speak....

Ye.M. Primakov: Why are you depriving me of that right?

Voice from the floor: (Inaudible). If the chairman provides a commentary every time, there will be no session.

Ye.M. Primakov: No, Comrades, one minute.... Let us come to some agreement, naturally, I will not take up too much of your time, but I do not see the work of chairman only involves giving someone the floor. Please....

I.P. Zelinskiy, rector of Odessa I.I. Mechnikov State University, Odessa City (Odesskiy-Leninskiy Territorial Electoral Okrug, Odessa Oblast): We heard the words "protection of citizens' rights" over and over very often during meetings with voters. Yet these words do no appear in the proposed titles of our committees and commissions. That is why I propose changing the name of the third committee on the list to read as follows: committee on questions of legislation, legality, law and order, and protection of citizens' rights. (Noise in the hall). I am proposing what my voters told me.

Ye.M. Primakov: So, thank you.

People's Deputy (unintroduced): I would like to touch on three things.

First: I do not agree that we should have a committee on economic and political questions because we should make policy by creating the relevant laws. That is our policy. We are not a party, we are a parliament. The party should tackle political questions. We—most of us are communists—will engage in policy within the party but we should deal with laws here. There should be a Law on the Press if necessary, and the law will provide for all policy on the press. That is my attitude. That is why the wording "Committee on Questions of Economic Reform" is correct, in my opinion.

The second thing that I would like to mention is this: The point is that we are once again stubbornly veering toward the sectoral principle. Have you noticed? We have added one sector, a second, and a third.... Unfortunately, that is still how we think at present. I believe that we should not strive for the sectoral principle, that it is not a mandatory principle in life. I think that we should choose questions that are of fundamental importance for our country today—sectoral and nonsectoral. In any case, none of us here imagines that we do not have the right to set up additional committees in the future if necessary. The arrangement is not meant to last forever. It seems to me that we only need elect those committees that are of fundamental significance for our country now. After 3 or 4 or 5 years some of these committees will fall by the wayside and new ones will be set up—that is progress.

My third question concerns chairmanship as practiced in parliaments. I categorically object to the present method of running the assembly. In my opinion, it is the chairman's job to ensure strict observance of the procedure of our sessions. In my opinion, the chairman has the right to sum up and, so to speak, express his opinion at the end of every question. But he does not have the right to correct everyone who expresses an opinion. I that case the chairman receives greater rights than any other deputy. I elected him only to moderate the daily work schedule correctly, and I do not give him any more rights than myself. Thank you.

Ye.M. Primakov: Thank you.

B.N. Nikolskiy, editor in chief of NEVA journal, Leningrad City (Smolninskiy Territorial Electoral Okrug, Leningrad City): Comrades, I think that the creation of a committee on questions of glasnost would be of fundamental significance under current conditions because glasnost is one of the main assets and achievements of restructuring and because the further deepening of the country's democratization is inconceivable without glasnost. That is why glasnost itself needs to be deepened today and legally defended. Glasnost still has no legal protection today. It depends in many respects on the individual rather than on the law. Comrades, it is surely no secret that we usually follow routine reshuffles in the Politburo with much more agitation and, I would say, trepidation in our hearts than, say, the appearance of any new resolution.

The most heated disputes are flaring up today namely around mass media organs and their role in the restructuring process. The most varied viewpoints are clashing here. Questions of creating new press organs affiliated to social movements and organizations are also assuming no mean significance. This question was frequently raised by voters during the election campaign. The Congress also raised the question of making the appointment of the chief editor of IZVESTIYA and the chairman of the USSR State Committee for Television and Radio Broadcasting the prerogative of the Congress or the Supreme Soviet. The committee on questions of glasnost could probably examine these candidacies. That is why I think that we should return to the question of creating a special committee on questions of glasnost and mass media organs. Thank you.

Ye.M. Primakov: Thank you.

A.A. Sobchak, chief of a Leningrad State University Juridical Faculty department, Leningrad City (Vasileostrovskiy Territorial Electoral Okrug, Leningrad City): I would like to voice my opinion on the committees' spheres of activity—without increasing their number. Questions of glasnost and the activity of the mass media are indeed such today (we Leningraders sense this particularly after recent combined Leningrad Oblast and city party committee plenums, where questions of glasnost and the work of the mass media were presented in a quite distorted form) that it is now the mass media that are in need of particular monitoring by deputies. I propose the following solution to this question. The committee on citizens' rights and appeals should be given the following title: committee on glasnost, mass media activity, and citizens' appeals. The question of citizens' rights should be transferred to the committee on questions of legislation, legality, law and order, and defense of citizens' rights. Then everything would be set to rights and we would encompass the most important questions of glasnost and mass media activity without increasing the number of committees.

Ye.M. Primakov: Thank you.

From the floor: Esteemed Chairman, Esteemed members of the Supreme Soviet, I would like to submit a proposal. I took part in the work of the Council of Elders session. Unfortunately, my proposal did not get through there. But I would like to repeat it here. The point that union republics, autonomous republics, okrugs, and oblasts will be represented in the work of the commissions. But, unfortunately, large administrative areas (on an oblast scale) which are the central link with our regional policy will not be represented at all in the Soviet of the Union. In my opinion, that would be incorrect. That is why I am proposing that a commission on regional policy and the economic and social development of krays, oblasts, and economic areas should be created within the Soviet of the Union to ensure that the Soviet of the Union takes part in elaborating regional policy and regional development policy and resolving various interregional problems and reflects the interests of the largest krays and oblasts.. If you consider my proposal impossible, then, in view of Yevgeniy Maksimovich's proposal, subcommissions should be created to consider this question somehow within the Soviet of the Union. Namely the fact that this kind of component falls outside our attention within the complex.

Ye.M. Primakov: Thank you very much.

D.G. Smirnov, engineer and designer at "KhEMZ" Production Association, Kharkov City (Kharkovskiy-Moskovskiy Territorial Electoral Okrug, Kharkov Oblast): Comrades, I can see that we are forgetting all the time that we are also the people who will set up these commissions and committees, make timely changes, and so on. Why are we discussing this now? Let us begin with what we have. If we do not like it, we will change everything at the next session. What about the Congress? It is the Supreme Soviet that creates its commissions. One thing, I would like to support Deputy A.A. Sobchak's speech: He formulated the name of the committee in a splendid fashion. His words should be used in the wording so that people can see right away what specifically the committee is engaged in and where to appeal.

Ye.M. Primakov: Thank you. Next.

From the floor: I would propose slightly amplifying this title: committee on human rights and citizens' appeals. Human rights incorporate, correspondingly, those rights that Comrade Sobchak mentioned. As for glasnost and the mass media, an individual committee, if any, should be created on these questions. Thus you can simply add to the title: committee on human rights and citizens' appeals. Analogies exist in virtually all Western countries' parliaments...

Ye.M. Primakov: I have been bullied too much to be able to react directly to all this. Please.

M.Y. Lauristin, director of a Tartu State University department (Tartuskiy Territorial Electoral Okrug, Estonian SSR): Since I was described as the author of the proposal to combine economic and political reform in a single committee, I will say first that I did not propose that. I proposed something else—I proposed including the contentious issue of glasnost in the mass media in the committee on questions of the work of the soviets, management, and self-management (as a subcommittee), because the problem of the development of the media and the development of glasnost and democratization is part of social management just the same. We can see now how important it is for the entire problem of feedback in our society and information flow to accord with democratization. This should be incorporated in a special committee rather than dispersed round various committees, as has been suggested to us. I consider the linking of this question to citizens' appeals to be wrong, because

citizens' appeals consist of letters, specific complaints, and so on. I am asking for it to be included in the committee on management so that problems of the press and the mass media and the development of glasnost are examined as a whole.

Ye.M. Primakov: Thank you. Please.

From the floor: I propose leaving the title of the committee on women as protection of the child and the mother. (Inaudible) Let us not forget those women who rear children. (Inaudible)

Ye.M. Primakov: Comrades! The last two speeches, because we agreed....

From the floor: Comrade Deputies, I fully support the speech (inaudible) arguing that management and self-management cannot be developed without glasnost and democracy. That is why other mass media must also be subsumed under the glasnost subcommittee.

Ye.M. Primakov: Thank you.

B.Kh. Blayev, director of Tyrnauzskiy Tungsten and Molybdenum Combine (Kommunisticheskiy Territorial Electoral Okrug, Kabardino-Balkar Autonomous Soviet Socialist Republic): I propose electing a commission presidium in every commission.

Ye.M. Primakov: Fine, a brief statement. You have another minute, please.

From the floor: I have a very short speech. Comrades! If we are saying that democracy is the voice of restructuring, we are depriving this democracy (inaudible).... We should create a separate committee subject to (inaudible).... Monitoring the mass media. Because (inaudible)...this is a problem relating to the separation of functions and is above all a problem for our deputies. State power should take this problem in hand. It is an important problem, the problem of democracy.

Ye.M. Primakov: So. Have you all had your say? Ivan Dmitriyevich, please.

I.D. Laptev: (Inaudible) However much monitoring of glasnost in the mass media is examined.... Our country's experience shows that any committee, as soon as we set it up.... (inaudible).

Let us consider this further. Let us have a look if we need to. But my own experience indicates that any new formation does not help but restricts....

Ye.M. Primakov: Good. A last speech. Please.

From the floor: We had a single commission for culture and education quite recently, comprising representatives of both chambers. We have today for some reason separated culture from education and switched them to one chamber alone. I reckon that problems of the Soviet person's culture and upbringing are directly linked with education. This even begins before education. The isolation of education from culture today... (Inaudible) Every Soviet person needs culture today, starting from the day he is born. This is a major factors, and we are seeing its results today—the lack of culture—even at our Congress. That is why, as a representative of culture, I consider that this question covers a kind of vast order opf creation encompassing great subspecies, including music, painting, culture, and literature. We now have millions of representatives in these fields. I believe that (inaudible) gradually, instead of giving culture greater significance we have somewhat belittled it.... Even in relation to the previous period of USSR Supreme Soviet activity.

Ye.M. Primakov: Thank you. Comrades, we have held a fruitful exchange of opinions and very many questions have been raised and answers followed. Since my instructions as chairman spoke of the need to seek solutions that combine all opinions, so to speak, and find compromises and so on, I would like to make certain changes in the light of our discussion.

But first let us agree to vote separately on the Soviet of the Union draft resolution on the permanent commissions and separately on the committees, if there are no objections. Right? Then I propose the following. You have the draft USSR Supreme Soviet Soviet of the Union resolution in your hands. There are the following amendments: The Budget and Planning Commission stays as it is and there were no serious objections to that. Next: the commission on problems of industrial development. A correct proposal was made here to exclude the words "industrial development" and the following title was proposed instead: commission on questions of the development of industry, power generation,. machine building, and technology.

The next commission is the commission on questions of transport, communications, and information science. Next, the commission for labor, prices, and social policy. Following our debate, that is the—amended—form in which it is proposed to ratify the Soviet of the Union draft resolution on the commissions.

I ask you to vote. Those in favor? Please lower your hands. Those against? Two against.

From the floor: A separate question—a question of fundamental importance: Information science is a broad concept.

Ye.M. Primakov: Yevgeniy Pavlovich (turns to Velikhov), despite the fact that you nominated me for this post, I will not allow you to reopen the debate. All right? Two people against. Any abstentions? No abstentions. The resolution is carried.

We now move on to voting on the USSR Supreme Soviet Soviet of the Union draft resolution on the formation of USSR Supreme Soviet committees. The following amendment has been proposed as the result of our debate...

I will read out first all the items where no change is proposed: Committee on International Affairs, Committee on Defense and State Security, Committee on Legislation, Legality, and Law and Order, Committee on the Work of Soviets of People's Deputies and the Development of Management and Self-Management, Committee on Economic Reform. Next—Committee on Agrarian Questions and Food. Next on the order paper: Committee on Construction and Architecture. Then, an amendment: Committee on Science, Public Education, and Instruction. Next, Committee for the Protection of the People's Health. The next committee title has also been amended: Committee for Women and the Protection of the Family and Children. (Noise in the hall). It was mother and child. People advocated introducing the concept of the family here. Let us render it as follows if there are no objections: committee for women and the protection of the family, mother, and child. (Noise in the hall).

From the Presidium: Family, mother, and child.

Ye.M. Primakov: There can be no mother and child without a family. So. Let us begin with the family. Protection of the family, mother, and child. Next—Committee on Veterans and Invalids, Committee for Young People's Affairs, Committee for Ecology and Rational Use of Natural Resources. The next committee name has been amended: Committee on Questions of Glasnost and Citizens' Rights and Appeals.

From the floor: Human Rights.

Ye.M. Primakov: No... rights. Republics can also have rights. Come on, human rights... There are also a citizen's rights and so on. Come on, in general... I am not proposing to amplify. It is proposed that the USSR Supreme Soviet draft resolution "On Committees" be adopted in that form.... What? The last. "Committee on Glasnost and Citizens' Rights and Appeals." What?

From the floor: (Inaudible) Let's vote on it. Let us vote for the first committee....

Ye.M. Primakov: No, Comrades. Well, alright. It is proposed that we vote on each committee. One minute, one minute.... We have received a proposal, let us vote on it. Who is in favor of this? I ask you to raise your hands.

From the floor: In favor of what?

Ye.M. Primakov: Voting on each committee in succession. Clearly no majority, Comrades. What? Another proposal? Yes, please.

From the floor: We have a democratic process; how is this possible. I may agree with this comrade, but not with others. But we are trying once again—on the whole. (inaudible)

Ye.M. Primakov: Allow me, Comrades. Certainly, your proposal is understandable... But I want to say that the name of the committee now, the elaboration of the names of the committees is, I believe—and maybe I am wrong and then you will correct me—but I believe that this is not the kind of question that requires, so to speak, voting by name or separate voting on every committee. We agree that there will be subcommittees and subcommissions. We are giving the maximum consideration to all the comments that have been made in the wording and names of the subcommissions and subcommissions. Well? Let us vote on the whole issue, especially since that is how the majority feel. Then we can announce all this right away. One moment, Comrades! Let us observe procedure. We will report everything just the same. We will tell the Soviet of Nationalities everything that we adopt now, and the Soviet of Nationalities will examine it, and we will then adopt it all at a combined session of the chambers. Understood? So let us nevertheless now give way to the minority, hard though it is—to those who are proposing a vote on everything. Right? You have a question? Please. Is it procedural? If not I will not give you the floor.

From the floor: It is procedural!

Ye.M. Primakov: Please.

From the floor: My question is more for Anatoliy Ivanovich. If our chambers vote differently, won't it be necessary to have a coordinating committee?

Ye.M. Primakov: Absolutely. If the chambers vote differently, one will be set up, and even if the commissions vote differently, Comrades, that is how I see this matter. Certainly Anatoliy Ivanovich also thinks that, if there are commissions that sit together on the same question, for instance, on the budget... and if these commissions have differences of opinion, a coordinating commission will be convened. Of course, this will enter into practice. But I don't think that there is any point now in convening and piling up these coordinating commissions on all questions. So... I will put it to the vote, Comrades. Who....

From the floor: (Inaudible).

Ye.M. Primakov: Well you realize, Comrades, that we have already finished our discussion—physical education and sport are of tremendous significance in our country, I realize, and we do also have other proposals of equally great significance. But when we speak about physical education and sport, we can direct all comrades to the Committee for Health Protection on these questions.

So, Comrades, your attention, please! Comrade Deputies! We are voting on the question of adopting the USSR Supreme Soviet draft resolution "On USSR Supreme Soviet Committees"; this question will then be passed on to the Soviet of Nationalities, because the first question falls within our competence and we simply have to acquaint them—the Soviet of Nationalities—with it. We will pass on the results of our vote here along with the document to the Soviet of Nationalities.

I ask those in favor to vote. Those against? One, two, three.... Three against.... Five against. Any abstentions? Seven abstentions.

The Supreme Soviet resolution is adopted. As I have already said, it will be handed on to the Soviet of Nationalities. I have a few announcements now. First, I have received...

From the floor: (Inaudible).

Ye.M. Primakov: A point of order, please.

From the floor: I have the following proposal to make: Several deputies spoke several times on the same question. Maybe we should introduce into our work the practice of not allowing repeat speeches on the same question until everyone who wishes to speak on all questions has spoken.

Ye.M. Primakov: That is a correct proposal.

From the floor: (Inaudible).

Ye.M. Primakov: I agree with you.

From the floor: (Inaudible). Second. It is very hard to work in an auditorium. It is sometimes necessary to simply ask a question. Is there provision for installing microphones at every desk?

Ye.M. Primakov: There is—as soon as possible, moreover. Now, any more points of procedure? Please.

From the floor: (Inaudible) I ask you to hand over there....

Ye.M. Primakov: Good. I will do that. Thank you. Now, since certain questions linked with the standing orders for our work have been raised I would also like to read out a note, signed by Supreme Soviet deputies; despite its anonymity it raises quite interesting questions, which I think are important: "We submit a request from members of the chamber asking deputies not to come to sessions wearing sporting gear in future. This amounts to disrespect for all of us." Let us introduce parliamentary norms for a truly respectful attitude for all of us and our voters. Now, Comrades, I think that we need to consider the standing orders for our work altogether, which should also include this proposal—to give those who have not yet spoken the right to speak first, observe the time allocated for speakers without fail, and then determine the time for debate in advance in order to keep within that time.

Comrade Deputies, the joint session of the Soviet of Nationalities and the Soviet of the Union will be held Tuesday 6 June at 1000 hours in this hall. There are plans to examine questions regarding the appointment of the chairman of the USSR Council of Ministers and also of the USSR Supreme Soviet committees at that joint session. I declare the Soviet of the Union session closed.

7 Jun Congress Proceedings Reported

Gorbachev Remarks on Fergana
LD0706170489 Moscow Television Service in Russian 1202 GMT 7 Jun 89

[Opening remarks by Mikhail Gorbachev, chairman of the USSR Supreme Soviet, at USSR Congress of People's Deputies session in the Kremlin Palace of Congresses—live]

[Text] Esteemed comrade deputies, may we proceed with the congress' work. Before we tackle the issues on the agenda, I would like to inform the congress, on behalf of the presidium, about the situation in Uzbekistan, how it is unfolding and developing, and what state it is in. The situation has been complex so far. The government commission is working; it has been set up in the republic under the leadership of Comrade Kadyrov, chairman of the Council of Ministers. Great explanatory work and work within the competence of administrative organs aimed at maintaining people's safety and public order is being conducted with the participation of all the local and republic organs and with aid from the country's administrative organs. Nevertheless, one way or another, here and there it bursts through, this situation, and it is accompanied by clashes which result in people being wounded or killed. Cases of arson, though fewer, are continuing. Anyway, although the situation is under control, let us put it this way, it has not acquired a stable character [Gorbachev corrects himself]...it is not changing for the better in a resolute way. Naturally, we all are very concerned about this, very concerned. This is yet another signal showing to what extent we should be patient, self-possessed, and attentive, to what extent we should adopt a responsible attitude to what we do in the country and all the regions and especially with regard to relations between nationalities. I would like to invite you to address once again the working people of Uzbekistan, on behalf of the congress, with an ardent appeal to heed our address, that of the deputies of the first congress, to keep self-control and calm, and most importantly, to do everything to keep these events under control, so that that group of people that is being incited now, one way or another—I must say this—and is using firearms—they are being incited to extreme methods—so as to take the situation firmly under control and to stop those people.

We hope the republic and working people have enough strength, and that they will hear this appeal of ours. In turn, I think, let's come out with the commission that the law and order bodies of the Soviet Union, working jointly with the republican commission and the working people of the republic, should do everything to ensure people's safety, and prevent them from coming under threat from these extremist manifestations that are taking place there.

I think that the working people will hear us in all republics, and will join with the congress in these words of appeal from the deputies of the first Congress of People's Deputies.

If you share this concern, and I am sure you do, I ask you to support this appeal and the commission we are coming out with, by raising your mandate papers. Please lower them. That is agreed. We shall keep the congress informed about the course of events.

Comrades, the first sessions of the USSR Supreme Soviet and its chambers have taken place, at which the basic organizational question were decided. The chairmen of the chambers have been elected, and the standing commissions have been formed. There has been an exchange of opinion on the committees common to both chambers; this remains to be definitively decided at joint sessions. Nevertheless, work in this direction continues. At a joint session today of the Soviet of the Union and Soviet of Nationalities, the chairman of the Council of Ministers of the USSR was appointed. The chairman of the Committee of People's Control was elected. The Supreme Soviet of the USSR has appointed Comrade Ryzhkov, Nikolay Ivanovich, chairman of the Council of Ministers of the USSR. [applause] Comrade Kolbin has been elected chairman of the Committee of People's Control of the USSR. [applause]

The floor is given to Deputy Ryzhkov, Nikolay Ivanovich, for his report on the program of the forthcoming activity of the government of the USSR. [unidentified voice from floor shouts "question"] Wait a bit. He's going to speak now, and then you can ask. Pardon? Later, later! [indistinct voice from floor] And it will continue. Yes, together, and I still intend to speak.

Ryzhkov Addresses Congress
LD0706181889 Moscow Television Service in Russian 1212 GMT 7 Jun 89

[Report by Nikolay Ryzhkov, chairman of the USSR Council of Ministers, to the USSR Congress of People's Deputies in the Kremlin Palace of Congresses—live]

[Text] Esteemed comrade deputies! Everything that is happening in this chamber, to which the attention of Soviet people is riveted, really does signify the beginning of a qualitatively new stage in the development of our society, and a transition to genuine people's power in one of the most ethnically varied states in the world. It is precisely thus, understanding the peculiarities and the significance of the current moment, with a feeling of immense responsibility and profound gratitude, that I perceived my nomination for the post of head of government.

In light of the sharp debates that have developed at the congress, it goes without saying that I need, apart from setting forth the basic guidelines for the forthcoming work of the USSR Council of Ministers, to give an analysis of the country's socioeconomic development. This will enable the deputies to penetrate further into the work of the government, and to make an all-round analysis of the steps which were undertaken to resolve the difficult problems which faced our economy and to get an idea of the platform of the new composition of the USSR Council of Ministers. Taking this as a premise, it will be evidently be correct to begin with an analysis of the economic situation in the country. It is not unambiguous and it can be assessed in different ways. Such assessments have been audible during the principled conversation on the topic at the congress.

The consumer market is in a complicated situation. Financial and money circulation are in an extremely disordered state. Agriculture and capital construction are emerging from stagnation too slowly, and there is no subtantial breakthrough in speeding up scientific and technological progress. That is one point of view, and it has a right to exist. There can be another; I would call it the traditional approach: The national income and the rates of growth of production are increasing, and to no small extent. The whole of the growth in industrial output has been achieved thanks to labor productivity, something that it has not been possible to achieve throughout the history of the development of our economy. Profit is increasing at an unprecedented rate. Wages and social consumption funds are growing, and we have turned a corner in speeding up housing construction, and in building of schools, hospitals and kindergartens. These are realities, and such an appraisal of them also has the right to exist. Finally, there is the third approach: The contrast between these processes, their contradictoriness and unusual properties, stem from the profound transformations upon which we have consciously embarked, from the immense complexities which are inevitable when society is in transition to a new qualitative level.

So the assessments vary. But it is only in combination that they can provide a real idea of the true state of affairs and that they will enable us to understand the sources of our difficulties and work out correct paths for further movement and, on this basis, determine both the urgent tasks for the coming year or 2 and those for the whole program for the new government.

People have a right to ask why the country is emerging from the economic crisis slowly. The reply to this and many other questions, whether we like it or not, is objectively contained both in our past and in the present.

During the debates on the report by Chairman of the USSR Supreme Soviet Mikhail Sergeyevich Gorbachev, we did not avoid the question of what we inherited up to April, 1985.

We must (?realize quite clearly) that the iceberg of colossal problems and difficulties which had amassed in the economy over many decades cannot be melted by 4 years of even the most active restructuring. Therefore, once again, I want to focus the attention of the people's deputies on the need to thoroughly weight the situation that existed when restructuring began. Facing the congress, we must admit with all frankness that the burden which was dragging the country to the depths of crisis turned out to be considerably heavier than the government had previously imagined. In the mid-eighties, the economy, because of its extensive development, was unable to guarantee the implementation to the equal extent of the three main tasks which faced the country at one and the same time: the raising of the people's welfare and the resolution of the social problems which had come to a head; the effective development of the national economy, allowing the tasks of the current period and also of the future to be resolved; and the guaranteeing of the high level of the state's defense capabilities. First, the development of the economy. It was held back by an insuperable barrier of the inertia of all economic systems, and the lack of receptivity to intensification, to scientific and technical progress. In all spheres of the national economy an expenditure-orientated mechanism prevailed. Mechanical engineering lagged behind. The economy's raw materials thrust and the underdevelopment of the consumer sector intolerably deformed the structure of public-sector production and set it aside for the solution of social problems. To this should be added the under-efficiency of the agroindustrial complex, and the country's growing dependence on imported foodstuffs.

The solution of defense tasks complicated the economic situation to no small extent. The need to guarantee the parity of the military potentials of the USSR and the United States demanded great efforts, the concentration here of the best specialists, and the most up-to-date technology and equipment: resources which were in short supply. Thus the expenditure-oriented economy and the defense complex swallowed up a considerable part of the national income. There was a constant shortage of resources for the main tasks connected with the satisfaction of people's demands. In the end result, by the middle of the last 5-year plan period the rise in the population's living standards had practically come to a halt, with complete stagnation of the social and cultural sphere. The financial deficit also rose continuously, although that circumstance was simply passed over in silence. Every year, the people were told that the budget income exceeded expenditures. In this very complex situation, the possibility had to be found primarily at least of halting or at the very least of slowing down the slide into the crisis. The country was, essentially, led into a dead end. There was no choice. Objectively, restructuring's time had come. Life pointed out to us the only true way: real economic reform. It rightly occupied the central place in the whole restructuring of Soviet society. We did not set about elaborating a program to implement it empty-handed. Ideas were gathered bit by bit, and we felt our way towards the theoretical foundations. Foreign experience was studied thoroughly, and experiments were carried out. I should say that at the beginning of that period, there was quite a bit of discord. But nevertheless, by 1987 we were able to complete that stage of work and to take up the creation of a new mechanism of economic management on a broad front.

The first steps did not come easily. Dogmatism and the residue from the periods of the cult, of voluntarism, and stagnation made it very difficult to move forward. There was no profound theoretical study of what we had to do. In many things we worked by trial and error, we learned and grew more mature for more radical decisions.

One of them was the working out of the law on state enterprises, a legal economic act of a fundamentally new kind. It has been the pivot for the modern system of management, and the foundation for its construction. Of course, not everything in the establishment of this system runs smoothly. Even the economic reforms are not going down a mirror-smooth road. There are examples of lack of coordination in specific elements of it. We are aware of them: Work in practice, and sometimes undesirable results, shed light on them. On the whole, the consistent application of the law on enterprises creates the essential conditions for changing the whole economic situation, and encourages the labor collectives to work efficiently.

It is clear that we have to seek an improvement in the economy persistently, overcoming one stage after another. The logic of the restructuring of production relations has led to it being essential to restore the cooperative movement in the country. In this sense one can, for example, speak boldly of the Law on Cooperatives of the USSR as another milestone on the road to renewal. It was a serious advance toward the further democratization of the economy. The cooperative movement is now suffering difficult growing pains: The future of the cooperative movement will depend to a large extent on how the healthy beginnings will develop in it, and what its prestige in society will be.

A year later, the Decree on Leasing. This shows that we are moving forward, consistently, step by step, to a new understanding of the role of various forms of ownership and management. We are making headway on questions about which, until not long ago, we still had such ossified ideas. What is particularly important is that the advance is happening not only on a theoretical level, but in concrete, practical deeds.

The consistent policy aiming at the democratization of management, the restructuring of the organizational structures in the national economy, and, the main thing, the social reorientating of the econmy, has brought us to the necessity of disseminating the principles of self-financing and self-recouping to the level of republican and local management.

Possible alternatives for implementing this idea have been worked out. The draft general provisions on the restructuring of the activity of the union republics has been published in the press, as is well known. In the process of debate, those provisions on the whole received support. But you know, comrades, the view of a number of republics on that question. It has been expressed more than once at the congress. I must say with all frankness, that a lot of how these republics see the problem in regional financial autonomy is attractive, and contains an element of healthy constructivism. At the same time, some of their proposals, which in many ways lead to economic self-isolation, and also a number of other fundamental provisions, are very debatable, and in our opinion will not be of help to the republics.

Throughout the world there are powerful integrational processes going on. This is an objective vital demand. So we have to search for the true path to success in the consolidation of forces, in deepening the distribution of labor while taking into account the specifics and potential of each one of the republics, the expansion of economic ties on a mutually advantageous basis, and the formation of an all-union market as quickly as possible.

Obviously there is no need to dwell on an analysis of the virtues and shortcomings of individual elements of the proposed mechanism of regional financial autonomy, the more so since much work lies ahead in drafting and debating the appropriate bill. The government's opinion on this question is that given the diversity of forms and methods of socioeconomic development of any region of the country, we should, on a political level, not violate the federative arrangement of the USSR, and, on an economic level, not permit splintering of the national economy complex in its new content. It would seem that these questions need to be examined only as a whole.

One must act in such a way that from 1991 all republics and regions may change to work under conditions of self-financing, and all law-making acts being drafted for the next 5-year plan period must be in keeping with these principles. But this does not exclude the possibility of working out in 1990 the most important elements of regional financial autonomy in individual republics.

I would like to speak in somewhat more detail about such a major section of the reform as perfection of the organizational structure of administration, to which the congress gave the closest attention. What has the government done here? Our efforts have been directed primarily toward the creation of various structures in the main link of the economy. For instance, about 800 new production and scientific-production and other associations of a similar kind have been created. There are already several state concerns, consortiums, and the first non-departmental corporations in operation. Here things have not proceeded without mistakes, either. Remember the sad experience of the state production associations: One thing was intended, but in fact what was created were offices. The provisions for them had to be cancelled. You live and learn.

Amendments in the primary link made it possible to start perfecting the upper echelons of administration. A number of ministries and departments have been abolished. Some of them have been transformed into all-union departments. The apparatus of state administration in the country as a whole has been reduced by 600,000 persons.

Undoubtedly, as the new forms of management are created at the level of the main link of production, the system of administration of the economy and the development of direct links in wholesale trade will be further improved. The number of industrial ministries will be reduced and their functions will undergo substantial changes.

In keeping with the USSR Constitution, the chairman of the Council of Ministers, endorsed by the congress, will submit to the Supreme Soviet specific proposals on this question.

To sum up what I have said, I would especially like to stress that while fully sharing the point of view of the comrades who have spoken here, radical restructuring of the economy is proceeding with difficulty. A number of adopted decisions, in connection with the real conditions of management, are half-baked. The reform is now at the most difficult and responsible stage. It is being tested for its durability under the complex conditions of the transition period, when methods of central direction and economic methods of leadership are coexisting. In many respects it is conditioned by the fact that while consistently advancing the reform and refining its main principles, we must not at the same time allow violations of the country's economic stability. In this connection, I wish to stress quite categorically and with all certainty my commitment to truly economic methods of management. I have already had occasion to talk about the fact that in the course of implementing the radical reform we will be drawing ever nearer to forming a new model of the socialist system of economic management. Now, among the scientific public and in the press, a great discussion is taking place on the main principles of this economic model. The position of the government is based on recognizing the role of the socialist market and competition in our economy. I am firmly convinced, however, that this market will be able to develop successfully under the new system of economic management, and will be serving for the good of man only if we create an efficient economic mechanism for regulating it, which ensures reliable protection of the interests of citizens from market spontaneity.

A most important condition for the development of the market is the overcoming of monopolism. It is still very strong, and is at the basis in many respects of the troubles and shortcomings that exist in our country, especially in questions concerning price formation.

Now more than a thousand major and super-large industrial enterprises dictate their conditions to consumers. It is clear that the policy aimed at developing competition in all spheres is exceedingly necessary. For this, in our view, anti-trust legislation will have to be developed. At present the Institute of Economics and the Institute of the United States and Canada of the USSR Academy of Sciences are working on a draft for this law. The draft will, it appears, be submitted to the Supreme Soviet as early as this year.

Giving a summary of the tasks of the new government in such an important sphere as the deepening of the economic reform, I believe that key directions here should become: First, the restructuring of the work of the union republics and local soviets on the principles of regional financial autonomy. I am putting this problem in the forefront as it is not only of economic but also of great political importance. Second, the improvement of the financial autonomy model on the basis of using various forms of ownership and new structural formations. Legislative bodies and the executive authorities will have to elaborate the forms of economic and judicial regulation—and in a number of cases even to opt for reconsideration of operating laws—with the aim of creating equal conditions for the development of all forms of economic management on the basis of competitiveness and competition. Third is the creation of up-to-date, effective methods of controlling market relations. State regulation under conditions of a developed market should be carried out with the aim of solving tasks of raising the well-being of the people and its social security. Fourth, the working out of new principles of taxation policy to ensure a just financial relationship between the state, the republics, local soviets, enterprises and the populace. Undoubtedly inherent in the process of deepening and perfecting the economic reform are its own dialectic, logic, and stages of development. Our task is to have full clarity and accuracy in all this. At the same time, comrades, it is perfectly obvious that the radical economic reform must be carried out simultaneously with the implementation of major measures for profound structural restructuring of the national economy. The structure of the economy's management that has come about remains extremely conservative and overweight. This can be gauged by the fact that in national economic complexes producing raw material, i.e. intermediate produce, there is a concentration of over 60 percent of all fixed industrial production assets, while in industries providing for people's everyday needs there is a paltry amount: Light industry has only 4, and the food industry 6 percent. Without breaking the trends which have come into being historically for primarily developing the production of the means of production, the economy cannot turn its face to the people. This is the reason for implementing a cardinal structural shift in the national economy. Another aspect of this important problem: For decades, since the times of the industrialization, we have had the idea that the production of technical potential of our country is one of the most powerful and up-to-date in the world. As for the power, it is truly so. It was precisely this which allowed the country to become one of the strongest and most influential states. As for being progressive and up-to-date, an analysis of the true state of affairs has shown that of the R1.9 trillion worth of fixed production assets, 40 percent are worn out. Unquestionably, such a situation has an extremely negative influence on the efficiency of the economy. It affects everything, starting from the mastering of progressive forms of production, productivity and working conditions, and quality of output, and ending with the ecological position in many regions of the country.

The technical re-equipment of basic assets will, of course, be one of the main questions. However, it is necessary to realistically evaluate our resources, because we cannot advance on a wide front to resolve this task at present time. Objectively, the necessary conditions for this do not exist in the country. The task consists in selecting the main directions—first and foremost the direction which is linked with people's life. To create the conditions for modernization and re-equipment of the national economy, we need a powerful and modern machine-building industry. Proceeding from this fact, it must be this industry which should be given a priority development in the future, too.

Comrades! The principal and, I would say, also the most difficult task was to make a structural turn aimed at the implementation of the social re-orientation of the entire national economy. For decades we had understood the development of our society mainly in the light of the prism of quantitative indicators; how much coal and ore was extracted, how much steel and cast iron were smelted, how many hectares of plowed fields were had, etc. We missed the moment when in the whole developed world it was not the arithmetical growth, but the qualitative content of these volumes which became the genuine yardstick for the achievements of the nations. As a result, we have arrived at extremely unsatisfactory social indicators. These are first and foremost the conditions of people's life. Behind these words lie the pictures known to all: the shortage of housing, the overloading of transport, the chronic shortage of goods, the disrepectful attitude toward people, and the growing social tension in society. The lack of good order in everyday life gives rise to the feeling of hopelessness in many people and puts an excessive burden on aged and disabled persons, children, and women. I should stress, in view of the huge scale of such a complex and inert system as is our economy, that the process of its improvement is not at all simple, but it was important to break the trends of stagnation. Certain positive shifts for the better were achieved only in 1988.

Let us take the distribution of the national income. In the past the steady growth of that part of it that was channelled toward the creation of production capacities

prevailed, and the poportion of the resources directed to consumption was correspondingly reduced. This situation has begun to change. This can be graphically seen in the expenditures of the country's state budget. While they have on the whole grown by 26.4 percent in 1989 in comparison with 1985, the expenditures on social and cultural measures have grown by almost 33 percent—including those on education, which have grown by 34 percent, on health care, by 45 percent, and on housing construction—counting of all sources of financing—by 37 percent.

Today it can be said with conviction that in the current 5-year plan period it has proved possible to overcome the residual principle in the development of the material base of the socio-cultural sphere. Rates of growth of investment channelled into non-production construction are more than two times outstripping the increase in production capital investment. The addition to the funds for this kind of construction as against the last 5-year plan period will amount in the years 1986-90 to some R80 billion. If, say, in the tenth 5-year plan period, as compared with the previous one, the commissioning of housing even fell by 17.5 million square meters, and in the eleventh 5-year plan period practically failed to grow, in the current 5-year plan period the growth will amount, however, to nearly 100 million square meters. A similar picture is taking shape also for the general education schools. In the tenth 5-year plan period commissioning of them was reduced by nearly 1.3 million places, in the 11th by 1.5 million places, but in the current one a growth of 2.5 million will be secured. The commissioning of hospitals in the two previous 5-year plan periods fell by 28,000 beds. In this 5-year period it will increase by 65,000.

It should be especially stressed that the housing program will undoubtedly be among the constant cares of the new government. For to cope with the set task it is necessary to build some 30 million apartments or houses. From this it follows that already in the next 5-year plan period it is necessary to ensure the commissioning of 850 million square meters of housing, against 650 in the current one. But it would be better still to go for 900 million square meters. This will make it possible to improve housing conditions for 18 million families.

The strengthening of the social bias of the economy has been given a substantial boost in the current 5-year plan period. To solve even the most acute social problem of society, it is necessary to embark on a major economic restructuring of the nature of investment structure, never before carried out in our country on such a scale. This will be a difficult and even an extremely painful process, but it has to be embarked upon.

Undoubtedly, the newly-formed Council of Ministers of the USSR will subordinate all its work to the achievement of the aims most important for each person and society as a whole, and the satisfaction of the requirements of food, goods and services, housing, health, and education, ensuring the possibilities for the spiritual growth of the people and preservation of the natural environment. Already in the current 5-year plan period the government's attention has been centred on questions of the production of nonfood goods. In the first 3 years their output has increased by 32 billion rubles, or by 18 percent, which is practically equal to the growth in the whole previous 5-year plan period. Nevertheless, this turned out to be insufficient for the normalization of the situation. The state of the consumers market was also affected by reductions in the import of nonfood goods, as a result of which their market allocations of 1988 were at the 1985 level. This called for taking additional measures toward increasing the production of goods, and for building up and improving the material base for their production.

A program for technically re-equipping enterprises of the light industry was drawn up and adopted in 1988. For the purchase of up-to-date equipment and technology for this industry we took the step of arranging credits abroad worth over R1 billion, despite our difficulties with foreign currency.

To speed up the normalization of the situation on the consumer market the decision was taken to redesignate many enterprises in operation. The conversion of defense plants is also aimed at this.

As calculations show, we need to increase the production of nonfood goods in 1990, as compared with 1989, by no less than R45-50 billion, or by 20 percent, which exceeds the average annual increases over the past 3 years almost fivefold. In preparing the draft plan for 1990, USSR ministries and departments and the councils of ministers of the union republics took as a target precisely the achievement of such an aim.

Preliminary studies show that next year an increase can be achieved in production against the plan for 1989 of washing machines by one-third, of sewing machines by 20 percent, of radio equipment and tape recorders by 16 percent, and of furniture by 12 percent.

Measures have been taken by the government to expand paid services to the population. Over the 3 years of the 5-year plan period their volume has risen by almost 38 percent and exceeded R62 billion in 1988, as against R58 billion under the 5-year plan. But we still virtually have to create a services industry.

The USSR Supreme Soviet chairman's report noted the efforts to develop public health and education. Sharp criticism on these matters was heard from people's deputies. Constructive proposals were voiced. The government, which is being formed anew, will undoubtedly take them as the basis in resolving urgent problems. I will only add that what we need to do is to bring the entire system of health protection up to qualitatively new limits. Calculations show that the concentration here of

resources, including through the reduction of expenditures on defense, are opening up possibilities for building new hospitals for 500,000 beds, polyclinics for 1 million visits per shift, for re-equipping treatment and prevention establishments, and for increasing by 2.5 times the supply of up-to-date medical equipment.

Questions of satisfying the population's needs for medicines, an acute shortage of which is now being experienced, are to be studied thoroughly. It must be said that our pharmaceutical industry is providing only 45 percent of the country's needs for medicines. We must implement a complex of major measures to develop Soviet pharmaceutics. Here serious efforts are needed on the part of the union republics, since at the present time the exacerbation of the ecological situation has led to a number of enterprises being shut down, which has aggravated the situation with medicaments even more. Nor do we exclude at the same time the possibility, for the purpose of solving the problem swiftly, of building, on a turn-key basis, three or four pharmaceutical factories as well seeking out a possibility for increasing import purchases of made-up medicines.

Now I would like to specially single out questions that have caused extraordinary concern among the people's deputies. This concerns those to whom no one can and should be indifferent. This is a question of supplying the material needs of certain groups of the population. During the years of the 12th Five-Year Plan a number of urgent, centralized measures have been put into effect, aimed at solving this problem. The wages of some categories of the working people have been raised. I must say that here, in spite of the unfavorable financial situation, we have to a considerable extent paid old debts, which were formed right at the time of the 24th party congress. We consider it exceptionally important to at least render partial assistance to families that are poorly provided for, to mothers and children.

In 3 years the per capita payments of benefits from the social consumption funds have risen by R87 and attained R613 in 1988. When speaking of a social policy, I consider it necessary—although a great deal has already been said about this here—to especially stress the question of the responsibility of society and the state for the material situation of the groups of the population that are the least protected socially, such as pensioners, invalids, and young married couples, and families with many children. Many people's deputies have made requests to me regarding this issue. The government understands that almost 40 million people are today living below the poverty line. Therefore, of all the varied social problems which have taken shape in the country, this is the sorest, testifying to social injustice, especially with respect to those people who have given everything for society. Therefore we attribute special importance to the law on the provision of pensions, on which active work is now being conducted. Here we take a firm stand.

We must wait a little for the solution of other social issues, but the problem of pension provision must be solved in the course of the 13th 5-year plan. [applause]

At the same time it is quite evident that some issues are pressing ones. This has been repeatedly emphasized at the congress with particular poignancy and anguish. The Central Committee Politburo and the government have thoroughly weighed the possibility of bringing closer the term for resolving some of the most acute and pressing problems, which should be resolved within the framework of the future pension law. I think the people's deputies will uphold the position of the Central Committee Politburo and the USSR Council of Ministers regarding the fact that it is quite possible that already from January 1 of next year the minimum pension of blue and white collar workers and collective farmers could be raised to R70 per month, with abolition of the differences in pension provision—that is, to the level of the minimum wage of blue and white collar workers effective at the present time. [applause]

This will enable us to improve the material situation of 20 million people, including 8 million collective farmers. [applause] To increase the minimum amount of pensions to invalids of the first group to R80, and invalids of the second group to R60—this is more than 1 million people. [applause] To increase the amount of pensions to widows of perished servicemen to R60 a month for losing a breadwinner, and also to give them the same status for privileges as participants in the Great Patriotic War—this is 800,000 people. [applause] To pay to war invalids supplements to retirement pensions, set by the legislations, [word indistinct] in the sum of R15 a month, regardless of their maximum amount—this is 300,000 people. [applause] To give the right of free medicines to participants of the Great Patriotic War and to widows of perished servicemen—this is 7 million people. To give the right to free public transport in towns to participants of the war, and also to people awarded orders and medals for unselfish work in the war period—this is almost 6 million people. [applause] As a result of this, almost 22 million people will be able to feel already next year the social changes in their lives. Taking into acount numerous requests, it is planned to remove from 1990 all earnings restrictions for workers and pensioners on payment for work, regardless of the amount of the pensions they are receiving. [applause]

For all this, comrades, almost R6 billion are needed. The Government will, in the near future, define sources, and will examine them jointly with commissions and committees of the USSR Supreme Soviet. At the same time it is quite obvious that the solution of the given problem is the concern of the entire society, of every enterprise and organization. Of course, all these and other acute social problems that have come to a head in the society will require great financial resources. They can be obtained only if there is a growth of efficiency of the economy; only then will their solution become a reality. One more question: In the course of the work of the congress, as

proposed by Mikhail Sergeyevich Gorbachev, a commission is to be set up of people's deputies to examine the complex of questions relating to the benefits system that has been created in the state. Taking this into account, the country's leadership is submitting the proposal that the distinction which exists in the upkeep of patients in different medical establishments, and also in departmentally run sanatoria and holiday homes, including the USSR Ministry of Health's fourth main administration, be eliminated right away, proceeding from principles of social justice. [applause]

Comrade people's deputies! I am touching separately on the issues of the development of the agro-industrial complex and food supply for the population. It is extremely difficult to speak on this topic. So much has been said about it, so many decisions have been adopted, that it would seem that they only need all be implemented, and the problem would disappear. However, it remains, and is even becoming worse. That means that for decades the measures adopted have not attained their goals; they have not matched up to the interests of the main link, and, first and foremost, of the peasantry. It appeared that the country was undertaking immense efforts to extract this sector of the economy from failure. More investment, equipment, and material resources were put into it, and so-called sponsoring assistance from the town for the country was organized. It seemed that it was all being done on a global scale, but the person working directly on the land was lost behind all this. Moreover, many initiatives originating from the center, and regional initiatives, led to the peasant everywhere being turned into the subject of all kinds of experiments, such as the consolidation and fragmentation of farms, settlement of farmsteads and small villages, cutting in half of subsidiary plots, elimination of cattle in the private farmyard, and so on. The rate of growth of output in rural areas started falling without restraint. While at the end of the 1960's the average annual growth was R27,000 million, and the hope emerged for Soviet people that some extra provisions would appear on their tables, later on this hope kept dwindling, and came to nothing. In the 9th 5-year plan period, the annual average growth fell to R20 billion, in the 10th 5-year plan to R15 billion, and by the end of the 11th 5-year plan to R10 billion. However, despite all this, the sorrows of the rural areas did not then truly become the sorrow of the whole state. They were spoken of everywhere, but they were perceived in abstract fashion at all levels of management. There began the ever more obvious manifestations of the extreme vulnerability of our agro- industrial complex. Because of the absence of sufficient reserves and insurance stocks, the state was compelled to opt for large purchases of food. In 1964, imports of food amounted to R1.4 billion.

In the midseventies it grew to R6 billion, and in 1981 it amounted to R15 billion. In 1985, of R111 billion of food products marketed by state and cooperative treade, about R16 billion were imports of food products. The food situation in recent years has not in practice improved. Imports have to be preserved as before, and alongside this, the unsatisfied requirements of the population for foodstuffs have increased, and are now assessed at more than R20 billion. The further exacerbation in this issue of late is evident from the following figures: While in 1987 the country was producing food products worth R134.4 billion, or an increase of 5.8 percent over 1986, in 1988 there was virtually no increase. It is perfectly clear that a serious improvement can be attained only on the basis of a radical further improvement in production relations and of further radical restructuring of the economic mechanism in the rural areas. I must stress, with complete conviction, that the interests of the peasantry must be put at the foundations of this most important matter. It is only here that there are realistic opportunities to substantitally increase production of food and raw materials using the already created material-technical base. At the same time, we have to attain a qualitative renovation of the material base of the agro-industrial complex, the supply to rural areas of the equipment and resources they need, and an improvement in the utilization of the achievements of scientific-technological progress. In this regard, I totally support the statements of the people's deputies concerning changes to legislation on land tenure and use.

The issues are truly topical. The criticism of the decree on lease contracting that has been heard from this rostrum has, in the main, been justified. The decree is a temporary document, and hence it could not, was not capable of solving all the problems connected with lease contracting. We need more extensive legislative acts, and I would like to hope that due attention will be paid to this issue in the new Supreme Soviet. But in my view, neither now nor in the future should we set up the collective or state farm in opposition to the independent peasant farm or the cooperative of leaseholders. The most important thing is to give the peasants the opportunity to manage their affairs independently on the basis of different forms of holding and managing property. [applause] Decisions directed toward this were also adopted in March of this year, concerning further improvement of the management of the agro-industrial complex. They match up to the new regional policy, and are aimed at expanding the rights and enhancing the responsibilities of local bodies for providing the population of territories with food.

Along with the changes in economic relations, overcoming the major shortcomings in the countryside's social development is the central, I would even say the fundamental issue for the countryside. Here, too, we also need fundamentally new approaches. The March plenum set the task of improving the provision of rural families with well-appointed housing in the near future. A number of specific measures regarding road construction have been determined. The volumes of capital investments for these purposes in the new 5-year plan must increase 2.4 times.

I also want to support the numerous statements by people's deputies which were heard from this rostrum to the effect that it is necessary to sharply raise the electrification and the level of gas supply to rural settlements and to radically change their entire social infrastructure.

For all this, in our view, over R120 billion of capital investments in the future 5-year plan must be used. This is 1.5 times more than envisioned for the current 5-year plan.

We must concentrate our efforts even more on the key problems of the country's agro-industrial complex, which are directly hindering our potential and the improvement of the provision of the population with food products, and are not allowing social tension in society to be removed. Above all this holds true for the transportation, processing, and storage of agricultural raw materials. Losses here are reaching astronomical figures. Up to one-quarter of what is grown by the countryside—this is according to modest calculations—does not reach the consumer. The extensive action program in this sphere is well known. It was the subject of a special examination in October 1987. The main aim which was set then is to ensure profound changes in the structure of the processing sectors of industry, to lay the main emphasis on strengthening its material and technical base. To implement this program in accordance with the government's decision it is planned to assimilate R77 billion. For all intents and purposes we must in many respects create anew the industry of processing, storage, and transportation of agricultural raw materials and food products.

I want to remind you that through the development of processing and the introduction of wastless technologies which rule out losses, output of up to R40 billion, or 60 percent of the entire increase in food goods in the country, should be obtaned additionally in 1995.

The question of land improvement in agriculture is now being completely revised. The system that existed for many years resulted in huge expenditures that did not yield the desired results, and was detrimental to nature in many respects. In this respect the criticism addressed to the former leadership of the Ministry of Land Reclamation and Water Resources is absolutely valid. The USSR Council of Ministers has drawn conclusions from this and believes that all questions of water resources should not be concentrated in the hands of a single organization. This ministry must become purely a construction organization.

As for construction projects, it is the collective and state farms and the union republics—those who know best what the land needs—who should be placing the orders. The center should be left to decide problems only of statewide and inter-republican significance. [applause]

Persistent work in all these areas will in the final analysis allow us already in the 13th 5-year plan to bring production of foodstuffs up to R200 billion a year, or increase it in comparison with last year by almost R70 billion. This is possible only with an annual increment of not less than 5 percent. Only in that case will there be a real change in the foodstuffs market.

I believe that the tasks of the new government to create conditions aimed at a radical improvement of the country's food supply should be directly taken from the appeal to the congress by the agrarian workers people's deputies. It is a code, the fulfillment of which should in effect transform the peasant, as he is all over the world, into a respected, prestigious figure. Everything must be done to ensure that he occupies a worthy position in our society. [applause] This concerns the social conditions of his life, including material supply, consumer services, medical facilities, education, and culture. It also concerns everything else covered in living conditions, production of the infrastructure, provision of machinery—in a word everything an urban resident has today.

For improvements in supplying the the populace with foodstuffs, a weighty contribution should also be made by other sectors of the economy. This applies first and foremost to such a powerful sector as fisheries, which is doing much to solve the tasks mentioned, but which also has quite a few problems. The main orientation in the government's activity in relation to the agrarian sector will be fulfilling the instruction from the people's deputies to turn the country's economy toward the need of the countryside. Only such concern for rural workers will provide the possibility to substantially change in a short period of time the state of affairs of foodstuffs on the consumer market.

Now to deal with the financial position of the state. Special attention was paid to this at the congress. The deputies should have exhaustive information at their disposal on this most important question. Over the three preceding 5-year plans, in connection with the drop in efficiency of social production, over R150 billion of income failed to be obtained, at a time when state expenditure was also above what was planned by R150 billion. Precisely here lies the source of our financial difficulties today. The shortage of financial resources at the time was made up from above-plan income from foreign trade to the extent of R103 billion. It was recovered due to the favorable situation of the world market for fuel and energy resources. At the same time there was a direct raise in retail prices of R54 billion, and about R20 billion came from a hidden price rise for consumer goods by means of lowering their quality.

A further R106 billion was borrowed from the banking system. Over that period, the issues of money reached unprecedented levels, and the amount of money in circulation increased by almost three times. Such is the actual picture. Superficially, all was well. The expenditures were equal to the revenues, and consequently there were no problems here. At the same time, against this favorable background of financial balance, enterprises and industries were stripped bare. They were in effect deprived of any chance of using the resources which they had earned. The vast majority of accumulated resources, with the exception of sums regulated by the plan, were returned to the budget.

Such was the economic system, one which superficially balanced overall the national economy, and actually stifled the economic initiative of work collectives. I ask you to pay special attention to this, because the financial situation which has formed today in the country can largely be explained by precisely a fundamental break with the principles which used to exist. This is the financial legacy with which the country entered the 12th 5-year plan. Much time was required in order to come to terms deeply and comprehensively with the state of affairs in this zone which was once secret and inaccessible for all. It became clear that if we would not implement radical measures to develop new principles for financial relations between enterprises and the state—and now the question of regions is also on the agenda—then we would not be able to achieve the necessary socioeconomic transformations and we would underine the economic reform.

Finding ourselves in such a financial position, we had to answer frankly the question: What strategy were we to select in order to get out of this most difficult situation? Various roads were proposed. The first was to cut social programs and to increase retail prices. The government had a firm position on this. It is the Politburo's position. That road is not acceptable from any point of view. The second was to take away from the enterprises the remainder of earned resources and to balance the state budget thereby, as was done previously. And this road was also rejected, because it directly undermines the foundations of the economic reform and violates the Law on Enterprises. The third was to increase the external debt. But that would have signified transformation of the domestic debt into a foreign economic debt. The latter had already reached a dangerous level, beyond which the country might end up in a most grave situation. Proceeding from all of this, a task was formulated: Relying on an increase in the efficiency of public-sector production and intensification of it, the growing expenditures of the state are to be covered only by increasing revenues, thereby stabilizing the financial situation in the country. And all this came against a background of a slump in world fuel prices which had already taken shape.

What are the results? Evidently, the 12th 5-year plan may turn out to be the first when the planned indicators for profit are achieved. An active process of recovery of the finances of enterprises has begun, and over half of profit now remains in their control. Currently, approximately R250 billion is concentrated in the hands of enterprises, taking into consideration the remainder of resources for economic incentive funds. This is the same amount as the Union Budget has this year.

However, it is necessary to note that, if we are seeing a strengthening of finances of the main production link, then the state of affairs with the state finances continues to grow worse. What is the reason for this? Overall, in the first 4 years of the 5-year plan, the state has not managed to receive the planned revenues and to stop the growth in expenditures. When working out the 5-year plan, the government expected a worsening in the state of the world market. However, the actual situation has turned out much worse than we had forecast. As a result, the revenues from foreign economic activity will be R30 billion less than was planned. The consequences of the antialcohol campaign which was forced along have also had an effect. As a result, state revenue, taking into consideration receipts from all sources, is expected to be R40 billion less. At the same time, over the years 1986-1989, expenditures will exceed those which were anticipated by R62 billion.

A significant portion of resources, in accordance with the decisions of the 27th party congress, has been allocated to implement measures for the country's social development. Could we have refrained from such expenditure? Judge for yourselves. I will name them for you.

The state has allocated over the 4 years R21 billion over and above what was estimated in the 5-Year Plan just in implementing the reforms in the health service and in general and higher education, in increasing to a minimum extent the pension provision of various population groups, in improving assistance to children in low-income families, and in improving the material provision of orphans, plus other expenditure. This, I stress, does not include capital investment in housing and other nonproduction construction.

Moreover, almost R10 billion has gone in additional assistance to agriculture. As you already know, more than R8 billion was required after the Chernobyl accident. The expenditure to eliminate the consequences of the earthquake in Armenia is also substantial. We spent approximately R5 billion annually in Afghanistan. The state of monetary circulation has deteriorated badly.

What is happening here? First, let us speak about the incomes of the population. In the first 3 years of the 5-Year plan they exceeded by R20 billion the plan figure, and almost the entire increment occurred in 1988. The growth in wages alone proved to be R14.5 billion more than was planned. The point is that, in availing themselves of the right granted them to manage the resources being earned, many enterprises lost an economically substantiated connection between work remuneration and labor productivity, thus violating a most important requirement of the law on state enterprises. The national economy was, of course, not ready to increase the production of goods and services which could compensate for such an explosion in incomes as happened in 1988. As a result, an extremely acute situation formed on the consumer market, particularly in 1988 and early in 1989. This has given impetus to inflation processes. Such, comrades, is the actual situation in finances and monetary circulation.

The government has examined a program for the financial recovery of the economy. It is to be implemented in two stages.

The first stage covers 1989-90. It is envisaged, as I have already said, to increase significantly over that period the production of goods, to reduce production, investment, and expenditure on defense, to reduce expenditure on the maintenance of the administrative apparatus, and to toughen the economic drive, along with a number of other measures. In particular, the problem of loss-making enterprises should be singled out. There were approximately 9,000 of them in 1988 in the spheres of material production. And that is not counting collective farms [kolkhozes]. More than R5 billion was required to cover the losses. But that is just one aspect of the matter, the purely financial aspect.

Another aspect, one which is probably no less important, is that the existing economic system, in which leveling tendencies are still preserved, enables such enterprises to live at the expense of work collectives which are working well, and about which Deputy Bunich has spoken here so graphically.

The government adheres to the firm position that 1990 must be the last year for such an economic phenomenon, which is inadmissible under our conditions. Comrades, all these measures will allow the budget deficit in the current year to be reduced by R29 billion and next year by R34 billion. In the second stage, in the 13th 5-year plan, the task is set not only to stabilize the financial position but also to overcome the budget deficit. In our opinion, it is necessary to draw up a program for making finances healthier in the 13th 5-year plan while preparing the concepts and main directions of the economic and social development of the country for the forthcoming period, to consider it in the USSR Supreme Soviet and discuss it at the second Congress of People's Deputies.

I cannot but speak about that situation that is taking shape in society around the cooperative movement. The processes developing here are being perceived by the people in different ways, since they are contradictory in many respects and have beneath them not only a healthy foundation, but also the completely negative strivings of individual categories of cooperative workers. This is doing irremediable harm to the very nature of cooperatives, to which elements such as self-seeking, unearned gain, personal enrichment, self-interest, and ignoring the interests of citizens are unacceptable. Unfortunately, all this exists in our cooperative movement and arouses the anger of working people. They are demanding that order be introduced. Things are getting to the state that demands are being put forward to close public catering and trade cooperatives and cooperatives carrying out intermediary activity, to leave them only in the sphere of production and domestic services. [applause]

I have to say, comrades, that nevertheless we need here a well-considered approach and painstaking consistent work to make cooperatives healthy [applause] and we need liberation from all the scum that has appeared during these 2 years of stormy development. And this work must be carried out locally in the most energetic manner, above all by the soviets of people's deputies, which give cooperatives the authorization to exist when their statutes are registered. The soviets have now been given the most extensive rights and possibilities to influence the establishment of new types of cooperatives that are necessary to society, of course in conformity with local conditions, and also to regulate their activity by means of an effective system of taxation. The basis in this matter is clear: the development of the cooperative movement on the principles of social justice.

Comrade deputies, the investment policy has been subjected to particularly sharp criticism. We should get right to the bottom of this matter and change the situation that has come about and bring the position into a healthy state. The principal peculiarity of the contemporary investment policy consists in the fact that enterprises, as a result of carrying out reforms, have received large financial resources. Thus, if in 1986 the proportion of investment from enterprises' own resources constituted approximately 3 percent of the overall volume of state capital investment, in 1989 it will reach 41 percent.

This fundamentally changes the whole organization of the investment process. The insistent need for substantial changes in the running of the construction complex has peaked throughout the country. Excessive centralization has fettered the initiative of republican and local bodies and has prevented fully accounting for their requirements and regional possibilities from being used.

No less important is the fact that the republics' responsibility has been sapped. Decisions were made on the decentralization of the management of construction production. Administrative functions have been transferred to the union republics. The only exception now is the Russian Federation, where the basic contract work is carried out by the union ministries. But facts have shown that here too a similar step must be taken.

The production of building materials has also basically been transferred to the union republics. This approach is in full accord with the principles of the new regional policy. Nevertheless, the situation remains difficult. The economic mechanism currently in operation in construction has not eliminated the former gross-output approaches and has only a feeble effect on the time-scale and quality of work.

At the start of the 5-year plan, in order to restrict the extent of construction, tough administrative measures were adopted as a forced step, but they produced only temporary results. Subsequently, during the changeover in economic methods, the situation of earlier years was repeated due to the imperfections of the economic mechanism. In 1988, as compared with 1985, the number of newly-started construction projects, the plans for which are now independently formulated and confirmed by ministries and enterprises, again rose by 31 percent.

Thus, the scattering of capital investment occurred once again. The time required to erect buildings today is more than double the accepted standard. Uncompleted construction is on the increase. Assignments relating to the commissioning of a great deal of capacity regularly fail to be made. As a result, the national economy is approaching the 13th 5-year plan with far less productive potential than was envisaged in the 5-year plan.

A future government will have to tackle highly complex tasks concerning investment policy. An assessment of the possibilities, bearing in mind the country's financial position, shows that realistically the overall volume of investment from all sources of finance during the next 5-year plan period can grow by no more than 10 percent.

At the same time, it is necessary to carry out major structural changes in the national economy, primarily in capital construction. First, we are to guarantee a fundamental turn-around in the economy toward the achievement of social tasks, which requires a major economic maneuver with the country's resources. This signifies, in effect, a need for outstripping growth in all kinds of capital investments which are directed at strengthening the material basis of the social and cultural sphere. Estimates show that their portion in the overall volume of investments in the national economy in real terms can grow in the 13th 5-year plan to 34 percent compared to 26 percent in the 12th 5-year plan, and the increment will be 1.5 times that in the current 5-Year plan.

Second, it is necessary to give priority to investments in the agrarian complex, and especially its social sphere.

Third, in the coming period, the main efforts should be concentrated on a radical reconstruction of branches in all spheres of the economy which are directly working for people. As for the reequipment of capital-intensive, basic branches of the national economy, the scale thereof will have to be substantially reduced; correspondingly, the efficiency of the existing production potential will have to be sharply increased, although here there are likewise problems which—and we must take this into consideration—could have an effect on the work of the entire national economy. Under such conditions, a tough approach will naturally be required in drawing up the investment program.

It will be necessary to stop or to postpone until a later date the accomplishment of a number of major projects and the fulfilment of a number of decisions on the development of certain branches and regions. It is difficult to do this, and this most difficult process will be most painful. Suffice it to say that preliminary estimates show that it would be possible to reduce the level of investment by R27 billion at individual major construction sites and installations alone. And it will be necessary, of course, together with the union republics, to carry out a package of vigorous measures to cut down the number of incomplete construction works. We need this very much, primarily because, given a slight growth in capital investments, it will be possible to increase in real terms the introduction of fixed assets.

Alongside the implementation of measures for structural reconstruction of investment activity, we are to pass over to using a fundamentally new economic mechanism which is directed at improvement in all qualitative features in the construction industry, because the currently operating mechanism has major inadequacies. Many troubles in capital construction are a consequence of the practice which has formed in financing whereby money for the erection of individual installations is not earned but allocated according to the desires of higher organizations. Of course, all this must resolutely be changed. To put it figuratively, money must have its master. Only then will it be used in a thrifty way.

The main provisions for the economic mechanism in construction have been elaborated. Of course, they must be clarified, taking into consideration the opinions of all the union republics. The new government will draw the right conclusions from the sharp but justified criticism which there has been at the congress. We must come to a civilized level in the sphere of capital construction. We are building installations which will live for decades and even centuries, and it is they which will reflect the intellectual and technical level of contemporary society.

Comrade deputies, let me speak briefly about the problems in the development of science and technology. An immense unevenness and degree of contrast are typical of the scientific and technical sphere of the national economy. On the one hand, there are great achievements in some spheres of science and technology, and on the other hand, there is a deep scientific and technical backwardness in many spheres, one which simply contradicts common sense in today's terms. The reasons here have an objective and subjective character, but the main reason is the economic management mechanism. It does not contain a motivational system that would stimulate any collective to seek new things and make it impossible to have material prosperity without mastering the achievements of science and technology. We must carry out in a precise way the policy for deepening financial autonomy and self-financing in the sphere of scientific and design activity.

Scientific establishments in 23 industries worked in 1988 under such conditions. This year all establishments are switching over, and this includes academies and higher educational establishments and the scientific organizations of the defense complex. Given this, it is exceptionally important to find a deep economic validity in the correlation between budget financing and business contract financing in the development of applied and fundamental research works. It is absolutely clear that, by switching scientific establishments over to working under the new economic management conditions, promising fundamental development work which has statewide, national and long-term significance must not in any way suffer. As previsouly, it must be financed mostly from the budget.

A year of work by industrial scientific organizations under the new conditions has shown that the principles contained in the economic mechanism are generally correct and efficient. True, it still shows some negative traits. Notably, an unjustified growth in wages and the setting of excessive prices for scientific-technical output are causing a reduction in pilot works and works to lay down scientific groundwork.

These impediments can be overcome, however. The main thing is to get the country engaged as quickly as possible in those development processes which are taking place today throughout the world. This concerns, primarily, the technological revolution which is objectively developing abroad. And great efforts and the concentration of our immense intellectual potential will be required here.

Comrades, problems connected with the creation of a favorable environment for human habitation are causing grave strains in the country. The movement which has developed in favor of environmental security is adopting a more and more acute social and political thrust. The vigor of the mass information media and of the population are totally understandable here. The practice of allowing the public to judge ecological issues in specific regions did not exist in the past. One must note that a considerable number of existing industrial enterprises—especially those which went into operation in the 1930's, 40's, and 50's—in the majority of cases, did not meet ecological standards. And technological processes at many industrial installations which have been freshly introduced lag behind contemporary requirements.

As a result, the ecological situation in a number of major industrial centers has proved very unfavorable. Emissions of harmful substances into the air alone now comprise approximately 100 million tonnes. During 1985-1988 decisions were passed by the government on the protection and the rational use of the natural resources of Lake Baykal and Lake Ladoga, and on additional measures to prevent air and water pollution in the towns of Chelyabinsk, Magnitogorsk, Karabash, Fergana, Kemerovo, Salavat, Sterlitamak, Tolyatti, and others. Work connected with the diversion of a party of the Northern and Siberian rivers and the construction of Rzhevskiy Hydro-Center and of the Volga-Chogray Canal has ceased. An all-embracing decision has also been made on nature conservation measures in the Aral Sea basin. Proposals on the Volga and Caspian Sea basins are being prepared. In comparison with 1985 the areas of reserves have increased from 18 to 21 million hectares.

As we can see, things are already being done. However, the burden of the accumulated problems is so great that it would be extremely difficult in a short period of time improve the current unfavorable ecological situation. Significant monetary and material resources are required for this. Thus, according to the preliminary calculations, R135 billion need to be assimilated, allotted and used during the course of three 5-year plans for implementing the long-term state nature conservation draft program while ensuring the necessary development of the productive forces of the country. That is an average of R45 million in each 5-year plan period as against the R15 billion of the current plan.

But it is not just a question of finances. To assimilate such resources, the specialized capacities of construction organizations need to be developed as well, and perhaps the most important thing is to create ecologically clean technologies and appropriate equipment.

Of all the acute problems which are being debated by the public today, the issues of atomic and hydropower engineering come to the fore. Many deputies' questions and addresses were received on them. The sources of such concern are understandable—they are Chernobyl, lowland hydroelectric power stations, and so on. The questions are so profound and so fundamental, they affect so directly the future development of the country, and so directly influence the living conditions of Soviet people that in our view, they deserve special scrutiny.

In our view, it is necessary to make suitable modifications to the USSR's current long-term power-supply program, to discuss it in the Supreme Soviet and to submit it for discussion by the whole people. [applause] It is also necessary to give special consideration once again to the whole package of issues associated with the situation in Belorussia, the Ukraine, and Russia that has arisen since the Chernobyl accident. In other words, the ecological problems confronting the country should be tackled by the whole production-technical and intellectual potential, including the scientific resources of the academies, higher educational establishments, and sectors of industry. It is essential to proceed toward improving the ecological situation, step by step, throughout the country's regions.

Comrades, the basis for the government's activities will always be a profound respect for the freedom and constitutional rights, the honor, and dignity of every Soviet citizen, and firm adherence to the principle of the consolidation of society and of the various social and demographic groups. This is very important. Centrifugal tendencies have intensified in the country; strikes and rallies for dubious purposes have grown more frequent; nationalist sentiments are being aroused. Here I would like to state definitely that one cannot permit flouting of human rights by virtue of national or any other indicators, anarchy and irresponsibility, interruptions in the labor rhythm, and rising crime and corruption. Strictly maintaining all democratic liberties on a legal basis, the new government will display firmness in creating an atmosphere of legality in public order in the country, including on the basis of strengthening and further improving the activity of law-enforcement bodies.

The process of democratization is growing rapidly in the country. Moreover, it is constantly embracing new spheres of people's lives. Democratic principles are becoming a stable part of our everyday life. This applies both to production and to culture, and to citizens' dealings with each other. Our whole political system, economy, and regional relations are becoming more democratic.

In a word, the healthy processes of the emancipation of the individual are going on more and more actively in this country, which is experiencing with difficulty the transitional period to a new quality of growth. However, the dialectics of this state in society mean that pseudodemocratic processes are developing alongside democratic principles. They are having an extremely negative effect on the stability of the situation in the state, eroding discipline and leading, contrary to common sense, to violations of order in society. Many good undertakings in the country are not being seen through to the end, because of laxity, irresponsibility and gross violations of elementary requirements.

We are being haunted by tragic cases accompanied by large numbers of human victims. Irresponsibility, an immoral attitude to the tasks, and sometimes even a gross deviation from elementary human duty are not infrequently behind all this.

We will undoubtedly succeed in eliminating phenomena of this kind from our society's life if literally the whole people engage in this cause. Having put forward the democratization of society as a primary task, the party put into this concept, first of all, the lofty sense of and need for well-understood discipline and order when the citizens of our huge country, in building a democratic society and state based on the rule of law and the principles of consolidation of efforts, do everything necessary so the country will advance surely along the path of progress in a stable and uninterrupted manner. Comrade deputies, the issues of ensuring state security, and of the overall guidance of the construction of the USSR Armed Forces, constitute one of the most important areas of the government's work. When forming the plans for 1986-90, because of the international situation prevailing at the time and our military doctrine, we were compelled to envision a traditional growth of defense expenses at a pace exceeding the growth of the national income. The peaceful initiatives of the Soviet state, the signing of a number of treaties on reducing and limiting individual types of armaments, and the principles of the new military defense doctrine, however, have made it possible to implement a truly revolutionary maneuver. Including the proposed reduction of expenditure for the forthcoming 2 years, the overall saving of defense expenses in relation to the approved 5-year plan will amount to nearly R30 billion [Russian: 30 milliardov]. No doubt, the congress has to have full information about the real defense expenses. Only in this case people's deputies will be able to have a notion about them that will enable them to participate actively in examining the formulation of military expenses. Thus, in 1989, out of the overall expenses amounting to R77.3 billion, the following allocations have been envisioned:

R32.6 billion for purchasing armaments and hardware;
R15.3 billion for research and development;
R20.2 billion for the upkeep of the Army and Navy;
R4.6 billion for military construction;
R2.3 billion for pensions for servicemen; and
R2.3 billion for other expenses.

I think there is no need to comment on these data. We intend to continue persistently along the path of disarmament and to strive for reducing by one-third to one-half the relative share of defense expenses in the national income by 1995. One assumes that this issue will occupy a special place in the activity of the USSR Supreme Soviet.

Taking into account the consistent reduction in spending on defense needs, the government will aspire to provide the Soviet Armed Forces with everything necessary while at the same time implementing the principle of reasonable sufficiency. The Army is a creation of the Soviet people and it deserves support with all the means at one's disposal. [applause]

There is a pressing need for a speedy conversion of military production, and for released capacities and resources to be directed to tackle social and economic tasks. These measures are creating the possibility to substantially increase by 50 to 100 percent the output of equipment for the agro-industrial complex, light industry, trade, and public catering. These sorts of measures have led this year to a change in the production structure of the defense complex. The pace of the output growth of civilian products and consumer goods is here double the growth of military output. Under the influence of the conversion, the production structure of the military complex is radically changing. While at present the relative share of civilian products is 40 percent of the general output of industry, in the current 5-year plan period, by the end of the current 5-year plan period, it will be 46 percent, and in 1995 more than 60 percent.

Guided by the decision on the reorientation of the national economy to meet social demands, defense industries have been instructed to ensure the speedy creation of new high technology types of civilian products and complex everyday goods. Above all, this applies to medical equipment. In 1989 its production by enterprises of defense industries will reach almost R240 billion [as heard] and in the longer term, annual output will reach not less than R1 billion. Taking into account special acuteness in the sphere of providing invalids with various medical equipment and also difficulties with providing prosthetic appliances, something which was discussed quite justly and with great sadness at the congress, the Council of Ministers has recently adopted a decision to hand over production in this sphere to leading enterprises engaged in the sphere of space. [applause]

The defense complex must make a much greater contribution in meeting the demands of the population for cultural and consumer goods. Now, defense industries are manufacturing this type of goods to the value of about 30 billion rubles, or 22 percent of the general output in the country. In 1990 their growth is to be 33 percent. We hope that in the 13th 5-year plan period the amount of such goods manufactured by the complex will be to the value of R250-270 billion, and will double the task of the current 5-year plan period. I consider it necessary to dwell also on the question of creating and using space equipment in the interests of defense and the national economy.

Clearly, just as is expenditure for defense purposes, information should also be presented to the congress about expenditure connected with the implementation of our space programs. So, what sums are being directed toward this? I will quote figures in thousands of millions of rubles. They are broken down as follows: national-economic and scientific space: 1.7; military space: 3.9; the Buran space shuttle system: 1.3; total R6.9 billion. The question arises: Is this expenditure justified? It is possible to say in this respect that the implementation of space programs of a military purpose alone, according to the calculations of Ministry of Defense specialists, will enhance the combat efficiency of our Armed Forces by 1.5-2 times. At the same time, the main thing is to place the achievements of space technology at the service of the national economy and to make them increasingly directed toward social issues. The possibilities here are immense. Let us take just one issue: the development of telephone communications. We will not be able to solve this problem in the conditions of our country by conventional traditional means for many years. Space will provide us with the opportunity to proceed along another, more rapid path, as was decided, for example, with television, which now reaches 94 percent of the population of our country.

I must also talk about the following. In the spirit of restructuring and the development of glasnost the procedure for working out and adopting decisions on defense questions will alter substantially. They will undoubtedly be examined in the same way as the state plan and budget. Our main duty before the people is to ensure peaceful living conditions for the present and future generations of Soviet people on the basis of the implementation of a foreign policy which has been profoundly considered and thoroughly adjusted. Soviet peace initiatives will undoubtedly increase. The policy toward a radical improvement in international relations will continue to be actively developed. The government sees as one of its most important commitments to persistently put it into practice and to serve in every way the noble cause of asserting the spirit of trust, mutual understanding, and cooperation between all countries.

Comrades, a few words about foreign-economic activity and the country's foreign currency situation. The measures which have been taken here have been directed toward making our economy more open and providing all enterprises, associations and organizations, including cooperatives, with the opportunity of participating in the international division of labor. At the present time, when all have been granted the right to enter foreign markets, over 2,000 participants in foreign economic activity have already been registered in the country.

About 460 joint enterprises have been founded on the territory of the USSR. Two thousand contracts or direct ties with partners from the CEMA countries have been concluded. A strategy has been elaborated for the development of the USSR's foreign economic ties. The main thing in it is the transition from traditional forms of trading to the most broad cooperation in science, technology, and production. We envision a substantial change in the structure of exports, and a sharp rise in the proportion of manufactured goods among them. In imports, the priority is being given to purchases of equipment for modernization and reconstruction. However, the situation in foreign economic activity at present remains very complex. In 1988, as compared with 1985, exports had fallen by 7.6 percent, and imports by 6.3 percent. We have not managed to compensate with an increase in incomes for export of manufactured products the losses connected with the fall in world oil prices, from R160 per tonne in 1985 to R60 in 1988, and that for petroleum products and gas, amounting to about R25 billion in freely convertible currency alone over the past 3 years. The situation does not permit us to avoid the purchase abroad of many kinds of production. Thus, over the first 3 years of the 5-year plan, we imported food products and raw materials for their manufacture worth nearly R31 billion. This year about R22 billion will be spent on import of consumer goods and food, including over R5 billion in hard currency for grain and food alone. The continuing high demand for imports along with restricted ability to pay has led to the USSR's hard currency debts being more than double the annual incomes from exports of goods and services. In connection with this, we have been compelled to take short-term credits, and to an ever greater extent of late. But even all the incomes from oil do not cover the interest payments. The government has calculated that the extraordinary hard currency debt is fraught with serious economic and political consequences. We have overstepped to such an extent, speaking figuratively, the red mark of the 25-percent correlation between payments for credit and currency incomes tolerated in international practice. It is clear that we must approach the questions of loans with the maximum circumspection. On the whole, I see the task in that the work of the new government must be directed toward decisively overcoming the alienation of our economy from the processes going on in the world economy, artificially created in the course of many years. As before, priority attention will be devoted to strengthening relations with socialist countries and to socialist economic integration.

In conclusion, I would like to say that we have to implement our work in a qualitatively changed political situation, and work with genuinely democratic soviets of people's deputies and their supreme organ of power.

The principal distinguishing feature of the government which will be appointed will be the fact that in new conditions it will really become a people's power organ enjoying the full rights. Only then it can be a reliable guarantee of the strict fulfillment of people's will. The party has made an irrevocable choice in favor of the Leninist concept of socialism as the living creativity of the masses, as a society developing on the basis of new genuinely humane goals. As of now, we can lean on all the experience and energy of people, the unbreakable unity between the policy and the everyday needs and interests of people. It was only yesterday when personal initiative, special regional features, cultural differences and nonstandard thinking were only obstacles for the bureaucratic management, but today they are the main sources for our hopes and optimism. I am convinced that by advancing firmly and consistently along the route of political and economic changes we shall at the end solve our urgent social problems. No matter how important is all that which will be done in the material sphere, we must not lose the most precious property—the cultural and spiritual heritage of the people—because people who lose their spiritual material have no historical prospects. On this level, I am supporting with all sincerity the position outlined at the Congress by the Deputy Dmitriy Sergeyvich Likhachev. He said that without culture in society there is no principled morality either, and without the elementary morality social and economic laws do not function. A low level of culture has a negative effect on public life, state work, on interethnic relations. The government will do everything possible to develop the material base of culture, press, and other mass information media and any useful initiatives and creative efforts to enrich the cultural heritage of the people; and the intellecutual potential of the society will receive our support. [applause]

Comrades! Many socioeconomic problems have accumulated in the country and this is also obvious from the discussion at the congress. All of them deserve the most serious attention. Their solution is only possible with intensive and very productive work of the entire national economy, every person. We have to consolidate ourselves for the solution of these problems. Only the cohesion and wisdom of the people can get the country out of the complex situation. We have ahead of us enormous work in the implementation of the party's course toward the renewal of the Soviet society. It is possible to fulfil it only under conditions of political stability in the state, and through the coordinated efforts of all peoples of our country. The new composition of the

USSR Council of Ministers will make use of all the useful things accumulated in the past years and all that which is being worked out by the Congress of People's Deputies, and on this basis will strive for a steady and dynamic movement of the country on the path of restructuring and progress. In this lies the entire essence of our work. Thank you. [applause]

Gorbachev's 7 Jun Closing Remarks
LD0706195589 Moscow Television Service in Russian 1340 GMT 7 Jun 89

[Closing remarks by Mikhail Gorbachev, chairman of the USSR Supreme Soviet, at USSR Congress of People's Deputies session in the Kremlin Palace of Congresses—live]

[Text] Comrades, at this point in the work of our Congress we need to consult with you. We in the Presidium have exchanged ideas and would like to report them to you. We would like to conclude this session of the Congress here, and, at 1800 [1400 GMT] resume the Joint Session of the Chambers of the Supreme Soviet in order to move forward. [Gorbachev laughs] Do you understand me? Heated discussions are going on there, too, and very substantive ones, too. That is the first thing. That is about today. But as for subsequent days, I repeat my request that you listen to me, dear comrades. How do we on the Presidium see the situation, and how do we propose to proceed? Tomorrow, on Thursday 8 June, there will be debates on the guidelines for the domestic and foreign policy of the USSR and the program of the forthcoming activity of the USSR government. Here I am responding to a question that arose. They will be held from 1000 to 1400 [0600-1000 GMT]. At 1400 we will have a break, of course, and at 1400, the Presidium will meet to discuss the list of matters to be included in the part of the agenda marked miscellaneous. This can be done now because many of the matters that were proposed at one stage for this part are already being resolved and are even being reflected in the main decision, the draft decision.

The evening session: What we have in mind—and the work is being conducted by the commission that we set up together—is to hand out the draft of the decision on the main areas of the domestic and foreign policy before the session, so the deputies have time to acquaint themselves thoroughly with it and work on it. Later on, during the evening session, we will examine the matter of confirming the chairman of the Council of Ministers, of electing the Committee for Constitutional Supervision, and on confirming the chairman of the Committee for People's Control, the chairman of the Supreme Court of the USSR, the procurator-general of the USSR, and the chief state arbiter. The evening session will be devoted to that.

Day thirteen, Friday 9 June: The morning session—the continuation of debates, but also the end of debates and the adoption of the Congress's decisions. That will all be from 1000 to 1400 [0600-1000 GMT]. The adoption of the Congress's guidelines for the domestic and foreign policy of the USSR and the adoption of the Congress's decision on the formation of a Constitutional Commission. Then the evening session will be held. Miscellaneous matters will be on the agenda. The Congress will conclude its work on Friday evening. [Applause]

For the Supreme Soviet—the second session of the Soviet of the Union will be held from 1000 [0600 GMT] on 10 June, at which the deputy chairmen of the Soviet of the Union will be elected. Both Chairmen of the chambers are now working with deputies to prepare proposals. Then, there will be the election of the permanent commissions of the Soviet of the Union and the examination of proposals on the composition of the committees of the USSR Supreme Soviet. The second session of the Soviet of Nationalities will be at 1300 [0900 GMT]. The agenda will be the same. And at 1600 [1200 GMT], the second joint session of the chambers will be conducted, as well as the election of the committees of the USSR Supreme Soviet, the examination of proposals by chairman of the USSR Council of Ministers and the composition of the government of the USSR, and also proposals on the composition of the Committee for People's Control, the Supreme Court of the USSR, and the Collegium and the Procuracy. But these are proposals that will be put forward.

Later, as we said today at the Supreme Soviet, deputies will evidently need a couple of weeks at the Supreme Soviet to examine the proposals, because all those in the commissions will have to meet and get to know each other, elucidate everything and then give their conclusions, in order to reach a decision. These will simply be proposals that are put forward. After the second joint session of the chambers, where these proposals will be heard, we will declare a break in the work of the Supreme Soviet until 20 June of this year. This will be from the 10th—in other words, for 10 days.

[Lukyanov] But the commissions will work.

[Gorbachev] But the commissions will work. Those are the proposals. Can we take them as a basis? Do we need to give you time to consider, or can we adopt this now? If something crops up in the meantime, we shall make corrections at the congress. You want to think about it? Perhaps we'll do it this way, comrades, if it is acceptable. I propose that what has already been said should be taken as a basis; the comrades can think about it, and if there are any substantial proposals about them, they can send their views to the Presidium. No, the debates will carry on, Andrey Dmitriyevich. The debates will continue. This is, as it were, the framework. You know, as far as miscellaneous matters are concerned, we shall be working in the Presidium tomorrow and reporting to you. The thing is that there are many different issues that have been submitted under miscellaneous, and we have already set up commissions on three of them on the most major questions. They have departed, and there remain a number of questions on regulations, and some others still remain, which are being submitted. The Presidium will submit these proposals for you. All I have done here is to set out the framework; as far as miscellaneous matters are concerned, these will be separate proposals.

Who is in favor of these proposals being taken as a basis? Please vote. Please lower your hands. Who is against? Please lower your hands. Any abstentions? They have been taken as a basis. Well, comrades, this basis will, so to speak, give us the chance to work in a creative way, to come up and to take into consideration possible serious and convincing proposals. Do yo agree? [sounds of assent from the hall] Fine! A break in the Congress until 1000 [0600 GMT] tomorrow. We request the Supreme Soviet to convene here where we have been working at 1800 [1400 GMT].

Lithuanian Deputies Walk Out 8 Jun in Protest
LD0806152289 Moscow TASS in English 1514 GMT 8 Jun 89

[Text] Moscow June 8 TASS—By TASS parliamentary correspondent:

The participants in the Congress of USSR People's Deputies on Thursday encountered an unusual situation when a considerable number of deputies from the Soviet Baltic republic of Lithuania walked out of the auditorium as a token of protest at the Congress' decision to set up the Committee for Constitutional Compliance in accordance with the constitution.

In these conditions the Congress postponed a final decision of the issue until to Friday, authorising Mikhail Gorbachev, president of the USSR Supreme Soviet, to hold consultations with those who disagreed and to report the results at the morning session on Friday.

The Committee for Constitutional Compliance is a new element of the political system of the USSR. Some representatives from the Baltic republics saw in the establishment of the committee the possibility of an encroachment on the sovereignty of the union republic.

Further on Baltic Protest
LD0806165289 Moscow TASS in English 1637 GMT 8 Jun 89

[Text] Moscow June 8 TASS—By TASS parliamentary correspondent:

At the afternoon session on Thursday the Congress of USSR People's Deputies was to elect the Committee for Constitutional Compliance, a new body in the political system of the Soviet Union.

The establishment of the committee is provided for by amendments to the Constitution. The amendments were adopted by the Soviet parliament in December last year after a country-wide discussion.

However, a congress decision on the issue had to be postponed.

Several deputies from Estonia, Latvia and Lithuania raised objections to the election of the Constitutional Compliance Committee and to the very idea of establishing it at today's session.

They argued, in particular, that the committee would become an instrument for pressure on the sovereignty of the union republics.

The Lithuanian delegation even warned that it would not take part in the vote. The following judgement was expressed: since the current Constitution is imperfect and is to be reconsidered, a decision on the item concerning the committee should be postponed until autumn.

Summing up the debates on the issue, Mikhail Gorbachev told deputies what the necessity to set up a Committee for Constitutional compliance had been motivated with.

This serious constitutional mechanism, which is being established by the congress itself and accountable only to the congress, must ensure the consolidation of the Constitution and of the line towards the application of the laws, so that no one, under the guise of the observance and development of this or that law, would devitalise it in the stage of realisation, he said.

The president of the USSR Supreme Soviet emphasised that the committee should stand guard over the constitution and law.

Gorbachev said the Presidium of the USSR Supreme Soviet exercised previously and continues to exercise control over the observance of the Constitution of the USSR and ensures the correspondence of the constitutions and laws of the union republics to the Constitution and laws of the USSR.

But with all its prestige the presidium not always covers the entire range of problems. The committee concentrates the best forces of Soviet jurisprudence that will help both the republics, citizens, collectives and central bodies, which would correspond to the policy of building a socialist state committed to the rule of law, Gorbachev said.

He put to the vote the question whether the Committee for Constitutional compliance should be elected at this congress or its formation should be postponed until autumn.

Out of more than two thousand deputies taking part in the vote, only 433 were against forming the committee at this congress. Sixty-one deputies abstained from voting, among them the delegation of Lithuania. However, the formation of the committee was not started because the Lithuanian deputies walked out of the auditorium.

The congress authorised Mikhail Gorbachev, president of the USSR Supreme Soviet, to hold consultations with those who disagreed and to report the results at the morning session on Friday.

Premier Ryzhkov Gives Interviews During Recesses

Stresses Consumer Goods
*PM0206154389 Moscow NEDELYA in Russian
No 22, 29 May-4 Jun 89 (Signed to Press 31 May 89) p 8*

[Interview with N.I. Ryzhkov, member of the CPSU Central Committee Politburo and chairman of the USSR Council of Ministers, as part of a center spread feature under the headline "The First Congress. Our Special Correspondents V. Gatov and A. Yevseyev Converse with USSR People's Deputies in the Kremlin Palace": "People's Deputy N. Ryzhkov"—no date of interview given]

[Text] [Correspondent] How does the head of the country's government feel now that the Congress of People's Deputies has begun discussing the domestic situation and our economic affairs?

[Ryzhkov] What can I say, a major, sharp, and highly interesting and useful debate is now under way, and I think that it will help us gain a deeper understanding of what is happening in the economy and how to solve our problems. Generally speaking, I have no doubt that this will be a useful discussion which we need.

[Correspondent] Just now you were talking to a Japanese journalist and you spoke of the economic reform, the acute problems in the economy, and the way to solve them. What do you think, is there some fine thread which, when pulled, could help to untangle the whole knot of economic problems?

[Ryzhkov] There is, of course, no such single thread. It is necessary to implement an entire package of economic measures. We know what is happening in the country, and we also know how to get out of the prevailing situation, who and where should get involved in solving the economy's problems. In this process, however, the line of improving the economy's health must be pursued consistently, firmly, and persistently. And all this is highly complex. When we talk about improving the economy's health in general, everyone agrees: Yes, of course, this is the way to do it, everything you propose is extremely necessary. But as soon as we get down to details, to strictly specific matters—after all, an illness can be cured only by using specific measures—people immediately become vocal: "Why are you bothering us? Why are you forcing us to do this? You'd better get the guys next door to tackle this, and please leave us alone...." This is a manifestation of diverse narrow interests—sectorial, territorial, or group interests. There are quite a few such instances. For example, this year we undertook to reduce capital investments by R7 billion with a view to somehow improving the financial health,

and right away we at the Council of Ministers were snowed under letters and telegrams from people asking that they should not be affected.

Of course, we realize what the nature of the process of improving the economy's health should be, but this is far from everything needed for success. The main point, I repeat, is that this will require a fair degree of persistence.

This is the only way out of the economic situation in which we have found ourselves today.

[Correspondent] You obviously know that the first few consumer societies and clubs are already functioning in the country. NEDELYA came forward with the suggestion that these societies be set up and is constantly covering this topic in its pages. And it expects assistance.

[Ryzhkov] You can count on my full support. Moreover, I am profoundly convinced that this is the path we must follow—the quality of goods and services can be improved only with the consumer's help. Monopolism is our undoing, and when monopoly enterprises produce something they are not, as a rule, too concerned about their consumers. But as soon as consumers unite and draw the producer's attention to the shabby quality of his goods, and furthermore start influencing him directly as it were, he will be forced to heed their voices. In my view, this is an altogether sound counterweight to the producers' diktat.

I am profoundly convinced that the result of measures like the setting up of consumer societies, the abolition of commodity producers' monopoly, and the various economic levers will be that people engaged in commodity production will properly get down to manufacturing modern and high-quality output.

In case your readers might be interested, let me add this: I am constantly following the development of the consumer movement and in my work as chairman of the USSR Council of Ministers I am pursuing a line aimed at its development. We must support its activity by all means. Let me repeat: This is something very good and extremely necessary for everyone.

[Correspondent] What are your plans? Are you preparing to become chairman of the Council of Ministers again?

[Ryzhkov] Yes, if the deputies were to decide so, I am prepared to take on this office again.

[Correspondent] The second bell has already sounded, and we obviously must end the conversation here... Could we count on a more extensive interview for NEDELYA? Some time in the future, of course.

[Ryzhkov] What can I say, you must realize that now this does not depend on me alone. I personally am in favor.

Discusses Economic Issues

PM0206142589 Moscow SOVETSKAYA ROSSIYA in Russian 1 Jun 89 Second Edition p 4

[Interview with N.I. Ryzhkov, member of the CPSU Central Committee Politburo and chairman of the outgoing USSR Council of Ministers, by own correspondents T. Karyakina and Yu. Nikolayev: "Interview During Session Recess: Planning the Stages of Development"; date of interview not given]

[Text] Moscow, the Kremlin—[Correspondents] Nikolay Ivanovich, in talking with deputies and listening to speeches from the rostrum you can see that deputies are worried by the content of the upcoming report on key economic problems. A collection of additions to and proposals for the future report is piling up, as it were. Will these various wishes affect your speech, is what has already been prepared being supplemented in the light of the realities of the congress?

[Ryzhkov] Of course, these realities are being taken into account. Above all, of course, the actual report delivered by Mikhail Sergeyevich Gorbachev. It mapped out the basic landmarks of our socioeconomic development and the basic guidelines of our society's further development. And they are all certainly being taken into account in the work on the Council of Ministers report. Everything said during the debate is also carefully taken into account. But there is a subtle point here. It is true: You always want to answer to some extent the questions which are asked and raised in deputies' speeches. But if you responded to every problem, the report could altogether simply come apart at the seams, split up into partial problems, and lose its integrity. The main thing therefore is to know how to group these problems and illuminate them with greater clarity. I think about this constantly. Otherwise, I repeat, you may get bogged down in detail and be unable to see the whole picture. That is the big problem today.

[Correspondents] Could you, if only briefly, give us your impression of today's speeches?

[Ryzhkov] Let us remember that today's debate was opened by agricultural workers and workers in the agro-industrial complex. In the performance of my official duty—although I am an industrialist myself—I have to concern myself very much with agro-industrial questions. I feel great sympathy for the speech made by Vasiliy Aleksandrovich Starodubtsev and the appeal to the congress that was subsequently read out, because we do after all have to solve the questions of the countryside some day. We have to solve the food questions. If we had solved them, 70 percent of the country's problems would not exist. The country's food supply is the basic thing today. As far as consumer goods, light industry goods, and consumer durables are concerned, I am convinced that within a certain time—2-3 years, say—we will find a solution. We can already discern the solution right now

and are beginning to get plants in various sectors, including defense sectors, involved in the manufacture of consumer goods and so forth. The questions concerned with developing the agro-industrial sector seem to me, however, to be the most complex. There is a very large and chronic ailment there. And it is not so easy to treat. I approach what the comrades said with understanding. And although there were perhaps overly harsh judgments and some extreme opinions, there were also very businesslike proposals, if I may put it that way. We will have to show a great deal of concern for the agro-industrial complex in the next 5-Year Plan. Notwithstanding the meager capital investments which are planned, I think that even so more capital investments will have to be allocated to the agro-industrial complex than to other sectors of the national economy.

[Correspondents] If it were only the countryside that needed investments.... We were talking with a group of servicemen deputies and not all of them, let us put it this way, take a sanguine view of the cuts in defense spending....

[Ryzhkov] Here one needs first and foremost to properly calculate and evaluate this breakthrough. I, at least, do not know at all whether our state ever before reduced its defense spending. The breakthrough started in 1987. In 1989 military spending will amount to R77.3 billion. A proposal has been submitted to cut it by another 10 billion in 1990-1991. And I think that most of the deputies understand this important step correctly.

[Correspondents] It is very clear that deputies constantly approach you with specific questions during the recesses. You just spoke with a woman who was clearly armed with a whole list of problems. Do you consider that this is natural during the work of the congress or something out of the ordinary?

[Ryzhkov] I think that it is ordinary work with people and their problems. It always existed before the congress and during the sessions of the old Supreme Soviet. It's just life, everyday practice. But the work is now becoming increasingly active. People do not just come up to you but also send heaps of enquiries, letters, suggestions, and requests. Many of them are, of course, pretty complex. But we carefully examine everything. If we can't solve them, we say so: We can't for such and such reasons. Because it is impossible to solve everything, otherwise, instead of the financial improvement which we are promising society, we can only worsen the situation. Yes, very large numbers of problems have built up in the country. They nevertheless need to be arranged in some order of priority. If we again adopt the broad-sweep approach, I am sure that we will only aggravate the situation. Certainly, one of the defects in the activity of yesterday's government was that, aware of the acuteness of vital problems and wishing to eliminate it, we sought to solve them at a stroke. But afterwards, when the time for analysis came, it turned out that acting from the best of motives, we had overstepped the bounds of the permissible in some places. And that had an impact on the financial situation. I fear that these contradictions will continue to have an effect. We want to solve specific problems. But when we do get down to them, we begin to see that things are not working out so well on the whole.

I think that the new Supreme Soviet's task is initially to decide in broad terms where to channel resources and how this is to be done, and then to resolve specific problems in crucial areas.

[Correspondents] Nikolay Ivanovich, does it follow from your critical tenor regarding the previous government that the new cabinet will undergo substantial changes?

[Ryzhkov] The chairman of the Council of Ministers, newly confirmed according to the constitution, will submit his proposal. We, the present government, have naturally thought about this and carried out the necessary preparation. I think that substantial changes are needed in the membership of the Council of Ministers. Although in general this process of collective deliberation is actually going on now at the congress. The exchange of opinions and all kinds of consultation signify that this process is under way. It forms part, incidentally, of the section of the state program which speaks of cutting spending on the management apparatus. The thesis of the Supreme Soviet chairman's report that the country should live within its means and needs material reinforcement touches on social aspects of our program for the near future. The savings on the management apparatus are, of course, details, but they amount to billions, which are swelled by further billions derived from other steps—the military spending cuts and the review of certain programs.

[Correspondents] What do you think: Is there not a tendency discernible in the speeches of some deputies to crush the executive altogether and confine all power solely within the Supreme Soviet?

[Ryzhkov] I think that both are dangerous. Yes, I also sense that some comrades are inclined to tackle every specific problem from here, without shifting from the spot. I think that is a mistake: Supplanting the executive by the soviets won't do any good. There should be a strict demarcation. The soviets—the legislative branch—should monitor the vital processes and participate in them, ensuring through their power the balanced development of the national economy at all levels, both union and republic. But supplanting executive power, that, I think, would be ruinous. Deputies would then be up to their eyeballs in the work which the executive committee deals with. The question of the demarcation of functions would then be revealed in a new light. This boundary should not be crossed. I think that the flurry of individual questions observable at the congress is simply due to the fact that many deputies today are still reeling from the elections and the heavy weight of the instructions they have received. They feel responsible to their voters and therefore endeavor to get their individual questions in.

[Correspondents] But, for all their specificity, they are closely bound up with the state of the economy. What kind of law now primarily needs to be adopted to improve it, in your view?

[Ryzhkov] To improve the economy we now need to have a whole range of priorities. The figure of 50 has been mentioned at the congress—50 laws demand promulgation. I think that there are 10 laws which could effectively regulate our life which need to be finalized right now. I am often asked, incidentally, what the Council of Ministers, our economy's supreme executive, administrative organ, thinks: Is it better for it to live under laws or without laws? I am firmly convinced that it is better for any executive organ to live under laws. Because sometimes, in the absence of a law, we are forced to adopt resolutions and certain decisions. And then it begins: We adopt them, they are implemented, and the criticism begins: On what grounds? Who is responsible? Okay. Someone has to make decisions in the country. The state cannot live any old way. The more laws there are, the fewer resolutions, orders, and instructions of all sorts there will be. These things are interconnected. Therefore I am in favor of laws.

[Correspondents] The term "socialist market" has come up time and again in reports and in debate, but it seemed to us that not everyone regards the actual concept in the same way. What does it mean? A market of consumer goods only or a capital market, a labor market?

[Ryzhkov] You also have to see definite stages here. What distinguishes the market in general from the socialist market? Many academics say that on the whole the socialist market is an invention. The market is the market. Socialist or capitalist...I disagree. If we just have a market, that will mean chaos, which will cast the country back into the 19th century. And I do mean the 19th century, because nowadays there is no pure market anywhere. Capitalists don't have one either. They have gone far beyond that time. That is why the socialist market is, in my view, a regulated market under which the country sets itself certain tasks. Social tasks, say—the provision of housing. The task determines the approach to it and includes the economic mechanism which will, in turn, steer the market in that direction. It is therefore a regulated market. That is the difference. Or, say, questions of pricing. One can of course leave everything to the market and let things develop as they will. But there are very few such states today, even capitalist countries experience a shortage of certain foodstuffs. They therefore regulate the market by means of subsidies or other mechanisms. I think therefore that our market will develop. And, in my view, it will develop first in the sphere of production—that is, wholesale trade. I think that it will gradually move into the consumer market. But I, for example, am firmly convinced that the consumer market should be regulated. If we do not regulate it now, we will place it the mercy of unrestrained market forces and will look back on our present talk of the population's living standards as a rose-colored dream.

Because inflationary processes will come that will have an immediate effect upon the population, particularly the poorest people. The development of the market should therefore be regulated.

[Correspondents] Do you have a clear picture of this regulatory mechanism?

[Ryzhkov] It is clear in principle, but it can only be actually achieved if every possible economic mechanism, including the tax system and tax policy, is involved. Much work still needs to be done here. The tax system, for example, has not been worked out, it simply does not exist today. We have been forced to revert to the past, to what existed until 1988, and to introduce a correlation between productivity and income into economic practice. An ideal instrument? No, I think not. But there is nothing else. Let's use this at least. It will in some way perform regulating functions.

There is much work still to be done by the new Supreme Soviet, the future Council of Ministers, and all of us citizens of the country.

Nationalities Chairman Nishanov Interviewed on Tasks
LD0606230589 Moscow Domestic Service in Russian 1800 GMT 6 Jun 89

[Interview by unidentified correspondents at press conference of recently elected Chairman of the Soviet of Nationalities Rafik Nishanovich Nishanov; date and place not given; recorded]

[Text] [Announcer] Immediately after USSR People's Deputy Nishanov was elected chairman of the Soviet of Nationalities, a small press conference took place during a short interval. Journalists accredited to this session asked quite a few questions. Rafik Nishanovich Nishanov said:

[Begin recording] [Nishanov] The position of the chairman of the Soviet of Nationalities obliges him to resolve all questions in the interests of all nations, of all ethnic groups. The essence of the question is to defend the interests of everyone in economic, social, and cultural development, in safeguarding legislative acts so that each people should feel its sovereignty.

And there is a second aspect to the question: Inasmuch as the representatives of many nations are living on the territory of the Soviet Union, in any part one must conduct such work as enables a person of any nationality to live well, and that he, wherever he might be, should enjoy all rights. This is the essence of our question.

[Unidentified correspondent] By virtue of certain reason, carrying out the mission of the Soviet states, you lost contact with Uzbekistan for 15 years. Are you not sorry to tear yourself away again for another 5 years?

[Nishanov] I didn't lose contact with Uzbekistan for 15 years. I lived and breathed Uzbekistan's concerns. And I think that, being here, I will naturally not forget Uzbekistan. Well, my position obliges me to treat everyone the same.

[Same correspondent] The more so as there are 10 more representatives of Uzbekistan in the Soviet of Nationalities.

[Nishanov] Absolutely right!

[Second unidentified correspondent] Rafik Nishanovich, a question from all-union radio. The deputies have now said that almost no institutes for interethnic relations exist in our country, so that we must set up such an institute. How do you see this work?

[Nishanov] Indeed, in the study of the development of nations and national relations we have no smoothly working institutes. But, in fact, we have now already formed the first such informal house. There was previously a Soviet of Nationalities but it existed somewhat formally. Thus, questions were asked, unanimous votes were cast, and the problems remained. Now, it seems to me, that a house is being set up which truly is a house of nationalities. But in order for the Soviet of Nationalities to operate effectively it needs the appropriate mechanisms: the study of the state of affairs, synthesizing, the drawing up of legislative acts, and others. It is natural that institutes are necessary for this. One of the delegates who spoke at the Congress was absolutely right in saying: We have an Institute of the United States, an Institute of Canada, an Institute of Oriental Studies, but we don't have an institute for the study of national problems. We obviously have a lot of work to do on this.

[Same correspondent] Well, and while such an institute does not exist are you planning to bring in sociologists, economists, lawyers, and scientists specialized in interethnic relations to work for you?

[Nishanov] That goes without saying. And only in close contact with representatives of scientific circles, of the intelligentsia which represents various sectors of our culture, art, by bringing in economic specialists, by bringing in historians, philosophers, sociologists, can we carry out this job.

[Third unidentified correspondent] In electing you as chairman the deputies said most of all that you should not be smoothing things out in your work, but be an innovator, perhaps generate new ideas in interethnic relations. What is your attitude to this?

[Nishanov] Well, first of all, I support this: One must be an innovator, asking questions which haven't been tackled for years and years. But in resolving them, one must nevertheless display patience and smooth things out. Because we have such acute questions, if one doesn't smooth them out and if one doesn't look for ways of resolving them calmly, these questions can acquire an insoluble form. Therefore acute questions must be asked. They must not be evaded. They must be solved, but in resolving them one must show wisdom.

[Fourth unidentified correspondent] What do you suppose the contacts of your house with the Soviet of the Union and with the commissions of the Soviet of the Union will be like?

[Nishanov] For the time being this mechanism has not been precisely developed but I proceed from the fact that we will have to have complete coordination, complete interaction. Without this, resolving questions is impossible.

[Fifth unidentified correspondent] Tell us please, it probably seemed to you today that you will not have an easy time with the deputies from the baltic republics here (?in future)?

[Nishanov] No, that is not how it seemed to me. Perhaps it seemed to you like that from afar. I have already established close contact with them and we have complete mutual understanding. [end recording]

Kolbin To Head People's Control Committee
LD0706111489 Moscow TASS in English 1104 GMT 7 Jun 89

[Text) Moscow June 7 TASS—By TASS parliamentary correspondent:

The Supreme Soviet, the new national full-time parliament, elected Kazakhstan Communist Party leader Gennadiy Kolbin, 62, by a majority of votes to head the People's Control Committee, a country-wide watchdog service consisting of volunteers combining efforts with government inspectors to fight red tape, inefficiency and sloppy management.

People's control groups are active at factories and organisations across the land.

Kolbin, a Russian, was born on May 7, 1927, in the city of Nizhniy Tagil in the Ural mountains and started working in 1942.

After graduating from the Ural polytechnic in 1955, he worked his way up from head of a technology bureau, a workshop superintendant and deputy chief engineer at a Nizhniy Tagil factory.

Kolbin has been in party work since 1959, elected secretary of a factory party committee, a borough party committee and a city party committee.

Between 1970 and 1975 he was a secretary and then second secretary of the Sverdlovsk Region party committee. From 1975 until 1983 Kolbin was second secretary of the Georgian Communist Party Central Committee and from December 1983 he was first secretary of the Ulyanovsk Region party committee.

He has been first secretary of the Kazakhstan Communist Party Central Committee since December 1986.

Kolbin Interviewed on Appointment
LD0806034289 Moscow Television Service in Russian 1700 GMT 7 Jun 89

[From the "Vremya" newscast; interview with G.V. Kolbin, chairman of the USSR People's Control Committee, by unidentified reporter, given during the interval after the 7 June afternoon sitting of the USSR Supreme Soviet in the Kremlin—recorded]

[Text] [Reporter] Gennadiy Vasilyevich, the Supreme Soviet has just approved the proposal made by its chairman. Great confidence has been shown in you, but the debate was heated. The whole country witnessed that. Considerations for and against were expressed. What is your attitude toward the debate that has just taken place?

[Kolbin] I consider that it was a very exacting discussion, the like of which for many years we did not witness or even permit ourselves to think of. Frank things were stated, both in my support and also the reverse. What is very pleasing is that I worked for many long years together with Comrade Yeltsin, and now suddenly we have been made, as it were, rivals in the settling of this cadre question.

I am grateful to all the comrades who made very serious criticisms of me. They will serve to help in my work. If the congress shows trust to the end in the solution of this matter, I shall have to adjust my actions a great deal, taking into account those criticisms that were expressed.

Biryukova Interviewed on Need To Help Poor
LD0806040189 Moscow Television Service in Russian 1700 GMT 7 Jun 89

[From the "Vremya" newscast; interview with A.P. Biryukova, deputy chairman of the USSR Council of Ministers, by unidentified reporter, given during the break between the 7 June afternoon and evening sessions at the USSR Supreme Soviet in the Kremlin—recorded]

[Text] [Unidentified reporter] Social problems are a painful matter for us and up to now they are, perhaps, the problems most difficult to resolve. In light of the debates that have been going on at the congress and here at the Supreme Soviet, in your view what is the chief link that needs to be grasped in order to get the chain moving in the near future?

[Biryukova] The debates that have been in progress at the congress, and not just at the congress—I have had occasion to have very many meetings with deputies— have confirmed again and again that our country's political leadership and the government have correctly determined the strategic line—namely, a radical turn of our economy toward tackling social issues and toward social problems.

First and foremost the chief problem is to solve, and solve forthwith, questions connected with improving the position of our pensioners and the poorly-off sections of our population—and their numbers are not so small. We now know that they number 43 million. We were intending to tackle these issues after we had adopted a law on state pensions. The debates at the congress have shown that the government and the political leadership immediately need to study the possibilities and find the resources—I mean both financial and other resources—in order, without waiting for the law on state pensions, to find a way to raise the standard of living of these sections of the population.

Many deputies in their speeches have very vigorously criticized that our administrative apparatus has been growing, but the administrative apparatus at the center is not growing. It has been considerably reduced. The administrative apparatus locally, at the middle management level—I have in mind those at production associations, at enterprises, and at combines—has increased over this period. It is necessary to raise the pay for labor resources not as a whole but for each person working in the administrative apparatus at the middle level and directly at the enterprises. The second direction that I think we should, or rather Nikolay Ivanovich in a few days' time will present the new composition of the gsovernment, and obviously we must set about further reducing the number of ministries and departments; and here, too, a saving has been obtained.

[Reporter] does it not seem to you—and people have been saying this at the congress—that women need to be brought a little more into the direction of affairs and the country's fate?

[Biryukova] I am wholly and fully in agreement with this view of yours and consider that women should be more broadly represented at all levels—in government bodies,

in ministerial posts, and in other official posts, too. During the years of Soviet power, women have developed very much in our country. They include very many wise, intelligent, bold, and energetic people, who are able to run things well in the most diverse posts.

IZVESTIYA Publishes Series of Opinion Polls

Poll on Expectations for Congress

PM2605133489 Moscow IZVESTIYA in Russian 26 May 89 Morning Edition p 2

[Unattributed report on telephone poll by USSR Academy of Sciences Institute of Sociology "congress sociology group," plus commentary by V.A. Yadov, director of USSR Academy of Sciences Institute of Sociology: "Expectations. Hopes. Doubts...."]

[Text] In yesterday's issue of IZVESTIYA we reported the results of an instant public opinion poll on the Congress of USSR People's Deputies carried out by sociologists of the CPSU Central Committee Social Sciences Academy and the All-Union Scientific Research Institute of Soviet State Building and Legislation. Sociological research on this very important event in our political life is currently being carried out by other organizations, too. In view of the wide public interest in the results of this research, the IZVESTIYA editorial office has decided regularly to brief our readers on it.

Today we give the floor to the "congress sociology group" set up at the USSR Academy of Sciences Institute of Sociology. On the evening of 23 May it carried out a telephone poll of the population to find out what citizens expect from the Congress of People's Deputies. The poll was carried out in five cities—Moscow, Leningrad, Kiev, Tbilisi, and Tallinn. In each of these cities some 300 people were polled by telephone. The telephone numbers were selected by random sampling, and the composition of those polled was controlled so as to represent the structure of the given city's population.

The figures are given in percentages of the number of those polled in each city, rounded up to the nearest whole percent. The proportion of those unable to reply is not cited.

	Moscow	Leningrad	Kiev	Tbilisi	Tallinn
1. I intend to follow the congress's work:					
All the time	55	55	56	65	52
Not all the time	28	24	29	21	26
I do not plan to follow the congress's work	12	12	8	8	14
2. The congress will adopt decisions exceptionally important to the country's future:					
Agree	63	53	53	46	47
Unsure	28	33	33	28	32
Disagree	3	5	1	5	4
3. The congress will discuss problems very important to the country's future:					
Agree	84	69	73	62	65
Unsure	13	17	9	16	21
Disagree	1	6	5	4	4
4. The congress will define ways of resolving economic problems:					
Agree	51	59	52	27	40

	Moscow	Leningrad	Kiev	Tbilisi	Tallinn
Unsure	31	11	25	34	42
Disagree	11	15	9	6	12
5. The congress will define ways of agreeing on solutions to national problems:					
Agree	55	47	50	23	33
Unsure	29	33	24	50	32
Disagree	9	14	12	12	17
6. The congress will reveal the positions of different population groups:					
Agree	59	57	63	50	52
Unsure	22	20	16	23	21
Disagree	7	4	6	4	7
7. The congress will be a decisive-step in the creation of a rule-of-law, democratic state:					
Agree	58	53	62	32	51
Unsure	27	23	23	27	32
Disagree	6	11	6	17	6
8. The congress will elect a competent and capable USSR Supreme Soviet:					
Agree	56	54	58	45	41
Unsure	32	26	26	25	39
Disagree	5	8	5	5	10
9. I believe that the congress's work will be:					
Successful, productive, useful	42	43	42	25	32
Intensive but with few results	37	33	35	43	44
I pin no great hopes on the congress's work	10	13	15	15	13

[Signed] "Congress Sociology Group," USSR Academy of Sciences Institute of Sociology

Commentary by V.A. Yadov, director of the USSR Academy of Sciences Institute of Sociology:

In general citizens intend to follow the congress's work intensively, believing that it will discuss problems that are very important to the country (65-84 percent). More than one-third of those polled in the various cities believe that the congress's work will be successful and useful, but another one-third (or even slightly more) do not believe that the congress will adopt useful decisions on important problems of the economy, national relations, or other questions. In all regions the majority expresses confidence that the congress will reveal the positions of different population groups.

People pin great hopes on the election of a competent USSR Supreme Soviet, although here, too, about one-third are skeptical.

There are significant differences in the positions of citizens in two republics (on the results of the poll in the cities of Tbilisi and Tallinn). People in Tbilisi, for the most part, are unsure whether the congress will be a decisive step along the path to creating a rule-of-law socialist state; people in Tallinn are particularly skeptical

about its success in defining ways of resolving economic problems. That reflects the real situation. In Tbilisi tragic events took place that cause perplexity from the viewpoint of observance of the rule of law. In Estonia one of the most acute problems is that of republican economic accountability and the republic's sovereignty in this sphere.

Initial Reactions to Proceeedings

PM0206114489 Moscow IZVESTIYA in Russian
30 May 89 Morning Edition p 2

[Results of opinion poll by the "Congress sociology group" of the USSR Academy of Sciences Institute of Sociology, with commentary by Professor V.A. Mansurov, deputy director of the USSR Academy of Sciences Institute of Sociology: "In an Atmosphere of Democracy"]

[Text] On 26 May the "Congress sociology group" of the USSR Academy of Sciences Institute of Sociology carried out an opinion poll in Moscow, Leningrad, Kiev, Tallinn, Tbilisi, and Alma-Ata. There were 1,832 people polled. They answered questions as follows:

[In following tables, cities are represented by initial letters as follows: M—Moscow, L—Leningrad, K—Kiev, Ta—Tallinn, Tb—Tbilisi, A—Alma-Ata]

	M	L	K	Ta	Tb	A
Are you following the proceedings of the congress?						
Constantly	39	38	47	27	56	21
More or less constantly	48	40	37	41	36	40
From time to time, irregularly	11	16	14	26	7	36
Almost never	2	6	2	6	1	3
How democratic do you find the proceedings of the congress?						
Completely democratic	41	31	50	22	17	52
More or less democratic	44	48	38	57	64	31
Undemocratic	7	13	6	10	15	15
Don't know	8	8	6	11	4	2
What is your opinion on the course of the congress at present?						
Much better than I expected	30	21	50	17	14	42
As I expected	37	39	25	33	32	33
At present it is not fulfilling my expectations	15	26	12	24	42	15
Don't know	18	14	13	26	12	10
In your opinion, is it expedient to combine party and state posts (party committee secretary and chairman of a soviet of people's deputies)?						
Yes	36	34	37	12	21	51
No	52	52	57	76	72	49
Don't know	12	14	6	12	7	0
What is your attitude to the election of M.S. Gorbachev as chairman of the USSR Supreme Soviet?						
I support his election unreservedly	65	66	71	57	41	65
I support it with reservations	28	20	22	33	40	20
I do not support it	5	12	6	6	17	11
Don't know	2	2	1	4	2	4

Commentary by Professor V.A. Mansurov, deputy director of the USSR Academy of Sciences Institute of Sociology:

The congress is evoking great interest among Soviet people, who are attentively following its proceedings. Judging by the results of the opinion poll, the inhabitants of Tallinn and Alma-Ata follow it the least constantly.

The majority of those polled note the atmosphere of democracy in which all matters are discussed. Nevertheless around 1 in 6 of those polled in Tbilisi, Alma-Ata, and Leningrad, and 1 in 10 in Tallinn, note a lack of democracy in the proceedings of the congress. If we compare the figures obtained with the figures from opinion polls of 25 and 26 May [as published; present poll was carried out 26 May], public opinion has become more positive about the democratic atmosphere at the congress.

The overwhelming majority of those polled (between 81 and 93 percent) support the election of M.S. Gorbachev as chairman of the USSR Supreme Soviet, with unreserved support of between 41 percent in Tbilisi and 65-66 percent in Leningrad, Moscow, and Alma-Ata.

As regards the debate on combining party and state posts, only in Alma-Ata did over half (51 percent) of those polled support this principle. In the other towns this idea is considered inappropriate by between 76 percent (in Tallinn) and 52 percent (in Moscow and Leningrad).

Is the congress living up to expectations? Despite the generally positive statistics (75 percent in Alma-Ata, 67 percent in Moscow, and 50 percent in Tallinn) it is noticeable that less than half of Tbilisi's inhabitants are satisfied with its proceedings, and furthermore, the congress is not yet living up to the expectations of 42 percent of the inhabitants of this town. This is also the opinion of one in six people in Moscow and Alma-Ata and one in four in Leningrad and Tbilisi on 26 May. Since that the opinion poll was carried out only 2 days after the beginning of the congress, it is not surprising that a relatively large number of those polled were unable to answer this question.

Deputies Polled on Congress

PM0206101789 Moscow IZVESTIYA in Russian 31 May 89 Morning Edition p 7

[Report by N. Betaneli, V. Lapayeva, and "Congress sociology group" leaders V. Alferov and S. Tikhonina under the rubric "Congress Sociology Group": "Deputies' Opinions...."]

[Text] Sociologists from the CPSU Central Committee Academy of Social Sciences and the All-Union Scientific Research Institute of Soviet State Building and Legislation have polled USSR people's deputies participating in the congress on how it is proceeding and what they consider most important in their activity. Taking part in the poll were 1,347 deputies.

The speeches by people's deputies have reflected a desire for a collective analysis of problems, broad dialogue, and consolidation. Conflicting opinions and open debate were noticeable on a number of questions. Although the correlation of opinions has no set or stable nature, it is possible to highlight a "least satisfied group with more radical expectations" (around 25-30 percent); a "group of balanced positions" (40-55 percent); and a "group of comparatively more moderate expectations and more cautious approaches, showing a greater degree of satisfaction" (15-20 percent). At the same time, the poll results convince us that on a whole number of issues deputies are predisposed to agreement, which sometimes covers 92 percent of those polled.

...On the Situation in the Country

Most deputies' views reflect acute concern for the state of the population's living standards and law and order in the country.

What is the most important thing for you all at the current time? (Deputies were asked to choose two points).

Maintaining law and order	56 percent
Greater participation by people in making important political decisions and further developing self-management	30 percent
Achievement of higher living standards for all	74 percent
Glasnost, openness, freedom of speech, the raising of the level of criticism and self-criticism	25 percent

How do you assess the current state of the process of democratization in the country?

The democratization process has become irreversible	21 percent
Additional measures are needed to guarantee the irreversibility of democratization	40 percent
Everything done has been half-measures, more resolute steps are needed	34 percent
Virtually nothing has been done, the democratization process has still not started	1 percent
Don't know	4 percent

...On the Congress's Influence on Solving the Problems Facing the Country

A large number of deputies (60 percent) expect congress decisions to considerably improve within the next 2-3 years the state of affairs as regards glasnost, openness, freedom of speech in the country, and opportunities for citizens to honestly and fearlessly voice their opinions on any problem. Some deputies (32 percent) make optimistic forecasts about increasing citizens' influence on state policy, on the state of affairs in society, and on the development of self-management.

...On the Conditions and Measures Needed for USSR People's Deputies To Successfully Carry Out Their Duties

The deputies consider the following to be among the priority measures:

The adoption of a USSR law on the status of USSR people's deputies	92 percent
The raising of officials' responsibility for failing to take measures on the basis of questions or appeals from people's deputies	74 percent
Free access for all USSR people's deputies to the information they need for their activities	70 percent
Guarantees of the independence of deputies' activities from local party and soviet organs	60 percent
Opportunities for all USSR people's deputies to take part in the work of the USSR Supreme Soviet and its commissions on their own initiative	57 percent
Mandatory consideration for the opinions of all USSR people's deputies in the adoption of legislative decisions by the USSR Supreme Soviet	57 percent
The provision to all USSR people's deputies of the equipment they need for their work	48 percent
The provision of working equipment for USSR Supreme Soviet deputies only	13 percent

The poll recorded the deputies' marked orientation toward increasing the level of information available to them and obtaining the broadest range of social information. In the deputies' opinion they need the following information right now:

On the state of public opinion on the most important state and social issues	60 percent
On statistics on the state of the national economy	36 percent
On Soviet legislation	36 percent
On foreign legislation	22 percent
On moral statistics	15 percent
On criminal statistics	8 percent
Other information	4 percent

In the opinion of most deputies (55 percent) the first few days of the congress on the whole lived up to their hopes and expectations. For 40 percent of those polled the congress had not lived up to their expectations on the whole. The following figures give a more detailed picture of deputies' positions:

Has the Congress of the USSR People's Deputies lived up to your expectations?

Yes	20 percent
More "yes" than "no"	35 percent
More "no" than "yes"	26 percent
No	14 percent
Don't know	5 percent

Talking about their first impressions of the congress, deputies indicated what they most liked about it:

The democratic nature of the congress, the plurality of opinions, and the open debate	37 percent
Deputies' boldness, initiative, their desire to defend their positions, and their frankness	13 percent
The glasnost in the press, TV and radio coverage of the congress	6 percent

A considerable number of deputies indicated their dissatisfaction with the resolution of procedural questions at the congress:

	A	B	C	D	E	F
Are you following the work of the congress?						
constantly	48	39	53	31	57	45
more or less constantly	33	35	35	43	32	40
occasionally, irregularly	18	21	11	20	11	15
practically not at all	1	5	1	6	-	-
How do you assess the course of the congress's work at present?						
Congress is proceeding far more successfully than I expected	24	17	39	14	43	45
Congress is proceeding as I expected	35	38	35	48	40	36
At present congress is totally failing to meet my expectations	32	36	26	23	8	13
I find it hard to answer	9	9	10	15	9	6
Do you agree with the stance taken at the congress by the deputies from your republic (oblast, city):						
Agree in full	36	42	27	48	71	37
Agree in part	32	31	25	31	8	25
Do not agree	5	10	7	2	2	13
I find it hard to answer	27	17	41	19	19	25

Commentary by Professor V.S. Korobeynikov, sector chief of the USSR Academy of Sciences Institute of Sociology:

The congress is continuing to rivet the attention of Soviet people. The inhabitants of virtually all cities are displaying a **high and steady interest** in the work of the forum of the people's elected representatives.

The progress of the congress's work as a whole is **justifying the voters' expectations.** It is true that there are substantial differences here according to region. Thus, in the opinion of over 40 percent of inhabitants of Tbilisi and Alma-Ata, the congress is proceeding far more successfully than they expected. At the same time almost one-third of Leningraders and Muscovites believe that the congress is so far failing to justify their expectations.

Satisfied	16 percent
More "yes" than "no"	27 percent
More "no" than "yes"	26 percent
Dissatisfied	28 percent
Don't know	3 percent

Third Public Opinion Poll

PM0106130589 Moscow IZVESTIYA in Russian 1 Jun 89 Morning Edition p 10

[Unattributed report under the "Sociological Service" rubric: "Congress Justifies Expectations"]

[Text] On 29 May the USSR Academy of Sciences Institute of Sociology's "Congress sociology group" held another public opinion poll, the third, in Moscow, Leningrad, Kiev, Tallinn, Tbilisi, and Alma-Ata. About 1,800 people were questioned. They were asked questions, the answers to which were as follows:

[In the following tabulation, column A represents Moscow, B Leningrad, C Kiev, D Tallinn, E Tbilisi, and F Alma-Ata]

Virtual **unity of the stances of deputies and the stance of the voters** has been revealed. A steady majority of those polled (from 52 percent in Kiev to 79 percent in Tbilisi and 80 percent in Tallinn [figure as published] agree in full or in part with the stance taken at the congress by the deputies from their regions.

PRAVDA Provides Congress Proceedings Coverage

Report on 1 Jun Congress

PM0206132489 Moscow PRAVDA in Russian 2 Jun 89 Second Edition pp 1, 5

[Reportage by "team of PRAVDA journalists" from the Kremlin Palace of Congresses: "Taking the Voice of the Voters Into Account"]

[Text] The Congress of People's Deputies, gathering pace, has entered its 2d week. You will agree that this is unprecedented, as is the interest that grows with each new day of work by the people's elected representatives. And whereas at first many people were watching to see how democracy and glasnost were being affirmed at the congress, now the time has come for the first interpretation of the work it has done. And voters are increasingly sending telegrams like this to their envoys: "Be more active, we expect from you not generalizations, but constructive proposals." The editorial offices are receiving similar calls.

"In M.S. Gorbachev's report there is criticism of the work of construction and planning workers," Moscow planner A. Zagorodnyuk said, for instance. "And that is quite right. But I wish to say that the departmental fetters that bind my colleagues cause us a lot of trouble. Therefore please tell our representative at the congress—USSR People's Deputy Yu. Andreyev, chief planning engineer—this: Let him fight for the preservation and further development of the principles of full economic accountability and self-financing in planning and research organizations and for the founding of a USSR planners' union, which will provide the opportunity to revive the integrated process of the design of equipment, technological and construction planning, and engineering and economic research, and make it possible to improve the technical standard of our enterprises and residential architecture."

But the voters should not think that the deputies are involved in state affairs only when they speak from the congress platform or to the television cameras. We have already described, for instance, the energetic activity of the agrarian deputies in the intervals between sittings. Television viewers saw the results of their work: At one sitting Deputy V. Gontar read out an Appeal to the Congress on behalf of 417 people's deputies representing the peasantry.

"Each day of the congress brings new lessons," A. Yablokov, corresponding member of the USSR Academy of Sciences, claims, "lessons that we deputies, and not only we, but society as a whole, must learn for ourselves. One of these lessons is the elections to the USSR Supreme Soviet. The USSR Constitution does not state what form voting should take on particular issues. By voting according to the majority system we robbed our parliament of many specialists in the sphere of economics, ecology, and so forth. This would not have happened if the elections had been held according to a proportional system: 30 economists would themselves put forward 6 deputies from their group, 20 ecologists— 4 deputies...."

Another organizational matter that is by no means trivial is that of information about deputies, the absence of which makes relations between them difficult. After all, many problems could be discussed and resolved in meetings behind the scenes, which would certainly make the sittings more productive.

But many people note that yesterday, for instance, there was more order than on the 2d or 3d day. Much here depends on the presidium.

This was acknowledged by Deputy V. Vorotnikov, with whom we spoke during one of the breaks.

"I accept the complaints against me and against the presidium," Vitaliy Ivanovich noted. "But there is a reason for everything. One reason was mentioned, incidentally, by Deputy Boris Oleynik: None of us has learned parliamentary protocol. We are all used to the excessive organization of our congresses and meetings to such an extent that it was hard to imagine anyone speaking without notes, still less forcing his way onto the platform out of turn. Naturally, in 'debates' like that there was only one danger for the chairman: that of falling asleep during the speeches. Now, as you can see for yourselves, the situation is different."

[Correspondents] "There are fears that the congress could drag on, because of the discussion of various procedural issues. And at the same time many deputies, in the view of some voters, are as yet only noting the negative factors that have accumulated in the country, and are not making any constructive proposals on rectifying the situation."

[Vorotnikov] "I do not agree. While in the fisrt days there were indeed few constructive proposals, since M.S. Gorbachev's report there has been no shortage. Much that is useful could spring from such an active and principled discussion. And that is what people expect from the congress. Therefore one would wish the deputies to adopt precisely this constructive tone and feel a sense of responsibility for their words and for the country's future."

We will not recount the deputies' main speeches—PRAVDA is publishing them virtually in full. Especially since each of them needs to be studied seriously by economists, lawyers, and sociologists. Only after this, in order to avoid doing damage by hasty decisions, can it be decided what to adopt and what to reject.

But it is necessary to dwell, if only briefly, on one proposition that is put forward in one way or another by nearly every deputy from the congress platform. This is the party apparatus. During the days of work by the people's deputies there have been many keenly critical and even, to put it mildly, unparliamentary remarks about it. But only some speakers have asked themselves this question: Can one manage without the apparatus entirely? In the party, in the state, at an enterprise, or in a scientific organization? No, of course not: And however justly we may criticize the party apparatus, that justice also demands that we acknowledge that restructuring is moving forward thanks in many respects to that apparatus. The restructuring that began on the party's initiative. Is there really any lack of party raykoms that are pushing through diverse mehtods of economic management literally by force? Or obkoms that campaign for the transfer of oblasts to economic accountability and cost recovery? Or party workers at various levels who seek direct dialogue with unofficial organizations and use their ideas for the democratization of life? Incidentally, this was spoken of yesterday by People's Deputy V. Kalish from Zaporozhye, a steel worker, and he was given an ovation.

But let us come back to yesterday's sitting. After a heated discussion the Congress of People's Deputies elected an editorial commission to draw up a draft resolution on the report of the chairman of the USSR Supreme Soviet. There were fierce arguments in the discussion of candidacies for the deputies' commission to investigate the circumstances surrounding the events in Tbilisi 9 April 1989. But the experience of the preceding days told: The debate was more organized and concrete. After amendments, the deputies approved the composition of the commission by a majority of votes.

A number of procedural questions also arose at the end of the morning sitting yesterday. E. Lippmaa, deputy from Estonia, proposed that the congress form a commission to formulate a political and legal assessment of the Soviet-German Molotov-Ribbentrop pact and the secret protocol to it.

Remember that this question has been raised over the years in the Baltic republics, and the attitude toward it is far from unequivocal. This was confirmed by the debates on the proposal put forward by the Estonian deputy, in which V. Yarovoy, Zh. Alferov, V. Ivanov, V. Semenov, V. Berezov, I. Kezbers, I. Gryazin, E. Inkens, Yu. Boldyrev, and R. Medvedev spoke.

M.S. Gorbachev supported the proposal to set up a commission to make a political and legal assessment of the 1939 Soviet-German pact, and gave some explanations on this matter.

The congress supported the proposal to form a commission and instructed the deputies of the Baltic republics and the presidium to submit a proposal on its composition.

At the evening sitting yesterday, the discussion of M.S. Gorbachev's report continued, and certain other questions were also examined.

Thus A. Lukyanov, first deputy chairman of the USSR Supreme Soviet, in response to deputies' questions and on the instructions of the USSR Supreme Soviet Presidium and the Congress Presidium, familiarized deputies with authentic documents—the texts of telegrams reflecting the dynamics of the development of events in Georgia that led to the tragic night of 9 April. These were three telegrams received at the CPSU Central Committee from Tbilisi 7-9 April and signed by the republic party leadership. The content of two telegrams on the situation in Tbilisi dating from 26 November was also cited.

M.S. Gorbachev noted that the documents read out confirm the correctness of the congress decision to set up a deputies' commission on this question.

Deputy F. Dovlatyan submitted a request for an answer to a question conveyed to the Congress Presidium by a group of deputies from Armenia.

The congress instructed the presidium to prepare an answer to the question from the Armenian group of deputies.

The congress heard B. Gidaspov, chairman of the Credentials Commission. He reported on the commission's conclusions on a question submitted at the congress by Deputy V. Alksnis, and also briefed those present on the Credentials Commission's activity in examining messages, letters, and telegrams sent to the presidium and the Credentials Commission.

On behalf of the Congress Presidium R. Nishanov submitted proposals to deputies on the composition of the commission to investigate materials connected with the activity of the USSR Prosecutor's Office investigating group headed by T.Kh. Gdlyan. Opinions were expressed on this question by deputies N. Ivanov, V. Shevchenko, E. Yusupov, N. Strukov, A. Mukhtarov, and others.

The commission was approved by a majority of votes.

In connection with Deputy A. Karpov's speech, A. Likhanov gave explanations on expenditure of the funds of the V.I. Lenin Soviet Children's Fund.

The congress will continue today.

Congress's International Dimension
*PM0506103789 Moscow PRAVDA in Russian
2 Jun 89 Second Edition p 1*

[Arkadiy Maslennikov commentary under the rubric "Notes of a Publicist": "Principledness and Dynamism"]

[Text] Hardly anyone would dispute today that the first Congress of USSR People's Deputies is a major event not just in our domestic life but also on the international scene. That is understandable, as the processes of restructuring, democratization, and glasnost which are taking place in our country have opened up new, unprecedented prospects for the whole of the international community.

Not everything in international affairs depends on us, of course. However, it will be no exaggeration to say that it was precisely the Soviet restructuring and the policy of new thinking which has been implemented by our country over the past 4 years which have made it possible to switch East-West relations from the rusty rails of position-of-strength confrontation and military-political rivalry to relaxation of tension and constantly expanding cooperation.

This is why people in all parts of the world are following the debates in the Kremlin Palace of Congresses so closely. They want to know whether the restructuring and democratization in the USSR, in whose success the whole world is interested today, will be consolidated. They want to be reassured that the policy of new thinking which has made it possible to mobilize new broad strata of the international public for active political creative cooperation and stave off the threat of a world nuclear conflict will be authoritatively reaffirmed and further developed at the highest forum of the Soviet Union.

It must be noted that this attention and this interest were not disappointed. In his report "On the Main Guidelines for the USSR Domestic and Foreign Policy" M.S. Gorbachev gave direct and unambiguous answers to all the main questions which are of concern to the international public.

The restructuring which is under way in the Soviet Union, he said, is inseparably and dialectically linked with the activities of the Soviet state in the international arena. The new political thinking—this dynamic concept which forms the basis of the Soviet foreign policy—is drawing its life force from both the humanistic ideals of the transformations which are being implemented in our country and the sober evaluation of the realities currently prevailing in the world. This fundamentally new approach to the formulation of foreign policy is based on the recognition of the priority of universal human interests and values; generally accepted norms of morality as an indispensable criterion of any policy; freedom of sociopolitical choice which rules out interference in the affairs of any state; and the need to deideologize international relations.

Naturally, the establishment of these principles in international politics is a complex matter and is proceeding with difficulty. People in NATO countries' government offices and military headquarters, and above all in the United States, are still convinced, or at least they are trying to convince others, that the positive changes which are currently taking place in the international arena are the result of the "position-of-strength policy" and of the nuclear "deterrence" of socialist countries which they are implementing. These ideas are also reflected, albeit in mitigated form, in the "Global Concept in the Disarmament and Arms Control Sphere" which was published on the results of the jubilee NATO Council session in Brussels.

Nonetheless, the gains of the policy of new thinking are indisputable. The general climate of international relations has become appreciably calmer than it was a few years ago. Before our very eyes more open, humane, trusting relations between peoples are developing. The process of real disarmament has finally been set in motion and is developing in several spheres. International cooperation in the solution of ecological, humanitarian, and other global problems is taking on increasingly tangible forms.

It does not matter if some of our Western partners are still interpreting these changes in their own way, if they do not accept our understanding of the relation between cause and effect on which these changes are based, and if they do not accept our terminology. Provided, of course, that these differences do not hamper cooperation, that they do not serve as a pretext for building up arms and intensifying mutual suspicions rather than working toward disarmament and the enhancement of the potential of mutual trust. In other words, it is the essence of the processes which are currently taking place in international relations which is important, and not the words in which they are clothed. When it is a question simply of the verbal framework in respect of the fate of mankind, it is possible and necessary to reach compromises.

As for the Soviet Union, its foreign policy is geared to the whole world, as M.S. Gorbachev noted in his report. It takes account of not only of individual countries' specific interests and the developing bilateral relations with them, but also key features of the regional and international situation. Its fundamental principles have always been:

ensuring the security of the country, above all by political means;

elimination of nuclear weapons by means of the negotiation process geared to disarmament and the reduction of the states' defense potential down to reasonable sufficiency;

exclusion from international practice of the use of force or threat of force;

rejection of confrontation and its replacement by dialogue with the aim of achieving a balance of interests as the only method of resolving international problems;

the incorporation of the Soviet economy in the world economy on a mutually advantageous and equitable basis, active participation in the formulation and observance of the rules governing modern international division of labor, scientific and technical exchanges, trade, and cooperation with anyone who is ready for this.

By enshrining these principles in laws, the highest organ of Soviet power will enhance still further the prestige of and confidence in the USSR's foreign policy which accords with the fundamental interests of the Soviet people and all mankind.

World Reactions to Congress

PM0606161589 Moscow PRAVDA in Russian
6 Jun 89 Second Edition pp 1,4

[TASS roundup dated 5 June under rubric "Abroad":
"In the Mirror of the World Press"]

[Text] Since the very first day of the Congress of USSR People's Deputies, its work has been the object of close scrutiny as far as the foreign mass media are concerned. Socialist countries and the West alike are unanimous that the new Soviet parliament is working in conditions of glasnost and openness uncommon in Soviet political life and that, for the first time, people's deputies have a real opportunity to influence democratic changes within the leadership and society, the conditions for conducting a frank, free discussion and exercising their right to legislative initiative, and so forth.

"By convening its first national assembly in 7 decades the Soviet Union has embarked on an experiment in the field of parliamentary policy," THE NEW YORK TIMES wrote the day the congress opened. A commentary on Austrian radio said: "This forum is a very important event in the life of Soviet society because it is concerned with urgent problems whose resolution can be delayed no longer. If there is any delay in overcoming the difficulties of restructuring, this will lead to social and political tension in the country."

The practice of the congress being broadcast live on television and radio has been interpreted by the foreign press as one of the most graphic signs of democratization in Soviet society. "The broadcasting of the congress sessions is clear evidence that glasnost is growing stronger," Poland's ZYCIE WARSZAWY noted. "Millions of viewers can see for themselves that a decisive end has been put to the tradition whereby everything followed a script from above. Now the scripts are written by the deputies themselves."

France's LE MONDE said: "These days virtually the entire Soviet population is glued to the television screen. While the congress has been at work the country has seen itself in a mirror—sometimes the reflection has not been flattering but it has always been true. An open discussion has been conducted on virtually every question that could be discussed." The opinion of Czechoslovakia's RUDE PRAVO: "The live broadcast from the sessions hall is convincing evidence that, despite the palisade of problems it is having to work through, the congress is an exceptionally important step on the way to an open policy. Such a school of democracy requires a great deal of time, energy, and patience."

A correspondent with the American CBS television company reported from Moscow: " 'Five years ago we could say nothing, and now everything is allowed,' one deputy admitted. This is the import of the 8 days of live broadcasting of the congress debates on television."

M.S. Gorbachev is the only leader who, in present Soviet conditions, can lead restructuring through to the end and prevent the unpredictable development of events in the country. This is the main theme of the overwhelming majority of commentaries on the results of the elections to the position of chairman of the USSR Supreme Soviet.

The Japanese MAINICHI said: "With the election of M. Gorbachev as the country's president, the Soviet Union is seeing the start of a 'presidential era' in which the policy of restructuring, designed to revive Soviet society, will be increasingly actively implemented." Another Japanese newspaper, YOMIURI, believes: "In conditions where resistance from the bureaucracy is growing, definition of the basic principles of the supreme authority belonging to M.S. Gorbachev will have a considerable impact on the course of restructuring. In this sense, his election to the highest state post in the USSR has important significance for both domestic and foreign policy. As chairman of the USSR Supreme Soviet, he has the right to appoint top officials and intervene directly in questions of how the country is run. Consequently, the development of restructuring will largely depend on Gorbachev." In the opinion of TOKYO SHIMBUN, with M.S. Gorbachev's election as chairman of the USSR Supreme Soviet "the structures for implementing restructuring are in place."

From the very first days of the congress sessions, a new term has appeared in the press: The birth of Soviet parliamentarism. Czechoslovakia's PRACE wrote: "Despite the purely outward confusion—loud exclamations from the auditorium, people rushing up to the rostrum, and the archaic counting of votes—everything points to the fact that a new standard of democracy is being born in Soviet society. It is a very promising start to the process of laying the foundations of parliamentarism, on whose experience subsequent congresses will rely." The newspaper ZYCIE WARSZAWY wrote: "Today no one has any doubts that the start of work by the congress has opened a new page in the history of Soviet parliamentarism."

The report read at the congress by M.S. Gorbachev has aroused enormous interest throughout the world. Britain's DAILY TELEGRAPH wrote that it showed confidence that the flourishing freedom of speech that has been apparent during the discussions at the congress will contribute to creating the conditions for reviving Soviet society. It is noteworthy that this is the first speech by a head of Soviet state to give full information on the Soviet military budget. The importance of providing this information shows the determination of the Soviet leader to channel financial resources from the military to the social sphere. Glasnost is the feature that distinguished the Soviet leader's speech to the congress. "Western countries," the British television company ITV said, "have expressed concern in the past about the lack of information on Soviet military expenditure, because without this information they have been unable to realistically assess the situation in any area. Now, in just one sentence in his speech, Gorbachev has presented proposals for arms cuts in a language comprehensible to the West that it will be hard to ignore."

In connection with the discussion which developed subsequent to M.S. Gorbachev's report, the Polish newspaper TRYBUNA LUDU offered the following reasonable opinion: "The lively, often mutually exclusive statements at the congress are a true reflection of the situation, the conflicts, the tension, and the concern present in Soviet society. However, despite all these differences, the parliamentary forum can be described as a congress of unity. Deputies are unanimous in their desire to speed up restructuring and bring mechanisms favorable to it into play. Deputies have rejected attacks on the party, expressed indignation with slogans which have appeared at some rallies, and defended the party apparatus. This defense has been necessary and well founded, because in the heat of the debate sweeping accusations have begun to be made against party workers, without properly assessing the conduct and stance of individual Communists."

"When it comes to making decisions at the congress, the last word certainly does not belong to forces striving for change," DAGENS NYHETER claimed. This situation, in the opinion of West Germany's DIE WELT, is giving rise to potential conditions for the formation of numerous fronts and factions among the congress participants.

Many Western newspapers are describing the discussion that has developed over A. Sakharov's interview with the Canadian newspaper THE CITIZEN as one of the most "furious and manifest" clashes, to quote THE WASHINGTON TIMES, between "conservatives" and "reformists." "Deputy S. Chervonopiskiy, who lost both his legs in Afghanistan, has called the accusations against the Soviet Army contained in this interview a lie," the U.S. newspaper THE BALTIMORE SUN wrote. "The standing ovation he received—the longest and stormiest in all the 8 days the congress has been in session—demonstrated that Chervonopiskiy touched deep feelings with his heartfelt defense of the military, the fatherland, and communism."

France's LE MONDE described as "sensational" the congress decision to set up a commission to investigate the historical facts connected with the 1939 Soviet-German Nonaggression Pact. An observer for the West German television program ARD stressed: "Setting up a commission to study the circumstances in which the Molotov-Ribbentrop Pact was concluded is further evidence of the development of glasnost in the Soviet Union."

Summing up the results of the Congress of USSR People's Deputies sessions held so far, the newspaper LE MONDE wrote: "In one week, the art of parliamentary debate, deputies' questions, proposal of legislative initiatives, political discussion, and public debate has appeared in a country which, one might say, knew nothing about this. The work of the forum is not confined to verbal discussions. Pledges are being made, which are becoming increasingly concrete with every speech and are already being followed up by concrete action."

Report on 6 Jun Congress

PM0706135389 Moscow PRAVDA in Russian
7 Jun 89 Second Edition pp 1, 6

[Report by team of PRAVDA and TASS journalists from Kremlin Palace of Congresses: "Responsibility for Restructuring"]

[Excerpts] Yesterday morning, when the congress met after a break for its 11th session, special composure and a businesslike approach could be sensed in the deputies' mood and in the course of the continuing debate. The tragedy in Bashkiria once again reminded the people's elected representatives of the complex, urgent problems facing the country and of the trust which the voters put in their emissaries when they in fact issued them with mandates to restructure and renew our society. This thought was central to Deputy A. Sokolov, chairman of Gorkiy Oblast soviet executive committee and a representative of the local soviets—the very ones whose sovereignty the political reform is designed to establish in the regions—who was among the first to speak. "Developing democracy," he supported one of the points in M.S. Gorbachev's report, "must in no way lead to a drop in discipline in all its aspects: state discipline, technological discipline, and, in particular, discipline of law and order." [passage omitted]

To judge from the audience's reaction, many deputies were moved by the congress speech of the writer Valentin Rasputin, particularly his genuine pain at Russia's national dignity, his concern for reviving and augmenting our society's moral values, and his sincere, heartfelt thoughts on the party's place and prestige in restructuring. It seems to us that his resolute words against "pluralism of morality" are also a weighty argument in favor of honest, conscientious labor, amicability in relations among people and peoples—in short, just about everything that can support human fellowship....

On behalf of the Congress Presidium, Chairman A. Gorbunov read out a draft statement on the events in the PRC.

The congress adopted this statement by a majority of votes. [passage omitted]

The first session of the chamber of the USSR Supreme Soviet Soviet of Nationalities began at 1600 hours in the Kremlin Hall of Sessions of the USSR Supreme Soviet chambers.

M.S. Gorbachev, chairman of the USSR Supreme Soviet, took the floor. After cordially congratulating the deputies on their election to the USSR Supreme Soviet Soviet of Nationalities, he emphasized that Soviet people expect of the new organs of power a real improvement in the work of all higher echelons. They associate the resolution of urgent problems, progress in restructuring, and real changes in our society with an improvement in their activity—at both the legislative and executive levels.

The deputies have felt during these days how attentively the people are following all the congress sessions and what a response this elicits. True, it is said that there is a negative aspect: As things stand, many people have even left their workplaces and are not working. This is not at all good. We have advised central television and all-union radio workers to increase the number of broadcasts from the congress during the evening and night hours, so that people employed at work during the day can follow the congress's activity.

Special features in the work of the Soviet of Nationalities, M.S. Gorbachev went on to say, are associated to a considerable, decisive degree with the fact that it is a question of a chamber of the Supreme Soviet of a federative state in which many nations and ethnic groups live. For decades they have been conducting a search on the paths of cooperation and interaction. Life, including the congress, convincingly indicates that we have achieved a great deal by marching together, helping one another, and strengthening and developing our cooperation. But, because of well known reasons connected to a considerable extent with the deformations that occurred in our history after October—in the economic, social, and political spheres—interethnic relations were also seriously deformed. And all this affected the implementation of the nationalities policy.

On the one hand, the USSR Supreme Soviet chairman pointed out, as a result of realizing the ideas of October our peoples have emerged onto a wide road and made great progress in their socioeconomic and cultural development and in education. Also associated with this is the formation of the national intelligentsia and the development of a sense of dignity by every people, every person, and every representative of every nation and ethnic group.

The existence of a large detachment of the national intelligentsia, including the scientific intelligentsia, results in every people taking a profound interest in their roots, their historical past, and all the ups and downs through which they have passed. This is perfectly understandable. Every people want to know their past, are concerned about the problem of the present, and want to forecast their future from the viewpoint of living conditions, the development of culture and language, and so forth.

All this is living reality. And we see how everything here is complex, how many problems are interlaced here. And, naturally, their resolution will be determined to a considerable degree by the level of our responsibility. And this presupposes a high level of work by the Soviet of Nationalities at this stage of restructuring, when we have embarked on the path of a truly Leninist nationalities policy in the context of present achievements and the present stage of our society's development. This is probably one of the chief sectors of restructuring.

M.S. Gorbachev declared the first session of the USSR Supreme Soviet Soviet of Nationalities open.

In accordance with the USSR Constitution, the question of electing the chairman of the Soviet of Nationalities was submitted for discussion by the chamber.

Deputy R.M. Khudaybergenova took the floor to put the proposal. On behalf of the Council of Elders she submitted for the deputies' consideration a proposal to elect Deputy R.N. Nishanov chairman of the USSR Supreme Soviet Soviet of Nationalities. He has great experience of work in party and soviet organs, was elected chairman of the Uzbek Soviet Socialist Republic Supreme Soviet Presidium and deputy chairman of the USSR Supreme Soviet Presidium, and spent many years in diplomatic work. R.N. Nishanov, the deputy emphasized, is a principled person, exacting toward himself and subordinates, he knows how to listen to others and to draw correct conclusions, and he is kind and responsive.

Deputy R.N. Nishanov took the floor to answer questions.

Answering, in particular, a question about the events that occurred in the Fergana valley, the deputy pointed out: Some 45 years ago the Uzbeks welcomed like their own brothers and sisters the Meskhetian Turks resettled in the republic and created all the conditions for their prosperous life. Approximately 60,000 Meskhetian Turks now live in Uzbekistan, including 12,000 in the Fergana valley. They all enjoy the attention of the republic leadership and take an active part in the national economy and in social life. In past years the Meskhetian Turks have asked to be permitted to return to their native places, and these applications have intensified recently.

The clashes began on purely everyday grounds. The first flareup was extinguished. Some time later, unexpectedly for party and soviet organs, groups of young Uzbek people began committing excesses, attacked Meskhetian Turks, beat them up, and set fire to their houses. Events ended tragically: Fifty people died, the majority being Meskhetian Turks.

For some time the situation was out of control. Emergency measures taken by union and republic organs made it possible to establish control over the situation. Some of the Meskhetian Turks have been evacuated and are safe. A curfew has been imposed in the regions of the clashes, and proper order is being ensured. On behalf of the republic's multinational population, the deputy emphasized, I have condemned what happened, apologized to the Meskhetian Turks, and expressed condolences to the relatives and friends of those who suffered. Uzbekistan's Communists and working people have learned the necessary lessons and will not allow a repeat of what happened.

Participating in the discussion of R.N. Nishanov's candidacy were Deputies G. Safiyeva, Ye. Rakhmadiyev, V.S. Shevchenko, G.S. Tarazevich, G.M. Magomedov, E.V. Bichkauskas, N.N. Medvedev, and others.

During the discussion a proposal was submitted to apply to the election of the chairman of the chamber the principle that the delegations of deputies from all the union republics should agree with his candidacy.

This proposal was rejected on a vote.

Deputy R.N. Nishanov was elected chairman of the USSR Supreme Soviet Soviet of Nationalities by a majority of votes.

The session was then chaired by R.N. Nishanov.

It was suggested that deputies examine the question of forming the standing commissions of the Soviet of Nationalities and also discuss a proposal to form the USSR Supreme Soviet committees.

A.I. Lukyanov, first deputy chairman of the USSR Supreme Soviet, took the floor on this question.

So, he pointed out, the Soviet of Nationalities has been formed finally as a constituent and equal part of the USSR Supreme Soviet. This chamber will resolve not only questions connected with ethnic affairs and interethnic relations. Any question under union jurisdiction will pass through this chamber and be given a national slant. These are, above all, questions of an economic nature, budget questions, and questions connected with the development of our culture and with services for the population. They are also questions connected with international relations. It is a very wide range of questions that will be tackled by the USSR Supreme Soviet, which is the highest legislative, managing, and controlling organ of state power. Such a broad forum as the congress simply cannot tackle very broad functions, many of them, in particular, in the spheres of legislation and the budget. They must be tackled by a narrower collegium. A collegium that resembles to a considerable degree Lenin's Central Executive Committee, which was elected in the past by the Congress of Soviets.

In this organism for exercising state power a very great role belongs to committees and commissions of the USSR Supreme Soviet. Realizing constitutional guidelines, our Congress Presidium has performed quite broad analytical work. When finalizing proposals we take very actively into account the comments and wishes of deputies themselves.

First, we proceeded from the premise that the chambers' composition is comparatively small—271 deputies in each chamber. And if we endlessly increase the number of commissions, we will simply be unable to ensure the necessary balance in order to observe proportion in every commission—half-and-half members of the chamber and deputies belonging to the congress.

Second, we proceeded from the premise that the commissions cannot be rigidly tied to sectors of state management, otherwise this will hinder the fulfillment of their parliamentary functions.

Third, subcommissions or subcommittees will undoubtedly be created under the commissions and committees and will analyze various questions in depth.

Finally, at the session of the chambers' Councils of Elders we were of the common opinion that when setting up commissions in one chamber we must take into account that different commissions will be operating in the other chamber. But the committees will be formed jointly. In other words, we must take a comprehensive approach to this problem.

At the session of the two chambers' Councils of Elders, we carefully went through the whole package of proposals as to what kind of commissions and committees the Supreme Soviet should have. This was followed by the first session of the Soviet of the Union, where these questions were discussed in detail in an atmosphere of quite pointed discussion.

It is proposed to form an equal number of standing commissions in each chamber—four in each. At the same time, as stressed at the 19th party conference, we must move away from the practice of functional depersonalization of the two chambers. In this respect the Soviet of the Union, which reflects national interests, must primarily focus its attention on questions of general state significance, while the Soviet of Nationalities must have its own special area of responsibility and concern itself with the development of nations, ethnic groups, union republics, autonomous republics, and other formations.

Compared with the original versions, the names of some of the commissions set up by the Soviet of the Union have undergone quite substantial changes. This is not merely a formal gesture but an attempt to more accurately define the all-union nature of their work or, in other words, encapsulate the powerful bloc of problems whose solution transcends republic-level competence and regional levels and which must be resolved by the union as a whole.

With regard to the standing commissions of the Soviet of Nationalities, they, too, are based on the conclusions of the 19th party conference. This chamber must primarily be concerned with resolving questions which have a direct bearing on the subjects of our federation, autonomous formations, and the development of Soviet nations and ethnic groups. That is why the Councils of Elders propose to bring the Commission on Interethnic Relations to the forefront. A great many questions have accumulated in this sphere, as shown by our session today. A great deal of work—and, I will be frank, very complex work—lies ahead.

The next commission is the Commission on Questions of Social and Economic Development in Union and Autonomous Republics and Autonomous Oblasts and Okrugs. This is rather like the republic, national side of the Budget and Planning Commission. These two commissions can work together, but each from its own standpoint.

Evidently this commission of the Soviet of Nationalities will have a series of subcommissions: In particular, we have discussed the advisability of having a special subcommission responsible for questions of the development of our country's smaller peoples. This is particularly appreciable here, it is here that all economic and economic management questions converge, and it is here that they must be resolved.

It is proposed to set up a commission concerned with the work of those sectors of the economy which are now being placed fully within the jurisdiction of the republics on the basis of the new concept published quite recently. This commission will be responsible for consumer goods, trade, municipal and consumer services, and other services for the population. There is a sea of problems in this area and they will have to be very thoroughly resolved—also from the standpoint of resolving ethnic problems.

The next commission was on questions of developing culture, language, and national and international traditions and preserving historical monuments. Here we proceeded from the basis that the roots of our multinational culture still lie in the development of every nation and ethnic group and that our multinational Soviet culture is made up of the different cultures of all our country's peoples. So it is proposed to set up four commissions in both the Soviet of Nationalities and the Soviet of the Union.

Now for the committees. As is well known, they will be established on principles of parity by the two chambers. Certain amendments have been made to the original plans in the course of discussing this question in the chambers' Councils of Elders and also at the Soviet of the Union session. It is proposed, first, to form a committee responsible for international affairs, which will embrace both foreign policy and foreign economic issues and concern itself with interparliamentary ties and questions of humanitarian cooperation.

Then there is going to be a committee on questions of defense and state security. These questions are so closely interconnected that they must be combined. As in all foreign parliaments, this committee will have special status.

The next committee will be concerned with questions of legislation, legality, and law and order. This is the main committee that will be responsible for legal matters. Of course, it will mostly be concerned with legislative work, fine-tuning the wording of legislation and statutes, but it is also very important for it to be in touch with the situation in the legal system and with law and order.

On the basis of many deputies' opinions, it is also proposed to set up a Committee on Questions of the Work of Soviets of People's Deputies and the Development of Management and Self-Management. It is absolutely necessary, because the Supreme Soviet is the top of the pyramid of our country's soviets and has to resolve a multitude of very complex questions.

The next committee will be concerned with questions of economic reform. It is being set up at the suggestion of deputies.

It is also deemed advisable to set up a Committee on Agrarian Questions and Food. We have reached the conclusion that it should be a general parliamentary committee which will be responsible not only for drafting laws in this sphere but also for monitoring the work of the relevant departments.

It is also planned to create a Committee on Questions of Construction and Architecture.

It is felt advisable to set up a single Committee on Science, Public Education, and Instruction, a Committee on the Protection of the People's Health, and a Committee on Women's Affairs and Protection of the Family, Mothers, and Children.

The speaker also proposed to set up committees on the affairs of veterans and invalids, on youth affairs, on questions of ecology and the rational use of natural resources, and on questions of glasnost and citizens' rights and appeals.

Of course, we will need to set up various one-shot committees and commissions will arise. The congress has already established three commissions to study specific current issues. In this connection, some deputies have said, in my opinion rightly, that there is no need to be in a hurry now to rigidly define the number of committees and commissions to be set up. We must reserve the right to flexibly change their purview if necessary.

The commissions and committees, the speaker stressed, will cooperate closely and bolster all the work of the Supreme Soviet and its chambers in the period between sessions and will actively perform control and legislative functions. They will undoubtedly make an important contribution to all the work done by our supreme representative body. A.I. Lukyanov then answered numerous questions from deputies.

The following deputies took part in the discussion: G.G. Gumbaridze, V.A. Ambartsumyan, M.L. Bronshteyn, V.I. Belov, N.V. Neyland, T.K. Ismailov, S.U. Kallas, I.O. Bisher, B.T. Palagnyuk, R.G. Salukvadze, A.I. Dubko, A.A. Likhanov, V.S. Advadze, B.F. Rakhimova, L.I. Batynskaya, and others.

The Soviet of Nationalities discussed the question of forming the chamber's standing commissions and also proposals on the question of setting up USSR Supreme Soviet committees.

On this point the first session of the Soviet of Nationalities came to a close.

A joint session of the USSR Supreme Soviet Soviet of the Union and Soviet of Nationalities will take place on 7 June.

IZVESTIYA Reports on Congress Proceedings

26 May Proceedings Described
PM2605190589 Moscow IZVESTIYA in Russian 27 May 89 Morning Edition pp 1, 3

[Special correspondents G. Alimov and A. Stepovoy "reportage": "Moscow, 26 May, the Kremlin Palace of Congresses"]

[Excerpt] [Passage omitted] The second session of the first USSR Congress of People's Deputies, with M.S. Gorbachev in the chair, began at 1000 hours 26 May. There was one question on the approved agenda: Election of the USSR Supreme Soviet. It was discussed in advance at a meeting of representatives of republic, kray, and oblast deputies. It was on behalf of this meeting that Deputy Ye.S. Stroyev proposed that the agreed candidacies be included on the secret ballot paper.

But even before the discussion of this exceptionally important question had a chance to begin, Deputy T.I. Zaslavskaya asked for the floor. Addressing the congress, she said that a meeting of Muscovites with deputies was due to be held in the center of the capital the night before. But the militia allegedly dispersed the participants in the peaceful demonstration. In this context, T.I.

Zaslavskaya proposed that the well-known decrees on rallies be suspended while the congress is in session, and addressed a deputy's question to V.V. Bakatin, USSR minister of internal affairs.

The reply to this question followed immediately. The minister said that rallies and meetings of voters to discuss progress at the congress had been held in many cities. There was also a rally in Moscow. But the militia did not prevent it being held.

Several deputies who spoke afterward backed the proposal to suspend the action of the decrees. But the congress declined this proposal by a majority of votes.

Thus, the unscheduled deviation from the agenda was resolved. There followed the discussion of what is perhaps one of the most important questions: How to constitute the USSR Supreme Soviet?

The main argument centered on the principle of nominating candidates for election to the Supreme Soviet: Should it be elected by the entire congress or should delegations assign their representatives there under a system of allocated quotas? The most diverse viewpoints were expressed.

The question of quotas, in other words a previously determined number of seats on the Supreme Soviet for different regions, produced many sharp and at at times contradictory opinions. Deputy F. Burlatskiy, criticizing this practice, drew the congress's attention to the fact that quotas for localities and organizations were last used at the Ecumenical Council in the 17th century. But since this archaic formula is still retained in our country, deputies deliberated on who should sit on the Supreme Soviet. In the opinion of a number of speakers, the proposed principle of constituting it is more suitable for the Soviet of Nationalities than for the Soviet of the Union.

It was explained that the bureaucratic principle of nomination, universally applicable in the past, is still being used in many places. Delegates to the Supreme Soviet are selected ex officio. Deputy V.P. Zolotukhin from Uzbekistan, for example, informed the congress of this. The republic's "quota" includes the first secretary of the Central Committee, the chairman of the republic Supreme Soviet Presidium, three oblast committee [obkom] first secretaries, and so on. Furthermore, there had been no democratic discussion of candidacies beforehand.

This situation, and this was clearly confirmed at the congress, became possible largely because there had been no absolute clarity: Would members of the Supreme Soviet become professional parliamentarians or would it be possible to combine this work with existing jobs? It was correctly remarked in this context: If we were to continue, as in the past, to send "dignitaries" to the Supreme Soviet, there would be an irrepressible rush there by all who hold high-ranking party and state positions. By no means all would agree to sacrifice their office for the sake of restructuring.

Following the course of discussion on the question of elections to the Supreme Soviet and the way some republics have filled their "quotas," we noticed two rather clearly distinguishable trends. The first involved a sort of unquestioning and blind faith by some deputies in the opinion of their superiors—they accepted without a murmur whatever was proposed. This was very well described by Deputy A.V. Minzhurenko from Omsk, who cited the following fact. The delegation to which he belongs contains several persons who, on virtually all matters, copy the opinion of one delegation member—the obkom first secretary. It appears, therefore, that one man has several votes at once, while others have no vote at all.

The other trend was the exact opposite—an a priori mistrust in everything that required discussion, no matter who had suggested it. Some people seem to sense, even before some unusual turn of events, some sort of dirty trick, a deliberate intention to infringe their interests. It seems to us that such an attitude would be the only reason why some people perceived a "secret design" in the Moscow delegation's proposal to nominate 55 contenders for the 29 "Moscow" seats. To have real choice. Let deputies themselves reflect on who is most suitable to work in the Supreme Soviet. The multiple candidacies idea was not in the least calculated to pack the Supreme Soviet with Moscow "intellectuals," as some people thought. As a matter of fact, Deputy S. Fedorov actually advocated from the congress rostrum that the Supreme Soviet should represent the "nation's intellect." After all, he said, we do not live in some fragmented country where everyone is concerned only with the interests of his own principality. This means that the work should be approached not from the selfish positions of the so-called region, but from statewide positions.

The congress lobbies are probably the only place from where there are no live television relays. Taking advantage of this, we took some brief interviews. Sheykh-ulf-Islam, mufti of all Muslims in the Transcaucasus and Central Asia, said:

"For the first time in all the years of Soviet power, clergymen are involved in the solution of the most important state tasks. This is why we must set a fitting example of wisdom, of tolerance for different opinions and beliefs. I would like to wish the congress participants more tolerance and the skill to listen to one another."

The congress is a crossroads of opinions. It would be strange if all toed the same line and held the same position.

Ye. Kabanov, deputy from the CPSU, captain-director from Petropavlovsk-Kamchatskiy: "In my view, the organization of the congress is unsatisfactory. The voting system has not been thought out. We have had 2 days to think over all the candidates, but we are still debating. I don't like this."

M. Fazletdinov from Bashkiria, deputy from the All-Union Collective Farms Council: "I wanted to speak yesterday, but when I realized that support for M.S. Gorbachev was guaranteed, I decided not to speak. It's all clear now: The choice that was made was the only correct one. Now we have to elect the Supreme Soviet. Our Bashkir delegation believes that every region should be represented on the Supreme Soviet. Our position is the same as that of the Baltic republics' representatives. Local deputies know better what is happening at local level."

M. Degtyarev, leader of a bricklayers' team from No 4 trust, Slutsk City, deputy from Belorussia: "Is the congress living up to my expectations? So far it is. We have started creating a rule-of-law state, and therefore we should be pleased rather than scared by the new aspects of the unusual working situation which are unfolding before the very eyes of deputies and millions of television viewers."

At the end of the morning session, the following question was put to the vote: Would it be mandatory for a deputy elected to the USSR Supreme Soviet to give up his previous job? The formulation proposed by M.S. Gorbachev was adopted by a majority of votes. A USSR people's deputy elected to the Supreme Soviet will, as a rule, be released from his fulltime work.

27 May Congress Proceedings

PM2705191789 Moscow IZVESTIYA in Russian 28 May 89 Morning Edition pp 1, 7

["Reportage" by special correspondents G. Alimov, A. Davydov, V. Kurasov, M. Kushtapin, and A. Stepovoy: "Moscow, 27 May, Kremlin Palace of Congresses"]

[Text] The scheduled session of the USSR Congress of People's Deputies began at 1100 hours. During the evening session the night before, on 26 May, the floor was given to Deputy A.I. Lukyanov. In his speech he described in detail the Presidium's conclusions on the remarks and proposals made during the morning session. He then spoke about the principles for forming the USSR Supreme Soviet chambers on the basis of the country's current Constitution, the way commissions and committees will be constituted, and the proposals to accept as a basis the lists of candidates discussed at representatives' meetings.

It was also noted that there will be an opportunity to add to these lists.

The floor was then taken by People's Deputy V.V. Landsbergis from Lithuania. He declared: The Lithuanian delegation objects to a general vote. The vote, in his opinion, should be taken within the actual delegations. Otherwise deputies from Lithuania will take no part in voting.

It seemed as if the congress's work had been deadlocked. And even session chairman M.S. Gorbachev described this as a crisis situation. He called on the Lithuanian delegation to rethink its decision.

The question is: Is it democratic to force the language of ultimatums on the congress? It is perfectly obvious that this is not the way. Deputy R.A. Medvedev unambiguously assessed such a policy as unacceptable. It can destroy the work on society's democratization which has only just begun.

His stance was backed by other deputies: A.D. Kuliyev from Azerbaijan, V.D. Romanenko from the Ukraine, S.P. Zalygin from Moscow. It was evident that many were also influenced by the speech by Deputy Ya.S. Kanovich from Lithuania, who said that he personally would vote according to both his conscience and his voters' mandates.

The congress took a 30-minute break in order to resolve the problem which had emerged.

After the break, Deputy V.V Landsbergis mounted the rostrum again. He expressed regret because his words had been misinterpreted. Essentially, as we understood it, this meant withdrawal of the initial proposal, which was perceived as an ultimatum by many deputies. Following this explanation, we felt that the atmosphere of trust was restored in the hall.

The discussion on the composition of the Supreme Soviet chambers continued. One deputy after another mounted the rostrum to make specific proposals and to submit additions and amendments to the list for the secret vote. We must admit, the nomination procedure takes an unusually long time. And we automatically noticed that some people in the hall get irritated by this. But the majority show understanding for procedures which are new in our practice. Demandingness is dictated by the fact that people are already taking a fresh look at the role played by the country's Supreme Soviet. And the self-nomination by some deputies is perceived as perfectly normal in the new conditions. G.M. Kurochka from Vorkuta, for example, nominated himself as a candidate for the Supreme Soviet. A deputy from Rostov-na-Donu expressed regret that not a single fellow resident from a city with 1 million inhabitants and three electoral okrugs appears on the list for the secret vote. Their seats were "distributed" among deputies from the oblast.

There was lengthy discussion about the candidacy of young Deputy A.A. Kiselev from Volgograd. His name was mentioned several times. The reason given was the fact that there were few young people on the proposed lists.

Many additional candidates were nominated by representatives of the Russian Soviet Federated Socialist Republic [RSFSR]. The congress was forced to give the 1,059 Russian deputies time to consult and decide who would be ultimately included in the lists for the secret vote. Russia's delegates were left alone in the sessions hall.

The congress resumed its work some time later. It became clear that as M.S. Gorbachev said, the "Russian faction" had run out of time. This is why the vote was taken before the full congress. The results were as follows: 726 Russian deputies voted in favor of the original list of 12 candidate members of the Soviet of Nationalities against a quota of 11. And the list with the proposed additions and amendments was supported by only 265 deputies.

In this way, many procedural questions associated with the election of the country's Supreme Soviet were resolved by the end of the evening session. But it was still not over. Following a lengthy break, during which ballot papers listing the names of many candidates were printed, the vote was taken.

The 27 May morning session began with an announcement of the results. The floor was given to [Tellers'] Commission Chairman Deputy Yu.A. Osipyan. He announced that 2,150 ballot papers had been distributed for the vote to elect the Supreme Soviet Soviet of the Union and Soviet of Nationalities. There were 2,149 ballot papers in the ballot boxes. They were all valid.

Yu.A. Osipyan then announced (by name) the results of the vote to elect the Soviet of Nationalities. The number of those voting against fluctuated between a handful and several hundred. All deputies gained the number of votes required for election. But since the RSFSR ballot paper had exceeded the quota (by one person, 12 instead of 11), it had to be decided who had gathered the smallest "harvest" of votes. Deputy B.N. Yeltsin, with 964 votes cast against him, was not elected to the Soviet of Nationalities from the RSFSR list. The Tellers' Commission minutes on elections to the Soviet of Nationalities was approved. Following a debate, the deputies adopted an amendment to the minutes.

The congress is continuing its work.

29, 30 May Information Report

PM3105104189 Moscow IZVESTIYA in Russian 31 May 89 Morning Edition p 1

[Unattributed "Information Report" "On Work of USSR Congress of People's Deputies"]

[Text] The work of the USSR Congress of People's Deputies resumed 29 May 1989 at 1000 hours in Moscow, in the Kremlin's Palace of Congresses.

M.S. Gorbachev, chairman of the USSR Supreme Soviet, chaired the congress session.

The congress elected A.I. Lukyanov first deputy chairman of the USSR Supreme Soviet.

The discussion of procedural questions continued at the evening session.

The congress will continue its work 30 May.

The work of the USSR Congress of People's Deputies continued 30 May 1989 in Moscow in the Kremlin's Palace of Congresses.

USSR People's Deputy R.N. Nishanov, member of the Congress Presidium, chaired the session.

M.S. Gorbachev, chairman of the USSR Supreme Soviet, delivered a report "on the main avenues of the USSR's domestic and foreign policy."

Then debates began on the report.

Speeches by people's deputies continued at the evening session.

At the end of the session the deputies held a secret vote on the candidacies for the Soviet of Nationalities from the Nagorno-Karabakh Autonomous Oblast.

The congress will continue its work 31 May.

29 May Proceedings Summarized
PM2905171789 Moscow IZVESTIYA in Russian
30 May 89 Morning Edition pp 1, 2

[Report by A. Davydov, V. Kurasov, M. Kushtapin, and V. Tolstov: "Moscow, 29 May. Kremlin Palace of Congresses. IZVESTIYA Special Correspondents Report"]

[Text] The people's deputies have resumed their places in the auditorium after Sunday's breather. However, many congress services continued to operate even on Sunday. A 10-page brochure entitled "On Citizen's Appeals to the USSR Congress of People's Deputies" was circulated in the lobby of the congress secretariat before the start of the morning sitting. It contains extracts from letters and telegrams (as of 29 May 21,300 of them had been received) from citizens and labor collectives.

The time was 1000 hours. M.S. Gorbachev reported to the congress that certain deputies believe that the live radio and television relay should be stopped, since some speakers are using it for purposes of self-advertisement. Mikhail Sergeyevich asked the authors of these notes not to press their proposal and to proceed from the interests of glasnost and openness.

Then the congress continued the discussion of the candidacy for first deputy chairman of the USSR Supreme Soviet. The floor was given to Deputy A.I. Lukyanov, who answered the questions put to him at Saturday's evening sitting. After this he briefly set out the main planks of his program. The ceremonial but essentially degraded status of the supreme organ of power in our country—the Supreme Soviet—must be ended, the deputy said; there must be no problems closed to discussion in the congress and Supreme Soviet; more attention should be paid to the work of local soviets; the congress and Supreme Soviet must be the epicenter of monitoring of the activity of executive and state organs; it is necessary to accelerate the implementation of the judicial and legal reform.

Deputy A.A. Shchelkanov mounted the rostrum. He disagreed with the procedure for answering the questions put to candidates for state posts. The questions should not be collected in a single package and held for a general answer, he believes, but each question should be answered immediately.

The chairman moved that congress agree with the deputy's opinion.

The question of congress procedures arose again in connection with the discussion of the candidacy for first deputy chairman of the USSR Supreme Soviet. On behalf of a group of deputies Deputy A.I. Konovalov proposed the following option for the procedure for electing the first deputy chairman: The congress accepts or rejects the candidacy proposed by the chairman of the Supreme Soviet; then the candidate presents his program and the congress discusses it and holds a ballot. If the candidate fails to muster the requisite number of votes, the procedure starts afresh. The proposal is that the chairman of the USSR Council of Ministers and other top state officials be chosen in a similar fashion.

M.S. Gorbachev moved that the deputies not accept this procedure straight off but ponder it and return to it in the fall, at the next congress.

Since opinions were divided, the question was put to the vote. The immediate formulation of the procedure was favored by 851 deputies, 1,130 voted against, and 47 abstained. Thus the motion of the chairman of the USSR Supreme Soviet was accepted. M.S. Gorbachev also moved that time be set aside later for deputies' speeches on procedural matters, in order to avoid delaying the course of the congress. The deputies also agreed with this.

During the discussion of the candidacy for first deputy chairman of the USSR Supreme Soviet Deputies V.P. Nosov, A.I. Demidov, A.G. Zhuravlev, and Yu.A. Koltsov not only spoke out in favor of M.S. Gorbachev's proposal but also told the congress about telegrams and opinions from their voters drawing attention to organizational shortcomings in the congress's work. For instance, many people cannot understand why deputies who are Politburo members and secretaries of the CPSU Central Committee sit in the auditorium on their own. Why do deputies spend so much time on voting? Do they always manage to maintain timely, well-documented contact with their voters?

At the same time Deputy Kh.A. Fargiyev used the platform to place before the congress the question of restoring Ingush autonomy, which was eliminated in Stalin's time. In the name of his Muscovite voters Deputy A.Ye. Sebentsov proposed that congress hold new elections to the Soviet of Nationalities from the RSFSR [Russian Soviet Federated Socialist Republic] in view of the nonelection of B.N. Yeltsin to the Supreme Soviet.

Whereas Deputy S.B. Aguzarova unreservedly supported A.I. Lukyanov's candidacy, noting his professionalism and knowledge, Deputy T.Kh. Gdlyan put to the candidate a number of questions relating to A.I. Lukyanov's previous activity as secretary of the CPSU Central Committee and first deputy chairman of the USSR Supreme Soviet Presidium and about his role and position in the fight against crime.

Judging by this speech alone, for instance, it can be seen that the acuteness of the problems that deputies are dealing with in the course of the congress is not decreasing. And at the same time it has to be noted that the debate is increasingly assuming a genuinely parliamentary character. Speakers are keeping their emotions in check, are becoming more correct toward their opponents, and are relying not so much on intuition as on arguments. The procedure for running the congress has also become more rational. There are no more lines of people waiting to take the platform, and the provisional standing orders are being more precisely observed.

The chairman gave the floor to A.I. Lukyanov to answer the questions voiced in the speeches of T.Kh. Gdlyan and other deputies (the answers will be published in the congress transcript).

Deputies N.V. Ivanov, I.N. Shundeyev, V.N. Kudryavtsev, R.A. Medvedev, R.Kh. Solntsev, and Yu.R. Yakubov also took part in the discussion of the candidacy for first deputy chairman of the USSR Supreme Soviet.

Continuing the discussion of the candidacy for first deputy chairman of the USSR Supreme Soviet, a number of deputies made criticisms of A.I. Lukyanov and put various questions to him. Thus, for instance, Deputy from the Komsomol [All-Union Leninist Communist Youth League] S.F. Kalashnikov noted that during the period of preparation for the congress, the USSR Supreme Soviet Presidium failed to take young deputies' wishes into account, and he proposed that A.I. Lukyanov hold a working meeting with deputies from the Komsomol.

Then the floor was again given to A.I. Lukyanov so he could answer the questions and the criticism. In this speech the deputy explained his position on the question of multiple candidate elections, stating that he views with respect the actual principle of such elections. Taking issue with Deputy N.V. Ivanov, A.I. Lukyanov noted that state policy is aimed at developing the fight against organized crime and that this process will be continued. A.I. Lukyanov expressed a principled position on the quesion of relations between the party and the USSR Supreme Soviet. "These are relations between policy and power," the deputy declared. "The CPSU Central Committee Politburo determines the direction of the policy of restructuring and there must be no dissension between the CPSU and the Supreme Soviet or between Communist deputies and the rest of the party. It is only thanks to the CPSU, which ensures unity in our country, that we can advance," A.I. Lukyanov said.

The Congress Presidium received motions that the discussion of the candidacy for first deputy chairman of the USSR Supreme Soviet be wound up. The decision was adopted by a majority of votes. But even after this deputies from Lithuania, Georgia, Azerbaijan, and Belorussia sought to speak on behalf of their delegations. The chairman of the USSR Supreme Soviet allowed them to speak. There ensued a further series of speeches in support of A.I. Lukyanov's candidacy, and also questions addressed to him.

After this Deputies G.I. Isayev, S.Kh. Negmatulloyev, G.A. Amangeldinova, R.A. Bazarova, and N.P. Kiriyak mounted the rostrum. On behalf of their delegations—Azerbaijan, Tajikistan, Kazakhstan, Turkmenia, and Moldavia—they supported A.I. Lukyanov's candidacy and called on the congress to vote for him. The floor was again given to Deputy A.I. Lukyanov to answer the questions contained in the notes handed in to the Congress Presidium.

M.S. Gorbachev, chairman of the USSR Supreme Soviet, asked the congress to support the candidacy he had proposed. Since the USSR constitution does not stipulate how the first deputy chairman of the USSR Supreme Soviet is elected (by secret or open ballot), the congress decided to hold an open ballot.

By an overwhelming majority of votes the USSR Congress of People's Deputies adopted a resolution on the election of A.I. Lukyanov as first deputy chairman of the USSR Supreme Soviet.

It was decided to devote the next sitting of the congress to the debate on procedural questions, and to hear the report of the chairman of the USSR Supreme Soviet Tuesday 30 May.

30 May Proceedings Reported

PM3105133789 Moscow IZVESTIYA in Russian 31 May 89 Morning Edition pp 1, 7

[Report by special correspondents G. Alimov, A. Plutnik, A. Stepovoy, and V. Shchepotkin: "Moscow, 30 May. Kremlin Palace of Congresses"]

[Text] The stormy debates of the first 4 days of the work of the congress, when some people insisted on a detailed discussion of procedural questions while others preferred not to linger on them too long and others still called for what was in their view empty talk to be ended as soon as possible and for work to be embarked upon, have ended. The day of 30 May was the day of the report of the USSR Supreme Soviet chairman, announced in advance and anxiously awaited by deputies.

On hearing M.S. Gorbachev's report, which opened the fifth day of the work of the congress, you probably noticed that applause was not heard that often in the auditorium, still less tumultuous ovations. And that in our view is the best assessment of its calm, businesslike nature and principled restraint.

In actual fact, the report contained nothing deliberately designed for effect, designed to strike the imagination or to extract applause, so to speak. It was a restrained consideration, appropriate to the moment, of the present complex stage of the profound transformations which have affected all aspects of social life, of the state of the national economy, and the social sphere which, as is well known, is far from brilliant, and of paths for the further economic and spiritual normalization of society.

As emerges from the report, these paths are far from simple. The state is continuing to live beyond its means. Wages are continuing to grow more rapidly than labor productivity. The market is unbalanced. It has nonetheless been deemed urgent to focus all efforts on very rapidly resolving problems described as blatant and causing an acute reaction in society: food, housing, services, health care, nature conservation, and the boosting of education, science, and culture.

We cannot expect instant fundamental changes in neglected spheres like agriculture, light industry, and the consumption sphere. And this quite joyless admission, even frankness, which, indeed, is characteristic of the entire congress, will, it seems to us arouse optimism more rapidly than the ideological and economic exaggerations and facile assurances and promises to rapidly rectify the situation which were so widespread in former times. Especially as the report was not simply a statement of the complex situation. It was rather a detailed program of activity based on an analysis of the real situation.

After the intermission the discussion of M.S. Gorbachev's report began. S.T. Melekhin, operator at the Nizhniy Tagil Lenin metallurgical combine and a people's deputy from the trade unions, paid a great deal of attention to problems of social and material protection, especially for the badly off strata of the population.

Deputy Ye.Ye. Sokolov, first secretary of the Belorussian Communist Party Central Committee, raised a number of serious problems in his speech. In particular he said that considerable harm had been caused to the republic's agriculture by the Chernobyl catastrophe and that it is making itself felt even now. The speaker's special attention was focused on the need for a more effective struggle against narrow departmentalism and on the elimination of the primacy of state law.

Deputy V.A. Masol, chairman of the Ukrainian Soviet Socialist Republic [SSR] Council of Ministers, who spoke next, noted that the congress is of enormous importance for the country and for future generations. In his opinion, key questions of economic reform should occupy the dominant place in the work of the USSR Supreme Soviet. The new government must follow more firmly the resolutions of the 19th party conference.

The speech by Academician D.S. Likhachev generated ardent support at the congress. His passionate speech was devoted to the general state of culture in our country. He drew attention to the fact that the overwhelming majority of deputies' election programs most regrettably do not even mention the word "culture." D.S. Likhachev recalled that without culture there is no morality. Many of society's misfortunes indeed come from the decline of culture. Yet to this day the notorious residual principle operates with regard to culture. Economizing on culture can lead to the sorriest consequences. The deputy believes that libraries and archives, architectural monuments and museums are in an extremely bad state. Even very important libraries in Moscow and Leningrad, to use the deputy's expression, are burning like candles and are being flooded. There is not a single library in our country provided with modern equipment.

In his speech Deputy A.P. Yanenko, rector of the Novosibirsk Construction Engineering Institute, raised the question of the need for the USSR Supreme Soviet to control the activity of the Council of Ministers and to hear reports from ministers. He stressed the importance of enhancing the role of the soviets of people's deputies of all levels.

A.P. Yanenko believes that the USSR people's deputies must know the true situation in the country. He mentioned several anthologies of documents prepared by the USSR State Committee for Statistics which totally fail to show the real state of affairs.

Deputy N.A. Nazarbayev, chairman of the Kazakh SSR Council of Ministers, said that the plan for the 12th 5-Year Plan was compiled in the worst traditions of the times of stagnation. Worshipping gross output rather than concern for real commodities has led to empty shelves in the stores. He sharply criticized the methods of departmental diktat and insisted on the need for the speediest adoption of a law on local self-management.

It seemed to us that with the start of the discussion of the report of the USSR Supreme Soviet chairman there was a substantial change in the tone of a number of speeches. Some speakers, above all republic leaders, began increasingly frequently to remind us of boring tradition, which was immediately obvious, inasmuch as it contrasted with the discussions of previous days. Incidentally, the deputies also noticed this—a note on the matter was sent to the Presidium.

The daytime session ended with a heated debate on the question of the representation of the Nagorno-Karabakh Autonomous Oblast in the Soviet of Nationalities, which began with a statement by deputies G.A. Pogosyan and V.D. Dzhafarov. Several deputies took part. It was decided by an overwhelming majority of votes to put three deputies on the list for the secret ballot: Z.G. Balayan, V.D. Dzhaforov, and G.A. Pogosyan.

At the evening session Deputy T. Kaipbergenov was the first to mount the rostrum. He spoke with pain and anger of a very major ecological catastrophe—the catastrophe which has occurred and is continuing to occur in the area around Lake Aral as a result of thoughtless economic management and departmental monopolism. This is a tragedy not only for the lake but also for the land poisoned with toxic chemicals and for the people who have died and who are suffering from serious illnesses.

Then the chairman gave the floor to Deputy T.V. Gamkrelidze, director of the Georgian SSR Academy of Sciences Institute of Oriental Studies. He gave the congress a detailed statement about the tragic events in Tbilisi on 9 April. In the deputy's opinion this was a massacre of people on an unprecedented scale. He assessed the breaking up of the meeting as a military operation and a punitive action. Deputy T.V. Gamkrelidze put the blame for the grave consequences on General I.N. Rodionov, commander of the Transcaucasian Military District.

In an answering speech Deputy I.N. Rodionov set forth his view of the 9 April events. He said that first of all it is necessary to give a political assessment of what happened in Tbilisi. And only after that should conclusions be drawn. The deputy believes that the tragic events are being presented in a one-sided, unobjective way.

After the hearings the congress deemed it necessary to adopt a resolution on creating a commission on the events in Tbilisi. The chairman suggested a list of members of this commission headed by Deputy V.V. Karpov. Debates began. During the debates Deputies A.M. Adamovich and Yu.F. Karyakin challenged individual members of the commission. V.P. Tomkus, a

deputy from Lithuania, and Yu.R. Boyars, a deputy from Latvia, said that something like the Tbilisi events had nearly happened in their republics. Deputy E.N. Shengelaya—producer at the "Georgia-film" studio—suggested a new composition for the commission under the leadership of A.N. Yakovlev, member of the CPSU Central Committee Politburo and secretary of the Central Committee.

Then deputies D.I. Patiashvili, Yu.A. Manayenkov, V.A. Voblikov, and others spoke on the issue.

The tension would mount and then subside for a little while. And although our attention, like that of millions of people, was constantly riveted on what was taking place in the auditorium, we nonetheless felt anxiety from time to time over some of the speeches. Forgetting that the proceedings were being broadcast all round the world, the deputies voiced not only statements which were in our view offensive to others but also expressions dangerous to the cause of democracy. And this was mentioned very correctly by Deputy V.A. Voblikov, who urged his colleagues to be more restrained, wiser, and more responsible. After all proposals had already been heard to halt direct broadcasting and this behavior merely strengthens the positions of the opponents of glasnost.

It must be said that Deputy R.N. Nishanov, first secretary of the Uzbekistan Communist Party Central Committee, who chaired today's congress sessions, coped skillfully, firmly, but tactfully with this difficult work—leading such an unpredictable, stormy meeting to fruitful results. He regulated the flow of those anxious to mount the rostrum and curbed emotions and at one moment by his imperturbable response, "never mind, everything's going well for us, comrades," caused spontaneous laughter in the auditorium and thus removed the tension. It is not surprising that at the end of the evening session a deputy approached him and on behalf of many of his colleagues thanked him for his skilled and good leadership of the congress.

7th Day of Congress

PM0206103989 Moscow IZVESTIYA in Russian 2 Jun 89 Morning Edition p 1

[N. Bodnaruk commentary: "Day Seven"; this and the next two items continue the series of reports published in the Soviet Union DAILY REPORT of 26 May, pages 30-31; 31 May, pages 67-70; and 1 Jun, pages 42-44]

[Text] The sensation you get from watching the development of topics at the congress is like a ride on a roller coaster—a dizzy ascent, followed by a plunge into the void which brings your heart to your mouth, and up again with sharp twists and turns to the right and the left.... From telephone calls to the editorial office I know that there are people who are tired of the stress and strain and others who are excited to the point of distraction by what is going on. Calm down! The Russian roller coaster is not for amusement, and even in the tragic wringing of hands it is necessary to know when to stop. It is time to realize that parliamentary debates are merely a job of work, one which unfortunately we are not too familiar with, but it is no tragedy if some things are a bit higgledy-piggledy at first. And in order to avoid getting dizzy at the sight of all the facts and viewpoints flashing past, it makes sense to take a step back.

Have you noticed that the congress is a unique phenomenon also because—unlike all the previous forums which have taken place during the period of restructuring—there has been no vilification of...glasnost. Incidentally, today in a number of statements old motifs reverberated hollowly, but there was no comparison with, say, the plenum held a month ago or any other prestigious assembly where literally almost every speaker considered it his duty to point to the news media virtually the main obstacle to restructuring.

This is a paradox: Here we have an outburst of glasnost of quite unusual force, yet there are virtually no reproaches on this account! Are the workers of the news media who, as Deputy V. Belov has said, allegedly wield real power to be credited with this outburst? Certainly not! The voice of the journalists is practically not heard today. Television, radio, and the press have merely put the airwaves and newspaper pages at the disposal of the people, in the shape of their representatives, and have provided them with the opportunity to speak out loud without editorial cuts or intervention. And as a result the truth has been revealed: It is not malicious journalists who shower people with problems, try to confuse them, or divert them from priority tasks.... It is the breath of the people that is felt in the hall. And the voices that ring out from the congress rostrum, whether you like it or not, whether you agree or disagree, are the voice of the people. And if people have stayed glued to their television sets over the past few days, if they carry portable radios close to their ears, and if people who are normally indifferent to official press statements are comparing what they have heard with what has been printed—if all this is happening, it means that we have reached the level of glasnost which the people need.

I ask myself: And what will happen later, after the congress? You may be sure that responsible comrades will emerge who will, at other forums, make "unambiguous" assessments of the level of glasnost at the congress and will try, each according to his wits, to define the desirable limits of glasnost. The foolishness of this course has been proved by both our history and the present state of society. I will make use of the metaphor of a ship which has been so popular with the deputies: You cannot set off on a voyage without knowing the force of the head wind or the tail wind, without being aware of underwater reefs and currents.... Worried by what you see? Dissatisfied with the picture revealed by glasnost? And what about sailing without knowing where you are going, unsure whether the crew is well trained or not, who is on deck and who is in the engine room, how much fuel there is in the tanks, and how much time you have left—does that not worry you?

We must be grateful to the congress if only for the fact that it has helped the people—from the head of the state to the peasant—to know themselves, to realize how complex the world in which we live is, and how difficult yet essential it is to reach consensus.

Here is one more detail that was in evidence also on the 7th day of the congress. It is the question of majority and minority. This is a problem which has always existed and will continue to exist, and consequently there will always be contradictions and confrontation. The drama of the many deputies who have found that they are in the minority at the congress is, in my view, the eternal drama of the Russian intelligentsia, which, in its noble quest, often becomes so divorced from the main masses that not just a militiaman trying to keep order at a rally, but even a deputy sitting in the next row cannot understand what is required of him, what is being proposed, and where, ultimately, he is being led. History has proved more than once that the majority can be wrong. I have no right to judge here who is right and who is wrong—time will tell. However, it is worth mentioning the value of doubt. Truth cannot be established by taking a vote. It is sought through joint efforts. However, it seems that some deputies have arrived at the congress with the firm conviction that they found the truth long ago, they are not weighed down by doubts, and they have no intention of making their brains work.

There is one thing I simply have to mention: I am amazed by the stubbornness with which those who are described as the minority insist, both in their election programs and after the dramatic voting at the congress, that referendums be held on all key questions (just recall B. Yeltsin's speech). I understand, this is a question of principles. But when insisting on these principles it would be as well to remember the aims and to try to guess the possible outcome. It would be interesting to know why they are so confident that the majority will vote for progressive solutions? What if the opposite happens? What if a specific referendum throws society a long way back—what is to be done with such a decision then, when it has been sanctified by the will of the majority, the will of the people?

So everyone, those who think they "possess" the truth, and those who are still seeking it, should face facts and listen to each other.

8th Day of Congress

PM0506132589 Moscow IZVESTIYA in Russian 3 Jun 89 Morning Edition p 1

[Commentary by E. Gonzalyez: "Day Eight"]

[Text] What ways have commentators not found to divide the delegates—into minority and majority, innovators and conservatives, maximalists and moderates, independents and those influenced by someone else, and, finally, by the territorial principle. After yet another day of debates on USSR Supreme Soviet Chairman M.S. Gorbachev's report, a new "classification" comes to mind.

It is based on the fact that there are only two ways to ensure the survival of society, a group, or an individual: to produce the requisite products or borrow them—one can, for instance, take, steal, elicit, in short, redistribute by any method. And gradually we appear to be realizing that for the sake of our well-being it is certainly important what the property situation is here, and even more important, what we do with it—increase it or just share it.

That is why the deputies who have addressed the congress can be divided up (theoretically, of course) in terms of their intentions regarding our common stock. Some have talked about how they would fill it to the brim, others about how to distribute fairly what is left.

It is not my task (it is not the task, in fact) to arrange the deputies on a ladder—who goes high, who goes lower, who is broad and who is somewhat narrower in his outlook. But one has certain doubts about the productiveness of questions like: What can peasants, young people, miners, architects, teachers, veterans, and many, many others expect from the congress? Understand me correctly: I do not doubt the authenticity and seriousness of the problems representatives of different strata and groups of the population have been talking about, but the fruitfulness of the speeches, often persuasive, graphic, and emotional, lending themselves, however, to a one-word precis: "Gimme!"

Unfortunately, this is now customary. Indeed, management organs (they alone?) have always been more assiduous, enthusiastic, and energetic about redistribution than about production. No wonder people, institutions, and even entire departments concerned not so much with the production of goods as with their distribution are more often than not in a privileged position.

Now, it appears, it is time to redistribute the privileges. Why, it is a noble and fascinating occupation, but, I fear, a very short-lived one. It could end before it has really begun and, having swallowed these crumbs, we would again be looking around for something else to redistribute. Alas, it was observed long ago that you cannot take something when there is nothing there to take. As one deputy said, it is pointless patching holes and switching resources from one social problem to another.

More promising is the approach of those deputies who would like to transform a society of redistribution into a society of production that is capable of feeding, shoeing, and clothing all its citizens. But what they sometimes propose one can be somewhat frightened not only to accept, but simply to listen to. Moreover, the radical reformers are clearly in a minority.

Yet we heed what they say. Because, in the first place, it would be odd and unnatural if such ideas were to pop up in the majority of heads—social development shows no similar examples. Second, I must point out that management is nearly always the function of a minority. As indeed is the congress itself, in relation to society.

In view of historical experience it would certainly be logical to adopt those decisions which have attracted not a majority, but a minority of votes. On condition, though, that the minority itself implements them. But that does not happen. Ideas must capture the masses, so to speak. And for this to happen as few as possible should be missed. The fact that some proposals will probably at the moment seem strange and unusual does not matter. The important thing is that they should be listened to and recorded. In time many of the things that seem too risky today will be as normal and as indispensable as the team contract, the lease system, economic accountability, and the market.

9th Day of Congress
*PM0706074589 Moscow IZVESTIYA in Russian
7 Jun 89 Morning Edition p 1*

[V. Nadein article: "Day Nine"]

[Text] The congress is quite confidently gaining experience of civilized parliamentarianism. There are fewer rally-style outbursts. The standing orders are being more precisely observed. The divergences in assessments have not disappeared, the sharpness of criticism has not abated, it is simply that the intensity of passions is increasingly often moving from the sphere of strong language to the sphere of businesslike argument.

People's Deputies K.S. Khallik and V.I. Yarovoy (both from Estonia) provided the congress with sharply contradictory and even mutually exclusive concepts of the events taking place in the Baltic republics. Both speakers cited a number of arguments that cannot be assessed on the primitive basis that one is right and the other wrong. Both approaches are all the more deserving of serious and attentive study in that the activity of responsible politicians cannot result in anything but rational compromise.

So far as I can judge, the public is not feeling tired of the protracted work of the congress. Maybe it is easier for us here on this side of the television screen than it is for the deputies in the Kremlin. For them there is no emotional escape in the form of young pioneer songs and delegations of soldiers marching colorfully beneath unfurled banners. So the cheerful animation during Deputy Kasyan's speech is understandable in human terms. The popular specialist in manual therapy may have been right in some respects in seeking the roots of the present procedural wrangles in N.S. Khrushchev's famous "shoe" speech in the United Nations. Or maybe not. But I thought that the applause with which the audience greeted the grating recommendations to switch ministers to driving combines and thereby solve the problems of economic restructuring was unjustifiably frivolous. There was plenty of advice of that sort at the 23d, 24th, and other party congresses. The results are well known.

Valentin Rasputin is brave and self-confident enough not to court general approval for what he says. Once again he harshly criticized the moral terror of the "restructurers," but on this occasion, too, he failed to indicate with total clarity exactly whom he had in mind. Since it is left to the public to decide the definition, it is for the public to decide the extent to which the writer is correct. But I think two points from his speech will attract particular attention. The first point: The natural right of Russians to conclusively defend their own national honor from direct or covert attacks, not leaving this right solely to noble representatives of other republics. The second: It is not only ordinary collective farm members or factory workers who are entitled to expect protection of their dignity in a proper state. This is the birthright of every citizen, including a Politburo member.

The numerous proposals on emerging from the financial, food, management, and other crises voiced on day 9 of the congress's work are united by a common sense of impatience, urgency, and exigency. That is probably all that unites them. The deputies who head oblast and kray party organizations and oblast soviet executive committees place more emphasis on tactical measures: the redistribution of capital investments and management functions, the harmonization of the "localities," and the "center." Scientists and writers pay more attention to systemic problems. In both cases the pictures that are drawn are motley and colored by personal experience.

But something that is criticized with mounting unanimity is the work of the mass media. Without digressing into now traditional reproaches (they didn't cover the labor holiday, they've filled the airwaves with pop music), I would note that the most accurate and fair criticism was voiced when neither newspapers nor television and radio were directly mentioned. Deputies' accounts of the disastrous position of small peoples (is it that long since we were singing odes?), the bogus autonomy of autonomous republics, and the collective egoism that flared up as a result of the Law on the Socialist Enterprise must be a serious reproach to us journalists....

It is absolutely clear that a considerable proportion of deputies will be unable to speak at the congress. This means that the ideas that they have been unable to voice will find their natural outlet: television and radio studios and newspaper pages. Will editorial collectives find the boldness to be as open and fearless as the congress platform? That is a question that time alone can answer.

Television Chief Comments on Congress Coverage

PM0606083589 Moscow KOMSOMOLSKAYA PRAVDA in Russian 3 Jun 89 p 1

[A. Khantsevich report under the "Phone-In" rubric: "About the 'Time' and About Ourselves"; first paragraph is editorial introduction]

[Text] By organizing the direct relay from the congress, central television has given us a unique opportunity to feel that we are direct participants in the political debate at the Kremlin Palace of Congresses. But we have thus also been made to shoulder a heavy burden of responsibility. There can no longer be any question of the slightest falsification or embellishment of the real course of events in the special congress publications, as happened in the past. People react avidly to every word and the slightest gesture on the television screen. They do not forgive mistakes on the part of the television journalists working at the congress. We saw this for ourselves when we invited Eduard Mikhaylovich Sagalayev, editor in chief of central television's news editorial office, to KOMSOMOLSKAYA PRAVDA's "Phone-In." The conversation was quite tough and point-blank questions were asked.

[Questioner] Aleksey Leontyev from Moscow. Eduard Mikhaylovich, what is happening to the "Vremya" program? During the day we see one thing on the second channel, and in the evening we see something else. A veil is pulled over one stance, while its critics are given full coverage....

[Sagalayev] I can comment on this, especially since Yuriy Vlasov also raised the question at the congress. We have carried out further checks on what happened 27 May. I can tell you that we reported Afanasyev's speech virtually in its entirety, part of Popov's speech, and an abridged version of Adamovich's speech. All this took 4 minutes. The speeches by Stepanov and Meshalkin took 2.5 minutes. I have a suspicion as to why you had the impression that we were encroaching on someone—you probably adhere to the first viewpoint. I can assure you of one thing: We television journalists simply swore a party, human, and journalist's oath to show the congress quite objectively. We are not concealing any of the sharp words that are being said at the congress; we are trying to bring it all to the viewer.

[Questioner] Fine. Another question. The cameraman is often too modest and does not show us how the Congress Presidium and how our Politburo are voting....

[Sagalayev] That is not quite so. On the contrary, we have received complaints that we are showing too much of the Presidium and are thus exerting pressure on the floor or demonstrating preference for the Presidium and insufficient respect for the floor.

[Questioner] Eduard Mikhaylovich, Turchina from Riga. I would ask you to hold a few more interviews with delegates during the recesses. I would like to hear all the delegations from the Baltic republics, Moscow, and Leningrad. Give them the floor, let them speak. One more thing: Ask Belov and Rasputin about their attitude to the "Pamyat" society, because very many rumors are going around about this.

[Sagalayev] Agreed. Although, in my opinion, there are very many interesting deputies from all republics and krays. We have been very wronged by people saying that we are devoting too much attention to the Baltic, Moscow, and Leningrad. There may still be people among the deputies—real, striking individuals—whom we have not discovered. But your wishes will certainly be considered.

[Questioner] A call from Balakov, Saratov Oblast: My name is Aliferenko. This is possibly a somewhat strange request. You realize that the elections were very difficult in our area. The municipal authorities put a spoke in our candidate's wheel. But he became a deputy nonetheless. We have not seen him once at the congress.

[Sagalayev] What is his name?

[Questioner] Eduard Sergeyevich Gams. You see, rumors have gone around the city in this connection that he was not admitted to the congress and was not issued with a mandate card. Is it impossible to show him somehow?

[Sagalayev] Well, I accept your request. We will certainly show him. But do you really believe these ridiculous rumors?

[Questioner] I am calling from Sverdlovsk. My name is Yevgeniy Valeryevich Lotash. Why, when deputies were shown the film about events in Tbilisi, did central television not also show it?

[Sagalayev] Because it was meant for the deputies. But I believe on the whole that it should have been shown on television. We will propose that to the congress.

[Questioner] Misha Petrov from Moscow. Eduard Mikhaylovich, what is your attitude to the proposal voiced at the congress for the congress to approve the chairman of the State Committee for Television and Radio Broadcasting?"

[Sagalayev] Unequivocally positive. I consider that a correct proposal from Yuriy Petrovich Vlasov. Television now thinks of itself as a government establishment, but it should be a state establishment, dependent on the congress, the Supreme Soviet, and thus on the voters and the whole people. Then it will be independent in the real sense of the word.

[Questioner] Mikhail Solomonovich Kozodoy, Khimki. The congress sessions take place in work time and many people cannot watch them. I ask you to show the unabridged video recording in its entirety at the close of the congress."

[Sagalayev] We will publish your viewpoint in KOMSO-MOLSKAYA PRAVDA and examine the reaction of other readers and viewers.

[Questioner] My name is Albina Ivanovna Khochunova, Moscow. Our collective Expresses its gratitude to you for your work at the congress. We ask you not to stop the direct relay although deputies have proposed doing that. Everyone needs it, you realize.

[Sagalayev] Albina Ivanovna, don't worry. The congress will be relayed until the end, I am absolutely sure of that.

[Questioner] Thank you.

Report From 6 Jun Congress Proceedings

PM0806115389 Moscow IZVESTIYA in Russian
8 Jun 89 Morning Edition pp 1-6

["Congress of USSR People's Deputies. Stenographic Report"—IZVESTIYA headline; for further reports from this session see the 7 Jun Soviet Union DAILY REPORT Supplement, pages 10-27]

[Excerpts]

Session 10

Kremlin Palace of Congresses. 6 June 1989. 1000.

USSR People's Deputy A.V. Gorbunov in the chair. [passage omitted]

A.A. Sokolov, chairman of the Gorkiy Oblast Soviet Executive Committee (Sergachskiy Territorial Electoral Okrug, Gorkiy City): [passage omitted]

Comrade deputies! There are many acute problems in our life today, and we are talking about them not just to savor them and demonstrate our bankruptcy but to find ways of resolving them. At the same time, the denial of what has been achieved and the besmirching of the past cannot conceal a clear-cut aim of trying to erode socialism and deny the party's leading role. Today's attacks on the party are aimed not at rectifying mistakes but at pooling forces to undermine confidence in the party and its organs and to break its ties with the people. In this respect we do not understand the point of the attacks on Politburo member Yegor Kuzmich Ligachev, whom we know as an active worker. Blasphemous words—I cannot call them anything else—have been said here with regard to the Lenin Mausoleum and the memory of Vladimir Ilich. (Applause).

Boldly revealing distortions and learning from mistakes, the party is restructuring the political system for the sake of Soviet people and to improve their lives. And I am sure that it will overcome the difficulties in the current period of restructuring. (Applause). [passage omitted]

D.N. Kugultinov, chairman of the Kalmyk Autonomous Soviet Socialist Republic [ASSR], Elista City (Iki-Burulskiy National-Territorial Electoral Okrug, Kalmyk ASSR): [passage omitted]

I have been thinking these past few days that yes, the congress, the first Congress of People's Deputies, will go down in history. I have even sensed the presence of great figures in history. To my mind, Peter I is seated somewhere here. He is watching with satisfaction and saying: "Well done, my descendants. You are speaking as I would have wished—not as if quoting from books, and with everyone able to see who's who." On the right I see Vladimir Ilich Lenin on the steps with his notebook. He is listening to us with alarm and sorrow, and he is saying: "How can there be no soap? How can there be no matches? How many years have passed?" He is told: "It's now

1989." And Lenin thinks: "What has happened, why is this so?—This is not what I taught them. How has it happened?" And it seems to me that he must be horrified by the idea that he had made a mistake. I heard about Lenin's mistake when I was 23—at that young age when the words "Lenin" and "mistake," or "Stalin" and "bad" would leave people in a mystical horror. But then in jail cells, on journeys, and in camps I heard about it again and again from old Leninist Bolsheviks. I realized that yes, Lenin had made a mistake, and his mistake was the following. I thought this when I was sitting in this auditorium on the first 2 or 3 days before the election of the chairman of the Supreme Soviet. His mistake, the old Bolsheviks told me, was that Lenin, working in the Council of People's Commissars, left everything else to Stalin, and in the space of 2-3 years Stalin concentrated power within his own hands to such an extent that even Lenin's note about the lover of hot dishes and the need to transfer him was not acted on at the well-known congress. And it was the Stalin years that prevailed in our country and led to all the problems that we now cannot resolve. That was the mistake. I am afraid now—in our transitional period when we are deciding what our state will be like—that we may be seduced by the beauties of democracy and suddenly distracted by highfalutin words, and say: "Comrade Gorbachev, deal with the soviets! Comrade (I don't know who), deal with the party!" And then something might suddenly happen again. [passage omitted]

I left on my seat a folder full of telegrams from the Crimean Tatars, from Germans from the Volga Republic, from Turks who were deported from the southern borders of Georgia, and from many peoples who tearfully turn to each of us, each deputy, to ensure that we are not complacent and that when we talk about the equality of all the peoples and about the brotherhood of all the peoples we also remember those who are not represented at this congress—those peoples whose lands have not been returned, those peoples whom Stalin condemned to long years of sorrow and long years of second-class citizen status. There must be no status in the Land of the Soviets—a socialist country, a communist country—whereby people are classed as the wrong sort just because of the shape of their eyes or the color of their hair. This should not happen! And I want to propose that we should do something about it at this very congress. We should adopt a law restoring the Crimea's autonomy. We should adopt a law restoring the Volga German Republic. We should adopt a law which would give each of them wings, and on these wings they would invisibly attend the congress tomorrow and applaud each of us, saying: "Yes, every deputy has a heart and understands the sorrow and truth of other people." (Applause). [passage omitted]

V.G. Rasputin, writer, secretary of the USSR Writers Union Board, Irkutsk City (from the USSR Writers Union): Esteemed comrade deputies! We have unwittingly revealed the contrast between us—between those who came through competitive, multicandidate campaigns, and those who were returned by social organizations. I have repeatedly heard it said over the past few days that the former are the people's choice, while the latter have been planted to impede the activeness of restructuring. I, too, think that the Law on Elections is imperfect and should eventually be altered to favor an okrug system only. Is it normal for some people to vote twice, three times, or even four times: in their own okrug, somewhere at the Cultural Foundation, at the Writers Union, and then again at the Academy of Sciences? Naturally, this should not be the case. (Applause). However, the further our discussions go, the more I am convinced that representatives from social organizations have been needed at the initial stage of our democratic elections. They have been needed for the sake of pluralism, which we have been discussing a great deal as a condition of democratic existence, because restructuring has now entered a stage of social development and reached a high point inhabited by hawks who are trying to monopolize it. And anyone who disagrees with them is called an enemy of restructuring.

The expression most commonly used at the congress has been "antirestructuring forces." We have heard that if restructuring is a revolution there is bound to be a counterrevolution too. The discussion about counterrevolution, as you yourselves understand, is a special one without any pluralism. When the hawks come to power they will try to set up a state system for suppressing counterrevolution, and now on the road to power a system of social suppression is being introduced—and quite successfully at that.

It is not a question of the differences which inevitably appear in the development process and which can be narrowed or removed as development proceeds. It is a question of something much greater: the fate of restructuring and democracy. I was pleased to hear Olzhas Suleymenov's idea: If you always row a boat on the left you invariably move to the right. That is not just an image but a law of action for any dynamic [povorotnyy] mechanism, including a social mechanism. The ancient Greek philosopher Plato had something marvelous to say about this. I quote: "Tyranny emerges, of course, from no system other than democracy. In other words, extreme freedom leads to supreme and brutal slavery." So in order to prevent this and ensure that democracy is established in our country once and for all, there is nothing reprehensible about society's needing to restrain the "madness of the brave." Singing the praises of this madness has led in the past to tragic consequences. Now it may propel us from the brink of one abyss to another. So we should treat antirestructuring forces more cautiously. By all logic, you, above all, should be included in that category. [passage omitted]

7 Jun Joint Session of Supreme Soviet Reported

Ryzhkov Council of Ministers Chairman
LD0806092889 Moscow Television Service in Russian 0600 GMT 7 Jun 89

[Relay of first part of the joint session of the Soviet of Nationalities and the Soviet of the Union of the USSR Supreme Soviet in the Kremlin—live]

[Excerpts] [Gorbachev] Comrades, first of all here is some information: Of the 271 deputies making up the Soviet of the Union, 262 have registered; and of the 271 making up the Soviet of Nationalities, 247 have registered. So we have every reason to begin our work. May I declare the first joint session of the two chambers of the Supreme Soviet open, and thus welcome the members of the USSR Supreme Soviet in its full composition on the commencement now of its regular work.

A statement from the USSR Council of Ministers has arrived for the examination of the USSR Supreme Soviet. I shall read it out: In accordance with Article 129 of the USSR Constitution, the USSR Council of Ministers considers its obligations at an end, and it lays down its powers before the newly elected USSR Supreme Soviet. The USSR Council of Ministers asks that this statement be made known to the USSR Supreme Soviet—Ryzhkov, chairman of the USSR Council of Ministers, 7 June 1989.

I think everything here is clear, and I submit the proposal that cognizance be taken of the statement from the USSR Council of Ministers on laying down its powers before the USSR Supreme Soviet. Are there any questions here? Who is in favor of such a decision? Please raise your mandates. Please put them down. Those against? None. Abstentions? It is decided.

Regarding candidacies for appointment as chairman of the USSR Council of Ministers, according to the Constitution, proposals on this matter are submitted and then presented by the chairman of the USSR Supreme Soviet. Taking account of the real position occupied in our society by the CPSU as the ruling party, consultations have taken place with members of the party's Central Committee concerning candidates for the post of chairman of the Council of Ministers. The CPSU Central Committee has discussed this matter and supported a proposal which I submitted for consent and consultation, and it expressed its opinion, which has been published. Relying on my own profound conviction and on the opinion of the party Central Committee, I hope that this also reflects the opinion of our people and the deputies, and I submit the proposal that Comrade Ryzhkov, Nikolay Ivanovich, be appointed chairman of the USSR Council of Ministers.

I would like to say a few words—although I have already expressed my views on this matter, in particular to the deputies at the party group—but nevertheless we have this question today, we have to decide on it, and I would like to add a few words to what I have said to present arguments in favor of the proposal which I have put before you.

This proposal stems from several principled considerations which I feel it is necessary to state here. In the first place, both in his political, business, human, and moral qualities, Comrade Ryzhkov is worthy of being reappointed chairman of the USSR Council of Ministers. That is the first thing. Second, in Comrade Ryzhkov we have a person, a Communist and a man of state, who, at a watershed stage in the development of our society, when in the party and in society in general we have arrived at the need to implement restructuring and renew socialist society, we have a man who is devoted on principle to this course; who occupies a firm, principled standpoint; who is a convinced adherent of the policy of restructuring and renewal in our society.

All that has been done over these years to expand these processes is to a considerable degree linked with his personal contribution. In this respect it is evidently of great importance that Comrade Ryzhkov has a good picture of the situation in the country, because all his preceding life makes it possible to see, in cross section as it were, all that has accumulated and the situation in which the country finds itself. For he was directly involved, for a considerable part of his life, in work in the industry and in rank-and-file work. Then for 5 years he was a chief engineer of Uralmash; for five years he was general director of Uralmash. Afterward he worked here in the Ministry of Heavy Machine Building. For 4 years he was first deputy chairman of the USSR State Planning Committee, and he worked in the Central Committee, so that he had an opportunity to accumulate experience and evidently to amass also his own understanding and his own thoughts with regard to the processes under way in society.

Evidently the conclusion from all this experience was his ardent desire to participate in the implementation and in working out the implementation of the policy of restructuring. Therefore in Comrade Ryzhkov's person we have—I would like to emphasize it first of all and this is the most important thing—a man dedicated to the policy of restructuring. Second—and this is no less important—our restructuring will not make progress if the processes of democracy are not expanded in it by systematically encompassing all spheres of life in our society. In the person of Comrade Ryzhkov we have a democratic man and a democratic leader. All that has been done in this respect both from the viewpoint of developing democracy and glasnost in society as a whole and from the viewpoint of expanding political process and political reform, I am able to say wholeheartedly that Nikolay Ivanovich shares these attitudes as a matter of principle.

This is imprinted on the drafting of the document concerning the economy. If you turn your attention to this, then the main core—I would say—of the proposals and documents relating to the economy is, all the same, democratization. It manifests itself. It has also manifested itself in the fact that on the initiative of the USSR Council of Ministers we have started working out the draft law on enterprise, which is the main link of our economy. This fact itself is important. Until now these reforms were as a rule initiated from above, with steps of one kind or another being taken in the top echelons, so that by the time all this reached the enterprises it had often lost steam and become emasculated and in this way, already in advance, as it were, this kind of outcome was laid down for many reforms. They existed, they were started in a legitimate

way, but this matter does not rest on this point alone. Comrade Ryzhkov's democratic approach was manifested in his active support for economic decentralization, naturally with the center retaining the key positions so as to harmonize our relations in the union and in our complex national economy. Nonetheless, the republics feel this and know this. Many documents have already been worked out and are now being drafted on this issue. Also, as far as the republics, and their independence, and embuing their sovereignty with realistic content, are concerned, and as far as local soviets are concerned, then solutions to these questions are being drafted with their active participation. This, too, is a very important element, for without this one cannot even talk about any kind of a power of the soviets. Nikolay Ivanovich not only shares this attitude, but he also heads the work on the drafting documents in this respect.

I think it can be said that Comrade Ryzhkov's democratic character has also been manifested in the fact that he has been an active champion of the development of new approaches, by way of unearthing new forms of organizing life, the economy, and socialist property. This was also manifested in the cooperative movement and in important decisions regarding leasing, and so on. I also think that even though the current 5-year plan still, to a significant degree, bears the stamp of the years of stagnation—because we have only just started to try to understand our economy, and on the basis of this understanding, to then embark on fresh decisions and approaches—nevertheless, even the drafting of this 5-year plan, which undoubtedly bears the burden of the past, and to a significant degree fetters the processes of the reform, too, was based on the important idea, the idea of reorienting our economy toward the individual and turning it toward social policy. This is also the position of the Council of Ministers and its chairman.

In describing Comrade Ryzhkov thus, I would at the same time like to say, of course—I have already spoken of this in the report—that far from everything that was intended has been done. Moreover, serious miscalculations have been made. However, I think that even that enables us to say that for all of us, and for the government mainly, this is a cause for serious lessons and for preparing for future approaches and solutions which will eliminate the problems already accumulated in the course of restructuring, which will remove the miscalculations, and which will set our economy on the road to development.

Comrade Ryzhkov is a self-critical person and has a party attitude to the results of government activity. It seems to me that it is now important for our confidence—which he received from the Central Committee—to be strengthened by the Supreme Soviet's confidence; for it to be shown; and to nominate him chairman of the Council of Ministers and thus give him the opportunity to continue to develop his plans, to rectify what has been allowed to take place, and learn lessons from the past. That is what I wanted to say to you in proposing Comrade Ryzhkov, Nikolay Ivanovich, for the nomination to the post of chairman of the Council of Ministers.

Naturally Nikolay Ivanovich is present. We can continue either by asking him questions or by discussing the candidacy. Are there any questions for Comrade Ryzkhov? Nikolay Ivanovich, please come a bit closer to us here. [Ryzkhov walks up to rostrum] We now have the tradition in this hall that people being put forward are invited to this rostrum. Please comrades, what questions do people have? Yes?

[Unidentified speaker] Esteemed chairman, you said that very serious errors had been made by the previous Council of Ministers. Can you be more specific about what errors are you talking about, please, Nikolay Ivanovich?

[Ryzkhov] I consider that on the strategic level, the Council of Ministers, in implementing our country's economic strategy, which was discussed at the 27th congress and at the 19th party conference, did not make errors in principle on the strategic level. As for individual theses which developed this strategy, in our opinion, when we evaluate the road we have traveled, we have indeed allowed several errors to be made which have had a negative effect on the development of the national economy, and on some of the reasons for social tension that have arisen in our society.

If I am to speak of errors of principle, I could dwell on the following: Having created at that time—and that was 1987—the law on state enterprises, which in our opinion was a progressive one, preparation on it started in 1986, and it was confirmed at the June plenum and then at the session of the Supreme Soviet of 1987. I believe it is progressive, and to this day this law has not lost its relevance, although I also have certain opinions—which deputies are expressing—that perhaps we will have to reconsider these laws to a certain degree. I consider that it was allowed to be left, well, unfinished in some ways, with some processes not fully thought through. I think that in parallel with the law on state enterprises, however difficult it might have been, we should immediately have worked out and ratified laws on tax liabilities, on the regulation of income, on how there should be a progressive direction of income of labor collectives. Since these questions were not worked through, there was an income explosion, if I can call it that, among the population in 1987, which the government was not in a position to make up for with consumer goods. Nor were we able to make up for it with services, and as a result very great social tension and an imbalance in the consumer market also emerged in 1988 and the beginning of 1989.

I think that for all its progressiveness the law on cooperatives—it is more progressive, more democratic, because it was adopted a year after the law on state enterprises—some of its provisions were evidently not worked out thoroughly, and today they have caused a sharp reaction among the people with regard to the cooperative movement. If we had worked through questions of regulating these processes a little more deeply in some way, I think there wouldn't be such a situation in the cooperative movement.

I think that one of the shortcomings, to speak on a large scale, was the fact that in tackling individual questions—individual necessary questions, like the law on state enterprises, on the development of the cooperative movement, on leasing—nevertheless, because of a lack of deep theoretical research and clearly drawn up ideas, we evidently at that time did not set out and delineate the final aim of our economic reforms. That is why particular decisions in the last resort sometimes contradicted each other, and of course created certain difficulties for us in the national economy.

For example, to this day four models of management exist: the first and second models are the two models of the state enterprise; the third is the cooperative movement, and the fourth is lease contracting. It is quite clear that we obviously needed to have a clearer idea from the start of the whole range of these models, and evidently bring them together under some single law, the question of which, by the way, comrades quite rightly, in my view, are raising at present, in order to have an integral concept and then deal with the individual elements. I think that this is one of the fundamental issues.

One can talk about individual, particular, local problems which have prevented us from moving forward. Take the issue of capital construction, which was mentioned fairly sharply in Mikhail Sergeyevich's report. This question was not, as they say, passed over in the speeches by people's deputies. When we were transferring from administrative methods...[Ryzkhov changes thought] As you know, previously absolutely everything was prescribed from the center, even down to the level of some barn—all this was written up in the plans, when to build it, how to build it, and so on. We considered this wrong; that in general it violates all kinds of principles of the independence of republics, enterprises, and so on, and for that reason we embarked on a democratization process, and we handed over the lion's share, or half, at least, to the union republics. The other half was the prerogative of the center, which kept in its hands the construction of the biggest projects. I think that the economic mechanism and the whole system in capital construction has brought us to a point where, alongside the fact that certain positive phenomena have emerged, we have nevertheless not resolved in a cardinal fashion the problem of investment in our country and that of capital construction. That is why, while there were positive results in the first 2 years, the second 2 years, these ones now, have, on the contrary, become worse, and it is quite evident that the economic mechanism in capital construction was not as fully worked through by us as it should have been.

I think that we have not done everything that is needed concerning the rural areas, either. I am not speaking today about material resources, I am not talking about the fact that there is a great deficiency in capital investment and in resources for resolving social issues, which there have been acute questions about at the congress and in the appeal made by our agrarians—I have to say that I support this appeal. But having formed the economic mechanism 3 years ago, it has resolved certain definite issues, but on the whole it has not made it possible to enhance productivity in farming sharply, and to improve the food supplies for our population. That is, we have evidently not found real approaches, and we think that the March plenum that was held recently laid a very serious foundation for our work; and I think that after the congress, when, as they say, we will have to think through it all, put everything in its place, I think we need to work through the decisions of the March plenum in the localities in a very serious manner and draw the relevant conclusions.

I could dwell on a number of other questions as well; there are objective ones, too; let's say it is possible to criticize the government, but there were objective reasons. Yes, a complex situation developed with the budget and the imbalance in the budget. However, in many ways it can be explained, of course, by how the national economy budget was shaped previously, and how it is shaped today. I have already said that if we used the old methods to shape the state budget of, say, 1989, we would definitely balance it. However, this is not the way and these are not the directions which are stipulated in the economic reform. If we traveled along this path we would undermine—undercut—all the roots of economic reform. We would be compelled—knowing the grave financial position. We were compelled to take certain decisions on certain social questions. Have we done this correctly, or not? I believe that, despite all the difficulties, we have done it correctly, because these problems were so acute that, in such a situation, there was no way we could simply walk away from them. Therefore, this aggravated the situation, but, in my view, this was an objective necessity which we just had to take into consideration.

That's what I would say in general terms about those shortcomings which, in my view, occurred in the government's work over the past years.

[Gorbachev] Yes, comrade. Yes, if you please. Just a moment, come up to the microphone.

[Unidentified speaker] Dzhezkazgan, Territorial Constituency [number indistinct]. Nikolay Ivanovich, what do you think? Will the country's economy improve in the course of a year? As future chairman, what measures are you thinking of taking to achieve that?

[Ryzhkov] I think that one must take a realistic view of things. I cannot promise that there will be fundamental changes in the country's economy within a year. That would be rash; it would be a deception. I think that in the coming year, as far as the consumer market is concerned, you can expect us to make certain radical changes. That is, certain economic situations will improve. But time, of course, time will be needed; time will be needed to resolve all the problems which exist in the country today, and we have been discussing this at the congress for many days now. Even a simple enumeration of them, as

they say, shows that there is huge number of them. However, we must proceed, must proceed so that these problems in the country can be removed step by step.

[Gorbachev] Go ahead, please.

[Unidentified speaker] Prunskiene, Lithuania. I have two questions for you, Nikolay Ivanovich. The first is that on more than one occasion you have said publicly that Lithuania is living at the expense of others. Do you consider that it is the same today, taking account of the shortcomings in pricing, subsidies and taxes, and in the economic mechanism as a whole? That is the first question. The second is this: 109 deputies signed a draft law on the economic self-sufficiency of the union republics, which as a draft was handed over to the congress. If you are familiar with this draft, how do you evaluate it, and the prospects for its adoption? Thank you.

[Ryzhkov] To the first question: I have never used the words living at the expense of others. You can check this. Such words have never been in any of my official statements. There has been economic accounting. This economic accounting exists. It may be submitted to the people's deputies. Such economic accounting was carried out, in actual fact, in order to create an objective picture of what is going on in our republics—all 15 republics.

As they say, imports were taken into the republic, all kinds of products and produce, and then goods—well, not goods but raw materials, materials and so forth—were exported from this republic. Such an economic accounting does exist. It shows that in this case Lithuania imports more than it exports. We asked for the economic accounting to be done in world prices because I agree that the current prices do not give an objective picture, a complete objective picture of our country.

This is a vast question and a great deal may be said here. We figured it in world prices and did the accounting according to world prices, not just in Lithuania, but in every republic; we calculated what it imports, what it exports, in world prices. The same thing happens—a rather interesting picture. Theefore, a realistic view must be taken of that, a realistic view and, as they say, there is no offense here. The structure, the structure of the national economy has taken shape in this way and that is why we must take measures, as they say, for the future. Likewise, for instance, Kazakhstan will say that it, being a republic, a large republic which produces raw materials—and in our country prices of raw materials are low—is permanently, as they say, theoretically speaking, unprofitable. That is the first part. That is why it is an objective picture and I never intended to say that someone was feeding someone else, and so on. We live in a single national economic complex and we must have a clear picture of those economic processes which are taking place in this complex and, as they say, draw long-term conclusions.

To the second question on territorial financial autonomy. I shall dwell in somewhat more detail, taking account of the fact that it worries many.

[Gorbachev] Sit down, meanwhile. [bustle in hall]

[Ryzhkov] When preparations were under way for the 1987 June plenum, this plenum and subsequently the Supreme Soviet session which adopted the Law on State Enterprises essentially summed up the results of 2 years of theoretical research. That means that for 2 years we went searching—for 2 years—and we formulated the principles of our economic reform. By June 1987 they had been formulated. I have to admit that there were very long arguments. But I can also openly tell you in confidence that in the Politburo these questions, let's say one question of economic reform, was discussed for up to 7 or 8 hours at a time.

Of course our talks were contentious but they were principled and they were in search of new ways. That was the case everywhere. Therefore, at the time when the concept of the economic reform was shaped, at that time it was written and we were at that time profoundly convinced that merely to limit ourselves to reform of the primary link—and that is our foundation, that is, the enterprise-association—and through that to change everything in our country, would be insufficient. Therefore the question arose that as well as the fact that we were taking this road, we needed to implement very major economic changes in the republics, in the regime of the country. If you look today at the documents of the June plenum—which contained a whole package of decisions from both the Central Committee and the Council of Ministers—this subject is covered in detail there, and it is stated that it is necesary to work out and introduce regional financial autonomy.

I was at that time profoundly convinced, and today I say firmly that without regional financial autonomy the economic reform will make no further headway. It will be half-baked. It cannot merely stay at enterprise level. Everything will remain as it was; the economic system which operated for decades will continue.

In November last year, when we saw that the process was under way, when the Baltic republics were preparing their model, and other republics were preparing their model, the central economic departments were not idle either; they were also preparing their definite model of financial autonomy for the territories. In November we assembled—the chairmen of the councils of ministers of all union republics, 15 republics, the 15 chairmen of the state planning committees, and all day we held our discussions on how we should build financial autonomy. At that time we did not have a single line written down. It was a blank page, and we asked everyone to have their say as to how they envisaged financial autonomy. The exchange of opinion was very good. A special commission was formed, you could call it a team, composed of 16 persons, 17 persons, 15 chairmen of the gosplans of

union republics headed by Comrade Maslyukov and his first deputy, Comrade Sitaryan. They were instructed to sit on the commission on a democratic basis and draft the provisions. They themselves said it was the first time in decades that they were all meeting together to work on a particular problem. At the beginning of the year, in January, this work was finished. We considered that the main principles were correctly formulated. So, it was examined in the Politburo, and the Supreme Soviet adopted the decision that these basic principles should be published in the press.

After this, after a short wait, we indeed received the documents from Estonia and Lithuania which differ from the principles expounded in the press. What can I say? This, of course, requires special analysis, and I think there will be an opportunity for this. I recently had a talk with Comrade Toome, chairman of the Estonian Council of Ministers. Evidently it is necesary to sit down at the table once again and weigh up all the pluses and minuses very carefully.

If I am to speak today of such a major fundamental plan, then firstly, I consider that in those proposals which were made and published and which were discussed in the republican supreme soviets, there are many constructive elements which can be kept and need to be carefully studied, and evidently they can enter the system of financial autonomy. That is the first point.

At the same time there are a number of questions which in my view, if they are adopted as they are formulated there, will not benefit those republics. Our question, our line, is integrational processes. It is necessary to integrate. However, there are some provisions which do not lead along the line of integration, but the reverse. I think that, considering the enormous links of the national economic complex, which sould not be underestimated, they will possibly exacerbate the situation.

There are also a number of provisions which are difficult to even introduce into our federative state today. Therefore, I would divide them up this way: there are both positive points, there are constructive proposals, but there are also proposals which both contradict the Constitution and sometimes go against our living in a united national economic complex in the new understanding of it. That is how I would reply.

[Gorbachev] Fine. [indistinct interjection] One minute, I shall finish and get back to you.

[Unidentified speaker] I'd like to ask the last question.

[Gorbachev] Never mind. Comrade Safiyeva, please go ahead. Just a moment, let the woman through. Perhaps we could have shorter questions, and incidently, perhaps Nikolay Ivanovich could be more brief, right? [laughter]

[Safiyeva] I have a question, Nikolay Ivanovich. I'm no economist, my understanding of these matters is poor, but I think that our obsession with huge economic projects [gigantomania] is by no means the last thing in the economic situation which our country is in. In his speech in Krasnoyarsk, Mikhail Sergeyevich spoke unfavorably about this obsession with huge economic projects, especially about the construction of electric power stations. We are amazed by something else—that the head of the state condemns this obsession, but the government allocates fantastic sums to construct these projects. An example of arrogant obsession with huge economic projects is the Rogun hydroelectric power station [GES] which is being built in Tajikistan. I would like to know what your attitude is to our errors in this kind of obsession in the past—what happened before—and your attitude to this kind of obsession in relation to electric power stations in the future. If we are going to go on living like this, what is this obsession with huge economic projects going to lead to? And what is your attitude to the Rogun GES?

[Gorbachev] I asked for questions to be shorter.

[Safiyeva] That's it, I've finished!

[Gorbachev] Fine. Nikilay Ivanovich, please.

[Ryzhkov] Well, first of all, my attitude in principle to this obsession with huge economic projects: I am against it. I believe that in the processing industries in particular we must not move in the direction of major enterprises; to the contrary, we must move toward medium-sized and small enterprises. As a rule these are more flexible and adapt better and more quickly to the requirements of the national economy and the consumer market.

As far as questions of power enginering are concerned, I must say, comrades, that this is a special question, and it requires special examination. The day before yesterday I gave my views when the Editorial Commission was sitting, and I would like to say now that we need, evidently, to have a proper discussion of the question of the development of power engineering in our country. The question is one of fundamental importance. The fact of the matter is that the long-term development of the national economy will depend on power engineering. An improvement in living standards and how to live better in the national economy—I mean the life of the people—will depend on power engineering. Therefore, I would say, a very intense situation has developed today around power engineering. Many people are opposed to nuclear power engineering— you have heard this at the congress. I must say that construction has ceased at many stations now. If we are talking about nuclear power stations, we had planned in this 5-year plan period to build nuclear power station capacities to the sum of 40 million kw of established capacity. Since Chernobyl we have amended this and it will now be only 30 million. However, I think that even 30 million will not be the figure; it will be much less.

And now on hydroelectric power stations. My opinion is that this is an ecologically pure form of power engineering. We utilize 20 percent of the theoretical potential of hydroelectric power. The United States has utilized 44 percent; Switzerland utilizes 65 percent. I may have made a mistake somewhere in these percentages as I am speaking only from memory. So we have to draw certain conclusions from those mistakes which we have made at one time or another on hydroelectric power stations, when we built stations on flat land [ravninnyye stantsii], and when we really disturbed the ecology and caused harm to nature. We must draw conclusions from this.

However, at the same time, obviously, to say that we must halt the construction of hydroelectric stations is, I think, clearly not right. The government's opinion is this. In all probability, after the congress—and the documents have already generally been prepared—we must have another look at this and make alterations to the power engineering program which has been approved and which is in operation today. You know that in the long term, power engineering is very much geared to the performance of the national economy. We must make certain alterations and examine with the Supreme Soviet questions of the long-term development of power engineering, for the next 10-15 years, and, I think, we must put it to nationwide discussion, and the people must tell us how they want to live in the future. That's my opinion.

[Gorbachev] Microphone No 5 please.

[Unidentified speaker] The economic situation of the country is very complex and continues to worsen. This is not only the consequence of the past. But in my view, the true way has not yet been found for a good manager to appear everywhere, that is, a more responsible leader with greater vested interest. So, here is my first question. What is your concept of the further development of the economy and how can a real manager be raised? The second question is this: What is your view of the decentralization of economic management, and does it contradict the process of integration? The third question: Do you think it is possible to carry out the experiment in the Baltic republics of giving them full economic independence; that is, the sovereignty as outlined in the constitution? Thank you.

[Gorbachev] Well, the next hour is taken.

[Ryzhkov] As to the first question of how I see the future role of an enterprise's manager: I see it in that we must gradually change our attitude toward the forms of ownership. I see that to a maximum degree there is the need for us to get away from the first model of economic management, to a maximum degree to change over to lease contracting and to give the possibility—well, to coordinate to a greater extent the results of man's labor at an enterprise and his end results. But for this it is required to work out very many provisions and above all questions concerning taxation and, I should even say, the use of taxation to regulate all correlations of reproduction and incomes and salaries, etc. I see a turn exactly in this direction, as a prospect. For this it is possible that we will have to reconsider, as they say, some provisions of the existing laws as well.

As to decentralization, I am an advocate of decentralization. I believe there will be a gradual reduction, especially in industrial ministries in the country, as economic conditions will be maturing in the primary link, that is at the level of enterprises, associations, and collective and state farms, and so on and so forth—as soon as we create economic conditions there that will enable work to be carried out without orders from above, without coordination from above.

In my view, we should have fewer and fewer ministries in this country. Of course, certain ministries will remain, and they exist in all countries. But the number of purely industrial ministries should I think be gradually reduced. But my view is that these are two...[speaker hesitates] well, these are communicating vessels. In other words, while gradually reducing their number it is necessary at the same time, as they say, to make it possible to develop the processes which it is essential to carry out at the bottom. This is the line that I support.

The third question is about the financial autonomy of the republics. The view of the government—and I feel that this is the view of people's deputies, too—is such that it is necessary for all the republics to change over to financial autonomy and self-financing from 1991. I am convinced that it is necessary to do this. If we fail to do this, the next 5-year plan period will not differ very strongly from this one. It is therefore necessary in the next 18 months to prepare a huge number of every normative document possible, so that we could use to a full extent, as they say, the financial autonomy of the union republics while forming the whole concept of the 5-year plan. I am in favor of this and I believe that it is an indispensable condition for our further development.

The question is being put that some republics should go over to financial autonomy in 1990. I think it could be formulated like this: It will be necessary to verify certain elements of territorial financial autonomy in some republics next year. Such proposals have now been prepared. They have undergone preliminary discussion with both the Baltic republics and with Belorussia, and for that reason I think that after the congress, we shall have to sit down and determine what can be done, in order to hold...[changes thought] to take a step in that verification. But on the whole the changeover must be in 1991.

[Gorbachev] Go ahead.

[Burachas] Nikolay Ivanovich, Burachas, Lithuania. I should like to clarify the criteria for loss-making by union republics. Specifically, the Lithuanian budget in the past few years was balanced, but this year we have a deficit, or state debt, of R285 million, added to the R700 million of all-union expenditure in a budget totalling more than R4 billion, and it is now not clear whether it will stand up [vyderzhan], so to say. Furthermore, R800 million was not returned to us for payment for milk and meat. So my first question is: How much must a republic pay for it not to be counted as an all-union loss-making one? My second question: Do you know that in the last few decades the situation of people living on the verge of starvation in our republic has scarcely changed? I'm talking about people who get only R30 [per month] and who live alone exclusively on the sum. Are you satisfied with the fact that the situation is not changing? My last question: Our microprocessor technology is developing at a fast rate, but networks are not being created, information data banks are not being created, and there is certainly no thought of information bases or banks. So I think that the great industrial and defense potential every year loses its value many times over. Thank you.

[Ryzhkov] The budget: I think, evidently, that the chairman of the Council of Ministers, if he is confirmed, if he is appointed by the Supreme Soviet, will evidently make a statement, a statement of policy, from the government which will explain this question, so that it should be perfectly clear what is happening with the budget in our country. [inaudible shouts from hall] I must say this, comrades, that there is altogether a certain paradox in our system, and we consider that territorial financial autonomy must, well, solve this problem, this paradoxical situation. The actual method for drawing up the budget of the country and the budget of the union republics, was that the union republics first of all detailed their expenditure, as it were, and then the union regulates the budget, as it were, and what happened was that all the union republics always balanced their income with their expenditure, but the state did not balance. For that reason—I'm not talking about specific figures at the moment—this year, when we published a R35 billion budget deficit, we were indeed obliged to spread some share of the weight of the deficit of the state budget proportionately around the union republics. For that reason I wouldn't like to dwell in detail now on those figures, all the more so since I don't have them to hand.

Your second question was about poverty. Yes, the government is aware that 43 million people, or 15 percent of the population of our country, live, if one can say so, below the poverty line.

Today our science has established R75 per person as the poverty line or limit. We know this. As for what needs to be done, well, as they say, we discussed this at the congress and, evidently, the future government will have to think very seriously about how to get out of this situation. The lion's share of these people are people of pensionable age—you know that the pension of a collective farm worker is R50, and the minimum pension is not much greater for city dwellers—and families with many children. These are the two main categories of people who have this low living standard.

The third question about microprocessor equipment. Yes, a special program for the computerization of the national economy was adopted by the government and the Politburo, and I think that alongside many shortcomings in our country, on this matter we are now, as they say, well, big changes for the better are taking place, a definite movement is beginning, and our task today is to secure the computerization program and also to set up special centers where people can be taught and where computer programs can be developed. The State Committee for Computer Technology and Informatics has been set up by us for this purpose and its main task is precisely to resolve these matters, and if it resolves them badly, then our task is to ensure that it does its work better. It was specially set up for this purpose.

[Gorbachev] Please, go ahead.

[Unidentified speaker] Mikhail Sergeyevich. First, I apologize for the lines that have formed here at the microphones. It is essential that everything be done as soon as possible to ensure normal work. Second, I have two questions for you, Nikolay Ivanovich, from myself and my electorate. First, do you believe yourself, oh, no, do you understand...the lack of the most essential consumer goods, do you understand that our country cannot afford the continued, planned construction of industrial installations, that this deflects enormous material and labor resources away from resolving some of the most topical problesm of the more rapidly efficient installations producing consumer goods, and that the reduction of construction by R8 billion planned in decision No 231 is a mere drop in the bucket in comparison with expenditure at the present time? The second question: Why is the Council of Ministers, headed by you, continuing as before, in violation of the Law on State Enterprises, to fulfill the plan according to gross volume of output? And does it understand that this is stimulating the production of expensive goods, not particularly necessary to the national economy, which hence causes additional expenditure, pay and material resources?

[Ryzhkov] The Council of Ministers has a firm standpoint on this issue and we believe that the matter of capital construction in industry should be sharply restricted in the next 5-year plan. But this has to be approached in a balanced way because there are certain things which the country cannot live without. Take, for example, the aforementioned power engineering. If there is no power engineering, we will come to a complete halt. But, I agree that we do have large reserves and that in the next 5-year plan, we should direct most of the increase in capital investment—and in our view this will not be a very substantial sum—into tackling social issues. Well, social issues or, say, the development of industry related to people. We have a firm standpoint on this and our future government will put it into practice in precisely this way.

As for approaches based on stressing gross volume and so on, well, comrades, we are at present at a very complex, complex stage of economic development, when the command method of management still exists, alongside the economic method of management, but we trying as far as possible to move away from this. There are indeed shortcomings in our economic mechanism which allow enterprises, when they have moved away, when they have stopped planning in detail one set of items or another—I mean, cheap goods are indeed forced out. We are fighting this, and where we see that an extreme need exists, as they say, we resort to, we introduce certain state subsidies. This is what we did in 1987 for the production of light industrial goods for children and with socially low prices for the elderly. Approximately R1 billion was allocated from the state budget for this purpose, in order to ensure that factories had the opportunity, as they say, or at least would strive to make these goods.

[Gorbachev] Please, go ahead.

[Unidentified speaker] Esteemed Nikolay Ivanovich, of course one misfortune cannot be compared to another and I would like to ask...[changes thought] We have put forward a proposal, signed by about 100 deputies, to regard the area around the Aral Sea as an ecological disaster zone. I would like to remind you here that when we speak of the area around the Aral, we are talking about the life of a population of 5 million, the population of Tashauz Oblast in the Turkmen Socialist Soviet Republic [SSR] Kzyl-Orda Oblast in the Kazakh SSR and Khorezm Oblast in the Uzbek SSR. What is your standpoint on this matter? That is the first question.

And the second one concerns the distribution of basic foodstuffs per capita, which is several times lower in Kara-Kalpak in comparison with the country as a whole. I would like to know what your precise position on this issue is. Thank you.

[Ryzhkov] My stance on the Aral and on this problem was absolutely precisely given in the governmental decision that was published on this question. We examined this problem very thoroughly, very thoroughly indeed. You know, there were many expenditions, we were instructing many commissions to examine the whole problem and find means to resolve this situation. It is not possible to say that this decision and these measures, which are planned, will return the Aral to us in its primary shape. Evidently, this is now an unrealistic matter. But it is necessary to halt the processes and to improve the situation.

Secondly, this decision—and you know this—places the main emphasis on creating normal conditions. This means at least a minimum degree of normal conditions for the life of the people who are in this zone. Life will show, as they say, whether we manage to do this with help of this decision. And if some questions are not finally resolved, I think that there will be an opportunity to return to this problem once again.

And with respect to foodstuffs, well, this is how the matters have developed in our country: that there is, indeed, a very great difference in foodstuffs consumption, particularly with regard to meat, butter etc. Here, there also exist historical roots, but on the whole this is, of course, of an economic nature. I think that we need to improve agriculture as a whole. If we do not improve agriculture and if we only—as they say—allocate who should get more and who should get less, we shall not resolve the problem. There will always be someone at a lower level. Therefore our task, and the task for all, is to precisely turn the attention to agricultural production. I think that of all social problems which the national economy faces today, they can be resolved quickly within 2 to 3 years, both consumer goods and so on—we can see this because we are involving the defense complex, we are altering the production program of the enterprises and this will yield results. However, the main thing these days is to improve the countryside. This will reduce by 70 percent the tension in our society.

[Gorbachev] If you please.

[Unidentified speaker] Esteemed Nikolay Ivanovich, I would like to turn to you with a specific question and at the same time with a request. How you satisfy this request will in many respects determine the attitude taken toward you by many inhabitants of Lithuania. As you undoubtedly know, an expedition to various places of Siberia to transfer the remains of those who died during Stalinist deportations between the years 1941 and 1953 is planned for this summer. Preliminary work in this connection were already carried out: the lists of those who died, specific places of their burial, the expenditure, etc. A question of transport has remained unresolved. We already appealed to the USSR Ministry of Railways, but we received a negative answer. As far as I know, this question had been raised in the Politburo, too. But we have not received a concrete answer, either. May we hope for your help in solving this question, which is very important for the inhabitants of Lithuania?

[Ryzhkov] Of course, I think that the question of transport is not necessarily the main issue in this matter. We all understand the tragedy that occurred in our country. This concerns Lithuania, this concerns all the union republics, the towns—all our people, and it is only for those positions that we can make an appraisal, and the Politburo is indeed giving its firm appraisal on this issue.

We must perpetuate the memory of those who died, and a very great deal is being done today in our country directly in the localities, in other words, in all regions. That is our position. The same may be said about Lithuania.

[Gorbachev] Nikolay Ivanovich, just a moment, I will take up two notes I have here. Some comrades are asking questions about the agenda. The impression seems to be that I have not read it out. But, comrades, I did this deliberately. If we raise one question and then see how long it takes to tackle it, then it will be clear whether we will be able to take up other questions. Therefore, as you will understand, I began with the statement followed by the question of the chairman. If we have time to deal with other questions—those which we must tackle in the Supreme Soviet—then we shall deal with them, and then we shall consult one another. Any objections to this approach? [indistinct utterings from hall] Oh? To whom should this time limit apply? To me? [further voices from hall] Okay! Just a moment, let's agree then that we'll set aside another half hour for questions and answers. Is that acceptable to everyone? [voices of approval] Commrades, or is it necessary to vote on this? Then, first of all, I will pass over written questions to Nikolay Ivanovich. Nikolay Ivanovich, that will be at the conclusion, then. Right, let's have brief questions and brief answers. One at a time, right? Nikolay Ivanovich, but what time limit, I don't understand! Ah! In other words, questions until what time? [more voices in hall] Right, let's agree on this: We'll ask questions up to 1130 [0730 GMT]. Every questioner can ask one question, and we will ask Nikolay Ivanovich to be brief. Those in favor of this proposal, please vote. Please lower your cards. Anyone opposed? Abstentions? Well, that approach is agreed by an overwhelming majority. Nikolay Ivanovich, yes, pelase, over to microphone number one.

[(Shcherbakiyev)] Esteemed Nikolay Ivanovich, Deputy (Shcherbakiyev) Is there a program of emergency measures to improve the ecological situation in the country, and least in the 100 hot-spots, the 100 towns, which are now in a most grave situation?

[Ryzhkov] Such a state ecological program is currently being worked out. It embraces questions of ecology as a whole, including 104 towns which are in a complex situation, and in the next few months it will be passed to the Supreme Soviet for nationwide discussion.

[Gorbachev] Comrade Sobchak, please.

[Sobchak] Esteemed Nikolay Ivanovich, what is your personal attitude to the proposal that, as of 1 July of this year, the law on the 12th 5-Year Plan and the Law on State Enterprises be brought into line, and that all the directive indicators of the 12th 5-year plan, in accordance with the Law on Enterprises, be declared not binding for enterprises, that is, giving them only guideline significance. And in connection with this, what is your attitude...

[Gorbachev] But that's a second...

[Sobchak] ...toward the idea that—this is the same question—all resolutions of the government and all the departmental acts of ministries and departments which contradict the Law on Enterprises and the Law on Cooperatives be recognized as not to be implemented from 1 July of this year?

[Ryzhkov] On the first question: In my view, today, with 1 and ½ years remaining until the end of the 5-year plan, I do not think it is expedient to adopt such strong, cardinal decisions concerning large changes in the economy. This would lead to very great destabilization in the economy. However difficult it may be, we have to see this 5-year plan through to the end, but in strict accordance with the laws. The second thing: Following the establishment of the Law on State Enterprises and on Cooperatives, a commission was formed which examined all the issues concerning how resolutions of the Central Committee and the Council of Ministers match up to these laws. Three thousand one hundred resolutions of the Central Committee and the Council of Ministers were annulled under the Law on State Enterprises, and, according to our figures, the republics—republican ministries—also annulled about 200,000 normative acts of all kinds. So we don't need it from 1 July; all these resolutions, in as far as they violate the law, have been cancelled. If they do crop up anywhere—they do indeed come up periodically—then we must get rid of them.

[Gorbachev] Comrade (Doga), [words indistinct]

[(Doga)] I would like to hear a reply on what can be expected from one of the models of the cooperative form of management, in the sphere of culture. A situation has now come about where cooperatives have been formed which have made tickets more expensive. Cooperatives are working at stadiums and concerts and sports complexes, the best artists have gone over to cooperative working, and the experienced philharmonic sector is falling apart. That is, the disproportion in social wages—so this is in connection with social justice—is terribly big, and there is thus a lot of antagonism. What is envisaged for this matter?

[Ryzhkov] This is a subject on which I have been criticized from both the right and the left. That is, the first criticism, very harsh criticism, came after 29 December, when the government resolution was issued, and the list was published banning types of activities for cooperatives—and this was in strict accordance with the Law on Cooperatives in which it was written that the Council of Ministers may adopt such decisions. We reckoned that alongside harmful production lines and so on, we had to have a very considered approach to the ideological sphere in our society. Precisely the ideological sphere. This aroused very great criticism. Our opinion is that we should not give ideology away into any hands, we must not. We must conduct ideological work, in our spirit, in the spirit of our values, directed precisely towards having a society in accordance with our socialist system. And so this very big dispute arose. We believe that the cooperative movement, in the ideological sphere—that is, in the press, and in concert work, too—should be implemented under the aegis of definite state bodies.

[Gorbachev] We'll let a lady speak, out of turn.

[Unidentified speaker] Nikolay Ivanovich, [words indistinct] my question. What [words indistinct] changes concerning rural areas and their workers do you see in the coming years?

[Gorbachev] This is on the rural areas, is it?

[Ryzkhov] I see real ways in the countryside. However, what was said at the March plenum—that is, of course, the development of economic relations, the further improvement of the material base—a great deal still has to be done there. But I see the main thing as the solution of the social problems of the countryside—that is housing, roads, culture, social amenities, and so on. In my opinion, the future government, well, especially in the forthcoming 5-year plan period, will have to give priority to the development of that question. Thank you.

[Unidentified speaker] Nikolay Ivanovich, do you intend to transfer ministries over to financial autonomy and thus to hand over power to enterprises and territories? And in connection with this, don't you consider the Kuzbass a zone of ecological crisis?

[Ryzhkov] I think that there is no need to transfer ministries over to financial autonomy. They are, all the same, bodies of state government. But some things are beginning to stir in these matters. Ministerial sectors are posing the question of leaving the ministries and setting up definite economic formations—associations and so forth. I consider this the correct path. It will advance. It will enable us to gradually reduce the number of ministries.

As far as the Kuzbass is concerned, I would not like to give any formula just now. It is much too crucial a business and, as they say, things must be thought out thoroughly. But I was in the Kuzbass recently and I have to say that there are most enormous problems there, most enormous problems. They must be resolved. One cannot live as the miners do in these rayons—Prokopyevskiy, (Kiselevskiy), and so on. Decisions must be made. Comrade Schadov [Minister of the USSR Coal Industry] is currently drawing up proposals to radically rectify the situation.

[?Gorbachev] Go ahead, please.

[Manko] Manko, Dushanbe City. Is the housing program up to the year 2000 borne out by material resources? Or does it only determine our need for housing? The felling of timber will increase with the two- to three-fold increase in housing construction. Won't that harm the ecology? And what measurs are being taken in our country to replace timber with other construction materials?

[Gorbachev] But, strictly speaking, just one question.... [bustle in hall; indistinct voices]

[Ryzhkov] Well, you know that in his report, Mikhail Sergeyevich said that we had recently increased housing construction by 15 percent. We regard this as one of the positive aspects of our country's activity. However, many problems were exacerbated immediately, including the problem of construction materials, furniture, and so on. We believe that the construction industry must be developed to a maximum now. Above all, that of course concerns the union republics to which, as they say, all these problems have been handed over. There are advances, but they are insufficient. As far as the forest is concerned, we are all sorry about the forest. Other forms of construction materials must be developed if we are not to fell trees, but there is something else: chemicals—but there are a whole lot of problems with chemicals, too. We believe that the chemicals industry must be developed to a maximum, for this would allow us to resolve both the question of consumer goods and many construction questions.

[?Gorbachev] Go ahead please, the fifth microphone.

[Engver] Nikolay Ivanovich, I am deputy Engver, constituency 658 of Izhevsk, Udmurt ASSR. In the election platforms of many deputies, including mine, there was the question of strict deputy control over the budget and over the appointment of the minister of finances and the chairman of the State Prices Committee. How do you feel about ministers accounting down to the last kopeck for the budgetary funds that the Supreme Soviet and the government allow them to spend? And will you take account of the will of the deputies in personal appointments of the minister of finance and the chairman of the State Prices Committee? Thank you.

[Ryzhkov] I'll start from the end. Concerning the appointment of ministers, and the minister of finance in particular. In accordance with the constitution, the new government, or the new chairman of the Council of Ministers, submits proposals for the structure of the government and the people who make it up. As far as we understand it, in contrast with the previous practice, there will now be, as they say, a very thorough examination of every candidacy in the committees, in the commissions, and evidently in the chambers of the Supreme Soviet. Evidently there will be a constructive dialogue. If the Supreme Soviet does not endorse some minister, then the chairman of the Council of Ministers can only go along with it. If, though, he is convinced that the minister can fulfil his functions, he has to prove to the deputies that that is the case. That is the only way, I think. As for the budget, comrades, it is clear that the situation wil change drastically compared to what has gone before. Of course we do not have the practical experience at the moment. We think that the draft plan, for instance, for up to 1990, including the budget, which is the chief component of he plan, wil be presented to the Supreme Soviet; the Supreme Soviet will study it—that is, the Planning and Budget Commission, as far as I understand it, will evidently be at the head of it, the coordinating body in this case, and the Supreme Soviet will endorse this budget. Then the endorsed budget will emerge and will serve as the foundation and, that is, the

letter of the law for the executive power. That is how I see it. But we must examine the budget thoroughly, as they say, and adopt specific decisions, on where to direct these or those funds.

[Gorbachev] Comrade Kugultinov. I am going according to the microphones, from one to six.

[Kugultinov] My question: The idea of the Volga-Chogray canal was linked to a transfer of the northern waters the northern rivers. They have given up that idea, but the 70 km of the Volga-Chogray has already been dug, without sufficient planning and survey documentation, approximately R100 million has been squandered, and, as in open-heart surgery, they have opened up the chest and left it. Will this open chest be left long to heal over by wind and sand?

[Gorbachev] Sit down please, Comrade Kugultinov.

[Ryzhkov] I do not think I need dwell in detail on the problem of Volga-Chogray. As far as I know, Central Television showed the session of the Presidium of the Council of Ministers which examined this problem, and the government adopted a decision to halt the construction of this canal. But we looked very carefully at all the proposals and comments, and most importantly, we sensed the pain of the Kalmyk people and of several areas in Stavropol Kray where people, as they say, are living without water, and we believe that these questions, the questions of water supply to these two regions, must be resolved. So a decision has been adopted to halt the construction of this canal, and we have instructed our country's leading scientists to provide an alternative by this fall on how to resolve these matters. We feel that it would be impermissible to leave both the people of Kalmyk and some parts of Stavropol Kray for the rest of their lives without somehow resolving the water problem. Let's wait until autumn to see what will happen.

[Gorbachev] Carry on.

[Smirnov] Esteemed Nikolay Ivanovich, I am Deputy Smirnov, Kharkov. Are you yourself prepared for the fact that some branches of our national economy will not only be developing further, but that they will even be considerably reduced? I have in mind the extracting and processing ones.

[Ryzhkov] Yes, I am prepared for this. Such are the realistic conditions of the next 5-year plan. If we start to solve the questions of the social sphere, if we start to increase investments in our rural agro-industrial complex, we shall be obliged to reduce the investments in heavy industry, whether we like it or not. It is our task is to find the correct solution as to how to get by.

[Gorbachev] That's all, that's all. [Word indistinct] at the microphone. Please.

[Orestov] Nikolay Ivanovich! Orestov, Chita Oblast. There is a long-term program for the Far East, Chita Oblast, and the Buryat SSR. What will happen to it in the future? Will the Council of Ministers deal with it?

[Ryzhkov] The Council of Ministers will deal with it. But I think that while we are gathered with you—and I stress this, the Supreme Soviet will now be an active participant in solving all socioeconomic problems of our country, as they say—we must very seriously weigh the reality of the 13th 5-Year Plan, but I think that there is no question about the fact that this program should be carried out.

[Grachev] Deputy Grachev, the town of Saratov. Nikolay Ivanovich, I have the following question for you: We are talking a lot about the independence of enterprises. It is correct, the enterprises should be granted independence. But at the same time, they should be granted independence in the redistribution of profits. I will give the following example: At our enterprise, 15 kopecks are left per 1 ruble of profit. It has already been planned for the year 1990 to earn R25 million of profits and to transfer to the state fund R23 million. What do you think? Is this correct or not? After all, what happens is that the labor collective has earned...

[Gorbachev, interrupting] Here is the same question again. It was already contained in the speeches.

[Ryzhkov] Be the transfers to the state budget as they may, in the future we should carry out transfers not only to the state budget, but also into the local budget. This means that when we change to conditions of self-financing there will be two transfers. They will differ. All depends on the kind, the work of the particular enterprise, as it were. Today it is impossible to provide a common method for transfers for the light industry and say, for the mining industry. Therefore, standard norms should be established in each individual case for each industry. What will they be like? Well, for this, it is necessary to sit around the table and solve it, as they say.

[Gorbachev] If you please.

[Sokolova] Nikolay Ivanovich, Deputy Sokolova, Soviet Women's Committee. The decision of the Council of Ministers on paid maternity leave until the child is 18 months old very much pleased millions of women. We expected this decision to come into force on 1 July. We now know that the date has been moved to 1 December. We are receiving anxious letters from women, asking whether this means that there is a possibility that the dates will be moved even further, or whether this threatens the whole fate of the decision.

[Ryzhkov] No, it does not. Indeed, we moved the date by several months, taking into account this situation. No.

[Unidentified speaker] Territorial district 553. Nikolay Ivanovich, there is double control over industry—the technical control department and state acceptance—at the majority of enterprises, in the technological process of manufacturing goods. This lengthens the technological process and requires additional resources. What is your view of the issue and the state of these affairs?

[Ryzhkov] I have a firm view on the issue. I think that state acceptance is a provisional measure. As soon as economic pressure on the quality of output starts to be felt—and for this, incidentally, we still have many things to finish off and, specifically, all sorts of monopolism—state acceptance will not be necessary, in my view, I believe, and we are now saying that the new government should adopt the following decisions: Collectives that pledge to produce high-quality output should be relieved of state acceptance. But there must be guarantees.

[Gorbachev] Please.

[Abdullayev] I am Abdullayev from Tajikistan. I would like to speak, Nikolay Ivanovich, about health care. For example, in our Republic, the development of health care is sharply lagging behind the growth and development of the population. As a result, many medical establishments are housed in primitive and ill-adapted premises. As a result, a very high rate of mortality among children and mothers is in evidence, along with a sharp and rapid rise in the incidence of contagious diseases. What are the plans for developing these spheres?

[Ryzhkov] Well, we are aware that you are in a very difficult and complex situation. Comrade Albert Anatolyevich Likhanov, who spoke at the Congress, mentioned this, and we regard this matter with great sympathy. We think that we should allocate more material and financial resources for health care—and, incidentally, this has already been done in this 5-year plan—and we think that we should substantially improve the situation in the coming 5-year plan with regard to the construction of hospitals and clinics, and especially the production of medicines, which have been in a very short supply in our country.

[Gorbachev] Next, please.

[Veyser] Veyser, deputy from the Komsomol. Nikolay Ivanovich, certain prominent economists see a large foreign loan as a way of taking our country out of the severe economic crisis. What is your view, as head of government, of this proposal?

[Ryzhkov] Yes, I know this view which consists of the following: To overcome the situation today, one should take major loans and solve, for instance, today's issues of removing social tension at the consumer market. Thinking in terms of today—and it would be just right for me to do this before today's conference, I mean, appointment—in general, one could opt for this move. But thinking about what we will have tomorrow, the day after tomorrow, or in some years, then I think that to incur such debts today would be politically wrong, in general, and very very dangerous. If I am to make a political statement today, I will try to answer this question. [applause]

[Matyukhin] Esteemed Nikolay Ivanovich, National Territorial Constituency No 6, Gorkiy town, Matyukhin. At the present time a program for the modernization of railway transport has been worked out. What is your point of view concerning your future as Chairman of the Council of Ministers if you are elected today? Thank you.

[Ryzhkov] Yes, such a program hass been worked out. We know that an enormous number of problems have piled up on railway transport, just as in other branches of the national economy, which cannot be ignored. We believe that this program must be examined in the autumn, or at least, around the autumn, when the positions with regard to the 13th 5-Year Plan have been finally formulated. We must, of course, conduct a thorough examination, and I am in favor of tackling these issues thoroughly.

[Gorbachev] Nikolay Ivanovich, thank you. It is 1130 but, you still have some questions.

[Ryzhkov] There are still some more, are there?

[Gorbachev] No [as heard], but you can have a look at them and then we'll think about them. I think that we'll finish the questions now, as we agreed. Nikolay Ivanovich, thank you. Pass him the questions.

[Ryzhkov] I thank you, comrades, for your attention. I thank you for those very, well, I wouldn't say particularly interesting questions, but at least, vital questions, and I feel that it is our common worry, our common concern, to find ways out of this grave economic situation which we are in so far today. Thank you.

[Gorbachev] Fine. [applause] Comrades, some comrades have sent in notes—I have four here—asking to speak on this question. The first note is from Comrade Druz, Petr Antonovich, from the Kuzbass, his was the first. He writes on behalf of veterans. Is Comrade Druz, Petr Antonovich, here? Please come up. He would like to speak on this question. Let's agree how long; 2-3 minutes: A maximum of 3—I shall act resolutely on this point—2-3 minutes, we're all agreed. Oh? Time for debate? How long; ½ an hour? Then, we'll finish at 1200. Right. We are starting to acquire experience!

[Druz] Esteemed chairman, esteemed members of the Supreme Soviet: For 2 weeks now the Congress of People's Deputies has had a very lively debate on political, economic, social, and moral problems of life in our country. It is laying the foundations for a new structure in which the role of the government is a very great one. The Kuzbass deputies have consulted one another and exchange opinions as to who could head the government in such an acute and crucial period. It is our common opinion that the candidature of Comrade Ryzhkov, Nikolay Ivanovich, put forward by the Party Central Committee, is the most suitable, and I support him. But, this does not mean that I am completely satisfied with the work of the Council of Ministers headed by Comrade Ryzhkov.

I believe that it is first and foremost the government and the ministers—who still hold the levers of centralized government, not the party, which was the initiator of restructuring and determined its concept—which should be answerable for the imbalance in the economy, the general deficit which has developed, the deterioration in the ecological situation and the deterioration in people's living standards. It was the ministers and the Council of Ministers who guided us in restructuring and who showed sluggishness and made miscalculations and errors. During the past elections the fire of criticism was directed mainly at the party, and the arrows of popular discontent rained on the leaders of local party and soviet bodies and industrial enterprises. They were there for the people to see, and they have taken the full blow.

However, the ministers, such as comrades Shchadov and Konarev, who still haven't even imposed order in their own industries and simply ignore party policy on the priority nature of the development of the social sphere of society, and through whose fault an unfavorable situation has developed in the Kuzbass, and in the country as a whole...these ministers themselves escaped the fire of criticism from the electorate. None of them, as you know, was put forward as a people's deputy candidate and they did not have to undergo a severe test by the people. This is grounds for serious thought.

Still, I would like to express my firm conviction that Nikolay Ivanovich Ryzhkov, having heard the kind of mental suffering now and the alarm and hopes for the future which have been expressd by the people's deputies of the congress over all these days, now fully realizes that the country's economic mechanism is not working and that the government must restructure its work and break down in practical terms the bureaucratic management apparatus by means of decentralization, mixed ownership, real financial autonomy, lease-contracting and handing over many functions to the local soviets. [sound of bell]

[Gorbachev] That's all!

[Druz] I think that Comrade Ryzhkov will cope with this job and will prove in practical terms that...

[Gorbachev interrupting] Thank you!

[Druz] ...the people are confident that our government will take restructuring to its logical conclusion. [passage omitted: Komarov from Tuva expresses support for Ryzhkov, disagrees with decisions on Ministry of Construction materials; Miloserdnyy will vote for Ryzhkov but criticizes some recent decisions; Igityan praises Ryzhkov's performance during Armenian earthquake; Trefilov supports Ryzhkov as great professional;

Lubenchenko says many of the reforms have only remained on paper; Ismailov says Ryzhkov is pillar of restructuring and deserves his post, economic shortcomings are the people's fault; Gritsenko Mukhametzyano supports Ryzhkov]

[Gorbachev] Deputy from the Ukraine.

[Unidentified speaker] Esteemed comrades, I know Nikolay Ivanovich from work with his colleagues in the Council of Ministers and I respect him very much. However, fateful questions are being examined here today and I, it must be said, am dispirited by Nikolay Ivanovich's answers to the questions today.

Well, comrades in our country the word "acceleration" has already been forced out of our vocabulary. It has been eroded groundlessly, groundlessly. Well, then, his ideas that the existing laws and existing trends should be preserved in this 5-year plan period and that not even gross output value should be abolished—that can be done immediately and can be done indeed. (?and there is) such a thought whereby Nikolay Ivanovich discussed, let's say, (?not restoring the Aral area), but it can be halted, the process can be rectified. This demonstrates that Nikolay Ivanovich, well, generally speaking, does not put the question in a hard and fast way, is not displaying his will here. And questions may be resolved here, to Nikolay Ivanovich.

It seems to me that generally in our sections we listened to your speech, report. Well, there was no section on the rehabilitation of the state's intellectual capacity. It is missing. A section is probably also missing on the urgent redistribution of financial resources, Nikolay Ivanovich. Further, the next section, you understand, is the strategic system of creating financial resources and the structural economic transformations in our industry. This is what I want to say, comrades: Bearing in mind what Mikhail Sergeyevich really recommends. I in principle, I would have abstained, would have listened, well, to the report, then my criticism would have been expressed, we'd have the concluding words of Nikolay Ivanovich and we, so to speak, would obviously have supported him. But nevertheless, I will now say that I will vote for Nikolay Ivanovich. However, I asked that I be given the floor so that I might express serious criticism of his speech and if possible examine the question of how the Budget Planning Commission could operate seriously. Mikhail Sergeyevich, these are very serious questions. The questions touched upon are really sore ones. They worried me, the answer worried me. Thank you for your attention.

[Gorbachev] Alright, comrades, I.... No, one moment. Well then, as we agreed, the time for discussion has run out. The requests here were mostly not met. Nevertheless, we have done as we agreed. Tell me, may I go on to determine if we will come to a decision now, or if we will continue the discussion? [bustle in hall] What is your answer?

[Saunin] Mikhail Sergeyevich [words indistinct]

[Gorbachev] Me? Go ahead please.

[Saunin] (?This question) is addressed to you and to the rest of the deputies. Saunin, Makeyevka Territorial Constituency No 443, Donetsk Oblast. On the first day, at the start of the Congress, I expressed the thought that a deputy gives the impression of chasing a departing train. We have been elected to the country's supreme Soviet. Do we intend to continue to decide highly imporant questions of state life in this way? I have a suggestion: Let those who do not have the time leave the hall. Why the hasty decisions? We are discussing the candidacy of one of the highest posts of state, the candidacy for the post of chairman of the USSR Council of Ministers. In any civilized country, debates on the government's program last several days. I consider that we have acted incorrectly. Nikolay Ivanovich Ryzhkov's report should have been heard out.

[Gorbachev] Well, we have already decided that question. Do you remember when the agenda was confirmed? It was then we decided

[Saunin] So that is what I am saying. We shouldn't have...

[Gorbachev interrupting] You don't have to speak out against...

[Saunin interrupting] ...shouldn't have decided in haste.

[Gorbachev] You don't have to speak out against that. Well that is your opinion. The congress made that decision. [bustle in hall]

[Saunin] But what is our hurry today? Where are we in a hurry to go to today?

[Gorbachev] You see that I am asking questions, and I want to clear up what we will do: Will we continue, or will we decide the question of the appointment? [bustle in hall]

[Saunin] Mikhail Sergeyevich, I came forward because I already felt the general mood. You set the questions and the general tone. We will finish the discussion on that.

[Gorbachev] Alright.

[Saunin] That is why I want to speak; I have an opinion of my own which differs a bit from that of other speakers.

[Gorbachev] Alright. Comrades, [words indistinct].

[Unidentified speaker] Mikhail Sergeyevich, we women here nevertheless suffered a great defeat at the elections. There is discrimination against women here, too. Men do not make way for women here. [bustle in hall] That is why [words indistinct].

[Gorbachev] The deputy feels that our discussion, its course, excluded the opinion of women, and she asks that to rectify that shortcoming, she be given 2 or 3 minutes to finish on that. Go ahead please, keep going.

[Same unidentified speaker] Much-esteemed deputies, much-esteemed Mikhail Sergeyevich! In my speech, I would first and foremost like to support the nomination of Nikolay Ivanovich Ryzhkov to the post of the chairman of the Presidium of the Supreme...[speaker corrects herself] to the post of chairman of the USSR Council of Ministers. I would like to support this nomination because I hold this man and our leader in high esteem first and foremost for his profound humane qualities, for his understanding of the interests of all stratas of the population, and first and foremost of us, the women. [applause] Still, I would like to turn to him with one question. Nikolay Ivanovich, I beg you, if possible, to respond either at the congress or in the course of your work—but I cannot but put this question to you Nikolay Ivanovich, I would like to know your view on the question of the pricing policy in agriculture and in particular in cotton growing, which is essentially a state monopoly, so to speak, and we are in essence in no way able to influence this policy. But our cotton growers and the entire rural population of our republic, which provides the major part of cotton for the country, 40 percent of whom live below the poverty level, await the solution of this problem. The fate of these people depends on this. All our voters in Uzbekistan expect an answer to this question. I have no time to go on, but in conclusion, I would once again like to give my support to Nikolay Ivanovich's nomination.

[Gorbachev] Thank you. I would like to voice one opinion which will perhaps clarify this situation. We are carrying out these exchanges, the questions and the exchange of views in connection with the appointment. If we appoint Comrade Ryzhkov, he will have to give a report. We handed to him all the questions which he was unable to answer. He will be preparing a report, and the debates will be continued after that, so that quite a few more deputies...[Gorbachev changs thought] a whole day at the congress will still be devoted to the discussion on these points. People will still speak and will still voice their thoughts. This is the first point.

Second: You have undoubtedly detected that the approval of the ministers will get under way after the presentation by the chairman of the Council of Ministers. The approval will evidently stretch over a week or two—half a month—time will tell. This means that at issue will be a serious discussion in the commissions and in the committees of all branches concerning all members of the government during their appointment. Well, the ice has just began to break, as they say. Perhaps this makes it easier to understand the fact that the Supreme Soviet will still be able to have a thorough discussion with the government, so to speak.

And so, comrades, shall we continue the discussion or not? Well, there is one proposal, or—as I understood—two proposals to continue the discussion. Then another comrade said not to continue it, to end on this point, and to commence the issue on the appointment of the chairman. Then there was another proposal to continue the discussion now, today. And what about you, do you also want to make a proposal or do you wish to speak?

[Unidentified speaker] (?I would like to) but I have already sent my notes.

[Gorbachev] Oh yes, I understand. You will find it (?here), I understand.

[Unidentified speaker] These notes should be read out during the discussion of Nikolay Ivanovich's report.

[Gorbachev] Yes, yes, yes....

[Unidentified speaker] And the one who wrote it should be given the floor.

[Gorbachev] Well, you know, the notes are there too...I glanced at Comrade Yemelyanov who so much wants to be registered. If we include these registrations, then we shall include him and the others who were registered at the congress. This evidently coincides with the fact that you were registered there, is it not so, Comrades? So that this question will be discussed. Yes, if you please.

[Unidentified speaker] I share the opinion of many of the deputies here. The presentation of one candidate by you is sufficient. Then specific proposals and observatons on the nomination should follow. Why is everyone taking the floor saying I support him, I support him? Once you take the floor it means that you support him; and if you are against, then stay put. [audience expresses approval] And if you want to voice your view, then you can say right away: I am against. [audience expresses approval] That means we need fewer words describing how good he is! We know from all the newspapers how good he is! But whatever you may have against him, you'd better take the floor and say so! And second, since I am standing up, I would like to put a question to Nikolay Ivanovich: Well, you have already started to say...will the discussion of each minister here at this....

[?Gorbachev, interrupting] I already answered this....

[Speaker] Did you?

[Gorbachev] I did. And it might take a long time.

[Ryzhkov] I said that, according to the Constitution, the chairman of the USSR Council of Ministers, appointed by the Supreme Soviet and approved by the congress, will at one of the sessions after the congress—and this must be assumed immediately—present the government personnel, [personalnyy sostav pravitelstva], the government personnel [Ryzhkov repeats himself] which will be examined, as Mikhail Sergeyevich has said, which will be specifically examined for 10 days, in both chambers, committees, and the Supreme Soviet. Each of them will be examined on an individual basis.

[Gorbachev] Never mind, never mind.

[Unidentified speaker] A remark. A remark, that means 30 seconds. Comrade deputies! I am addressing you all. You know, I can understand that not everyone has gotten used to being members of the Supreme Soviet, and probably there is a leading tone in what many have to say. Let's leave this out, we are the real power, because we want to have the real power. But you come and plead: Esteemed Nikolay Ivanovich, help! Let's solve these matters ourselves, and not be pleading with people!

[Gorbachev] All right. I think that everything that has been heard here is useful. So, there is the first proposal, to restrict the discussion in connection with appointment to the post of chairman of the Council of Ministers to this and get on with voting. Please vote, those in favor of this. Put your cards down. Who is against? Put them down. Against? Shall we count them, or not? It is an overwhelming majority. The question is settled, we'll cut it off. I will put the question to the vote. I have to consult here. [Gorbachev to Lukyanov] We're voting together, yes?

[Lukyanov] Yes, the two chambers make the decision.

[Gorbachev] Good, I will put the question to the vote: Who is in favor of appointing Comrade Ryzhkov, Nikolay Ivanovich, to the chairman of the Council of Ministers of the USSR? Please raise your madates. Please lower them. Who is against against. Count. In total, nine against. Abstentions? Thirty-one abstentions. So Comrade Ryzhkov, Nikolay Ivanovich, has been appointed chairman of the Council of Ministers of the USSR. [applause]

[Ryzhkov] Esteemed people's deputies, I sincerely thank you for the support you have just shown me in appointing me to the post of chairman of the USSR Council of Ministers. I am very well aware of the responsibilities that lie today with the head of the government; I am very well aware of what a complicated time we now live in; but I am very well aware that it is only moving forward that will enable us to solve the urgent tasks that face our society.

I think that the new government which you will confirm will put all its efforts into solving the problems that face our country, the problems that face every Soviet person. This, evidently, will not be an easy path, nor easy work. I am counting on the help of the people's deputies of our country, on the body of deputies, which is radically different today from the old body. I am placing my hopes on the intelligence and wisdom of the deputies, and I am hoping for the great support of our Soviet people, because I shall give all my strength to serving them. Thank you. [applause]

[Gorbachev] We have already adopted decisions on two questions. The first question: We took into consideration the statement of the Council Ministers on the delineation of its powers; we have appointed the chairman of the Council of Ministers. But things are continuing here, and we have a need—as we have done by tradition—before approving the new composition of the government, the new one will continue to carry out its duties. Right, comrades? Thus, our final decision will be this: First, to take cognizance of the statement of the USSR Council of Ministers on the delineation of its powers before the USSR Supreme Soviet; second, to appoint Comrade Ryzhkov, Nikolay Ivanovich, chairman of the USSR Council of Ministers, and to instruct him to present to the USSR Supreme Soviet the proposal on the composition of the USSR Council of Ministers; and third, the USSR Council of Ministers will continue to carry out its duties until the formation by the USSR Supreme Soviet of a new USSR Council of Ministers. That's it. [Gorbachev confers with someone in hall] Before the formation by the Supreme Soviet—this will depend on the Supreme Soviet, what debates are held. Therefore, I put this draft decision to the vote. Members of both chambers vote. Those in favor or adopting this decision please raise your cards. Please lower them. Anyone against? Any abstentions? One against and two abstentions. Fine. We have decided, comrades. Now we have time, we still have 1 hour and 40 minutes in hand. We will now have a 20-minute break, so we have 1 hour and 20 minutes. Then we have to consult on whether we need to continue the agenda—we can then, we will have the time. At this joint session we should have elected the chairman of the USSR People's Control Committee, the chairman of the USSR Supreme Court; appointed the USSR procurator general; appointed the chief state arbiter of the USSR; and formed the committees of the USSR Supreme Soviet on the basis of the debates which have already been held in the chambers.

So, that is the agenda. All questions about elections and appointments except, of course, the committees—these are the questions that must then finally be decided at the congress, both the chairman of the Council of Ministers and these comrades that we must also endorse.

Well, comrades, shall we take a break and deal with these questions?

[Unidentified speaker] Yes.

[Gorbachev] A 15-minute break then. Twenty minutes.

[Unidentified speaker] Twenty.

[Gorbachev] Twenty, excuse me.

Second Joint Session
LD0906081489 Moscow Television Service in Russian 0844 GMT 7 Jun 89

[Relay of second part of joint session of the Soviet of Nationalities and the Soviet of the Union of the USSR Supreme Soviet in the Kremlin—live]

[Excerpts] [Gorbachev] Shall we start, comrades? I hope that you have now acquainted yourselves more closely with the constitution's provisions relating to the activity of the new bodies, the supreme bodies of power and, therefore, do not read anything into the fact that I, in my capacity as chairman, continue to act and make proposals here. According to the Constitution, candidates for the positions I have mentioned are proposed to the USSR Supreme Soviet by the chairman of the USSR Supreme Soviet. About the chairman of the committee of people's control. You remember, perhaps, I spoke about that and touched on these issues at a party group for the purpose of information. This was long ago but I would like to recall. The information given then has already prompted preliminary discussions and some new proposals, so to speak, on this account have already emerged. Currently, Comrade Sergey Iosifovich Manyakin is chairman of the committee of people's control. Comrade Manyakin has asked us to allow him to retire. And in connection with this another candidate, Comrade Gennadiy Vasilyevich Kolbin, has been named. You have the materials, and I can say some words to introduce Comrade Kolbin in this position. We think that he is the right choice, because we are talking about an experienced man both from the point of view of life experience and from the point of view of carrying out important functions within the party and the state. And what I am going to say next is very important: He is a man full of initiative, a progressive man, and a man with strong adherence to principles.

What we know about Comrade Kolbin permits me to assert this, comrades. Comrades know him very well by his activities in Sverdlovsk where he spent a considerable part of his life—he is from Sverdlovsk and I remember that when I met him he was the first secretary of the Nizhniy Tagil City Party Committee. Comrades in Georgia know him, too, as a very open and considerate man, and he was valued there. They were even sad when we took him away. I remember that situation and Eduard Amvrosiyevich [Shevardnadze], at least, conveyed not only his own opinion when he asked whether or not it was possible that we...[changes thought] Comrade Kolbin had good relations and good contact with Georgia's working people and did a lot of useful things with Comrade Shevardnadze there. He worked actively, too, though for a short time, in the Ulyanovsk Oblast Party Committee where matters were very seriously neglected, and he did a lot of useful things there. Precisely that makes it possible, taking account of his life and party experience and of his political and human qualities, to recommend him for the post of first secretary of the Kazakh Communist Party Central Committee. I do not want to anticipate the opinion of the comrades from Kazakhstan, this is something they should tell us, as we should ask all the comrades where Comrade Kolbin has worked, although I have information at my disposal and, based on it, I am putting forward this proposal. But it seems that large-scale and concerted work is now being conducted in Kazakhstan, too.

And the fact that a lot has now been done to turn attention toward caring for people over there, in what relates to the food complex and housing construction—and you know about that, and also the issues of social justice—this fact can be explained, to a great degree, by Comrade Kolbin's principled position. Therefore, I make this proposal with a clear conscience and hope that in this committee, where a man of firm principles is required on the whole, a serious and independent man loyal to restructuring, that Comrade Kolbin's candidacy seems to me to be suitable if judged by such strict criteria. What questions do you have for me or Comrade Kolbin? Please.

[Unidentified deputy] What did you proceed from, primarily, when selecting a candidate for the post of the chairman of the USSR Committee of People's Control? Of course, you are using your constitutional right in accordance with the basic law. When selecting, did you think of an alternative candidate before submitting this one for discussion here or, suppose, at the May plenum?

[Gorbachev] Yes, I did.

[Deputy] Could you tell us what other candidates you considered with Kolbin?

[Gorbachev] You know, when Comrade Manyakin asked to be allowed to retire—he had worked a lot in Siberia, he is a man of merit—well, I had a great deal to think about then, and I proceeded, first of all, from the fact that in that case the question was of an important position indeed, one that pertains to all society, frankly speaking: control. And the people—for the people can have real influence on processes through this organization by taking all of society under its control. Therefore, this question presented itself and it was not a simple one, not a simple one. I did not discuss it with anyone but in my mind I reviewed about 10 or 15 people, those from here, from Moscow, secretaries of the party Central Committee or oblast committees; also we considered the deputy corps and, however, one, Comrade Kolbin, was chosen. Comrades supported me but then we had to talk because it is a question of a secretary of the Kazakh Communist Party Central Committee. We seem to have found mutual understanding both with Comrade Kolbin and with comrades from Kazakhstan, so that is it. This is our opinion.

[Sukhov] I am from district 519, Kharkov.

[Voices] Speak up, please!

[Gorbachev] Comrade Sukhov, come up to the microphone.

[Sukhov] Mikhail Sergeyevich, would Comrade Boris Nikolayevich Yeltsin's candidacy be suitable for your work? This will reflect our people's desires, and if it coincides with your view, I will propose his candidacy. Thank you. [applause]

I must say now that we have discussed these issues with Boris Nikolayevich; they are part of the context of practical processes, as it were, which are in progress. We have talked to Boris Nikolayevich...I have talked with him on this account, proceeding from the fact that he has to engage in the Supreme Soviet's normal activity, so to speak, and for that one needs, so to speak, to make it through the first stage and to eliminate both the wholly understandable uneasiness and say, the arguments and opinions that have emerged around this subject. We have agreed—and I asked Borish Nikolayevich to respond to that and we seem to have understood one another—that he should head a large and important committee for the issues of construction and architecture in the Supreme Soviet. There are huge problems encompassing the whole country, there are many problems involving, in essence, the development of all industries. Many shortcomings have accumulated there; he has experience in that area, he has proposals on that account, and he has already put them forward, and proceeding from that, it is supposed...[Gorbachev changes thought] This is a large committee, and, as a matter of fact, it will maintain links with the whole country, all the commissions, and all the republics. Its stance will have influence on the investment policy to a great degree, and so on and so forth.

That was the preliminary conversation that we had—Boris Nikolayevich, since the situation has emerged—and I asked him to agree to that. Comrade Sukhov, have I answered your question? It is another matter whether or not it coincides with your view, but I have told you about it to let you know. We proceed from the viewpoint that Boris Nikolayevich should engage actively and normally in the Supreme Soviet's work.

Great and new life is beginning, so to speak, in our upper echelon, that is it. But what lies ahead is whether or not we are going to keep that committee. We will examine it when we start electing its chairman. But since the question has been raised, I am speaking about this now, in a preliminary fashion. Next, please.

[(Skakar)] (Skakar), territorial district 291. I have a question for Gennadiy Vasilyevich. We know what sort of events took place in Kazakhstan in 1986. Has everything been good and normal since then to a great degree, or is he himself unprepared to work in the new capacity? What is his opinion?

[Gorbachev] Please.

[Kolbin] Regarding my preparedness to work, a Communist must work and be prepared to work everywhere he has been offered a job, be it small- or large-scale. This is the first thing. Second, about the situation in the republic today: Please, understand me correctly, comrades. In all the events that emerge, such as the 1986 events, or yesterday, one of our deputies raised a question requiring examination. Believe me, I did not generate the events of December 1986, but I had to do a lot to stabilize the atmosphere, to bring people closer together, to do everything to ensure that today people solve questions which unite and not divide them. The solution of such questions as the improvement of food supplies, the improvement of the housing problem and consumer goods, and a whole range of other aspects has contributed greatly to that, too. And if I tell the esteemed comrade deputies that over the 3 years since the 5-year plan started, in Kazakhstan the meat consumption per capita has risen by 10 kilograms, from 58 kilograms to 68 kilograms, then, this is, perhaps, an appreciable and obvious result. This is the first thing; here is the second.

Describing the solution of the housing problem, I would say that today few people practically, or nobody at all, are trying to be put on a waiting list, because in the past 2 years the waiting list has been reduced by 41 percent and over 3 years it will be reduced by 60 percent. In over 5 years people will be given accomodation. This is a program that is in progress and it imbues people with confidence and creates the corresponding mood. The third thing is that I have been working not on my own but with comrades-in-arms, my colleagues from among the Politburo, and I am confident that today each of us can be nominated for work in another area without damage to the cause. As regards work in the committee of people's control, I have not worked within the system, and this can be seen from my curriculum vitae, yet I have been constantly in touch, beginning from my work in the Georgian party organization when, following the 1972 decision on the Tbilisi City Party Committee, I had to work with Comrade Shevardnadze and other party colleagues in the republican party organization. We waged an active struggle against all negative phenomena through the prism of the commission of party control and through the system of those organs. Later, the same work was conducted in Ulyanovsk Oblast and in Kazakhstan, though in every region, this work has its own features and pecularities.

And the last thing. I had a chance to acquaint myself, in quite a lot of detail, with the work of the Union Committee of People's Control some 2 and ½ years ago when I was head of the commission of the Supreme Soviet deputies for checking the effectiveness of the work of the USSR committee with my report at the Supreme Soviet session. Now I manage to follow the course of the work. I can see positive changes in the course of restructuring, in the work of the committee. I can also see to a certain extent a certain desire with respect to improving the activity of this committee. But I am getting the impression that in particular the law on the committee of people's control will have to be changed, taking into account the political reforms that are being conducted and the importance of heightening of the functioning of the status of that big body of the committee of people's control. Many other questions are arising in this respect. This is what I would like to reply.

[Gorbachev] Let's go on. Comrade (Povalenko), you have a question, don't you? Go ahead.

[(Povalenko)] (Povalenko), 243d constituency. Well, there is no need to hide the fact that the influence and authority of the committee of people's control, especially on sport, have declined over the last few years. In my opinion, they could not get any lower. Then we, a group of deputies, approached Mikhail Sergeyevich, and Antoliy Ivanovich, and, as it were, proposed, or perhaps recommended—requested—that Boris Nikolayevich Yeltsin be appointed to that post, knowing that his authority and influence among the masses would help to raise the people's control to the necessary high level. But now since there is no longer any question of that...[changes thought] We have incidentally only heard good things about you in the central press, although we are not personally acquainted with you. Do you have sufficient strength and energy, if we put it like that, to boost the influence of people's control to the necessary high level?

[Kolbin] Well, the formulation of the question is such that I should swear honestly that if I am alive and well I will overcome everything. But the only thing I can say about such assurance is that no matter where I have worked I have given myself to my work from the beginning to the end. It will be just the same here, if you put such trust in me. As far as the effectiveness of the work is concerned, I believe it has to change.

[Gorbachev] Go ahead with you question.

[Unidentified speaker] I would first like to say I did not quite like...[reply is drowned by protesting noises from the audience] Do you have a question or....

[Unidentified speaker, interrupting] Question. I would like to say....

[Gorbachev] Yes.

[Unidentified speaker] A microphone?

[Gorbachev] A microphone, please.

[Podziruk] 9th territorial constituency, Podziruk. The question consists of the following: You said that if a Communist is sent, he should work. But don't you think first and foremost that the competence of a Communist should determine his preparedness for the job? [audience noises]

[Kolbin] Well, you are putting the question approximately like this: Do you understand anything about this matter? This means that if I state that I have gone into all the details, it would probably not be true, since I have not yet entered that office except for the purpose of checking it over, in my time. In this case it would be like you're asking if I think I'm cut out for this? But as far as competence is concerned, that is, as far as raising the

level of the committee's work is concerned, I think that one has to add that restructuring in the committee system is not going ahead sufficiently fast. That is the first thing.

Second, the experience of work abroad by state control committees is not being generalized. There are state committees. In this connection, let's say, I could cite the following example. In England, not a single minister can release a financial document to be issued as orders or a decree until it has ben passed by a representative of the state control committee.

Is he spending money correctly? The picture is just the same in many other countries.

[Gorbachev] But the Supreme Soviet won't let you do that. [laughter]

[Kolbin] But the presidium is also under the supervision of the Supreme Soviet, Mikhail Sergeyevich. But I think it is quite possible to exchange experience with countries abroad regarding questions of the oganization of their control departments. Mikhail Sergeyevich, 150 countries are united, in an association, with conducts exchanges and meets three times a year. I am saying this because there is something useful in other countries, too, which one can arm oneself with and which can help. [passage omitted: deputies query appointment procedure]

[Volkov] I am Volkov from Sverdlovsk. Gennadiy Vas-ilyevich, the issue of social justice is one of the most sore issues of our society. How are you going to solve this issue within the framework of the committee of people's control?

[Kolbin] There are two issues here. Well, to ensure social justice in distribution, one needs to have something to distribute, otherwise there will be no justice at all later. Therefore, it is a question of increasing production in accordance with the constitutional provision, and the committee of people's control should carry it out. As regards social justice, I think that it should be strictly observed regardless of any positions. I understand it is a question of privileges of whether or not it is possible to examine certain things closely, to sort things out and to unseat certain persons, those who, perhaps, are enjoying them unlawfully. I think that there is a very correct proposal in Mikhail Sergeyevich's report to set up a special commission on privileges and to sort everything out.

The authorized privileges should not be regarded as a violation, whereas unauthorized privileges should be regarded as a violation and the corresponding measures and actions should be applied. Regarding some questions that have been asked: I would make no secret, comrades, of the fact that I have reviewed many speeches at the congress, remarks and stenographic reports, and many people put forward such ideas as, for example, to hand over the establishments of the fourth department of the ministry of health to child care institutions, and so on. I think this is within the competence not of people's control but of the commission that will be set up by the congress of people's deputies.

In other words, if you test my strength in issues of social justice, I can say only that I had to deal with this in Georgia for nearly 9 years, 3 years in Ulyanovsk, and now in Kazakhstan. I have said that there are different approaches in different regions. In Kazakhstan we chose the following principle that people should know: We are waging an uncompromising struggle against the organizers of abuse, with full measure of responsibility, but in relation to those whom the organizers, using their positions of seniority, had involved in criminal activity and those involved who had left a little in their pockets and who had given a little to their bosses, we promulgated the following principle: All should voluntarily return what they have misappropriated and then such a measure of punishment will be fixed which will not involve deprivation of freedom if one takes account of the coefficient of families in Kazakhstan. Someone must be around to bring up the children. I must inform you, comrades, that in 1987 alone, without criminal proceedings instituted against them, 17,000 people pleaded guilty and came to state banks where they returned voluntarily R12 billion. I think that we should combine severity in observing social justice with sensible measures aimed at humanism in the conditions of restructuring. [applause] [passage omitted: question on the commission's subordination]

[Gorbachev] Comrade Medvedev, please.

[Medvedev] Well, I must say that I did not quite like the reply by Comrade Kolbin, who is being recommended for the post of chairman of people's control, that the party recommended him and was placing him in this post and that he must bow to the decision of the party. We must, however, make the people's control committee a most independent body which must act primarily at the dictate of conscience, according to state interests and the requirements of the people. And I get the impression that we will not get such independence with such a leader. I would never recommend Boris Nikolayevich Yeltsin as chairman of the USSR Council of Ministers. I think his qualifications for that post are insufficient. We have a ruling party. We have an opposition, and I don't think we need an opposition party. But some element of opposition should be represent in the people's control committee. And, therefore, although I have many complaints about the personality of Boris Nikolayevich Yeltsin—he is too quarrelsome, he too often criticizes that which perhaps should not be criticized—it is the people's control committee which should have such a leader. And, therefore I, too, support the proposal to elect Boris Nikolayevich Yeltsin as chairman of the people's control committee. [passage omitted]

[Gorbachev] Please, you [word indistinct].

[Unidentified speaker] Excuse me, my question is not to Gennadiy Vasilyevich but to you, Mikhail Sergeyevich. It is a general question about the candidates presented to us. Today out of five proposed candidatures—I speak both as deputy and as physician—there were as many as three persons of pensionable age. I think there should be a rejuvenation of the leading bodies. What is your position on this?

[Gorbachev] I do not see any great cause for alarm here. They are all doing tremendous work, they are getting on with their jobs. I do not think there is any problem here. [passage omitted: deputy asks about a successor for Kolbin in Kazakhstan, asks what happened to the money returned by the criminals, cadre appointments]

[Gorbachev] Now let's exchange opinions. Who wants to speak? Go ahead.

[Boykov] Sergey Boykov, National Territorial Constituency No 693. I consider that the canditature of Boris Nikolayevich Yeltsin shoud be included without his consent. Why do I say this? I do not want to be suspicious of anyone. But, nevertheless, we do have such a concept as party discipline. I think you will understand me correctly: I do not say that you put pressure on him or anything, but I think we placed him in a difficult position and we should nevertheless leave this candidate as an alternative.

[Gorbachev] Good. Who wants to be next? Please.

[Voskoboynikov] Deputy Voskoboynikov, Novyy Urengoy Territorial Constituency No 324. I had misgivings about the part of the speech by Gennadiy Vasilyevich in which he said that he agreed to take the post in which the party had placed him. Deputies have repeatedly talked about this. They have spoken about and stressed this point. I will stress the same thing. I consider that given this way of looking at the question and given Gennadiy Vasilyevich's views, he will bow, so to speak, to the decisions of precisely the party bodies. But the committee in our country is nevertheless a people's one. Mention has already been made here of the contradiction. It has been stressed. I want draw attention to this. I cannot trust a person in such a situation. I think that there should really be a person in that position who is capable of clearly expressing his point of view. And I support the the proposals that have been made concerning the candidacy of Boris Nikolayevich Yeltsin.

[Gorbachev] Yes, go ahead.

[(Samsev)] Deputy (Samsev), constituency No 345, Yaroslvavl. I support those comrades who have proposed that Comrade Yeltsin, Boris Nikolayevich, be appointed to this post. I consider that he is a leader with a wealth of political experience and independent attitudes, a leader who has given a good account of himself in the fight against Moscow corruption and the mafia. He is a leader who is very popular among the people:

Virtually the whole of Moscow voted for him. He was nominated in more than 100 constituencies in the union, and we must reckon with that reality. It has already been said repeatedly at the congress that we must give this man sufficient opportunities to display his potential. Involving him in this work will enable him to capitalize on that potential in practice. I think this appointment will be welcomed with gratitude and enthusiasm by many electors in our Soviet Union and in particular by electors in my constituency. Thank you. [applause] [passage omitted: deputy says deputies have no right to nominate]

[Gorbachev] Well, there, the comrades have been explicit. Although they don't claim to be great professors or jurists, although I feel that Comrade Sobchak...[changes thought] In this case, I have invited him here to give a professional opinion and now he has started to maneuver, I see. We must not maneuver. According to the Constitution, proposals on all these posts come from the chairman of the USSR Supreme Soviet. You may accept them or not accept them and send me back to the drawing board to think again and to propose again. These are your rights and mine, the demarcation of rights. And let's not get confused, let's remain firmly on constitutional ground. I don't want to deprive—not that that would ever be easy and it will not happen—that I should try to stop you fulfilling your role. But I ask you to approach my power, too, in that same spirit, with respect. I think I had to give you this explanation, comrades. And that puts no one in a difficult situation, to the contrary, I'm clarifying the situation. That's the first thing.

Now the second. Has my opinion changed or not as a result of the discussion that has taken place here, in respect of my proposal to nominate Comrade Kolbin? It has not changed, comrades. It has not changed. And now the deputy who spoke last—from Azerbaijan or where? [indistinct response] From Uzbekistan, from Uzbekistan, pardon me. He was right. There is a situation, and we have been encountering it recently, in which a person succeeds in expounding his thoughts more literately, in a better form, and in general we should welcome and encourage that gift. If this is additionally combined with a person being able to do things, to perform great and constructive work, to unite people, then that is doubly valuable and very important.

Consequently, I would like to say this. I, too, listened to Gennadiy Vasilyevich's answers. I didn't meddle in the process: You asked him whatever you wanted. Some of the answers were clumsy, and I would simply not have attempted to answer some of the questions had I been in his place, because he still needs to go into these matters carefully. But as such an energetic man, you know, and that's how Kolbin is, he thinks that he should answer everything right away. The comrades earlier, who are sitting over there, I saw how they behaved. In one case it was not clear and there was something they didn't understand well enough; they needed to think it over;

they told you and themselves and others that the thing had to be studied. Gennadiy Vasilyevich wasn't satisfied with that. But that does not detract, comrades, from Comrade Kolbin's chief qualities, his political qualities. His experience, his great industry, his responsiblity. It doesn't detract from the fact that the man works in his style—very accessible to people, close to them, not indifferent to people's lives but quite contrary: He feels things with them.

We have seen him everywhere. Incidentally, in Sverdlovsk I've spoken to the people, and in Georgia I know the opinion, and in Kazakhstan this comrade has been accepted, too. And in Ulyanovsk, too, he was well thought of. So we've seen him at work and he's a man who immediately welcomed the restructuring policy. I'll tell you that at times he's even, so to speak, used go-getter methods. I'll tell you that's no bad thing, either, because so far we're still at the beginning, our restructuring is still at the beginning, and people like him are not stereotyped and are sometimes even challenging. I include Comrade Yeltsin in that category: He doesn't always behave tactfully, not at all, I'd say. That is, he can't be overlooked as a person. The more so in that we have to overcome great obstacles and barriers, and so on. So, comrades, I'll tell you bluntly, I perhaps share the dissatisfaction. And it was because of this dissatisfaction with the answers that the comrades wanted to submit that he is not a suitable candidate. That is their view; I'm not accusing them; I'm just discussing. I'm just discussing. But just the same, as the main criterion for judging whether Comrade Kolbin should or should not be the chairman of the People's Control Committee, I would take his lifelong aggregate, his position today, his political....[changing thought] He's a mature man on whom you can depend; a progressive man, a champion of restructuring, a champion of decisive methods of overcoming and eliminating shortcomings. He has those qualities and I am confident that we can rely on him. I, comrades, ask you, as the man who made this proposal and after the discussion—I don't think it disadvantageous to any of us or to Comrade Kolbin—but I ask you to support my proposal. We, I assure you—I say this sincerely—will not allow mistakes. Don't think I would be very reluctant for you to acquire some measure of distrust toward me. I would be very reluctant for you to acquire some measures of distrust toward me. Well, that is, the chairman of the Supreme Soviet can't just stand here rigidly, and not move either way. No, he can't. The thing is that these proposals are cropping up; it's not just that it's not convenient for me, so I make these proposals. I notified Comrade Kolbin recently. When he was first secretary in Ulyanovsk and first secretary of the Central Committee of the Kazakhstan Communist Party, I became familiar with him and looked at him more closely. I was following affairs there and so I approach the assessment of this proposal especially seriously. That is what I thought I had to tell you. [passage omitted]

[Gorbachev] Allright. Comrade Burlatskiy, please.

[Burlatskiy] Comrade deputies, my name is Burlatskiy. Our parliament is taking its first steps, and we have to be guided by or rather to take into consideration, the experience that we can see in international practice. You know the way in which, for instance, the team is picked in the United States, when the president nominates candidates. Moreover, he always nominates a single candidate. That is his right. And the proposal that someone made here that the issue should be submitted to alternative voting deprives the president of this right. It violates a constitutional principle. This is a quite well-defined presidential practice in any country.

Discussions are another matter. Remarks can be made and different views can be expressed, but all this goes back to the president, if we are calling Mikhail Sergeyevich Gorbachev president and have entrusted him with this role. I should, therefore, like to oppose alternative voting. As far as Comrade Kolbin is concerned, I do not know him very well, although I have followed his biography. When he spoke here he gave me, personally, the impression that he was a humane and decent person. Humane—this is very important in that job. Of course, there are two factors which cause one a little trouble: on is that he is still not very competent in this work, and the other is the age factor. I think that when voting everyone has a right to take these factors into consideration. But I am personally prepared to rely on the view expressed by Mikhail Sergeyevich Gorbachev and to support this viewpoint. [passage omitted]

[Passage omitted] [Gorbachev] Boris Nikolayevich [Yeltsin], please! Boris Nikolayevich has asked to speak. Come closer Boris Nikolayevich.

[Yeltsin] In this situation I must voice my opinion about Gennadiy Vasilyevich. We have known each other since the 1950s, working together for about 20 years. Our paths then separated. Nevertheless, we have continually, I would say, been both comrades and friends. In general, I know him very well. I believe he is a person who, from a political point of view and from the point of view of his experience, his business qualities, his adherence to principle, his attitude toward people, is completely suitable to be entrusted with this post. [applause]

[Gorbachev] Also, comrades, let us wind it up, all right? [indistinct cry from deputies] Well, that is all, now the last speaker.

[passage omitted]

[Gorbachev] All right, the debate is concluded. Before the vote, there was a proposal on how to vote. [loud commotion] I am putting it to a vote. Well, we have it written that only the chairman of the USSR Supreme Soviet is elected by secret vote, and the reminder is at the discretion of the Supreme Soviet. So, since we have proceeded on the premise that we are doing it openly, just as we elected the chairman by open vote, all the same, I have to put the other proposal to the vote, a proposal to hold a secret vote on....[deputies shout out about order of proposals]. Well, yes, as they come, very well. I am taking the amendment. The first proposal is open voting, the second is to have a secret vote. Who is for holding open voting on the election? Put them down. Who is against? Put them down. Abstentions? Well, that is an overwhelming majority for open voting. And so, comrades, I am putting it to a vote. Who is in favor of electing Comrade Kolbin, Gennadiy Vasilyevich? Please vote. Put them down, Please. Who is against? [pause as voters are counted] Well, there have been two tellers, Comrades Lukyanov and Nishanov. Thirty-four have been counted against. Please, those against put down [your cards]. Who abstains? You comrades that have raised passes, are you members of the Supreme Soviet or guests? Members? Have you forgotten your cards? Very well, let this be a reminder to you! [Lukyanov tells him "53"] Fifty- three? Thus, comrades, of 509 present, 34 have voted against and 53 have abstained. Comrade Kolbin is elected chairman of the People's Control Committee. [applause] [passage omitted]

[Gorbachev] Comrades, I think we should now have an interval until 1600. when the congress will resume, the congress. Thank you.

[Moscow Domestic Service in Russian at 0840 GMT on 7 June in a similar report adds:]

[Gorbachev] A group of deputies has been to Chelyabinsk Oblast, to the disaster site. They regard it as their duty to report to you on their visit in 3 minutes. Please forgive me, my mistake. Comrades, the report by Comrade Ryzhkov is to come next, and we just will not get around to this otherwise. And we now have the full Supreme Soviet in session; everything is switched on and the information will be conveyed to the people.

[Naumov] Esteemed comrades, people's deputies, and members of the Supreme Soviet: We, representatives of the delegation of USSR people's deputies from Chelyabinsk Oblast—three of us, Aleksandr Nikolayevich Penyagin, Andrey Vladimirovich Logeyko, and I, Sergey Yakovlevich Naumov—went home to the city of Chelyabinsk on 5 June on the instructions of our delegation because we considered it necessary to be on a spot and to see what happened there, in a purely human way. [passage omitted] Esteemed comrade people's deputies, the state commission to eliminate the consequences of the accident is doing its work. It is unquestionable, there is no doubt, that the true causes of this tragedy will be established. But there is a grave question that must be asked. Why is it that in recent years our country has been shaken by terrible blows, why has our country been grieving? The reply could be that what is to blame is the frequently irresponsible attitude—as Mikhail Sergeyevich said on 5 June—the frequently irresponsible attitude of individual officials toward their official duties, their lax attitudes and irresponsibility. And I call on you all, comrade people's deputies, at your places of work and in your production areas, in the fulfillment of your official duties, to step up accountability and exactingness. I am completely convinced that the success of restructuring will only be ensured by the strictest exactingness, discipline, and order in each and every place. And then we will not have days of mourning.

[Gorbachev] Comrades, allow me to thank the deputies for their initiative in acting in this very humane way, to acknowledge what they have reported, and to ask Nikolay Ivanovich to give immediate instructions for everything necessary to be done on the specific matters to do with saving lives. I think that it will be done. [speaking to a deputy who wants to speak] Go ahead.

[Unidentified deputy] Please excuse me. I don't want to say many thanks to the comrades who went there, but I want to dispute the point they made, the call for officials to be called to account. Comrades, we cannot base either the security of our country or the safety of our people on the question of whether this or that person is responsible. At the end of the day we are all human. Everyone's health has to be considered, everyone has a nervous system. There is a technical term, foolproof [previous word in english]. We as a legislative body must take all possible measures to foolproof all systems that could be a threat to people's health and the security of our country. This is what we were talking about from the very first day, procedures and standing orders. In other words, we must think through every system, both in our Supreme Soviet and at the congress, in order to make things foolproof. We must not have to rely on the good will, the state of health, the honesty, and the reliability of individuals. That is my appeal to you.

[Gorbachev] An interval until 1600 is declared.]

Gorbachev Defines 8-10 Jun Agenda for Congress
PM0906143589 Moscow IZVESTIYA in Russian
9 Jun 89 Morning Edition p 8

[Stenographic Report: "Congress of USSR People's Deputies. Eleventh Sitting"]

[Text] The Kremlin Palace of Congresses. 7 June 1989. 1600.

M.S. Gorbachev, chairman of the USSR Supreme Soviet, is in the chair.

M.S. Gorbachev: Esteemed comrade deputies! Let the work of the congress continue. Before we tackle the questions on the agenda I should like, on behalf of the Presidium, to inform the Congress about the situation in Uzbekistan, how it is shaping up and developing, and what state it is in.

The situation at the moment is complex. The government commission set up in the republic under the leadership of Comrade Kadyrov, chairman of the Council of Ministers, involving all local and republic organs and with the help of the country's administrative organs,

is at work. Much explanatory work is being done, measures are being taken within the sphere of the administrative organs to safeguard people's security and to maintain public order. Nevertheless, one way or another, this situation erupts in one place or another and is accompanied by clashes which lead to injuries or deaths. Instances of arson, though fewer, are continuing. In any event, even though the situation is under control, it has still not acquired a stable character and is not changing resolutely for the better. This worries us all very much, of course. This is yet another signal that we must be patient, restrained, and attentive and that we must show responsibility for our actions and for the situation in the country and in all the regions... Especially with regard to interethnic relations. I should like to invite you all once more on behalf of the Congress to issue to Uzbekistan's working people a fervent appeal to remain composed and calm, and most important of all to do everything necessary to ensure that these events do not get out of control, that the section of the population which, one way or another, and I must say this, is now being incited to extreme methods and using firearms in the process, that the situation is taken firmly in hand and these people are stopped [sentence as published]. We hope that the republic and working people have sufficient strength and that they heed our appeal. In turn, I think, we should issue an instruction that the law enforcement organs of the Soviet Union in cooperation with the republic commission and the republic's working people should do everything to protect people's lives so that they are not threatened by the extremist manifestations that are taking place there.

I believe that working people in all republics will hear us and will align themselves with the Congress and these words of the appeal of the first Congress of People's Deputies. If you share this concern, and I am sure that you do, I would ask you to support this appeal and the instruction which we are issuing here by raising your mandate cards.

Please lower them. That is agreed. We will keep the Congress informed of events.

Comrades, the first sittings of the USSR Supreme Soviet and its chambers have been held and have resolved the main organizational questions: The chairmen of the chambers have been elected, the standing commissions have been formed, and opinions have been exchanged on the committees common to both chambers. This still has to be definitively resolved at the joint sittings. Nevertheless, the work in this direction goes on. At the joint sitting of the Soviet of the Union and the Soviet of Nationalities today the Chairman of the USSR Council of Ministers was appointed and the chairman of the People's Control Committee was elected.

The USSR Supreme Soviet has appointed Comrade Nikolay Ivanovich Ryzhkov as Chairman of the USSR Council of Ministers. (Applause)

Comrade Kolbin has been elected chairman of the USSR People's Control Committee. (Applause)

I give the floor to Deputy Nikolay Ivanovich Ryzhkov for the report on the forthcoming activity of the USSR Government.

From the floor. (Inaudible)

M.S. Gorbachev. He will speak, then ask your question. The discussion will continue... And I intend to speak again.

(N.I. Ryzhkov's report is published on pages 1, 2, and 3).

M.S. Gorbachev. Comrades, at the stage that we have reached in the work of our Congress we need to consult with one another. We in the Presidium have exchanged opinions and want to convey our thoughts to you. We would like to end the sitting of the Congress at this point now and resume the joint sitting of the Supreme Soviet chambers at 1800 hours. There are impassioned and very meaningful discussions there, too. That is the first point, that is for today. As for subsequent days, I would ask you, dear comrades, to listen to how we in the Presidium see the situation and how we propose proceeding subsequently.

Tomorrow, Thursday June 8—debates on the question of the basic guidelines of the USSR's domestic and foreign policy and the program of the USSR Government's forthcoming activity. This is my answer to the question which arose before the report. We shall work from 1000 hours to 1400 hours. At 1400 hours we shall have a recess and we in the Presidium are going to discuss the list of questions for inclusion on the agenda under the heading "any other business." This can be done right now because many questions which were proposed for discussion in this section at some point are already being resolved and are even being reflected in the main decision—the draft decision. It is our intention, and the Commission which we created together is working toward that, to issue before the sitting a draft resolution "On the basic guidelines of domestic and foreign policy" so that deputies have the time to work on them thoroughly.

After that, the evening session will examine the question of the confirmation of the Chairman of the Council of Ministers, the election of the Constitutional Oversight Committee, the confirmation of the chairman of the USSR People's Control Committee, the chairman of the USSR Supreme Court, the USSR Prosecutor General, and the Chief State Arbiter.

Day 13. Friday, June 9. The morning sitting—the debates continue. But the debates will end, too, and the Congress resolution will be adopted. That is all from 1000 hours to 1400 hours. The adoption of the Congress resolution "On the basic guidelines of the domestic and foreign policy of the USSR" and the adoption of the Congress resolution "On the formation of the Constitutional Commission." The evening sitting's agenda: items under "any other business." And the Congress will finish work on Friday evening.

For the Supreme Soviet: The second sitting of the Soviet of the Union is to be held from 1000 hours, 10 June, at which the deputy chairman of the Soviet of the Union will be elected (both chairmen of the chambers are presently working with deputies to prepare proposals). The election of standing commissions of the Soviet of the Union. Examination of proposals on the composition of the committees of the USSR Supreme Soviet. At 1300 hours there will be the second sitting of the Soviet of Nationalities. The same agenda. And at 1600 hours the second joint sitting of the chambers. The agenda as follows: Election of committees of the USSR Supreme Soviet, examination of the proposals of the chairman of the USSR Council of Ministers on the composition of the USSR Government and also of proposals on the composition of the USSR People's Control Committee, the USSR Supreme Court, and the collegium of the Prosecutor's Office. These proposals are just being submitted now, but subsequently, as we have already said today, to examine these proposals in the Supreme Soviet deputies will clearly need a couple of weeks, because it is necessary to meet with everyone in all the commissions, to get to know one another, to elucidate everything, and to produce a conclusion in order to reach a decision. After the second joint sitting of the chambers, where these proposals will be heard, a recess is declared in the work of the Supreme Soviet until 20 June this year. That will be on 10 June, that is to say, for 10 days.

A.I. Lukyanov: But the commissions will be working.

M.S. Gorbachev: They will. These are the proposals. Can we take them as our basis?

Deputies: We can.

M.S. Gorbachev: Do you need to be given time to consider this or can we adopt it right now? And if something arises in the meantime will we introduce modifications at the congress? You need to think about it?

From the hall: Yes.

M.S. Gorbachev: Perhaps we'll resolve it this way, comrades, if it is acceptable? I propose that this be accepted as the basis. Comrades can think about it and if they have any substantive proposals, they will send them to the presidium.

From the hall: (inaudible).

M.S. Gorbachev: No, discussion will continue, Andrey Dmitriyevich, discussion will go on. This is the framework of our work.

From the hall: (inaudible).

M.S. Gorbachev: But, you know, as far as "any other business" is concerned, we will be working in the presidium tomorrow and report to you. The point is that many questions have been submitted under "any other business," but we have already set up commissions on three of them, the most important ones. And a number of others questions remain: On Standing Orders, and several others which are being submitted. The Presidium will submit these proposals for your discussion. I have only set out the framework here, and as far as "any other business" is concerned there will be another separate proposal on this question.

Who is in favor of adopting these proposals as the basis? Please vote.

Please lower your hands.

Against?

Lower your hands, please.

Abstentions?

Carried. Well, comrades, this basis will give us the opportunity to work and creatively approach and consider possible serious, cogent proposals. Okay?

From the hall: Yes?

M.S. Gorbachev: Fine. A recess in the Congress work is declared until 1000 hours tomorrow. The Supreme Soviet sitting starts here, where we have been working, at 1800 hours.

8 Jun Congress Proceedings Reported

Shmelev Urges Draconian Measures
PM0906131189 Moscow PRAVDA in Russian
9 Jun 89 Second Edition p 2

[Speech delivered by N.P. Shmelev (from the USSR Academy of Sciences) at the 8 June morning session of the Congress of USSR People's Deputies]

[Text] I want to start by saying that as an economist I am not greatly worried about our long-term development prospects. I believe that we are not as a nation and as a country about to commit suicide and, having tried in our history every conceivable and inconceivable means of organizing economic life, we cannot fail to take the road which Vladimir Ilich Lenin determined in the twenties, in the last 2 years of his life, and formulated as one of his fundamental ideas. Strictly speaking, throughout our 70-year history we have only had 7-8 years of a really effective economy and we simply cannot fail to return to that path—we have no alternative. But it takes time to do this. Some 8-10 years on average are needed in the

West to turn a bankrupt nonviable firm into a flourishing concern once again. Of course, much longer periods are needed for such an enormous economic mechanism as the Soviet economy.

But I am very concerned by our short-term prospects. I have decided to voice my misgivings here: If we do not stop our snowballing inflation, the decline in the consumer market, and our monstrous budget deficit—which constitutes a world record (in relation to our gross national product)—we may within 2-3 years suffer economic collapse.

What is in store for us in that case? The script for this train of events was written 200 years ago at the time of the French Revolution. It repeated itself on several occasions later in history and we are repeating it with the same consistency as before. We are faced with the prospect of a universal rationing system, a drastic depreciation of the ruble, the wild rampage of the black market and the shadow economy, the collapse of the consumer market, and an enforced—I stress, enforced—return for some time to rigid administrative-edict discipline in our national economy.

After Nikolay Ivanovich Ryzhkov's report I saw once again that the government and the country's leadership realize that we are faced with this danger. But I have grave doubts as to whether they realize how acute this danger is. The Council of Ministers has mapped out measures to even out the market and reduce the budget deficit but, in my opinion, these steps are insufficient and too protracted in terms of time. Whereas our budget deficit is somewhere in the region of R100 billion plus, the austerity measures this year and next year will reduce it by less than R30 billion and barely more than R30 billion respectively. The remainder will once again be obtained by printing money and take the form of enforced loans from our savings bank depositors and our enterprises. I am afraid that our economy will not withstand such a gigantic mass of new money in addition to what we already have.

Why has this situation developed? The popular explanation is that the rapid increase in wages is to blame for everything. That is unjust. We saw yesterday from the report that wages have increased R14 billion in the last year while the budget deficit has topped R100 billion. Moreover, comrades, whether we like it or not, irrespective of our conditions, our specific conditions, a great historical process has started up. Our country has the highest level of work force exploitation of all industrial countries. We spend approximately 37-28 percent of our GNP on wages, while in industrial countries this figure is more than 70 percent. Our working class has a moral right to increase its share of our GNP and it is setting about resolving this task. This must be reckoned with in the future and this process cannot be halted. The second popular explanation that we have also heard here from the Congress platform is that cooperative workers are to blame for everything and are turning money on paper [beznalichnyy] into ready [nalichnyy] cash. That is quite an ignorant explanation. The population's income in our country is somewhere in the region of R430 billion per year. All the income that cooperative workers pay out on wages totals approximately R2 billion, of which more than R1 billion simply involves the redistribution of existing money. Thus, cooperative workers are less than 0.25 percent to blame for the operation of our printing presses.

What has brought about this situation? Nikolay Ivanovich Ryzhkov yesterday rightly spoke about the grave legacy we inherited. That is true. We inherited the traditional factors of the budget deficit and they have been preserved to this day. But one cannot overlook the situation whereby the budget deficit was R20 billion on average during the three 5-year periods referred to by our premier, whereas it now exceeds R100 billion. This constitutes an altogether new quality and new reasons, reasons that have arisen in the last 3-4 years, and I would like to point out the main ones. First, something that has already been mentioned here on several occasions, the totally incompetent action regarding the sale of alcohol. This was a noble action but, as the saying goes, naivety is often worse than a theft. With our good intentions we have inflicted tremendous damage on market equilibrium and the equilibrium of the budget deficit. Our second mistake was the shortlived but extremely painful campaign of 1986 to combat so-called unearned income, which hit our agriculture hard. The third mistake, which we could also have avoided committing, was forced on us by the fall in oil prices, a sharp fall in oil prices, and our enforced reduction in imports. But we preferred not to reduce grain imports nor imports of machinery and equipment—we slashed what we most needed, something that shored up our state budget. We slashed imports of consumer goods, where the budget received an income of R8-10 for every ruble's worth of hard currency spent on imports and—given the requisite sensible import structure—this could have been raised still further. Lastly, there was our our last mistake, which I am unable to explain by any reasonable arguments. Whereas last year our budget deficit was somewhere in the region of R50-60 billion, this year it has soared to R100 billion plus. Our capital investments have soared at the same time. Where has this money come from? So, the government from the very outset set about covering all this expenditure by printing money. There was no other source for this increase in capital investments. This was a deliberate inflationary step.

Of course, I do not envy Nikolay Ivanovich Ryzhkov's position: He is being hard pressed by some not very competent ministers, who see gold stars looming vaguely before their eyes, and in these cases, as the saying goes, grab everything they can with both hands. But do we have a central authority or not? Could Nikolay Ivanovich and Boris Ivanovich Gostev not have said: No, there is no money, we will not print any more money. I think that they could have said so.

In order to avoid financial catastrophe and a financial crash, we need to restore our economy to health, and this applies, above all, to our financial system. This involves smoothing out the market and evening out the commodity supply and the monetary supply and, above all, eliminating the budget deficit. Why do we need to do this? Above all to boost the living standard of our population—workers, peasants, intelligentsia, and pensioners. If we created a commodity situation in our country whereby everyone could spend their rubles on what they really want, that would involve an increase of approximately 50 percent in the standard of living of all population groups. Second, we need to do this to ensure that the ruble finally begins to operate within the economy so that people want to earn rubles. Third, we need to create a situation where supply exceeds demand so that all the incentives provided within the new economic system and above all the incentive afforded by competition between production workers are brought into play.

How can we improve our financial system and restore it to health? As I understand it, the government is pinning all its hopes on a sharp increase in consumer goods production this year and in 1990. Without going into details, I can say that this envisaged increase is inadequate. It is scarcely sufficient to cover the increase in the money supply. This increase cannot touch the vast sum of available [neotovarennyy] money that has accumulated among the population.

There is also another suggestion—namely, to implement a radical reform of consumer prices. That is a correct idea per se. But in the present situation where the social situation is so tense, I believe that we cannot take the risk of such a step for some time. At least until the market is—albeit only slightly—saturated with goods. It is no coincidence that when polled only one-third of the population agree to reform of retail prices and only on the condition that everything would appear in the stores.

There is one other desperate proposal. The proposal to confiscate surplus money from the population. From this rostrum I would like to appeal to Deputy Viktor Afanasyev, chief editor of PRAVDA. I ask him and his editorial collegium what they were thinking of when they published Chekalin's article, in which PRAVDA openly called for surplus money to be removed from the population. Truly no CIA, no class enemy could do us as much damage as we do to ourselves through our own foolishness, so to speak. Such calls in such a heated situation, when everything is disappearing from the stores and when people, sensing a rise in inflation, are grabbing all they can, is tantamount to adding further fuel to the fire and increasing alarm. It's bad enough having all these shortages of soap, salt, or matches, without PRAVDA—a central organ—whipping up people's feelings (contrary to government assurances, incidentally) by telling them to spend money before it turns into mere scraps of paper. And of what benefit is the confiscation of money (I am not even considering the moral aspect) under present-day conditions? It can fill a hole in the budget for 6 months, and then we'll be back where we were. Not to mention the extent to which this will undermine people's feelings about and confidence in restructuring.

Thus, like it or not, we must resort to normal economic measures in improving our financial situation. We should use not confiscation in whatever form, but those commodity-money relations that currently exist.

I am trying to put forward a program that seems realistic, comrades. If I could beg your indulgence for a couple of minutes, permit me to elucidate. I would warn you straightaway that many people will not like this program and it is hardly likely to win government support.

What measures do I think are needed now? First, a return to a normal trade in liquor. It should not be the militia (they are powerless in this respect) but economic measures that are used to suppress moonshiners who, first, have siphoned off state income, and, second, are undermining our society's entire social stability. I want to turn to the writer Vasiliy Belov in this respect. If I were to call him an ideologue of the Mafia, of the black economy, and rampant speculation, he would probably be terribly offended. But that is exactly the case. Currently, even if one refers to official publications, half of all the liquor in the country (you have this reference material to hand, comrade deputies) is being produced by moonshiners. And this is using sugar alone, not counting hooch made from tomato paste, "taburetovka" [meaning unknown], all kinds of filthy concoctions [tarakanyi zhidkosti—possible reference to line in Anton Chekhov's play "Three Sisters" spoken by the character Solenyy in which he refers something being consumed at a dinner party as being made from roaches (tarakany)], and so forth. We are not drinking any less. That is an illusion. And people don't drink because of rising prices. People drink because of sadness, lies, and having time on their hands. We should seek ways of solving the problems in this area, rather than destroying one source of commodity and budgetary equilibrium in the country.

There is a second factor in equalizing the situation in the market. We now have around R150 billion in "hot" money in the country, according to specialist estimates. This is money waiting for goods to come onto the market, it isn't savings for the future: As soon as goods appear on the shelves, the money materializes to gobble them up. In order to mop up and provide goods for this R150 billion, we need approximately $15 billion in one-shot consumer goods imports. Additionally, for the next 2-3 years, while the economy is in this unbalanced state and while there is fear of a slump, we need artificial—I emphasize, artificial—imports of the order of $5-6 billion a year to maintain a commodity balance. Where will this money come from? Yesterday we heard a very serious report from Nikolay Ivanovich Ryzhkov stating that there is no such money in the country. I make so bold as to claim that the money could be found should the occasion arise.

First: Could the government at some point seriously put it to our collective farm chairmen that if they produce grain and meat above a certain normal level they would be paid in foreign currency with the right to spend that currency where they want? And ours are modest people. I am sure that we do not need to pay them $200 per tonne of grain. Seventy-five dollars would do—they will sell for that. So this is the first source of colossal savings of foreign exchange. The second source is the following: Every year our carryover stocks measured in dollars of uninstalled machines and equipment is around $10 billion. Perhaps we could halt imports of equipment for all our giant projects for 5 or 10 years?

Source three: Here I am regrettably forced to use foreign assessments, we do not publish the figures. It is reasonable to ask whether anyone has ever thought how much our interests in, for instance, Latin America cost us. According to professional U.S. estimates it is $6-8 billion every year. A considerable amount of that in hard currency. And, bafflingly, we spend a considerable proportion of this sum on, for instance, paying four times the going rate for Cuban sugar (compared with the world price), and we pay in hard currency. This source alone would be enough to keep the consumer market in balance for the few years we need in order to turn ourselves around somehow and really embark on the road of reform.

Finally, loans: Nikolay Ivanovich says that he does not want to leave his grandchildren any debts. I can understand him, but there is nevertheless something provincial in this. Nowadays the whole world borrows with one hand while giving with the other. Everyone lives in debt, so to speak. And if we borrow some sum (less than the debt which now hangs over us, but, if we again utilize Western sources [of data], a net debt somewhere in the region of $30 billion hangs over us), nothing dreadful will happen. How do you pay it back? If you are talking in business terms (every financier will understand me), no one pays back nowadays. You do not have to. It is necessary only to sustain the payment of interest, and to service the additionally borrowed money any of the the three sources previously mentioned by me will suffice. These are, I repeat, the reduction in the import of agricultural produce, the reduction in the import of heavy equipment, and cuts in our expenditure on international commitments.

Next, we need, if we are thinking about smoothing out the market, to make up our mind to sell land or at least make it available on perpetual lease to anyone who wants. This constitutes an enormous money-generating source. We need to make up our minds not just to talk about but to actually right now sell apartments, sell trucks, sell tractors, sell everything that lies in stock. Let the state sell all it can to equilibrate the market. And, finally, a factor like share ownership, shares and a high-yielding 30-year government bond (normalnyy zaem). This would also tie up a substantial part of the population's unstable money.

But what I would like to stress again is that the funds which we can obtain from the increased import of consumer goods—this money needs to be disposed of, written off. Only then will we obtain excess of supply over demand and a situation which will enable us to switch to normal economic conditions and normal competition. One can and must remove surplus money from enterprises and also write that off and dispose of it. How? Through auctions. By all means, sell a car to your neighbor, if he wants it, at 10 times the price, but then you put half that selling price into the budget, and the budget will dispose of that money. And, of course, there are state loans: Idle money, money not converted into goods in the possession of enterprises can also be brought into the stable state structure by selling high-yielding state bonds to the enterprises.

We have already talked here about other means of reducing our expenditure. Of course it is necessary to reduce production capital investments. I, for example, was gratified to hear yesterday that we will, thank god, at last be increasing pensions. But does anyone even realize that if we stopped just one of the "projects of the century"—the Tyumen project—that the money would suffice to increase pensions and increase payments to all the disadvantaged strata of our population this very year? And how many such "Tyumen projects" are we still implementing now or just on the point of planning to do? It has to be understood that the state is ruined and that there can be no "communism construction projects" for the next 10 years and that we can construct only that which produces a rapid consumer impact. No "communism construction projects"! And I think that banks should also curb enterprises' capital investments through increased interest rates.

Defense spending has already been mentioned here, too. There is another factor—a very sensitive one. I do not know whether our agrarian workers will support me or not. Of course, our agriculture needs extra injections of state resources, it needs support. But we have thought up the most inefficient and most absurd form of state aid to agriculture whereby we pay the good worker R1 per kg of output but pay R2 per kg to the worker who couldn't care less. This must be stopped. And this expenditure is no trifle, it represents almost one-third of the state budget deficit. This kind of expenditure must be terminated as quickly as possible. I do not mean to say that we should put a brake on the economic reform for 3 years while we ameliorate and restore our financial position to health. No, both the improvement and the reform must proceed in parallel. But the most urgent thing now is not the long term, the most urgent thing is the immediate future. In that connection I am going to submit several proposals.

First of all, it seems to me that the budget is such an important and urgent matter that when we meet in October or November the adoption of the budget must be within the competence of the Congress of People's Deputies.

The second point. Nikolay Ivanovich Ryzhkov promises to eliminate the budget deficit some time in the mid-nineties. I believe that this date can and must be brought forward. It is unrealistic to do it this year, of course. But if we take draconian, radical measures for next year we can reduce the deficit to at least the level which was usual in our country for 15 years—around R10 billion to R20 billion, for example—unlike the colossal figure which exists now. Therefore, I propose: That the Congress' recommendations should envisage the elimination or fundamental reduction of the budget deficit not at the end of the next 5-year plan but in 1991.

Furthermore, so that we can understand where we are, what is happening to us, and the position that the state is in, I believe it is absolutely necessary to publish the real scale of the state debt. For many years we took hidden loans from the population and from enterprises. The state debt is enormous but we do not acknowledge it. We must know the true picture of how much the state has taken, how much it owes to the population now including the amounts taken from savings banks and from enterprises' savings. Just as it is absolutely essential to publish our foreign debt and our balance of payments. At the moment we are all guessing, groping our way along, but do not fully know the real situation.

And, finally, one last idea and there I shall stop, the last proposal. The country's Central Bank cannot be in the position in which it finds itself now—the role of a department of the Ministry of Finance or of the Council of Ministers. In the prevailing situation the Central Bank must take the whole problem of money issue and inflation into its own hands. In all normal states the Central Bank is as independent as the Supreme arbiter or Constitutional oversight. The President of the Central Bank must not be subordinate to anyone, including Nikolay Ivanovich Ryzhkov, he must be subordinate to the Congress alone.

Gumbaridze Addresses Congress

LD0906033389 Moscow Television Service in Russian 0843 GMT 8 Jun 89

[Speech by Givi Grigoryevich Gumbaridze, first secretary of the Georgian Communist Party Central Committee, to the Congress of People's Deputies at the Kremlin Palace of Congresses—live]

[Text] Esteemed comrade deputies, our dialogue with each other is first and foremost an open conversation with the people and the country. The value of the uttered word has probably never before been so high. As I think about this I constantly see the faces of my fellow countrymen, for whom everything that is said from this platform is not simply direct speech but is a matter of their dignity and honor, of their hopes and faith in the future. The atmosphere of our congress in many ways reflects the complex and sometimes contradictory picture of the state of our society. We gathered here to discuss the immediate and long-term prospects of the domestic and foreign policy of the country, and the constructive program presented by the government. That means that we gathered to determine the most rational methods for our movement forward, so that the anomalies of the economy, in social and spiritual life, demography, ecology, relations between nationalities, and matters of the political, legal and cultural sovereignty of nations do not become insurmountable obstacles in the path of restructuring. They are all making themselves felt in the life of Georgia as well. I have something to say about them and I intended to do so, but the content of preceding discussions and the political situation in the republic force me to review and restructure my speech. There is a whole series of weighty circumstances which impels me to return again to the April events in Tbilisi.

For us, profound personal anguish is enclosed within the Tbilisi tragedy. Nevertheless, we must rise above emotions and examine all that has occurred in the broad political context. For this is a matter not only of the authority of power but also of the prestige of our restructuring itself. We have boldly laid bare the rotten springs of the authoritarian regime, but precisely for this reason, the high humanitarian and moral standards that determined the foundation of the theoretical quests of Vladimir Ilich Lenin should from the very start be placed at the very basis of our new political model. From such standpoints, this conclusion is unavoidable. Under conditions of democracy, the decision made in the republic which led to such grave consequences—a crisis of confidence and to moral and political damage—can under no circumstance be acknowledged to be politically correct, and every one of us feels his responsibility for this. It is incorrect, and at least politically naive, to qualify the April rallies and demonstrations in Tbilisi as a public carnival [narodnoye gulyaniye]. They were a political act which the demonstrators in the main tried to link with the issue of self-determination by the nation. The assertion to the effect that there were no slogans and appeals of an altogether extreme nature is likewise incorrect.

However, all this cannot justify the bloody tragedy that occurred that night. It is not hard to accuse a 70-year-old woman and a 10-year-old adolescent boy of extremism, but such an approach has no future and we have convincingly seen what it can lead to. It is also irresponsible to attribute anti-Russian feelings to a whole people. There have been and are no such feelings of Russophobia in Georgia. We know that the Russian people, the Russian intelligentsia, just as all the fraternal peoples, are gravely upset, together with us, by the pain of the Tbilisi tragedy. Indignation over the bureaucratic diktat really should not be confused with anti-Russian feelings.

The congress has adopted a decision on an investigation of the reasons and circumstances of the events of 9 April. An authoritative commission has been set up. I am sure that it will thoroughly study all the material and will establish the full truth, as was demanded by Mikhail Sergeyevich Gorbachev, and that the culprits, no matter what post they occupy or where they work, will receive the punishment they deserve. All the deputies from Georgia are convinced of this, deputies Mikhail Sergeyevich found time to meet during the work of the congress, something that served as a characteristic example of a truly open, honest, and so necessary dialogue. When the inability to carry on a dialogue leads to counting on force, this is a blow to restructuring, and without speaking this truth, we will find no other truth.

In creating a law-governed state, we are under obligation to teach citizens, particularly young people, to respect the law, and it must be the first duty of party bodies and state institutions to set an example of scrupulous observance of it. Decisions made noncollectively, hastily, and in circumvention of the standards of party and official ethics are always fraught with fateful errors and violations of the law. Public order is the concern of society, and in extreme cases there is the militia and the public law and order enforcement bodies. It is hard to find even an explanation, let alone justification, which some people are trying in vain to find, for the involvement of assault subunits in this kind of civil act for the carrying out of uncharacteristic functions. Had this not happened we would not all be upset now about the participation of the Army in the tragedy, and the military procuracy would not have to institute legal proceedings, all the more so since it has now turned out that the instructions to the Army subunits and their commanders only stipulated the implementation of protection measures.

Even the introduction of the curfew, which was announced to the public only 4 minutes before it came into force, also resulted in grave consequences. A phrase to the effect that the Army must not be deployed against the people was also heard here. I would say the same thing. We are all obliged to protect our Army, not laying the political problems we have failed to solve on its shoulders. My fellow countrymen, whose grandfathers and fathers fought worthily on the battlefield at Borodino and in the battle of Stalingrad, sacredly honor this tradition. Neither have our mothers been spared the funerals of the Afghan war. That is why a number of inadmissable appraisals and expressions made from this platform by former so-called Afghan soldiers were perceived so keenly and with such pain by the whole republic. I speak of this with particular personal feeling as a person who grew up in the family of a Soviet officer and political worker.

Indeed, elementary ethics and humaneness obliged Colonel-General Rodionov, who allowed himself to call the Tbilisi tragedy the Tbilisi provocation and the Georgian version of restructuring, to search out in his vocabulary words of at least some kind of regret and sympathy for the victims and their near and dear. [applause] One can take his speech in various ways. However, how can one justify the cruelty of the excessive zeal, demanded by no one? Was excessive zeal not also the reason for the subsequent insincerity and misinformation? How can one justify one's actions by citing publications in the newspaper ZARYA VOSTOKA during the days of the curfew, if the real facts were distorted even to official bodies? Only on the third day was the use of sappers' shovels ascertained, and only on the fifth the use of gases, and only almost a month later their chemical composition became known, although this was extremely important for the treatment of the casualties.

These facts were stubbornly denied at daily meetings not only to us, but also to the two representatives of the Politburo of the CPSU Central Committee, Comrades Shevardnadze and Razumovskiy, to the top leadership of the country. Maybe not everyone knows this, but only their persistance and only the principled approach of Mikhail Sergeyevich Gorbachev made progress in the search for the truth possible. We also bring him our gratitude for the help in sending to the republic highly-qualified medical specialists from Moscow, Leningrad, and other cities in the country, and also from abroad, and representatives of the Soviet and the International Red Cross.

Restructuring of society should be accompanied by restructuring of the institutions of power, primarily the perfection and sometimes a radical change in the style, forms, and methods of work of party organisations. It is unthinkable without renewal. It cannot be decreed by willful decisions. Under conditions of glasnost, attempts at forcible suppression of any unsanctioned manifestations of thought and word of national feelings must be condemned. We must consistently overcome the gene of authoritarianism which is deeply entrenched in us. We must learn to talk to people, to find weighty and exact arguments in any difficult matter. When the fundamental provisions of restructuring take on a declarative nature, the public initiative which it has provoked, unable to find a natural way out, starts to acquire the form of open protest, as happened with us.

So, consolidation, reasonable compromise, and integration of all the potiential of society, is the only way of avoiding the process of revolutionary violence and unnecessary intellectual and physical victims. Experience confirms that one of the most effective assets for this is constructive dialogue. Society must not be divided into the official and unofficial, especially when investing these concepts with profound political meaning. We must, if only henceforth, work to convince by our sincerity even those who have lost confidence in the future of such dialogue, convince them that we stand together with the people, not in words but in deeds, that we share their social and political ideals, that we are entirely devoted to them, not thinking about our own official well-being. Restructuring has expanded the framework and forms of showing national feelings and interests.

It is time to remove from our ideological baggage many obsolete stereotypes. Recently in the republic, for the first time since Lenin's time, the day of restoration of Georgian statehood was marked. That is natural. Historic dates are a tribute to events, and they do not disappear from the memory because of anybody's whim. When we deprive the people of them, we dislodge their spiritual and moral supports; we violate the continuity of their historically formed political orientation. It is simplest to explain events like those in Tbilisi by an outburst of national emotions. But surely to some extent they also showed the results of the known deformations of socialism, and particularly of the constitutionally enshrined federal foundations of Soviet statehood which for many decades were committed in the country. The centuries-old traditions and ideas of Georgian statehood, which are identified with the natural aspiration of the people for cultural, linguistic, and physical survival, and to whose defense have been devoted the political and fighting energy of tens of generations, have been laid waste. In the years of repression the flower of the Georgian nation was destroyed. Tens of thousands of innocent people were thrown in prison and shut up in camps. Among the fabricated court trials there were the so-called cases of the Georgian writers, of theatrical figures, of scientists and technical intelligentsia, and many others.

The waste of the thirties, forties, and fifties jumped across like a shadow and [words indistinct] Stalinism in 1956 on those same Tbilisi streets deceived young people were killed. All of this cannot fail to be considered in political work in the age of glasnost. Now when the party is consistently carrying out the rehabilitation of slandered names and fundamentally filling in the blank spots in our history, we must everywhere objectively look into our past, especially the recent past, not elevating scientific research and disputes (?to the level of grand policy).

The rapid growth of national consciousness testifies to the fact that the people have placed their faith in restructuring and are seeking to realize, through it, their innermost aspirations. What is needed now in my view is not so much recipes as a constant interpretation of all the processes without haste or prejudice of any kind.

Thus matters of political sovereignty are perceived with particular acuteness by the public. One has to consistently develop work to create the reliable economic and constitutional basis for it, and the sociopolitical mobilization of the population along constructive lines.

The elaboration of the concept of republican financial autonomy with the aim of the more rational ownership, command, and use of local natural resources has been started, albeit belatedly. Yet work on the draft constitution of Georgia, in our view, should be directed at the harmonization of relations with the center, and at combining them properly with the republic's real political and economic sovereignty.

In our view the need has arisen to work out the matter of ensuring a balance, in multinational republics and regions, between interethnic interests and the interest of the indigenous nation, above all through language, culture, and other national values. This will without doubt facilitate the deepening of trust.

I want to stress that the republic has every opportunity, given mutual agreement and respect, to resolve all interethnic problems, above all those which concern the Abkhaz people, with which the Georgian people have blood ties stretching through centuries of fraternal interrelations.

There are also problems currently of particular concern for young people and the republic as a whole, which are at the stage of being resolved in the near future. We all have to learn to tackle matters in such a way that society is not driven down a blind alley and that damage is not done to the progress of our common cause. In order to actually advance restructuring, we must elaborate a fundamentally new concept of the national question. National energy is an enormous potential which we must learn to channel properly. That is why today consolidation on the basis of the genuine pluralism of political, economic, and national interests is as necessary as the air we breathe, so that the collective intelligence of our party and of the soviets triumphs over grayness and conservatism.

There is another matter I would like to address from this rostrum. None of us change our moral perception in order not to discredit the political force, thanks to which both the 19th party conference and our congress have adopted a specifically democratic path. I consider our attitude to the party's prestige at the current decisive phase to be a choice, too—either in favor of restructuring or not in its favor. The party is the initiator of the renewal of our society: it should also stand in the vanguard of restructuring. Thank you. [applause]

Suleymenov Speech to Congress
LD0806115889 Moscow Television Service in Russian 0956 GMT 8 Jun 89

[Speech by Deputy Olzhas Omarovich Suleymenov to Congress of People's Deputies at the Kremlin Palace of Congresses—live]

[Text] I have abbreviated what I could. So, we literary figures do not just talk about flowers, but now more about the fruits. Among the many aspects of restructuring, the main one for me is the continuation of the process of decolonialization, frozen during the twenties. It is taking place with all the manifestations characteristic of this process. The originality of the historical situation lies in the fact that the former metropolis, Russia, on a par with the other republics, has itself become a colony of the center. We are reexamining the familiar in a new light. The interests of the state have always been higher than the interests of the people and the individual.

I was elected in Semipalatinsk Oblast, in a land of ancient historical tradition. Great Kazakh writers were born there. Those steppes and mountains are our Yasnaya Polyanas, Mikhaylovskoyes, and Tarkhanys [homes of Tolstoy, Pushkin, and Lermontov]. These places are precisely where the nuclear test site operates. There is one test site in the United States, there is one in China. Other countries test charges thousands of miles from their territory, paying compensation to the residents of atolls. There are several test sites in the USSR. The oldest is at Semipalatinsk and it is the most active. Eighteen explosions per year. It is situated virtually in the center of the country. For 15 years, open tests have been carried out on the land and in the atmosphere. According to the most modest calculations, charges have been exploded with a total capacity of 2,500 Hiroshima bombs. Could this possibly take place without having any effect on the health of the population of rayons surrounding the installation? Even if official specialists say yes, we do not believe them. Experts of the Nevada-Semipalatinsk public movement have other, more frightening data. The Third Main Administration of the USSR Ministry of Health keeps research material secret. Hiroshima and Nagasaki are today, perhaps the highest indicators in the world of the average life expectancy, as a result of deliberately raising the standard of health care and the social care in these cities, and from them to Japan as a whole.

It must be admitted that our state has shown less sympathy and respect for its citizens. Over the 40 years of testing, not one health center has been built or one rural hospital equipped at the expense of the center [of the country] in the rayons surrounding the test site, not to mention anything else. The consequences of open explosions will continue to affect the health of the whole country for a long time to come. In 1963, an agreement was finally signed on halting tests in several spheres.

For the sake of fairness, the stance of our scientists, and especially Academician Sakharov, who convinced the government to insist on this agreement, should be given its due. [applause] This happened following the test of the most powerful hydrogen bomb of 600 megatonnes. Scientists saw what a nightmare their invention was preparing for the world, in which both genius and villainy were combined, with the increasing predominance of the latter.

This combination can now be seen even in the fact that the organizers of the Semipalatinsk test range were ordered to be under Kurchatov and Lavrentiy Beriya. Underground explosions are not safe, either, as is shown by the emission of radioactive gases on 12 February this year. Similar things have happened in the past, too—last summer, for example. Thousands of children one day went down with a hasty diagnosis of acute respiratory disease, nosebleeds, giddiness, and other signs very characteristic of something besides a bad cold.

The world is changing. We are beginning to have fewer enemies in the West and in the East, and that means less defense expenditure. The Soviet and world arsenals are overfilled. The nuclear shields of the superpowers are colossal in size and are capable of crushing those they are supposed to protect. The statement by Mikhail Sergeyevich Gorbachev in the London Guildhall that the country is closing down production of plutonium has added to hopes for a nuclear-free 21st century, and adds to confidence that we are becoming a peaceful state [applause]; that there is a new situation in the country. We know that the center is now hearing us because of the following fact: The formation of the Nevada-Semipalatinsk movement has led to a halt in tests. The test ranges have been silent for over 3 months now. It is a brittle silence, but we very much hope that the governments and the public antinuclear movements in the countries in the nuclear club will hear us, will understand and give support, and will create the conditions for signing a final agreement on banning tests in all environments. [applause]

Following the 19th party conference it is now particularly obvious that our development will depend more and more on the degree of openness, of dialogue between the people and the state. The process (?must sometimes be refined from) various standpoints, and so it is worth remembering that the country's troubles began at the end of the 1920s, with the persecution of dissident thought. In order for democracy and glasnost to continue, it is important to express in legislation the state's attitude to dissident thought, to recognize it as a creative factor and not a hostile one. [applause] In the resolution and in separate documents it is necessary to condemn the crimes of the Stalin clique against socialism, in particular those such as the physical extermination of the opposition. [applause] The extreme left theory and practice of rapid development, which manifested itself in the rate and methods of the notorious reforms, must be declared criminal.

How often have the fresh winds of change, propelled in ignorance, turned into crushing hurricanes. In the war the Kazakhs lost 350,000 lives. But in the so-called peace years, in the periods of rapid acceleration, we lost more than 4 million. Every people can apply this model to its biography. History repeats itself pointlessly if we do not learn its lessons. We must at last publish a white, or rather a black paper on Stalin's tyranny, with figures for all republics. We do not want to dismiss all our history in the round. After all, apart from the dark areas of it, we have gained common spiritual values, and alongside the sad experiences there are some positive ones which must be preserved and continued. It is precisely because of this that we must separate the clean from the bloody.

Yes, millions died without publicity. Today the memory of them is crying out. Today we are in a position to condemn tyranny against individuals. This is evidence of the speed of development of our morality and awareness of the law. The Alma Ata students and workers were the first in the country to stage unsanctioned meetings. If the Alma Ata events of December 1986 had been discussed as widely and democratically discussed and understood, perhaps the 9 April tragedy in Tbilisi would not have occurred. I consider that it would be correct to examine the circumstances of the Alma Ata tragic incident in the light of the new, humane approach. I am passing on all the cables and letters to the relevant Supreme Soviet commission where I am prepared to deliver a report on this issue. I call upon my fellow countrymen, Kazakhs, Russians, Germans, Ukrainians, Uighurs, Koreans, Turks, the people of Kazakhstan that have experienced everything, to realize the gravity of the moment, to have faith that justice is possible if we manage to hold on and understand the value of our common interests.

How much pain has built up in the country, and how powerful the result is. There is not a single people in whose awareness there are not wounds which bleed. Many of us will remember the crying demands of the Meskhetian Turks, the Crimean Tatars, the Abkhazians, the Ingushetians and Chechens, the Gagauz. The Supreme Soviet commission on interethnic relations will have a vast amount of work, and at least some of these difficulties must be overcome by the time of the next congress. The knot of Karabakh is drawing ever tighter, and ever bigger factors, ethnic and religious and others, are becoming involved.

Academician Likhachev rightly spoke of the role of culture in interethnic disputes. This role is restricted without a full and capacious knowledge of the history of the issues. The one-sided, targeted knowledge that peoples have been educated in is the cause of many national grudges and ambitions. We have to issue a special series of anthologies of documents on the hottest topics. Culture presupposes steps toward one another. Such an anthology, apart from objective historical information, should also include the cruel truth about Sumgait, and a report on the crash of the aircraft from Baku, when 50 Azerbaijani soldiers were flying to help those who suffered in the earthquake, having been called out to give a hand to their neighbors in trouble. These boys wanted to make their contribution to the cause of restoring friendship, and they gave all they could—their lives. They have no monument, their names have not been heard in a play, it is only their mothers that know their fate. There are probably many such such unknown facts of nobleness on both sides. They must be constantly made public so that we can learn to empathize with each other. [applause]

What happened in Uzbekistan, what happened in Bashkiriya are not coincidences. They are portents of a depressing and heavy metaphor that we have to read. One thing is clear: We cannot raise the pressure when there are so many leaky pipelines in the country. The vicious fuel of national and social dissatisfaction is flowing toward the tracks along which the trains carrying children are traveling. May our children and grandchildren not inherit increased harshness. We have earned the right, while they are simply obliged to be happy. Thank you. [applause]

Lithuanian Walkout Reported
LD0806212789 Moscow Television Service in Russian 1200 GMT 8 Jun 89

[Relay of the Congress of People's Deputies, held in the Kremlin Palace of Congresses—live]

[Excerpt] [passage omitted] [Gorbachev] So, comrades, the first proposal is that the Committee for Overseeing the Constitution [Komitet Konstitutsionnogo Nadzora] should be set up now. Would those in favor of commencing this raise their cards? [responds to indistinct shout] Yes, without fail. We're voting on whether to set it up in principle or not, and then we'll deal with all the rest. Please raise your cards. Please lower them. Those against?

Well, comrades, we probably don't need a count; there's a clear minority against. [responds to indistinct shout] What, you don't know what we are voting for? I'll say it again. I thought I had put it precisely. We are now to decide whether to go about setting it up, or to postpone it until the fall. The first proposal is to set it up now. Who is in favor of doing it now? [responds to indistinct shout] There'll be a third one, too. Fine. That concerns the essence, the essence. Yes, yes, the comrade backs the proposal, but with different powers. [addressing an unseen deputy or deputies amid commotion] Comrades, don't abuse the procedures.

So the first proposal is to set up the...[Gorbachev changes thought] to go about appointing the members of the Committee for Overseeing the Constitution. Those in favor of the proposal please raise your cards. Please lower them. Who is against? Well, comrades, it's clear. Do we need a count? No? We need to? Hold a count then! [video shows tellers counting and collating the show of cards]

[Tellers' official] Esteemed deputies, 433 deputies have voted against.

[Gorbachev] Who abstained? [video shows a further count]

[Tellers' official] Sixty-one deputies have abstained in the vote.

[Gorbachev] So, the decision has been adopted.

[Tellers' official] Fifty deputies from the Lithuanian republic did not take part in the vote.

[Gorbachev] Out of how many?

[Tellers' official] Comrades, how many deputies are there in the Lithuanian delegation? [indistinct shouts] A total of 58 are present. [more shouts] Excuse me, please raise your hands so we can count how many are present.

[Unidentified speaker] Fifty-four deputies are taking part at the moment.

[Gorbachev] But that is of no significance under the circumstances. [video shows teller counting the Lithuanian delegation, which appears to be seated together. One of the deputies stands up and shouts an indistinct remark to Gorbachev]

[Gorbachev] No, quite the reverse, quite the reverse. I'm just saying that we have been dealing with procedural matters, and in this case...[he stops speaking as the Lithuanian deputies who have just been counted stand up and file out toward the back of the hall; camera dwells on the exiting deputies]

[Gorbachev] Comrades, comrades, please be calm, because all this is no simple matter. We must not simplify things, and I would not turn it in this instance into...[Gorbachev changes thought] All this is no simple matter. We must now consult on what to do next. [there is a pause of almost 30 seconds as Gorbachev is shown waiting for a response from the hall, where deputies are seen in a state of some agitation] What are we to do next, comrades?

[Unidentified deputy, from rostrum] Dear comrade deputies, one of the important issues is that we are setting up a committee which does not have a statute. We can't—we don't have the right to set up the committee until such time as its statute is drawn up. As was said here, a compromise decision is needed, and such a compromise is becoming all the more important now—let us not set up the Committee for Overseeing the Constitution today. [applause] Let's set up a commission to draw up the statute for the committee, perhaps with the same membership, but it whould be a commission, and when it is in operation it can then be transformed into the Committee for Overseeing the Constitution. That is my proposal.

[Fedor Burlatskiy, from rostrum] Comrade deputies, I'm from the Soviet Peace Fund. We must take a wholly responsible atttude to the present moment in time. We must have a wholly responsible attitude because we...[Burlatskiy changes thought] Our leaders have convened this congress in the name of democracy, in the name of the development of restructuring and in the name of unity. And we must seek ways of achieving such a unity. I propose that discussion of this matter be postponed until tomorrow and that the Congress Presidium, and Mikhail Sergeyevich Gorbachev personally, be asked to enter into talks with representatives of the Lithuanian delegation [applause] and to report on this matter to the congress here tomorrow. [applause]

[Moshnyaga, from rostrum] I'm Moshnyaga from Kishinev, National-Territorial Constituency No 257. Esteemed comrade deputies, the Committee for Overseeing the Constitution is, from our delegation's point of view, the most important body for the Congress of People's Deputies. This is because it will be overseeing the Constitution, which is the country's basic law. And the country's basic law lays down the noninfringement of the interests of any other republic, the noninfringement of the interests of any other Constitution, of any other republic. As a consequence, this body to oversee the Constitution will, at the same time, examine matters to do with the constitutions, the observance of the constitutions of the union republics. And in view of the fact that there are differences of view about the adoption of such...[Moshnyaga changes thought] about the vote concerning the principle and the membership, it seems, I propose that consideration of this matter be deferred at least until, as has just been proposed, consultations have taken place again. Thank you.

[Gorbachev] Perhaps we won't extend the debate after all? I would adopt Comrade Burlatskiy's proposal. Despite the fact, comrades, that there may be certain emotions and certain attitudes among us—there have been many of these emotions, undoubtedly, and they will be displayed on more than one occasion in the future— this is not the worst thing. The worst thing would be if we end with our congress failing to find solutions which match up to the spirit and policy of restructuring and the harmonization of relations between nationalities, with all points of view being harmonized. The simplest thing, it appears, would be to decide now. But I think that the wisest decision would be to adopt Comrade Burlatskiy's proposal and to instruct the presidium to hold consultations with the Lithuanian deputies and report on the results tomorrow. All right. That's all right, comrades, is it? Do we need a vote? [chorus of no] Fine, that's agreed then. [indistinct voice] What? Well, with the deputies who left. [indistinct voice continues] What? I don't understand. Oh, to set it up or not, you mean? Yes, yes—carry on. [video shows deputy who has been speaking going to rostrum]

[Bredikis, from rostrum] Deputy Bredikis, from Lithuania. May I say this. As we travelled to the congress our mood was of course such that we understood that in a vote there can always be a majority, and our standpoint, although we shall doggedly defend it, may not always be heard. That is what has happened now. I agree that we need further discussion. The idea of deferring it would of course, in my view, be the most logical way to proceed. But I have a question to ask. Are the results of the vote just taken being annulled until tomorrow?

[Gorbachev] Er, no—I think for the moment the question of the results of the votes is not being taken off the agenda. We're going to hold talks, talks. And naturally, the talks will also be with the deputies from Latvia. [responding to the deputy asking to speak] You want to speak on this issue? Comrades, we've decided by and large. Do we need to continue the discussion? [shouts] [video shows a woman going up to the platform who exchanges some words with Gorbachev] Comrades, let's consider the matter settled. That's enough, that's enough, comrades. I shall conform, and you must conform. But let's not have suspicions that some people are Leninists, and others are not Leninists. That way we could end up going too far. We still have many issues, and I should like to ask you about this. Let us have an interval until 1500 and then do some more work. Let's have an interval until 1500.

Sukharev Appointed New Prosecutor-General
LD0806191989 Moscow TASS in English 1842 GMT 8 Jun 89

[Text] Moscow June 8 TASS—By TASS parliamentary correspondent:

The Congress of People's Deputies endorsed on Thursday a number of personnel decisions taken on Wednesday [7 June] by the USSR Supreme Soviet.

It endorsed the election of Yevgeniy Smolentsev to the post of chairman of the USSR Supreme Court. The 66-year-old lawyer headed until recently the Supreme Court of the Russian Federation.

The congress confirmed the authority of Gennadiy Kolbin, 62, who had been elected chairman of the USSR People's Control Committee. Kolbin is heading the Central Committee of the Communist Party of Kazakhstan.

The congress endorsed the nomination of Yuriy Matveyev, 49, to the post of the chief state arbiter. Previously he was chief arbiter of the Ukraine.

The endorsement of Aleksandr Sukharev, 66, on the post of the USSR prosecutor-general took a lot of discussion. Deputies expressed varied opinions of the performance of Sukharev who has held the post since 1988. Many people regard him as a person who firmly protects the law. However, others, specifically the investigating officers Telman Gdlyan and Nikolay Ivanov (they have been criticised of late for using illegal methods for obtaining evidence) are critical of Sukharev. They maintain that the prosecutor-general is conniving with "high-ranking criminals."

After analyzing all pros and cons, deputies endorsed by the majority of votes the appointment of Aleksandr Sukharev to the post of the USSR prosecutor-general.

Council of Ministers Chairman Ryzhkov Profiled
LD0706093589 Moscow TASS in English 0852 GMT 7 Jun 89

[Text] Moscow June 7 TASS—TASS parliamentary correspondent reports from the Kremlin:

Nikolay Ryzhkov, who was appointed chairman of the Council of Ministers of the USSR today, was born in the village of Beleyevka, Donetsk region of the Ukraine, on September 29th, 1929. His nationality is Russian. He joined the Communist Party of the Soviet Union in 1956.

Nikolay Ryzhkov began his working career in 1950 at the Urals heavy machinery plant after graduating from a technical school. Many pages of his biography are linked with this enterprise. He continued to work there after graduating from the Urals Polytechnical Institute in 1959, discharging different engineering duties. Then he was appointed deputy director of the enterprise. He headed the plant from 1965 to 1970. In 1971-1975 he was director-general of the "Uralmash" production amalgamation, leader of the Soviet machine-building industry.

In 1975 Nikolay Ryzhkov was transferred to Moscow as first deputy minister of heavy and transport machine building. Starting from 1979 Nikolay Ryzhkov discharged the duties of first deputy chairman of the State Planning Committee of the USSR.

In November 1982 he was elected secretary of the CPSU Central Committee, concurrently heading the Economic Department of the CPSU Central Committee. At the April plenary meeting of the CPSU Central Committee in 1985 (the first plenum after Mikhail Gorbachev's election to the post of general secretary of the CPSU Central Committee) he was elected member of the Politburo of the Soviet Communist Party Central Committee. Nikolay Ryzhkov became head of the Soviet Government as of September 1985.

New Supreme Court Chairman Smolentsev Profiled

LD0706165289 Moscow TASS in English 1633 GMT 7 Jun 89

[Text] Moscow June 7 TASS—By TASS parliamentary correspondent:

Yevgeniy Smolentsev was elected today chairman for the Supreme Court of the U.S.S.R. by a majority vote of the Soviet parliament, the Supreme Soviet of the U.S.S.R. Before the promotion he was chairman of the Supreme Court of the Russian Federation, the largest of the 15 Soviet constituent republics.

Yevgeniy Smolentsev was born in 1923. He is Russian. In 1953 he graduated from the Law Institute in the city of Sverdlovsk in the Urals and worked in the Sverdlovsk regional court till 1972, starting as member of the court and working his way up to chairman of the court.

From 1972 to 1977 Smolentsev headed the collegium on criminal cases at the U.S.S.R. Supreme Court, and was then, for ten years, deputy chairman of the Supreme Court of the Russian Federation. He headed the Russian Federation Supreme Court since 1987.

New Chief State Arbiter Matveyev Profiled

LD0706165789 Moscow TASS in English 1631 GMT 7 Jun 89

[Text] Moscow June 7 TASS—By TASS parliamentary correspondent reporting from the Kremlin:

A 49-year-old doctor of law was appointed chief state arbiter of the USSR at today's session of the national parliament.

The new arbiter, Yuriy Matveyev, who served as chief state arbiter of the Ukraine, received backing from the majority of the Supreme Soviet deputies.

Upon graduation in 1962 from the Kiev University School of Law, Matveyev worked at the arbitration office for the Kiev region and then as teacher at the Kiev Higher School of the Ministry for the Interior.

He served two terms on the UNESCO Secretariat: First in 1967-1973 and then in 1981-1983. After returning home from Paris, he held the position of dean of the Kiev University School of Law.

Matveyev was appointed chief state arbiter of the Ukraine in 1987.

USSR Supreme Soviet Committees Listed

PM0806085789 Moscow PRAVDA in Russian 8 Jun 89 Second Edition p 1

[USSR Supreme Soviet Resolution "On Committees of the USSR Supreme Soviet"]

[Text] The USSR Supreme Soviet resolves:

1. To create the following USSR Supreme Soviet committees:

International Affairs Committee;
Committee for Defense and State Security Questions;
Committee for Questions of Legislation, Legality, and Law and Order;
Committee for Questions of the Work of Soviets of People's Deputies and of the Development of Management and Self-Management;
Committee for Economic Reform Questions;
Committee for Agrarian Questions and Food;
Committee for Construction and Architecture Questions;
Committee for Science, Public Education, Culture, and Upbringing;
Committee for the Protection of the People's Health;

Committee for the Affairs of Women and of Family, Mother, and Child Protection;

Committee for the Affairs of Veterans and Invalids;

Youth Affairs Committee;

Committee for Questions of Ecology and the Rational Use of Natural Resources;

Committee for Questions of Glasnost and Citizens' Rights and Appeals.

2. Pending the adoption of a legal act regulating the committees' activity, to extend to USSR Supreme Soviet committees the operation of the Statute on Standing Commissions of the USSR Supreme Soviet Soviet of the Union and Soviet of Nationalities as regards basic principles, working procedures, and committees' rights and duties.

Soviet of Nationalities Commissions Listed

PM0806085589 Moscow PRAVDA in Russian 8 Jun 89 Second Edition p 1

[USSR Supreme Soviet Soviet of Nationalities resolution "On Standing Commissions of the Soviet of Nationalities"]

[Text] The Soviet of Nationalities resolves:

To form the following standing commissions in the Soviet of Nationalities:

Commission for Nationalities Policy and Interethnic Relations;

Commission for Questions of the Social and Economic Development of Union and Autonomous Republics and Autonomous Oblasts and Okrugs;

Commission for Consumer Goods, Trade, and Municipal, Consumer, and Other Services to the Population;

Commission for Questions of the Development of Culture, Language, National and International Traditions, and Protection of the Historical Heritage.

Deputies View Congress Proceedings Through 2 Jun

PM0506132989 Moscow PRAVDA in Russian 3 Jun 89 Second Edition p 1

[Report from the Kremlin Palace of Congress by PRAVDA team of journalists: "Man and Restructuring"]

[Text] Everyone—journalists, sociologists, foreign commentators and so on—is talking and writing about the fact that the Congress of USSR People's Deputies is arousing lively, informal interest among the people who elected it. This is explained by the novelty of the elections themseves, genuine and democratic, and the nature of the debate at the congress—open, uninhibited, and sincere. But perhaps the main reason why people of all

nations, ages, and professions are glued to their television sets and radios day and night and are reading newspapers intently is the enormous expectation of long-awaited changes that have built up during the years of restructuring.

One can approach the deputies' speeches in different ways, their temperament amd style of utterance, but what clearly and favorably distinguishes them from the speakers of past years is their genuine sense of responsibility to the electorate, their ardent and sometimes even feverish desire to restore people's dignity and well-being and the country's honor and prosperity.

The aim of restructuring is man. This leading idea has dominated every day of the congress and every speech, no matter what the topic. Whether it was the clash between the acute polemical ideas of well-known farmer Vasiliy Starodubtsev and trade union leader Vladimir Shcherbakov on how to feed the country; the pain felt by Albert Likhanov for homeless children alienated by society, and by Zoya Pukhova for the working conditions and meager existence of our women, which went straight to the hearts of the audience; the intensifying debate about ethnic problems and conflicts—all this inspired the delegates to find ways whereby everyone in the country can have a comfortable and free life and work with joy and inspiration....

How do the people's deputies themselves see this important connection? No doubt you have heard the congress speeches on the television and radio, and they have been published in PRAVDA, too, at the request of our readers. What we are offering is deputies' views expressed to journalists during breaks between sessions.

G. Klimova, plasterers' team leader (Engels, Saratov Oblast):

"Restructuring has given me faith in the true renewal of life. But it is increasingly clear to me that we must work better to ensure that it does not get bogged down in words. We must not simply go to work to waste time, but put all our creative efforts into the job and treat all that is going on around as something in which we are personally involved, something that concerns us directly. Only then will there be more apartments and kindergartens, only then will the country stop squandering its wealth, in small and large chunks. Many deputies have made constructive proposals. But there have been rather few concrete proposals on how we are to get out of the crisis."

V. Shmotyev, heat specialist at the Verkh-Isetskiy metallurgical plant (Sverdlovsk):

"The elections themselves were a gain for restructuring. In contrast to past campaigns the people's masses were really active. What has restructuring given to our particular enterprise? Perhaps it has not percolated through to the very bottom yet, but it is putting out shoots. But everyone now has the chance, depending on his contribution, to increase both his pay and the profits of the plant as a whole. But the lion's share of what is earned still goes to the state budget, the enterprise being left with very small resources. So workers still do not feel they have a major stake in increasing the effectiveness and quality of their labor. It is still largely a matter of appeals for people to be more conscientious. There should be a material incentive, too!

"As for the debate on M.S. Gorbachev's report, the speeches by some senior leaders responsible for oblasts and republics have been accounts of successes achieved. We do not need that right now; it only takes up precious time."

...Deputies have focused attention on interethnic problems practically from the moment the congress started. This is understandable: Without solving them it is impossible to unite the efforts of the multilingual Soviet community in the cause of restructuring. G. Kolbin, deputy from Kazakhstan and first secretary of the republic's Communist Party Central Committee, expressed his thoughts on the subject in conversation with us:

"Everyone senses the acuteness of the problem of interethnic relations, yet few, unfortunately, know its parameters, so to speak, in each individual region, its depth and specific qualities, and its social and historical nature. Ethnic problems by and large are based on feelings and emotions above all. And the social circumstances merely intensify or reduce the acuteness of the emotions.... For that reason it is no good trying to patch things up—either seizing on the 'creative intelligentsia' factor or sending food and industrial resources into the 'high-temperature' region.... None of it works. The solution of this or that interethnic issue, as we realized in Kazakhstan, demands in the first place a comprehensive approach. And I would stress that the 'recipe' absolutely must not be prepared somewhere in the center, but in the actual region in question, by highly authoritative people in the working class and peasantry, among the body of elders, among the creative intelligentsia...."

[Questioner] "But does this approach not result in a certain trend toward self-isolation?"

[Kolbin] "This thesis is fundamentally wrong. All our republics, as a rule, are multinational. Life itself predetermines a policy of dialogue. The fact that the center is dragging its feet on a number of issues is a different matter. In particular, the lack of a unified concept of a state language has created conditions for the establishment of the monolingual concept in a number of regions. There is no question that the language of the indigenous people of a republic must be the state language. But what about the language of the union? What is its status, then? There is also controversy in connection with the concepts of citizenship, republican currency, and so forth.

Of course, there is going to be a CPSU Central Committee plenum on the whole range of issues. But the congress has already given food for serious and urgent thought."

...A man is inseparable from the land which bore him—that is indisputable. There is also no doubt that man cannot be detached from the land completely. That is why one of the chief topics at the congress is the topic of return to the land. Here is the opinion of V. Krivorotov, chairman of the "Rossiya" collective farm [kolkhoz] in Crimean Oblast:

"I very much like Deputy Starodubtsev's speech. It is time the farmer finally got his freedom. Why maintain a wall of instructions between the kolkhoz member and the land? Restructuring has untied our hands, but many of my comrades are saying that local officials are forcing them virtually to a man to switch to lease contracts. What if it is to someone's disadvantage? For example, our "Rossiya" kolkhoz gets R7-9 million net profit a year, we have our own sanatorium and dispensary, and average pay is R242. A kolkhoz member pays 6 kopeks a day to keep a child in the kindergarten, although the child's upkeep costs the farm nearly R2. What kind of cooperative is a person going to leave this kolkhoz for? He may get a lot of money there, but where are the goods to spend the money on? Who is going to provide him with the consumer and social services for such a nominal sum? But I am a strong supporter of cooperatives and the lease contract. We need them in order to keep the kolkhozes 'on the ball.' Of all the kolkhoz' indicators we are most proud of the fact that there are 160-170 new USSR citizens born here every year. Are we not working for them today?"

The standing orders at the congress have become markedly stricter since the emotionally turbulent initial days. And although nearly every speaker has asked for "one or two minutes" more, he has not managed, as a rule, to get everything off his chest. That is why we decided to interview people behind the scenes after their speeches. Sh. Amonashvili, a well-know teacher and innovator, agreed that he had been able to say by no means all the things he wanted to say.

"The 15 minutes at the rostrum passed like a flash. There was a great deal I wanted to say and, although I packed things in, I did not manage to say everything. Today's young people are often accused of a free-loading attitude," the deputy remarked. "There is a lot of bitter truth in this. But we forget that these children grew up in the years of stagnation. So their free-loading attitude, if it exists, is a product of stagnation. But the generation which has taken shape during the period of restructuring will be altogether different—more enterprising, open, and bold. At the moment everyone is demanding more resources for the social sphere, in particular for education. This is correct, but in my view it is not just a matter of money. In order to produce someone who makes a contribution he must have a worthy teacher. Both literally, in the school sense of the word, and in the metaphorical sense—the moral example of today's deputies springs to mind."

Ideas about people's welfare continued to be expressed at the congress. For example, Deputy V.P. Shcherbakov noted that we are proud of the great achievements of October, but the potential of socialism is not being fully exploited. It is increasingly difficult to explain why the people's living standards are declining. The main reason for the economic mess, in the speaker's view, is the fact that economic accountability has not yet started working in teams and in shops, and enterprises do not yet have proper independence.

There are articifial limits on pay rises at enterprises, whereas there are no restrictions in cooperatives, the speaker stressed. I am not against high wages, but pay must correspond to the labor input. The development of the cooperative system is essential, but it is a bad thing when it is not controlled. One deputy voiced the fear that cooperatives, by "draining resources" out of enterprises, could lead the country to financial ruin. In the first 5 months of this year, he said, Moscow cooperative workers have taken R976 million out of the bank and put only R38 million in. The money taken out by the cooperatuve workers would be enough, for example, to increase the paid leave of all working people in the country to 24 days. The working class wonders whom this benefits.

According to the deputy, another reason why restructuring has not yet picked up the necessary momentum is that economic experts are so far merely subjecting everything to sharp criticism. It is necessary now for them to pool their efforts to elaborate an economically substantiated outline plan for restructuring, rather than "swinging" from one side to another.

In order to develop the economy, V.P. Shcherbakov proposed urgent measures to improve the financial situation, including the implementation of a monetary reform which would not affect the interests of honest workers but would confiscate ill-gotten gains, the accelerated introduction of a progressive income tax, the placement of state enterprises and cooperatives on an equal footing, and the settlement of accounts with cooperatives only from material incentive funds.

In his speech the deputy also touched on the problem of saturating the market with high-grade goods. He spoke about the need for a redistribution of funds from the state budget in favor of the development of Group "B" sectors and the introduction of a mechanism which would provide an incentive for enterprises in other sectors to get involved in the production of consumer goods.

Much criticism at the congress has been leveled at ministries and departments. It was noted that they are paying little attention to the social sphere and to people's needs. We asked O. Anfimov, USSR minister of the electrical equipment industry, who was present in the hall, for his opinion on this problem.

"I agree with those speakers who have sharply criticized the serious shortcomings in the development of the social sphere from the rostrum. At the same time, a sharp turning point has already been achieved in our ministry this year in respect of social problems. In cooperation with the collegium of the Central Committee of our trade union a program through the year 2000 for providing the sector's workers with housing has been elaborated. More than 130,000 families will have moved into new apartments by 1995. At present we are commissioning approximately 820,000 square meters of housing per year. If we manage to maintain this pace, we will fulfill our program. This will be assisted by the active development of the direct labor method in construction. The money allocated in the past for the 5-year period is clearly insufficient. We are trying to make fuller use of the right to switch part of the industrial fund resources to the nonproduction sphere. I think it would be hard nowadays to find a minister who does not want to ensure normal living conditions for the workers. And if there are problems, they are due to the shortcomings of the economic system itself. We would like to hear proposals from the people's deputies on how these problems can be overcome."

Deputy S. Chervonopiskiy, a former internationalist serviceman, spoke about the difficulties encountered by former servicemen who have discharged their international duty in Afghanistan. It has come to direct accusations being leveled at internationalist servicemen for nonexistent atrocities. This is how the speaker evaluated the, in his opinion, totally unfounded claims in the foreign press made by Deputy A. Sakharov. In this context S. Chervonopiskiy read out a message from the collective of the "60-year Soviet Socialist Republic" airborne unit. In connection with Deputy S. Chervonopiskiy's statement A. Sakharov gave an explanation. His remarks on events in Afghanistan were condemned by Deputies P. Shetko, V. Ochirov, A. Eyvan, V. Yakushkin, S. Akhromeyev, G. Kravchenko, N. Polikarpov, T. Kazakova, and others.

Toward the end of the evening session the congress approved the lineup of a deputies' commission to draw up a political and legal assessment of the 1939 Soviet-German Nonaggression Pact and associated documents.

A. Lukyanov, who chaired the session, briefed deputies on questions submitted to the congress Presidium and Secretariat and on messages and statements addressed to specific leaders of ministries and departments.

Deputies' Views on 'Atmosphere of Openness' Noted

*PM0706135189 Moscow TRUD in Russian
7 Jun 89 p 3*

[Special correspondents N. Kishkin, V. Konstantinov, and B. Leonov report: "In An Atmosphere of Openness. TRUD Special Correspondents Report from Kremlin Palace of Congresses"]

[Excerpts] The discussion on the main document at the Congress of USSR People's Deputies is drawing to an end. As a result the supreme organ of state power will define the main avenues of the country's domestic and foreign policy and further ways to develop restructuring. The deputies' speeches have already voiced proposals on the main socioeconomic problems. Priorities such as the food problem, the immediate improvement of the position of poorly paid sectors of the population, the bringing of order to the cooperative movement, and other matters of concern to our people have been mentioned. How do deputies themselves assess the course of the congress?

Yesterday morning all of them and the press received the results of a poll conducted by the sociological service that is operating here. Replying to the question: "Has the congress lived up to your hopes and expectations?," half of the deputies expressed satisfaction on the whole. An approximately equal number believe that the congress has lived up to their voters' expectations too. Deputies are noting the positive changes in the psychological atmosphere of the congress, the increased level of democratic discussion, and the way in which decisions have been worked out. At the same time, they are concerned about the low standard of the discussions and the inadequate level of agreement between the positions of different groups of deputies.

It is now clear that many of the almost 500 people who registered for the debate on the report were unable to speak. Admittedly, some further speeches [povtory] have now started, but it is not ruled out that some new ideas will remain unspoken. In the preceding days deputies had a chance to avoid this, but they "failed to notice" or to assess the situation. Several days ago a group of deputies submitted a proposal to set aside a special period for brief speeches at the end of each session. It would be enough to put forward a specific idea. There was also another opportunity: The poll has shown that deputies need to consolidate right now on the basis of similar positions and interests. Most of those polled (81 percent) consider it permissible to unite deputies in groups to work out general proposals based on unified positions. But this realization has probably come too late. Yet that is precisely the route that was proposed by a number of deputies in the very first days of the congress.

During the recess we talked with Deputy I.I. Zaslavskiy from the capital.

"To a certain extent the discussions are held on the old territorial principle," he said. "Yet we are not discussing the problems of the regions but statewide problems. And it has turned out that specialist deputies have been poorly represented in the debates. We have missed out on a lot because of this." [passage omitted]

In front of the entrance to the Kremlin Palace of Congresses a group of foreign and Soviet journalists asked Deputy B.N. Yeltsin for his impressions of the Congress' work.

"The Congress is not over yet and it is too soon to give a full impression of its work. Let us wait until it ends," he said. "But even now I feel a certain dissatisfaction at its progress. I particularly do not understand the 'outbursts of anger,' such as occurred after A.D. Sakharov's speech concerning the Afghan question. It is necessary to learn to receive any opinion or viewpoint calmly and thoughtfully..."

The matter is not one of emotions in themselves. But sometimes they do not simply emphasize the lack of a parliamentary culture but, by drowning out logic and reason, they prevent the thorough and objective discussion of urgent questions and divert the Congress from the essentials.

Hero of the Soviet Union Lieutenant Colonel R.S. Aushev, a veteran of Afghanistan, told us that he receives a lot of letters from young men who have returned from Afghanistan. Each letter contains pain, despair, and indignation at the fact that they, especially the invalids, have to suffer taunts and humiliation when it comes to enjoying the privileges granted by the government. Not only do officials use any pretext to refuse them priority in the provision of housing and of work appropriate to their state of health, they also resort to insulting arguments of the "I didn't send you to Afghanistan" type. This very problem—our society's still-bleeding wound—was discussed from the Congress rostrum by former internationalist servicemen S.V. Chervonopiskiy and P.V. Shetko. They spoke about the difficulties of the social rehabilitation of the young men who came back from that war but most importantly about the moral agonies and the attempts to shift the blame and responsibility onto yesterday's youngsters from those who gave the order almost 10 years ago to send the soldiers into Afghanistan... Misfortune must never be a pretext for all kinds of fabrications and false beliefs. Only the truth, albeit the most bitter truth, can take away the pain. And the facile talk about "helping a neighbor," help which cost not only billions of rubles but also thousands of our young men's lives, like Academician A.D. Sakharov's comment that Soviet helicopter pilots had allegedly been ordered to annihilate Soviet soldiers who had been surrounded, are more salt to bleeding wounds... Unfortunately the wave of emotion has so far considerably sidetracked the discussion on the "Afghan theme," including the most important problem of the social rehabilitation of those who were carrying out their military orders...

In the opinion of a number of the deputies with whom we talked at the Palace of Congresses, many speakers have been rightly noting our clear shortcomings in the economy and the consumer market and criticizing departmental diktat. But unfortunately, few of them are making constructive suggestions or pointing out specific ways to restructure our economy. It is possible that such speeches are still to come, after the report by the chairman of the USSR Council of Ministers. But the economy is the paramount question for the further course of all restructuring and the solution of social problems. And the more ideas and proposals that are put forward and discussed, the more guarantees there will be that the Congress will adopt the only correct concept in our conditions for the economic development of the Soviet economy.

IZVESTIYA Continues Series of Congress Reports

10th Day of Congress
*PM0806142189 Moscow IZVESTIYA in Russian
8 Jun 89 Morning Edition p 1*

[A. Plutnik commentary: "Day Ten"]

[Text] I feel that an observation made by one of the deputies to his colleagues—regarding the pleading tone in which they speak with contenders for responsible state posts—is absolutely correct. It is indeed true that representatives of the highest authority still far from always see themselves as such. But their attitude to themselves and to their responsibilities is changing before our eyes. The path trodden by contenders for the highest state posts is becoming increasingly thorny, as they are having to answer not only questions which are essentially political arithmetic but also questions which represent the higher mathematics of politics and morality. It seems that the approval of N.I. Ryzhkov's nomination for the post of chairman of the USSR Council of Ministers was the last in that series, which, from the very outset, was more like a press conference of a leader who had already been elected than merely that of a contender for this position.

However, if it were not for the fact that nine days of congress work lay behind us, with their sharpness and unpredictability, we would probably have given this public discussion a quite different appraisal. We would have been elated by the fact that it had been possible at all in our social life. But now we have a different point of reference—the congress, the very pithy discussions which are being conducted there, and the fearless speeches of those who take the floor.

Have the proceedings in the Supreme Soviet during the discussion of nominations reflected the mood of the congress? And the congress itself—how far does it reflect the public mood and the present state of our society? It undoubtedly reflects them to a considerable extent. Trying to pinpoint public opinion, sociologists are conducting selective surveys. In their findings there is much that is incidental, but nevertheless the end result "by and large" gives a fairly accurate picture of what is happening in our society. A picture of our life is also being given by the congress—a picture of the state of social thinking, those forces which have taken shape and are at work, and those trends which are developing or dying out.

And if a note of sycophancy can be discerned in a deputy's question with regard to a contender for a high post, if, in another question, inflexibility in the struggle for the truth and for the interests of the cause clearly comes across through the enormous nervous tension, and if someone, losing his nerve, decides not to rise from his seat, then behind all this there lies our life, its present state, and the prevailing frames of mind.

The congress is a microcosm of our society. Those assembled are not a homogeneous mass. Their many different strata are clearly in evidence at times. When, in a burst of exultation, some delegations spring from their seats as if at some command, frantically applauding the speaker, others maintain a marked unreceptiveness, denying any cause for jubilation, and remain as one in their seats. Thereby making it clearly understood that condemnation can also be expressed in this way—by not registering approval.

But should we feel affronted if in some deputies the hankering after the old ways is stronger than the desire for new ideas? If, despite the fact that they are in the majority, they are not becoming more charitable? Surely this reflects certain social trends? Should you feel affronted by those assembled if they do not think as you do? After all, their lack of democracy often stems from the vexatious belief that only someone who thinks the same as I do is thinking correctly. In any case, the hall is a reflection of life and an inalienable part of it. And life takes different forms. People are different. The audience is like life. We are fortunately no longer afflicted with the disease of unanimity.

Two important ideas have been voiced by deputies. The first: There is a strict logical pattern as regards precisely which buildings remained standing in Armenia during the terrible earthquake—it was those of which the names of the architect, the client, and the builder are known. The buildings which collapsed were anonymous, while those for which people had taken responsibility remained standing. The second: If everyone knew exactly what he was responsible for, society and all of us would always know who to blame.

There must be no impersonality—this, in my view, is the most important lesson we must take with us to day 10 of the congress. But unfortunately there is still a great deal of impersonality in our life. (Anonymity of labor, anonymity of ownership: common ownership, the people's property—what does this mean? Is this not the most widespread form of ownership in our country—no one's?) There is also a great deal of anonymity at the congress. Even today, many do not even give their names when questioning candidates. And remember how on previous days many speakers gravitated toward impersonal statements. They did not speak in their own name but "under cover." They spoke on behalf of the miners of Vorkuta or the farmers of Non-Chernozem Zone, people of their nationality, or people of their generation. Please do not think, they seemed to say, that I have thought all this up myself.... Even this is a kind of "pleading tone." However, one would be hard put to suspect that certain speakers are speaking on their own behalf. They forget that they have been elected—to represent the trade unions, say, and not just the chairman of the All-Union Central Council of Trade Unions (AUCCTU), to represent the All-Union Lenin Communist Youth League (Komsomol) and not just the first secretary of the Komsomol Central Committee, to represent a certain territory and not just the local "top man."

At one of the first congress sessions, without even having established the correlation of forces, so to speak, some deputies apparently decided to observe complete neutrality for the time being—and abstained when any decisions were being taken. But then the chairman gently pointed out that, comrades, you should vote "for" or "against"—we need you to take a stand.

We need you to take a stand—that is the whole crux of the matter. We need certainty that will rule out all anonymity. Every word must have a name attached to it, and every deed even more so. The congress and life have an increasing need for fearless people who are incapable of using a pleading tone.

11th Day of Congress
PM0806193789 Moscow IZVESTIYA in Russian 9 Jun 89 Morning Edition p 1

[E. Gonzalyez commentary: "Day Eleven"]

[Text] The present congress has not yet adopted any cardinal decisions, but it has already changed our views on life (if not life itself). We are looking at literally everything from a slightly different angle now. And that includes the congress itself. And we see that the deputies are not equally ready, not just for work under conditions of democracy, but also for the role of member of government. The impartial television screen shows that this role fits some people as if it were made to measure, while in the case of others there is plenty of growing room, so to speak.

This situation is only natural, and there would be no need to even mention it, if only the deputies could see themselves from a distance. They would, I am sure, themselves focus on a certain lack of restraint which, in my view, does not befit state officials, on emotional outbursts, applause for totally unsuitable reasons, support not so much for ideas as for the people who are expressing them, and a selective desire to listen contrasting with an almost boundless desire to speak.

It is no so bad when the explanation for the irrepressible attraction of the microphone is long abstinence. It is worse if the speech at the congress is an end in itself, and worse still if it pursues group or territorial interests and ambitions only. We have already seen a scrupulous and naive totaling up of how many people have spoken on behalf of union republics and how many on behalf of autonomous republics. What for? Are there people among the deputies who believe in the power of words to that extent? Is not the solution of the problems which are being discussed the main thing?

Voices have already been heard complaining about the seating arrangements, about having to sit in the wrong row, or the wrong corner. It is not quite clear whether the deputies in question are complaining about not being able to see properly what is happening "on the stage," or about not being seen by people in Central Asia or the Far East.

Frankly speaking, what we want to be able to see is the development of ideas, rather than the expression on people's faces. And last week when there were arguments, clashes of opinion, when one speech brought forth the next, this was just about possible, albeit with difficulty. On Tuesday the thread broke—self-praise came wafting from the screen. It would have been surprising, of course, if there had not been any at all—people lack that sort of education, so to speak. However, I want to draw attention to something else: Obvious self-praise met with the same (if not even louder) applause than the most original, bold ideas.

The report by N.I. Ryzhkov, chairman of the USSR Council of Ministers, redirected the attention of the congress back to the serious problems which lie ahead of the country. Out of inertia, I wrote "problems which lie ahead" but then I thought: Have not many deputies asserted here that what lies ahead is in fact the **solution of problems**, whereas we are getting more and more bogged down in the problems themselves.

In the debate on the report "On the Program of the Future Activities of the USSR Government" concern for the "development of individual krays, oblasts, or regions" was also frequently expressed and there were attempts to divert deputies' attention to individual sectors. However, in my opinion, the main issues were also addressed—why the solution of problems still lies ahead of us, why we are struggling in our unenviable position marking time, why we lack the courage to make a breakthrough.

And there were proposals. Serious proposals, on the scale of the country. Their analysis must be just as serious. Meanwhile I would merely like to say the following: It is possible to question the expediency of convening a workers' congress, argue about ways of curing the financial situation, or view the demand for republican independence as a false bottom. But it is impossible to deny that all these proposals are specific, precise, well-weighed, and novel.

And most important—they are implementable as distinct from the usual decisions "to accelerate," "enhance the responsibility of," or even "set up a commission." However, not for nothing are merits regarded as a continuation of shortcomings and vice-versa. The novelty and unprecedented nature of the proposals may do them a disservice. It is not just a question of conservatism here, but also of an objective risk inherent in experiments in such a complex and vast economy which, incidentally, lived for many years exclusively by the rules of precedent.

The proposals have one more shortcoming—they are unfamiliar to the very departments which have to implement them. The experience of introducing even the simplest production rationalization proposals indicates that this can frequently be an insurmountable obstacle.

It is somewhat reassuring, though, that as regards the departments themselves, a consensus seems to have emerged at the congress—there should be as few of them as possible. Well, that, too, would be an unprecedented decision which would pave the way for many others.

Another thesis, which was expressed by several deputies, is probably also unquestionable: The new tasks must be implemented by new people with new thinking. Incidentally, this question also arose at the USSR Supreme Soviet session during the elections to various posts. Up to now leaders of a certain rank were virtually shuffled around in a circle. This was motivated by a shortage of cadres. Where can you find a ready-made leader? people asked. This is another thing to the credit of the congress—it has shown how many people there are in our country who are not just ready to exercise leadership, but who also know how to do it.

6 Jun Soviet of Nationalities Afternoon Session

PM0906100189 Moscow IZVESTIYA in Russian
8 Jun 89 Morning Edition pp 6-10

["First Session of USSR Supreme Soviet: First Session of Soviet of Nationalities. Stenographic Record"—IZVESTIYA headline]

[Excerpts] Hall of sessions of the USSR Supreme Soviet chambers in the Kremlin. 6 June 1989. 1600.

Comrade M.S. Gorbachev, chairman of the USSR Supreme Soviet, is in the chair. [passage omitted]

V.S. Shevchenko, chairman of the Ukrainian Soviet Socialist Republic [SSR] Supreme Soviet Presidium, Kiev City (Kiyevskiy Rural National-Territorial Electoral Okrug, Ukrainian SSR): Esteemed comrade deputies! The most diverse problems have been voiced a great deal at our congress. But it seems to me that the problem of interethnic relations is not simply being voiced, it is crying out and calling on all of us to help. That is no coincidence. Clearly this is because very many centers of tension based on interethnic relations have emerged in various parts of the country recently. And that causes Soviet people great concern. It causes concern for our common home, our union.

It seems to me that the solution of interethnic problems—of the republics and all the nations and ethnic groups in country—depends to a considerable extent on how they are examined in our chamber. I would say that our chamber has a special role to play. A colleague from a Baltic republic has said that a very respectful attitude is needed here to the opinion of the representative of each nation and ethnic group, a respectful attitude toward culture, language, traditions, and problems. And very much will depend on who is going to conduct our chamber's sittings and who is going to direct the activity of all the deputies of this chamber.

I think that Rafik Nishanovich is probably the most suitable candidate for the post of chairman of the chamber of the Soviet of Nationalities. I know Rafik Nishanovich from our work together in the USSR Supreme Soviet Presidium. He is a man of very high culture, great tact, and deep knowledge, who has experience of party, soviet, and diplomatic work. I think that in this situation Rafik Nishanovich is perfectly equipped to listen to a large number of opinions and reach a compromise, a compromise in the interests of everyone and of our entire multinational socialist state.

Under the conditions of the further reform of the political system, democratization, glasnost, and the restructuring of the USSR Supreme Soviet's activity, I think that these qualities of Rafik Nishanovich's are of exceptionally great significance, and we fully support his candidacy for the post of chairman of the Soviet of Nationalities. I urge you all to vote for him! I do not think that we shall be making a mistake!

M.S. Gorbachev: Comrade Tarazevich! I see Comrade Vizirov over there; I shall call on him later.

G.S. Tarazevich, chairman of the Belorussian SSR Supreme Soviet Presidium, Minsk City (Molodechnenskiy National-Territorial Electoral Okrug, Belorussian SSR): Comrade deputies! I also know Rafik Nishanovich well from working with him in our country's Supreme Soviet Presidium. I should like to stress that Rafik Nishanovich is a very learned man with a good fundamental grounding in the humanities and education. He is a man with great experience of leading work—party and soviet work—a diplomat who has been very favorably mentioned in the countries where he has been and fulfilled a mission on our country's behalf. Furthermore, Rafik Nishanovich possesses lofty human qualities. I should like to note first of all that he has the ability to unite people around him. He understands people. He knows how to get on with people; he attracts others to him. So it seems to me that these human qualities will play an important role in the great work which awaits our chamber.

Rafik Nishanovich is a man of principle. This is confirmed by the fact that, when he had been secretary of the Uzbek Communist Party Central Committee but found himself transferred to diplomatic work, he did not abandon his principles. He is a man who really knows how to lead people. We have seen and witnessed for ourselves how he chaired the congress. Therefore our delegation, I mean the Belorussians, will vote unanimously for Rafik Nishanovich and we urge everyone to support his candidacy.

From the floor: We haven't known Rafik Nishanovich as long but I saw him for the first time at the conference conducted by the party Central Committee in Tashkent recently. There were some quite awkward situations there, too. He was able to conduct the conference in a very simple and accessible way and he made a very good impression on all those present. But since the Council of Elders had examined this question, we studied Rafik Nishanovich's biography in depth, and then spoke with comrades from Uzbekistan and Tajikistan. Then we discussed among ourselves, within our Bashkir delegation (yes, his answer on the autonomous republics pleased us very much) and reached the conclusion that he clearly has a very good, sober view of this matter. Therefore, we fully support his candidacy and think that we could not want a better man as chairman of the chamber of nationalities. I think that all the autonomous republics and all the deputies will also support us on this question.

I disagree with the comrade from the Baltic who proposes complicating this question again with more procedures of some kind. What for? There is no need for that!

Here is another suggestion. Even in this situation we should surely observe the standing orders and talk about the candidacy, not about anything and everything.

Thank you for your attention!

G.M. Magomedov, first secretary of the Sergokalinskiy CPSU Rayon Committee [Raykom], Dagestan Autonomous Soviet Socialist Republic [ASSR] (Izberbashskiy National-Territorial Electoral Okrug, Dagestan ASSR): Comrades! We small ethnic groups are sometimes unlucky. At the congress we are sitting in the corner at the very back, and here, too, we have also been placed in the corner even though the hall is semicircular. (Animation in the auditorium)

Even though I have heard Comrade Nishanov's name several times before, I did not get to know him personally until the congress, and I am very glad to have been able to make his acquaintance. I saw him several times before the congress, at conferences and meetings of the party group, and I saw him elected a member of the Congress Presidium. I recall how he conducted the congress and chaired a sitting of it. It was gratifying and very pleasing for us to listen to him. His words came to mind: "Everything is in order here, don't worry! Everything is proceeding normally." His tone and style of speaking are good. He chaired the congress skillfully and, when necessary, harshly removed from the rostrum speakers who had come up to speak without his permission.

I also attended the sitting of the Council of Elders. Quite a few questions were put to Comrade Nishanov there. In a speech of about 15 minutes he described how he sees the Supreme Soviet Soviet of Nationalities. Here too, comrades, I realized that I did not want to see any other candidacy for the post of chairman of our Supreme Soviet's Soviet of Nationalities.

Our Dagestan group—there are four of us here and our neighbors in the auditorium at the congress and here—the Buryat group—fully support Comrade Nishanov's candidacy, and I would ask all the colleagues sitting here to cast their votes for him. Furthermore, comrades, I am sure that Nishanov will be elected chairman of the Soviet of Nationalities. And I would ask him to join with us all in paying special attention to the development of our autonomous republics.

Our colleagues from Estonia have put forward an attractive proposal on regional economic accountability here. We have given much thought to this question and reached the conclusion that our autonomous republics still have a long way to go to catch up with the Baltic republics. I should like to quote one example to demonstrate that to you.

Over 100,000 able-bodied people in our republic have no work at the moment. For that reason they have to leave in spring to earn a living in Central Asia, Kazakhstan, Orenburg Oblast, Gorno-Altay Oblast, and other parts of the country. There are probably comrades from Smolensk Oblast here. I have met with them at the congress. Last year we leased from them a state farm [sovkhoz] in

Kalininskoye village, Glinkovskiy Rayon. We are to ensure the well-organized resettlement of families from Dagestan to there, take over neglected and deserted villages, and revive the sovkhoz.

We have many proposals for ministries and departments. We ask them to build plants and subsidiaries of plants in our area. I think that the Soviet of Nationalities will help us on this question. We cannot understand it when some deputies speak out and say: We do not want an asphalt plant, a cement plant, or any other plant. We ask, we beseech that plants be built in our area, that our people be given work and can earn a wage so that they do not abandon their families and leave Dagestan to spend 5, 7, or 8 months elsewhere.

Comrades, I consider the question of the Caspian to be of considerable significance also. In the past few years the water level in the Caspian has risen by 135 cm. This is a major calamity. Our coastal towns are simply in a hopeless position. Therefore I think that this question will be resolved in the Soviet of Nationalities. Thank you for your attention. I hope that everyone will support the proposal of my comrades and me and vote unanimously for Comrade Nishanov.

M.S. Gorbachev: Please go ahead....

Voice from floor: (Inaudible).

M.S. Gorbachev: Comrades are drawing attention to the essence of the question. (Noise in hall).

L.A. Arutyunyan, chief of department at the Yerevan State University, Yerevan (from women's councils united by the Committee of Soviet Women): Esteemed chairman, esteemed deputies! I would not have spoken had I not heard the reply to the effect that Rafik Nishanovich intends to organize his activity in such a way as not to offend anyone. In my view, the Soviet of Nationalities is not being set up in order not to offend anyone, but to provide the legislative foundation for our parliament's work.

I am very glad that our future work is going to be calm and emotionally relaxed, but I would very much like not to believe that our work will remain at the level of such mutual relations. And the Supreme Soviet Soviet of Nationalities draft resolution "On Standing Commissions" proves that I am not mistaken. See, the words "law and policy" are not mentioned here. I am absolutely amazed by this fact. Why do we, when citing the names of the commissions, not once use the word "law" and not once use the word "policy"? Is it an accident, or is it a bid regarding the future content of the work of the Soviet of Nationalities? If it is a bid regarding the future content I would like to draw Rafik Nishanovich's attention to the fact that he will be required to show the quality of a reformer in his work. Is he prepared to totally reform the tradition of discussion of nationalities problems?

We are faced today with serious interethnic conflicts; we are faced today with a cumbersome pyramidal machinery, a pyramidal mechanism of ethnic relations which constantly malfunctions. As you will appreciate, plugging the holes will not help, because the river has already burst its banks and it will sweep away the dam. We need to very significantly modify the entire mechanism and to bring it into line with international norms. So there can be no question of good or bad relations. It is a question of innovation, of a new system of relations between nations. And from this viewpoint the future chairman of the Soviet of Nationalities must be aware of his serious task and be an innovator in this respect.

Finally, I want to say that at the moment we essentially lack a mechanism for representing nations' interests. We still do not even know who is the subject of federation; we do not have a consensus mechanism. Essentially we lack a system for arbitrating on interethnic conflicts. We entirely lack the mechanism.

So a great deal of work has to be done to create a mechanism. Fine words about peace in our common home are an anachronism today. This peace must be safeguarded by law, legislation, and sanctions, not by wishes alone. I wish the chairman of the chamber good, effective work, but I want to assure him that the work can only be effective if he is able to take a critical look at what we have and if he appreciates that the future can only be built on a legal foundation. Thank you.

M.S. Gorbachev: I want to ask you this: Are we going to continue the discussion? There are many who want to, comrades. I notice that despite the diversity of opinion, the deviations from the matter under discussion, and the widening of the issues raised, everyone has supported the proposal that was put forward. Even Comrade Medvedev, when putting forward and justifying approaches to the way we should act when electing the chamber chairman, nonetheless was positive in his reaction to Comrade Nishanov. Perhaps someone has other opinions? Yes. Comrade Starovoytova, please go ahead.

G.V. Starovoytova, senior scientific assistant at the Center for the Study of International Relations under the USSR Academy of Sciences Presidium, Moscow (Yerevanskiy-Sovetskiy National-Territorial Okrug, Armenian SSR): Esteemed comrade deputies! In my view, we are present at the exceedingly important procedure of electing the chairman of the Soviet of Nationalities. In my opinion, this chamber is more important than the Soviet of the Union in our two-chamber parliament. Everyone knows now that ethnic issues are the third component of restructuring, without which the two other components—socioeconomic and political reforms—cannot happen in our country. Therefore I would like to hear a more serious discussion of the problems which the chamber and its esteemed chairman have to tackle.

I would like to say one or two words about how I view these problems, since, unfortunately, this has not been addressed today and I did not hear in esteemed Comrade Nishanov's answers solutions to some very important questions that we will be dealing with for 5 years.

First of all, our Congress of People's Deputies includes representatives of 65 nationalities—so we were told by the Credentials Commission. We know that, according to the latest population census figures, there are representatives of more than 120 nationalities in our country (these are just the amalgamated groups recorded in the census). Thus one-half of the country's peoples are not represented in today's parliament. And some peoples, particularly those who do not have their own forms of national statehood, such as the Crimean Tatars, Germans, Jews, Kurds, and others, are obviously inadequately represented. This is a very important issue. I believe the chamber's deputies will have to confront it and offer prescriptions for solving it.

The second problem is that of renewing our union treaty. As is well known, the Treaty on the Formation of the USSR was concluded on 30 December 1922. An entire historical era has gone by since then. The composition of the sovereign subjects that signed the treaty back then has also changed. The very content of the functions (social, economic, and political) which the republics, as sovereign subjects of the treaty, delegate to the central federal government has also changed. The catalogue, the list of functions clearly needs renewing and overhauling. I believe this is another issue that will face the chamber.

Some problems have already been discussed here—our multitier, four-level national-state structure, and legal guarantees of a nation's right to self-determination. There are definite contradictions here. For example, according to Article 72 of the USSR Constitution, a people representing a union republic have the right to self-determination, even withdrawal from the USSR, but small peoples with other forms of statehood—autonomous oblasts, autonomous republics and okrugs—cannot change their national affiliation even within the context of the union or switch from membership of one union republic to membership of another. That is, people's rights are differentiated to a certain extent in the existing structure. I fear that these problems will crop up in the chamber's activities and they will require highly competent expert appraisal.

The entire past year has demonstrated to us that there is a serious lack of readiness to solve these questions and there is a serious fear of setting a precedent. This fear is understandable, because for 65 years we said that the nationalities question has been solved here once and for all. Even today, during the congress, the press has objectively been fueling interethnic tension in certain regions.

Unfortunately, at the moment we do not see a sufficiently competent independent expert appraisal of all these questions; we do not see adequate knowledge of foreign ethnopolitical experience in solving similar problems. I was pleased to hear that Rafik Nishanovich is a candidate of historical sciences, because this chamber must have many specialists, and its chairman above all must be a competent specialist. I would also like to know—I did not have the opportunity to ask this question before—the topic of your dissertation. I have a personal interest, if you like.

Voice from the floor: (Inaudible).

G.V. Starovoytova: Me too, me too.... Are you asking me a question? Yes, if you open the USSR Constitution you will see that I have the right to participate in the chamber's sitting with a consultative vote. Please give me a couple of minutes to finish my speech, because I have been interrupted.

M.S. Gorbachev: Yes, Comrade Staorovoytova. Particularly as the agenda is the election of the chamber chairman, and only then will the chamber decide how to arrange its work and what kind of hierarchy to set up. That is all in the future....

G.V. Starovoytova: What I want to say about this is that I am also happy with—I personally liked the way Comrade Nishanov has chaired a number of sittings, although I cannot speak for my voters. I have received many complaints, but I think that today the simple ability to smooth rough edges, the ability to find a compromise, is a very important ability in general, particularly in the activity of this chamber. A valid scientific program and action platform are needed. Who would be the ideal chamber chairman, I wondered? Possibly, say, a representative of a little people, one that does not have its own statehood, perhaps. Certainly it must be someone in whose republic things are in good shape, where interethnic relations are in good shape. And a number of other conditions, it would seem to me, in abstract terms, must be met.

M.S. Gorbachev: That's it. Let's finish now.

G.V. Starovoytova: I think this problem can be....

M.S. Gorbachev: Comrade Starovoytova, there's no need to introduce an element....

G.V. Starovoytova: ...can be solved by means of rotation, which has already been discussed here by a comrade. I propose rotation.

M.S. Gorbachev: You have exercised your right as an invited guest; you have been given the floor. Do you have a contrary opinion? No. We agreed that if someone had a contrary opinion that person would be given the floor. According to the Constitution, we are gathered here to elect a chamber chairman.

Do you have a contrary opinion? Please go ahead.

E.V. Bichkauskas, investigator for particularly important cases at the Lithuanian SSR Prosecutor's Office, Vilnius (Shilutskiy National-Territorial Electoral Okrug, Lithuanian SSR): [passage omitted]

R.N. Nishanov, chairman of the USSR Supreme Soviet Soviet of Nationalities, is in the chair.

R.N. Nishanov: We are continuing the work of our sitting, comrades. Before we move on to the next question on the agenda, I would like to express to you my tremendous gratitude for the fact that you have entrusted this high, responsible post to me. I will try to make the maximum effort to ensure that the tasks facing the Soviet of Nationalities are resolved in a well thought out and successful fashion, and accord with the interests of all nations and ethnic groups.

Comrades! At this sitting it is proposed to examine the question of forming the standing commissions of the Soviet of Nationalities and also to discuss proposals regarding the formation of USSR Supreme Soviet committees. Comrade Deputy A.I. Lukyanov has the floor on this question.

A.I. Lukyanov, first deputy chairman of the USSR Supreme Soviet: Comrade deputies! So the Soviet of Nationalities—a component part of the Supreme Soviet—has finally been formed. It is an equal chamber and will, of course, not only resolve questions linked with our nationalities affairs and interethnic relations: any question within the competence of the union will pass through this chamber and be viewed from a nationalities perspective. This means above all economic questions, budgetary questions, and questions linked with the development of our culture and services for the population. It means questions linked with international [mezhdunarodnyy] relations, that is, the broadest spectrum of questions to be tackled by the USSR Supreme Soviet, which is the supreme legislative, administrative, and monitoring organ of state power. These are very broad functions, and you yourselves realize that many of these functions, in particular, both in the sphere of legislation and in the sphere of the budget, simply cannot be resolved by such a broad forum as the congress. They must be resolved by a narrower collegium, a collegium which should resemble to a considerable extent Lenin's Central Executive Committee, which was once elected by the Congress of Soviets. USSR Supreme Soviet committees and commissions play a very large role in this organism of state power. I want to recall that Article 122 of the USSR Constitution indicates that the Soviet of the Union and the Soviet of Nationalities elect from the members of the USSR Supreme Soviet and other USSR people's deputies the chambers' standing commissions to conduct legislative drafting work and the preliminary examination and preparation of questions within the jurisdiction of the USSR Supreme Soviet, and also in order to promote the implementation of USSR laws and other decisions adopted by the Congress of USSR People's Deputies and the USSR Supreme Soviet, and to monitor the activity of state organs and organizations.

Under the Constitution the Supreme Soviet chambers can also create USSR Supreme Soviet committees on a basis of parity and, in addition, a whole series of commissions, including investigative and auditing commissions.

Our Congress Presidium has carried out quite extensive analytical work in implementing these constitutional directives. As you know, all deputies were given a questionnaire and a draft resolution listing the commissions and committees that could be formed at the USSR Supreme Soviet. We asked every deputy to express his opinion as to which commission he would like to work in. Approximately 1,800 deputies responded to this questionnaire. Four-fifths of them supported the proposals regarding the named commissions and advocated participating in a commission. Some comrades indicated that they could take part in two commissions. Others named two commissions and said that they agreed to be involved in either of them. Approximately 12 percent of the responses contained proposals for refining the list and the work assignment of the Supreme Soviet commissions and committees. So we took these proposals from deputies most actively into consideration when putting the finishing touches to the proposals.

On what premise did the Supreme Soviet Presidium, the chambers' Council of Elders, who received a report on this, and the Congress Presidium proceed?

First. We proceeded on the premise that the membership of the chambers is not very large, comparatively speaking: Each chamber has 271 deputies. If we increase the number of commissions ad infinitum we will simply be unable to ensure the requisite balance, which envisages that each commission complies with the following proportion: One congress deputy to every member of the chamber.

Second. We proceeded on the premise that the commissions cannot be rigidly tied to sectors of state management. Otherwise they will duplicate ministries and departments even in their titles, which will, of course, impede their parliamentary activity and the fulfillment of their parliamentary functions, and distort the parliamentary assignment of commissions and committees.

Third. Subcommissions or subcommittees will undoubtedly be set up within the commissions and committees. It is here that questions of interest to the Supreme Soviet and your chamber must be analyzed in depth. That is, every committee will have within it a subdivision dealing with particular issues.

Last, at the session of the chambers' Council of Elders last Saturday we arrived at the unanimous opinion that, when setting up committees [as published] in one chamber, it is necessary to take into account the fact that commissions with a different assignment will operate in the other chamber, but committees will be formed jointly. That is, we must have a comprehensive approach to this problem. So when we talk about Soviet of Nationalities commissions, we must see without fail what commissions the Soviet of the Union has set up. Therefore at the sitting of the chambers' Council of Elders we carefully went through the whole package of proposals, so to speak, as to what commissions and committees the Supreme Soviet should have.

Then, as you know, the first sitting of the Soviet of the Union was held and discussed these questions in detail in an atmosphere of quite keen debate, after which a resolution was adopted regarding the formation of Soviet of the Union standing commissions; this has been published. You have seen it.

So permit me to briefly inform you how work on these documents went and what amendments have already been submitted and are being submitted for your examination. Okay, first a word about the Soviet of the Union standing commissions. It is proposed to form an equal number of standing commissions—four each—in each chamber. At the same time, the 19th party conference stressed that we should abandon the functional depersonalization of the chambers. The Soviet of the Union, which reflects nationwide interests, should concentrate above all on questions of statewide significance, and the Soviet of Nationalities should have its own profile, linked with the development of nations and ethnic groups and the development of union and autonomous republics and other autonomous formations. Proceeding on this premise, the Soviet of the Union formed the following commissions. A Planning, Budget, and Financial Commission. As you can see, this deals with the USSR's entire plan and entire budget. The Commission for Questions of the Development of Industry, Energy, Equipment, and Technology also constitutes a statewide question. A Commission for Transport, Communications, and Information Science Questions. Once again an all-union question. Lastly, a Commission for Labor, Prices, and Social Policy Questions. Here the perspective that was chosen is that labor relations and labor should be regulated on a countrywide scale, identically with regard to every citizen; this constitutes equality of rights for citizens. Prices are of most fundamental significance in general for the whole market and for all commodity turnover. Lastly, the main directions of a strong social policy are, indisputably, a statewide question.

You have obviously noticed that, compared with the original versions distributed to deputies, the names of some commissions have undergone changes, and quite substantial changes, too. This is no mere gesture to form, but an endeavor to more precisely define the all-union essence of the sphere of work, that is, to encapsulate a mighty set of problems whose resolution transcends the bounds of republican competence and the regional level and which must be resolved by the union as a whole.

As for the Soviet of Nationalities standing commissions, the conclusions of the 19th party conference that this chamber should primarily resolve questions with a direct bearing on the subjects of our federation—the republics and autonomous formations—and the development of Soviet nations and ethnic groups were also used as the basis here. That is why the Council of Elders propose moving the Commission for Interethnic Relations to the foreground here in this chamber. There is certainly no need to comment in detail on this proposal. Very many questions have accumulated in this sphere, and our current sitting attests to this. A very great deal of, let us be blunt, very complex work lies ahead of us here. The next commission is the Commission for Questions of the Social and Economic Development of Union and Autonomous Republics and Autonomous Oblasts and Okrugs. This constitutes, as it were, the republican, nationalities aspect of the Planning, Budget, and Financial Commission, but with its own perspective. These commissions can work together. But the Soviet of Nationalities commission has its own perspective, which should be reflected as much as possible when elaborating the plan, the budget, and other economic programs—namely the perspective of consideration of ethnic relations. This is a most serious commission. It would certainly be right to say that this commission does indeed by and large resemble the Soviet of the Union Planning, Budget, and Financial Commission, but only with regard to the republics. Obviously, this Soviet of Nationalities commission will have a number of subcommissions; in particular, the Council of Elders discussed the fact that it would be advisable to have a special subcommission within this commission dealing with questions of the development of our country's small peoples. All economic and management questions meet here and must be resolved here.

Next. It is proposed to establish a commission linked with the work of those sectors of the economy which are now—according to the new concept published not so long ago—being completely transferred to republican jurisdiction. This is the Commission for Consumer Goods, Trade, and Municipal, Consumer, and Other Services to the Population. As you know, there is a mass of problems here. They must be very thoroughly resolved, including from the viewpoint of solving ethnic problems.

The next commission is the Commission for Questions of the Development of Culture, Language, National and International Traditions, and Protection of Historical Monuments. The opinion expressed by both chambers' Councils of Elders and deputies' proposals on this question were based on the fact that the roots of our multinational culture are found here, in the development of every nation and ethnic group. It is from the cultures of all our country's peoples that our multinational Soviet culture takes shape. That is why it is proposed to have this commission among the commissions within the USSR Supreme Soviet Soviet of Nationalities. Thus it is proposed to create four commissions within the Soviet of Nationalities, just as within the Soviet of the Union.

Now a word about the committees. Is is well known that they will be created by both chambers on a basis of parity. Certain amendments to the original outlines handed out to deputies were made during the discussion of this question in the chambers' Councils of Elders and also at the sitting of the Soviet of the Union.

I will comment on them in brief. Thus, it is proposed to form an International Affairs Committee, which will encompass both foreign policy and foreign economic questions and will engage in interparliamentary ties and, to some extent, questions of humanitarian cooperation and so on. In my opinion, everything is clear here.

Next, a Committee for Defense and State Security Questions. The Soviet of the Union discussed these questions for a long time and decided that they are so closely interconnected that they should be linked together. The Soviet of the Union sitting also raised the question of whether this committee will monitor the activity of state security organs. It certainly will. The KGB falls within the purview of this parliamentary committee. But, as Mikhail Sergeyevich Gorbachev pointed out, it will, of course, have a special status, as in all foreign parliaments.

The next committee is the Committee for Questions of Legislation, Legality, and Law and Order. It has been said here that there is no mention of the legal principle when forming the committees. But this is the main committee which will deal with legal questions. Of course, this committee will be most involved with legal drafting work and fine-tuning the wording of legislation and statutes. But it is very important to ensure that it is linked—and this was stressed, you will remember, at the congress itself—with the state of affairs in the sphere of legality and with law and order. It must be able to supervise the practical implementation of laws, study this work, and monitor the activity of law enforcement organs. Without this, there would be no point to pure legislative work, especially as other committees—all the other committees—will also engage in legislative work, with this committee's participation, of course. Practice shows that the Legislative Proposals Commission cooperated very closely with other USSR Supreme Soviet commissions.

Next: Also on the basis of many deputies' views, it is proposed to create a Committee for Questions of the Work of Soviets of People's Deputies and of the Development of Management and Self-Management. I must say that this is a new committee and is absolutely necessary because the Supreme Soviet is indeed the apex of the entire pyramid of our country's soviets and must resolve a host of questions—most complex ones, I can tell you. That is why we received so many proposals regarding the creation of this committee from the localities and literally from soviets at all levels—rural, settlement, rayon, municipal, oblast, and kray soviets. All the soviets were in favor of creating this committee.

The next committee whose proposed creation has been submitted for your examination is also linked with deputies' wishes and the conclusions of Mikhail Sergeyevich's report at the congress. I am talking about the Committee for Economic Reform Questions. There was no mention of this committee in the material you were given at first. The Soviet of the Union Planning, Budget, and Financial Commission, the Soviet of Nationalities Commission for Questions of the Social and Economic Development of Union and Autonomous Republics and Autonomous Oblasts and Okrugs, and the Committee on Economic Reform Questions, will in fact work in the closest contact. Such is the specific nature of these parliamentary institutions, and it is important, of course, that their chairmen coordinate their work in this very important area.

The next committee which the chambers' Councils of Elders deemed it advisable to establish is the Committee for Agrarian Questions and Food. It was first entitled "for Agrarian Policy and Food," but then it was decided that policy is a somewhat general sphere, as it were, and we will have specific—agrarian and food—questions of a parliamentary type. As you know, it was first proposed to set up this committee in one of the chambers, but then we reached the conclusion that this must be a general parliamentary committee—a committee set up by both chambers on a basis of parity. As you know, this coincides with the opinion of the more than 400 deputies specializing in the agrarian sphere who signed the appeal to the congress, although I must say that they conceive of the committee somewhat differently—cluttered with a corresponding apparatus.

M.S. Gorbachev: Anatoliy Ivanovich, comrades have approached me here and some of them are worried; they think that everything has been eliminated at government level. But here, on the contrary, as you will hear, a proposal is going to be submitted, and there will be a first deputy chairman of the Council of Ministers who will head this whole complex. All this will also be studied at government level. So that this is at the level of the Supreme Soviet, and at the government level—everything will be considered there, too.

A.I. Lukyanov: And there will be this committee. Its main function is not just to draw up laws in this sphere but also to monitor, above all, the departments concerned with these questions. This is the specific feature of a parliament, of parliamentary monitoring.

Now the Committee for Construction and Architecture Questions. There were many proposals for it. Some people said that its title should refer only to urban planning, but in that case we would have been forgetting agricultural construction. Others said that a Committee for Architecture and Construction is necessary, and they are still not withdrawing their proposal. But everyone agreed that it would be most apt if we call this committee the USSR Supreme Soviet Committee for Construction and Architecture.

The question of the Committee for Science and Public Education was thoroughly discussed. We could have taken the course of splitting it into two parts—science and public education. But it was deemed expedient—and deputies at the sitting of the Soviet of the Union and the chambers' Council of Elders advocated this—to combine these elements in one parliamentary organ, since it is simply impossible to separate science, particularly VUZ [higher educational institution] science, from education.

Moreover, during discussion of this question at the sitting of the chambers' Council of Elders, it was also considered necessary to include questions of upbringing here, because education had been divorced from upbringing, as it were. This addition is highly significant. Thus the title now reads the Committee for Science, Public Education, and Upbringing. Although clearly a minimum of three autonomous subcommittees may be necessary here.

Now for the Committee for the Protection of the People's Health. Proposals were submitted on this question by the Academy of Medical Sciences. Given the present state of health protection, it is clear that this committee will have a very, very great deal of work.

The next committee is the Committee for Women's Affairs and Family, Mother, and Child Protection. Initially the idea was to have two committees—a committee for women's affairs and a committee for the affairs of the family and children. But eventually all deputies came to the common conclusion of having a single such committee.

At the sitting of the Soviet of the Union (as compared with the version of the chambers' Council of Elders and deputies' proposals) a new, very important and substantial element appeared in the definition of this committee—the family, protection of the family. This derives from life; the deputies proposed this themselves. We are very concerned now by the not altogether satisfactory, to put it mildly, situation regarding the family, divorces, single mothers, orphans, and so forth. And it is directly enshrined in our Constitution that the Soviet state concerns itself with and takes care to strengthen the Soviet family.

Next the Committee for the Affairs of Veterans and Invalids. Then one more committee—the Youth Affairs Committee. Here no one had any doubts that these committees are necessary and that they are confronted with quite a few complex questions. Matters regarding the setting up of a Committee for Questions of Ecology and the Rational Use of Natural Resources are exactly the same. Dozens of speeches at the Congress of People's Deputies and numerous publications in the mass media have revealed the full acuteness of this problem, although I should tell you that, unfortunately, when deputies were asked, not very many of them signed up or offered their services as participants in the work of this difficult committee. Finally, the Committee for Citizen's Rights and Appeals. I should tell you that the question of whether there should be a separate committee for rights was examined. Deputies, however, came to the conclusion that a committee which will be closely linked with the proposals and complaints received by the USSR Supreme Soviet must be set up. And, comrades, there are around half a million statements, proposals, and complaints to the Supreme Soviet each year.

The possibility of directly reacting to breaches of citizens' rights should be created. And here the Supreme Soviet is called upon to firmly adopt a stance of strictly protecting Soviet people's legitimate rights and interests. A substantial addition was made to the committee's title during the examination of this question at the Soviet of the Union sitting, and the committee is now entitled the Committee for Questions of Glasnost and Citizens' Rights and Appeals. Just a single word—glasnost—was added, and the committee's functions immediately took on a more profound meaning. These, comrades, are the committees, 14 of them, which it is proposed be formed jointly by the two chambers of the USSR Supreme Soviet. Thus, while the question of the Soviet of Nationalities standing commissions can be resolved today, right now, the question of committees, if the chamber approves the submitted list with or without amendments, will be referred to the joint sitting of the USSR Supreme Soviet chambers and finally decided there. I would like to add to what has been said that we will of course need to set up various, so to speak, ad hoc committees, commissions, and so forth.

The congress has already set up three commissions on specific current questions, and in this regard certain deputies, in particular Deputy Revenko at the Soviet of the Union sitting, said, correctly in my view, that there is no need to be in a hurry now to rigidly define the number of committees and commissions to be formed. We need to reserve the right to flexibly alter the assignment of commissions and committees if need be. Especially as it will often be quite difficult in practice to drawing any kind of insuperable dividing line between commissions in the different chambers or with different assignments. However, constantly increasing the number of commissions makes no sense either. They will operate, as a rule, in close contact and it is therefore impossible to draw sharp boundaries between them.

As you know, it is proposed that each commission will consist of 40-45 deputies, roughly half being members of the Supreme Soviet and half USSR people's deputies. They will cooperate closely, will bolster the whole work of the Supreme Soviet and the chambers during recesses,

will be very much concerned with monitoring and legislative functions, and will undoubtedly make their own contribution to the whole work of our supreme representative organ. These are the proposals which I have been instructed to report to you on behalf of the the USSR Supreme Soviet Presidium and our chambers' Council of Elders, and I ask you to carefully examine this very important question which will determine the area of activity and the actual course of the work of the Soviet of Nationalities in the upcoming period.

R.N. Nishanov: Will there be questions, comrades, for Anatoliy Ivanovich?

From the floor: (Inaudible).

A.I. Lukyanov: No, questions now.

R.N. Nishanov: No, questions for the moment, then we will proceed to discussion.

From the floor: I would like to know where the Constitutional Oversight Committee comes in.

A.I. Lukyanov: The Constitutional Oversight Committee is elected by the Congress of People's Deputies separately. The members of this committee are not Supreme Soviet deputies and it has different functions, which may, among other things, be connected with evaluating laws and acts which the chambers adopt.

R.N. Nishanov: Please come up to the rostrum, to the microphone.

From the floor: I would like to know the following: What is the future procedure for determining who serves on the commissions and committtees? How is this planned?

A.I. Lukyanov: We plan that the composition of committees should be the concern of the chamber itself, above all the chairman of the chamber, who will carry out consultations with deputies and take account of the proposals which were in the questionnaires, and the committees will be formed in this way.

The committee chairman will certainly be someone released from all other functions. He will be concerned only with the work of the committee. Clearly the deputy chairman, who does not have to be a member of the chamber, and the committee or commission secretary will also certainly be released for the whole period, unless they are replaced on rotation. This constitutes great, serious, and permanent work in the Supreme Soviet. That is how the creation of committees is conceived. Of course, the questions and wishes of the actual deputies and consultations with the chairmen will play a predominant role here. After all, you will appreciate that there cannot be, for example, a Committee for the Protection of the People's Health made up solely of doctors. Soviet workers and the directors of enterprises which have their own polyclinics, hospitals, and so forth are also necessary there. There must be a broad spectrum there. A committee should not be narrowly professional.

Therefore it is necessary to show restraint here, to work within the bounds of reason, so to speak, and show moderation. All the deputies' potential must be invested in the committee's work.

R.N. Nishanov: So, Comrade Safiyeva.

G. Safiyeva, poet, chairman of the Tajik Republican Department of the Soviet Culture Foundation, Dushanbe City (from the Soviet Culture Foundation): Did I imagine it, or have they dropped such an important committee as the Committee on Literature, Culture, and Art? What happens to us?

A.I. Lukyanov: Yes, this question was discussed very thoroughly in the Soviet of the Union, and it was deemed appropriate for cultural matters to come under the commission of the Soviet of Nationalities, because that is where culture has its roots. That does not mean that the Planning, Budget, and Financial Commission will not be concerned with culture. It will also deal with appropriations for culture and so forth. It does not mean that the other commissions, on, say, education, will not be concerned with culture. But all the same, it was decided to place the emphasis here and form a commission in your chamber.

R.N. Nishanov: Right, your question, please.

From the floor: Anatoliy Ivanovich, is it possible for one deputy to participate in the work of both a committee and a commission? Or is that ruled out?

A.I. Lukyanov: We did not envisage that. We wanted each deputy to concentrate his efforts in one specific place. But if he is interested in the work of some committee or commission to which he does not belong, it is now enshrined in the standing orders, and we want to make provision for it in the Law on Status, that a deputy has the right to a consultative vote at the sittings of these committees and commissions. But he himself belongs to one particular committee. In all, comrades, there will be 800-850 deputies taking part in the work of committees and commissions, which means that we are immediately taking nearly half of the Supreme Soviet for permanent work in these important organs of our....

M.S. Gorbachev: No. Not of the Supreme Soviet. Of the commissions.

From the floor: (Inaudible).

From the floor: Anatoliy Ivanovich, I would like to add to, or rather, enlarge on the propositions put forward by Comrade Safiyeva. Is it the case that questions of culture, language, and other nationality problems, so to speak, are the concern of the Soviet of Nationalities?

M.S. Gorbachev: Yes.

From the floor: The Soviet of the Union is virtually abandoning cultural matters. Especially since the committee of both chambers, where it says "Committee on Science, Public Education, and Upbringing," omits the most important thing. All this—science in a civilized world, public education, upbringing—it is all based on culture. So how can the word "culture" be omitted? The Soviet of the Union automatically avoids discussing cultural problems and issues. Thus language, culture, and other—so to speak—problems become solely the prerogative of the Soviet of Nationalities. I would like to propose that all this be given proper consideration. In my opinion science, public education, and upbringing cannot be divorced from culture, and cultural matters should form part of the functions of that committee.

A.I. Lukyanov: If I am allowed also to express my own position as a deputy, I would in that case propose another solution. We have a Commission (in the Soviet of the Union) for Labor, Prices, and Social Policy. So perhaps we should advise the Soviet of the Union to add an element to the title, and say: "sociocultural policy." Then we will take everything into account. If you want to tie culture solely to science, public education, and upbringing, then it seems to me that the approach will be too narrow.... I would like to say, comrades, that practice shows that as soon as a contentious issue falls within the sphere of activity of two commissions, the situation that arises is that "everyone's business is no one's business."

R.N. Nishanov: Does anyone wish to speak on this question, on this specific question? You want to speak on this question? Go ahead, please.

A.I. Lukyanov: Let's hear the questions, so that we can answer everyone.

From the floor: On the question of culture.

B.S. Safarov, shift engineer at the aviation technology base at Kulyab Airport, Kulyab City (Kulyabskiy National-Territorial Electoral Okrug, Tajik SSR): The point is that formerly this question of culture came under the jurisdiction of the Soviet of the Union. But that did not help. For nearly 45 years now we have been excavating an archaeological monument which is of enormous value to all mankind, because it has a thousand years of history. But to this day no one is willing to help us. So we think that cultural matters should come under the Supreme Soviet and its Soviet of Nationalities, so that the opinions of all nations and the interests of all peoples are taken into account.

R.N. Nishanov: Right, questions please.

From the floor: (Inaudible).

A.I. Lukyanov: I propose—in the Soviet of Nationalities.

R.N. Nishanov: One moment, I am giving the floor to the lady. And then you. Go ahead.

From the floor: If you want to finish, I will give way to you.

R.N. Nishanov: Fine.

From the floor: Let us resolve the question of setting up a Culture Committee. We have unionwide problems. In particular, the creation in Moscow of an all-union aesthetics center, the creation of an all-union museum of children's art, the creation of a museum of modern art. All these problems cannot be tackled only in the subcommissions and commissions that exist within the Soviet of Nationalities. I believe a Culture Committee is abolutely essential. Experience shows that for many years the USSR Ministry of Culture has failed to cope with one of our country's deficiencies, the culture deficiency. That is why I propose that an emphasis be placed on culture.

R.N. Nishanov: Right, any more questions? Go ahead.

From the floor: I would like to ask a question that was already raised at the session of the Council of Elders. In particular, about the Commission for Socioeconomic Problems of Development. The question was raised of how the interests of autonomous oblasts are to be taken into account, if we do not refer at all here to the formation of which they form a part administratively, that is, the kray. If they are to resolve matters in isolation from all the problems of the kray, I do not think they are likely to resolve them at all. Yet krays as national formations incorporating an autonomous oblast already exist. What is your opinion on this?

A.I. Lukyanov: My opinion is that sometimes an autonomous oblast really needs defending from the kray. The chamber will do this. That is the first thing. Second. It is my opinion that there has long been an urgent need for the autonomous oblast's budget and plan to appear as a separate item approved by the republic (specifically for an autonomous oblast), because unfortunately very many violations have emerged in this connection in the course of preparations for the CPSU Central Committee plenum on interethnic relations.

R.N. Nishanov: Your question, please.

From the floor: The economist deputies from Lithuania have proposed that instead of the Commission for Consumer Goods and so forth, a Commission for the State Structure of the USSR be formed. There are questions that must be resolved: representation, the voting procedure, the state structure of a multinational country.....

A.I. Lukyanov: I can comment on this question as follows. If we are to set up a Commission for State Structure, that is, on virtually the entire wide spectrum of questions of relations within the USSR, these functions could be exercised by only one commission, which

we are already proposing (as we have heard in deputies' speeches) to set up at the congress. This is the Constitutional Commission, which will be set up at the congress and will draft a new USSR Constitution. All the other questions relate in one way or another either to interethnic relations, or to economic relations, and so forth. Here the main question is for the competence of the union to be defined absolutely precisely and exhaustively, and for all other questions that are outside the competence of the union to be resolved within the union republic. That is the principle. This can only be resolved in the constitution, and nowhere else.

From the floor: We have a Commission for Trade, and so forth. Why do we need it?

A.I. Lukyanov: Comrades, practice shows that we do. I do not know whether the Baltic republics need such a commission in the Supreme Soviet, but questions relating to trade and services to the population will certainly arise in your chamber, there is no avoiding them. And incidentally, this will not be a matter of the union interfering in your affairs, in the republic's affairs. The point is that the union could help the republic.

R.N. Nishanov: Comrade Gamkrelidze, please.

T.V. Gamkrelidze, director of the Georgian SSR Academy of Sciences Institute of Oriental Studies, Tbilisi City (Akhalshenskiy National-Territorial Electoral Okrug, Adzhar ASSR): It appears that the last two commissions of the Soviet of Nationalities—the Commission for Questions of the Development of Culture, Language, National and International Traditions, and the Protection of Historical Monuments, and the International Relations Commission...

R.N. Nishanov: Interethnic Relations.

T.V. Gamkrelidze: ...the Commission for Interethnic Relations overlap to some extent. You cannot examine interethnic relations or study them without examining questions of culture, language, and national traditions. It seems to me that it would be more expedient to form a Commission for Questions of Culture, Language, National Traditions, and Interethnic Relations—for one. And the second should be the Commission for the Protection of Historical Monuments, because a Commission for Interethnic Relations cannot exist without examining questions of culture, national traditions, and language.

A.I. Lukyanov: The practice we have today has shown, comrades, that it is simply impossible to reduce interethnic relations to questions of culture, language, or national and international traditions. Interethnic relations are much broader and deeper: They include economic relations, political relations, and so forth. If we want to study questions of culture and language specially, then of course such a commission is expedient. A

Commission for the Protection of Historical Monuments will cover, in my view, too narrow a range of questions. But that is for the deputies to decide.

R.N. Nishanov: Fine. Your question?

From the floor: (Inaudible).

A.I. Lukyanov: Certainly, but not only that.

R.K. Odzhiyev, deputy chairman of the "Internatsionalist" Cooperative Association, Tajik SSR, Dushanbe City (from the Leninist Communist Youth League [Komsomol]): Please explain to me: What is the basis of the relations between our chamber and the commission that has now been set up on the events in Tbilisi?

A.I. Lukyanov: I think that is an ad hoc commission, not a standing commission. It was set up by the congress, not the chamber. And I think that commission has its own, limited range of questions that it has to answer. Interethnic relations and so forth is a permanent range of questions that must be worked on. Someone has mentioned this range of questions, the number of "hot spots" alone that we have, is approximately 18-20. These will have to be studied constantly. But the commissions on Georgia and other matters are temporary; that is how they were conceived.

R.N. Nishanov: Comrade Ambartsumyan, please.

V.A. Ambartsumyan, president of the Armenian SSR Academy of Sciences, Yerevan City (Ashtarakskiy National-Territorial Electoral Okrug, Armenian SSR): I agree that each deputy can belong to no more than one commission. But it would be good—because deputies have wider interests—if he had the right, say, to receive materials from another commission too, in order to study them. For him to be able to declare this interest, and the materials would be sent to him regularly.

A.I. Lukyanov: Viktor Amazaspovich, this right will be guaranteed. A deputy wishing to participate in the work of a given commission should receive materials from that commission.

R.N. Nishanov: Right, your question. And then yours.

M.L. Bronshteyn, faculty chief at Tartu State University, Tartu City (Tartuskiy-Sovetskiy National-Territorial Electoral Okrug, Estonian SSR): I and a number of deputies see no point in setting up a Commission for Consumer Goods, Trade, and so forth. It duplicates the Commission for Socioeconomic Questions, especially since according to Maslyukov's draft these questions are transferred to the competence of the republics. But it is extremely important to have a Commission for Interethnic and Interregional Economic Relations, or a Common Market. We could be united by a common market, if we carry on trade between republics. This is a factor that could act in the direction of unity. This question is not covered anywhere at present: neither in the Soviet of the Union nor in the Soviet of Nationalities. It seems to me that it is extremely important to have such a commission.

A.I. Lukyanov: If you want to know what I think, let me tell you that in effect two commissions will be concerned with these questions. First, the Commission for the Development of Republics which we have named—the second commission of the Soviet of Nationalities. And interethnic economic relations will undoubtedly to some extent come under the Commission for Interethnic Questions. Otherwise—without a market, without direct ties, without all the rest of it—this commission too, is, inconceivable.

M.L. Bronshteyn: But that will be a very concrete area of work; it will differ from all the others.

A.I. Lukyanov: Yes, we must at all costs set up a subcommission there on these very sensitive, subtle, but very necessary questions of economic reform.

M.L. Bronshteyn: Nonetheless we ask to raise and consider this question.

A.I. Lukyanov: As regards trade, services for the population, and so forth, I must say that there was no objection from deputies demanding its exclusion, and we are proposing that it be set up precisely in the Soviet of Nationalities, since these questions have been placed entirely within the jurisdiction of union republics.

R.N. Nishanov: Your question.

From the floor: My proposals are about creating a Commission for Land Use. For some reason the Council of Elders ignored these proposals. However, I believe, and many deputies believe, that a Commission for Land Use is very necessary. We have all kinds of committees here and all kinds of commissions, but we are not reflecting land use anywhere. (Noise in the auditorium) No, pardon me, but this question does not concern agriculture alone, it concerns industry, protection of the environment, and nationalities questions as well.

A.I. Lukyanov: I agree with you, and questions of land use in the agro-industrial complex will be dealt with.... These questions will be dealt with by the agro-industrial complex, but that is not an end to the issue. The point is that, in my view, to the maximum extent possible (if we want to protect the interests of the lessee, if we want to protect the interests of land users in general) all questions of land use must be placed within the charge of the commissions dealing with the soviets of people's deputies. They must have maximum competence in the sphere of land use, and maybe at some stage there will be such a subcommission or subcommittee.

R.N. Nishanov: Right, your question please.

N.V. Neyland, Latvian SSR deputy foreign minister, Riga City (Darztsiyemskiy National-Territorial Electoral Okrug, Latvian SSR): I would like to ask you, Anatoliy Ivanovich, about the second committee, although you have already said that defense and state security questions have much in common. Naturally, they have secrecy in common. But there are secrets and secrets. I think that if we look at the military-political problems that are being discussed in Geneva, Vienna, and so forth, these actually contain more of foreign policy than of state security. What are we losing? First, there is international practice. In both Britain and America—everywhere has different committees and commissions for defense and for state security. State security is often examined by hearings behind closed doors. If we close the doors on defense questions in the same way as on state security, we will also lose out with regard to the trust that we are now gaining. Glasnost is developing on questions of military building, but it's having a hard time. Two years ago we promised we would say what our military budget is. Mikhail Sergeyevich has just announced it. Last year we spoke of the structure of our Navy from the UN platform. But I am sure that in our country no one knows this, although the whole world knows it. What we had in our country was a tiny little report on Petrovskiy's speech from the UN platform.

That's not all. Today we do not know how many weapons we sell and how many we give away. At any rate, the Defense Committee has plenty of work. And I am very much afraid that the glasnost that is gradually spreading to questions of military building in our country will take refuge behind state security (where hearings must naturally be in camera).

A.I. Lukyanov: I can go along with you in saying that a gradual expansion of glasnost is needed here, and I do not think that the KGB can block defense problems. On the contrary, we certainly did not proceed from questions of secrecy in defining this committee. The point is that the sphere of the protection of our border is most closely involved with defense. This is approximately half of what the KGB does. That is the point one.

Two. A considerable proportion of international security questions—arms reduction and so forth—will be dealt with not only by the Defense Committee but also by the Committee for International Questions. That is, once again there will be an interface, once again there will be joint studies and hearings. And on such international questions they will mostly be open hearings. Open.

M.S. Gorbachev: And subcommittees can probably also be created later, in order to learn.

A.I. Lukyanov: So inside the committee there should probably be some kind of narrow subcommittee that will deal with totally secret questions, and as for the rest, neither the Supreme Soviet nor, I think, the Supreme Soviet Presidium is interested in engaging in excessive secrecy here.

R.N. Nishanov: Right, your question please. You're next.

From the floor: My question has to do with the fact that I can see in neither the commissions nor the committees how questions of religion and religious buildings will be resolved. This is a very sensitive question; there are already hunger strikes, people are asking that churches be opened, and so forth. I don't see these issues here.

A.I. Lukyanov: Without mentioning religion, in view of the separation of church from state, we specifically assigned these questions to the commission that is to deal with traditions. That's where religion comes in.

From the floor: I've got another question. It says here: "protection of historical monuments." We have long had such a law in our country—it is passive in form: if a monument is standing, then ostensibly it is being protected. I would think it would be better to say here: "preservation of cultural monuments." That is an active form of restoration. Of both preservation and restoration.

A.I. Lukyanov: You have a point; it's just that I'd prefer it not to be a long title, that's all.

R.N. Nishanov: Okay, your question please. You're next.

From the floor: What I want to raise is the title of the first commission, what you describe as the main one—that is, the Commission on Interethnic Relations. I support the deputy who said that the word "policy" is missing here. Indeed, in my view the phrase "interethnic relations" sounds merely like a fire extinguisher. I would propose the following: "Commission for Nationalities Policy and Interethnic Relations." Because in my view interethnic relations are, first, the result of policy.

A.I. Lukyanov: I was simply proceeding on the basis that, as a specialist on the state, I believe that here it is a question not of policy but of specific decisions.

M.S. Gorbachev: Of the law, of legislative activity.

A.I. Lukyanov: Of legislative activity. But in principle....

From the floor: Well, I don't know. I have another proposal about the committees. The Committee for Questions of Glasnost and Citizens' Rights and Appeals. I think our colleagues from the Soviet of the Union have already added the word "rights," or was it "glasnost"?

A.I. Lukyanov: "Glasnost."

From the floor: "Glasnost." I want to add one more word. If there are questions of glasnost and rights, I think the term ethics should also be added here. That is, the Committee for Questions of Glasnost, Ethics, and Citizens' Rights and Appeals. I think that wherever there is glasnost, there must be some kind of....

A.I. Lukyanov: Thank you. I want to answer you, comrades. This question arises every time, no matter how much we have discussed it in the Councils of Elders and the Soviet of the Union. Okay, an ethics committee. The congress has shown that this is an urgent question! Various parliaments abroad are creating so-called general committees or ethics committees. But most parliaments nevertheless entrust their presidiums—that is, chairmen and their deputies—with examining ethical questions. First, the two chambers often combine here. For the moment these questions have not flared up very acutely in our country, so to speak, and we have no need to set up a parliamentary police, as they do in some parliaments, so for the moment the examination of these questions could be left to the chairmen of the chambers and their deputies. And if this doesn't work out, we will create a special Ethics Committee.

R.N. Nishanov: You have a question, please go ahead. Sergey Aleksandrovich will be next.

D.A.A. Kerimov, chief of department at the CPSU Central Committee Academy of Social Sciences, Moscow City (Shakhbuzskiy National-Territorial Electoral Okrug, Nakhichevan ASSR): Anatoliy Ivanovich! I will venture to return again to the question of culture. I feel a kind of inner dissatisfaction. You're quite right that the Soviet of Nationalities must naturally have a Commission on Culture, on Language, and so forth. But, as someone has already correctly noted here, this is also of all-union significance. So I would propose a compromise solution. Keeping the commission in the form in which is now exists, but in the title of the Committee for Science and Public Education throwing out the last word, "upbringing," and replacing it with "culture." Upbringing a priori must be implemented everywhere.

A.I. Lukyanov: Just between ourselves, I can tell you that it was originally like that—the word "culture" was taken out.

R.N. Nishanov: Right, Sergey Aleksandrovich, please go ahead.

From the floor: I want you to give us an answer about the Committee for Defense and State Security Questions. I'd like to know your opinion. In many countries of the world it is customary for the defense minister to be a civilian. I think it would be good for the chairman of this committee in our country also to be without fail a civilian without military rank, and for the committee's membership also to include people without military ranks.

A.I. Lukyanov: I think this has been taken into account. If you want to know our opinion, we subscribe to a similar position.

R.N. Nishanov: Your question, please.

From the floor: I'm from Tajikistan. As a territorial deputy, I am a member of neither the Soviet of the Union nor the Soviet of Nationalities. I have been allowed to attend the sittings of the chamber. I have the following proposal: These committees have already been discussed in the Soviet of the Union, today we are discussing.... I think it makes no real difference if we move a word forward or back. We can change the titles in the process of our work.

A.I. Lukyanov: Of course.

From the floor: We can change the titles or form new commissions in the light of proposals submitted by comrades.

R.N. Nishanov: Okay, do you have a question or a proposal, please?

From the floor: I propose that it be approved.

R.N. Nishanov: Fine. We accept your proposal. Go ahead, please.

T.K. Ismailov, general director of the Azerbaijan SSR Academy of Sciences Space Research Science and Production Association, Baku City (Nakhichevanskiy National-Territorial Electoral Okrug, Azerbaijan SSR): Anatoliy Ivanovich, I suppose I have a philosophical question. A colleague who spoke here talked of a passive form of protection, protection in general, so to speak. I would like to develop this point a little. I think we do not always use this word correctly: As soon as discussion turns to health or any dynamic processes, we immediately employ it. But first we ought to create normal conditions for the functioning and development of the sphere. Then, in that process, a need for protection may arise. Take the Council of Ministers Committee for the Protection of the Environment, for instance. What's the point of protection? We should create conditions for the normal functioning of this committee, whereby protection will be just one of its functions. That is, the way in which the word "protection" is used must be active.

And we have a Committee for the Protection of the People's Health. But we must not protect the people's health, we must create conditions conducive to normal health. You know, I'm not a medic, but it is not a matter of diagnosis and treatment. I am simply asking that this question be considered—can the word "protection" be included in the titles of our committees and commissions when the use of it in a dynamic, functioning sense has been forgotten?

A.I. Lukyanov: I agree with you. But when we proposed calling this committee the "Committee for Public Health Protection," the medics exploded, saying: Public health is too narrow a concept (though, as you can see, the word "protection" features here too)—let's call it the "Committee for the Protection of the People's Health." That is, they wanted to embrace the whole range of problems—ecological, mother and child health protection, and so forth. This will really be protection of the people's health.

R.N. Nishanov: Right, your question, please.

From the floor: It ought to be called the Committee for Questions of the People's Health, the Committee for the Family, the Maternity Committee. Why "for the protection"?

A.I. Lukyanov: You know, what I would say to you is this: We have too many committees "for questions" and too few committees for answering them.

R.N. Nishanov: Your question, please.

S.U. Kallas, deputy editor of the newspaper RAHVA HAAL, Tallinn City (Rakvereskiy Severnyy National-Territorial Electoral Okrug, Estonian SSR): I have three short remarks. First, about the Committee for Questions of Glasnost and Citizens' Rights and Appeals: There are two aspects here: On one hand the press and glasnost, on the other citizens' letters and appeals. Won't this be too much for one committee? Won't one aspect get overwhelmed by the other?

Second: Wouldn't it be advisable for us to set up a Commission To Formulate and Improve the Standing Orders and Procedure for the Work of the Supreme Soviet? After all, such a commission will work virtually constantly, because at every step we are all wasting time and we may get bogged down in these unsolved questions.

Third: Where will questions of space research end up? Which commission will deal with them?

R.N. Nishanov: Go ahead. You can submit proposals from the floor or from the rostrum.

I.O. Bisher, professor at the P. Stuchka Latvian State University, Riga City (Stuchkinskiy National-Territorial Electoral Okrug, Latvian SSR): Already at the sittings of the Council of Elders and Soviet of the Union I have sensed a desire to create as many committees as we have problems in the country. But we certainly have a lot of problems, and we certainly don't have enough deputies for them. It has to be said that not all problems always have to be solved at the all-union level and necessarily by parliamentary methods. We must also take this into account. Thus, for instance, there has been a lot of talk of education here, which is clearly something that indeed we must not ignore. But probably we here will not be able to do for the Academy of Pedagogical Sciences what it has been unable to do so far for itself. So I think that we must proceed from the real functions entrusted to the Supreme Soviet and from the problems that we must solve without fail. And also from the real packages of proposals which we have already received and on which

we are to work in the immediate future. The commissions and committees must be formed on the basis of all this. I think that the list of them is basically in line with reality.

At the same time I still want to raise here one question that several comrades have raised at the congress before me, and that has also been broached here. That is the question of ethics. I don't entirely agree with Anatoliy Ivanovich's assessment that everything is fine in our country in this regard. True, we have not yet come to blows, and, as he said, such committees have to be created where people have already come to blows. I think we should go further; we should prevent this. But at the same time there have already been a number of statements that certain deputies, organizations, and even entire union republics have seen as discrediting and slandering them. There have also been attempts to resolve such questions. But the way in which they have been resolved cannot be regarded as the optimum method. The method of resolving them was strongly reminiscent of the old Novgorod assembly: a question of who outdoes whom when it comes to shouting and applause. I think that this method is not altogether correct, that such questions must be precisely analyzed, and that each person must bear responsibility for what he says, whether he is a Hero of the Soviet Union or a hero of Afghanistan. If we want to demand that others display responsibility, first of all we must raise our own responsibility. And clearly we must have a method of resolving such questions. The proposal has been made here that they be referred for examination by the presidium. I think that it will have plenty of work even without that. I have no objection to one of the deputy chairmen of the chambers heading such a commission, but I believe that the presidium obviously should not be in the business of finding out where a particular deputy was in 1968—Czechoslovakia or the United States. Probably someone else should do this sort of thing.

I think that we must also formulate specific rules on ethical questions. As is well known, other parliaments in the world have quite detailed rules of this kind. They apply not only to remarks, but also to a number of other questions. We must not close our eyes to this. After all, we once believed that we needed no rules on ecology—everything was splendid in this sphere in our country—and that we needed no laws on combating the mafia, because it simply does not exist. But it subsequently emerged that we start feeding the dog only when the wolf is already among the sheep. That is a Lettish proverb.

I think that we ought to create right now a commission to formulate specific ethical rules and sanctions both regarding the aforementioned remarks and regarding other questions of deputies' conduct. For instance, I have now been included in the commission on a well-known case (I don't recall the commission's precise title) and I think that its members, too, should behave according to certain ethical rules. If we have such rules, it will be very useful.

Now for our internal standing orders. We have wasted a very great deal of time at the congress because many questions of the standing orders were not formulated, and we have tried to resolve them directly at the congress. Clearly, we need to set up a special group to define all the principles of our activity: how commissions work, what their rights are, and so forth. This is a new task, of course, but a necessary one. I propose nevertheless that one more committee be created—for ethics and the standing orders.

R.N. Nishanov: There is food for thought there. Maybe we should confer with the chairmen of both chambers. How should this be organized? Perhaps we should submit a specific proposal tomorrow?

Please come up here. And I implore you, keep it brief. Just one minute per proposal, comrades.

From the floor: I think we're taking rather a strange approach toward the creation of our commissions, that is, toward the content of their work, which is reflected in the title. For instance, the word "culture" was mentioned and we began (though no one had any objections) to wonder where it should be inserted. It doesn't seem to fit anywhere. Clearly, this is the wrong way to resolve this question; we should not be wondering where to put this word. Culture is an exceptionally important matter. But we are trying to tack it on somewhere: maybe in this line, or maybe in that....

R.N. Nishanov: Do you have a proposal?

From the floor: Obviously culture merits a separate, independent committee. That is my proposal. Incidentally, the same thing happened with the word "glasnost." I am very grateful to our colleagues from the Soviet of the Union who mentioned this word when the question of committees came up. But there, too, a search immediately got under way: Where can we tack on glasnost? They found somewhere to "tack it on": the last committee, ahead of citizens' rights and appeals. The effect is rather eclectic. But you can find a connection, an interconnection between anything you like. Glasnost is such a broad and important concept (and this is precisely confirmed in the special resolution of the 19th party conference) that other equally important questions should not be "dragged in" and attached to it. Today glasnost needs to be developed, but it is in equal need of defense, because a definite attack is being mounted on it.

I propose that citizens' statements and appeals be transferred to the third committee—for questions of legislation, legality, and law and order. For citizens' appeals are precisely about violations of legality. So it will be appropriate here.

R.N. Nishanov: So let us proceed in order. Please. It will be your turn after this comrade.

B.Y. Palagnyukh, director of the 60th Anniversary of the USSR Pedigree Poultry Sovkhoz, Rybnitskiy Rayon (Rybnitskiy National-Territorial Okrug, Moldavian SSR): I submit a proposal to create a subcommission for language on the basis of two commissions: the Commission for Questions of the Development of Culture, Language, National and International Traditions, and Protection of Historical Monuments, and the Commission for Interethnic Relations. Why do I submit this proposal? In connection with the fact that the status of the state language which gave the republic its name has recently been adopted in a number of republics, including ours. But other nationalities also live in the republic, including a Russian-speaking population. Why do I want you to listen attentively to what I am about to read out to you? Talking in the spring of 1945 with the priest Morelli and with Washington's representative in Switzerland, Allen Dulles, the leader of U.S. intelligence, said: It is a ludicrous venture to send saboteurs into the future Russia to blow up plants. But if our propaganda proves in a precise and well-reasoned way to Russia's nationalities that each of them can exist and converse only in its own language, this will be our victory and the Russians will be powerless to counteract this victory. Yulian Semenov, "The Position," volume 1, page 144.

This problem affects not only our republic. It affects the Baltic republics and other republics. A Russian-speaking population of inside 80 million lives in the republics, and so I consider it necessary to create a subcommission for language precisely within the Interethnic Relations Commission, and to give Russian the status of a state language. It must, of course, be protected. Vladimir Ilich Lenin once said: Of course, there is no need to decree the Russian language, for it will itself find its road and take its place. Yes, it did find its road and take its place. But now such relations are taking shape: When republics give their own languages the status of a state language, the Russian-speaking population remains outside the language. Therefore, on behalf of deputies from a number of republics, more than 25 people signed an appeal which I wish to read out and pass on to the congress. We consider it necessary to give Russian the status of a state language. This is very important for us. I myself am Ukrainian, but, I repeat, some people have already had their say here today and earlier—esteemed Comrade Oleynik and esteemed Comrade Drutse. One spoke of duplicity, ashamed to speak of bilingualism and the great Russian language. But others, when preparing USSR laws, do not even mention in the draft the Russian language, in which the majority of the USSR's peoples converse, the language of our interethnic communication.

R.N. Nishanov: I apologize, comrades. I feel that we are digressing from the agenda. One moment. Hear me out, I will let you speak, just wait. We are digressing from the agenda. We will be in session much longer, and every time we must adhere to a definite agenda. This is the first point. Second, I ask the speakers to have their say specifically on these questions, and then we will vote. Third, we will work until 2030. At 2030 we will end our session.

From the floor: I propose forming a subcommittee for inventions within the Committee for Science, Public Education, and Upbringing, and calling the committee itself the Committee for Science, Technology, Public Education, and Upbringing.

R.N. Nishanov: Your question, please. You may approach the microphone.

R.G. Salukvadze, director of Sukhumi I.N. Vekua Physicotechnical Institute (Sukhumskiy-Leninskiy National-Territorial Electoral Okrug, Abkhaz ASSR): I propose—not just for the sake of an alternative, but as a matter of principle—creating independently a Committee for Science. I say this because science has recently found itself in straitened circumstances in connection with the transfer of sectoral science to economic accountability and the upcoming transfer of academy science also to economic accountability. Sectoral institutes are suffering in particular today from the viewpoint of the development of fundamental research. I believe that VUZ science, which receives far less from sectoral science, is already suffering no less today. Therefore I believe that there are no grounds today for saying that science is a sector of culture or the economy. Science, as I said long ago, although this did not happen in reality, is a sector and it must be a foremost sector. And we will not bring science into foremost positions just by acquiring licenses and "knowhow" or by creating joint ventures. Therefore, for fundamental science to develop properly, it is necessary to create a committee with a special status.

R.N. Nishanov: Your turn, please. Comrade Likhanov will be next.

A.I. Dubko, chairman of the "Progress" Agro-Industrial Kolkhoz-Combine, Grodnenskiy Rayon, Grodno Oblast (from the kolkhozes united in the Union Kolkhoz Council): First of all, allow me to say, Rafik Nishanovich, that you, too, are to blame because our work is taking a long time. The standing orders should have been defined at once when you were elected.

R.N. Nishanov: We will take account of this.

A.I. Dubko: And the second point. Anyone who read the recent statement by the FRG ambassador to the Soviet Union will remember that he said: Prior to 1956 the Germans engaged not in politics but in economics. Today we are all endeavoring to be politicians and are working very badly in economics. As a result, even today I alone am speaking for the kolkhozes.

Specifically—the Committee for Agrarian Questions that is proposed for the Supreme Soviet in no way satisfies us. We approach again with our yardstick, for agricultural affairs virtually remain at the same level as before. Or still worse. That is, in practice this committee will not protect us, and the three people who will be working just won't be able to keep on top of things.

Therefore we still insist on our solution: It must be a working committee, and when elaborating questions it must report to the government its agreement or disagreement. Thank you for your attention. In other respects we probably have no need to complicate matters unnecessarily. We said at the beginning that a commission is not frozen dogma. They will be developed and perfected. We will not find a prescription for all eventualities in life today.

R.N. Nishanov: Comrade Likhanov. Then you, Comrade Rakhimova.

A.A. Likhanov, writer, chairman of the board of the V.I. Lenin Soviet Children's Fund (from the V.I. Lenin Soviet Children's Fund): Comrade women and men! I address the men in particular. And as such I address precisely you, comrade deputies. Statistics attest that our entire productive labor in the course of a year amounts to approximately 200 billion man-hours. And, of course, a large share of this belongs to women. In addition, statistics assert that housework takes up in excess of a further 100-billion man-hours. And all of this is shouldered by women. In some regions today, so sociologists claim, a woman spends approximately 20 minutes a day bringing up children. And in some regions even less. So, comrade men, let us finally try to share with the women responsibility for the family, for children. Why have we again lumped together, so to speak, such categories as women's affairs and protection of the family, mother, and child? This is a colossal business, a colossal affair. And again we are thinking in the old way.

Incidentally, I tell you, this question already has quite a long history. And we, the Children's Fund, put forward this proposal on the eve of the congress. And we are continuing to do so.

Anatoliy Ivanovich! After the sitting of the Soviet of the Union and, when this information came, this morning, almost 200 deputies put their suggestions to the secretariat. To agree, all the same, to this idea of ours. For it is a good, noble, restructuring idea. Let us create two committees: a Committee for Women's Affairs and a Committee To Defend the Interests of Families and Children. I earnestly beg you to support my proposal.

R.N. Nishanov: We will approach these questions when preparing proposals. It must be borne in mind that the Soviet of the Union approved these committees with amendments and comments. Of course, we have the right to make our own suggestions, but the aforesaid must be borne in mind. Comrade Rakhimova, please. You wished to speak? Comrade Rakhimova next.

From the floor: Still it seems to me that the Commission for Consumer Goods, Trade, and Municipal, Consumer, and Other Services to the Population is, nonetheless, on a republic, oblast, and local level. There seems to me no need to create it. On the other hand, I see no other commission that will examine general principles relating to problems of economic accountability, as well as the materials submitted by the Baltic republics. Which commission will examine problems of republic economic accountability, Anatoliy Ivanovich? The commission for reform?

A.I. Lukyanov: For economic reform.

From the floor: And the third point. People here have spoken of ethics. What kind of ethics, comrades? When the congress gave a tumultuous ovation blaspheming those who died 9 April and insulting the soul of the Georgian nation and human conscience in general? What kind of ethics?

R.N. Nishanov: Deputy Rakhimova, please. We now give the floor to the women.

B. Rakhimova, secretary of Leninabad Tajik Communist Party Obkom (from the women's councils united in the Committee of Soviet Women): Today we have been discussing the creation of a Commission for Questions of Socioeconomic Development and Interethnic Relations in the chamber of the Soviet of Nationalities. I believe that this is perfectly correct. It must be precisely in the nationalities chamber, because many of our interethnic problems are associated precisely with the failure to resolve socioeconomic questions. I wish to raise one problem in this connection.

I realize that maybe this question should have been raised at the congress. But taking advantage of the opportunity to speak here, I would like to say this. Comrades, virtually the entire history of the development of our country and of our republic in particular, and maybe of the whole of Central Asia, testifies that throughout the time of stagnation, before and after that period, the state capital investments allocated for social, cultural, and consumer service projects were kept to an absolute minimum. It is no accident that our republic is the only one to run a three-shift system of teaching in schools. Only 4 percent of children in our republic attend preschool institutions, there is a shortage of maternity homes, and we have the highest mother and infant mortality rate. Let me tell you bluntly, comrades, that the mortality indicator—45 per 1,000—is double the average for the Soviet Union. I believe that this is a tragedy. Therefore in the commission where we will discuss socioeconomic development—and all regions are now switching to self-financing—we must take into account the starting position of the republics and regions switching to self-financing. In this context, and in order to equalize conditions, I believe that our chamber, or maybe the Supreme Soviet, should have a corresponding state fund which would be used to equalize conditions in our regions, primarily in Central Asia, and maybe even in Kazakhstan.

I wish to raise another question. Comrades, there was talk of women's problems here today. We are setting up a Commission for Women's Affairs and Mother and Child Protection. I support Comrade Likhanov's statement to the effect that mother and child protection would be better assigned to the Commission for Protection of the People's Health. After all, mothers and children are also part of the people. And then, comrades, women's problems are very specific. Therefore I believe that, at worst, the Commission for Women's Affairs should have a subcommission for problems of mother and child protection specifically in Central Asian regions.

And one last wish addressed to our chairman of the Soviet of Nationalities chamber—I already mentioned this at the Council of Elders, in which I took part. I realize that now we have had democratic elections and we women, bluntly speaking, have lost, because now there are only one-half as many of us as there were in the Supreme Soviet previously. But let us, now that we have so many wonderful women in the chamber—maybe we were acting according to the principle 'better fewer but better'—let us elect one woman as deputy chairman of our chamber from among these, the best of our women. (Applause)

R.N. Nishanov: I beg your pardon, but we have only 5 minutes left, you are the last one to speak, and then let us consult. We will have further sittings.

L.I. Batynskaya, editor of the newspaper KRASNOY-ARSKIY KOMSOMOLETS, RSFSR, Krasnoyarsk City (From the USSR Journalists Union): I would really urge the esteemed deputies and the chairman to support me and my journalist colleagues in the view that it is necessary to set up in the USSR Supreme Soviet a Committee on Questions of Glasnost and the Mass Media on a basis of parity between the two chambers. Questions of the mass media are questions of content, structure, technical issues, journalists' rights, and society's rights in the face of the mass media.

Speakers from the congress rostrum have come up with various similes for our democracy and glasnost. I'm not going to add to this series of images; let me say only that glasnost—even today, in the 5th year of restructuring—is still being divided into central and regional. The degree of the latter depends on the regional leader's personality and the editor's ability to stand up to pressure from various officials. I am convinced that as the power of soviets expands and strengthens, their leadership of the press will be transformed from a formality to a reality.

If the esteemed deputies do not find it possible to set up such a committee—which we journalists will really regret—we would ask that the words "mass media" be placed in the following context: Committee for Questions of Glasnost, the Mass Media, and Citizens' Rights and Appeals. Thank you.

R.N. Nishanov: Please, your question. I apologize, of course, for commenting on the fly, but a Law on the Press is due to be adopted and many questions will be solved there, comrades. Please go ahead.

From the floor: We all lack brevity and precision. I want to make a specific proposal.

I believe that the first commission ought to be called Commission for Interethnic Relations and the Development of Culture, Language, and National and International Traditions. All this is interlinked.

The second commission, in my view, ought to be called the Commission for Matters of the Development of Union and Autonomous Republics and Autonomous Oblasts and Okrugs and Protection of Historical and Cultural Heritage.

And the Commission for Consumer Goods and Trade, I think, ought to be given a different name. Let us get away from this stereotype and call it Commission for Protection of Consumer Rights and Improvement of the Quality of Services and Output.

And finally, there is an opportunity to form another commission which is lacking—a Commission for the Affairs of Voluntary and Unsponsored Societies, Associations, and Social Self-Management Organs.

A few proposals as regards the committees. I believe, as an architect by profession, that the Committee for Construction and Architecture Questions ought to be named Committee for Questions of Construction, Architecture, and Organization of the Habitat.

The Committee for Women's Affairs and Family, Mother, and Child Protection, I think, would be more aptly named Committee for the Defense of Childhood Rights, Protection of Motherhood, and Women's and Family Affairs.

And the last committee. Instead of "Glasnost and Citizens' Appeals" it should be named Committee for the Defense of Citizens' Rights and Appeals and the Study of Public Opinion.

R.N. Nishanov: One moment, comrades. I don't think that this is our last sitting, and we will have further opportunities to say everything. Let me voice a few considerations. Keep your seats for a minute or so. After all, this is not our last sitting.

First. Many proposals merit serious attention. Like the proposal on ethics, for example. I will consult the chairman of the Soviet of the Union and we will draft a proposal on this question. We will examine this matter at one of our sittings in the near future.

Second. A number of proposals submitted here merit attention. But maybe in order not to overextend the list of our committees and their titles, we should take a series of these proposals—which are really pressing—into account when subcommittees or commissions are being set up. We will certainly inform you of the form in which we intend to do this. Now, on the basis of this broad exchange of opinions, I would like to propose three amendments for your attention.

Among the standing commissions of the Soviet of Nationalities, that the Commission on Interethnic Relations, which was proposed to be set up first, be named Commission for Nationalities Policy and Interethnic Relations.

That the final part of the title of the commission which talks about historical monuments be as follows: International Traditions, and Protection of Historical Heritage. This covers these matters on a broader basis.

Since very many deputies here urged that the committee's title should include the term "culture," maybe we ought to set up a Committee for Science, Public Education, Culture, and Upbringing.

We have thus taken the more global proposals into account.

From the floor: A subcommittee for invention work.

R.N. Nishanov: And a subcommittee for invention work. That was on the fly. Just a moment, Comrade Gamkrelidze. Here we have a deputy who asked for 1 minute, please let me give him the floor and we'll call it a day. Please, let us adhere to the standing orders.

From the floor: As far I can make out, four commissions will be set up—no more and no less. Absolutely nothing about agriculture; there is not a single word in our national commissions. Look, what are we going to protect, sell, and enjoy if there is absolutely nothing about agriculture? You see—the most important point—we could still add to the Commission on Questions of Social and Economic Development, if we cannot set up a new commission or eliminate one, something about land use. At least this question. No, it will not go away, it will indeed not go away. There is a committee but there is no commission. My proposal: We should nonetheless include the question of land use in this commission.

R.N. Nishanov. There have been several proposals on this question. Just one moment, we have given the floor to the last comrade. Just one moment. Comrade Gamkrelidze, please.

T.V. Gamkrelidze: I have a remark to make on your proposal. Language is disappearing from the commission's title. Your wording for the commission no longer contains the word "language."

From the floor: Language is there.

T.V. Gamkrelidze: Which commission says language? You have reworded it so that there is no language.

R.N. Nishanov: I read out only the final part of the proposal, not the beginning. Here we are, we have a Commission for Questions of the Development of Culture, Language, National and International Traditions, and Protection of the Historical Heritage.

T.V. Gamkrelidze: So everything stays the way it was.

R.N. Nishanov: Of course. In this form. So, comrades, we'll do some more work together, we'll work things out, questions may arise, and so on. And now the last proposal. It was made several times. We have a Committee for Agrarian Questions and Food. This covers all agricultural questions. We shall consult with the Soviet of the Union chamber over whether or not to include land use, and we'll inform you of our views later.

Many thanks for your active participation. The next sitting will be the USSR Supreme Soviet's sitting tomorrow at 1000 hours, in this hall. Goodbye.

7 Jun Supreme Soviet Evening Joint Session Noted
PM0906163189 Moscow IZVESTIYA in Russian 9 Jun 89 Morning Edition pp 9, 11

["First Session of the USSR Supreme Soviet. Stenographic Record."—IZVESTIYA headline]

[Excerpts]

Joint Sessions of Soviet of the Union and Soviet of Nationalities

The USSR Supreme Soviet Hall of Sessions, the Kremlin. 7 June 1989. 1800.

Comrade M.S. Gorbachev, chairman of the USSR Supreme Soviet, in the chair.

M.S. Gorbachev: Currently 466 deputies are registered. Shall we begin?

Deputies: Yes.

M.S. Gorbachev: We are continuing, as agreed, to work through the agenda which we agreed after the appointment of Comrade Ryzhkov as chairman of the USSR Council of Ministers.

On the candidacy for the post of chairman of the USSR Supreme Court. I want to brief you, comrades, since this is my duty. Many of you took part in the party group sitting when Comrade Lebedev, chairman of the Moscow City Court, was put forward as a candidate. Many lawyers spoke then and said that they have nothing against Comrade Lebedev and value the work he has done and is doing here in Moscow's courts. Nonetheless, it was the general opinion—we then discussed the matter again and consulted with comrades—that someone with more experience both of life and of the judiciary should be nominated for the Supreme Court. So you see, sometimes it is said that people are past pensionable age, sometimes that they are too young. Those are the dialectics. I think that Comrade Lebedev will understand that. Let him go on working, there is no question of a lack of confidence in him or of undervaluing his work. It is simply the general view that the Supreme Court should be headed by someone who is weightier in every respect—well prepared and with greater experience. The role of these organs of ours will grow immeasurably as we proceed toward a rule-of-law state and, clearly, this approach is justified.

Here is Comrade Yevgeniy Alekseyevich Smolentsev. You know him. You even know him so well that the question has already arisen as to whether cadres from Sverdlovsk are beginning to dominate things. Such coincidences probably do happen.... Comrades, we have looked at all the cadres whom we have available. And in this respect we have another great need—to set up a constitutional committee. It will require very major judicial figures. We also have a commission or a committee on questions of legislation, and so forth. I won't give its precise name, but there, too, people will have to do a great deal of work within the framework of the Supreme Soviet in connection with the forthcoming volume of work that is veritably hanging over us, so to speak. It will require the mobilization of all forces in our corps of deputies—and to that end it will be necessary to set up and arrange these forces more correctly. But, naturally, both the Supreme Soviet and everyone else will rely on help from experts and involve them in their activity. There is no doubt about that. Now to turn to Comrade Yevgeniy Alekseyevich Smolentsev. He is currently chairman of the Russian Soviet Federated Socialist Republic [RSFSR] Supreme Court and has great experience. Furthermore, he is familiar with the activity of the USSR Supreme Court. You should note that he has worked there for several years. From 1972 through 1977 he was a member of the USSR Supreme Court and chairman of the USSR Supreme Court Judicial Collegium on Criminal Cases, and from 1977 through 1987 he was deputy chairman of the USSR Supreme Court.

Is Comrade Yevgeniy Alekseyevich Smolentsev here? Come on down. We'll surely discuss things with you. I have asked comrades from Russia and Sverdlovsk—everyone who has been connected with him—to give their opinions. This is apart from the fact that we have studied how Comrade Smolentsev has worked at the Supreme Court. The opinion expressed on all sides—from all points of view, so to speak—was positive, highly positive.

Yevgeniy Alekseyevich Smolentsev is before you. What questions do you have for him, comrades? Go ahead.

From the floor: Yevgeniy Alekseyevich, if there were an oath at the USS'. Supreme Court, what would you say?

Ye.A. Smolentsev: I would say that I have prayed all my life and will continue to pray to one God—the strict observance of legality. I cannot say anything else.

I.N. Gryazin, chief of the Estonian Soviet Socialist Republic [SSR] Academy of Sciences Institute of Philosophy, Sociology, and Law, Estonian SSR, Tartu City (Pyarnu Rural National-Territorial Electoral Okrug, Estonian SSR): Highly esteemed colleagues! Forgive me, this is a legal question, but the post is such that we have to talk about legal matters. Yevgeniy Alekseyevich, as you know, the USSR Supreme Court plenum issues and has issued guiding resolutions interpreting, among other things, articles in the criminal and civil codes of the RSFSR, which is a union republic. This was a violation of the RSFSR's sovereign rights. Does the Supreme Court under your leadership intend to continue this practice, whereby the all-union court does the work of a union republic—the RSFSR?

Ye.A. Smolentsev: Comrades, however sophisticated we make our laws, life and practice raise lots of questions of all kinds, and one of the USSR Supreme Court's main duties is to give explanations on the numerous issues arising in judicial practice to ensure that new laws are applied properly.

The current Law on the USSR Supreme Court clearly states that the USSR Supreme Court gives explanations only on those laws which are all-union laws. As for republican laws, explanations as to the practice of their application should be provided by republican courts. But the point is that republican laws are based on all-union laws, on main guidelines, and on other all-union laws. So the Supreme Court is entitled to provide explanations in such cases, on this sort of law. But the Supreme Court plenum has no right to provide explanations on purely republican laws if there is no all-union law.

M.S. Gorbachev: I had also understood it to be the case, Yevgeniy Alekseyevich, that we are moving down the road of expanding and supplementing the real sovereignty of republics. Perhaps a clearer definition is needed in this sphere, too?

Ye.A. Smolentsev: Quite so. I think that the functions of union republics' supreme courts will be considerably expanded. That is indisputable. And, naturally, the USSR Supreme Court should not interfere in all those laws that are issued in the union republics.

From the floor: Yevgeniy Alekseyevich, what is your attitude to trial by jury?

Ye.A. Smolentsev: Comrades, Mikhail Sergeyevich already said last time that we should take a look at trial by jury. I cannot agree with the viewpoint that it is necessary to introduce trial by jury. The point is that trial by jury was progressive when society was passing from feudalism to capitalism. At that time trial by jury was really progressive and that, naturally, gave it great importance. But let us take a look at today's practice. After all, practically all the capitalist countries where trial by jury exists, have essentially abandoned it: In America O.5 percent of cases are tried by jury, in Britain around 4 percent, and in other countries even fewer. Not so long ago, France has given up trial by jury altogether, describing it as "street justice." I believe that our society will not agree to the introduction of trial by jury because, from my viewpoint, it would be a step back. I believe that our people's assessors have a wider range of powers in court proceedings than a jury. After all, a jury has no say in the court proceedings and essentially decides only one question: Guilty or not guilty? All the other questions are decided by the court. Our people's assessors, on the other hand, decide the whole range of questions, including the question of guilt and the measure of punishment, and they determine the nature of a particular crime.

So why has this question arisen? The problem is that in recent years the corps of people's assessors has not been made up of particularly good people. In my view it should consist of people who have a good experience of life and have learned from it, prestigious, and well-educated people. Why make a secret of it—sometimes we send people who can be most easily released from production to people's courts as people's assessors. If we staff courts with people's assessors who are real, well-educated, experienced citizens, the prestige of our courts will be considerably higher than it is at present.

This is my stance. I don't know, perhaps a decision to introduce trial by jury will be taken, as many scientists now favor this option.

K.V. Moteka, attorney at the No 1 Vilnius Legal Advice Office, Vilnius City (Varenskiy National-Territorial Electoral Okrug, Lithuanian SSR): I would like to ask how many acquittals have been passed in courts of the first instance presided over by you during the past 10 years?

Ye.A. Smolentsev: Comrades! Both the USSR Supreme Court and the republic' supreme courts are trying to deal with as few cases as possible. We seek to ensure that cases are dealt with at local level by people's courts, especially oblast courts. There have been a number of acquittals in the cases dealt with by the Supreme Court of late, and there have been partial acquittals. Quite recently I was able to lodge protests against two sentences in North Osetia with a view to dismissing the cases. A major swindler who was brought to trial for embezzling large sums of money, around a million, out of fear of capital punishment, incriminated a number of senior officials—a minister and a deputy minister. When these cases came under investigation, it emerged that apart from his testimony there was no other evidence. He declared: "I am willing to go down on my knees and beg forgiveness of these people, I have slandered them." I was able to lodge protests in these cases. One case has already been dismissed by the prosecutor's office, the other is being reviewed. Personally, in connection with the transition to the Supreme Court, in connection with the great volume of work, I did not investigate any cases directly in the first instance, that is, I did not preside over any during the past year.

K.V. Moteka: I asked how many in 10 years.

Ye.A. Smolentsev: Well, there have been cases in the last 10 years, but I do not remember the acquittals, because we still take the kind of cases which are of great public interest. But if you take the RSFSR as a whole now, in the last year the number of acquittals has more than doubled and the number of cases submitted for further investigation has approximately doubled. The courts are making much tougher demands with regard to preliminary investigation material.

Yu.V. Golik, dean of the law department at Kemerovo State University, Kemerovo City (Tsentralnyy Territorial Electoral Okrug, Kemerovo Oblast, RSFSR): Yevgeniy Alekseyevich, the need for legal reform is much talked about at present. Could you please give us your theories on legal reform as you see it.

Ye.A. Smolentsev: Comrades! Evidently, 15-20 years ago, until the 27th congress, our courts were in a submissive position. Since Stalin's time, when the USSR Prosecutor's Office was created in 1933, it has been accepted, for example, that the public prosecutor will oversee the law courts in the carriage of justice. Very great importance has thereby been attached to preliminary investigation material and, in fact, it has been given primacy. Wherever the courts have demonstrated principle and consistency in strictly abiding by the law, these judges have usually been called liberals and often condemned for this in party respects as people who are impeding the fight against crime. From my own point of view, the most important thing now is for our Soviet court to play an appropriate role within a rule-of-law state and become the supreme body of social protection that it is intended to be under the Constitution. In this respect, we must all, the whole of our society, do everything possible to ensure that the court of law is really independent, really has full rights, has the final say in all cases, and has the opportunity to assess preliminary investigation material. So that investigators cannot say that the court has taken the wrong decision. We have a potential medium for rectifying mistakes made by the courts: If someone does not agree with a decision, he should make the appropriate representation and appeal to the higher authorities, who have the right to appeal against a wrong decision. Consequently, the most important point in the implementation of legal reform is to raise the court of law to the level at which it should be. That is the most important point.

I also think that when carrying out legal reform, we should give very serious thought to our investigative apparatus. For several years now, our investigative apparatus has been in a state of limbo, and I must say with all frankness that the best, the very best cadres are now leaving the investigations departments, just as they are leaving the courts, because people do not feel they have any prospects. As far as I am concerned, neither the Prosecutor's Office nor the Internal Affairs Ministry (MVD) should have an investigative apparatus. We have discussed how one body cannot be responsible for supervision, investigative work, and also special supervision of this work. I think we will be making a big mistake if we concentrate the investigative apparatus in internal affairs bodies, and I also think that there is still a great danger here, a possibility that the operations service and investigative service will merge. This could lead to very sorry consequences. From my point of view, the opinion now being voiced—that an independent investigations committee should be set up, which would be responsible for these questions from top to bottom—is correct. This is the second problem. I do, of course, think we should strengthen prosecutor's office supervision by releasing it from its investigative responsibilities. These are the main problems we need to resolve in the context of legal reform. I am not going to touch on smaller issues, such as improving our legislation. A great deal is now being said on the question of whether we should retain the death penalty, how we should resolve questions concerning members of the legal profession, legal protection, and so forth—I do not think all is well here either. At present, the accused can only invite a counsel for the defense when the investigation has been completed. Surely this cannot be right? We must take action to ensure that anyone accused, any alleged offender has the right to a counsel for the defense at an earlier stage, at least from the point of his arrest, from the point when criminal charges are brought. I believe our legislation must develop in this direction; I feel that our justice and social fairness can only benefit from this. There are a whole series of other questions I will not go into here, as much can be said in detail about them.

From the floor: How do you feel about the establishment of a patents court?

Ye.A. Smolentsev: You know, comrades, some countries do have patents courts. I do not think there is any point in our considering this at present. We need to strengthen our civil court and the civil collegiums in oblast courts and supreme courts so that they consider these cases. But I think that with the development of our relations, and particularly with the establishment of joint enterprises and so forth, we cannot rule out the possibility that at some stage we will evidently have to come back to this question and set up a special patents court. We do not have this practice at present and I do not feel we need to decide this question now.

M.S. Gorbachev: Go ahead, comrade.

From the floor: (The deputy does not give his name). Yevgeniy Alekseyevich, you have talked about strictest possible observance of legality, but I have a problem in this connection with regard to the concept. After all, the words "strictest possible" as applied to the law and legality have existed in our country since 1917, but there is still very little legality in our country and sometimes none at all. Perhaps we could drop the words "strictest possible"? If we have legality, then that is all there is to it. I have another question in this connection: What happens if you are faced with a law which positively sanctions lawlessness? For example, what will you do with the words "strictest possible legality" if faced with a law containing article 11 point 1?

Ye.A. Smolentsev: I see what you mean. I believe that the question of the validity and correctness of any law must be decided by you, esteemed people's deputies. A judge must abide by the law and not think about whether that law is correct or incorrect. But if such a question should arise, then the USSR Supreme Court and the republics' supreme courts have the right of legislative initiative and, evidently, this right can sometimes be exercised. But I think that we must very strictly educate our judges so that they do not ponder over the question of whether a law is correct or incorrect. As long as a law exists, its word is sacred. Otherwise we will have anarchy and it will lead us into the situation we had here in 1937 and subsequent years.

V.Ya. Medikov, prorector of the Siberian Metallurgy Institute, Novokuznetsk City (Novokuznetskiy Territorial Electoral okrug, Kemerovo Oblast, RSFSR): Yevgeniy Alekseyevich, tell us please about your attitude toward mass amnesties and the fact that people are being sent to do time in Siberia.

Ye.A. Smolentsev: For a long time I have advocated that we should not practice one-shot releases or mass amnesties. I advocate that the law is enforced and that sentences are firm. That someone who has been given 5 years should know that he will be serving his punishment through these 5 years. But now there are too many proposals associated with the need to pass harsher sentences. Some people, ignorant of the real situation, believe that we can solve the problem of the struggle against crime by means of harsher sentences. This opinion is incorrect. For too long a time we passed too many harsh sentences on people. And, comrades, many of you here know that until quite recently our places for deprivation of freedom were like, you know, a boiler full of steam. Periodically, a few times a year, we opened the release valve of this boiler in order to release people from these places. I believe that this is a clearly incorrect situation. It is a wrong situation, it is a harmful situation. My stance is that we must be very cautious, very thoughtful, and very sparing as regards punishment taking the form of deprivation of freedom. People who have committed for the first time a non-dangerous offense, and even more so an offense of negligence, have nothing to do with places for deprivation of freedom. They are not the perfect places where man can be reeducated, on the contrary, we often some up against a different situation. But at the same time I must emphasize that under no circumstances should there be any lenience toward persons who have committed serious crimes which are dangerous for society. And this is path now being followed by judicial practice. I can cite the following figures for the Russian Federation. Especially since 1982, when the legislature adopted a whole series of measures which the courts could apply in sentencing people to punishment not involving deprivation of freedom.

This might appear to be a liberalization of punishment. But now we have seen the results. Deprivation of freedom declined from 55 percent to 35 percent since 1972, and at the same time there were harsher measures of punishment involving, say, deprivation of freedom for between 3 and 15 years. Back in 1982 this accounted for, say, 35.5 percent, and the present figures stands at 45.5 percent. In other words, the courts have taken a position of cautiously punishing persons who have committed crimes of lesser importance for society, and harshly punishing persons who have committed serious crimes like murder, robbery, rape, and so on. I think that this is the only correct practice to be followed not only by the courts but also in our legislation.

M.S. Gorbachev: Please.

V.A. Karpochev, chairman of Volzhskiy Rayon's "Put Lenina" collective farm [kolkhoz] (Zvenigovskiy National-Territorial Electoral Okrug, Mari Autonomous Soviet Socialist Republic [ASSR]): The way I understood your answer, you are not an advocate of making our laws any harsher. Tell us then, what is the cause of the fact that the number of breaches of the law has increased and there is growing crime today? It seems to me that labor collectives and our society will be unable to cope with this unless the laws are made harsher. Many people speak of this today.

Ye.A. Smolentsev: Comrades! This year did indeed produce very bad and lamentable results. There has been a serious growth of grave crimes in our country. Crime in the country as a whole increased 3.8 percent. But the especially lamentable fact is that serious crimes increased: A 14-percent increase in premeditated murder, while other increased further still—by up to 23 percent. If we were to depict the dynamics of crime in linear form, the result would be a very irregular line. In some years it rises, in others it falls. If we were to look at the crime level for this year, it would not be the highest in all preceding years. But I must say that crime has sharply declined since the introduction of the measures adopted at local level in association with the need to combat drunkenness. There was a very sharp decline in the 2 years of 1986 and 1987. Moreover, while at present one in every three crimes in our country is committed in a state of intoxication, during the 2 years following the adoption of the decree and the implementation of serious measures at local level only 16, 20, or at most 25 percent of persons sentenced in our country had committed serious crimes.

Now we have a fresh boom as it were. People have learned to replace vodka with moonshine and—and this must be bluntly said—people are now distilling it even in places where there had not been even a whiff of moonshine earlier, like in the Far East or the cities for example. There are no regions where people have not learned to distill moonshine. And this naturally furthers the growth of crime.

Therefore, the problem facing our society now is to wage a most serious struggle against drunkenness and the dissoluteness associated with it.

There is another very serious problem. There are hundreds of thousands of people in our society who are doing nothing. Nowadays, one in every five or six of those who receive sentences is a parasite, in other words someone who is not engaged in socially beneficial labor. There is a vast amount of work to be done here by the militia, by all our law enforcement organs, and by the public.

Juvenile crime is also a serious problem. You know that 1 in every 10 crimes today is committed by an adolescent. This may be more or less insignificant when compared with other countries, but the evil of it all is that almost one-third of these crimes are aggressive group crimes like rape, murder, robbery, hooliganism involving knife fights, and so on. This is why now, if we intend to take decisive measures in the struggle against crime, we must give attention primarily to juvenile crime and juvenile delinquency. We cannot resolve this problem by applying only the measures available to law enforcement organs. These are serious questions of upbringing, these are serious questions of employment, of amending our school education. I recall my own childhood: After lessons we got down to airplane model building and other study circles. Nowadays nobody does anything of the sort at schools.... In other words, this a major and multifaceted problem, and it must be tackled by our entire society. This is it, in brief.

M.S. Gorbachev: Comrade Medvedev, please.

R.A. Medvedev, writer (Voroshilovskiy Territorial Electoral Okrug, Moscow City): I have the following question: What is your attitude toward enhancing the Supreme Court's independence and totally eliminating what our press has dubbed "telephone law," and—maybe not now but in 5 or even 10 years' time, at the next stage of the new political system's operation—introducing the practice of electing the Supreme Court for life? So that a judge may leave it only by submitting his own resignation. And something else: How do you view the suggestion that Supreme Court members should resign from the party while in office?

Ye.A. Smolentsev: I have no objection as regards us having judges for life. I think that we will evidently come to that. In actual fact, it is necessary to create conditions whereby someone—if he is properly doing his duty—should not think that a time might come when he may not be elected or he might be somehow influenced.

As for judges resigning from the party, I categorically object to this. I personally would never agree to work on the Supreme Court had I suddenly been told today: Resign from the party. Ours is a communist party, and I think that judges—provided we create the proper conditions for their work—will pursue an independent line. As a matter of fact, let me tell you frankly that now nobody exerts any pressure on the union's Supreme Court—and I have been working on it for 10 years. True enough, there have been attempts by individual officials, and some quite high-ranking ones at that. For example, Comrade Aliyev and the former first secretary of the Kirghiz Communist Party Central Committee made attempts to intervene in specific cases, but the party Central Committee drew their attention to the impermissibility of such interference in judicial affairs. In any case, I do not advocate that judges be nonparty people as an obligatory requirement, even though a certain percentage of them are, and there may even be more of them in the future.

M.S. Gorbachev: Please.

V.V. Khmura, chairman of Olginskiy Rural Soviet of People's Deputies Executive Committee, Olginskaya Village, Primorsko-Akhtarskiy Rayon (Timashevskiy Territorial Electoral Okrug, Krasnodar Kray): Yevgeniy Alekseyevich! I have two questions. First. It happens at times that a rayon court hears a case and a person is not satisfied. The case is heard by the kray court, the person is again dissatisfied, appeals to the RSFSR Court, and the latter remits the case again to the kray court. And you end up in a vicious circle. Do you consider this right? The second question. A kolkhoz chairman was sentenced for engaging "moonlighting" teams to do building work on the farm. He was given 5 years without the right to take positions of authority or work in positions of responsibility....

From the floor: And he was dismissed from leadership work....

V.V. Khmura: But the kolkhoz members, recognizing his merits, reelected him kolkhoz chairman. He even told them words like: Comrades, under me you'll be working 16 hours a day. I'll work your fingers to the bone. And the kolkhoz members, recognizing his merits, voted for him.... What do you think, can the court's decision be set aside at the kolkhoz members' request?

Ye.A. Smolentsev: On the first question. Some cases get as high as the republican supreme court and even the USSR Supreme Court. I think that this is a perfectly normal situation in a rule-of-law state. If someone fails to have his problem resolved elsewhere, he can go as high as the Union Supreme Court. If a mistake has occurred, it must be corrected come what may.

And now about your specific question. If there is such a case, when a deserving chairman is respected so much that he has been elected chairman despite the existence of a court decision banning him from holding office, let us take a look at this case. You tell us which case this is, we will request and obtain it, we will look to see how justified it was to decide to ban him from holding leadership office.... But this is a specific case and I would not like to comment on it now.

M.S. Gorbachev: Please.

V.A. Nozdrya, leader of a team of fitters and installation workers at the "S. Ordzhonikidze Sevastopolskiy Morskoy Zavod" Production Association, Sevastopol City (Sevastopolskiy Territorial Electoral Okrug, Crimea Oblast): I know that in the United States and in other countries there are judges sentencing criminals to a total of 100 and more years. Do you think that this practice is correct and should it be introduced in our country?

Ye.A. Smolentsev: Every state adopts the law that it thinks most correct. I would not like to criticize America for the fact that there are sentences there amounting to hundreds of years. I would not like to criticize America for the fact that they have people sentenced to death waiting for decades to be executed. I believe that there is no need for us to introduce this kind of indefinite imprisonment. You know that academics' sociological studies have shown that confinement in places of deprivation of liberty for up to 8 years alone plays a role in reeducating man, and then it ceases to play that role.

M.S. Gorbachev: Let us spend another 10 minutes on this and then bring this question to a close. Please, Deputy Medvedev. Let's have a brief question and a brief answer.

N.N. Medvedev, chief of a Kaunas Radio Gauge Institute sector (Kaunasskiy-Panyamunskiy National-Territorial Electoral Okrug, Lithuanian SSR): We are well aware that the best changes within the state are in effect those that stem from an improvement in morality. This was what Aleksandr Sergeyevich Pushkin said. That is why I was very disquieted by your statement that a judge must not think. Phenomena in life are analogous, while the law is discrete. It is trial by jury that ensures that this analogous form of the essence of life is taken into consideration. Herein lies the dialectical contradiction.

M.S. Gorbachev: Lawyers feel as if they are speaking from a judge's chair here.

N.N. Medvedev: That is why, in connection with your speech, I was particularly interested by the following question: What is your attitude to the death penalty?

M.S. Gorbachev: Be brief with your questions and answers.

Ye.A. Solomentsev: Our country now envisages the death penalty for 15 corpora delicti. It is enforced virtually only for murder under aggravating circumstances. While throughout this norm's existence it has never been enforced for such crimes as, say, counterfeiting and so on. It is not applied to women or for economic crimes. It is my firm conviction that the death penalty must be preserved for people who have committed serious murders involving rape, multiple killers, and so on.

P.A. Druz, pensioner, Belovo City, Kemerovo Oblast, (from the All-Union Organization of Veterans of War and Labor): Yevgeniy Alekseyevich, what is your attitude to the death penalty? You have not answered the question. Moreover, what is your attitude to the fact that most convicts are even now sent to serve their term of imprisonment in Siberia?

Ye.A. Smolentsev: Comrades! I am not aware that most convicts used to be sent to Siberia. Comrade Bakatin knows this problem better than I. We have a system of places of deprivation of freedom and lawbreakers are sent there—the convicts' personal features are, of course, taken into consideration. There are no special-regime colonies in Moscow. Naturally, they are sent to Vladimir and Kalinin or somewhere else. But in principle, I believe that people are sent to those oblasts where there are the appropriate correctional establishments and not to Siberia. At one time there was a law whereby prostitutes and people without fixed abode were exiled to Siberia, but this law no longer exists and no one sends anyone to Siberia.

A.A. Likhanov, writer and chairman of the V.I. Lenin Soviet Children's Foundation, Moscow City. (From the V.I. Lenin Soviet Children's Foundation): Yevgeniy Alekseyevich, what is your attitude toward family courts? Such courts exist, as you know, in many countries of the world.

M.S. Gorbachev: Be brief, there are only 7 minutes left.

A.A. Likhanov: How should we create family courts to stop the number of divorces.

Ye.A. Smolentsev: I do not believe that we need to set up any family courts. We need to ensure that our courts occupy the requisite position in society and are indeed an organ providing effective social protection. Then they will resolve all questions, including family questions.

M.S. Gorbachev: Please, your question. No, I have already promised, there are still 5 minutes left, comrades.

From the floor: In the last 3 and one-half years Uzbekistan's courts have pronounced more than 450 acquittals. This was mentioned last fall at the Uzbekistan SSR Supreme Soviet session. Tell us, please, Yevgeniy Alekseyevich, have any workers from law enforcement organs, particularly investigative organs, who have permitted violations that fall under the operation of the articles of the criminal code section on crimes against justice, been punished?

Ye.A. Smolentsev: I work in the Russian Soviet Federated Socialist Republic [RSFSR] and you are talking about Uzbekistan. Only the USSR minister of justice can answer your question.

M.S. Gorbachev: Good. Your question.

A.L. Pershin, excavator operator at Kungradskiy Rayon Production Repair Service Association, Kungrad City (Kungradskiy National-Territorial Electoral Okrug, Karakalpak Autonomous Soviet Socialist Republic]): Yevgeniy Alekseyevich, have you made any mistakes in your official judicial activity and how have you rectified them?

Ye.A. Smolentsev: What, what?

A.L. Pershin: Have you made any mistakes in your official judicial activity and how have you rectified them?

Ye.A. Smolentsev: My mistakes personally? I do not recall any serious mistakes that would affect the sentences that I passed at the time and cause them to be repealed. In particular, no sentences where strict measures of punishment were enforced have been repealed. But it is not impossible that some of the sentences that I passed when working in the oblast, in the people's court may have been repealed. At any rate I do not recall any such sentences among my recent decisions.

From the floor: Yevgeniy Alekseyevich, do you think that some of the directives adopted by the USSR Supreme Court plenum exceed the constitutional powers of the Supreme Court, when the scope of the civil law's operation is restricted, say, on questions of residence permits—in particular the directives of 1987—or when picketing is equated with demonstration, thus giving a broad interpretation of a Supreme Court Presidium decree legislative act. Would it not be better in such cases to display legislative initiative? Would it not be more correct to act in this way when building a rule-of-law state?

M.S. Gorbachev: Keep your question brief.

Ye.A. Smolentsev: Comrades, first a word about the law involving strikes and so on. We hid the fact that we have strikes, rallies, and other public manifestations for a very long time. People said: These things do not exist in our country, they cannot exist under socialism—that is why no law was adopted. Was this really a good thing? A law has now been adopted. It may be imperfect but in any civilized country there are laws which regulate this kind of public manifestation in order to safeguard society above all. I do not want to assess all these laws. I believe that this lofty deputies' forum will decide how far they are justified and legitimate. I confirm once again that the law is binding on a judge.

M.S. Gorbachev: Your question?

Ye.A. Gayer, scientific staffer at the USSR Academy of Sciences Far East Branch History, Archaeology, and Ethnography Institute, Vladivostok City (Dalnevostochnyy National-Territorial Electoral Okrug, RSFSR): Yevgeniy Alekseyevich, I want nonetheless to supplement the question asked by my comrade from Siberia. In Komsomolsk-na-Amure and the Far East you encounter convicts from the European part of the USSR, who are serving their term of imprisonment there and who then remain in our area after their release. Many voters ask that these comrades be sent back to the places where they were sentenced after their release. What is your view of that and how will this be resolved?

Ye.A. Smolentsev: I ask you to ask Comrade Bakatin this question when you approve him as minister. I am a judge and we only determine the nature of the colony. It is the minister of internal affairs who decides where to send a person.

M.S. Gorbachev: Last question.

D. Khudonazarov, first secretary of the Tajik SSR Cinematographers Union Board, Dushanbe City (Khorogskiy National-Territorial Electoral Okrug, Gorno-Badakhshan Autonomous Oblast): Yevgeniy Alekseyevich, did you take part in the work of our morning sitting?

Ye.A. Smolentsev: Morning sitting? Yes, of course, I did.

D. Khudonazarov: Then I would like to find out your opinion—as a professional and skilled jurist—of the actions of Kazakhstan's leaders.... As Gennadiy Vasilyevich mentioned.

Ye.A. Smolentsev: Gennadiy Vasilyevich?

D. Khudonazarov: Yes, when we were talking about money....

Ye.A. Smolentsev: You realize the point here. I understood him to be turning a blind eye. In principle, comrades, I consider this kind of action illegal. Nonetheless we should not force a person to hand over money. Then is he suddenly not guilty? The court must conduct an investigation. Is he or is he not guilty? I understood Gennadiy Vasilyevich to mean that since there were too many cases of people feathering their nest in all manner of ways in the republic, the following appeal was made:

"Hand over what you have stolen!" And if a person voluntarily handed it over, let...I do not think that we will be any the worse for this. But in principle, I believe that money can only be exacted from a person following a judicial ruling.

M.S. Gorbachev: Good. Sit down, thank you. Shall we open the debate?

Hall: No!

M.S. Gorbachev: No. I will put the question to the vote. Those in favor of electing Comrade Yevgeniy Alekseyevich Smolentsev as chairman of the USSR Supreme Court please raise your mandate cards. Lower them. Anyone against?

From the floor: Three.

M.S. Gorbachev: Lower your mandate cards. Any abstentions? (Votes are counted).

From the floor: Three against and seven abstentions.

M.S. Gorbachev: Comrade Yevgeniy Alekseyevich Smolentsev is elected chairman of the USSR Supreme Court. (Applause). [passage omitted]

M.S. Gorbachev: Fine. Who is in favor of appointing Comrade Aleksandr Yakovlevich Sukharev? Please raise your documents. Please lower them. Who is against? (The votes are counted). Against—27. Please lower them. Who abstained? (The votes are counted). Abstentions—36. Thus, Comrade Aleksandr Yakovlevich Sukharev is appointed USSR general prosecutor by a majority of votes. (Applause).

Now, if a discussion does not arise, let us talk briefly about the Supreme Soviet committees. We have already discussed them with regard to the chambers. So these are the committees that were suggested, stemming from the discussion in the chambers:

For International Affairs
For Defense and State Security Questions
For Questions of Legislation, Legality, and Law and Order
For Questions of the Work of Soviets of People's Deputies and of the Development of Management and Self-Management
For Economic Reform Questions
For Agrarian Questions and Food
For Construction and Architecture Questions
For Science, Public Education, Culture, and Upbringing
For the Protection of the People's Health
For the Affairs of Women and of Family, Mother, and Child Protection
For the Affairs of Veterans and Invalids
For Youth Affairs
For Questions of Ecology and the Rational Use of Natural Resources

For Questions of Glasnost and Citizens' Rights and Appeals.

I am sure that comrades will not find some things among those I have named. It turned out here that a compromise had to be found.

A.I. Lukyanov: There are the commissions, too....

M.S. Gorbachev: Well, the commissions, yes. I am talking about the committees now, as regards the Supreme Soviet as a whole, for the committees will serve both chambers and the Supreme Soviet as a whole.

Of course, I have listened to all the discussion, sitting to one side, so to speak, and I liked the discussion in general, as deputies questioned both Comrade Lukyanov and others and themselves said a very great deal. I have drawn the conclusion for myself that we probably have not achieved the optimum at the first attempt. I have this feeling. We are getting away from what used to happen in the Supreme Soviet, and we want the committees to express the new height and the new level of work and the status and role of our Supreme Soviet. We seem to have made solid progress. But, at all events, all the time everyone wanted to find in the discussion a mention of his own sector, sphere, and so forth. This happened. But, probably, it must not. And again. Someone said that there really is, nonetheless, maybe, a certain eclecticism. Yesterday this was said in the Soviet of Nationalities. The "adding on" of questions gradually increased and increased.... There was "science and education," and then "upbringing and culture" was added. But, in general, what approach is to be taken here? Culture in the broad sense is culture, so to speak, both material and spiritual, and if a sphere more closely linked to spiritual criteria, then, perhaps, this is quite possible, science and education—this is a process taking place—and culture of upbringing.

Why am I saying this?... I thought: How are we to get out of this situation? Perhaps, as many people said, we still have some more work to do, probably—let us see what will happen. Probably this is the correct approach, comrades.... Now we have reached a certain stage, and now we must start working. First, we ourselves must work out—who is to join a particular committee or commission must understand whether or not he has ended up there [sentence as published]. And we must find forms of work, and it will probably come to light whether something either is not covered or is simply mechanically attached to some committee or commission. Therefore I would not consider that you and I will adopt such a perfectly ideal document now. But, comrades, we must probably do this and start work. The rest is in the hands of the chamber and in the hands of the Supreme Soviet. Moreover, the bulk of the Supreme Soviet will work here. Yes, people rightly say that it is still possible to express some aspect of domestic and foreign policy through a subcommission, through a subcommittee. It will, probably, be possible to take account of this. Well, comrades? This is what I think—if we now continue making comments, they, too, will probably be substantial. But since we have synthesized everything that we accumulated during the preliminary work with regard to these committees, it would be possible to vote now. Well, comrades? Can we vote?

The hall: Yes.

M.S. Gorbachev: And begin allocating forces, so to speak. Then, comrades, with regard to our mutual understanding, I put to the vote the question of adopting a decision to have the below-mentioned [as published] committees under the Supreme Soviet. Please raise your documents. Please lower them. Any against? No. Abstentions? No.... So the road has been opened up for improvement; this is the most important point.... This is the first compromise, let us say, in the Supreme Soviet....

Comrades, I thank you for your work and your active participation. This has been a very important period of time in the work. I wish you all the best. Yes, one minute, please sit down. Tomorrow, I have already announced, we meet at 1000. But I would like to ask something. Should we not, given the situation that has taken shape in Uzbekistan (we wanted to decide this at the congress, but the Supreme Soviet must, perhaps, take on more and more), should we not in this situation, Rafik Nishanovich and the comrades from Uzbekistan, send the most respected and authoritative deputies in the Uzbek delegation there now, to the republic, so that they can be on the spot? Well, comrades, is that right?

The hall: Yes.

M.S. Gorbachev: This question has arisen here from Uzbekistan itself, and there has even been a telegram. Comrade Kadyrov probably needs support, advice, and assistance. And comrades at the congress—Popov and Poltoranin—have sent a note that we must back up the appeal that we have made by having the most authoritative people set out right today or tomorrow morning and help to defuse the situation there on behalf of the Supreme Soviet. Is that so, comrades?

From the hall: Yes.

M.S. Gorbachev: Let Comrade Nishanov and his comrades from Uzbekistan (this all coincides both within the framework of the chamber and within the framework of the republic) decide. Not the whole delegation, of course. You will find someone....

All the best, comrades.

8 Jun Congress Procedings Reported

Yemelyanov Addresses Congress
*PM1006131189 Moscow PRAVDA in Russian
9 Jun 89 Second Edition pp 3-4*

[Text of speech delivered by A.M. Yemelyanov of Leninskiy Territorial Electoral Okrug, Moscow City, RSFSR, at 8 June morning sitting of the USSR Congress of People's Deputies]

[Text] Comrade deputies! Esteemed voters who are pinning your ultimate cherished hopes on our congress! The fate of restructuring and the destiny of the whole country largely depend on our congress. Restructuring has now reached a critical point. Four years have not produced an improvement in the population's real living standards. Latterly a number of negative trends have been observed in society's democratization. The situation now, in generalized terms, is as follows: Either we go further down the road of the revolutionary democratic renewal of society, or we start something we know well from the past—moving in a new circle with an inevitable period of reactionary revenge.

Of course, it would be wrong to pin the blame for existing difficulties solely on the current leadership. The legacy we inherited was too grave and the abyss in which we found ourselves was too deep. But for the sake of objectivity it must be said that our current difficulties can largely be explained by the inconsistency of our policies. We have talked a very great deal about new thinking. But we have probably only really put it into practice in foreign policy, where we have had real results. As for the development of the economy and the social sphere, in these areas former approaches prevail; we have been moving away from what we have achieved, and papering over the cracks, and therefore there have been no special results. Nikolay Petrovich Shmelev has already cited specific examples of this. I would like to quote a couple of examples from the agrarian sphere. Indeed, why do we find enormous foreign-currency and natural resources every year in order to buy masses of grain and meat yet there are insufficient resources to reduce the losses from our own harvest? Why do we have enough oil for grain purchases, yet when the harvest starts combines and trucks stand idle because fuel quotas have been used up? What kind of policy do we need here? These are questions which any ordinary worker or peasant could resolve if they were in charge, but are beyond the comprehension of our high-ranking officials.

Probably the main thing is that over the past 4 years we have made very little progress in resolving the main issue of setting up a political system and political mechanism which would really put the people in charge of the country. It is clear that if the people were in charge we would never have gotten into our present state. Now, unfortunately, the tendency is that the further you move away from the people towards the top, the more democratic principles tend to be compromised. This, indeed, is understandable. Our restructuring (the initiators of restructuring—the Politburo—have long stated this in their documents) is a revolution, and any revolution is a fundamental change of power and a struggle for power. But history teaches that the ruling class and ruling elite have never voluntarily or enthusiastically relinquished power. And our four years of restructuring are graphic confirmation of that.

The administrative and bureaucratic apparatus at all levels, particularly in the upper echelons of power, has mustered its defenses and is doing everything to retain the monopoly under which it has only rights and no duties. Under which it determines and decides everything but bears no responsibility to lower-level links and, ultimately, the people, for the consequences of its decisions. And I can imagine how difficult it is for the initiators of restructuring—the general secretary and other democratically minded leaders in the upper echelons of power—to more or less consistently implement the idea of restructuring and the idea of the democratic renewal of our society.

In particular, we have been talking a great deal recently about the independence of the grass roots and enterprises. But it is elementary that it will not be possible to do this unless the functions of higher bodies are limited. You can't please everyone at the same time. But look at what is actually happening. Models of economic accountability are a dime a dozen, but only isolated enterprises have been given more or less genuine economically accountable autonomy. And which enterprises, you may wonder? Those enterprises which consistently prove that they are not just loss-makers but are already dying and on their last legs. Only then do officials assemble to discuss the matter, and some of these enterprises are given relatively full economically accountable autonomy. But while an enterprise still shows signs of life, our concrete state and bureaucratic mechanism will work on finishing them off. Why isn't economic accountability introduced in good time? What kind of science can compensate for these basic absurdities? It is necessary to extend the elementary principles which have proved their worth in the cooperative system—vested interest and autonomy—to state enterprises, and this, in my view, needed to be done and could have been done long ago. Because these principles are not just cooperative principles, they are the principles of basic normal economic management. And they should exist at any state enterprise.

I can understand why this is not done. If all state enterprises were given this autonomy, the superfluousness of our entire vast bureaucratic superstructure would be immediately apparent. And who wants to sign his own death warrant? It seems to me that we need to fundamentally alter the principles of our approach to the restructuring of the administrative system. We should not go from top to bottom—changing signs, papering over cracks, and repainting the exterior—we should start from the bottom and move up. At each administrative

level there should only be administrative organs whose functions and apparatus numbers are needed by the grass roots. The existence of any administrative organ is only justifiable if the need for it is dictated from below by the interests of developing production.

This principle—in my personal view, admittedly—was timidly included in the agrarian workers' appeal, an appeal which is a cri de coeur from our peasantry reflecting their sorrow. I think that this principle should perhaps be introduced not only in economic management, but also in the system of party leadership. Then we would be able to construct an administrative pyramid in our country based on a firm foundation whereby the entire administrative apparatus is at the service of the people—rather than the people being at the service of the apparatus, as is to all intents and purposes the case at present.

The survival of the administrative and bureaucratic apparatus is largely ensured by the existence of social privileges in the distribution of material and spiritual benefits. This is not a new issue; it was also raised at our congress. It is not possible for me to dwell on this point in detail. I want to stress one point: When certain leaders tell us that these privileges allegedly do not exist, then—put in plain language—it follows that they think that the whole people live and are provided for in the same way that they are. So what kind of policy can we consider or count on? We have talked here about setting up a commission on this. I do not oppose a commission, comrades, but commissions have one powerful feature—they can spin out the resolution of any issue. I propose that our congress resolution include a binding decision on the elimination of these privileges as a principle. Let the commission determine the specific mechanism for implementing this congress directive.

Within the framework of this major problem I would like to stress one specific issue which is, nonetheless, of general importance. I am a deputy from the capital's Leninskiy Electoral Okrug, which takes in Leninskiy and Kievskiy Rayons. Few Muscovites and even fewer non-Muscovites know that 40-60 percent of inhabitants in the historic center of the capital are born, raised, and die in communal housing. When the time comes for them to obtain an apartment, they are allocated one in the capital's outlying regions. Comfortable apartment blocks for the Council of Ministers, the Central Committee, and other highly important departments are being built here. This is not just disregard for the population's interests, it is, I think, a blatant challenge to the people. And I, as a deputy, convey an insistent demand—not a request (our people are tired of begging for indulgence from their leaders)—I convey the voters' insistent demand that apartment blocks currently at various stages of completion be given not to those for whom they were intended, but to the inhabitants of this residential district.

In principle we should strive to ensure that on the basis of self-management no department should be entitled to do anything on the territory of a particular rayon or territory without the consent of the inhabitants of that region. Otherwise there can be no self-management.

I fully support the proposals put forward here in connection with the need to assist socially disadvantaged sections of the population. I would merely like to emphasize that students ought to be added to this category since their grants, just like old-age pensions, have been devalued as a result of galloping inflation and do not cover the existential minimum.

There is a multitude of economic and social questions. However, their solution depends ultimately on the creation of a democratic political system. Not everything has always been bad in our country. There have been glimpses of light in between cults after the replacement of the main political leader of the country—the general secretary. This applies approximately to the period of 1953-1957, and the eighth 5-year plan (1966-1970). But why, 4 or 5 years later, did the economy and the social sphere slide go downhill?

Above all because the political mechanism changed. There was a transition from relative democracy and collective leadership to a regime of personal power and authoritarian rule. There was no political mechanism here to protect the democratic life of the country. And there still is no such mechanism; even now we do not have anything to guarantee the irreversibility of restructuring. Therefore the formation of such a mechanism is the number one task.

It is often being stressed now that the party itself is the guarantor of the irreversibility of restructuring. Allow me to question this proposition. We have always had a party, and despite this we have arrived in our current situation. Strictly speaking, the people did not arrive in the present crisis situation by themselves. They arrived under the leadership of the party, frequently implementing its course under duress. We must bear this in mind if we are to soberly assess the past and draw lessons from it for the present and the future. A one-party system presupposes also one-party responsibility. We have already taken considerable steps in the formation of the new political mechanism. What more is to be done? That's the first question. Separation of state and party functions and hence the issue of holding more than one post. Comrades, we must not adapt the system to a particular leader, but make the leader fit in with a system which is based on democratic principles. And the principles are as follows: A one-party system already means a monopolization of power, and if the leader of that one party is simultaneously also the president, that is monopolization of power squared. And if, at the moment, we temporarily need to combine these two posts (and I understand why, because transferring power from the party to the people is a very difficult and protracted process), we must not present this temporary solution as a principle of socialism. We must enshrine this in the congress documents and return to the solution of this

question again and again. People are asking, but who is to head the party? What sort of party do we have if everything hinges on the leader alone? And later, if there is no such leader in the Politburo, it we will have to look further afield. And in principle, what sort of a system, what sort of a mechanism is it if we do not know the members of the Politburo well? After all, they are virtually all of them in the same political mold; frequently they express practically the same ideas, and sometimes they even use the same expressions. It was different under Lenin. And we should put an end to it, too.

As for combining party and state power at lower levels, we must firmly enshrine in the congress decisions that this is impermissible because otherwise there will be an even greater unforeseen monopolization of power.

Next question. We must approach the next elections to republican and local soviets with an improved system.

First, the elections of all deputies must be equal.

Second, we must not allow single candidates to run because this is a loophole to facilitate the election of a number of functionaries as deputies.

Third, we must be prepared to switch in the future to the election of the president by a direct ballot of the entire people on a competitive basis from more than one candidate. I fully support the proposal put forward here in connection with the direct elections of the chief editor of IZVESTIYA and the chairman of the State Committee for Television and Radio Broadcasting. I support the proposal to publish a "Remembrance" book featuring the names of all those who died in Afghanistan. But I would like to add that the names of those who made the decisions on Afghanistan should also be recorded in this book, showing who voted on this question and how. Somehow this question has petered out. Voters are asking—they asked me, for instance, last night—why no commission has been set up on Afghanistan and why this question has been kept quiet.

Last, the transition to genuine people's power greatly changes the position of the party in our social and political system. I must make a reservation straight away. Esteemed party and political leaders, let us understand each other correctly. Otherwise any attempt to raise this question is immediately interpreted (as has happened here at the congress too) as virtually an attempt to drive a wedge between the party and the people, to belittle the prestige of the party. But that is not so. The prestige of the party has declined, of course, that is a fact. However, it has declined above all as a result of its activities in the past. And it must be stated frankly that even now the democratization of intraparty life is lagging behind the democratization of society. That applies, for one thing, to the elections from the party (I am referring to the 100 [candidates] for the 100 [seats]). It also applies to the decrees about which much has been said here, and to the decision of the March plenum on

Comrade Yeltsin, a decision which had a major impact on the final stage of the election campaign in Moscow, and clearly not only in Moscow. The people gave their assessment of this decision, among other things, by their rallies. It is only a pity that the members of the Politburo and members of the Central Committee did not join the people at these rallies bringing along with them the, in their opinion, outstanding representative of the working class Comrade Tikhomirov. So that, as was done in Lenin's time, they could themselves explain to the people the essence of their decisions, rather than delegating this task to rayon committees and grassroots party organizations.

In conclusion I would like to underline the main thought once again. Since we are moving toward people's power (and that is the main purport of restructuring) it is necessary to redefine the place of the party in the social structures. Voters are asking: What can you, deputies, do? Almost all of you are Communists. The Central Committee will adopt a decision and you will have to vote in accordance with the Party Statutes and all your will of the people will be snuffed out. This question is cropping up at virtually all the meetings. I believe it is based on the old notions, when the party held complete sway. And the people were essentially deprived of power. However, the situation is radically changing now with the transfer of power to the soviets. The people rank above the party. Our congress ranks above the party congress. The Supreme Soviet ranks above the party's Central Committee. The Constitution ranks above the Party Statutes. The party operates within the framework of the Constitution drawn up by the representatives of the people. And this determines our priorities. Each of us is first a deputy and then a party member. This determines his or her conduct. This correlation between party and people's organs must be reflected in the USSR Constitution, the Party Statutes, and the documents of our Congress.

And we have to give expression to the priorities that have been set out in everything, including the order in which organs are listed in the various documents. Voters asked me yesterday, for instance: "Why was the Central Committee listed first and the Supreme Soviet second in a recent information report?" That, too, is a vestige of the past and here, too, we must replace the stereotypes which have taken shape.

In conclusion I would like to say: Comrades, we are living in a time of restructuring when objectively speaking, and I stress, objectively, all roads lead to genuine people's power. And we must do everything to remove all obstacles from these roads, irrespective of who put them up. Only then will we be able to avail ourselves of the last chance which history has granted us to rehabilitate ourselves before our people and before the world community.

Deputy Prunskene Speaks

PM0906114589 Moscow PRAVDA in Russian 9 Jun 89 Second Edition pp 2-3

[Speech delivered by K.D.P. Prunskene (Shyaulyayskiy Territorial Electoral Okrug, Lithuanian Soviet Socialist Republic) at 8 June morning sitting of USSR Congress of People's Deputies]

[Text] The many years' practice of partial economic reforms has convincingly proved their unsoundness under the conditions of the overcentralized management of the economy of a great power such as the union has become. The normalization of this gigantic economic organism and its extraction from stagnation or even the overcoming of decline are inconceivable with the old methods of long-distance management from a remote great-power center, however strong or even wise it may be.

The Baltic concept of economic reform contains the principle of the localization of the solution of the problem, its transfer to the level where economic and social processes take place, where there is real information, and these processes are accomplished by committed people. We view the republic's economic autonomy as a primary and essential condition for restructuring the management of the economy both of individual republics and of the union as a whole. The need for this is determined by a whole series of circumstances.

First. Decentralization and democratization of the economy can take place only in all the economy's sections, they cannot be implemented selectively, that is we cannot seek the independence of enterprises and leave the republics as a whole and their local soviets without rights. Otherwise the point of the appeal "all power to the soviets" is lost.

Second. The so-called unity of the national economic complex implemented at the center's will and through it—everyone knows the results—must be replaced by direct ties between republics and above all between their enterprises. Nothing so unites peoples as their economies, as the market.

Third. The development of the economy of any republic and region must take into account the principle of regionalism, that is the centuries-old traditions of economic thinking and motivations of the actions of a specific people and the nature of their collaboration with a specific social and natural environment. Ignoring this, trying to seek and apply standardized solutions in the center causes enormous, quite irreparable harm to all peoples of the union and tears out the natural roots of development and participation in the international division of labor with their own unrepeatable character. Is it not this which has led to the death of Lake Aral and many other ecological catastrophes?

Fourth. Restructuring can be implemented only by a committed person, not simply by the work force of an enterprise or department. In production collectives this commitment is one-sided, it does not encompass ecological, sociodemographic, cultural, or national aspects of life which can and must be regulated within the framework of a socially discernible territorial community. The small republics capable of becoming masters of their own lives and directing the economy's development responsibly for the benefit of man and the people of the republic and the union as a whole are just such communities.

Fifth. Restructuring is proceeding unevenly both in individual republics and in regions. Nor is there an equal readiness to switch to self-management. This unevenness is natural and it must be admitted. Artificially holding back the processes of socioeconomic activeness and economic enterprise leads to the underuse of the internal potential of republics and regions and produces nothing but loss—both to each region and to the entire union. Marching in step can take us only toward the abyss, and we can only extricate ourselves from the routine of stagnation by unleashing initiative.

Sixth. The republics' right to the independent management of their economies is as natural as the right of a people or person to existence and self-determination. The actual absence of rights in the sphere of the economy, and not just the economy, and the question of the return of these rights is in my view a most painful and urgent task. Even if we do not touch on those specific circumstances connected with the deals between Stalin and Hitler over the Baltic states. If these rights are passed over then democratization itself and the idea of a rule-of-law state and a union become speculative.

Finally, to attract people to invest their labor and money in an individual peasant farm—even in the lease, which shows little promise in the Baltic republics, or in the acquisition of shares—and to other forms of the demonopolization of the economy, the rights of people and enterprises must be defended and there must be guarantees and trust with regard to the laws. Restoring lost trust in the laws and authorities at the level of the republics is far easier than on the scale of the union. Today the Lithuanian peasant is already prepared to trust his deputies, but will he trust the voting of the congress? That is a big question. As yet even we will be unable to persuade him without going against our conscience, because what is automatically comprehensible to the majority of people of the Baltic republics is still incomprehensible or unacceptable to many congress deputies from other republics. But can the entire Lithuanian, Estonian, or any other people be wrong or irrationally emotional? And who can assume the mission of assessing this?

Briefly about the actual content of economic autonomy set forth in the draft law which has been submitted to congress and has already been handed to the deputies. I note that the law was elaborated on the basis of an integral concept. If only individual parts are applied or removed then the mechanism will simply not work. Under the draft the republics have been assigned control over the adoption of legislative acts to regulate the republic's economy and to adopt, use, and dispose of the republic's state property, and that means the decentralization of state ownership itself. The republic becomes the full master of its own land, subterranean resources, forests, and other resources created not only over the years of Soviet power—and it thus finally acquires a committed owner. The republics' organs of state power conduct state regulation of all spheres, including the monetary and credit and financial systems, the formation of the republic's state budget and of local budgets, foreign economic activity, the determination of the bases for the remuneration of labor, pensions, and grants, the procedure for price formation, and the principles of enterprises' economic activity, equal for all sectors including the cooperative sector, whose defects have been caused by the economy itself and the lack of a normal market.

One argument from the center and other opponents of the idea of the independent republic is the fear that regional differences may be intensified. It seems to me that it is better to live well and differently than for everyone to live equally badly.

We have already experienced leveling down, it not only holds back the more developed but also helps to perpetuate the weakness of the laggards. Many deputies from the Baltic republics were surprised, to put it mildly, by Comrade Ryzhkov's statements which have generated hostility toward us from other republics. More advantageous conditions have allegedly been created for us and, taking advantage of cheap raw material, we are appropriating the final product and deriving great advantage. Under inaccurate price assessments, Lithuania is being "sentenced" to a minus balance in the interrepublican commodity exchange. Consequently we are becoming dependents. I cannot believe that the prime minister does not know the real state of affairs regarding who is ultimately appropriating a substantial profit from industry. After all about 95 percent of deductions from the profits of enterprises of union subordination are accumulated by the center. Prices for agricultural output, over half of which Lithuania is compelled to deliver to union funds, are extremely disadvantageous. Is it not a paradox that the growth of deliveries to the union fund is leading to an increase in the republics' debts—now approaching R1 billion—to the union coffers? If we produced less we would have no debts. After all, prices, state orders, limits, and other instruments of economic rule are established not by us but by the center itself, using office-based methods. For instance, if Lithuania, because of unsubstantiated prices, underpays Uzbekistan or Tajikistan for cotton, then under economic autonomy agreements will be adopted on mutually advantageous prices. And this cannot lead to any isolation of the economy, which some leaders fear so much, but merely to the rectification of irrational, sometimes distorted structures and links imposed by the center. Integration will finally acquire a natural basis.

We realize that under the conditions of shortage a certain amount of time will be needed to create an effective interrepublican market whereby there will not longer be any need for the state to interfere directly in trade deals between enterprises. Our concept provides for the maintenance of existing interrepublican ties for a transitional period. It is planned to implement these ties through mutually advantageous agreements and contracts between individual republics and also between republics and the union apparatus, while representing some of the special interests of producers and consumers in the form of a consolidated order and the republics' proposal for equivalent commodity exchange. When all republics and regions switch to self-management, the process of the establishment of independent, self-financing enterprises collaborating in the union market will be considerably accelerated.

The republic's economic autonomy can in no way be combined with the existing principle for the formation of the union state budget, nor with that proposed by the USSR Council of Ministers. Mutual relations should be structured as follows: republic budget-union budget, because the union unites not economic enterprises but sovereign republics. They have the right to know and to jointly determine what budget is needed, how we form it, how much we spend and on what, including on the idle running of the departments' bureaucratic apparatus, the excessive needs of the Armed Forces, the development of space, and so forth. People's plight obliges us to become sensibly thrifty and to resolve questions of the budget—both of the union and of the republics—as people want.

The people of my republic, like many other peoples, are capable of constructive creation and are industrious and are aiming for a better life. They do not want to appropriate other people's labor, to live on handouts from the center. And where does the center take them from? We insist on the universality of the principle that if you work better you have the right to live better. That is not an exceptional but a universal right for every people. To fail to recognize this as applied to the people of Lithuania or any other republic is to deviate from the most sacred thing that a person or people has—the right to free self-determination.

We have ventured to voice the initiative for the transformation of the union from a suprarepublican, republic-controling powerful center into a community of sovereign republics with an interrepublican apparatus which they have formed and which represents their interests. That also applies to economic mutual relations in the union. The center's wisdom and democratizing, restructuring strength can be assessed by whether it will be able to step across selfish interests of self-preservation and promote the process of democratization or whether it intends to continue the tradition of deciding the fates and even petty economic affairs of great and small peoples.

Connected with this is the point of the so-called Baltic problem, which even as the congress proceeds is inevitably turning into a universal problem of the building of the union and its long term. So far neither in Comrade Ryzhkov's report nor in the government's actions can we see advances toward constructive solutions of the question of recognizing economic autonomy, and there is mention of increasing only a few rights for republics whose peoples have expressed their firm will in this respect. The solution of the problem cannot be put off even until fall. The people cannot remain for a long time in the political tension which is becoming heated because of the dilatoriness and obstacles from the center, which is acting under the auspices of protecting the gains of socialism and internationalism. We state that the economic models elaborated by the Baltic republics are very close to the statements of Moscow scientists and contain far more socialism than we have today. The Baltic republics are prepared to assume responsibility—and responsibility is required toward our own people, not toward the great-power center—and to become experimental, if you like, turning the economy toward a natural, healthy path of development. We simply have no other way out and nor, it seems to me, does the center.

Afternoon Session Reported

LD1006022289 Moscow Television Service in Russian 1200 GMT 8 Jun 89

[Relay of the Congress of People's Deputies, held in the Kremlin Palace of Congresses—live]

[Excerpts] [Gorbachev] Esteemed comrade deputies!

We continue the work of our congress. As we agreed yesterday, we are proceeding to the examination of the following items on the agenda. The item on confirming the chairman of the USSR Council of Ministers. As you know, the USSR Supreme Soviet has appointed Comrade Nikolay Ivanovich Ryzhkov as chairman of the USSR Council of Ministers. Yesterday, we heard his report and began its examination. I am submitting for your discussion a proposal to confirm Comrade Ryzhkov in the post of chairman of the USSR Council of Ministers. Do the deputies have questions for Comrade Ryzhkov?

[Unidentified deputies] We do!

[Gorbachev] Yesterday, as you may remember, those of you who followed that debate, quite a substantial conversation took place at the Supreme Soviet. And today, as far as I can see, the participants of the debate still have quite a lot to say today and tomorrow. Too, perhaps, addressing to the government—and not only to the government—their ideas, critical remarks, assessments. But nevertheless, in the framework of all that, in the context of this approach to this issue, I would like to ask you whether I can put that proposal to a vote, or there will be any...here...[unidentified deputies] [words indistinct]

[Gorbachev] Ah, so it is so? That is what you want? Very well.

[Unidentified deputy] [Words indistinct]

[Gorbachev] There was some on the report, right? I think that as we have agreed, we shall give Nikolay Ivanovich the floor at the end of the debate to let him answer the questions which were asked in connection with his report.

[Unidentified deputies] That's right!

[Gorbachev] Is that right, comrades! Right. If that is the general frame of mind, I will put this issue to a vote, comrades. Those in favor of confirming Comrade Nikolay Ivanovich Ryzhkov as the chairman of the USSR Council of Ministers, raise your credentials, please. Lower them, please.

Those against. Count them, please.

[Gorbachev] While the comrades tally the results, we in the Supreme Soviet have already come to an agreement that the chairman should conduct the meeting in a sitting position, as is generally accepted.

And here, too, wishes were expressed addressed to me—and not only addressed to me—that this is one of the elements which must be taken into account, and the chairman is not to loom over the hall, I apologize, so to speak lean over it. What do you think, comrades? [approving shouts heard in the background] Here we must come to an agreement so that there are no false interpretations. So you agree?

Good.

[Unidentified teller] Esteemed deputies, 59 voted against.

[Gorbachev] Who abstained?

[Teller] Eighty-seven deputies abstained.

[Gorbachev] Thus Comrade Ryzhkov is confirmed by the Congress of People's Deputies. [applause]

Comrade Ryzhkov asks for the floor.

[Ryzhkov] Esteemed Mr Chairman, people's deputies.

Allow me to express sincere gratitude for confirming me in this high state office of our country. It is the second time that I have been appointed to this office, but I must say that this appointment which took place at the present, yesterday and today—is sharply different from the old way of being appointed to high posts in our state. I regard this as the result of the very huge changes which have been taking place in our country in the past few years, in the years of restructuring which have enabled us to discuss precisely on a democratic basis, as they say, all questions of our life and our society, and, as they say, appoint the leaders of our state.

The discussion of questions at the congress, the numerous meetings, the numerous questions which we received during the past days show that a vast number of problems have come to a head which must be resolved and I think that the congress will outline the main directions along which our society, the whole of our country, needs to advance. I understand in what a difficult time I am coming to head the government, I am aware of the scale of the tasks facing the country, and I know how difficult it will be to resolve them.

But I am profoundly convinced that if we manage to choose the correct direction, the correct policies—both strategic and those on a tactical plane—we will find ourselves capable of resolving the principal issues, the impending issues of our society of which this congress has spoken with so much ardor over the last few days. I hope that we will work in a close rapport with the Supreme Soviet which is going to be in session permanently, and with the commissions, the committees, and all people's deputies. The executive will carry out smoothly the policy line approved by the supreme legislative body of our country. I firmly promise you that.

And in conclusion, I would like to thank you again, I would like to thank the entire Soviet people which is vesting so much trust in me today. Thank you. [applause]

[Gorbachev] Next item is the election of a USSR Committee for Overseeing the Constitution. In accordance with the USSR Constitution, the Committee for Overseeing the Constitution is elected by the USSR Congress of People's Deputies for a 10-year term from among experts in the field of politics and law, and includes a chairman, a deputy chairman, and 21 committee members with each union republic represented.

Dear comrade deputies, we have paid a great deal of attention to the fact that this very important body, formed by and directly responsible to the congress, should be made of respected and competent people, because we associate the success of the cause toward forming a law-based socialist state with the activities of that body.

Many of you—not only Communists but also non-party deputies—were present at the meeting, at the conference of the party group where this subject as well as the composition and the chairman—proposals on the chairman—came into focus. Sufficiently persuasive arguments were put forward concerning the need to place an authoritative and competent person at the head of that new and very important body.

That is why I would now like to propose electing Comrade Vladimir Nikolayevich Kudryavtsev, who is a vice president of the USSR Academy of Sciences, as chairman of the Committee for Overseeing the Constitution and Comrade Boris Mikhaylovich Lazarev, a sector chief at the State and Law Institute of the USSR Academy of Sciences, as deputy chairman. You have received documents relevant to the candidacies for inclusion on the committee and a copy of the draft decision on electing the Committee for Overseeing the Constitution, and, I hope, you have been able to acquaint yourselves with them.

As you can see, it is proposed that representatives from all the union republics, top specialists in the sphere of politics and law, be included in the committee. So that's my brief report. Do the deputies have any thoughts, observations or views? If so, let's hear them.

[Vorontsov] Deputy Vorontsov from the scientific societies. I would like to say that I have no objections against any of the list of members and head of the proposed new body individually. As far as one can judge from their curriculum vitae, they are specialists either in jurisprudence or in history. So this is all fine. But I do have one fundamental observation regarding the make-up of this important body and of subsequent bodies. Our society consists both of members and of the leading Communist Party and of non-party members, but among the members of this...among these nominations I do not see a single non-party member. I ask myself whether there are any doctors of juridical science in the country or not? Are there any specialists in the sphere of state and law that are not members of the party? I am not in the least attempting to question this list, indeed I am going to vote for it. But I would like these observations of mine to be taken into account when subsequent congress bodies are being formed. I think that when forming the leading bodies we should at least to some extent...we do not have a single non-party minister in the USSR, we do not have, or virtually do not have, as far as I know, any non-party deputy ministers, we have hardly any non-party directors of major enterprises. This does not in the least signify any disrespect on my part toward the majority of party members here, but we have to take into account our society's diversity, and we have to bring out this diversity, if only to a small degree, in the make-up of the country's leading bodies. Thank you.

[Kolotov] Kolotov, Electoral Constituency No. 61. I am not personally acquainted with Vladimir Nikolayevich Kudryavtsev, but I got to know him at a distance, so to speak, a long time ago, particularly during the election campaign and in connection with the so-called Gdlyan-Ivanov affair. One can see that Comrade Kudryavtsev is

a man with a solid legal training behind him, and his curriculum vitae testify to this. But what seriously perturbs me is that in his speeches on television and his press articles, Vladimir Nikolayevich clearly displays a desire to oblige the authorities unfailingly, to be unfailingly in tune with the official view. And it seems to me that you can't cover this up with any kind of outwardly strong and allegedly independent talking. For this reason I disagree with the nomination and have no confidence in Comrade Kudryavtsev. We have all been fed up with yes-men. A man with a character like his—this is a view based on my observations—cannot chair such an important body as the Committee for Overseeing the Constitution, even if he has a superb legal brain. That's my opinion. [applause]

[Gudaytis] Gudaytis, Constituency No 235, Lithuania. If I were to propose that you, esteemed deputies, should not set up the Committee for Overseeing the Constitution, I would probably be accused of obstructionism or of attempting to impede the previously-planned scenario for the congress finale. But nonetheless, articulating the will of my voters and the citizens of Lithuania, I declare that a hastily-created committee will without fail become a tool for pressuring the ethnic revival of the union republics, to press against their sovereignty. Nor shall we be consoled by the exalted legal qualifications of the chairman and members of the committee, including the authoritative Lithuanian specialist (Stachokus), whom we respect. In your apologetics for centralism and a unitary state which retains the main features of the Stalinist imperial model, reassure us by saying that the USSR Committee for Overseeing the Constitution will not become a legal—in quotation marks—guarantor for the forces that want to control the ethnic problem with an iron glove. Reassure us by saying that the committee will not speak out against the creation of new democratic institutions in the republics nor question a nation's right to its land and, most importantly, its self-determination. No outside force has the right to interfere in the constitutional situation in any of the republics; no institution can set itself above the interests of the people of my Lithuania, not to mention suspend the laws of a sovereign republic, in particular, the recently adopted amendments to the Constitution of the Lithuanian Soviet Socialist Republic. As a test, we could propose an amendment to Article 125 of the Constitution: The Committee for Overseeing the Constitution should be elected from among law specialists and consist of 15 chairmen and 15 members of the committee from the 15 union republics. The committee should be run according to the principle of strict alternation. If the sovereignty of any union republic is restricted it has the right of veto. Let this be food for thought for the future; we find the present formula unacceptable.

The overwhelming majority of the Lithuanian delegation together with a large group of deputies from Latvia and Estonia address the following statement to the congress. Given that: First, the congress has revealed a constitutional crisis in the form of inner contradictions in the

Constitution of the era of stagnation and the need to create a new USSR Constitution rather than supervise adherence to the obsolete one. Second, there is as yet no law on constitutional supervision in the USSR as such. Third, the powers of the Committee for Overseeing the Constitution in the USSR, as stated in the Constitution with the relevant amendments, allow that body to infringe the sovereign rights of the union republics. Fourth, by collective protests which gathered around 4 million signatures, the population of Latvia, Lithuania, and Estonia expressed as far back as last autumn its disapproval of the latest undemocratic amendments and addenda to the USSR Constitution. Fifth, the voters have now instructed us to work for the sovereignty of our republics, we consider the election of the Committee for Overseeing the Constitution in the USSR inexpedient and refuse to participate in it. Thank you. [applause] [passage omitted]

[Balayan] Balayan, the 729th national territorial constituency, Nagorno-Karabakh. The Constitution, the basic law, is written in a lapidary way, as is known, and only those things can be squeezed onto it, so to speak, which have a certain meaning.

Naturally, to be able to make sense of all the details, one should turn to the appropriate legal codes and commentaries on the Constitution which exist. The 1982 publication carried by the Politicheskaya Literatura Publishing House has, on page 250, the following text. The title of the publication is "The USSR Constitution, Political and Legal Commentary."

An autonomous oblast derives its name from the name of the people which chose the autonomous oblast as an implementation of its right for self-determination.

Vladimir Nikolayevich Kudryavtsev, Vadim Konstantinovich Sobakin, Anatoliy Ivanovich Lukyanov are among the authors of this legal publication of political and legal commentary on the USSR Constitution.

Seven years have elapsed since then. As you know, Nagorno-Karabakh Autonomous Oblast is the only autonomous oblast which is named not after a national distinction but on geographical grounds. As you know, there is no such nationality as Nagorno-Karabakhers. There are Armenians there. I would like to ask Vladimir Nikolayevich....

[Unidentified deputy] And Azerbaijanis!

[Balayan] There are Armenians, Azerbaijanis, Kurds, Talyshis, Greeks, and Russians there. However, in accordance with the Constitution, and I quote again: An autonomous oblast derives its name from the name of the people which chose the autonomous oblast as an implementation of its right for self-determination. I would like to ask Vladimir Nikolayevich Kudryavtsev,

nominated for the post of the chairman of the Committee for Overseeing the Constitution, professor, vice president of the Academy of Sciences, who has been director of the State and Law Institute for 10-15 years, to clarify this issue. Thank you. [passage omitted]

[Yakovlev] I am Aleksandr Maksimovich Yakovlev of the Academy of Sciences. I really do, comrades, understand the entire concern being displayed in the hall from the point of view of both the composition and the function of the Committee for Overseeing the Constitution. But I would immediately like to dispel any suspicions that the Committee for Overseeing the Constitution will somehow stand in the way of positive and constructive changes in our Constitution.

Comrades, one must not confuse two things: Respect for what is accepted within the Constitution and the possibility of it being changed in a purposeful and regulated way by democratic means. These are two functions which exist equally of their own right. I therefore wanted to immediately dispel any suspicions about this committee that it might stand in the way of improvement. We will vote simultaneously for a commission to elaborate a new Constitution. It is impossible for it to appear in the capacity of an anti-constitutional commission, so to speak. That is the first point. The second is that I have known Vladimir Nikolayevich for not so long, approximately since 1954. I myself am a fairly elderly person, as you see. I must tell you that I was offended by the words that he is a sycophant.

I will tell you frankly. Of course, we are all, as they say, children of our times. What point is there in us concealing our sins? But I have never known Kudryavtsev to lie, or Kudryavtsev to be sycophantic or to be dishonorable either in respect of his colleagues or on matters of principle. We have not always mustered the courage to speak the truth in time. We have not always raised ourselves to the level of Academician Sakharov, for example, who was perhaps the only one to tell the truth when we were all silent. All that is true. And we are perhaps all to blame for that. But there was never an instance when he said something against his conscience or against the truth and honor. I will recount just two episodes to you. Back in the times when the current president of our republic was not general secretary of the party, Vladimir Nikolayevich Kudryavtsev, myself, and a number of other colleagues raised the issue of how shamefully things stood in our country with the fight against crime. We sent a memorandum to the current president, who was not yet the general secretary, in which we wrote what we are now at last beginning to overcome, that crimes are not being reported, that the militia is doing nothing, that the courts are powerless, that two people's assessors headed by a judge form the same troika with which we dashed through the terrible years. We raised all those matters even then. Well, excuse us for raising them in a memorandum, because naturally nobody would have written such heresy. And the current president at that time appended instructions, and I think that it is no longer an official secret. I think that the questions which have been raised here are questions of honest Communists on fundamental issues relating to our system of justice, and there have been instructions to the minister of the interior, to the procurator-general, and to the chief justice to look into things and elaborate specific proposals for improvement of the work of our criminal justice system. Well, as always is the case, something, of course, has been done, and something has not been done. You remember that an improvement has begun to happen with reporting at least. The idea has emerged of creating a joint investigatory committee, something we will decide now. That is the first episode.

Now to the second episode. You know all of our notorious decrees and the shameful Article 11(1). And I will tell you one more secret. Of course, it would be correct to get up and immediately tell the whole world what an unconstitutional article it is. But I should tell you that our future—that is, naturally, if he is elected—chairman of the Committee for Overseeing the Constitution said on the second or third day at the supreme party forum in our country, at the Politburo, that this article is not good enough and needs to be removed, whereupon he received immediately either oral consent or blessing. I think that the members of that supreme party forum who are present here can confirm this episode to you. In brief...[indistinct interruption from behind]. There, you see. I have a witness behind me, as they say. In a word, I think that, in Kudryavtsev, we are acquiring a person who is made for occupying precisely this post, in terms of the logic of his mentality and his entire biography and his scientific prestige. Such is my opinion. [passage omitted]

[Unidentified deputy] Esteemed deputies.

I apologize to you for the delay, but I would like to put forward my view on the question under discussion. One of the previous speakers from the Baltic region claimed to be speaking for all three republics and all the voters that exist there. One can clearly perceive a desire and effort to shorten the arms of a committee which has yet to be created, to prevent it investigating affairs in the union republics. The implication is that somebody's rights might be infringed. It seems to me, however, that this committee is being set up to provide a guarantee to everyone across the country against infringements of their rights. In this connection, I want to tell you that even now the rights of many inhabitants of those very same republics are being infringed. Such laws have been adopted, and I would like this Committee for Overseeing the Constitution to begin its work by looking at the Baltic region [applause], particularly Estonia. I would like the committee to examine whether the amendments adopted in Estonia on 16 November are in conformity with the USSR Constitution. I would like it to examine the constitutionality of the concepts adopted on the basis of those amendments to the Constitution. I would like the committee to analyze the legality of our so-called laws on languages, in which education in one language is guaranteed while that in another is permitted. And in addition to that, knowledge of a language forms the basis for the concluding and extending of work contracts. There are smaller points, too, but that's the most important thing. [passage omitted]

[Boldyrev] Deputy Boldyrev, territorial constituency No 54, Leningrad. It has been said here that some comrades are attempting to torpedo the election; I think that it is those who have prepared this election in this way that are torpedoing the election of the Committee for Overseeing the Constitution. [applause] I think that most of you went through the election campaign, which lasted for several months. Now we are suddenly being invited, in the course of a single day, to vote for people whom many of us do not know. Here I am wholly in agreement with the view expressed somewhat earlier by the Lithuanian delegation that this is fundamentally immoral, and that we do not have the right, being accountable to our voters, to vote for people we do not know. This is particularly important when we are electing a body like the Committee for Overseeing the Constitution for 10 years.

Why is this happening? Why has this come about? I think that to a considerable extent the cause is that as was said at the party group meeting, I think, the Committee for Overseeing the Constitution is a political tool. As long as it remains a political tool this kind of thing is going to go on. Moreover, you probably noticed that during this debate on the election of the Committee for Overseeing the Constitution issues concerning, in effect, the mechanism of power are being brought up, i.e., issues that we have not managed to discuss.

I believe that we must not by any means elect the Committee for Overseeing the Constitution in such a way, nor must we elect it until we have seriously discussed issues concerning the mechanism and structure of power in our country. These are issues that we have still not seriously debated at this congress. Thank you. [applause]

[Sandulyak] Leontiy Sandulyak, territorial constituency No 544, Chernovtsy. Highly esteemed chairman, highly esteemed peoples deputies of the USSR, the Committee for Overseeing the Constitution is a very important state body and the elections to it are perhaps the first steps toward a law-based state. I solemnly promised my electors that when I had to make responsible state decisions, that is, to use the power given to me by my electors, I would without fail study the question by consulting specialists and asking the opinion of my electors. It seems to me that is precisely a case when we can make this decision only after studying the opinion of our electors. I am not talking about a referendum. Therefore, I propose that this question be postponed until the next congress as it is an unprepared question [applause] because like all of you I received the document one hour before the voting. [passage omitted]

[Yevtushenko] Yevtushenko, Constituency No 520. Comrades, I have never been charged with a criminal offense and I have never asked Comrade Kudryavtsev to defend me. Moreover, I am not even personally acquainted with him and I have never had any contact with him in my life. However, this is what I would like to say: It seems to me that we should elect to the Committee for Overseeing the Constitution the most honest and purest people. This does not mean that I suspect Comrade Kudryavtsev of anything dishonest, but I think that proof of the professional purity of people of his profession should be provided by the behavior of these people at the time when human rights were being violated. I know many people, who are not professionals in this line, including writers and scientists who came out in defense of the so-called dissenters or, putting it more simply, simply free thinking people, defended them, got them out of jails and mental hospitals. I never heard the voice of Comrade Kudryavtsev in this struggle.

All the same, I would not come out [changes thought] and I think that if he will, if we are to vote for him, he should reply to my inquiry and tell us what he did to save people from prisons, from camps, and from mental hospitals. [sentence as heard] Another thing I would like to say is this: Recently LITERATURNAYA GAZETA published a letter sying that a former assistant of (Ryumin)—if I am not mistaken his name is (Grishayev), forgive me if I have gotten it wrong—is still teaching law and so on and jurisprudence. Why have I not heard the voice of Comrade Kudryavtsev raised in anger over this right now?

Nevertheless, the main thing I wish to tell you is that I do not know what Comrade Kudryavtsev says in the Politburo lobby, and I do not think that this is of decisive importance for me and for the people while we are determining whether he should or should not be elected for this senior post. Just as it is of no importance whatsoever what I whisper in my wife's ear or what I talk to my mother-in-law about in the kitchen. I heard the way Comrade Kudryavtsev commented on the law, rather the decree of 28 April, which includes this well-known Article 11/1 which has aroused the indignation not only of my Kharkov electors but also of all the working people, the working class, and the intelligentsia. Practically disguised as a soft criticism of this decree he was actually advocating this decree of Article 11/1, whereby criticism of a director by his workers, of the Central Committee secretary by rank-and-file party members, and so on and so forth can be declared a case of discreditation, that is criminally punishable discreditation.

This is why I would like you to pay attention to these qualities of Comrade Kudryavtsev, to his inclination to advocate this sort of very dubious decree. I believe that the purest kind of person should take this post. Purity includes a fight in which one does not spare one's head. Another thing, Mikhail Sergeyevich: I am going but I wish to say, Mikhail Sergeyevich, we would like [changes thought] I am 56 years old. At one time, when I was 30, I was battling to become the editor of the journal, but now I will not take it. Mikhail Sergeyevich, it is necessary for this commission to be headed mainly by people even younger than you are. We should take this into account as well. [applause] [passage omitted]

[Lautsis] Esteemed comrade chairman, comrade deputies. Here previously serious shortcomings in the life of our state were due to the fact that in the system of the Soviet socialist state there was no special body that supervised correct and consistent implementation. Now when we are setting up such a conceptional body, various voices can be heard explaining things in various ways and generally reducing the matter to the fact that it is necessary to wait to create this committee and see what it will be like and so on and so forth. I do not agree with this point at all. I think that at this first congress we should indeed create this Committee for Overseeing the Constitution with the membership that has been proposed to us. As for Comrade Vladimir Nikolayevich Kudryavtsev in particular, the vice president of the USSR Academy of Sciences, although I am not a lawyer and although I am not acquainted with him personally, but as a modern man and an enlightened one—I hope you will not take this as lack of modesty on my part—by following the events in the country, I have known him from a distance for at least 15-20 years. Obviously recently when the question was tackled about strengthening the leadership of the USSR Academy of Sciences, it was probably not in vain that he was elected for the post of the vice president, who is engaged in tackling questions concerning development of social sciences including judicial ones in this country. I think that he is a very worthy candidate for this high post. I propose comrade deputies, to vote for him. [passage omitted]

[Gorbachev] I do not take the entire burden of responsibility upon myself for finding a solution. Let us seek one together. I will merely share a few thoughts. Let us think a bit. I think, oh, yes, Comrade Kudryavtsev wanted a word. Go ahead. Excuse me.

[Kudryavtsev] Esteemed comrades, I want to reply to the questions which were asked of me. Well, it is necessary to say something about how I construe that difficult work. You see that the work—if one is to speak about me and the committee—is generally exceptionally difficult. That is evident from these debates. Well, I would like to make a few responses to specific questions. First of all, there is Comrade Balayan who made quotations from the political and legal commentary about the name of an autonomous oblast. He is right. One must say that there it is incorrectly and badly written. I do not recall that text but you probably quoted it correctly in saying that an autonomous oblast is named after the people who lives there. This, as you see, is not always the case, and does not always correspond with reality. Therefore, one has to admit here that this is a mistake. I will not go into who is the author of that text. There is no need to applaud, because it was not I who wrote that bit. I do not know who was the author of that bit but I was a member of the editorial board, and I naturally should have noticed that. That is evident.

The second point is about Yevgeniy Aleksandrovich Yevtushenko and his major and detailed reproach of me. I also wish to dwell, Yevgeniy Aleksandrovich, on some of your remarks. As to voices about saving people from prisons, then what should one say about this? People act in different ways in such cases, proceeding from their different opportunities. One person does this by speaking at a meeting and by calling for people to be freed. Another does this in the form of letters to a newspaper or by some other means of speaking out in a public way. If this concerns a lawyer, particularly the director of the Institute of State and Law, then naturally he has some other channels for this purpose.

Well, I cannot now (?deal with) Aleksandr Maksimovich Yakovlev who spoke just now. It was once estimated during his election campaign how many people he—well, we cannot say that he liberated them—helped in getting out of prisons because 45 or 46 people approximately, so we counted, apply to him every month. Generally, about 20 people make applications to the institute every month, and we in most cases help them, because, I would put it this way, about 50 percent of applications are justified, unfortunately. Unfortunately in the sense that as we see things, people are being held in prisons illegally or unfairly, as it seems to us. [passage indistinct]

This is what I will say. This is about legislation, including legislation about political prisoners. [Yevtushenko shouts from audience] You are not a professional, Yevgeniy Aleksandrovich; one also needs to know a few details here. You possibly do not know that a year ago a decision was made about psychiatric hospitals. It was quite a solid document, though I feel, and it is our view, that it was not 100 percent complete. We battled to ensure that it was 100 percent complete, all the way, or to international standards; but, at least as it was it represented a major step forward. But after all, you don't know how much I or my colleagues were involved in it, so I'm not going to go in for self-advertisement here, so to speak. I could mention another document, for which I simply headed the commission—the draft foundations of the criminal legislation of the USSR and the union republics. It was published in the press and is now being criticized for its humanism, as you probably know, since, alas, this has been quite widespread in the press.

Now, as for the decrees of 8 April. I have just received a note here saying: On instructions from voters, I would like to be informed of whether Kudryavtsev was one of the authors of the 8 April decree on criminal liability for state crimes, Article 11-1. I would say, to begin with, that I was not the author, and second, I would like to explain the situation a bit to clarify it to all the deputies. That decree of 8 April is a fragment, or—I would say—an element of another document: the draft law on state crimes. That draft law was drawn up over approximately 1 and ½ - 2 years, and many lawyers were involved, including some from our institute. As I don't happen to have the text with me at the moment, I can assure you that the draft was fairly democratic in its make-up, and its main aim was to replace the former law on state crimes, which was based in the past on Stalin's legislation. That was the main aim, and I consider that the group achieved this in its work. I'm talking here about the draft that existed before the decree of 8 April. This can all be confirmed; there are no state secrets or classified information here.

When the decree came out on 8 April it was as much of a surprise to me as I imagine it was to everyone here. Anatoliy Ivanovich Lukyanov spoke about the decree when he was being questioned. And I was the first to comment on it, as Yevgeniy Aleksandrovich Yevtushenko said, though he mistakenly mentioned that I spoke about Article 11-1. I did not, in fact, talk about it at that time, and this is not difficult to check. I saw the failings in that Article 11-1, but I said nothing of them in my commentary. That may have been wrong—I cannot maintain that it was correct on my part to remain silent on the matter, but on that same day, first, I spoke about it to several top officials. It may be again that I (?would have acted differently) and not gone to the rally. And then, just as Aleksandr Maksimovich said here at the sitting of the political body, I also spoke openly about the shortcomings of that article. So judge for yourselves whether I acted correctly or not. [Words indistinct] it's probably not for me to judge. I would just like to say that a discussion in the Politburo is quite a different matter to a chat over the dinner table. [applause]

Well then, there is another of your comments which I fully accept, Yevgeniy Aleksandrovich; it is about age. A bad age; I am already old, born in 1923. There is nothing you can do about it. I would, of course, also consider that it is much better to be young in the make-up of this committee. But here, well, if this trust has been placed in one and if one is still alive, one must work. That is the way I understand this matter. [applause]

Right, now I would like to say a few—excuse me, Mikhail Sergeyevich, this may go on a bit longer—but I must say a few words of a more general nature. I, too, consider that this is an indispensable institution, that properly speaking it is an element of the law-governed state and a continuation of the policy of dividing powers, or if you like, of creating those restraining counterbalances we do not currently have in the political mechanism. I think that it is not easy to work and not easy to oppose the various forces we have heard even now in this hall. The committee does have some possibilities here, specifically independence. As you will recall, according to the Constitution the committee is subordinate only to congress. It is not subordinate even to the USSR Supreme Soviet. Thus, in essence there is one organ to which the committee is answerable: the congress. I think that the committee must, of course, pursue a policy of legality, democratization, observance of civic rights, and of combating departmental lawmaking.

There is a difficult issue here. It was raised by deputies from the Baltics, and it must not, of course, be evaded, either. The difficulty lies in the fact that the Constitution is old while the legislation is being renewed. Esteemed comrade deputies from the Baltics, you could, after all, have cited a different example. For instance, say, a law on leasing is promulgated, but the Constitution does not contain anything about leasing. Does this mean that the Committee for Overseeing the Constitution must put an end to the law on leasing and deem it to be anticonstitutional? This question is not a simple one either, after all. For this reason it is probably necessary to create a practice of rational activity here. As far as republican legislation is concerned, I think that it must transfer to a new federalism, restoring the Leninist principles of federal relations between the union and the republics. It has seemed to me—this is my point of view—that in this complex situation with regard to republican and all-union constitutions it is quite possible to find rational juridical solutions which are not at all as unattainable as they seem to some people, and to find a normal solution to this issue that satisfies both the union and the republics, as it seems to me.

The last thing I must say here is that the committee is, after all, a collegial organ. It is not the chairman who decides something—indeed, he cannot decide; it is 23 people. Moreover, I think that the committee must work in an authoritative manner and rely on the will of congress and on the resolutions congress will adopt, and on the laws it adopts. Of course, a law on overseeing the Constitution, which does not now exist, must be created. Obviously, the congress must also charge some part of the committee and the Supreme Soviet with doing this. I consider that the issue is not one of official position, so to speak, but of the responsible work which in this form or that composition must nevertheless be done by someone, because this body is, all in all, a step forward along the path of a law-governed and democratic state. Thank you.

[Gorbachev] Allow me to sum up the discussion of this question. On the whole, comrades, it seems to me that suspicion among us is arising here to no purpose, and between deputies and republics as well. I would like to remove this immediately. After all, before we had no constitutional committee and we got on all right. The USSR Supreme Soviet Presidium formerly carried out and now carries out—after the addenda to the Constitution—overseeing the USSR Constitution and ensures that the constitutions and laws of the union republics correspond to the USSR Constitution and laws. This was the case before the addenda in November, and this is the case since the addenda in November. So it is possible, generally speaking, to withdraw the question of a constitutional committee altogether. But let us remember why it came up.

It was planned through this mechanism, this very serious, constitutional mechanism—created by the congress itself and responsible to it alone—to create a kind of instrument to strengthen the Constitution and strengthen the course toward realizing and implementing laws and statutes; and that this committee, this instrument, should operate in such a way that no one, under the guise of carrying out and developing one law or another, should drain the law of blood at the implementation stage.

You and I already have such experience, and remarks on this score have resounded here at this congress. There is the law on enterprises and there are decisions. Comrades even named examples—I do not know to what extent they were—that the government has in some places in this instance undermined the law in some way, although the government was the author of that draft law submitted for discussion. Departments have created many instructions and interpretations for their application where they have limited even more the existence, or one might say, held in check and bridled that law. Well then, such a juridical body is a most important instrument to stand sternly in defense. This is most correct because the Supreme Soviet Presidium, for all its broadness and opportunities, and for all its prestige simply does not always take in the entire range of problems to work through these issues in detail.

The debates were considerable because the issue of the constitutional committee and, you remember, the constitutional court were discussed. What form, as it were, should be found to strengthen this part of our legal mechanism that would strictly guard the Constitution and the laws? For this reason, it seems to me, the fact that we are moving towards setting up a constitutional committee will only reinforce the opportunities of our whole federation—of all the other citizens, collectives, labor collectives, republics, autonomous formations, and so on—to clear up their worries through this mechanism, to use it as a competent body that is, moreover, made up democratically thus, and to use it as an independent body to clear up and attain a correct, consistent implementation of the provisions in the Constitution. I think, comrades, that to argue on this issue—even more to repudiate, to place in doubt the need to form a constitutional committee—is simply to cut off the branch we are all sitting on. For this reason, dear friends from the Baltic republics [murmurs from the crowd: autumn, autumn]

Just a minute. What does it matter, in the autumn or summer. That is the next question. Let us look into the essential points. Perhaps we will not do this at all. Let's decide. This is already [changes thought] I am speaking about how we came to the necessity, because after all we have the Supreme Soviet Presidium, which has the same functions. But in this committee the best forces of our jurisprudence will be concentrated. We are taking the most mature lawyers, authoritative people who will help the republics, the citizens, the collectives, and the central bodies to resolve this very important task. This corresponds to our policy of forming a socialist law-governed state.

Now, as far as your anxieties are concerned, and this includes the formulas, as it were, some people gave as to how it should be here, here are the signatures of Comrades Gorbunov, Bisher, Bresis, and others. This proposal was heard here. I think, comrades, that naturally we stand before the necessity of what we need: a new Constitution. The draft decisions you received, I think this has been distributed. In the main, decisions on the issues of internal and foreign policy and the formation of a constitutional commission are already envisioned.

This is the first point. The second point is that the commission will begin to work. This means that one can refer matters to it and it will work simultaneously. This is the second point.

We will probably not get by until the constitutional commission prepares a draft and puts it up for consideration to the congress, and then evidently when the congress deems it necessary it will put it up for a referendum or for countrywide discussion. We will decide that later. We must cover a certain path to get to that point. Then we will proceed on it. Evidently, the need to move along the path of political and economic reform, along the path of restructuring, will set questions before us that must be decided by preparation and introduction of amendments to the Constitution. Proposals born from this process must be incorporated in the entire system of the institutions we are now creating. This is to make sure, of course, that old laws—and I am speaking in this instance not only of the Constitution—do not stand in the way.

Law is always a little behind. That is an old rule, so to speak. It is natural. At the same time, however, I think we cannot express things in such a way that we have some kind of Bacchanalia with respect to our Constitution, whatever it is like. If proposals required for restructuring emerge, then we will need amendments and changes in the Constitution. This means that if we have drawn up certain proposals and are ready for them, then we will formulate them and introduce them according to the established procedure. We now have a mechanism that can quickly and competently develop and introduce a question about amendments to the Constitution.

In other words, first, we have not come to the idea that we need such an important idea by coincidence, and second, I think that in proceeding along the path toward implementing restructuring and engaging all the mechanisms—meaning the Supreme Soviet and the Constitutional committee, plus a constitutional commission that will be working—we will find a way of latching onto questions that are becoming urgent, and of finding a correct solution for them. I think, comrades, that if we

are committed to renovating and strengthening our federation according to Leninist principles and proceed along that path, then we will discover and resolve all the issues.

In this respect I would agree with those comrades. Let us not address to each other questions, any question at all in such a way that it looks like a diktat or an ultimatum. This, this is what I think has caused indignation among other deputies. We will have to juxtapose in one way or another the essence of questions, any proposals, whoever they came from. This is the way it should be. This is a normal judicial process, regardless of whether it corresponds to present laws or not. If it does not correspond, it must be further improved, and if we adopt correct and well-founded proposals, new proposals connected with advancing on the path of reforms [sentence incomplete as heard] Therefore, I think that setting up a constitutional committee will only provide opportunities for us to tackle even better the issues that have become urgent. This must not, I think, worry anyone in this sense. This must not cause any sort of doubts suddenly among people regarding the fact that there might be something here that can once again stand in the way of the reforms.

Now there are two proposals left: to create it now or in the autumn. [noise in hall]

Why do people have to be elected for 10 years? Oh, I see. I am asked why 10 years, since deputies are elected for 5 years. Well, comrades this is a generally accepted practice to give stability, so to speak. As a rule, incidentally, as was said yesterday at the Supreme Soviet, all over the world they try to put the wisest and most competent people on the institution in question, and on the supreme court, as well. [noise in hall]

Incidentally, everyone who will be a member of the constitutional committee must resign from the deputy's post. None of them may be deputies, none of them. This is also a clear matter. So it is left for us to decide. Why did I think it possible to introduce this proposal, comrades? I would ask your attention. I understand that this issue is a burning one and is arousing discussion, but one can only work in a hall where there is order. Otherwise this will be a Novgorod veche [popular assembly in medieval Russian towns]. I do not know whether it was like this in Novgorod.

I think and am convinced that we acted correctly and put forward a proposal today to resolve the issue. Why? I will tell you. After all, nothing gets done if it is not weighed and thought through beforehand. The question of the composition of this body has already been studied by the Presidium in the course of preparation—as the Presidium of the USSR Supreme Soviet received the task of preparing the congress—during the last 3 months. The proposals from the republics took shape as a result of the discussions. These are the proposals of the republics themselves. If out of 21 people the representatives of the republics are taken away, then a small part, we are talking about 6 people, remains. That is the chairman, his deputy, and some representatives of the center.

In point of fact, this is an issue that has been carefully thought out and studied. No distrust of the opinion of the republics arose here, did not arise at all. I do not think that anyone put [changes thought] With regard to Belorussia, there arose Comrade Tarazevich who withdrew this question on behalf of Belorussia, I understand. [sentence as heard] For this reason I think we can resolve this issue. But I am prepared to say the same thing, taking into consideration the statements and reasonings here of all the comrades who put forward a question about a second proposal. Yes, I would just like to say, comrades, that I am forming the perhaps mistaken opinion that someone is hurrying to finish the congress more quickly. I think we were working normally and there was none of this. I, too, am beginning to wonder whether there is a desire to drag it out by any possible means. [noise in the hall] To foist these discussions on us as well. [shouts from the hall] Come, we are speaking frankly with one another. Why speak like that? [shouts from the hall] All the more so as I saw that one and the same speaker was doing the rounds. [noise in the hall] Comrades, let it be like this. Let no one suspect that we want to finish the congress in a hurry. We may even announce a break in the congress's work if this is the opinion of the congress, and return again after a few days or so.

It seems to me that we could have, on the basis of collegiate exchange, come to the conclusion yesterday that we had resolved the main task that we had put forward for the congress. But we will not resolve all of the tasks. We should be realists. The first congress has thrown up so many proposals, we still need to digest what has been said. It is good that we have agreed that the next congress will be in the autumn, which is soon. Let us not be suspicious of one another and drive each other into corners.

Let us, all the same, work together, as the last comrade, from Estonia I think, said. Let us work amicably; let us do things amicably. I am in favor of this; I am in favor of this. No one should consider himself the victor or the vanquished at this congress. Our democracy wins, the process of political reform wins. Through this congress we are coming out of a difficult battle of opinions with the fact that we may not be satisifed with everything, but we are already at a new stage in the development of democracy and glasnost and of the political processes in the country in general. Well, excuse me for discoursing in front of you, but you should know my opinion and now have the right to decide for yourselves. So there is a first proposal to postpone it. Yes, compromise, a compromise.

[Unidentified male deputy] We will vote. Do not worry needlessly.

[Gorbachev] Yes.

[Unidentified male deputy] I have this to say. I propose electing this committee now, but as a committee for preparation of its own status—it does not have one, after all. We will see how they work and perhaps in the autumn we will confirm them in the capacity of this committee. [applause]

[Gorbachev] Let us finish, comrades.

[Korniyenko] I am deputy Korniyenko from the city of Gomel. Deputy Tarazevich spoke here on behalf of the Belorussian delegation. I wish to make the following statement: The Belorussian delegation did not discuss the candidacy of Comrade (?Yermilov), and I think, therefore, that he has no right to express the matter in such a way. That is all.

[Gorbachev] Let us first decide how we are going to build the bridge, lengthwise or breadthwise, then we will move on to individual matters. So, comrades, the first proposal is that the Committee for Overseeing the Constitution [Komitet Konstitutsionnogo Nadzora] should be set up now. Would those in favor of commencing this raise their cards? [responds to indistinct shout] Yes, without fail. We're voting on whether to set it up in principle or not, and then we'll deal with all the rest. Please raise your cards. Please lower them. Those against?

Well, comrades, we probably don't need a count; there's a clear minority against. [responds to indistinct shout] What, you don't know what we are voting for? I'll say it again. I thought I had put it precisely. We are now to decide whether to go about setting it up, or to postpone it until the fall. The first proposal is to set it up now. Who is in favor of doing it now? [responds to indistinct shout] There'll be a third one, too. Fine. That concerns the essence, the essence. Yes, yes, the comrade backs the proposal, but with different powers. [addressing an unseen deputy or deputies amid commotion] Comrades, don't abuse the procedures.

So the first proposal is to set up the...[Gorbachev changes thought] to go about appointing the members of the Committee for Overseeing the Constitution. Those in favor of the proposal please raise your cards. Please lower them. Who is against? Well, comrades, it's clear. Do we need a count? No? We need to? Hold a count then! [video shows tellers counting and collating the show of cards]

[Tellers' official] Esteemed deputies, 433 deputies have voted against.

[Gorbachev] Who abstained? [video shows a further count]

[Tellers' official] Sixty-one deputies have abstained in the vote.

[Gorbachev] So, the decision has been adopted.

[Tellers' official] Fifty deputies from the Lithuanian republic did not take part in the vote.

[Gorbachev] Out of how many?

[Tellers' official] Comrades, how many deputies are there in the Lithuanian delegation? [indistinct shouts] A total of 58 are present. [more shouts] Excuse me, please raise your hands so we can count how many are present.

[Unidentified speaker] Fifty-four deputies are taking part at the moment.

[Gorbachev] But that is of no significance under the circumstances. [video shows teller counting the Lithuanian delegation, which appears to be seated together. One of the deputies stands up and shouts an indistinct remark to Gorbachev]

[Gorbachev] No, quite the reverse, quite the reverse. I'm just saying that we have been dealing with procedural matters, and in this case...[he stops speaking as the Lithuanian deputies who have just been counted stand up and file out toward the back of the hall; camera dwells on the exiting deputies]

[Gorbachev] Comrades, comrades, please be calm, because all this is no simple matter. We must not simplify things, and I would not turn it in this instance into...[Gorbachev changes thought] All this is no simple matter. We must now consult on what to do next. [there is a pause of almost 30 seconds as Gorbachev is shown waiting for a response from the hall, where deputies are seen in a state of some agitation] What are we to do next, comrades?

[Unidentified deputy, from rostrum] Dear comrade deputies, one of the important issues is that we are setting up a committee which does not have a statute. We can't—we don't have the right to set up the committee until such time as its statute is drawn up. As was said here, a compromise decision is needed, and such a compromise is becoming all the more important now—let us not set up the Committee for Overseeing the Constitution today. [applause] Let's set up a commission to draw up the statute for the committee, perhaps with the same membership, but it whould be a commission, and when it is in operation it can then be transformed into the Committee for Overseeing the Constitution. That is my proposal.

[Fedor Burlatskiy, from rostrum] Comrade deputies, I'm from the Soviet Peace Fund. We must take a wholly responsible atttude to the present moment in time. We must have a wholly responsible attitude because we...[Burlatskiy changes thought] Our leaders have convened this congress in the name of democracy, in the name of the development of restructuring and in the name of unity. And we must seek ways of achieving such a unity. I propose that discussion of this matter be postponed until tomorrow and that the Congress Presidium, and Mikhail Sergeyevich Gorbachev personally, be asked to enter into talks with representatives of the Lithuanian delegation [applause] and to report on this matter to the congress here tomorrow. [applause]

[Moshnyaga, from rostrum] I'm Moshnyaga from Kishinev, National-Territorial Constituency No 257. Esteemed comrade deputies, the Committee for Overseeing the Constitution is, from our delegation's point of view, the most important body for the Congress of People's Deputies. This is because it will be overseeing the Constitution, which is the country's basic law. And the country's basic law lays down the noninfringement of the interests of any other republic, the noninfringement of the interests of any other Constitution, of any other republic. As a consequence, this body to oversee the Constitution will, at the same time, examine matters to do with the constitutions, the observance of the constitutions of the union republics. And in view of the fact that there are differences of view about the adoption of such...[Moshnyaga changes thought] about the vote concerning the principle and the membership, it seems, I propose that consideration of this matter be deferred at least until, as has just been proposed, consultations have taken place again. Thank you.

[Gorbachev] Perhaps we won't extend the debate after all? I would adopt Comrade Burlatskiy's proposal. Despite the fact, comrades, that there may be certain emotions and certain attitudes among us—there have been many of these emotions, undoubtedly, and they will be displayed on more than one occasion in the future—this is not the worst thing. The worst thing would be if we end with our congress failing to find solutions which match up to the spirit and policy of restructuring and the harmonization of relations between nationalities, with all points of view being harmonized. The simplest thing, it appears, would be to decide now. But I think that the wisest decision would be to adopt Comrade Burlatskiy's proposal and to instruct the presidium to hold consultations with the Lithuanian deputies and report on the results tomorrow. All right. That's all right, comrades, is it? Do we need a vote? [chorus of no] Fine, that's agreed then. [indistinct voice] What? Well, with the deputies who left. [indistinct voice continues] What? I don't understand. Oh, to set it up or not, you mean? Yes, yes—carry on. [video shows deputy who has been speaking going to rostrum]

[Bredikis, from rostrum] Deputy Bredikis, from Lithuania. May I say this. As we travelled to the congress our mood was of course such that we understood that in a vote there can always be a majority, and our standpoint, although we shall doggedly defend it, may not always be heard. That is what has happened now. I agree that we need further discussion. The idea of deferring it would of course, in my view, be the most logical way to proceed. But I have a question to ask. Are the results of the vote just taken being annulled until tomorrow?

[Gorbachev] Er, no—I think for the moment the question of the results of the votes is not being taken off the agenda. We're going to hold talks, talks. And naturally, the talks will also be with the deputies from Latvia. [responding to the deputy asking to speak] You want to speak on this issue? Comrades, we've decided by and large. Do we need to continue the discussion? [shouts] [video shows a woman going up to the platform who exchanges some words with Gorbachev] Comrades, let's consider the matter settled. That's enough, that's enough, comrades. I shall conform, and you must conform. But let's not have suspicions that some people are Leninists, and others are not Leninists. That way we could end up going too far. We still have many issues, and I should like to ask you about this. Let us have an interval until 1500 and then do some more work. Let's have an interval until 1500.

9 Jun Congress Proceedings Reported

Ryzhkov Speaks at Congress
LD0906215289 Moscow Television Service in Russian 0754 GMT 9 Jun 89

[Speech by Nikolay Ryzhkov, chairman of the USSR Council of Ministers, at Congress of People's Deputies session in the Kremlin Palace of Congresses—live]

[Text] Comrades, I will try to keep to the scheduled time.

Comrade people's deputies, in the debate that unfolded at the congress an objective appraisal has been given of our country's domestic and foreign policy, including the government's forthcoming activities. In our view, these debates have been very fruitful. We have received a good foundation for the elaboration of further steps to rectify the state of affairs in the economy both at the present stage of national economic development and in the long term. Of course this dialogue of people's deputies with the government both from this rostrum and via direct contacts during the congress has been in many respects very instructive and has taught us a great deal. It has been at first glance an unusual opportunity to see problems not only from above but also, as they say, to get a feeling for them from below—that is, directly from the people. Unfortunately, I have not been able to meet many of the deputies I wanted to meet to discuss various problems. You have seen how compressed our time has been. However, I am certain that there will be such an opportunity in the future, and I consider, of course, that it is necessary to follow the practice of personal exchanges of opinions. It will only be of great benefit.

During the meetings that have occurred there have been—in addition to the questions that hae been raised from this rostrum—very many questions, letters, and notes from people's deputies. Many of them have of course been repetitive and deal with various problems.

For this reason we obviously do not have the opportunity today to give a specific answer to every question. I would like to formulate a few positions of principle and express my thoughts on these matters.

As regards specific individual questions, they are connected with the development of the economy of particular regions of the country and the solution of various social problems.

They concern the allocation of resources—equipment, capital and production investments, construction—or on the contrary the cessation of construction. All of them will be without exception thoroughly examined. Instructions on many of them have already been issued and the government was instructed to find the best possible positive solutions.

I want to say that a great number of questions came in on halting the construction of chemical plants and production, and on the construction of nuclear power stations, such as the Krymskaya, Yuzhno-Ukrainskaya, Gorkiy Rostov, Tatar, and nuclear heat supply plants, etc. On the whole I spoke about the situation in the country's power generation industry at the Supreme Soviet session. The situation developing in this respect is extremely serious and should, frankly speaking, be a cause of worry for us. The country may find itself in a very serious situation with regard to power generation. Therefore, competent groups of specialists are now working on the individual power stations that comrades mentioned here. And, as final conclusions become available, appropriate decisions will be adopted and will be brought to the attention of both people's deputies and the public.

I would also like to dwell on some questions that to a greater degree touch on people's interest. This is in the first place the issue of ecology. In my report I made certain generalizations on this issue; I outlined the government's views and stances in the sphere of ecology. But seemingly, the length of the report and the time allocated for the report did not make it possible to cover this problem in depth. I agree with Comrade Yablokov, deputy, who spoke about this issue, that on the whole all of us must become ecologically minded—all of us! Starting from the chairman of the council of ministers [applause] right up to each individual. [applause] I think that the proposals that were voiced here with regard to organizational forms, in my view should be—this is what I think—they should be as follows: Of course, there should be a very powerful committee in the govenent that should deal with these issues and there should, of course, be a committee or commission of no lesser power in the Supreme Soviet. It is precisely upon these principles that we should start looking into all contradictions in the ecological sphere. In deciding any particular issues.

As far as the money is concerned, the R135 billion for 3 5-year plans or beyond, I think right now there is no need to argue; we have to sit around the table and look into the matter.

Comrades, I would like to answer two specific questions related to ecology. The first question worries very many people. I received a lot of notes on this question, and the speakers touched on it, too. Of late, this problem is being very vigorously touched on by mass media. The conversation...[loud noise from the hall]

[Lukyanov] Comrades, I ask you, I ask for your attention. Hand all your speeches in to the Congress Secretariat. [noise from the hall]

[Lukyanov] I am sorry, Nikolay Ivanovich. [noise from the hall]

[Ryzhkov] What's the matter?

[Lukyanov] Go ahead, Nikolay Ivanovich.

[Lukyanov] Please go ahead, Nikolay Ivanovich. [calls from the audience asking for an interval] Nikolay Ivanovich, what will we do? Shall we announce an interval?

[Ryzhkov] Please do. [audience says "no"]

[Lukyanov] No. The text will be published and that's it. [bell sounds] Please go ahead.

[Ryzhkov] I do not understand. This means that I can go on? All right. Thank you. Now I understand what is required of me. So, I have said that the issue of the construction of the gas and chemical complex in West Tyumen, in the Tyumen Oblast of West Siberia, is giving rise to many questions. And I should evidently give an exhaustive reply now. Let us decide together how to resolve this problem. The first principle-based question is that of whether or not we can go on managing without the development of the chemical industry in our country. My opinion is firm: Without the development of the chemical industry, the country is not in a position to progress any further, not in agriculture, in consumer goods production, in construction, or in industry. Without the chemical industry we will not move ahead. We will fell the forests, we will spend a long time on construction, and so forth. Therefore, the question is a principle-based one. And I think that we should take on this.

Second, certain scientists, specialists—and that was mentioned first and foremost in the press—proposed an option under which capacities should not be created, should not be built in Tyumen Oblast, but should be carried out—the processing of chemical raw materials, of gas and other hydrocarbon elements—should be carried out in the European region. I ask you: Is it possible today—I am speaking to you; I am speaking to the towns,

to the people of Volgograd, Dzerzhinsk, Gorkiy, Ufa, Sterlitamak; I can list very many towns and cities where there is more than enough of the chemical industry today—can one seriously ask whether we should build new plants there or expand the existing ones? I believe that is not a legitimate formulation of the question. [applause] If these towns agree to this, I will be the first to agree to do away with that problem.

Second [as heard]: Why is it that we think this should happen in Tyumen Oblast? Comrades, over a period of 25 years we have invested absolutely enormous amounts; we have created an infrastructure. We have set up towns there. And today West Siberia is a resource region, a raw materials province. There is no processing industry there today. Therefore, that gas that we extract is six, it contains six percent ethane. Today it is considered normal in the world to extract ethane if there is 1.5 percent in an area. We leave this ethane in the gas, as they say.

We burn it and disrupt the ecological environment in the Soviet Union. Foreigners are more clever: They receive our natural gas, collect the ethane, make plastics and other chemical products, and sell them to us ten times dearer. So we are obliged to do it.

Second [as heard]: 15 billion cubic meters of gas are being burned today in western Siberia. It's burned in flares. I will tell you that this generates 10 million tonnes of soot, and burns up 30 billion cubic meters of oxygen. Can one really permit such a squandering of our means, our natural resources? For that reason, the government really has been thinking for a long time. And it was, incidentally, an initiative from the localities that, step by step, production facilities should be built there that would enable chemical products to be made on the spot. The program is to cover 15 years. During the next 5-year plan period, the maximum that can be built is to extend the Tobolsk factory and make chemical products there, and in Surgut, too. That is the maximum that the country can do. There are no financial resources in the country today.

But the main thing is that we have no ecologically clean chemical technology today. So we are obliged to negotiate with foreigners. We have only the wish, and we have the natural resources. We have nothing else. That's why we hold such talks. But we have imposed very rigorous economic terms. We have imposed very rigorous ecological terms, and when, in the fourth quarter, or in the first quarter of next year, the two projects about which talks are being held today are submitted to us, well, if necessary, let's set up an international ecological situation, as they say, and see whether it is or is not in accordance with ecological cleanliness.

The second question concerns the construction of the Katun hydroelectric power station. On this, claims have been made to the government and to me personally in connection with the project, about what the media are supposed to have reported. I want to quote, comrades, what the newspaper PRAVDA said on 15 March, when I was in Altay Kray: Ryzhkov was informed, I quote, that, following repeated consultation with experts, the USSR Academy of Sciences rejected the fear that the ground water would carry into the reservoir dangerous concentrations from the mercury deposits found here. There was nothing to support the fear that the water balance of the Ob would be disrupted by the damming of the Katun. Nor does the dam threaten the local landscape. The canyon is virtually free of woodland. However, the head of the government, after listening attentively to these new arguments, refrained nevertheless from making a final decision. It can be made, he declared, only on the basis of in-depth study, bearing in mind the views of the population and proceeding from all the ecological consequences and the economic effect. End of quotation. I still maintain that point of view. [applause]

Comrades, there have been a great many notes and personal addresses and speeches here concerning the fact that, well, the government, they say, has broken the law on state enterprises and introduced very stringent regulatory measures on wages and labor productivity. I have to report to the congress that in this respect the government has not broken the law. If the law is evoked, those who have a copy of it look under Article No 14, point 4, where it is stated clearly. Therefore, we realize that the regulation of wages and of labor productivity and the production of consumer goods is not really effective; is not the ideal way. And in this respect I agree with Comrade Popov. And it is my opinion, too, that it is not the ideal way. But then, let's find the ideal system, the ideal system of taxation—I am not speaking of citizens' personal taxation, I am speaking of the taxation of expenditure on wages, reproduction [as heard], and so forth. We do not have such a system today. Well, let us create such an effective system of taxation. I think that it must be effective for state enterprises, for leasing, and for cooperatives. We must find a universal system of taxation, then we would not require the measures that we are taking today to regulate these processes to some extent.

Now the pricing question. A great many questions were also raised about this. Obviously, I am repeating myself. As far as retail prices are concerned, I support the position expressed recently by many scholars. And I say recently because it was completely different in the beginning. You know the Politburo's position, the government's position, on this question. We consider that for the next 2 or 3 years there is no need for us at present to embark on considering retail prices. The consumer market must be balanced to a certain extent, and then this issue may be approached, but it is necessary to think within the framework of the next 5-year plan period.

As far as wholesale prices are concerned, there are questions here. After the congress, we obviously will have to carefully evaluate and weigh everything again. There are many problems. Among these, the problems of purchase prices on agricultural raw materials are acute. Among these, the question of the purchase price of cotton is very acute—and there was talk of that there today. Incidentally, I will give you some information. We sell for freely convertible currency 100,000 [unit not specified] of cotton, in order to buy from Egypt the same 100,000, but long-fibred ones, to make threads. We do not earn anything in hard currency on cotton. Delivery is made only to CEMA member countries. That is why we must thoroughly think things through as far as wholesale prices go, and decide once and for all. But, obviously, we still have to work a bit on that.

I am giving information. When I said in my report that restrictions should be abolished on wages for retired workers, I said workers but the next day very many notes appeared. I would like to confirm again that just as in Moscow, that refers to unskilled and skilled workers. Comrades, yet another question. With regard to teachers, yes, we have received a question. It is a new one for us. It needs to be studied thoroughly; we will return to it.

Comrades, I want to dwell on yet another question, excuse me, on two questions. I have evidently already gone over the time allotted me. I would like to request the time to deal with two more questions.

[Lukyanov] Shall we give him the time? [audience roars yes]

[Ryzhkov] Several people, comrades who have made speeches, have asked a principle-based question: Should we end the 5-year plan in 1989, even in the next few months? I am convinced that during the 1 and a ½ years that remain until 1991 we must concentrate every effort, both of science and of those doing practical work, of absolutely all the economists and sociologists, to work out an efficient economic mechanism for the next 5-year plan. The errors that we have been allowing, have allowed to happen, must be taken into account. We must take into account the fact that we have accumulated experience. The main thing is that we should transfer the republics over to complete financial autonomy. To carry out such absolutely enormous groundwork—which will radically change our situation even for those principles, economic principles that is, which are in effect today—we need time and we need to concentrate efforts.

If we now allow ourselves, in the middle of 1989, to be drawn into breaking up this perhaps imperfect economic management model, we will first of all be wasting time and, what is most important, today every working collective is engaged in and knows that it has its norms, good or bad, on which it has made all its plans until the end of the current 5-year plan.

If we disturb this today, we will disturb our economic stability, and I think that will do more harm than good.

And the last question: Very many notes—proposals—were submitted and there were speeches, too—Comrade Shmelev spoke—to the effect that when taking into account the difficult situation which has arisen on the consumer market, it is necessary to take foreign credits, not to be afraid to increase foreign economic debt in the name of balancing the consumer market. I would like the people's deputies to be fully informed and clear on our opportunities in this direction. I will cite some data:

So I do not use foreign sources of information on our foreign currency debt, I—perhaps for the first time today—report that the country's foreign debt is now R34 billion. [uproar in the hall] I am convinced even now that it is necessary to approach the problems of the growth of debt and in particular of taking credits in a very carefully weighed manner. For many years we have been living in debt. How is the hard currency situation developing in the country? I am talking about freely convertible currency. For example, it is expected that in the current year the foreign currency revenue will be approximately R16 billion.

That's all we have: R16 billion. And now I would like you to turn your attention to the following figures. Of that amount, more than R5 billion goes to purchase grain and foodstuffs—that's one-third. Can we make a reduction here? Can we? [noise in hall] Well, then it is necessary. If we make a decision like that, taking into account the situation that nowadays still persists in our agriculture, then I think we will sharply worsen the supply of foodstuffs in our country. We will sharply worsen it! Second, R2.5 billion goes to acquire equipment and new technologies; R2.6 billion goes to purchase chemical materials. We are forced to buy them abroad. R1.5 billion goes to purchase raw materials for light industry. R2 billion goes to purchase rolled metal, especially cold-rolled metal, and special pipes, etc. Thus, even a simple calculation will show that approximately R2.5 billion remain. And simply to service the debt that we already have, taking into account that we have to pay interest [kredity] on this debt, we need R12 billion. This means that we are again taking on debt. Is it possible to further aggravate things? Comrades, I think, that we need a very well-balanced position regarding this question.

And in conclusion, esteemed comrades, I would like to say that the government, in close cooperation with the USSR Supreme Soviet and the people's deputies, will do all to ensure that our country embarks upon the path of stable development. The support in this is the trust of the people—the enormous credit which it gave us today. Thank you. [applause]

Gorbachev Gives Final Speech

LD0906184589 Moscow Television Service in Russian 0840 GMT 9 Jun 89

[Speech by Mikhail Gorbachev, chairman of the USSR Supreme Soviet Presidium, at Congress of People's Deputies session in the Kremlin Palace of Congresses—live]

[Text] Esteemed comrade deputies! We are completing the examination of the main areas of domestic and foreign policy at the first Congress of People's Deputies.

The work of the congress is drawing toward its conclusion. Using the right of rapporteur, I would like to share my most preliminary impressions of the work of the congress. I think that we are still going to have to do a lot of thorough work on its results and the discussions that have taken place here, and anyone who was to try now, during the congress or immediately after it, to take upon himself that kind of mission, then I think he would be displaying arrogance, all the more so in view of the fact that many comrades who have not spoken are giving their speeches to the Secretariat. Overall, as a result of the discussions we are receiving an enormous amount of material which requires an appropriate, profound, and serious attitude and study.

Nevertheless I think—I am convinced of this, moreover—that this present congress of ours takes us into a new stage of the development of democracy and glasnost in the country, into a new stage in the development of restructuring itself. No doubt each one of us has his own opinion about the congress, his own observations, and his own assessments of the various sessions, the various discussions, and the various decisions. I consider that to be perfectly normal and natural. But you will evidently agree that this congress, notwithstanding all our differences in its assessment, can, nevertheless, be regarded as a major event in the whole history of the Soviet state [applause]

I know that there are different opinions about the character and the content of the discussions that have been taking place at the congress, but you must agree that we are the living witnesses and participants in the free comparison taking place in the atmosphere of the congress of views and points of view on the processes taking place in our society, on its past, present, and future.

This gives us a unique opportunity, not only us deputies but all the working people who are observing the work of the congress, the whole of our society, to have a clear idea of the real state of affairs, of the achievements and shortcomings, the reasons for this or that phenomenon taking place in the country. And this is very important. It gives us the opportunity once again to confirm what I already mentioned before: That in the framework of broad democratization and glasnost, there are real possibilities opening up for taking account of and for implementing the most varied interests of all strata of society. It is in precisely such an atmosphere of democratization and glasnost that our principle of pluralism of views is being put into practice. And this shows the enormous potential of our political system and our social system.

I felt it necessary to emphasize this at the very beginning in sharing my impressions of the congress, since as the congress has proceeded, guided by the discussions at the congress and assessing them, some people are throwing up the idea of a constructive opposition, of political pluralism, not pluralism of views, but political pluralism. I think that the congress, the entire work of the congress, is a convincing argument in favor of this, that in the framework of our political system and social system, but along the paths of democratization and glasnost, it is possible to have broad discussion and opposition of views, dissent, the elaboration on the basis of the comparison of points of view and agreed decisions, finding compromises, on all questions dealing with the fate of the country and the fate of the people.

Our congress is showing enormous possibilities for collective searches for the necessary decisions both for accelerating restructuring and accelerating socioeconomic development. And if anything should be said again about anything, comrades, it is that we must go further along the path of democratization and glasnost, towards people's power, along the path of deepening the revolutionary transformations. I have formed the opinion—and I want to tell you—that the congress, as I see it, firmly takes this line. [applause] And another thing, comrades. To tell the truth, many of us were psychologically and perhaps intellectually unready for such a turn of the discussions at the congress.

This also concerns the problems of social life as they have been raised here, and economic and political reform, and legislative activity, the essence of and the prospects for our union state, and an assessment of certain events in our distant and recent history. But I would not overdramatize all of that, in so far as everything that is happening is a reflection of the powerful democratic flow which is gaining speed in our country. We must delve into everything calmly and in a well measured manner, evaluate everything and, on the basis of collective discussions, come to coordinate conclusions, and we must transform them into a policy and into practical action.

We must seriously evaluate the critical remarks and proposals that were made in the speeches by the delegates of which I have already spoken at the beginning of my speech. Everything that is wise, innovative, constructive, and useful must be made use of without any prejudices. There is only one criterion here: the interests of restructuring, the interests of the people.

Probably something else needs to be spoken of once again: Any time of change requires search; it requires a breakthrough in thinking, in science and practice, and nonstandard decisions. Restructuring precisely sets the task of finding new ways to ensure the renewal of society. We must seek out these ways together, not fearing novelty and boldness if it moves us forward along the path of restructuring and solving urgent probems in our society.

Over the past few days, we have heard sharp, harsh, and emotional speeches by deputies and, over and over again, one can sense the burden of problems, their vast weight, and the fact that for the most part, the main and essentially the most important work still lies ahead of us.

The deputies have brought to the congress rostrum major and specific issues, a critical spirit, fresh thinking and, I would say that this is perhaps the most important thing, dissatisfaction with the state of affairs in the labor collectives, in the regions, in the industrial sectors, and in the country as a whole.

True, opinions have been expressed that too much has been said at the congress about unresolved problems, but a lack of concrete proposals can be felt. I have even seen that in some telegrams coming in to the congress, there is very much criticism leveled at the center and little self-criticism. What would be my attitude to such judgments? I rather think that the merit of our congress has precisely been that on the basis of a broad discussion we are, as it were, obtaining a full idea of the real processes taking place in all the spheres of our country's life and of the moods among the people. That is the first point. Second, the congress makes it possible for us to see how restructuring is faring in life itself, how the political directives and decisions adopted by central bodies are being implemented, how the people themselves are appraising this restructuring and what stands in the way of an implementation of the reforms, lowers their effectiveness, and slows down or else simply puts the brake on our transforming activities. All of this, comrades, provides us with the knowledge, which is essential to tackling problems fruitfully and successfully, moving ahead, and improving our work. This knowledge then—and the debate provides us with considerably more in this regard than other meetings and forums—gives us the opportunity to assess our past work, detect shortcomings, draw lessons, and take all this into account in the elaboration of policy and where decisions have already been taken, they need to be adjusted to make these adjustments.

People's deputies have been saying sharply and uncompromisingly that there can be no talk of restructuring unless radical changes occur in the sphere of production and consumption, unless foodstuffs and goods appear on the shop shelves in sufficient quantity, and unless there is an improvement in housing, the provision of pensions, and in the sphere of health care and services, and so on. I do not regard as a shortcoming the fact that the discussion of these matters was the main theme both in the reports and in the speeches of deputies, although I am aware that many deputies are dissatisfied with both reports, in that they were too down to earth. I feel that even taking into account the debate that has taken place here, that indeed the reports were obviously directed nonetheless at what is concerning society at the present time.

It would be incomprehensible if in the context of the acute problems existing in our country at the moment and in the context of what troubles the people and creates great social tension in society, we should now engage in discussing how we envisage the nature of the renewed society, how we see it, what its main features are, and how and what stages we must go through to reach this goal, leaving without due attention and consideration all that is the subject of primary concern of the people today.

I believe that discussion of all these vitally important and urgent issues increases our conviction that the solution of these urgent—or as we say "crying out"—tasks is possible in the near future. Why am I talking about this? You see I haven't found, overall, any great divergences of principle on these matters. The subjects raised here were in fact the ones we have grown accustomed to and which have long been at the center of attention in discussions at previous congresses. Although—and this is very important and should be noted, so that it should not be understood from this that the congress has somehow not produced anything—there is a difference in approach, particularly with regard to the level of radicalism of the measures proposed by the government and of those proposed by the deputies. And this difference is quite substantial and deserves very serious political and scientific analysis and assessment.

From this, I feel, comrades, there follows just one thing: Work must be continued on a program of urgent measures for resolving pressing, vitally important socioeconomic problems and improving the economy as a whole. This must be done, moreover, without delay both by the USSR Supreme Soviet and the government, involving scientists, economists, and practical workers. I do not want to repeat myself comrades, but the exchange of opinions on approaches to the solution of tasks of developing our economy which took place here at the congress makes it necessary, in my view, to speak my mind on one or two, or three issues.

At the congress the deputies said a lot about shortcomings in the development of our economy, the national economy. This concerned labor collectives, regions, branches of the national economy, and the principle of economic management itself. I personally take all of this seriously and evaluate it as an important contribution to the search for solutions. But I would like to say the following: We will not move resolutely forward and we will not be able to achieve the goals that have been set if we do not carry out a cardinal restructuring of socialist property relationships. We need restructuring of a kind under which the person, the labor collective, is put in real terms into the position of the master of production with all the deep and serious consequences that flow from this. [applause] Without that, comrades, we will not solve anything, and our structural measures, the reorganization of management, and all our slogans will not produce anything either. But if we breathe a living spirit into the economic activity of people and collectives, then the situation will change radically. This is something of which I am deeply convinced and I share the opinions of those who hold this position. And overall I think that this is not just the fruit of scientific and intellectual exercises, it is also the result of certain experience that has been built up.

Here I have to say that so far we have been feeling our way with difficulty toward ways of solving this cardinal problem. The search for the most efficient forms of financial autonomy and progressive models of it is proceeding with difficulty. But it seems to me that a general approach toward the reforming of socialist property is nevertheless gradually appearing in outline. I would support the ideas expressed here by deputies about regenerating the social character of state property, uniting it with the person and the collective via relations of socialist leasing in the very widest meaning of the word. In other words, the issue is this: society remaining the proprietor of the property of the whole people places it at the disposal of labor collectives and individual people through various kinds of leasing relationships—and they assume utter and complete responsibility for its use, they bear definite economic obligations to the state, they run their enterprise independently, on their own account and with the help of credits, and they form the income of the collective according to the result of their economic activity.

In doing so they act on the socialist market as independent producers of goods. [applause] The substantial difference between public and cooperative enterprises are being overcome with this approach, although, of course, the forms of management can and will be different. On this basis, on the basis of the large-scale introduction of leasing relations and the development of cooperatives, incentives will be created for the effective, dynamic, interested running of the economy.

I would only say once again—we have nevertheless heard the topic, even though it was not covered as frankly as it was on the eve of the congress during the past few months: How are we to approach resolving the problem of the market? I firmly think and I speak for this, for the market. [sentence as heard] I have already said so. But I think that it is impossible to agree with the comrades who believe that everything needs to be left to the market. Almost dropping all questions of regulation—naturally, regulation not within the framemwork of the administrative system but within the framework of new approaches, using economic methods. It seems to me that such reliance on the market which, so to speak, automatically must decide everything, I think that this is not serious. Even the capitalist market does not accept this. Doing things in this way means demolishing this entire market tomorrow and creating even greater strain, and then tomorrow we will talk—then already all will be on the streets and at meetings—with the working class, with all working people of the country.

So, we must follow our road to the market, preserving plan regulation, preserving economic methods of influence on processes taking place on the market, while at the same time stimulating the economic independence of primary production collectives as much as possible.

Comrades, evidently we have come right up to a fundamental turning point in the development of the economic reform. We must recognize this. We have positive experience, we have negative experience, we have accumulated quantitative—so to speak—experience, and we must understand all this in order to take a decision of principle on how to act further.

In this sense, I highly appreciate the discussion and the exchange of views that has taken place on these matters here at the congress. Taking account of the broad exchange of opinions that has taken place here at the congress, the government needs to thoroughly work through these issues and present them for the consideration of the USSR Supreme Soviet. That is the first thing that I would like to emphasize.

Further, improving the finances of the national economy is of decisive importance for the fate of restructuring the implementation of economic reform. While supporting the government's proposals in this respect, at the same time I think it expedient for the thoughts expressed here by deputies on this issue to be attentively considered by the government and the Supreme Soviet. It seems to be that here, too, as a result of the more in-depth considerations, taking into account the proposals that have been expressed, we shall be able to reach optimal solutions which will answer the real situation and the tasks of stabilizing the monetary and financial situation in the country. Indeed, those deputies who have been saying that half measures will not do in this regard are correct, and for this they have justly been criticizing the government and our economic departments. Much of what has been said on this matter by the economists deserves the most attentive consideration.

Comrades, I would like to say something further about the agrarian issue. Serious things have been heard at the congress on this issue, and not just because all of us, the entire country and the people, are concerned over food supplies in the country but also because of the energetic stance that the agrarian deputies have presented to the congress. In principle, I would like to support them, but, as people say, words alone in this respect are not very much support. This issue is of such a scale, since it concerns the fate of the peasantry and, in general, if you like, the fate of the country, that it needs to be approached in that way in the formulation of policy and in the carrying out of practical work.

We have been saying, and have been saying for a long time now, that the revival of the agrarian sector and its transformation into a highly developed sector of the economy capable of providing the country with everything needed is a task involving the whole people, but nearly always we have the peasant, the agricultural worker, and the rural inhabitant to face many problems on their own, the lack of amenities in rural life and the lack of the necesary funding for the conduct of agricultural production. The March plenum of the Central Committee, I am convinced, chose the right path. We must, on the basis of a radical restructuring of economic relationships in the countryside, finally remove all the fetters from the collective and state farms, from agricultural workers. We must provide them with wide opportunities for independence, that is how we must act. At the plenum, we recognized that it was necessary first and foremost to also solve the question of providing the countryside with social amenities. Moreover, large resources are to be directed to those ends. Already in the near future, people should start feeling real changes in their living conditions, and they should be firmly assured of a reliable prospect for life in the countryside. The accelerated development of storage and processing bases in the countryside has been recognized as one of the important and urgent tasks; for any efforts to increase agricultural output, agricultural produce, and the production of agricultural goods simply lose their raison d'etre unless these questions are solved urgently. Here, too, much has been determined in advance and is already being done. But, as I have understood from the speeches of the agrarian deputies and from their appeal, the needs of the agrarian sector to strengthen the material and technical basis require additional attention and examination both by the government and the Supreme Soviet.

But in general they require the attention of the whole of society, and this is how we must approach it—at the rayon, town, oblast, and republic level. We must make sure a change. [applause] Comrades, using all the economic power of our economy, we must go for a speedy solution of all these vitally important problems of the development of the countryside. I understand that on this account we have a common opinion here at the congress. [applause] We are all agreed, comrades, that we must resolutely carry out, more resolutely carry out the process of economic and political transformations. But this requires great legislative work, and it has started. I agree, as deputies have said here, and primarily Deputy Alekseyev, that it would be useful to work out and be guided in it by a defined strategy. That is correct. It even seems to me—not just seems, I am convinced—that a lagging behind in this area of the activity of the legislative organs is already hindering the advance of the transformation processes in our federal state.

Hence we get artificial clashes between the center and the republics; some seem to get the feeling they are misunderstood and others, in the center, that they are being pressured, without being given the opportunity to understand. All this demonstrates that life is leaving us behind, so to speak, with regard to our legislative work, and embarking on new legislative acts to correspond with the current stage of restructuring. And this stage is a very important one—both economic reform is a crucial stage, and political reform has reached its second stage, touching now upon issues of our federation, sovereignty of republics, autonomous formations, the life of national okrugs, and so on. Also of local soviets. Local soviets as well.

Clearly comrades no issue has been discussed as broadly at our present congress as the issue of interethnic relations. We have all clearly felt this, and felt it strongly, experienced quite a few uneasy moments even during the congress. There is much that troubles us here. It is essential to resolve these issues in an integrated way, an all-embracing way, boldly and at the same time tactfully and respectfully. But this also presupposes at the same time, comrades, that we cannot allow any compromise with attempts to resolve these generally very important, vitally important issues—without which restructuring will not go forward—affecting, to put it plainly, all peoples and nations of our country. We cannot agree, even for a single moment, with attempts by certain groups to resolve these problems, to settle, so to speak, the interethnic issues by criminal methods, disregarding morals and laws, and sometimes embarking on the road to anarchy.

This is unacceptable not only in interethnic issues, but in restructuring, in our lives as a whole. We must steer a constructive path, through democracy and glasnost, through mutual understanding and cooperation. These are essential prerequisites. And especially, frankly speaking, through dialogue.

And therefore, I, as chairman of the USSR Supreme Soviet, appeal to you, dear comrade people's deputies, and to all the citizens of our country, let us show wisdom, responsibility, restraint, and farsightedness in tackling these very important questions. [applause] Let us not allow outbursts of spur-of-the-moment emotions to gain the upper hand over concern for the future of our peoples, our children, grandchildren, and great-grandchildren. And only on the soil of wisdom and the law—and I repeat once again—of a broad dialogue, is it possible to solve—and we certainly can solve—all the problems which have accumulated in this important—and now acute—sphere of human relations. We must firmly and resolutely apply the law with regard to those who do not heed the arguments of common sense and the norms of the law.

In the deputies' speeches, questions were asked on the correlation between the center and the republics which are fundamental for our federation. As a result of the discussions which took place one may state that there is accord on two positions, it seems to me. First, on the vital need to strengthen the USSR as a multinational socialist state within the framework of which the free development of all the peoples which make up its population is ensured. And second, we must fill the Soviet federation with real content and ensure the sovereignty of the union republics, broad independence, and autonomy, and the rights of the individual whatever his national affiliation. [applause]

In the debates, in a general sense, we have been all the time in one way or another been discussing cardinal questions and new questions. At the same time, we have been returning to questions which are, as it were, ordinary ones. But their importance lies in their ordinariness. I have in mind questions of law and order and discipline. I would like to again say a few words on this question. Restructuring and democracy are unthinkable without discipline and self-discipline and without a high sense of responsibility. Everywhere and in everything, and at all times, one of the bulwarks of democracy has been a developed civic sense, inseparable from the ability and readiness to control one's own actions, and to answer for them to oneself and to society.

In recent years the public has witnessed more than one tragedy which has stunned the country. Many human lives have been lost, mainly because of basic slovenliness and criminal dereliction of one's direct duties on the part of someone. That was the case with Chernobyl, with the "Admiral Nakhimov," at Sverdlovsk and Arzamas, near Alma-Ata, and in other places—and the latest tragedy with the trains in the Urals. These, comrades, are only the most glaring examples—and how many are there of the kind that you and I have become accustomed to? And behind every catastrophe are human lives, not to mention economic losses.

What we need is firm production and technological discipline. We must get rid of slovenliness and irresponsibility. It is our duty to work toward developing a conscious sense of discipline in society. I believe that the attention of the congress and all its bodies should be constantly drawn toward this. That is what I feel, and in my recent visit with Comrade Ryzhkov to Bashkiria and Chelyabinsk Oblast, that was the mood of the people, comrades. The people are very worried by this.

Closely connected with the viability of democracy, discipline, and self-discipline, is the problem of crime. The growth in crime gives rise to just anger among Soviet people, and all of us, especially in the localities, must direct maximum efforts to fighting this plague, especially against such a challenge to the very foundations of our society as organized crime.

The government and the law-and-order bodies, and all of our public, are obliged to adopt exhaustive measures on this question. That was the opinion of the congress, and I would just like to support that opinion. [applause]

Comrades, the urgency of solving many problems must not, of course, push restructuring—the future of restructuring—into the background, unless we want to repeat a deadlocked verion of development. Immediate and urgent decisions today must serve as a bridge to tomorrow, a bridgehead for the advance of restructuring and the success of further transformations.

I listened with great interest to Comrade Shmelev's speech, but as for his phrase—he spoke too lightly—that I am not interested in what we do tomorrow, only today, I think he was wrong in treating this subject in such a light-hearted fashion!

A policy that concentrates only on short-range objectives and does not combine the present and the future is not going to be of full value. Party policy is, to use an expression from the Marxist classics, tactics that never lose sight of the great obectives. This is a serious matter, comrades. Ever since it became a science, socialism has demanded to be treated as a science. That was Lenin's view. Trenchant, publicist phrases and poetic metaphors will not help here, although it is always interesting. Serious scientific analysis is necessary, and the party carries it out as it tackles the new problems confronting the theory of socialism. We must conduct our scientific investigations and discussions even more intensively, as we interpret the society in which we live. What have we built? What are we restructuring? Finally, what are the social aims and intentions of restructuring? How do we see the new targets of the revolutionary renewal of society and of socialism?

We have been long accustomed to taking as our starting-point the view that we have created the best of all possible social systems. This conclusion emerged from the idea that there was only one model of socialism, an idea that was formulated by the fact of building social-ism in one country. We now know that this is not so. We have both seen in practice and recognized in theory the diversity of the roads of socialist development. We have discovered the real dangers of deviations from the essence of the socialist idea and of its distortions through dogmatism and impracticable, speculative plans, to say nothing of arbitrary rule and lawlessness.

But we also see something else: the inexhaustible riches contained in the idea of socialism, riches that can only be revealed by a diversity of practical solutions, united by the humanist ideas of service to mankind. I believe in the boundless possibilities of socialism—and this is not just a belief, but a matter of my own knowledge—and I think we must seek answers to all the questions that modern life has posed for us and which the broad discussion of all problems will pose within the framework of our system, on the roads of democratization and glasnost, rather than seeking somewhere from which to borrow other values in order to resolve our own problems. I think that that is the wrong road. I wanted to state my own position on this categorically at the congress. [applause]

We do not yet know the full richness of the forms of the society toward which we are moving. But we do know that these forms will continually arise from practice, from past, present and future knowledge, and through assimilation of all the achievements of human civiliza-tion.

When Marxism was formed as a theory it did not stay aside from all the processes taking place in the world, nor did it arise on the roadside of the development of human civilization but on its highway of it. And all the more so, today it cannot but draw upon all the achievements of human civilization. That is why we cannot embark upon the path of isolation from the world and of restricting ties and cooperation with the world. No, that would contradict Leninist ideas.

We know that this society in all its relations and mani-festations will be oriented toward man. It will be shaped and developed by the initiative of the masses, will be created by their creativity, and will open up vast expanses to man. Colossal forces are latent in socialism and we must give them an outlet on the basis of democ-racy and glasnost, the humanization of social relations, the recognition of values common to all mankind and of simple standards of morality and justice, the social and legal protection of the individual, of course, on the basis of an efficient and dynamic economy relying on eco-nomic methods and a diversity of forms of social own-ership, and on the basis of professionalism, competence, conscientiousness of work, discipline, and self-disci-pline. That means on the basis of culture, comrades, in its broadest interpretation.

In essence, it is the problem of the spirituality of society. This has been spoken of at the congress, although not a very great deal. Socialism by its nature must be a society of spiritually rich, genuinely intelligent people, no matter what they do, no matter what social group they belong to. We must be extremely sensitive and attentive to spiritual problems. Otherwise, comrades, the renewal of society will not succeed. For everything is through man, and the main deciding force, and the main acting figure of restructuring is man. [applause] Many characteristics of the future are being formed in the course of restructur-ing.

It has taken us 4 years to recognize in the atmosphere of democratic discussions the real state of society, to elab-orate new approaches in the economy and in the political sphere, and to begin restructuring in practice. I think that this work should be deepened, supported by what the present stage of restructuring gives us, and especially by what the present Congress of People's Deputies has given. As I see it, this is a major direction of party work on the threshold of the 28th CPSU Congress. In this sense the first Congress of USSR People's Deputies has worked well for restructuring, and therein lies its great service in the revolutionary renewal of socialism. [applause]

Comrades, I accept the criticism addressed to me, addressed to the political leadership, first and foremost over the slowness that has occurred in carrying out reforms. We have been late in many respects. This has had a serious effect on all the transformation processes. I think that there would have been fewer shortcomings and omissions if the Central Committee had displayed more exactingness in the execution of the instructions both of the party congress and of the 19th party confer-ence. This also applies to no less extent to the USSR Government. One of the gravest omissions has been the slow dismantling of the obsolete management structure, the attempts to solve pressing questions—and many of them have acquired a chronic nature—with old methods which have already more than once doomed us to failure.

In approaching a number of problems there has not been enough due principledness and timeliness in reacting to this or that topical problem of internal life. Today we are all better aware that restructuring is a fairly long-term matter. It is a historic transitional period in the development of socialism. It is necessary to stress once more: We are against skipping stages, losing touch with reality, even for the most noble of motives connected with an understandable impatience in society. But we must fight, and fight resolutely, also against gradualism, against Oblomovite [passive] behavior, against voluntary or involuntary application of the brakes on restructuring. In the last analysis the two extremes, both conservatism and ultra-leftism meet. The result, if one places either of these extremes at the basis of political activity can be the same: an irreparable blow to restructuring. I favor a vigorous, but at the same time balanced, realistic policy. The CPSU proposes it, without claiming infallibility and the absolute truth. On the contrary, it is inviting all our society, all the intellectual forces of our society to enrich it. We must self-critically—we are becoming increasingly successful at this—analyze every step we make, subjecting to public discussion the party's activity.

Restructuring has not been, nor will it be beyond criticism, and that is why it is restructuring. However, analyzing its lessons in the most impartial way, one cannot forget a good saying: Don't throw the baby out with the bathwater. It is unlikely, comrades—let's be realists and honest to ourselves and to our working people—it is unlikely that this congress would have taken place but for the April plenum of the Central Committee, the 27th party congress, and the 19th conference. [applause] Notwithstanding all the diversity of opinions, judgements, and proposals which there have been at the congress, one cannot be blind to this or fail to realize it, provided, of course, one does not take a biased stand. That has happened here, too.

One of the obvious results of restructuring consists in the fact that we have attained a normal and open political life after long years of despotism of the administrative-command system. Or perhaps I will put it like this, mostly normal. This is an achievement gained through hard suffering. We would have ruined restructuring had we not preserved it, and would have cut off its air.

Comrades, I would like to speak about another matter, too. There have been heated disputes at our congress and opposing opinions have been expressed. This is a natural phenomenon strengthening the constructive basis of restructuring. I, and probably many deputies, too, cannot agree unconditionally with all the criticial pronouncements. But for all that, there is discussion. We cannot agree particularly when one or another individually-adopted reason, phenomenon, or aspect of life which really do exist are made absolute. I think that such an approach is capable of distorting our view, of negatively influencing our appraisals and conclusions, thereby giving rise to new errors.

In the first few days here, quite a few sharp and scathing words were said about the apparatus. I do not want to defend bureaucracy, inflated staffing levels, or negligent and incompetent workers. Moreover, I think that we are waging the battle against bureaucracy without the necessary resoluteness and are resolving slowly the cadres questions which are dictated by restructuring itself. [applause]

However, I am convinced, convinced that the breaking of the command-administrative system must not be identified with a struggle against the apparatus. The overcoming of bureaucracy will not bring us success if it is confined to a campaign directed against the apparatus in general. Without a qualified, competent, well-organized apparatus of government in the center and in the provinces, we will not achieve anything sensible, comrades. And, incidentally, those who criticize and who speak on these problems, are themselves preparing generally to enter a new apparatus [applause]

So, overall this is what is at issue. [applause] And I am adding nothing surprising here, either. Let's put it like this; we need a new apparatus. I agree with that. [applause]

Comrades, I shall touch on yet another question which is worrying all of us. It also worries me. Because of historical reasons and distressing experience, we are especially sensitive to the question of excessive concentration of power in the hands of one leader. And this has been heard here at the congress; this concern is present. Since the question exists, I think it is necessary clearly and unambiguously to express one's attitude to it. You would probably simply not understand if I did not react to this theme which was present both on the eve of the congress and at the congress.

As a Communist I categorically do not accept the hints expressed - if not very plainly—alleging that I am trying to concentrate all the power in my hands. This is alien to me, to my views, my outlook, and indeed my character— I hope that you are already somewhat familiar with my style and character. It was not for this that the sharp about-turn to the new policy was made at the April plenum. It was not for this that the party and people embarked on the hard work of democratization, glasnost, cleansing, and renewal of our society and public life. As general secretary and chairman of the Supreme Soviet I have no other policy than that of restructuring, democratization, and glasnost and I declare again to the congress, to the working people, to the entire people my unwavering loyalty to that policy, for it is only on the basis of that that we shall be able to consolidate our society and resolutely accelerate movement along the path of restructuring. [applause] I see the meaning of my life and work in this. [applause]

Comrades, Marx and Lenin considered a critical attitude to one's own activity to be essential for a revolutionary party. I think that we can say in our party and society this is becoming a norm of life. But in this connection, as a Communist, I categorically reject attacks on the party. [applause] I repeat, so that it will be clear: I consider that we have raised the question at the very beginning and thus it must stand, and that must be our approach. The party is at the service of the people. That is the main thing. It is responsible for its policy, and it cannot be beyond the criticism, judgement, and assessments of the people. [applause]

But it is quite a different thing when it is a matter of attacks on the party simply as a party, a political party. Of course, in its history, the party's history, there have been various pages, including also tragic ones.

Our party has honestly owned up to the mistakes made, and soon there will be something more to tell you when we conclude on these matters in the near future. The party has assumed responsibility for them, has acted as the initiator of restructuring, of the radical renewal of society. I am confident that the 20 million Communists and the Central Committee will be to prove, in restructuring, that they are equal to the difficult tasks of the time and are capable of fulfilling in the future also the role of Soviet society's political vanguard.

Yes, the party, just as society as a whole, must restructure itself. As general secretary of the Central Committee I wish to tell the deputies that the Politburo firmly intends to put into effect the line of the 27th congress and the 19th party conference toward restructuring in society. I think that we must carry out a vast amount of work in preparing for the 28th party congress, a vast amount of work.

But the comrades have, evidently, been right in saying that the party is lagging behind and if it wants to be the vanguard of society and fulfill this mission—and society needs such a vanguard force, a bearer of program goals—the party must also restructure itself more quickly than society. [applause]

Comrades, I want—alarming rumors of what is supposedly taking place in the Central Committee and in the Politburo have been heard here—I want to say: The Central Committee holds the same position which I stated when describing the position of the Politburo, and I assure you that dangers of coups or of something similar do not at all exist here. This I state firmly. [applause] Let us be finished with rumors of all kinds, for in 4 years I have died 7 times and my family has already been slain 3 times. [laughter]

And all this is rife, going around you understand. And they bring me family trees [skhemy rodovyye] of some kind and I look at them.

Comrades, let us be finished with these rumors, and above all the deputies and people involved in state matters should not rely on all this chatter which they are frequently being fed with. [applause]

There is a task facing us, comrades, which is exceptionally important in scale and newness, and that is to unite in an organic way the efforts of renewed Soviet power and the political work of a renewed party, so that the gigantic potential to be found in the socialist social system can be fully revealed. Yes, we are in a complex situation, but we are not in gloom or darkness. I want to say this bluntly, not in gloom and not in darkness, as it might seem to some people, even among those sitting here in this hall. We have a clear policy. The party will succeed in fulfilling its historic mission—the renewal of socialism—by working out a policy and offering it to society and I am sure that the Soviet system which is being regenerated on new principles of democracy will make its decisive contribution to the implementation of the tasks which we have drawn up.

At the congress, and many comrades have probably drawn attention to this, little has been said about foreign policy. It has been said that at the present stage of restructuring we have truly achieved considerable results which are welcomed by our people and the public throughout the world, results which have changed in many ways not just the image of the Soviet Union but the situation in the world, too. This is indeed so. What has been accomplished in the field of foreign policy is not as a result of a change in notions, concepts, or even doctrines. From what we have inherited, much that is musty, harmful, and vicious has been discarded.

But nobody will bring us positive changes in world affairs as a gift, any more than to other peoples. No, comrades, each step on the path to a new and more civilized world must be conquered in a difficult struggle, even though outwardly it may not always be so noticeable.

Let us take note of one other thing: In order that the positive advancements in international affairs may become irreversible, we must always remember that we are speaking with partners who take account of facts and facts alone, and we must always present them with facts which will convince them, for a long time I hope, that it is better to get along well with us, just as we hope to get along well with all neighbors, near and far. [applause]

And so, comrades, a difficult yet clear path lies ahead, if we assess it in a composed and stately manner, as we—people's deputies—are expected to do. Power to the soviets, comrades, means creating a system of democratic institutions, a system for the sovereignty of the people—orderly, efficient, and functioning in all conditions and under all circumstances. Power to the soviets is unattainable without the return of the land to the peasants. Power to the soviets cannot be unless each one of us feels himself to be a part of society and nature, health care and the education service, prosperity and well-being. The sovereignty of the people will not become firmly established until it displays a higher degree of efficiency than any other form of power. It follows from this that in politics, we shall have to learn much, assimilate much, and get used to much. The congress that has taken place has taught us a lot. We shall, no doubt, derive the necessary lessons from it and will part all the wiser. There is also no doubt that we shall come better prepared to the next congress. In short, all of us together have to become familiar with the school of soviet sovereignty of the people. I am sure that we shall manage this.

Allow me to express the conviction that by combined effort and through the deeds of each deputy, we shall cope with the obligations that have been placed upon us by the people and by our common fatherland. [applause]

9 Jun Congress Continues Work
LD1006193389 Moscow Television Service in Russian 1203 GMT 9 Jun 89

[Relay of the Congress of People's Deputies sessions held in the Kremlin Palace of Congresses—live]

[Excerpts] [Passage omitted: Gorbachev passes deputies' written questions to editorial commission for draft document; Minsk deputy says there are too many control bodies; deputy calls for better state information system and planning changes; Deputy Zaslavskiy calls for aid to the disabled; Deputy Stepakov makes suggestions for reorganizing banks; Deputy (Shelkanov) proposes improvements in social security; Deputy Burlatskiy talks about amending human rights provisions and preventing another Afghanistan]

[Gorbachev] We give the floor to Deputy Mikhail Sergeyevich Minasbekyan, and the next speaker will be Comrade Mikhail Nikiforovich Poltoranin. [indistinct interruption from hall] Go ahead.

[Minasbekyan] Esteemed comrade chairman, esteemed comrades and people's deputies: I want to make the following proposals. The first one is on Nagorno-Karabakh. This has already been talked about here frequently. Why has this problem not been solved to this day? In my view, this will not happen until the very concept for examining important problems concerning virtually the whole population of the oblast is changed. The point is that to date they are trying to solve them, instead of the people of Karabakh; it should be the other way around. If our goal is sovereignty of the people, and this is not simply a declaration, we have to embark boldly on the path to self-determination.

In his report, Mikhail Sergeyevich Gorbachev stressed, when talking about the acuteness of the nationality issues, that restructuring creates the basis for rectifying any mistakes and deformations that were committed in the past. Thus, let us give the people of Karabakh the opportunity to rectify these themeselves and determine their own destiny. This will make it possible to stabilize the situation in Nagorno-Karabakh and will create the confidence that the principles of justice are being restored in our country.

The following would also indisputably serve to stabilize the situation. The country has embarked on a correct course to eliminate the blank spots in history. It is important not only to state the facts but also to give them a worthy assessment. It is well known that in 1915 in western Armenia, Ottoman Turkey, about 1.5 million Armenians were annihilated or deported. Therefore, I propose that the congress acknowlidge and condemn this incident as genocide. I am sure that if this had been done before, many of the negative things that have already been mentioned here could have been prevented. However, it is not too late, even now. There is no statute of limitations for crimes against humanity. [passage omitted: Minasbekyan calls for law on informal organization]

[Grigoryan, not further identified] [passage omitted] Allow me, first of all, to respond to the speech by Deputy Suleymenov from Kazakhstan who said, inter alia, that in the difficult days for Armenia after the tragic earthquake, a plane with soldiers that flew from Baku crashed in the disaster zone, and alleged that the memory of those who died has remained only with their mothers. At that time, a plane flying to us from Yugoslavia also crashed. The republican press has written about these catastrophes frequently with sorrow and pain. Piles of fresh flowers have been laid every day at the place where people perished who were rushing to the aid of Armenia. The collection of money began at that time throughout Armenia for the construction of monuments to those who died. A design competition was announced and a decision was made on this by the Armenian Communist Party Central Committee and the republic's Council of Ministers.

There is no need to stir passions once again without knowledge of the real state of affairs, particularly as gratitude is one of the characteristic features of the Armenian people, who have experienced too much grief in their tragic history not to understand the grief of one's neighbor, particularly at this time when the world shares our grief. If the speaker was not pursuing other aims, why did he not approach us before the speech and clarify the facts? How can such things be said about a people who have been recovering bodies from the debris for more than 6 months now, and who are restoring their destroyed homeland today with the help of fraternal people? [passage omitted: on need for legislation against ecological crimes]

I want to dwell on the role of the intelligentsia in such a fundamentally important and delicate issue as relations between ethnic groups. We are not thinking about condemning the Azerbajani people for what happened and what is happening in the Azerbaijan Soviet Socialist Republic, or for the atrocities in Sumgait. The young people who went out into the streets yesterday, and who do so today, are unfortunately brought up to do this. We think that [shouts from hall, some applause] it has been decided—1 minute—we think that the decision on the just demand by the Nagorno-Karabakh Autonomous Oblast, as it has been entered in the draft, is quite all right. It only remains to be implemented urgently. Thank you for your attention. [passage omitted: Deputy Ginzburg calls for publication of all the deputies' proposals]

[Deputy Yashar Abbasov, steel worker from Azerbaijan] [passage omitted: criticizes people not well-versed in Nagorno-Karabakh issues for voicing their views] Certain deputies are insisting that the Nagorno-Karabakh issue be examined at the congress itself and that a commission be set up to investigate the events in Sumgait. But there is also a proposal from deputies from Azerbaijan, who are also demanding that the circumstances be examined which led to all Azerbaijanis leaving the Armenian Soviet Socialist Republic, and the resulting deaths of many people. I think that these issues are acute and difficult; they require the most serious, profound and comprehensive examination. You understand that we have a lot to say in connection with this. [Gorbachev rings bell] However, I feel that in the common interests, in the interest of getting to the truth [applause], the presidium's proposal—to pass on all these issues to the relevant commissions and committees of the Supreme Soviet—is correct, and we must get down to this right away.

[Passage omitted: vote is taken on whether Obolenskiy should be allowed to join the constitutional commission; the results are as follows: 934 for, 903 against, and 114 abstentions; he therefore fails to gain a majority of the total and is not elected; Gorbachev reads out other proposals for this commission]

[Deputy Roald Sagdeyev, USSR Academy of Sciences researcher] I have a proposal to strengthen somewhat the nonparty layer—if there is such a thing—on this commission, and I hope to strengthen its moral authority appreciably by proposing Academician Andrey Dmitriyevich Sakharov. [applause]

[Gorbachev] Thank you. Is that all? Are there any objections, comrades, against this inclusion? [hall replies "no"] No. There is no need to vote? [hall replies "no"] Shall we vote? [hall replies "no"] No. We will vote as a whole afterwards. [passage omitted: various deputies speak for and against Deputy Samsonov's inclusion as a member of the constitutional commission; Samsonov speaks in his own defense; Gorbachev puts the Samsonov nomination to a vote; the teller reports: 500 support the withdrawal of his nomination, 1188 oppose the withdrawal, 101 abstain]

[Borodin] Borodin from Yakutiya, constituency No 690. We have analyzed the list of candidates for this commission. This is what we have learned. There are 17 first secretaries of oblast party committees and [members] of the CPSU Central Committee. There are another 31 employees and members of the Central Committee who are linked with the highest party leadership, as it were. It turns out, comrades, that 55 percent of the commission members are from the highest party leadership. I have a question. What are we trying to create: new party rules or

a new Constitution? [applause] Second, no one consulted me, a member of the Yakutiya delegation, as to whether it was necessary to include the secretary of our oblast party committee, Yuriy Nikolayevich Prokopyev, on this commission. I have nothing against this. But this is also a violation of our democracy. I propose that people with real life experience should be on this commission. That is the first thing. Second, I propose that an alternative commission should be set up altogether, and that there should be two draft constitutions to choose from. I propose Yevtushenko for the second commission, first and foremost. He has already formulated very well one point in the new Constitution. That is all I wanted to say.

[Passage omitted: a deputy from the Komsomol proposes that the commission has a youth representative; the proposal is accepted; Deputy Sukhov calls for attention to be paid to all opinions and proposes Yevtushenko and Vlasov as members to the commission; Gorbachev puts Yevtushenko's nomination to a vote]

[Sakharov] I suspect that I will be in the minority on all the fundamental issues that arise during the drawing up of the text of the constitution. This puts me in a difficult position if it is not agreed in advance that the commission will present two alternative drafts which will be examined on an equal basis. This seems very important to me. [applause] [Sentence indistinct]

[Passage omitted: Gorbachev announces that the vote is against Yevtushenko; the deputies then vote on Vlasov, who is also rejected; Deputy Mikheyev comments on Borodin's earlier comments; deputy says that since some candidates have been voted on, all should be; Gorbachev says the question is settled; Gorbachev moves on to the editorial commission; Gorbachev asks whether the constitution commission should be voted on as whole or whether each individual should be voted on; Gorbachev then announces that the commission membership is approved]

[Gorbachev] Dear comrades, last night we left one question undecided: the question of the Committee for Supervising the Constitution. In order to get out of the situation which arose here and which we all witnessed, we had conversations last night—this morning I had a meeting with the deputies from Lithuania. In the same way, we had conversations with and proposals were made by Estonia, by the deputies from Estonia.

The following proposal is submitted and I ask you to support it, to proceed in the following manner: to set up a commission to prepare a draft law on supervising the Constitution of the USSR. [applause]

It is proposed to include on the commission the following comrades: Alekseyev, corresponding member of the USSR Academy of Sciences, Urals, Sverdlovsk—you heard his speech; Comrade Akayev, vice president of the Khirgiz Academy of Sciences; Badamyants, chairman of the Armenian State Security Committee; Buachidze, chairman of the board of the Georgian Culture Fund; Golik, dean of the law faculty at Kemerovo University; Gryazin, head of a department of the Institute of Philosophy, Sociology, and Law of Estonia; Yeremey, chairman of the Moldavian republican trade union council, from Kishinev; Kalmykov, head of the department at Saratov Law Institute; Kirimov, head of a department of the Academy of Social Sciences under the CPSU Central Committee; Kryuchkov, first secretary of the Odessa Oblast party committee; Kudryavtsev, vice president of the USSR Academy of Sciences; Negmatullayev, president of the Tajik Academy of Sciences; Ovezgeldyyev, president of the Academy of Sciences of the Turkmen Soviet Socialist Republic; Pavlov, head of the state and legal department of the CPSU Central Committee; Rustamova, member of the Syrdarya Oblast court of the Uzbek Soviet Socialist Republic; Semenka or Semenka, excuse me if I am not pronouncing it correctly, chairman of the Ivanovo Oblast court; Skudra, minister of justice of the Latvian Soviet Socialist Republic; Smaylis, head of a laboratory at the Januskievicius cardio-vascular system physiology and pathology research institute, Lithuania; Sobchak, head of a department at the law faculty at Leningrad State University; Sultangazin, president of the Academy of Sciences of Kazakhstan; Sukharev, procurator of the USSR; Tarnavskiy, procurator of the Belorussian Soviet Socialist Republic; and Yakovlev, head of a sector at the state and law institute of the USSR Academy of Sciences, Moscow.

Are they suitable? [hall says "yes"] Can this be put to the vote? [hall replies "yes"] I ask all those in favor of forming this commission, made up of these people, and to present their work to the congress in autumn, to raise their cards. Please put them down. Are there any against? Please take a count. [passage omitted: there are 10 votes against and 25 abstentions; Gorbachev announces a break]

Afternoon Session Proceeds

LD1106153189 Moscow Television Service in Russian 1417 GMT 9 Jun 89

[Relay of the Congress of People's Deputies sessions held in the Kremlin Palace of Congresses—live]

[Excerpts] [Gorbachev] Comrades, before moving on to the next matter, we have to agree on something. I think that deputies will have a perfectly natural interest in ensuring that we don't get a situation where we don't seem to have ended up with the adoption of the main document, where we seem to have broken up without voting for the whole document. But we have already voted on the fundamentals of the document, on the main things that were drafted and taken into account as we went along; we have adopted them.

All the same, we feel a certain awkwardness and sense that it's a rather delicate situation. We could ask you to vote for the decision as a whole, while instructing the

presidium and commission to finish refining the decision. Let it be as it will. If you, the deputies, are saying that it would be better to handle things that way, if you are of that view, then we could do it that way.

Or, as I was saying, do it as follows. We have already adopted the main fundamentals. There are many supplementary points, very many. In the course of a week we could carry through the whole process to the end in the commission and the presidium, and within that week we would send out to deputies the new refined draft, incorporating remarks from deputies, and we would then get your agreement. Somewhere in a week, or in 10 days at the most, at the most—because this is a voluminous decision altogether, embracing all the fundamental issues—it would be published.

So there can be two options. Either we stick to the option we agreed on—that no later than 10 days hence it would be completed and published, with the final draft of the decision being unfailingly communicated to deputies; or we could adopt different instructions, voting for the decision as a whole and instructing the drafting commission and the presidium to take maximum account of the proposals that have been voiced, and after that work is completed to publish it. [shouts from floor] Comrade Boldyrev, the third—go ahead—there is also a third proposal.

[Deputy Boldyrev] Comrades, I draw your attention to the fact that by virtue of our status we cannot and should not empower the drafting commission to decide something on our behalf. The drafting commission is a purely bureaucratic body whose job is only to propose options to us, and it is up to us to vote on the proposals that we submit. Thus the third proposal is the only acceptable one in my view, namely that the main disputed proposals must be put to a vote. Otherwise it will not be a congress decision; it will merely be a decision of the drafting commission. [applause]

[Gorbachev] So from this third proposal it follows that the proceedings of the congress would have to be extended. [indistinct shouts] No, no, no. I'm talking precisely of the first option, but under Comrade Boldyrev's I understand we would have to continue the congress proceedings. Is that right, Comrade Boldyrev? He didn't follow it through, but I always have to follow things through, to make sure things are clear. [laughter] So it would mean an extension of the congress proceedings until the decision is adopted. So we have three proposals. The first proposal is the one we arrived at during the previous session. Who favors going about things the way we agreed, with the rider that the document should be published no later than 10 days hence—please raise your cards. [some confusion] What isn't clear? The first proposal is the one we agreed on—to instruct the commission and the presidium to work up the decision, to send the worked-up document out to deputies, and to get it all done and published within a week, and not later than 10 days from now. And deputies would have to suspend their normal work, of course. Who is for the proposal—please show! Please lower. Who is against? Let us perhaps have a count. It is a fundamental issue. [vote counting taking place]

[Teller] Would the 10th sector report, please! [counting continuing] [video shows Sakharov going up to the platform and talking to Gorbachev]

[Gorbachev] Andrey Dmitriyevich Sakharov asks me to say that, when the comrades receive the draft after it has been updated with the remarks and all that has been expressed which are to be added to it, each deputy will be able, so to speak, on each amendment to express his thoughts and put his name to them. But it is necessary- ...[Gorbachev is interrupted by conferring] Okay, we are agreed. If you please!

[Teller] Esteemed deputies, 121 deputies have voted against.

[Gorbachev] Are there any abstaining comrades? It seems to me that there are none. No, there are some abstainers. [more counting under way] Comrades, while the count is under way, the deputies nevertheless consider as follows. It is proposed that what we have already discussed here and adopted as a basis be voted upon—or should we consider that these provisions have been accepted? [some animation in the hall] But I do not see the sense of it. [even more animation in hall] Okay then. Therefore the version remains as we agreed with you. What I think is this. We shall be told the figures there, but the question has been decided. If you please!

[Indistinct question from the hall]

[Gorbachev] What was that?

[Further indistinct words from hall]

[Gorbachev] That is precisely what I think.

[More indistinct words from hall]

[Gorbachev] Yes, definitely. That is all definite. You have in mind that there will be many repetitive and coinciding proposals? We have already been discovering them during yesterday's work and overnight.

[Teller] Thirty-two deputies abstained.

[Gorbachev] It's settled then. Comrades, now I shall let Comrade Lukyanov give a brief introduction to the other remaining business. He will speak on behalf of the presidium—we have discussed this matter two or three times.

[Lukyanov] Comrade deputies, in the period leading up to the congress and during the congress proceedings, the delegations and people's deputies from republics and regions submitted proposals that the congress should consider a whole set of issues that did not enter the preliminary agenda. As you will recall, a decision was adopted on this at the first session of the congress—to add "any other business" to the agenda. The Congress Presidium has considered all the proposals very closely—more than 20 different proposals came in. Three times the Congress Presidium went through these matters before reaching a conclusion.

It has to be said first of all that many proposals have already been resolved at the congress in one form or another. Many questions that deputies have raised have come to be incorporated. Thus, in the decision on the main guidelines for domestic and foreign policy that has been adopted by us in its basic form, the relevant instructions are given to the Supreme Soviet, government and other bodies concerning a whole set of issues having to do with the implementation of economic reform and the development of the social sphere; provision is made for the radical updating of legislation on the soviets of people's deputies and for the consolidation of the fundamental principles of the law-governed state; and the preamble embodies proposals that, it had been suggested, should be framed in the form of a congress decree. The decision reflects, among other things, deputies' proposals on the need to check whether certain decrees of the USSR Supreme Soviet Presidium are in conformity with the Constitution—and that has also been embodied in a specific provision of our decision.

Considerable attention was devoted to issues connected with proposals from the republics. In particular, this was reflected in our basic decision, and the question of setting up a special commission on this will also evidently have to be dealt with. What is involved is regional financial autonomy and the implementation of reform in the republics.

In connection with the deputies' request concerning the insertion of changes and additions into the existing Constitution and the drafting of a new Constitution, a constitutional commission which was instructed to study carefully all questions which were put by the deputies and to submit corresponding proposals was, as you will know, established today.

You also know that the commissions on the evaluation of the 1939 Soviet-German treaty, on the investigation of the circumstances connected with the events in Tbilisi, and on the inspection of the documentation concerning the activity of the investigation group lead by Deputy Gdlyan and others, have been established by the congress, and that they are already working.

Taking into account what has been said, the Congress Presidium has, after long discussion, arrived at the conclusion that it would be possible, taking into consideration the proposals of the deputies and delegations, to examine the following questions under miscellaneous business.

First. On working out a draft law on the status of the USSR people's deputies. You know that the proposals on this subject were voiced in the speeches of many USSR people's deputies. Some people's deputies submitted their proposals in writing. For example, deputies (Olubenchenko), Nazarenko, Koltsov, and Sebentsov. They presented their ideas in the form of entire drafts of a USSR law on the status of USSR people's deputies. This was already discussed here. As is known, basic rights and duties of people's have been determined by the law on the status of the USSR people's deputies, which is in force. But many clauses of this law can already now be applied and implemented, because they are not in contradiction with the new provisions of the Constitution, and apply to all deputies, all bodies—the represetative bodies of state authority. This concerns such things as a deputy's immunity, contacts between the deputies and voters, the deputies' enquiry, the right to initiate legislation, and a number of other clauses of this law.

At the same time the USSR people's deputies are rightly raising the question of the necessity to draw up a new law on status. And the presidium completely agrees with it. This law—and it should be drawn up—should contain increased guarantees of people's deputies' rights; it should define more precisely legal bases of relations between the deputies and the bodies of state authority and management; it should provide detailed rules for all questions related to the implementation of a deputy's authority. Taking this into account, a draft decision of the congress proposes to instruct the USSR Supreme Soviet to work out a draft law of the USSR on the status of people's deputies—with the intention of adopting it at the upcoming USSR people's deputies congress at the end of this year. This draft has been submitted for our examination and has been handed to you in advance.

In the decision it is also proposed to set up several additional provisions immediately, for the so-called transitional period before the new law is adopted. These provisions are aimed at creating for people's deputies the conditions in which they can efficiently perform their functions as deputies. It is, specifically, a question of supplying the deputies with the relevant material and of ensuring the people's deputies' priority right of access to the mass media. It is envisaged that a deputy may have a secretary, paid from funds featuring in the USSR Supreme Soviet budget estimates. The decision also states that deputies must be given the premises necessary for carrying out of their obligations as deputies. It establishes that officials failing to perform their duties in relation to USSR people's deputies are liable to disciplinary action and even to dismissal.

Naturally, these provisions, which are brought together in the draft that has been distributed to you, are of a temporary nature, pending endorsement by the next USSR Congress of People's Deputies of a new law on the status of deputies, which will be drawn up by the Supreme Soviet and submitted for your consideration at the next congress. It goes without saying that these provisions of a temporary nature will also be appropriately reviewed in the light, evidently, of the practical experience which we will accumulate. I have had to talk to many comrades. On this draft, too, they have already submitted several views, and I think that they are fair views. The only thing is that our law will have to gradually incorporate the experience of the 2,250 deputies—USSR people's deputies—elected to take part in our congress. The congress's draft decision of the preparation of a draft law on the status of people's deputies has already been given to you, and I hope that you have had the opportunity to read through it.

Now, for the second question. A sizeable proportion of deputies' proposals for inclusion in the "any other business" section of the agenda was linked with the need to draw up the laws that are required to ensure the active working of our congress and also of the Supreme Soviet, the committees, the commissions and, in general, of each people's deputy. Thorough work is necessary here, as on the law on status. Accordingly, the Congress Presidium proposes that, following discussion, a decision on this question should be adopted concerning the preparation of several draft laws to regulate the working procedures of the USSR Congress of People's Deputies, the Supreme Soviet, and its organs. The draft decision has been distributed to you. It provides for making the Supreme Soviet responsible for drawing up, and submitting for consideration by the second congress, drafts of the standing orders of the USSR Congress of People's Deputies and the USSR Supreme Soviet, a law on the reimbursement of USSR people's deputies for expenses incurred during their work as deputies, and a law on the procedure for recalling USSR people's deputies. We only have a law on the procedure for recalling deputies of the Supreme Soviet, while there is as yet no such procedure for a USSR people's deputy.

As far as—and another law was mentioned there, you have seen it—as far as drawing up the draft law on overseeing the USSR Constitution is concerned, we could charge the special commission which has been set up today with it. We have given these instructions today. That is why it appears that it would not be appropriate to include this draft law in the text of a general decision on instructions to the Supreme Soviet—on drawing it up, although some comrades today have put forward quite an interesting proposal that a schedule of legislative work should be drawn up and the results also reported to the people's deputies congress. I, for my part—I think it is a useful course of action.

And, apart from that, during our debates, a very substantial proposal was voiced. A number of delegates expressed the view that the USSR people's deputies congress should adopt an appeal to the world's peoples, in the framework of which we could describe our attitude to restructuring and the principles of our foreign policies.

These are the three major issues which we could examine in the item "any other business" on our agenda, the kind of work which is included in "any other business." I would like to stress again that all remaining issues which we very thoroughly worked through in the presidium have been more or less reflected in the main decision of the congress, including a number of decisions on the ethnic issue, which make mention of certain sore points, so to speak, which we have in tackling the inter-ethnic relations issue.

It was this proposal that the Congress Presidium had instructed me to bring to your attention.

[Gorbachev] Comrades, such is the body of proposals submitted for discussion at this session of ours by the presidium. You have a question?

[Zubkov] Comrade Zubkov.

[Gorbachev] Go ahead, please.

[Zubkov] We have received the text of a draft law on taxation [words indistinct].

[Lukyanov] Comrades, you have received the texts of several draft laws today: on taxation, on the activities of inventors, etc. You have, probably, noticed that....

[Gorbachev, interrupting] This was a request.

[Lukyanov continues] ...all these drafts were subject to a wide public discussion, a wide one. Some of them have been finalized taking into account the public discussion, some of them have not yet been finalized. We were proceeding from the belief that all deputies should receive the text of all these draft laws for their personal use, just as we agreed to provide you with the knowledge of what exactly the Supreme Soviet is going to deal with. These are the drafts which will be submitted for discussion by the Supreme Soviet and its commissions. For the time being, there is no need to examine them at the congress.

[Gorbachev] Therefore....

[Antifeyev, interrupting] I have a question.

[Gorbachev] Just a moment—go ahead, please. [passage omitted: Antifeyev reports receiving numerous cables from the voters supporting the proposal to elect the IZVESTIYA SYEZDA at the congress]

[Gorbachev] Comrades! Go ahead, please. You have something to add, right? To the agenda, right, to the agenda?

[Levykin] Yes. Deputy Levykin, the 39th constituency. I believe that the congress could also examine the issue of repealing Article 11 (1) of the 8 April decree. The fact is, I believe that there is already a sufficient body of opinion

and, as a matter of fact, it has been expressed in the final decision itself. That is why I believe that we could make that decision right now. And that is not only my view, but also that of the thousands of people who signed the appropriate appeal. I move to submit that issue as a legislative initiative, so that a decision could be reached. [applause]

[Nikolskiy] Deputy Nikolskiy, Smolnenskiy constituency, Leningrad. Even before the opening of the congress, the Leningrad group of people's deputies suggested putting the issue of setting up a commission to investigate all circumstances leading to the involvement of the Soviet Armed Forces in the Afghan war on the congress agenda. It has transpired from the congress proceedings that this issue remains topical, and one of the most dramatic moments at the congress came when this issue was discussed. That is why we, the people's deputies from Leningrad, put forward the following proposal. I think it would be difficult at this late stage of the congress to set up a commission—that is why a draft of the following decision is being offered: to instruct the USSR Supreme Soviet to set up a commission on investigating and assessing the circumstances which led to the participation of the Soviet Armed Forces in the Afghan war. [applause] [passage omitted: Deputy Martirosyan on the practical needs of deputies: accommodation, etc.]

[Gorbachev] Good comrades, let us first of all finish drawing up the agenda, since debating proposals has already begun. One minute now. Are there other addenda to the agenda? Please, you were first.

[Zhuravlev] Deputy Zhuravlev, Minsk Soviet, 566th Territorial Electoral Constituency. I propose that the question of amendments that are necessary to introduce into the law on elections be included in the agenda in "any other business." Many of us experienced personally all the deficiencies of this law. We are now approaching the elections to the local soviets, and we do not have the right to leave unchanged at least some parts of the law in operation. In particular, I would propose that one part be abolished by our voting on it—we have the right to do this—the part about the constituency electoral commissions. [applause] In addition, I consider that we must make a quite definite statement about the inadmissibility of carrying out a substitution of elections with voting. That is, we must make a definite statement on the inadmissibsility of elections on the basis of no alternative candidate. Finally, my third and last point—in doing this we could discuss the question of what prevents us in general from holding elections on the basis of alternative candidates. I think that one of the deficiencies, one of the reasons for this, is that we we do not have this kind of experience at the lower levels. It seems to me that we are now ready, at least in many regions of our country, to start the elections of the first leaders of the regions on the basis of alternative candidates by means of direct, secret elections by all the population. That is all I have to say. Thank you for your attention.

[Sanchat] Deputy Sanchat, constituency 47. Comrade deputies, in the KOMSOMOLSKAYA PRAVDA newspaper for 2 June of this year, a number of people's deputies of the USSR, comrades Batynskaya, Yemelyanenko, and you, Sokolov, reminded us about the events in Novocherkassk in 1962. In connection with these events death sentences were passed on seven people, and a significant number of people were condemned to various periods of imprisonment. I propose that a decision of the congress be included in the agenda, under "any other business," by which we would instruct the USSR procurator general to dispute the aforementioned judicial decisions and to take measures to rehabilitate the corresponding people. [applause] [passage omitted: Deputy Plotnikov from the Komsomol; first part of Deputy Andreyeva, Union of Designers, on the need for deputies to be kept informed about the plans and agendas of the Supreme Soviet sessions]

[Andreyeva] We did not finish the discussion of questions of the state of affairs so far as the decree of 8 April—the law on internal troops—and other recent legislative acts is concerned, which have aroused doubt in many deputies' minds and given rise to fears about how they will be used. For that reason I have this proposal: I would like to include in the agenda, to put forward for discussion under "any other business," the possibility of these laws being used before their wording has been changed—and at the same time to ask the question about the period of time it will take to change their wording, about the use of these laws and this decree only with the permission of the USSR Supreme Soviet or of the USSR Congress of People's Deputies. Thirdly, I consider that it is necessary, in confirmation of what Anatoliy Ivanovich [Lukyanov] was just saying, to give to all people's deputies a list of those immediate draft laws which are literally knocking at the door, as Comrade Lukyanov said, so that people's deputies may determine their degree of priority, and so that this degree of priority serves as a basis for the work of the Supreme Soviet.

Finally, my last point—I consider that it is necessary for us, under "any other business" at the end of the agenda, to allot time—this is a request from deputies, which I have just been given—to allot time for notices and announcements from groups of deputies, if groups of deputies or individual deputies have such. Thank you. [passage omitted: another deputy submits proposal on help to the poor]

[Shamshev] I'm Deputy Shamshev, constituency No 345, Yaroslavl. Comrades, I support the proposal of the Leningrad delegation that the Afghan war should be discussed—but in a slightly different form. I think that we should not be talking of a commission, since we can talk in terms of a commission on Tbilisi, where around 19, say, people died, and where there were several hundred casualties, whereas tens of thousands and even millions of people died there—around a million Afghans died; what is needed here is not a commission, but there should be open hearings in the USSR Supreme Soviet on the emergence, course, and results of the war. Those guilty of unleashing it must be identified, and a Supreme Soviet report should be presented to the second Congress of People's Deputies. Aside from that, it seems to me that the congress should perhaps even today condemn the war, which was begun by decision of a narrow circle of the country's leaders, and which was waged illegally and was against the USSR Constitution, unsanctioned by the Supreme Soviet. In addition, I think that we should adopt a decision that the congress categorically prohibit the dispatching of contingents of USSR Armed Forces beyond the borders of the USSR without the matter being discussed in the USSR Supreme Soviet and a decision being carried by a two-thirds majority, with the vote being taken by name. [applause] [passage omitted: Deputy Kirilov wants regional referendums on ecological matters]

[Antanavichyus] I'm Antanavichyus, National-Territorial Constituency No 228. Deputies have proved themselves indefatigable. I still think that we should continue considering the problems of economic reform. We submitted for consideration a draft law on the economic independence of the republics, signed by 109 deputies. We have had no response on this matter. Instead, it is being proposed to us that consideration be given to general principles of the restructuring of the management of the economy and the social sphere, and so on. We have already been considering that from early January, and before. This is indeed only about the restructuring of management, and this cannot satisfy anyone. There is no question of any kind of independence here, and the main point is that there is no mention here of economic reform, the reform of economic relations. The relations stay as command-type relations, just as they were. So I propose mandatory inclusion on the agenda of a discussion of the draft law on economic independence, including the reform of economic relations.

Similarly, Academician Sakharov proposed on the 1st day that the congress should consider and adopt a decree 'All Power to the Soviets.' I believe that we cannot leave such a matter undiscussed. And also—and this is in line with a previous speaker—Deputy Rasputin submitted the issue of looking into having a referendum on nuclear power stations. I think this issue also needs to be included. Thank you.

[Yanayev] On the rule of procedure!

[Gorbachev] Go ahead, please. [to someone else] Just a moment. We are giving the floor to Comrade Yanayev, who is going to speak on the rules of procedure—out of turn. As he sees that people keep lining up, there are 20 to 30 people more, I believe.

[Yanayev] Esteemed comrade delegates! I am Deputy Yanayev. Would comrades in the line excuse me for asking for the floor out of turn, on the rules of procedure.

Mikhail Sergeyevich, my first question is to you. Unless my memory fails me, and I hope that it does not, you said that we had up to 8 hours to discuss the matters under "any other business."

[Gorbachev] That is right.

[Yanayev] In that connection, my proposal would, perhaps, help the comrades to get oriented, for even now we already have such a mass of proposals to be discussed under "any other business" that the discussion of each of them would take about as long as the debate which we have had up to now. [passage omitted: Yanayev calls for realism on the part of the deputies]

[Gorbachev] Just a moment. Let us consider the proposal of Comrade Yanayev. [agitation] Just a moment. His proposal boils down to the following: to stop registration of items. Just a minute. To stop registration of items and to proceed to the examination of the proposals made by the comrades, whether they should be put on the agenda or not. Is the motion clear, comrades? I put the proposal—those in favor of adopting this proposal and embarking on the examination of the issue of inclusion of the items that have already been registered to the agenda, vote, please. Lower, please. Those against? Lower, please. Any abstentions? The registration closes, the issue has been resolved. Thank you. Thank you.

[Yanayev] Mikhail Sergeyevich, what I meant was not that it was necessary to put on the....

[Gorbachev, interrupting] Wait a minute, please. If you wish to speak on the items that have already been included, you will take the floor later. But now, we will get on with it. Otherwise, we will waste the rest of our time. [rings the bell] That is it, comrades, that is it.

Now, I would like us to discuss what we are going to leave—our time, indeed, is ticking away; it has been 55 minutes already—and I would like to discuss what we are going to leave for discussion.

So, the first item on the status of the deputy. Will we leave it for discussion?

[Voices in hall] Yes!

[Gorbachev] Very well. Item two, on drawing up the laws necessary to ensure that the congress works actively. What is meant is the one on the standing orders of the Congress of People's Deputies, the law on reimbursing the costs associated with the activities of a delegate to the congress, the law on the procedure of recalling a USSR people's deputy. Will we leave it? We will.

Item three is the issue of the appeal; that proposal was made shortly after our congress opened. Now, I would like to list your [other proposals], both from my memory and from my notes; the wording will not be, perhaps, exactly the same as given by their authors, but the gist will be clear.

The comrades moved: to examine the issue on confirming the editor of the IZVESTIYA daily and of the radio and TV head—that is one. To resolve the issue of Article 11, that is, to include also the decrees—that is two. On setting up a commission on Afghanistan. Well, on the services to the deputies, their offices, etc., that will be stipulated by the status and by everything it envisions, that is four. On amending the law on elections. On the events in Novocherkassk. On the decrees—I have spoken on this one already, to allot time for making statements. Now, to examine a draft of the decision about those who are poorly off, as the comrades suggest. They believe, comrades, that what has been proposed by the government is not sufficient.

Now it is being suggested to resolve the issue of referenda on ecological issues, even before the law on referenda is adopted. The eleventh one is on an economic reform, and I understand it is the initiative of the Baltic republics and Belorussia. Am I right, have I understood it correctly?

So, these are the issues. Let us have a look at what we are going to leave for discussion.

[Unidentified deputy, speaking from the floor] First three, the first three items!

[Gorbachev] Right, there are proposals made by the presidium—three of them. There are also issues put forward by the comrades here.

[Lukyanov] Estonian comrades. [noise in the hall throughout his intervention]

[Gorbachev] I would not rush things, comrades, and I would pay attention to this, after all. There are many substantive issues here.

[Unidentified deputy] These issues have been proposed for discussion!

[Gorbachev] But this is exactly what I—you have got my meaning—that is exactly what I mean. I believe that...I have now set them out in order. [laughter in hall] There are some questions, I will name them...I do not consider that we need to resolve the issue of the newspaper editor and of the radio and television chief at the congress. One is a member of the government and is in the committee, and the other will be higher than the government. The government and all of the others are approved by the Supreme Soviet, and this is even above the Supreme Soviet, the editor is higher than the Supreme Soviet. Here we have something which is such that we need to look into it again. [noise in hall] I do not think that it is necessary to do everything according to mood. As far as the formation of a commission on Afghanistan is concerned, we could—I will say it straight—I would make such a proposal, instruct the Supreme Soviet with resolving this issue. [noise from hall] And make the...and we will decide then what sort of hearing should be conducted. On changes in the election laws. I do not think that we need to open debates at the congress. In my opinion, this is altogether an illusion. We should instruct the Supreme Soviet to deal with this and prepare a draft law which would take everything into consideration. This is very serious, after all, comrades. Such issues are not resolved by making a noise and stamping one's feet. I am sure that we need to have an election law which is more perfect that the one we had during this election campaign.

[Unidentified voice] (?And they will resolve the republican ones themselves?)

[Gorbachev] And they will pass the republican ones themselves. Now I have already spoken about the decrees. I think to set aside time for declarations—that is already outside the possibility of this congress, I think. Yes, and the Novocherkassk events—I would also hand this issue over for examination by the Supreme Soviet. [noise from hall] With such explanations I would do this. On this group of issues, that is how things appear to be shaping. Additionally, Article 11 remains; I will leave it separate. I would hand over all of these issues, by our decision, enumerating them in succession, for examination by the Supreme Soviet, for the resolution of these issues: Where there should be a commission, where there should be preparation for a new draft election law, and so on. That is, on all of these issues...[shouting from the hall] Just like that. [voice can be faintly heard shouting a question] In a minute, in a minute. I—in my opinion, if you had listened attentively, if you had read our basic decision—it starts with that, that the Congress of People's Deputies takes power into its own hands. [shouting from the hall] Yes, open it, read it. [noise from the hall] That is our basic document. [voice asks an inaudible question from the floor] What? [question repeated, still inaudible] Just a minute, just a minute. Andrey Dmitreyevich.... [video shows Sakharov has stood up and is shouting inaudibly] [noise from the crowd] Yes, and in this way we will resolve the issue of what to leave under "miscellaneous business." That is, the first three questions—I would propose—which the presidium made. And a commission to be set up to resolve the issues connected with republican financial autonomy and economic independence, as included in the basic draft, adding Belorussia, but already forming a commission for this work. There are four issues to be included. [shouting from the hall] As far as—and also to include the issue of Article 11(1), resolving it now, and examining what sort of decision we will take; and handing over all of the remaining issues to the Supreme Soviet [noise from the hall] with appropriate comments and the instructions about which I spoke. [noise from the hall] Do you agree, comrades?

[Voices shouting from the floor] Yes.

[Gorbachev] I request that those in favor of such an approach vote. Please put your hands down. Who is against? Abstainers? Passed. And so, according to the agenda, comrades, on the status of the deputies, Comrade Krayko, if you please. As far as the time limit is concerned, this comes under remarks from the floor, so just one or two minutes, comrade.

[Krayko] Three minutes, please. So, comrades, it is proposed to introduce the following changes in the draft which we have here. Article 9, in which it is written about the secretary, to replace it with the following article: To fulfil his duties as a deputy, the USSR people's deputy may free himself from his basic work and rely on helpers who act as his agents and also on consultants and technical specialists. Their labor and also postal expenses and spending on duplicating documents and so forth will be paid for from the deputies' budget, the upper limit of which is prescribed by the USSR Supreme Soviet. That part of the deputies' budget not spent in the current year is to be returned to the state budget and cannot be spent on the personal needs of the deputy. A USSR people's deputy carrying out his work as deputy is entitled to transport provision. Local soviets are to make available permanent premises, fitted with communications facilities, where a deputy and his assistant can work. Now another important point that has repeatedly been raised at the congress here—the so-called party-state collision. Let me recall an incident from Lenin's experience. At the eighth Congress of Soviets, a preliminary Central Committee decision was being adopted on a particular issue, and the deputies asked Vladimir Ilich what would happen if they voted against it. Vladimir Ilich cited the party rules, and replied—and here he quoted from the party rules: On matters of its internal affairs and day-to-day work, the party faction [fraktsiya] is autonomous. I'll continue with Lenin's words: Thus, all members of the party faction have the right and obligation to vote according to conscience, and not on instructions from the Central Committee. In line with this, it is proposed to add a 14th point to the existing provisions, to read as follows: At the Congress of People's Deputies and in the Supreme Soviet, people's deputies are guided only by the law, the will of their electorate, and by their convictions, and are autonomous with regard to other state, political and public bodies.

Finally, the following wording is proposed for the first point, in line with what I have said: The USSR Supreme Soviet is to be charged with drawing up a new draft law on the status of the USSR people's deputies for consideration at the USSR Congress of People's Deputies in the fourth quarter of 1989. This law, along with what follows—and then all the points are listed—is to provide for the separation of the jurisdiction of deputies of soviets of different levels; the right for collective and individual investigation of the actions of state and public organizations and their representatives; modern information support, including the right to use printing and duplicating equipment; and criminal accountability of officials for giving deputies deliberately false information. The draft law is to be sent to USSR people's deputies in September 1989.

What I have set out is the result of the work of a large group of Moscow deputies. I ask for all of these points to be put to a vote. [applause]

So how much our proposal will be worth depends on what budget will be given to us. Two hundred rubles is too little for us. That is for sure.

[Gorbachev] Just a minute, just a munute. On the strength of the fact that this [proposal] is already of a well-considered nature, so to say, we will consider these questions. Let us...they are of a principled nature. I think that we are running ahead of ourselves here. How can the congress...[changes thought] If we proceed in this way along such a path, and in general make decision in this way, then I guarantee you that we will produce such decisions that no one at all will be able to report back on them. If we have discovered that we have [had] many serious shortcomings in the process of preparing and making decisions and carrying them out in the past, then approaching matters in this way, without due preparation, will not do, comrades. I think and am convinced that we must start from the following premise: We must prepare a good, well-founded law on the status of the deputy and table it at the congress. Moreover, I think that this law must be thoroughly prepared, so that the deputy is both put on the proper level and protected and provided for. I will speak frankly: There must be all these points. [applause] Now...now, I think, the question is being resolved in the draft: First, already today, and in addition to what there is in the provision on the status of deputy, since we have deputies who are in the Supreme Soviet and deputies who are not, to resolve these questions and to maintain, so to say, the lofty position [of the deputy], a series of matters are being added and are being consolidated. Incidentally, this is from the proposal made by Comrade Krayka and his comrade deputies. Incidentally, on the whole this is taken from there. They want only for the whole draft to be brought about now, but we cannot do this straight off, you understand. Although I must say, I do not want to reject this out of hand. But to give you now...or for us to take it upon ourselves to accept all this, I tell you, our people will say: Just look, that is how they are pulling the country apart. [laughter] One, two, three, finished, you understand, a lively bunch of people has appeared and that is it, finished. [applause] I am certain that it is necessary to resolve the question about material conditions without delay; the [the deputy] must be provided with transport without fail, he must have a permanent office for receiving people; he must have a secretary on a permanent basis; he must receive general information from any body—that is already sufficient for the time that it takes

for the law to be passed. [applause] Incidentally, transport, of course, transport but not an individual car, but transport is to be ensured and [the question of] expenditure on transport must be resolved. For that reason, comrades, there are two approaches, two approaches—let us do it this way. In my opinion all this is very important, and we do not need to look ridiculous in front of our people, you understand.

For that reason, I would put the issue this way: Let us use from these proposals everything that relates to the question, to the questions of an immediate solution, in order to ensure the working conditions of deputies. Let us use all the rest in the preparation of the draft law. Shall we do it like that, comrades? Well, Comrade Krayko has anticipated me, that is, he has made the proposal and we should either accept or reject his proposal. Those in favor of accepting now, in their full form, the proposals that he made, I ask you to raise your identity cards. Please lower them. Those against. Well, in sum, on the whole, the whole congress is against Comrade Krayko. But nevertheless, I assure you all the proposals will be used, because there is much that is valuable here. [to deputy on rostrum] You've got something to say on status, yes?

[Minzhurenko] I'm Deputy Minzhurenko, from Omsk. I have more modest proposals, and I think they could be adopted without delay. [passage omitted: anecdotal detail] I think we could now, without much trouble, confirm that since many of us go on trips, and we're busy doing other things, too, that we can leave our agents—lawyers, say—legally certified power of attorney, and they could carry on with our work on our behalf. I think it would not be very difficult to do.

[Gorbachev] All right. The proposal is clear. Your proposal is clear.

[Minzhurenko] Clear, is it?

[Gorbachev] Comrades, I don't know if this comrade is giving up his powers voluntarily [laughter from hall] or do we want to have three, four or seven deputies in one constituency? [more laughter] Comrades, these are special powers that we obtain from the people, via the election campaign, and we must not simplify things. It'd be no good. It is simply unacceptable. And I don't think we need a vote on this: We simply need to clarify the issue. It would simply be a scandal. No, no, no—let the agent help you, but we have only one people's deputy, and that's all there is to it! [applause] [passage omitted: Deputy Zubanov raises further points about deputies' affairs]

[Gorbachev] Comrades, I'd like to say something on an issue which, I think, we have already gone into. First, deputies who work in the Supreme Soviet, in the commissions and committees, have equal rights with members of the Supreme Soviet engaged in these commissions and committees. [sentence as heard] Moreover, those involved in permanent work in these commissions will be eligible for the same material provision as permanently working members of the Supreme Soviet. But all this has to be resolved, so to speak—and it will be. Now, deputies who consider it necessary, when certain questions of special interest to them are being discussed, to take part, will, as we have said, be provided with information about the sessions of commissions and so on, and they should send a telegram to the USSR Supreme Soviet Presidium. And on the basis, so to speak, of coordination with the presidium, they can set off. As for people who work, people who work in a factory—they will get everything—he will be reimbursed average earnings from the budget. That is written into the provisions on status. As far as transport is concerned, let us leave the wording in its present form, and I think that locally people will take care to sort out these matters, since this is in the congress wording. After these 3 or 4 months, I think the situation will be clarified—and then the law will enshrine provisions that will resolve all the matters and any difficulties that arise.

[Shapovalenko] I'm Shapovalenko, constituency No 243, Orenburg. [passage omitted: points about deputies' affairs] It was said that there would be no time for statements, but since I have a whole minute left, I'll make a statement. The first USSR Congress of People's Deputies is coming to an end. The debates at the congress were unprecedentedly open and exerted a strong influence on public awareness and on the entire domestic situation in the country. At the same time, the preparations for and conduct of the congress contained much that has left a feeling of dissatisfaction and alarm. We believe that the congress has failed to create a mechanism for eliciting, comparing, and bringing together different points of view. Many key problems concerning the affairs of the country were either not examined at all or discussed at high speed. Many valuable proposals went unnoticed, or were rejected without sufficient grounds.

The main source of the difficulties that the congress has come up against is, we believe, first the lack of preliminary preparation, and second the absence of due mutual understanding among deputies, and the impossibility of discussing and preparing...[Shapovalenko changes thought] and unwillingness to understand alternative points of view. We must learn lessons for the future from this.

Taking cognizance of the experience of the work of the Moscow Deputies' Club, which carried out substantial preparatory work prior to the congress, and also the experience of the agrarian deputies', Komsomol deputies', public education employees' and ecologists' groups, which managed to do a lot during the congress, we wish to establish close contacts and mutual understanding between deputies from different regions of the country.

Desiring to create favorable conditions for dialogue and accord based on compromise, we announce the establishment of an interregional group of people's deputies.

The chief purpose of the group is to start preparations for the next congress in the fall of 1989 and to draw up proposals and draft documents, above all in the following spheres. [bell rings] All right, I'm just finishing. This announcement has been signed by more than 150 deputies. Those interested can stay after the evening session, and we'll carry on the discussion. Thank you. [applause]

[Gorbachev] Comrades, on status, please—be precise and specific.

[Samarin] I'm Deputy Samarin, Orel constituency No 249....

[Gorbachev, interrupting] Comrades, just a moment. Because this deals with our internal matters, there is a proposal to thank the media and to get down to our own business. All right? Who is in favor of the proposal, please show? Please lower your hands. Who is against? Who abstained? The decision is adopted. We thank the comrades and guests. [applause]

Congress 9 Jun Closing Session
LD0906222689 Moscow Television Service in Russian 1545 GMT 9 Jun 89

[Unscheduled relay of the Congress of People's Deputies held in Kremlin Palace of Congresses—live]

[Text] [Lukyanov] The Supreme Soviet Presidium, after thoroughly studying the question of Article 111, considers it possible here and now to propose to the congress to abolish this article, and at the same time, if such an element should be required in the future, it will be examined during ratification—and evidently these are to be ratified by the congress—of the fundamentals of criminal legislation and of a law on state crimes. [applause]

[Gorbachev] But that is a legal point. We have to vote, comrades. Yes, go ahead.

[Ryabchenko] Deputy Ryabchenko from Kiev. All the same, I would like to add a minor detail to what Anatoliy Ivanovich has said. I believe that what he said was about the Supreme Soviet Presidium considering it possible to abolish the article. But I should like the words: At the insistence of the congress, to be included. [applause]

[Gorbachev] Yes, but I think that, as it happens, that has been stated. There is complete understanding and a unified stance here. Everyone in favor of the proposal that has been made—for adoption of the decision on this matter—please raise your mandate. Please lower them. Anyone against? Please count them.

Comrades, I would ask you to bear in mind that after the congress is closed there will be announcements. Life goes on.

[Teller] Esteemed deputies, there were seven against.

[Gorbachev] Abstentions?

[Teller] Six deputies abstained.

[Gorbachev] The issue is settled. The decision to abolish this article has been adopted. [applause] [passage omitted] Comrades, I should tell you—since the presidium and I cannot presume to decide this issue—that Deputy Andrey Dmitriyevich Sakharov has persistently been asking to be allowed to speak. [commotion in hall] Just a minute. We in the presidium have consulted on this. During the debates there was no such opportunity, particularly since Deputy Sakharov has already spoke several times, seven times, in fact. We had to take this into account. That was the joint opinion of the presidium. But I have to inform you that there has been this request from Deputy Sakharov. Moreover, he has asked for 15 minutes. [commotion in hall] One moment. Comrades, let's do it this way: Let's establish our position. Will we give him the floor? [mingled shouts of yes and no; as Gorbachev speaks Sakharov is shown making his way to and slowly mounting rostrum]

Andrey Dmitriyevich, one moment. This is the way I see it: Let us ask Andrey Dmitriyevich to put forward and set out his thoughts in 5 minutes. [commotion in hall; a bell is rung] Andrey Dmitriyevich, one moment. Take your seat for the time being, or just stand there. One moment, comrades. [unidentified woman is seen approaching Gorbachev in the presidium and remonstrating with him]

Don't do that. No. Don't do that, don't do that. You're not helping. Now isn't the time. Comrades!

There's another request here: that, for example, the Society of Theatrical Workers does not consider it right that despite persistent requests Comrade Lavrov of the Soviety of Theatrical Workers has not been allowed to speak once. [uproar in hall] That's the situation. [woman is seen striding toward Sakharov]

[Woman] Seven times, you've...and not once....

[Sakharov] Comrades, I have not spoken seven times. I had 5 minutes at the opening of the congress. The other times were mere rejoinders. Those weren't speeches. Speeches are when...[woman turns and leaves]

[Gorbachev, interrupting] All right, let's resolve the matter. Comrades, let's resolve the matter this way: I want to put forward a compromise suggestion. Anyone in favor of allowing Deputy Sakharov 5 minutes to make his speech, please raise your mandates. [many hands are raised; Lukyanov is seen reaching into his pocket]

There has to be a count. Who is against? A minority, clearly a minority. Please go ahead, Andrey Dmitriyevich. Five minutes. [ripple of applause]

[Sakharov] That's it then, comrades. One can't always manage this. I have not made a speech outlining my ideas. I should say that my position is, in fact, somewhat exceptional. I am aware of this, and am aware of my responsibility. And therefore I will speak as I had intended to speak.

Esteemed people's deputies, I am speaking to explain why I voted against the concluding document that was submitted, despite the fact that it contains an exceedingly large amount of very important ideas and is highly useful. Nevertheless, I believe that the document reflects the proceedings of the congress, and the congress failed to perform its main task: that of establishing power, a system of power which will ensure that other tasks are performed, the economic task, the social task, and the task of overcoming ecological madness.

The congress elected a chairman of the USSR Supreme Soviet on the very first day without a broad political discussion and without even a symbolic element of alternative candidacies. In my view, the congress made a serious mistake by considerably reducing its ability to influence the shaping of the country's policies, thus performing a disservice to the elected chairman as well. Under the existing Constitution the chairman of the USSR Supreme Soviet has absolute personal power that is virtually unlimited by anything. The concentration of such power in the hands of one man is highly dangerous, even if this person is the initiator of restructuring. I personally have the greatest respect for Mikhail Sergeyevich Gorbachev, but this is not a personal matter, it is a political one. One day it will be someone else.

The construction of the house of state has started with the roof, which is clearly not the best way of going about things. The same thing was repeated in the elections to the Supreme Soviet. As far as the majority of delegations were concerned, there was simply a process of appointment and then formal endorsement by the congress of people, many of whom are unprepared for legislative activity. The members of the Supreme Soviet are as a rule to leave their former work, according to the imprecise formula that was employed, and as a result of which more than 50 percent of the Supreme Soviet comprises wedding-reception generals [people invited to make up the numbers at a social gathering].

Such a Supreme Soviet, it can be feared, will merely be a screen loyal to the power of the chairman of the Supreme Soviet and the party and state apparatus. In the country, in the context of an impending economic catastrophe and tragic exacerbation of interethnic relations, powerful and dangerous processes are taking place, one of whose manifestations is a general crisis of confidence in the country's leadership on the part of the people. If we are to swim with the current, comforting ourselves with the hope for gradual changes for the better in the distant future, the growing tension could smash our society, with the most tragic consequences.

Comrade deputies, an enormous historical responsibility falls to your lot. Political decisions are needed, without which the strengthening of local soviet bodies and the resolution of economic, social, ecological, and ethnic problems are impossible. If the Congress of People's Deputies cannot take power into its hands here, there is not the smallest hope that the soviets can take it in the republics, oblasts, rayons, and villages.

[Gorbachev] One minute left!

[Sakharov] Without strong local soviets it will be impossible to have land reform or any effective agrarian policy at all that will differ from the senseless transfusions designed to resuscitate unprofitable collective farms [kolkhozes]. I'll drop the further arguments, and I'll cite the text of a decree on power, which I propose for adoption:

Decree on Power

Proceeding from the principles of power by the people, the Congress of People's Deputies declares:

First. Article 6 of the USSR Constitution is to be repealed.

Second. The adoption of USSR laws is the exclusive right of the Congress of People's Deputies of the USSR. [bell rings, deputies clap] On the territory of a union republic USSR laws assume juridical force following endorsement by the highest legislative body of the union republic.

Third. The USSR Supreme Soviet is the working body of the congress.

I'll skip a point to save time.

Fifth. The election and recall of the highest USSR officials, that is, chairman of the USSR Supreme Soviet, deputy chairman of the USSR Supreme Soviet, chairman of the USSR Council of Ministers, chairman and members of the Committee for Overseeing the Constitution, chairman of the USSR Supreme Court, USSR procurator-general, the USSR chief arbiter, chairman of the Central Bank, as well as chairman of the KGB of the USSR, chairman of the State Committee for Television and Radio Broadcasting, and chief editor of IZVESTIYA, are the exclusive right of the congress. The officials listed above are accountable to the congress and independent from decisions of the CPSU and its bodies.

Sixth. [bell rings, commotion in hall] Candidacies for the post of...[Sakharov changes thought] I'll miss out another point.

Here is the final, seventh point. The functions of the KGB should be restricted to the tasks of protecting the USSR's international security.

I request that a drafting commission be set up, and that this decree be examined at an extraordinary session of the congress.

I appeal to the citizens of the USSR with the request to support this decree individually and collectively, in the way they gave their support when there was an attempt to compromise me and deflect attentions from responsibility for the Afghan war.

I'll miss out some further arguments. I'll continue. [bell rings, commotion in hall] For a long time now there has been no danger of a military attack on the USSR. We have the biggest Army in the world. [clapping becomes louder] It is larger than the USSR...[corrects himself] er, the United States and China put together. I propose that a commission be set up to draft a decision on the reduction by about half of the period of Army service for privates and sergeants, with a corresponding reduction of all types of armaments, but with a substantially smaller reduction of the officer corps, with the long-term prospect of transferring to a professional army. Such a decision would be of vast international significance for the strengthening of confidence and disarmament, including the full prohibition of nuclear weapons....

[Gorbachev, interrupting] Andrey Dmitriyevich!

[Sakharov] ...and also of enormous economic and social significance.

[Gorbachev] Enough. Enough.

[Sakharov] My speech is of fundamental significance.

I will continue. [commotion in the hall; bell keeps ringing; clapping]

Now to ethnic problems. We have inherited from Stalinism a national constitutional structure that bears the stamp of imperial thinking and imperial policy of divide and rule. [clapping increases] The small union republics and the small ethnic formations that form part of the union republics on the principle of administrative subordination are the victims of this legacy. For decades they have been subjected to ethnic oppression. These problems have now dramatically erupted to the surface. [rising chorus of shouts] But to no lesser extent the large peoples have also been victims, and that includes the Russian people....

[Gorbachev, interrupting] The microphone, the microphone.

[Sakharov] ...who have had to shoulder the main burden of imperial ambitions and the consequences of adventurism and dogmatism in external and domestic policy. Urgent measures are required. I propose a discussion be held on the transfer to a federative, horizontal national-constitutional system. This system would provide for the granting of equal political, juridical, and economic rights to all existing national-territorial formations, irrespective of their size and present status, with the present borders being preserved. With time, a clarification of the borders will be possible and probably necessary....

[Gorbachev, interrupting] Finish now, Andrey Dmitriyevich. Come on! You've had two time periods, two time-periods.

[Sakharov] I'm finishing. I'm dropping all limitations [as heard]. I'm dropping a very great deal. [bell rings constantly]

[Gorbachev] That's enough. Your time's up. You've had two time periods. Please excuse me. That's it.

[Sakharov] Just a moment. At the moment the attention of the world is riveted on China. The resolution that we have adopted does not reflect the full tragedy and the full depth of the problem of the internationalist feelings of our people who sympathize with democratization in China.... [Sakharov is seen continuing to speak but his microphone is apparently not working]

[Gorbachev, ringing bell three times] That's it! That's it! That's it! Comrade Sakharov! Comrade Sakharov! Do you respect the congress?

[Sakharov] I respect the congress, but I also respect the people who are listening to me at the moment. I respect mankind, which...[Sakharov changes thought] I have a mandate that extends beyond the bounds of this congress.

[Gorbachev] Very well, very well. O.K. (?For glasnost.)

[Sakharov] I would ask Deputy Starovoytova to read the address adopted by the group of deputies. If she finds this physically difficult, then I will read it myself.

[Gorbachev, ringing the bell] Enough. Enough. Enough.

[Sakharov] This is extremely important. It is the...[words indistinct, drowned by ringing bell] and bloody repression of it. The last thing, we ought to demand the recall of the Soviet ambassador from China, where this bloody action is taking place.

[Gorbachev] Please end now. Please finish. Very well. Enough. Take your speech with you, please. Take it. Take it. [prolonged applause; many deputies stand] [passage omitted]

[Gorbachev] Please sit down! Please sit down! Switch on a microphone, the No 3 microphone. What do you want?

[Troitskiy] Troitskiy. I want to express a certain amount of surprise that for some reason the presidium is dividing us, equal people's deputies, into those who can speak seven or eight times. And why must we listen to Comrade Sakharov? Why must we hearken to him, so to speak? Why do we allow Comrade Sakharov to use the platform of this congress to appeal to the peoples of the Soviet Union? Is he not taking an awful lot upon himself? That is all I have to say. [applause]

[Gorbachev] Let us continue with the congress proceedings. Allow me to ask People's Deputy of the USSR Valentina Andreyevna [as heard] Kiseleva to read a draft...[Lukyanov whispers something] What? Valentina Andreyevna Kiseleva. Adamovna, is it? Must be a misprint!... A draft appeal, a draft message to the peoples of the world, as we agreed.

[Kiseleva] A message to the peoples....

[Gorbachev interrupts] Switch on the microphone!

[Kiseleva] A message from the USSR Congress of People's Deputies to the peoples of the world. We, USSR people's deputies, have convened for our first congress in order to lay the legal foundation for the all-round democratic renewal of our socialist society in an atmosphere of glasnost and openness. As plenipotentiary representatives of the many-million-strong Soviet people, we fully acknowledge the historical responsibility that falls to us. We are aware that the problems that our homeland faces today are enormous, and we proceed from the premise that there is no alternative to the radical restructuring of all the spheres of its life. We have chosen this path in a considered and firm manner, and we shall not depart from it.

At the center of our attention are people, with their joys and sorrows, cares and hopes. We are convinced that a socialist society does not and cannot have any other moral guideline than the interests of the people and the aspirations and rights of the free individual. Restructuring is the internal matter of the peoples of the Soviet Union. It has been engendered by the country's vital needs. But we do not separate ourselves from the world community and from the processes that define the shape of contemporary civilization, while taking the freedom of the individual, democracy, and social justice to be the fundamental values on which the life of our society should be built. We regard restructuring as a part of the increasing democratization of the whole world order, as the Soviet Union's contribution to tackling the global problems that have loomed over mankind. They are all closely interrelated and tied into a dangerous and tight knot. It can and must be untied, but the joint efforts of the world community in the name of its survival are needed for that.

Restructuring is fundamentally altering our attitude to the world about us. Today we are open to the world, we are prepared to cooperate with all to whom human life and dignity are the highest values, and we count on mutual understanding.

In today's rapidly changing world, one cannot live by the old rules and standards. One cannot count on strengthening one's security and achieving prosperity by disdaining the interests of others. It is pointless to turn international relations into an arena of ideological wars. It is criminal to allow the arms race to be a drain on the world economy and to disparage concern for the conservation of man's environment. Whatever barriers may divide us, we are all children of mother earth, and we have a single common destiny. Thus, we call for an end to be put to enmity and discord between peoples.

A peaceful new period in the history of mankind is possible, and this opportunity must be made reality. The congress solemnly assures the peoples of the planet that it is assuming responsibility for the strict observance by the Soviet state of the principles of peaceful coexistence with regard to all the states and peoples of the world.

Drawing on the new political thinking, the USSR Congress of People's Deputies has endorsed the principles by which our state should be guided in international affairs. They amount to the following: The security of our country needs to be ensured above all by political means as an integral part of universal and equal security in the process of the demilitarization, democratization, and humanization of international relations, with reliance being placed on the prestige and resources of the United Nations. Nuclear weapons must be eliminated as a result of talks geared to disarmament and the reduction of the defense potential of the state to the limit of reasonable sufficiency. The use of force and the threat of force to achieve any sort of political, economic, or other goals are inadmissible. In relations with other countries, respect for sovereignty, independence, and territorial integrity is immutable. Not confrontation, but dialogue and talks aimed at a balance of interests, should be the sole way of resolving international relations and settling conflicts.

The Soviet economy should organically plug into the world economy on a mutually advantageous and equal footing, and should play an active part in drawing up and observing the rules of the modern day international division of labor, scientific and technological exchange, and trade.

As the supreme organ of state power, our congress declares that the Soviet Union intends to rigidly adhere to these principles in its foreign policy. From now on and forever that is our foreign policy strategy. That is the open and honest line of the Soviet Union and of restructuring on the international scene. That is the choice of the Soviet people.

We issue an appeal to the peoples of the world and to world public opinion to do their utmost to develop the exchange of ideas, peoples, cultural and spiritual values, and contacts and dialogue at all levels and in all fields, and jointly to search for and find mutually acceptable compromises for the sake of maintaining peace on earth, and for the sake of the prosperity and progress of the whole of mankind. [applause]

[Gorbachev] That can be discussed. How do you view this, comrades? If anyone having heard that can think of anything that requires clarification or improvement, please come up to the presidium so that it might be implemented. In principle, I could put it to the vote—to adopt the draft message as read. Anyone in favor of doing this, please raise your documents. Please lower them. Against? Abstentions? Two. It is adopted. [applause]

Dear comrades! The congress is ending the 13 days of its work. Once again I want to thank you, the people's deputies of the USSR, for the enormous contribution which you have made to the preparation and holding of the congress. We all of us agree with what—and here I reject the negative opinions of Deputy Sakharov aimed at belittling the congress, at belittling its role and its landmark significance in the destiny of our country. [applause]

Nevertheless, I welcome the open and direct dicsussion which has taken place here, perhaps for the first time in the whole of our history, of all problems which disturb both our own people, our peoples, and the peoples of the world. [applause]

No doubt with the first congress—as we predicted—we have not been able to exhaust all problems, and many of them therefore remain outside the congress. But then we are only just beginning our work. Following the congress, and on the basis of its instructions and the decisions that have been taken, the USSR Supreme Soviet is beginning work as a permanent organ, a permanent legislative body, with its committees and an enormous number of deputies. This is opening up great opportunities for the ideas that have been expressed here and the proposals that have been made here to receive the most deep and careful consideration and embodiment, either in acts of legislation or in the activity of the executive authority, or for discussion of them to be continued in subsequent stages of activity, both of the Congress of Soviets and the Supreme Soviet and the bodies which they set up.

I am extremely satisfied with the fact that, thanks to openness and pluralism of opinions, we have felt for the first time the whole range of problems which is characteristic of the current state of our society, and we realize perhaps for the first time at this congress the enormity, the importance, and the large-scale nature of the tasks which the new bodies of Soviet power are faced with, the bodies that have now been created as far as the upper echelon is concerned and which are going to be created under the new approaches, under conditions of openness, democracy, and glasnost, in the next stage of the political reform.

We are armed with the best knowledge, and this gives us hope and confidence in working out correct solutions and in functioning better in order that restructuring might move forward resolutely in all areas, and primarily in those sectors that are linked with—whose activity is linked with—the satisfaction of the vital needs and requirements of our peoples. We are confident that all the main ideas that have been expressed here—including those put forward during the discussions—will find their resolution in the further acivity of the bodies of Soviet power.

Please allow me to wish you great successes, comrade deputies. You have before you an enormous amount of work, and we are confident that our congress will take upon its shoulders concern to ensure that the cause which we have started in renewing our society in the interests of the people, upon the principles of democracy and glasnost, and in the interests of making the life of our people more human—we are confident that this congress, this corps of deputies, will be up to it. [applause] I wish you great successes! The agenda is exhausted! [applause continuing with Gorbachev speaking over it] The first Congress of People's Deputies is declared closed. [there follows the music of the Soviet national anthem, after which Gorbachev continues]

Dear comrades, as I mentioned before, a few organizational matters.... [relay ends at this point]

10 Jun USSR Supreme Soviet Proceedings Reported

Soviet of the Union Session
LD1106194189 Moscow Television Service in Russian 0600 GMT 10 Jun 89

[Relay of the Soviet of the Union session held in the Kremlin Palace of Congresses—live]

[Excerpts] [passage omitted] [Yevgeniy Primakov, session chairman] The next candidate is Nodar Mikhaylovich Mgaloblishvili, a Georgian born in 1927. He has a higher education and graduated from the Moscow Institute of Architecture in 1952; member of the CPSU since 1955; people's deputy of the USSR and deputy of the Supreme Soviet of the Georgian Soviet Socialist Republic. He has been a chief architect in Tbilisi and administrator at the Tbilisi Academy of Arts. Now Nodar Mikhaylovich is chairman of the board of the Union of Architects of the Georgian Soviet Socialist Republic and secretary of the board of the Union of Architects of the USSR. [passage omitted]

[Mgaloblishvili] Perhaps I could say a few words to deal in advance with some questions, because it is no doubt important for the deputies to know the stance held by the people they are going to elect. I have jotted down a few words here; perhaps it will simply reduce the time taken by our elections. I must say that Eduard Amvrosyevich Shevardnadze said in one of his talks that it was the greatest surprise to him when he was appointed foreign minister. Please do not take this comparison to mean a lack of modesty on my part, but for me this was the same kind of absolutely unexpected proposal. I am an architect, chairman of the Union of Architects of Georgia, as you have heard. I graduated from the Moscow Institute of Architecture. I worked in Moscow for 13 years. I had an apartment here and a job. My wife is a Russian. She is an architect from Moscow, from the Ulitsa Vorovskogo. [passage omitted]

Academician Yegveniy Maksimovich Primakov precisely defined the tasks facing the Soviet of the Union at the last session. I believe that our main task is to create a state with real laws, establishment of the rule of law. First, it seems to me that it is the task of the deputy chairman of a chamber of the Supreme Soviet to listen carefully to all sides, both the right and the left, to draw together all the material received from the people and to resolve all issues together with the Soviet—and only with the Soviet and no one other than the Soviet.

Second, it seems to me that many questions in the Supreme Soviet will fall away of their own accord when there is complete economic independence in all republics, and real sovereignty. Every republican supreme soviet and every people will themselves decide 80 percent and more of all the issues that now arise here. Then only the cardinal inter-republican issues, and not every trifling manner that is quite capable of being resolved on the spot, will reach the USSR Supreme Soviet. Third, it seems to me that there is no need to kill off the all-union ministries; they will die on their own, or at any rate they will become much smaller when every republic, including the Russian Soviet Federated Socialist Republic, has economic sovereignty and decides all its own issues. For this is indeed what is being proposed by the Baltic republics. We will all remain in a united community. And if misfortune strikes anywhere, then we will be able to help together, as we helped Armenia during the terrible earthquake. Let us be patient and look at the results of the experiment in Estonia and the Baltic republics at the end of 1990. If it is necessary, we will all help them, for we provide aid to the countries of Latin America. It might be that Estonia and Lithuania will themselves be able to help us like Finland, for examaple. That would be a fine example for all the republics. I think, therefore, that our task is to listen to each other very carefully, all together, without shouts and noise. We must take—without haste, but without dragging things out—the decisions that are the very best and most useful for the people.

A few words about the USSR Congress of People's Deputies: I am absolutely convinced that this congress is a turning point in the history of our country. I would like to believe—and I do believe—that our people, a patient and long-suffering people, will begin to live better. I rejoice overall in the flowering of democracy at the congress. Out of many thoughts I would now like to express just three observations which lie on the surface, as you might say. First: It bothers me very much when a carefully thought out and well-prepared proposal submitted by our colleagues from the Baltic republics in a refined and utterly parliamentary form is received by a certain part of our congress with ill-becoming howling, hissing, and direct unparliamentary insults. [applause]

Second: I feel ashamed when loutish people—I cannot use any other word—insult the two most outstanding people in our country, on the whole planet, indeed: Gorbachev and Sakharov. If the attacks on Mikhail Sergeyevich can be explained by the lack of education and culture on the part of those speakers, the heart-rending shouts and hysterical outbursts against the words of Andrey Dmitriyevich—which may well indeed be questionable—cannot be explained. [applause]

Third: It was simply dreadful for me when that same section of deputies in the hall provided what was virtually an ovation following the speech by the commander of the punitive expedition in Tbilisi on 9 April, who had reported that there were anti-Russian slogans there and that that was why women and girls had been savagely killed. I can state with complete responsibility that there is no anti-Russian feeling in Georgia. Not one—I repeat—not one single Russian has suffered on account of the fact that he is Russian. But how immoral it is to applaud before the eyes of the whole world a statement that peaceful women have been killed on account of nonexistent anti-Russian feeling. That was dreadful. No, that was not the reaction that we expected from some of our deputies, colleagues, and friends. But I am an optimist. And I repeat: Our profoundly democratic congress is an enormous victory for restructuring. I am confident that in time we will also have economic successes and that the people will begin to live better. We must all of us try hard to work effectively. Thank you for your attention. [passage omitted]

[Primakov] Thank you. Please go ahead, Roy Aleksandrovich.

[Medvedev] I support the candidate nominated for the job of second deputy chairman of the Soviet of the Union but I want nevertheless to make one observation about what he said on the subject of Tbilisi. I myself have been elected to a commission dealing with a no less delicate and difficult matter: the case linked with Gdlyan and Ivanov. As I am going to announce at the joint session that I have been elected chairman, [I will tell you that] the first thing we did was to agree that until the commission finishes we will not comment [applause]; we will not comment. [shouts of "quite right!"] We will not give any interviews and we will call on the press not to publish material on the subject. Perhaps this is not binding on people who live in Tbilisi, but for delegates who have elected a commission on Tbilisi which has not yet delivered its decisions and has not drawn up its findings I do not think it is ethical for delegates to express themselves in categorical terms on this matter. [applause]

[Primakov] Taking advantage of this proposal, I would like to ask all comrade deputies not to exchange opinions on this problem now while the commission is at work.

[First unidentified speaker] I accept that observation and we therefore are not commenting.

[Primakov] Good. About this?

[First unidentified speaker] Permit me, I....

[Primakov] Please go ahead. You have a question?

[Kulikov, not further identified] Kulikov. No, it is not a question. I want to express my opinion....

[Primakov] We will be expressing it in a minute...

[Kulikov] Then I will ask a question: The much respected comrade whom we wanted in good conscience to put forward as deputy saw himself what happened in Tbilisi during those very difficult days....

[Primakov] Let us....

[Second unidentified speaker] We must return to this question once again....

[Primakov] Comrades, I also consider...comrades, let us....

[Kulikov] Then I want to say why did you, in getting this important post, or in putting yourself forward for this post, why do you in advance call this some kind of special expedition or campaign and so on, thereby putting yourself in an awkward situation and providing grounds for inciting passions? I am going to vote against you.

[Second unidentified speaker] Permit me....

[Primakov] Your proposal, please.

[Second unidentified speaker] Once again, I ask everyone...[changes thought] deputies, we must not deal with the Tbilisi question until [words indistinct]. [passage omitted]

[Primakov] Thank you. Please go ahead now, Sergey Fedorovich.

[Akhromeyev] I want to say this about the candidate's address. It is right and it is a good thing that he expressed his position frankly. This reflects well on him because before elections people can have short-term considerations in mind. He puts these short-term considerations to one side and he set out his position. That reflects well on the comrade. On the other hand—and moreover I am going to vote for him insofar as you are proposing him, Yevgeniy Maksimovich, and you are the chairman—I am going to vote for him, but I would like to say this: We have been elected deputies, comrades, and throughout the whole congress, although we have had a lot of shortcomings and imperfections in our work, the line has taken shape. We must understand each other; we must understand each other's position. We have to bear in mind, say, that if someone is expressing the opinion of the majority at any particular moment, then we have to listen carefully to the opinion of the minority and think about that opinion and form a united opinion which is subsequently worked up into a united decision.

And so the comrade spoke and expressed his stance from very extreme standpoints; I would say that he did so aggressively. When he talks about his own position, his own position personally, that is the case, but he should also have the wisdom to accept that his own position is neither the only one nor the most correct one. In some way he also must take into account the positions of others. And from that point of view, as deputy chairman, he must be more patient with regard to the opinions of other deputies; he must be more patient altogether regarding opinion which is being shaped. I would like him to take this into consideration.

[Primakov] Thank you, Sergey Fedorovich. [passage omitted]

[Third unidentified speaker] At the congress, one of the people's deputies said that the space budget should be cut and...handed over for social needs. What is your view?

[Vladimir Kurtashin] This is a very difficult issue. In my view...I, as the general director of the Kriogenmash scientific production association, have a vested interest in space development, since our association makes a very major contribution to that industry. The second issue is that we do not make use of space technology. If the United States has obtained $3 profit for every dollar, we are only today starting to open up the package of advanced technologies for the national economy. I think the industry has to be...[Kurtashin changes thought] We have fallen behind a little in this industry. Good prospects are emerging for the sale of our space technologies abroad—as the comrades here know—for large sums of money. If we can put into effect everything that has been achieved in this area, we will earn large profits and have priority in the development of the industry.

Soviet of Nationalities Session
LD1106224889 Moscow Television Service in Russian 0927 GMT 12 Jun 89

[Relay of the USSR Supreme Soviet Soviet of Nationalities session held in the Kremlin Palace of Congresses—live]

[Excerpts] [passage omitted: candidates for deputy chairman named]

[Genrikh Igityan] The situation in the country today is very grave. We are all aware of that. Moreover, I cannot fail to say, Rafik Nishanovich—because my heart has been torn asunder these past few days—I cannot fail to reproach you, because in Uzbekistan there is a situation of the greatest complexity, and we know that something monstrous is going on there, because correspondents whom we have met have told us about it, and all the while you sit there calmly as Central Committee secretary of the Communist Party of Uzbekistan, and you say: "Keep calm, comrades. It will be all right. We will sort it all out. We will see to it all. I know this: I have an ideal of a leader of a nation. So far as I am concerned, one such man was (Masherov) in Belorussia, who, with squads of partisans, helped liberate his land of fascism. A most extreme situation. Another example: Nikolay Ivanovich Ryzhkov, who worked around the clock during an emergency. I simply cannot understand if we have assembled today to introduce any serious changes to the essence of the country and to the state it is in. Because we are all concerned.

[Nishanov] What is your proposal?

[Igityan] My proposal is that either we all work in earnest, or else have the dignity and honor to say, "Comrades, we are disillusioned. Apparently this is not what we expected and not what the country's press had prepared us for—all the mass media. Let anyone with any conscience creep quietly home." This is my proposal: that you should fly immediately to Uzbekistan.

[Nishanov] Sit down.

[Igityan] Anatoliy Ivanovich can conduct the session of the Soviet of Nationalities.

[Nishanov] Sit down, please.

[Igityan] Thank you. [applause]

[Nishanov] It is by your will that I am here. You elected me, and that is why I am here. It is my duty to conduct this session, in order to form our top bodies, to elect the deputy chairman, and to form our commissions. Then again, I am fulfilling my duty: For your information, I went there for 2 days—that was as long as it was feasible to stay. I visited all the places and had meetings with all sides—the Meskhetian Turks and the Uzbeks. Those steps that had to be taken in the republic, I took in the republic, while those things I had to do here, I did. I have had numerous meetings here with Meskhetian Turks, including this morning. Together with the union bodies we are tackling many issues. Therefore I would refute that part of your complaint. As for whether we are engaged in serious work or not, I would ask you yourself to be more serious. We are discussing serious business. [passage omitted: Boris Yeltsin nominated]

[Nishanov] Comrades, first I should explain that when we were holding the Council of Representatives and the Council of Elders, Boris Nikolayevich (?raised a point) and Mikhail Sergeyevich, who was chairing our sessions, spoke of the agreement that existed between them on the question of the recommendation to the post of chairman of a committee. You know the committee. Therefore I did not bother noting that down here, because we were as one in the Council of Representatives. Yes, Boris Nikolayevich, please explain this yourself.

[Yeltsin] In the first place, regarding that conversation: It was very provisional, and I gave no agreement since it is the deputies of the chamber or else of the Supreme Soviet as a whole who decide. [passage omitted: Yeltsin withdraws in favor of Gayer; Bisher is nominated and elected; Tarazevich nominated chairman of commission on inter-ethnic relations]

[Nishanov] Your question, please?

[Unidentified deputy] My question is, I would like to draw attention to one point. Now that we have two very good speakers, we have started talking about the essence of the question. I have the very greatest doubts about the candidate proposed in connection with the fact that we know the attitude of a certain part, at least, of the Belorussian leadership to the democratic processes taking place in that republic. This makes me extremely wary. [passage omitted: importance of the post]

I wish to make a specific proposal: to elect Klara Semenovna Khalik chairman of the Commission on Nationalities Policy and Inter-Ethnic Relations.

[Nishanov] So. Are there any questions....

[Tarazevich] Well, I understand that the comrade deputy who has just spoken had in mind some specific complaints against my candidacy, personally, and not against the republic as a whole or the Belorussian people. That being so, I would ask the comrade to say precisely what complaints he has about my candidacy, against me personally.

[Deputy] It wasn't a question, it was a new candidate being put forward. I am not expecting (?any reply), for heaven's sake! Please do not reply.

[Tarazevich] Well, you started by saying that. [passage omitted]

[Nishanov] Your question?

[Second unidentified deputy] Esteemed Deputy Tarazevich! You, as has already been said, as a member of the USSR Supreme Soviet Presidium, it seems to me, bear some responsibility for the decrees which have been criticized of late and which the congress has confirmed are unconstitutional to some extent. They violate the constitutional rights of the individual, and moreover they were adopted with the crudest infringement of Article 119 of the Constitution. What responsibility did you bear for adoption of the anti-constitutional acts, and how do you feel about this now, since the Congress has to some extent confirmed the dubiousness, to put it mildly, of these decrees?

[Tarazevich] Well, in asking this question—I have in mind the part concerning responsibility—you know the answer full well. So I do not think there was any need to ask this question. As far as my attitude toward these decrees is concerned, I agree with the decision of the congress, and I voted for this decision. [passage omitted: Eduardas Yono Vilkas is nominated chairman of social-economic development commission]

[Nishanov] Deputy Ishanov, please.

[Khekim Ishanov] Deputy from National-Territorial Constituency No 439, town of Nebit-Dag in the Turkmen SSR. Esteemed colleagues, my question is, that every region has its own issues. The supreme issue for the republics of Central Asia, especially Turkmenia, Uzbekistan and Tajikistan, is that excess manpower has emerged or, to be more precise, unemployment has appeared. For example, in the Republic of Turkmenia there are today 6,000 to 7,000 unemployed for every 100,000 population. Do you see a solution to this problem?

[Vilkas] Well, to begin with, proposals must come from the republics themselves. I do not think the commission should busy itself with, so to speak, examining complaints. It should organize economic cooperation and assistance—internationalist assistance, if one can put it like that—for social issues. But the main thing, I feel, is that the commission should organize mutually beneficial economic cooperation between republics. Naturally, the question of, so to speak, setting more or less equal starting conditions for all republics will, in the initial stage, also be very topical. In particular, the issue of unemployment falls under such topics. [passage omitted]

[Nishanov] So, next please, Deputy Geda, your question.

[Sigita Geda] Like Deputy Shtoyk, I have a very brief question for Comrade Vilkas. I would like to know his point of view on the introduction of special monetary units when republican financial autonomy is brought in. What is your point of view?

[Vilkas] All right. If I were to say that they must be introduced and not explain why, that would be quite a poor answer. I will reply thus, that this option of introducing republican monetary systems is one of the most realistic options for getting out of the union's financial difficulties. [passage mitted]

Ryzkhov Addresses Joint Chambers

LD1006212189 Moscow Television Service in Russian 1207 GMT 10 Jun 89

[Speech by Nikolay Ryzhkov, USSR Council of Ministers chairman, at a joint session of both houses of the USSR Supreme Soviet in the Kremlin; Ryzkhov is introduced by Anatoliy Lukyanov, chairman of the USSR Supreme Soviet session—live]

[Text] [Lukyanov] Comrade deputies: I declare open the joint session of the Soviet of the Union and the Soviet of Nationalities of the USSR Supreme Soviet. I would like to inform you that at the two preceding sessions of the chambers of the USSR Supreme Soviet, the majority of questions regarding the setting up of these chambers' commissions was discussed, and it was agreed that the chambers should be guided by the regulations of the USSR Supreme Soviet since they do not contradict the Constitution of the USSR in its new wording. At today's session, it is proposed that two questions should be examined. The first question deals with the proposals of the USSR Council of Ministers chairman regarding the composition of the government. As you recall, the instructions to submit these proposals were given by the USSR Supreme Soviet to Nikolay Ivanovich Ryzhkov, who was appointed Council of Ministers chairman and confirmed in that appointment by the Congress of People's Deputies. The second question is the election of the committees of the USSR Supreme Soviet. It there any objection to an agenda like that? Shall we vote on it? No. It is adopted. The floor is then given to Comrade Ryzhkov, Nikolay Ivanovich.

[Ryzhkov] Esteemed members of the USSR Supreme Soviet: The Congress of People's Deputies has put forward tasks that are exceptionally significant. Guided by the will of the people and relying on their creative potential, we are obliged to do everything necessary in order to bring the country out of a complex economic situation, fundamentally transform the political system of the state, and create the conditions for a steady rise in the welfare of Soviet man and for the spiritual enrichment of the individual—all in a short period of time. These are the central tasks which predetermine the principled demands which must be made the basis for forming the new government. What is their essence?

First of all, it is our duty to proceed, in all our actions, from the main aim—the satisfaction of the needs and requirements of Soviet man. Second, to ensure development of the economy, in its new socially oriented capacity. Third, to manage not by administrative-command methods, but by economic ones. Fourth, to strictly observe the principles of economic democracy on the basis of pluralism and equality of forms of ownership. And fifth, to fully reveal the creative potential of socialist federalism. Only with these approaches is it possible to achieve radical changes in production relations, a diversity of forms of economic management and genuine equality of these forms, the economic emancipation of the basic sector of production, and the successful implementation of a new regional policy.

On the other hand, all this means that the object of government is itself changing radically. This gives rise to the need to lend genuinely democratic content to centralist principles in government.

There is a legitimate question: What organizational structure of state government must objectively correspond to all these conditions? Before answering this question it is necessary to fully grasp the essence of the structure of national economic management which has formed. All in all, it is typified by a clearly expressed—I would even say hypertrophied—branch orientation, by an overweight multitier system, by an unwieldy list of narrowly profiled ministries and departments, and by the lack of correspondence to the economic conditions of such very important management functions as finance, pricing policy, banking operations, and so on.

All this was created over decades, on the basis of theoretical dogmas and the desire to accomplish isolated separate tasks by setting up more and more new links of management. This was done in order to regulate absolutely everything from the center. The de facto unlimited command permeated the entire management hierarchy, from the top tiers right down to the ordinary worker.

The system of economic leadership which existed directly reflected the economic principles on which the state's relations with the basic production sector and with the regions were constructed. In the course of implementing economic reform, we began restructuring the management system. We are consistently cleansing it of all that is ineffective and that contradicts the free development of production forces.

The need for more radical changes in the structure, functions, style, and methods of operation of the government and the bodies of state administration has ripened. There was a major and principled discussion of this at the congress, too, and the people's deputies voiced quite a number of severe, critical assessments and constructive proposals about the role and place of the ministries, departments, and state committees in the new model of the socialist management system.

Summing up everything that has been said, we may conclude that we now have to create a structure that will make it impossible for any of the subdivisions of the upper administrative stratum to interfere in the operational activities of the main production link. The center should retain only those functions inherent to it and the opportunity of concentrating fully on strategic tasks at the national economic, inter-industry, and inter-regional levels, without being distracted by day-to-day business. We have begun to move strongly in this direction; in particular, we have somewhat adjusted the administration system; we have reduced the number of links, and we have decisively gone in for the creation of new production, scientific-production, and other kinds of financially autonomous associations which have helped to intensify the integration of science and production. During that work itself, economic conditions have begun to emerge which have objectively led to the abolition of a number of union and union-republic ministries and committees.

What has been achieved so far? First of all, practical experience—albeit not very much—has been accumulated in combating the command-administrative system of management, and objective preconditions have been created for taking more practical steps in the shaping of a qualitatively new national economic management structure. Thanks to all this, we can now get down in earnest to effecting radical changes in the makeup and functions of state bodies. There are still, however, various points of view regarding the role and place of state bodies in the management of the economy. Some people are insisting on the immediate and complete abolition of industry ministries on the grounds that they have exhausted their purpose and function as the present economic reform continues to develop. Others take a different view, that we cannot get by without the ministries in their present composition, since control over the economy would otherwise be lost and it would become impossible to manage the national economy on a nationwide scale.

What can we say here? These are issues of extraordinary significance for our economy, both now and in the future. They cannot simply be tackled and resolved at once. There has to be sensible rationality and consideration for the realities of our life, for the extent to which economic methods are being mastered in practice and their impact on economic processes. The evolution of the new production relations is proceeding with difficulty, of course.

But this is precisely the reason why it is extremely important to have a well-considered assessment and clear forecast of what could be the result either of premature reorganizations or of dragging them out. In a word, comrades, rushing forward and running ahead of events, just like marking time on the spot, are equally dangerous. The experience that has been built up over the years of restructuring, the reform of the country's economic and political system, and the work on further improving the management of the economy which has unfolded in all areas of the national economy have had a direct influence on the formation of the proposals on the composition of the USSR Council of Ministers. Upcoming major changes in regional policy, whereby a considerable part of the economy located in the republics, krays, and oblasts is transferred directly into the management of the republican and local bodies, have been placed at the foundation of the new management system; the system of two-fold subordinations and responsibility in the form of the union-republican ministries and departments is thereby abolished, and the extent to which there exists a number of stages in management is being reduced—hence the independence and the responsibility of the localities for satisfying the vital requirements of the national economy and the population is being raised.

Deep changes in the activity of the bodies belonging to the upper echelon are becoming one of the urgent tasks in the further improvement of management. First and foremost, this concerns the central economic departments. Their importance and responsibility in accomplishing the basic tasks of the economy and in speeding up the economic reform which is being implemented is extraordinarily great. This brings with it an obligation to assess very critically the work of the departments in question, since many shortcomings in the economic reform which is being carried out, and the slow development of the process of the improvement of the economy, are directly linked with their activity. The State Planning Committee, the Finance Ministry, the State Committee on Prices, the State Committee for Statistics, and other departments were subjected to the sharpest criticism at the congress. It was correct criticism and fair, and the newly elected government will draw the appropriate conclusions from it. We also have to take into consideration the fact that the role and the importance of the central bodies in regulating economic processes will grow as the qualitative restructuring of industrial management and the strengthening of economic independence of enterprises and regions proceeds.

The composition of the state-administrative bodies that is suggested to you was drawn up bearing in mind the great diversity of the functions performed by the government, which could be notionally reduced to two fundamental directions. The first comprises the functions that are inseparably inherent in the government as the supreme executive-management organ of state power. They are well known. I shall not describe them in detail; I shall just list them briefly. First and foremost, they are the functions connected with the overall economic regulation of the development of society. The government performs them through the central economic bodies. The area of these obligations also includes directing the diverse social sphere, guaranteeing the defense of the sovereign rights and interests of the socialist state and its citizens, as well as monitoring the whole complex of nature-conservation measures both in individual regions and in the country as a whole.

In these spheres, it is intended to place government activity and the tasks of state administration on 25 committees and ministries. They embrace the whole varied package of problems of state administration.

Another fundamentally important area of the work of the government is the implementation of functions to develop the material and technical base of the production sphere. Here, as a result of the unfolding of the economic reform and the increasing of the economic independence of enterprises and territories, and also in connection with the forthcoming changes in the activities of ministries and departments, the most substantial transformations of the administrative system and reduction of the number of union bodies are planned. Thus, it is planned to reduce the overall number of ministries dealing with the basic branches of industry, construction, transport, and the agro-industrial and defense complexes from 50 to 32, [Moscow PRAVDA in Russian on 11 June 1989, in its Second Edition, publishes on pages 1 and 4 a version of this address entitled "Report by N.I. Ryzhkov," which gives the preceding figures as 52 and 32, instead of 50 and 32] that is, by almost 40 percent in comparison with those functioning currently. For instance, machine-building will be left with 4 ministries, instead of the 11 ministries that existed at the start of the current 5-year plan. In the metallurgical complex, the ministries of ferrous metallurgy and nonferrous metallurgy will be reconstituted into a single USSR ministry of metallurgy. In the chemical and timber complex, only three out of five ministries will be left. In the fuel and energy complex, three ministries are being abolished, and two in the defense complex. In the construction complex, where previously there were seven all-union ministries, only two are left. Moreover, the construction ministries functioning on the territory of the Russian Soviet Federated Socialist Republic [RSFSR] are being placed under the jurisdiction of the RSFSR, as was done earlier for other union republics. Thus, a proposal is being made to set the number of ministries and committees in the USSR Council of Ministers at 57, with 25 bodies of administration currently functioning being abolished.

The above-stated number of ministries and departments, given the changes in their role and functions at the present stage of the development of the economy, is the most acceptable to our way of thinking. It is clear that as the economic reform goes deeper, the conditions will also be created for the further integration of the functions of the corresponding state management bodies as well.

The question may arise of whether we are not opting for the creation of superministries, which will strengthen even further their monopoly position and their departmental diktat. I wish to stress once again that we are talking of ministries of a new type that are qualitatively different from the old ones. They will be stripped of many economic management functions, apart from one—the active fostering of the creation of an economic environment that will allow the potential of the main production link to be fully opened up. This is perhaps their main task. They are to lay the main stress in their work on the development of the priority areas of scientific and technological progress, on defining the long-term development of the industry, and on pursuing an investment policy that is in the spirit of the demands of the social reorientation of the national economy. The task of developing and deepening the radical reform, and the need for a day-by-day, in-depth, and all-around

substantiation of successive steps in economic transformations pressingly dictate the desirability of setting up a state commission of the USSR Council of Ministers on economic reform as a permanent body of government.

Proposals are also being made about the formation of a state commission of the USSR Council of Ministers on extraordinary situations. The need for it has been dictated by life itself. The task of the commission will consist in ensuring that we are ready to act in emergency situations; in coordinating and supervising the work of ministries and departments in the work of organizing, in an ordered way, emergency relief work and search-and-rescue work; in preventing such situations or eliminating their consequences; and in providing vital services to the population.

Comrades, the USSR Council of Ministers is being substantially renewed. I want to inform you that, of the government which was formed in 1984 and numbered 100 people—without counting the chairmen of the union republics' councils of ministers, who are included in the composition of the government because of their position—only 10 people remain in the composition which is being proposed today. More than half of the members of the currently working composition of the Council of Ministers are being relieved of their duties, mostly in connection with their retirement on pension. In effect, one in three members of the government is being proposed for appointment for the first time. It is planned to conduct substantial changes in the composition of the Council of Ministers Presidium. Half of it is being renewed.

In order to decide current issues urgently, the office of first deputy chairman of the government for general matters is being introduced. It is proposed to appoint Comrade Lev Alekseyevich Voronin to this post, he being a major organizer and an experienced leader who has worked in many important areas of the system of administration of the state. It is proposed that Comrade Yuriy Dmitriyevich Maslyukov be confirmed as first deputy chairman of the USSR Council of Ministers and chairman of the USSR Gosplan [state planning committee], he having had in the past good experience in industry and having been one of the leaders of Gosplan, and who, in the post of deputy chairman of the USSR Council of Ministers, was responsible for the work of an important national economic complex.

Taking into consideration the particular significance and the urgent nature of resolving matters pertaining to the development of the agro-industrial complex, it is proposed that the post of first deputy chairman of the Council of Ministers and chairman of the State Commission of the USSR Council of Ministers on Foodstuffs and Procurements be created. It is proposed that Comrade Vladimir Ilyich Kalashnikov be appointed to that office, he having worked over a lengthy period in various posts in agriculture. At the current time he is first secretary of the Volgograd Oblast party committee. It is proposed that for the first time famous Soviet scientists be appointed deputy chairmen of the government—Comrade Academician Leonid Ivanovich Abalkin, who will lead the State Commission for Economic Reform which is being formed, and Comrade Nikolay Pavlovich Laverov, vice president of the USSR Academy of Sciences, who is being nominated for the post of chairman of the USSR State Committee for Science and Technology.

These people are well known for their progressiveness and for their devotion to the ideas of restructuring, and they possess profound theoretical knowledge. It also proposed to confirm as deputy chairmen of the USSR Council of Ministers Comrades Igor Sergeyvich Belousov, to the State Commission of the USSR Council of Ministers on Military Industrial Matters; Aleksandra Pavlovna Biryukova, to the Bureau of the USSR Council of Ministers on Social Development; Vladimir Kuzmich Gusev, to the Bureau of the USSR Council of Ministers for the Chemical and Forestry Complex; Vitaliy Khusseynovich Doguzhiyev, to the USSR State Commission of the USSR Council of Ministers for Extraordinary Situations; Vladimir Mikhaylovich Kamentsev, to the State Foreign Economic Commission of the USSR Council of Ministers; Pavel Ivanovich Mostovoy, to the USSR State Committee for Material and Technical Supplies; Lev Dmitriyevich Ryabev, to the Bureau of the USSR Council of Ministers for the Fuel and Energy Complex; and Ivan Stepanovich Silayev, to the Bureau of the USSR Council of Ministers for Machine Building. I can say of each of them that they are leaders who are distinguished by a high degree of professional training and by great practical experience of work in various sectors of the national economy. All of them have done much for the implementation of the policy of restructuring of economic management. One should bear it in mind that, due to the nature of their duties, the deputy chairmen of the Council of Ministers are, as a rule, simultaneously the leaders of the corresponding standing bodies of the USSR Council of Ministers. The composition of the presidium of the USSR Council of Ministers, in accordance with the law about the USSR Council of Ministers, also includes the USSR minister of finances and the administrator of affairs of the Council of Ministers. It is proposed that Comrade Valentin Sergeyevich Pavlov, doctor of economic science, be appointed as USSR minister of finances. He has obtained the experience of practical activity in the financial sphere which is needed for a leader of such rank. He has worked his way up from inspector of a rayon financial department to first deputy minister of finances and chairman of the USSR State Committee on Prices.

It is proposed that Mikhail Sergeyevich Skhabardnya, doctor of technical sciences, who has been working as minister of instrument-making and automation equipment, be appointed administrator of affairs of the Council of Ministers.

More details of the biographies of the presidium members and also all heads of committees and departments that are being submitted for endorsement are in your possession, and so there is evidently no need for me to dwell on each candidacy.

I would like to add that of eight deputy heads of some state bodies who were confirmed in the rank of USSR minister—I refer to the present government—it is planned to have only two such posts in the new government: first deputy chairman of the USSR State Planning Committee, and chairman of the State Committee for Light Industry attached to the USSR State Planning Committee.

The principle of selection will, I think, be clear from the new composition of the government that is submitted for your consideration. Well-known and authoritative leaders have been picked here. A combination of people of high academic qualifications and a wealth of practical experience has been achieved.

Among the proposed candidacies, there are six academicians and corresponding members of the USSR Academy of Sciences. Twenty-three have academic degrees, while 37 were major economic managers. Among the recommended members of government, 5 are under 50, 21 are 51-55, 31 are 56-60, and 13 are in the 61-65 age group. Thus the average age of the proposed government members is 55.

Comrade members of the Supreme Soviet, I ask you to examine the structure of the organ of state government and the personnel composition of the USSR Council of Ministers. You have the draft documents on these issues. As for the appointment of the chairman of the USSR State Committee for Nature Conservation, the candidate for that post will be named later. The procedure for forming a government—henceforth enshrined in the Constitution—providing as it does for a preliminary consideration of proposed candidates by commissions of the chambers and commitees of the Supreme Soviet, will enable the proposals submited to be thoroughly examined from all angles. I ask you to endorse the proposals that are being submitted for your consideration.

Supreme Soviet Session Continues
LD1106133189 Moscow Television Service in Russian 1200 GMT 10 Jun 89

[Relay of the joint session of both houses of the USSR Supreme Soviet in the Kremlin chaired by Anatoliy Lukyanov—live]

[Excerpts] [Passage omitted] [Lukyanov] Do any deputies have questions? Questions? [passage omitted: a deputy asks Ryzhkov why there is no body on inventions, and is told it would be inappropriate; another deputy asks about the responsibilities of the central and republican building materials supply ministry]

[Lukyanov] Deputy Bronshteyn, please.

[Bronshteyn] Nikolay Ivanovich, tell me—do you consider it right that the man who is directly responsible for the country's dire economic situation should be left in the important post of first deputy and chairman of Gosplan? Moreover, a man who essentially is not a professional, whose background is engineering but who has been working in Gosplan since 1982?

[Ryzhkov] I believe the personnel composition of the government will be discussed in the committees and commissions, which will air their views. And therefore, the new Constitution, so to speak—the new laws are, as it happens, intended to ensure that the composition is not endorsed at once, but that there is an opportunity to work on it.

But if we are to speak about Comrade Maslyukov—and the subject has been broached—I should tell you this: Comrade Maslyukov has very great experience of life. Yes, he is indeed a mechanical engineer and has occupied many posts. But those sectors where he has worked—both in Gosplan, for you know that he has worked in the USSR Gosplan as first deputy chairman of Gosplan, and in the Military Industrial Commission, where he also worked as chairman and where, of course, he came up against not just technological matters, but economic matters, too; and of late he has worked as chairman of Gosplan—I consider that this is a perfectly well-qualified man. And to heap all the blame today on Comrade Maslyukov for the economy being in the state it is—I would not draw those conclusions. In my opinion Comrade Maslyukov is the very person to work in Gosplan. He has the range of interests, the economic mind required, great organizational flair, and therefore—well, of course, it is up to the deputies of the Supreme Soviet—you are the ones who will decide! But as for my opinion—since I've put him forward, those are my firm views on Comrade Maslyukov. [passage omitted: a deputy asks about republican transport ministries and the need for central coordination, an idea which Ryzhkov rejects]

[Primakov] Deputy Velikhov, please.

[Velikhov] Nikolay Ivanovich. Given the present severity...[Velikhov changes thought] of the atomic industry, of atomic power stations and also of other types of accidents, is it in fact appropriate to merge the two supervisory bodies—the State Committee for Supervision of Safe Working Practices in Industry and for Mine Supervision, and the State Committee for Safety in the Atomic Power Industry? And second, do you not think that in the future it might be best to restructure or redesign the ministries themselves, their apparatus, and somehow hand things over to the actual enterprises, which would set up, in effect, societies for the production of different kinds of product? They could then...[Velikhov changes thought] they know better what functions they require, they would preserve the necessary contacts that exist in those minsitries, and at the same time elect

the collegium, perhaps even the minister, and finance that structure. [passage omitted: indistinct complaint from the hall, sorted out by the chairman]

[Ryzhkov] I haven't replied to Yevgeniy Pavlovich. As far as the monitoring bodies are concerned, I think it was stated quite straightforwardly at the congress that we have very many monitoring bodies, very many—this was during the debate on setting up the People's Control Committee. We therefore believe that one body could handle the monitoring functions for industry as a whole, encompassing mining supervision, atomic power supervision, chemical supervision, etc.

If we go ahead with creating committees in the atomic, chemical and the mining spheres, and on machine-building and so on, we shall create a very unwieldy system of monitoring. Therefore in our view one body of this kind for monitoring industry has a certain logic. Of course there will be separate experts within it on atomic power engineering, and mining and chemical experts, for instance. This is natural.

The second question. I can only voice my thoughts, which are based on an analysis of those trends that are beginning to run in the national economy. In my report I have already said that the present management structure corresponds with the present stage in the development of the economy, only the present stage. It is quite obvious that there will be another structure for managing the national economy at the next stage. One thing is clear, that the ministries and committees which are carrying out overall economic regulation of the country's life will continue to exist, of course. They are the Ministry of Finances and so on. As for industry, I have already said and I can say now, that I think that there will be fewer and fewer ministries. I think that there will be one path. First large associations will be set up which will join together on the basis of their interests, not into monopolies, but precisely on the basis of their interests. And I should inform deputies that a question is being worked on at present to create an association for the production of mineral fertilizers on a democratic basis.

Probably...we will back this to the hilt. I think there will be such an association. Right now they are thinking about an association of the clock industry and others—for instance, other directions of machine building. Therefore, as such associations are set up, as two intersectoral associations have been set up in Leningrad and in Moscow, and so on, of course there will be increasingly fewer ministries. I think that, for instance, at some time there will be a state committee for machine building that will be only be responsible for certain regulatory processes. But this is a process. [passage omitted: deputy asks about the Ministry of Water Conservancy; Ryzhkov says the ministry must be preserved but used wisely, it will not decide policy; Ryzhkov opposes the idea of a single transport ministry; a deputy complains that there is no agriculture minister; Ryzhkov replies that the republics have responsibility for agriculture and that a state commission will attend to unavoidably central matters; a deputy complains about the poor quality of agricultural equipment; a deputy recalls criticism of the ministry of biological industry and criticizes an individual proposed as minister; Ryzhiov says individual ministers will be discussed elsewhere]

[Mikhail Aleksandrovich Bocharev] First. Nikolay Ivanovich, how might we nevertheless learn the functions of ministries, at least as they are designed to be? We talk about them them a great deal, and have been doing so for more than just 1 year, but in general, the new functions are not really evident. Enterprises' mutual relations with the ministries will naturally depend on this.

The second question: about the banks. Do the Zhilsotsbank, Promstroybank [expansions unknown], and so forth remain within the structure of the bank credit system, or are they and the banking system itself changing their structure?

A final question. I am going to talk about the ministries, the mergers and divisions there. A great many questions could have been asked here, incidentally, but I would still like this final question. What do you consider to be the transitional period from today to the next point—this is purely as a guideline, and perhaps there is no precise answer, but nevertheless—1, 2, or 3 years? Why? Because here one might really have thought about combining ministries of the industrial and construction complex, and the transportation complex, about which a correct comment has been made. The Ministry of the Gas Industry, after all, worked magnificently at one time. True, the volumes were small when the construction ministries, or rather construction issues, were within the composition of the ministry.

[Lukyanov] We agreed to put the questions in brief.

[Bocharev] Yes, there you are, those are the questions.

[Ryzhkov] I understand there to be two questions. The first question is about the functions of ministries. I have spoken briefly about this, and I would like to say once again that as economic reform becomes deeper, and as we work out all the elements and deepen economic reform, the functions of branch ministries will sharply change. They are changing even now, and they will change in the future. What do we consider to be the main orientation of future branch ministries? First of all, they must, of course, determine the basic strategic directions of scientific-technical progress; what direction we are to move in. That is the first point.

The second point: They must create an economic environment. What is involved here will also largely depend on the development of our economic reform. If we reach a point where there is a single norm, say, a standard national economic norm for industries from 1991, then the ministries will participate very little in this matter. If,

however, we go down the road of differentiated norms then they will participate in this, like it or not. This is about it: In our view, operational activity must pass away. We consider that as wholesale trade is developed—1992 has been set as the target and the development of wholesale trade will, I think, largely depend on how rapidly we adjust our market, including the market in production, and the correspondence between money and material resources—the functions of supply will gradually pass away from our ministries. Those are approximately the directions, so to speak, that the work of branch ministries will take.

As far as the banking system is concerned, we consider—and this is stated in the document which has been issued to you—that only one bank, the USSR State Bank, belongs to the government. The branch banks, or rather the specialized banks, do not belong to the government system. They exist today; as you know there are several specialized banks. Here, however, we are of the firm opinion that alongside the specialized banks we must create—no, it is not we who must create them—a large number of all kinds of banks must and will be created: branch banks, cooperative banks, and so on, even though you have also heard criticism in this direction, at the congress. This is our opinion. It may differ from that of certain comrades who made the very strong criticism a year ago that it was very good when there was one unified bank in the country, and that it became bad when five banks were set up. We consider that there are too few banks in the country. Too few. There must be an opportunity to have more banks, and to give every enterprise an opportunity to go to the bank which it considers it needs to go to. Not to impose some particular bank on it. In our view, this is the direction in which the banking system must move. You need the state bank; you cannot do without it. After all, it regulates all economic life in our country, credit policy, monetary policy, and so on. It is, of course, the main bank which must use economic levers to regualte all of the banking system and the other economic systems. That is, the bank must be woven into the economic fabric of our national economy.

[Lukyanov] Deputy Yeltsin.

[Boris Yeltsin] Two questions, Nikolay Ivanovich. The first question. Of course, thirteen deputy chairman have been proposed. That is a considerable number, but I would like to know who will be engaged in matters of capital construction.

[Ryzhkov] In connection with the fact that capital construction ministries formerly subordinate to USSR Gosstroy, that is, the four union ministries operating in the Russian Federation—two ministries in the European part and two in Siberia and the Far East—are now being transferred to the Russian federation by us, we believe that Gosstroy must undergo change and that its functions must be radically revised. We believe that there is no need for it to have a deputy chairman of the Council of Ministers. The USSR Gosstroy must be headed by a USSR minister—we are submitting a proposal on this. Comrade Serov from Gosplan has been proposed by name.

[Yeltsin] Does this mean that Gosstroy will not have production management functions?

[Ryzhkov] Yes.

[Yeltsin] Given this, you will not have a deputy chairman dealing with construction?

[Ryzhkov] No, there will not be one. There will be a USSR minister who must engage in coordination, scientific-technical progress, the development of economic mechanisms, and who must at the same time coordinate, to some extent, the specialized ministries: the Ministry of Installation and Special Construction Work, the Ministry of Transport Construction, and so on. [passage omitted: on deputy proposing discussion on commissions]

[Unidentified deputy] Nikolay Ivanovich, be so good as to tell us whether, in the structure as it has been proposed, the government commission to eliminate the aftermath of the accident at the Chernobyl nuclear electric power station is retained, and if not, why not?

[Ryzhkov] The government commission is today part of the bureau for the fuel and energy complex. It is our opinion that if the Supreme Soviet endorses the structure of the government that I have today suggested, we believe that those sore points that there are today—in this instance Chernobyl, Armenia, and several other points where work must be carried out—should fall within the sphere of the government commission on emergencies. Control should be maintained there. That is our opinion. [passage omitted, Ryzhkov replies to question on need for two timber industries; question on who is responsible for baby food]

[Unidentified deputy] Nikolay Ivanovich, given what I see as the administrative-command system of administration that endures to the present day, to what extent can you guarantee that the structure of the Council of Ministers proposed will lead to a substantial reduction in the administrative apparatus? Approximately what sort of reduction will there be, and where would these people be sent?

[Ryzhkov] We believe that, if this scheme is adopted for the management of the national economy, we believe that the ministries' personnel must be cut by at least 30 percent. [passage omitted: deputy calls for water conservancy to be completely abolished; Ryzhkov says the Supreme Soviet has the power to do this but careful thought should be given to it; next deputy asks about the

long-term plans for the Soviet Far East and the Non-Chernozem Zone; next deputy asks about resolving a passport question; next questions concern gas and geology ministries]

[Lukyanov] Thank you, Nikolay Ivanovich. Comrade deputies, as has been stated, in accordance with Article 123 of the USSR Constitution the appointment of officials to the Council of Ministers occurs once the relevant standing commissions of the chambers and the USSR Supreme Soviet committees have reached their conclusions. Therefore you are asked to consider the following Supreme Soviet draft decision:

—First, that the USSR Supreme Soviet should accept for consideration the suggestions put forward by Comrade Nikolay Ivanovich Ryzhkov, the USSR Council of Ministers chairman, on the structure and composition of the USSR Council of Ministers.

—Second, that the relevant committees of the USSR Supreme Soviet and the standing commissions of the chambers be charged, in accordance with Article 123 of the USSR Constitution, with providing their conclusions on the candidates proposed for appointment to the USSR Council of Ministers. That is the draft decision. [passage omitted: Lukyanov recapitulates this for the benefit of a deputy]

Now I would ask you to prepare to vote on this draft. I put it to the vote of both chambers at the same time. Everyone in favor of the draft decision as proposed, please raise your credentials. Please lower them. Against? Two. Abstentions? One. The decision is passed by a majority of votes. [passage omitted: commissions' work begins 19 June; government membership will be discussed for a week; a joint session on 26 June will adopt decisions on this]

[Lukyanov] We are dealing with the question of the selection of the committees of the USSR Supreme Soviet. This question was initially discussed in the system of committees by both chambers, and then at a joint session of the chambers, and the chairmen of the Soviet of the Union and Soviet of Nationalities were entrusted with the task of consulting carefully on this question with deputies, with groups of deputies from the republics and regions, and then, taking in account the ideas expressed by the deputies on their participation in the committees and commissions, of putting forward their proposals. This work has been done by Comrades Primakov and Nishanov, the chairmen of the chambers. This has been done as a preliminary because in some respects the membership of the committees will be sorted out later. So let me give the floor on this question to Comrade Yevgeniy Maksimovich Primakov:

[Primakov] Esteemed comrade chairman, esteemed comrade deputies! As has already been said, the chairmen of the chambers were entrusted with the work of forming committees and of making the committees' composition agree with many people. This work [of selection (selektsiya)] has, I would say, been completed, so far as the heads of the committees are concerned. Before reading out the candidates being proposed for the posts of chairmen of committees, I would like to make few preliminary remarks.

First, comrades will realize that some 800 people can work in these committees and in the commissions of the standing chambers: 400, roughly speaking, from the Supreme Soviet, and 50 percent from other deputies who did not get into the Supreme Soviet, that is to say another 400, making 800 in all. Roughly speaking, that is one-third of the whole number of people's deputies. On the basis of rotation people will be changed, and the contours of these committees will constantly be changing, in their numbers perhaps, and in the quality of their membership, but let us start out with the idea that all those who work well in the committees will be consolidated there, and those who are just there on paper will leave, to be replaced by those who really want to work. That is my first preliminary remark. The second is that the list which has been handed out to you on the committees is a preliminary one, a basis, so to speak; it will be modified as a result of the proposals that will be made, and are already being made, and we are taking all these proposals into account as far as possible, so there will be some castling [chess term referring to a particular move], shifting from one committee to another, an increase in the membership of the committees, and so on. So I would ask that our discussion now should not be concentrated on questions connected with the membership of these committees; we will resolve this in working order, and we must not now distract ourselves from the more important question of the chairmen of the committees.

After we had conducted our preliminary conversations, discussions, and talks, which were possible over a period of a few days—naturally, we dealt with these questions only for a few days, because otherwise you would have reproached us with having made an apparatus-type preparation of this matter, and would have said that the preliminary list was prepared beforehand and given to us; this was not the case—we came, therfore, to this conclusion: the Committee on Foreign Affairs. We have so far not managed to select a chairman. Obviously the chairman will have to be confirmed or chosen by all of us at the next session of the congress, or in connection with the work of the next session of the congress, because there will already have been a certain rotation, and evidently some new candidates will by then have emerged.

On the question of defense and state security. You will realize that this is a very important committee, which will hold part of its discussions in camera, which is the common practice in all countries of the world, without exception; as a rule, not all questions connected with defense and state security can be discussed openly, and

therefore, along with open sessions—and there will certainly be some—this committee will also hold a number of closed sessions. This is natural practice. After lengthy reflection, after discussion and so on, we settled on the candidacy of Comrade Lapygin. [passage omitted on reasons for selecting him because of his background, opinions; Alekseyev selected to chair committee on legality and law and order; review of his background and opinions, as expressed during the congress; Pivovarov is being put forward for chairman of the commission on matters of the work of the soviets of people's deputies; he is very familiar with the workings of soviets of people's deputies and is a firm advocate of strengthening local government and decentralization; Vologzhin is proposed for the commission on economic reform; he has implemented economic reforms at his own works]

In this committee on matters of economic reform we held talks with many scientists, too, and decided to strengthen its leading group and make recommendations. Because I want to say that in order to observe fully the democratic nature of the election of the bureau, of the presidia, or simply the cabinets, as you like, of every committee, we decided—when I say that we decided, I mean Rafik Nishanovich Nishanov and myself—to turn to this practice. We shall not recommend right now to you, or to any of the committee chairmen in advance, any specific comrades. But if people turn to us for advice we are ready to do this. In this committee, for example, we are prepared to recommend Comrade Bunich, Comrade Tikhonov, and others for work in the leading group of this committee. [passage omitted: remarks about agrarian committee and recommendation of Veprev as its chairman]

As for matters of construction and architecture, the post of chairman of the committee was offered to Boris Nikolayevich Yeltsin, taking into account his professional profile and taking into consideration the public profile which he has. Evidently, he will be a good chairman of the committee, one who will work genuinely in this area. He, too, will form the composition of his assistants. [passage omitted: nomination of Ryzhkov to chair science committee; of Borodin to chair health protection committee; of Matviyenko to chair family protection committee; of Bosenko to head committee on affairs of veterans and invalids; of Tsybukh to chair committee on youth affairs; of Salykov to head committee on matters of ecology]

Finally, Comrade Vladimir Konstantinovich Fotcyev is proposed as chairman of the committee on matters of glasnost, rights and applications from citizens. He is currently first secretary of the Checheno-Ingush Oblast CPSU committee. He is described as a person who in this respect may prove very useful precisely because he is working there, has proved himself from the viewpoint of the reports of his comrades. He has proven himself as an official who reacts extremely sharply to incoming critical remarks and who generally knows that criticism and self-criticism are the motive force in our society. And in this respect, say the comrades, he will be here the figure whom we need.

At this point I would like to complete my report, Anatoliy Ivanovich Lukyanov. [passage omitted: Lukyanov asks for questions; Primakov replies to a procedural question; question on formation of defense and security committee. Primakov replies: The deputies' wishes regarding participation in various particular committees were taken into consideration when the proposed lists of members were drawn up; the task of the committee is to monitor activity of the relevant industries and draw up plans and budgets. Deputy rises to support previous deputy on the defense and state security committee: Does the lack of Baltic representation mean the start of the demilitarization of the Baltic Republics? That he would welcome. Further deputy rises to make a point; Primakov replies: We cannot now set up a large number of committees, we could set up a commission to look into the committees issue, then we could continue with out work, which is the main thing—let's get on to the discussion of the candidatures for the miniterial posts. Deputy rises to stress the importance of the defense and state security committee, and suggests that professional military people and arms people ought to be excluded from membership of it; the committee exercises civilian control over the Army. Primakov replies that there shouldn't be any discrimination against deputies who have been elected for any reason—though the military shouldn't dominate. Deputy in military uniform rises to say there are no serving officers on the proposed committee—and there should be; he suggests his own candidacy. Estonian deputy says his group put him forward as a candidate for the defense committee; he recalls his own years of military service, his role in the Chernobyl cleanup operation. Primakov says amendments will be made in the light of what he has said. An unnamed deputy—in military uniform—says that there are so many wanting to take part in the defense committee that another committee should be formed. Primakov says that no one is trying to deceive anyone over these matters; there cannot be an unlimited number of members of this committee; so let's discuss it reasonably. Deputy from Moldavia rises to propose that there ought to be military specialists on the committee, but no more than one third of its composition—the remainder should not be military people. Unidentified deputy rises to complain of the unrepresentative nature of the Chamber of Nationalities element in the proposed list. Primakov says this is a committee of the Supreme Soviet. Primakov replies to another military deputy who asked for an explanation of certain procedures in the selection of nominees for the committee. Deputy makes a further point on procedural matters and rotation—to which Primakov again responds with his view. The deputy wants to know how people are chosen to replace those who leave a committee under the rotation procedures. Unidentified deputy laments the lack of a Georgian representative on the ecological committee. Deputy

Shevchenko takes the floor: We are ready to propose amendments; on the defense committee we share the view that defense industries should switch to consumer goods production, but we must not forget about the country's security and the provision of a reliable defense. Lukyanov proposes that the question section of the agenda be considered completed—and makes a statement about various procedural issues. Lukyanov announces a 20 minute interval in the session]

Afternoon Session Continues Work
LD1006181189 Moscow Television Service in Russian 1434 GMT 10 Jun 89

[Relay of the joint session of the two chambers of the USSR Supreme Soviet in the Kremlin—live]

[Excerpts] [passage omitted] [Yakovlev] I have this question for Boris Nikolayevich [Yeltsin], Boris Nikolayevich....

[Primakov] Introduce yourself.

[Yakovlev] Yakovlev. Tell me, please, several suggestions were put to you both in the Supreme Soviet and at the congress which you, well, obviously did not refuse, but to which you did not assent. How do you view the situation at the moment, and the proposal that you should work in this committee [the Commmittee on Construction and Architechture]?

[Yeltsin] Concerning these proposals, I weigh up my chances realistically. That was why I withdrew before. And now, of course, there is still some doubt, but if the deputies give me their confidence, I will work conscientiously. [applause] At the same time, I would like to ask literally for 3 minutes of the chairman, given that yesterday, at the end of the session of the congress, I did not have a chance to speak because of what happened over Comrade Sakharov's speech. Nevertheless, I would like to explain my attitude and perhaps continue this theme for literally 3 or 4 minutes.

And so, while in no way wishing to minimize the significance of the congress itself or to belittle its qualities, or the political significance of the issues of democratization, glasnost, and so on, nevertheless now that the congress has ended and the [Supreme Soviet] first session is drawing to a close, I must say that I am not fully satisfied with the congress because many of the issues that we deputies awaited—or at any rate, I speak for myself—remained unresolved. The proposals concerning amendments to the Constitution were not passed—proposals that could have been passed quickly and that could have enabled the congress to proceed with its work considerably faster, rather than marking time for 3 days.

Second, the proposal that there must of necessity be alternative candidates in each election was not passed.

Third, the proposal calling for a referendum to be held, if not every year than at least after 2 years, on nationwide confidence in the chairman of the USSR Supreme Soviet, that was not passed. And on a number of other matters.

And of course, I am not particularly satisfied that economic and financial measures that really could get our country out of the deadlock in a fairly short space of time have been put together and presented to us. These were fairly run-of-the-mill reports, and therefore there is no confidence that, sure enough, in 2 years we will have improved the economic and financial position of our country. I could not but say this before you make your decision. Thank you.

[Primakov] Any questions?

[Unidentified speaker] This is my question, Boris Niko-layevich.

[Lukyanov] Do you have a question on the candidacy or on substance?

[Unidentified speaker] On substance.

[Lukyanov] Go ahead, then. [voice from hall shouts "I propose that we begin voting"; others in hall agree] But there are questions. [passage omitted: further slight interruption from hall]

[Unidentified speaker] From the reports and the analyses that have been made at the congress, all have indicated that lately there has been a sharp increase in uncompleted production in capital construction. Will the committee that you will head be able to have an impact on this in the space of a year, 6 months, leading to a sharp decrease in uncompleted production work?

[Yeltsin] In terms of legislation....

[Unidentified speaker, interrupting] In accordance with the article [indistinct interjection by Yeltsin]—it is a very good article—it was also stated there that we should also be looking for money there, too.

[Yeltsin] I understand the question and here is my answer. By changing investment policy legislatively, it is possible to resolve this matter.

[Unidentified speaker] But how are we to have an impact on supplying full sets of equipmint in capital construction? After all, we know that the increase in capital construction has occurred largely because the equipment supplies to construction sites have virtually gone beyond the control of builders.

How will the committee bring influence to bear on this? Today at my combine, for example, full sets of equipment are not supplied for all construction work. Will we have an impact on this or not?

[Yeltsin] First of all, the committee is probably not an executive body, but the legislative and supervisory body. That is the first point. Second, my idea, if you listened to my speech at the congress, was this: To ensure that supply for builders exceeds demand in our country, it is necessary to reduce the volume of centralized capital investment for industrial construction in the first years at least by 30 percent. So there you have the supply of complete sets of equipment, there you have the cadres, and there you have construction materials for retail trade for the building of garden sheds, dachas, and repairing apartments and so on. And there you have the strengthening of the ruble's rate, because it is necessary to withdraw this centralized money, simply withdraw it, reduce it by R30-40 billion, and withdraw them from circulation altogether.

[Lukyanov] Good, that's clear. Another question: Please go ahead.

[Rogozhina] Rogozhina, from the women's councils. Esteemed Boris Nikolayevich, for many years you have been the number one in construction. The trouble with the quality of construction is seismically active regions has been shown by the destruction for the second time of the town of Gazli. Please tell us what measures you have taken, as the person in the state responsible for construction, in order to increase, improve the quality of construction in seismically active regions.

[Yeltsin] First of all, I have not been the number one in construction for many years.

[Rogozhina] Excuse me. I am going on the information in our files.

[Yeltsin] Pardon?

[Rogozhina] I am going on the information in your files. You were secretary of the Central Committee for Construction, and then you moved to deputy chairman.

[Yeltsin] I was Central Committee secretary for 6 months, and I have spent a year at the USSR State Construction Committee. Furthermore, for the time being, our State Construction Committee is divided into two sections, a managerial and administrative section, which is engaged in this whole field, and a second section, which Minister Bidin runs. And the second section is the old part of the State Construction Committee that is involved with quotas, standards, and construction norms and specifications. That is the kind of paper work that I loathe.

[Rogozhina] Excuse me, Boris Nikolayevich, I have to disagree with you. I am acquainted with the norms and specifications that regulate construction in seismically active regions. There is nothing wrong with them. What is wrong actually is the observance of these construction norms and specifications, and I still think that someone who is responsible for construction both in the Central

Committee and in the Construction Committee should probably have paid attention to the fact that the document that regulates construction in particularly dangerous regions, in regions which are exposed to catasprophes that we cannot avert, should be fulfilled. In connection with this, I have this question: Can you say, if you are elected to this post—and I do not doubt that this will happen—what measures you will take to ensure that catastrophes of this kind are not repeated?

[Yeltsin] First, in our country there is in fact no regulation with regard to the determination of seismic forces. There is not even any with regard to this disaster, so to speak. When work was done on it with Academician (Lader), they determined that even there, it turns out, they were all independent, chance documents. For instance, they went and established that the seismic forces were measured in nine degrees. At the request of the republic, they went and lowered it to seven degrees. Someone did it in accordance with some kind of decision, and so on and so forth. Therefore, having asked Comrade (Lader's) advice, they agreed that at the present time a seismological map—a macro-seismological map and a microseismological map, so to speak, of the whole of our country—must be specially published with the involvement of the republics and naturally with the involvement of geologists and other specialists. That is the first thing. Second, all the standards must be revised. Am I answering the question? [murmur in hall] And so forth. That's all; thank you.

[Rogozhina] May I be so bold as not to agree with what you said last, because there is nothing wrong with our maps?

[Yeltsin] There is no doubt about that. We saw for ourselves that in those apartment blocks that were destroyed, for instance, in the concrete there was 50 percent of what is required—the amount of cement. The iron reinforcing in the concrete did not hold. It could quite simply just be pulled out by hand. What happened to that cement?

[Lukaynov] Are there any more questions, comrades? Take a seat please, Boris Nikolayevich.

[Primakov] Of course, I cannot agree with the assessments made of the congress here, either. I think the congress is a tremendous and important event. In order to implement the program that we have planned, efforts will have to be made by all of us, every deputy, though some of the issues raised by Boris Nikolayevich are just. I ask those in favor of electing Comrade Yeltsin chairman of the Commission for Construction and Architecture to raise their identity cards; deputies of both chambers should vote. Who is against? One, two, three, four...four, five—there are five against. Who has abstained? Ah, sorry I didn't notice you there—seven against. [voices from floor] Well let's count them, then. Who is against? Please count them...eight people against. Who has abstained? According to my calculations it's

four people. [unidentified voice: five] Five. [voice: What's the difference?] Well, we have to be precise. So, comrades, by a majority vote Boris Nikolayevich Yeltsin has been elected chairman of the commission. [applause]

The next nomination is that of Yuriy Alekseyevich Ryzhkov as chairman of the Committee for Science, National Education, Culture, and Upbringing [vospitaniye]. You know him, right? The rector of the Moscow Aviation Institute. Questions for Yuriy Alekseyevich, please. Are there any questions? [voices: no] No, then those in favor of electing Comrade Ryzhkov please raise your identity cards. Down again. Those against? Abstentions? One person, two—two. Comrade Ryzhkov is elected chairman of the committee. [applause]

[Lukyanov] Comrades: Very many comrades have asked my to say a little bit about the arrangements for our further work so that it is perfectly clear. Well, we have formed the committees; and the greater part of the commissions, with the exception of two commissions from the Soviet of Nationalities, have been formed.

We propose that the work of our session be broken off now for 1 week, for 1 week, until next Monday, the 19th of the month. You have been given material about the composition of the government, about the structure of the government, and so on. We want the committees and the comrades who will be members of the committees— and you will receive the latest details about the committees from the chairmen of the chambers—we want them to come here on the 19th of the month for 1 week in order to work in each committee on the composition of our government and to listen to the ministers. I think that that could perhaps be very useful work in order to see, even, what the volume of the work is, what is being done in the country, and to take a critical look at this. And on the 26th of the month we want you to gather for a joint sitting of the chambers of the Supreme Soviet— that will be 1 week later—in order to settle issues concerning the confirmation of our government as far as its personnel composition is concerned.

Those deputies who have not joined the commission— those members of the Supreme Soviet who have not joined the commissions—can arrive on the 26th, by the 26th, if they do not have an interest in the work of any of the committees and if they do not want to listen to these issues. [indistinct remarks from floor] I will repeat it once again: The commissions and the committees, those who are not on the commissions and committees, if they do not want to come to participate in their work, then they should come on the 26th.

It is planned that as soon as the government is formed we will be faced with a whole series of issues which have been entrusted to us by the congress. The first rough sketches suggest that if we work in an organized way it will be approximately 1 month and 10 days. And then, given that the composition of the commissions and the committees will already have been determined—that is to say, the chairmen, the deputy chairmen, the secretaries and the leaders of the sub-commissions—it will be clear at the session which of the members of the Supreme Soviet will be working permanently in Moscow until the time of the rotation. Only then will it become clear. That is why we cannot answer that question now, you understand. The plan is that approximately 80 percent of the comrades will be working here.

I have just spoken to Mikhail Sergeyevich on the telephone. He asked me to convey this greeting to you once again, and he asks you to meet with your voters, tell them about our congress, tell them about the first session of the Supreme Soviet which will be continuing both in the commissions and in the work of the chambers. Bring home to them the whole democratic fire of the congress, as he put it. [applause]

At this point, I declare the joint session of the chambers closed.

What are we going to do about the Soviet of Nationalities?

Remain behind? Remain behind, comrades!

Congress Constitutional Commission Members Listed
PM1006191189 Moscow PRAVDA in Russian
10 Jun 89 Second Edition pp 1, 2

["Resolution by the USSR Congress of People's Deputies: On the Formation of the Constitutional Commission"—PRAVDA headline]

[Text] The USSR Congress of People's Deputies resolves:

To form a Constitutional Commission composed as follows:

Commission Chairman:

Gorbachev, Mikhail Sergeyevich—chairman of the USSR Supreme Soviet, general secretary of the CPSU Central Committee.

Commission Deputy Chairman:

Lukyanov, Anatoliy Ivanovich—first deputy chairman of the USSR Supreme Soviet, candidate member of the CPSU Central Committee Politburo.

Commission Members:

Akayev, Askar—USSR people's deputy, vice president of the Kirghiz Soviet Socialist Republic [SSR] Academy of Sciences, Frunze City.

Aleksandrin, Valeriy Grigoryevich—USSR people's deputy, chairman of Yoshkar-Ola City People's Court, Mari Autonomous Soviet Socialist Republic [ASSR].

Alekseyev, Sergey Sergeyevich—USSR people's deputy, corresponding member of the USSR Academy of Sciences, director of the USSR Academy of Sciences Urals Department, Sverdlovsk City.

Ambartsumyan, Sergey Aleksandrovich—USSR people's deputy, rector of Yerevan State University.

Arutyunyan, Suren Gurgenovich—USSR people's deputy, first secretary of the Armenian Communist Party Central Committee.

Barabashev, Georgiy Vasilyevich—USSR people's deputy, chief of department at the Moscow State University named for M.V. Lomonosov Law Faculty, doctor of juridical sciences.

Berger, Arnold Vladimirovich—USSR people's deputy, director of the Kustanay Agricultural Institute Training and Experimental Farm named for Gagarin, Kazakh SSR.

Bikkenin, Nail Bariyevich—USSR people's deputy, chief editor of the journal KOMMUNIST.

Bisher, Ilmar Olgertovich—USSR people's deputy, professor at the Latvian State University named for P. Stuchka, Riga City.

Bogdanov, Igor Mikhaylovich—USSR people's deputy, school director, Gorkiy City.

Bogomolov, Oleg Timofeyevich—USSR people's deputy, director of the USSR Academy of Sciences Economics of the World Socialist System Institute, Moscow City.

Brazauskas, Algirdas-Mikolas Kaze—USSR people's deputy, first secretary of the Lithuanian Communist Party Central Committee.

Bunich, Pavel Grigoryevich—USSR people's deputy, corresponding member of the USSR Academy of Sciences, chief of department at the Moscow S. Ordzhonikidze Management Institute.

Burlatskiy, Fedor Mikhaylovich—USSR people's deputy, political observer of LITERATURNAYA GAZETA, Moscow City.

Vagris, Yan Yanovich—USSR people's deputy, first secretary of the Latvian Communist Party Central Committee.

Vezirov, Abdul-Rakhman Khalil ogly—USSR people's deputy, first secretary of the Azerbaijan Communist Party Central Committee.

Velikhov, Yevgeniy Pavlovich—USSR people's deputy, vice president of the USSR Academy of Sciences, Moscow City.

Vilkas, Eduardas Yono—USSR people's deputy, director of the Lithuanian SSR Academy of Sciences Economics Institute.

Vlasov, Aleksandr Vladimirovich—USSR people's deputy, chairman of the Russian Soviet Federated Socialist Republic [RSFSR] Council of Ministers, candidate member of the CPSU Central Committee Politburo.

Volskiy, Arkadiy Ivanovich—USSR people's deputy, chairman of the Nagorno-Karabakh Autonomous Oblast Special Administration Committee.

Vorotnikov, Vitaliy Ivanovich—USSR people's deputy, chairman of the RSFSR Supreme Soviet Presidium, member of the CPSU Central Committee Politburo.

Vyalyas, Vayno Iosipovich—USSR people's deputy, first secretary of the Estonian Communist Party Central Committee.

Gamzatov, Rasul Gamzatovich—USSR people's deputy, writer, chairman of the Dagestan ASSR Writers Union Board.

Golik, Yuriy Vladimirovich—USSR people's deputy, dean of the Kemerovo State University Law Faculty.

Grossu, Semen Kuzmich—USSR people's deputy, first secretary of the Moldavian Communist Party Central Committee.

Gryazin, Igor Nikolayevich—USSR people's deputy, chief of department at the Estonian SSR Academy of Sciences Philosophy, Sociology, and Law Institute.

Gumbaridze, Givi Grigoryevich—USSR people's deputy, first secretary of the Georgian Communist Party Central Committee.

Yevtyukhin, Yuriy Alekseyevich, docent at the Kemerovo State University, candidate of juridical sciences.

Yeltsin, Boris Nikolayevich—USSR people's deputy, Moscow City.

Zalygin, Sergey Pavlovich—USSR people's deputy, chief editor of the journal NOVYY MIR, secretary of the USSR Writers Union Board.

Zaslavskaya, Tatyana Ivanovna—USSR people's deputy, academician, director of the All-Union Center for the Study of Public Opinion on Socioeconomic Questions under the All-Union Central Council of Trade Unions [AUCCTU] and the USSR State Committee for Labor and Social Problems.

Zvonov, Sergey Nikolayevich—USSR people's deputy, director of Ivanovo's No 2 Motor Vehicle Passenger Transportation Enterprise.

Iskhaki, Yusuf Bashirkhanovich—USSR people's deputy, rector of the Tajik State Medical Institute.

Kalmykov, Yuriy Khamzatovich—USSR people's deputy, chief of department at the Saratov D.I. Kurskiy Law Institute.

Kerimov, Dzhangir Ali Abbas ogly—USSR people's deputy, chief of department at the CPSU Central Committee Academy of Social Sciences, Moscow city.

Kiyamov, Nurgaziz Vagizovich—USSR people's deputy, chairman of the Tatar ASSR Vakhitov Collective Farm [kolkhoz].

Kolbin, Gennadiy Vasilyevich—USSR people's deputy, chairman of the USSR Committee for People's Control.

Kosygin, Vladimir Vladimirovich—USSR people's deputy, own correspondent of Kamchatka Oblast Committee for Television and Radio Broadcasting, Koryak Autonomous Okrug.

Kryuchkov, Vladimir Aleksandrovich—chairman of the USSR KGB.

Kryuchkov, Georgiy Korneyevich—USSR people's deputy, first secretary of the Odessa Oblast Ukrainian Communist Party Committee [obkom].

Kudryavtsev, Vladimir Nikolayevich—USSR people's deputy, vice president of the USSR Academy of Sciences, Moscow City.

Kutafin, Oleg Yemelyanovich—rector of the All-Union Extramural Legal Studies Institute, doctor of juridical sciences.

Kyabin, Tiyt Reynkholdovich—USSR people's deputy, scientific secretary of the Estonian SSR Academy of Sciences Presidium Social Sciences Department.

Laptev, Ivan Dmitriyevich—USSR people's deputy, chief editor of the newspaper IZVESTIYA.

Lizichev, Aleksey Dmitriyevich—USSR people's deputy, chief of the Soviet Army and Navy Main Political Directorate.

Likhanov, Albert Anatolyevich—USSR people's deputy, chairman of the V.I. Lenin Soviet Children's Foundation Board, writer.

Marchuk, Guriy Ivanovich—USSR people's deputy, president of the USSR Academy of Sciences.

Masaliyev, Absamat Masaliyevich—USSR people's deputy, first secretary of the Kirghiz Communist Party Central Committee.

Matveyev, Yuriy Gennadiyevich—USSR people's deputy, USSR chief state arbiter.

Makhkamov, Kakhar—USSR people's deputy, first secretary of the Tajik Communist Party Central Committee.

Medvedev, Vadim Andreyevich—USSR people's deputy, member of the CPSU Central Committee Politburo, secretary of the CPSU Central Committee.

Mironenko, Viktor Ivanovich—USSR people's deputy, first secretary of the All-Union Lenin Communist Youth League Central Committee.

Nechayev, Konstantin Vladimirovich—USSR people's deputy, Metropolitan Pitirim of Volokolamsk and Yuryev, chairman of the Moscow Patriarchate Publishing Department.

Nikonov, Aleksandr Aleksandrovich—USSR people's deputy, president of the V.I. Lenin All-Union Academy of Agricultural Sciences.

Nishanov, Rafik Nishanovich—chairman of the USSR Supreme Soviet Soviet of Nationalities.

Niyazov, Saparmurad Atayevich—USSR people's deputy, first secretary of the Turkmen Communist Party Central Committee.

Ovezgeldyyev, Orazgeldy—USSR people's deputy, president of the Turkmen SSR Academy of Sciences.

Pavlov, Aleksandr Sergeyevich—USSR people's deputy, chief of the CPSU Central Committee State-Law Department.

Platon, Semen Ivanovich—USSR people's deputy, chairman of Kagul City Soviet of People's Deputies Executive Committee, Moldavian SSR.

Platonov, Vladimir Petrovich, USSR people's deputy, academician, president of the Belorussian SSR Academy of Sciences.

Pokrovskiy, Valentin Ivanovich—USSR people's deputy, president of the USSR Academy of Medical Sciences.

Polozkov, Ivan Kuzmich—USSR people's deputy, first secretary of Krasnodar Kray CPSU Committee.

Popov, Gavriil Kharitonovich—USSR people's deputy, chief editor of the journal VOPROSY EKONOMIKI.

Primakov, Yevgeniy Maksimovich—chairman of the USSR Supreme Soviet Soviet of the Union.

Prokopyev, Yuriy Nikolayevich—USSR people's deputy, first secretary of Yakutsk CPSU Obkom.

Pukhova, Zoya Pavlovna—USSR people's deputy, chairman of the Soviet Women's Committee.

Razumovskiy, Georgiy Petrovich—USSR people's deputy, candidate member of the CPSU Central Committee Politburo, secretary of the CPSU Central Committee, chief of the CPSU Central Committee Party Building and Cadre Work Department.

Rustamova, Zukhra Karimovna—USSR people's deputy, member of Syrdarya Oblast Court, Uzbek SSR.

Ryzhkov, Nikolay Ivanovich—USSR people's deputy, chairman of the USSR Council of Ministers, member of the CPSU Central Committee Politburo.

Sagdiyev, Makhtay Ramazanovich—USSR people's deputy, chairman of the Kazakh SSR Supreme Soviet Presidium.

Salayev, Eldar Yunis ogly—USSR people's deputy, president of the Azerbaijan SSR Academy of Sciences.

Salykov, Kakimbek—USSR people's deputy, first secretary of the Karakalpak Uzbek Communist Party Obkom.

Samsonov, Aleksandr Sergeyevich—USSR people's deputy, director of Moscow's No 1 Timepiece Plant named for S.M. Kirov.

Sakharov, Andrey Dmitriyevich—USSR people's deputy, academician, chief scientific associate of the USSR Academy of Sciences P.N. Lebedev Physics Institute, Moscow City.

Sbitnev, Anatoliy Mitrofanovich—USSR people's deputy, steel worker at the Kommunarsk metallurgical combine, Voroshilovgrad Oblast.

Sergiyenko, Valeriy Ivanovich—USSR people's deputy, chairman of Krasnoyarsk Kray Soviet of People's Deputies Executive Committee.

Simonov, Sergey Borisovich—USSR people's deputy, fitter and assembly worker at the Ufa motor-building production association.

Skudra Viktor Yanovich—USSR people's deputy, Latvian SSR minister of justice.

Slyunkov, Nikolay Nikitovich—USSR people's deputy, member of the CPSU Central Committee Politburo, secretary of the CPSU Central Committee.

Smolentsev, Yevgeniy Alekseyevich—chairman of the USSR Supreme Court.

Sobchak, Anatoliy Aleksandrovich—USSR people's deputy, chief of department at the Leningrad State University Law faculty.

Sokolov, Yefrem Yevseyevich—USSR people's deputy, first secretary of the Belorussian Communist Party Central Committee.

Suleymenov, Olzhas Omarovich—USSR people's deputy, writer, first secretary of the Kazakh SSR Writers Union Board.

Sukharev, Aleksandr Yakovlevich—USSR people's deputy, USSR general prosecutor.

Sychev, Nikolay Yakovlevich—USSR people's deputy, chairman of the Moscow City War and Labor Veterans Council.

Talanchuk, Petr Mikhaylovich—USSR people's deputy, rector of the Kiev Polytechnical Institute.

Tarazevich, Georgiy Stanislavovich—USSR people's deputy, chairman of the Belorussian SSR Supreme Soviet Presidium.

Tarnavskiy, Georgiy Stepanovich—USSR people's deputy, Belorussian SSR prosecutor.

Tkachuk, Vasiliy Mikhaylovich—USSR people's deputy, chairman of the "Prapor Kommunizmu" Kolkhoz, chairman of the "Prut" Agrofirm, Ivano-Frankovsk Oblast, Ukrainian SSR.

Topornin, Boris Nikolayevich—director of the USSR Academy of Sciences State and Law Institute, corresponding member of the USSR Academy of Sciences, Moscow City.

Umarkhodzhayev, Mukhtar Ishankhodzhayevich— USSR people's deputy, rector of the Andizhan State Language Teacher Training Institute.

Fokin, Vitold Pavlovich—USSR people's deputy, deputy chairman of the Ukrainian SSR Council of Ministers, chairman of the Ukrainian SSR State Planning Committee, Kiev City.

Khallik, Klara Semenovna—USSR people's deputy, leading scientific associate of the Estonian SSR Academy of Sciences Philosophy, Sociology, and Law Institute, Tallinn City.

Chebrikov, Viktor Mikhaylovich—USSR people's deputy, member of the CPSU Central Committee Politburo, secretary of the CPSU Central Committee

Shalayev, Stepan Alekseyevich—USSR people's deputy, chairman of the AUCCTU.

Shakhnazarov, Georgiy Khosroyevich—USSR people's deputy, corresponding member of the USSR Academy of Sciences, aide to the general secretary of the CPSU Central Committee, Moscow City.

Shevardnadze, Eduard Amvrosiyevich—USSR foreign minister, member of the CPSU Central Committee Politburo.

Shevchenko, Valentina Semenovna—USSR people's deputy, chairman of the Ukrainian SSR Supreme Soviet Presidium.

Shinkaruk, Vladimir Illarionovich—USSR people's deputy, director of the Ukrainian SSR Academy of Sciences Philosophy Institute, Kiev City.

Shinkuba, Bagrat Vasilyevich—USSR people's deputy, poet, Georgian SSR.

Shlichite, Zita Leonovna—USSR people's deputy, attorney with the Klaypeda Legal Advice Service, Lithuanian SSR.

Shcherbitskiy, Vladimir Vasilyevich—USSR people's deputy, first secretary of the Ukrainian Communist Party Central Committee, member of the CPSU Central Committee Politburo.

Yakovlev, Aleksandr Maksimovich—USSR people's deputy, chief of section at the USSR Academy of Sciences State and Law Institute, Moscow City.

Yakovlev, Aleksandr Nikolayevich—USSR people's deputy, member of the CPSU Central Committee Politburo, secretary of the CPSU Central Committee.

Yakovlev, Veniamin Fedorovich—director of the All-Union Scientific Research Institute for Soviet State Building and Legislation, doctor of juridical sciences.

East Bloc Leaders, Others Congratulate Gorbachev
PM0206094189 Moscow PRAVDA in Russian
28 May 89 Second Edition pp 1,3

[TASS report: "Greetings Telegrams to M.S. Gorbachev"]

[Text] In connection with his election as chairman of the USSR Supreme Soviet, Comrade M.S. Gorbachev has received greetings and congratulations from party figures and statesmen all over the world.

In his telegram T. Zhivkov, general secretary of the Bulgarian Communist Party [BCP] Central Committee and chairman of the Bulgarian State Council, said:

"Esteemed Comrade Gorbachev,
"On behalf of the BCP Central Committee, the Bulgarian State Council, and the Bulgarian people and from myself personally, I send you the most cordial congratulations on your election as chairman of the USSR Supreme Soviet.

"The decision of the Congress of USSR People's Deputies to entrust you with this new, top state post accords with the supreme interests of the Soviet state and reflects the trust and active support which the Soviet people give to the CPSU's historic course of revolutionary restructuring and the fundamental renewal of socialism in the Soviet Union and to the policy of new thinking in the international arena. The Soviet people link their hopes and their belief in the irreversibility and success of this historic cause with the revival of the Leninist idea and practice of full power for the soviets, with the activity of the Congress of People's Deputies, and with the new USSR Supreme Soviet.

"We invariably appreciate highly the relations of fraternal friendship and international collaboration between our two countries. We are deeply convinced that, through joint efforts, we will continue to even more fully reveal and more effectively utilize the potential of all-around Bulgarian-Soviet cooperation in the interests of our peoples and for the sake of our common aims and ideals.

"With all my heart I wish you, dear Mikhail Sergeyevich, the Congress of People's Deputies, and the USSR Supreme Soviet fruitful work and success in the fulfillment of the large-scale, creative tasks of the socialist renewal of the Soviet Union, and wish the fraternal Soviet people happiness, prosperity, and peace."

In his greetings telegram K. Grosz, general secretary of the Hungarian Socialist Workers Party [MSZMP], wrote:

"Dear Comrade Gorbachev!
"On behalf of the MSZMP Central Committee and from myself personally, I congratulate you on your election as chairman of the USSR Supreme Soviet at the Congress of USSR People's Deputies. I wish you, dear Mikhail Sergeyevich, a great deal of strength, good health, and great success in your responsible work in this post."

In his greetings telegram Bruno F. Straub, president of the Hungarian Presidential Council, said:

"Please accept cordial congratulations on your election as chairman of the USSR Supreme Soviet.

"With all my heart I wish you great success in this high state post in the name of the revolutionary renewal of Soviet society and the prosperity of your country. I am sure that the close friendship and all-around cooperation between our countries will continue to steadily develop in the interests of our peoples, socialism, and peace."

Nguyen Van Linh, general secretary of the Communist Party of Vietnam [CPV] Central Committee, Vo Chi Cong, chairman of the SRV State Council, and Do Muoi, chairman of the SRV Council of Ministers, wrote:

"We send you the most sincere, ardent congratulations on your election as chairman of the USSR Supreme Soviet.

"The Congress of USSR People's Deputies is an important event in the sociopolitical life of the land of the soviets and clear evidence of the Soviet people's determination to overcome all obstacles in order to successfully implement the 27th CPSU Congress course of restructuring.

"Your election as chairman of the USSR Supreme Soviet at the Congress of USSR People's Deputies is an expression of the people's respect for you as an outstanding leader of the party and the Soviet state.

"The party, government, and people of Vietnam highly appraise your contribution to the struggle for peace and progress on earth and to the task of strengthening the bonds of friendship and solidarity between the USSR and the SRV and enhancing the effectiveness of Soviet-Vietnamese cooperation in line with the policy taken by our parties and states to implement restructuring and renewal.

"The Vietnamese people ardently welcome and fully support the new Soviet peace initiatives and approve of the results achieved by the recent Soviet-Chinese summit meeting and the normalization of relations between the USSR and the PRC, considering them to be an important contribution to the cause of peace, security, and cooperation in the Asian and Pacific region and the rest of the world. We are deeply confident that under the leadership of the CPSU, the Soviet people will successfully implement the historic decisions of the 27th CPSU Congress and the 19th All-Union Party Conference.

"We wish you good health and further great achievements in your important, responsible work."

In his telegram E. Honecker, general secretary of the Socialist Unity Party of Germany [SED] Central Committee and chairman of the GDR State Council, said:

"Dear Comrade Mikhail Sergeyevich Gorbachev!
"In connection with your election as chairman of the USSR Supreme Soviet I send you most cordial congratulations on behalf of the SED Central Committee, the GDR State Council, and the people of the GDR.

"This decision of the highest popular forum in the USSR is fresh confirmation of the great authority you have won as the highest representative of the Leninist party and the Soviet state. This election is also a high appraisal of your enterprising work for the good of peace, which is so dear to all people.

"I am deeply convinced that the tested combat alliance and inviolable friendship between our parties, states, and peoples will continue to develop and grow stronger in the interests of socialism and peace.

"With all my heart I wish you, dear Mikhail Sergeyevich, creative strength, good health, and great success in your responsible work."

Kim Il-song, general secretary of the Workers Party of Korea [WPK] Central Committee and president of the DPRK, wrote:

"On behalf of the WPK Central Committee, the DPRK Government, and the Korean people and from myself personally, I send you ardent congratulations on your election as chairman of the USSR Supreme Soviet at the Congress of USSR People's Deputies, thanks to the deep trust of the Soviet people.

"The Soviet Union has formed a new supreme body of state authority and you have been elected chairman of the USSR Supreme Soviet. This reflects the will of the CPSU, the Soviet Government, and the Soviet people to implement the decisions of the 27th CPSU Congress and the 19th all-union party conference.

"We wish you new successes in your future work designed to accelerate the pace of restructuring, bring prosperity to the Soviet Union, and defend peace throughout the world.

"I would like to take the opportunity to express my confidence that the traditional relations of friendship and solidarity between our two parties, countries, and peoples, which have firmly developed during our common struggle against imperialism and for the triumph of the great cause of peace, socialism, and communism, will continue to develop and grow stronger."

Yang Shangkun, president of the PRC, wrote:

"I cordially congratulate you on your election as chairman of the USSR Supreme Soviet and wish you success in this high, responsible position.

"You recently visited the PRC, which was an event of historic importance. Your meeting with Chinese leaders put an end to the past, opened up the future, and led to the normalization of relations between China and the Soviet Union.

"May relations between China and the Soviet Union constantly develop and grow stronger."

In his telegram J. Batmonh, general secretary of the Mongolian People's Revolutionary Party [MPRP] Central Committee and chairman of the Mongolian People's Great Hural Presidium, said:

"Dear Mikhail Sergeyevich,

"On behalf of the MPRP Central Committee, the Mongolian People's Great Hural Presidium, and all the working people of our country and from myself personally, I cordially congratulate you on your election as chairman of the USSR Supreme Soviet at the Congress of USSR People's Deputies.

"We regard your election to this, the highest state post as fresh confirmation of all the Soviet people's determined support for the CPSU course of consistently implementing revolutionary restructuring. The highest body of state authority in the Soviet Union—the Congress of People's Deputies—is a historic step on the way to renewing the Soviet political system, creating a socialist rule-of-law state, and steadily developing democracy and glasnost.

"I express deep confidence that Mongolian-Soviet relations of fraternal friendship and close, all-around cooperation will continue to develop and grow stronger in the spirit of our glorious traditions and the new times.

"Allow me to wish you, dear Mikhail Sergeyevich, good health and great, new successes in your tireless work for the good of the Soviet people and the sake of peace and security on earth."

In his greetings telegram W. Jaruzelski, first secretary of the Polish United Workers Party [PZPR] Central Committee and chairman of the Polish State Council, said:

"Deeply esteemed Comrade Gorbachev!

"In connection with your election as chairman of the USSR Supreme Soviet at the Congress of USSR People's Deputies, I send you cordial congratulations on behalf of the Polish people and the Polish State Council and from myself personally.

"I wish you, dear Comrade Gorbachev, great success in all spheres of social life in your high, responsible position as head of the Soviet state, where fundamental, revolutionary transformations are now being effected.

"I am deeply convinced that, inspired by the CPSU Program and with the active support of the USSR Supreme Soviet headed by you, the Soviet people will consistently continue the great task of restructuring for the good of the development of the land of the soviets, the renewal of socialism, and universal peace. The process of far-reaching, democratic changes, glasnost, and new thinking in international relations are having an enormous impact on the strengthening of socialism and the building of a world free of wars and violence.

"Your election to the post of chairman of the USSR Supreme Soviet inspires confidence in us that our ties as allies, which are strong as never before, and the partnership relations of friendship and cooperation between our states and peoples will continue to grow stronger and successfully develop in our common interests. The consonance of the aims and aspirations of Soviet restructuring and Polish renewal is contributing to the deepening and mutual enrichment of these historic processes.

"Please accept, dear Mikhail Sergeyevich, cordial wishes of further success in your work for the good of the Soviet people and state and in the task of restructuring international relations. I also wish you good health and success in your personal life."

N. Ceausescu, general secretary of the Romanian Communist Party [RCP] and Romanian president, wrote:

"Dear Comrade Gorbachev,
"It gives me particular pleasure to convey to you on behalf of the RCP Central Committee and the Romanian State Council and from myself personally cordial congratulations and very best wishes on your election to the high post of chairman of the USSR Supreme Soviet.

"Taking satisfaction in noting the ascendant course of relations between our parties, countries, and peoples, I express the firm belief that the meetings and talks held in Bucharest and Moscow and the accords we have reached will give new impetus to Romanian-Soviet relations by still further strengthening friendship and all-around cooperation between the RCP and the CPSU and between Romania and the USSR in the spirit of the Treaty of Friendship, Cooperation, and Mutual Assistance and in the interests of, and for the good of, our countries and peoples, the cause of socialism, and peace throughout the world.

"I would like to take the opportunity to wish you good health, happiness, and success in the fulfillment of the highly responsible mission with which you have been entrusted. I wish Communists and all working people in the Soviet Union new and even greater achievements in the implementation of the 27th CPSU Congress and 19th All-Union CPSU Conference decisions and in the struggle for disarmament, cooperation, and progress throughout the world."

In their greetings telegram M. Jakes, general secretary of the Communist Party of Czechoslovakia [CPCZ] Central Committee, and G. Husak, president of the CSSR, wrote:

"Dear Comrade Gorbachev!

"On behalf of the CPCZ Central Committee and the people of the CSSR, we sincerely congratulate you with all our hearts on your election to the post of chairman of the USSR Supreme Soviet. Your election in the period of the deepening process of democratizing Soviet society is an expression of the people's trust in the policy of restructuring being implemented by the CPSU and a recognition of your tireless work for the good of the Soviet people and your services in the task of strengthening peace and international security and developing cooperation between countries and peoples.

"We wish you, dear Comrade Gorbachev, good health and great success in your responsible work."

INDEX OF SUBJECTS AND PERSONS MENTIONED

INDEX OF SPEAKERS